Readings and Cases in Educational Psychology

Readings and Cases in Educational Psychology

Anita E. Woolfolk
Rutgers University

ALLYN AND BACON
Boston • London • Toronto • Sydney • Tokyo • Singapore

Library of Congress Cataloging-in-Publication Data

Woolfolk, Anita.
  Readings and cases in educational psychology / Anita E. Woolfolk.
    p.   cm.
  Accompanies the author's Educational psychology. 5th ed.
  Includes bibliographical references.
  ISBN 0-205-13821-7
  1. Educational psychology. 2. Educational psychology—Case
studies. I. Woolfolk, Anita, Educational psychology. II. Title.
LB1051.W746 1993
370.15—dc20   92-37249
                                                           CIP

CREDITS

1) Gage, N. L. (1991). The obviousness of social and educational research results. *Educational Researcher, 20,* 1:10–16. Copyright 1991 by the American Educational Research Association. Reprinted by permission of the publisher.

2) Killion, J. P. & G. R. Todnem (1991). A Process for personal theory building. *Educational Leadership 48,* 6:14–16. Reprinted with permission of the Association for Supervision and Curriculum Development. Copyright 1991 by ACSD. All rights reserved.

3) Sparks-Langer, G. M. and A. S. B. Colton. (1991). Synthesis of research on teachers' reflective thinking. *Educational Leadership, 48,* 6:37–44. Reprinted with permission of the Association for Supervision and Curriculum Development and author. Copyright 1991 by ASCD. All rights reserved.

4) Fischer, K. W. & C. C. Knight. (1990). Cognitive development in real children: Levels and variations. In R. McClure (Ed.) *Learning and thinking styles: Classroom interaction.* Reprinted with permission by the National Education Association.

Credits continue on p. 298 which constitutes an extension of the copyright page.

Contents

CHAPTER 8

CHAPTER 9

CHAPTER 10

CHAPTER 11

Subject Guide

The articles and cases in this reader provide information about many specific topics in education and educational psychology. Use the guide below to locate material on topics that interest you. Many articles cover much more than is indicated below, but this guide should give you some direction in your reading and research.

Preface

TO THE READER

Many of you reading this book are studying educational psychology for the first time. Others may be taking an advanced course or a graduate seminar. To all of you, welcome to some interesting reading and exciting ideas. I have been teaching and learning about educational psychology for over 20 years and have witnessed many developments. But of all the times to study educational psychology, this is the most fascinating. The field has been changing rapidly. There is renewed interest in how the mind works, how children and adults learn, what motivates students, and how excellent teaching happens. Educational psychologists have more useful information for teachers than ever before, as you will see in the coming pages.

This volume has two parts. In the first section is a collection of readings selected from professional journals and magazines. Some of the articles are reviews of research on important topics prepared for practicing teachers and administrators. Other articles take a position or make an argument for a particular approach to teaching or testing. Finally, a few of the entries report results of research. These give you a firsthand look at how educational psychologists study teaching and learning.

In the second section are five original cases written for this book by experts studying the teaching and learning of school subjects. These cases show principles of educational psychology in action in actual classrooms as students attempt to learn math, reading, or history.

TO THE INSTRUCTOR

This book is divided into two parts. The first is a collection of articles chosen from professional journals and magazines. Many of the articles are summaries of research in a given area—some written for researchers and others for practicing teachers and administrators. Other articles take a position on a controversial issue. These reviews and position papers are taken from *Educational Researcher, Phi Delta Kappan, Educational Leadership, Harvard Education Letter,* and *Educational Psychologist.* A few selections are primary sources—reports of research from such references as the *Journal of Educational Psychology* and *Sex Roles.* The statistics in these research studies are very basic and descriptive. Even introductory level students will find these studies easy to understand. I have included a few examples of research so readers can see firsthand the sources of knowledge in educational psychology.

All of the readings in this volume are cited in my educational psychology textbook (*Educational Psychology*, 5th edition, published by Allyn and Bacon), but I have chosen the articles to complement any text, even if these sources are not directly cited. The articles are grouped by topics that are consistently found in most educational psychology books.

The second section of the book contains five original case study analyses, written by educational psychologists who study the teaching and learning of specific school subjects. These five analyses represent the most current thinking and research in educational psychology and reflect current attempts to understand how the principles of educational psychology are manifest as students learn math, reading, or history. Each analysis includes some case material—slices of life from real classrooms. This material may be in the form of interviews with students or descriptions of class events or experiences of a particular teacher. What distinguishes these "cases" from the many others currently available is that *each is based on actual events and each is derived from a program of research.* Thus, in reading and analyzing the cases, your students not only learn about the realities of classroom life and how principles of educational psychology look in action, they also get a glimpse of how research is conducted in educational psychology and how information from research can inform practice. Some of the contributors have included extensive analyses of the case material while others leave this analysis to the reader. Each case includes questions to stimulate students' thinking about the situation.

Hilda Borko's contribution, "Ms. Daniels: Strengths and Limitations in a Novice's Teaching," describes a student teacher's more and less successful attempts to make difficult concepts in mathematics understandable to her sixth grade students. In the process, she shows readers what the term "pedagogical content knowledge" means in a real teaching situation. Borko's case can be assigned when your class is studying research approaches in educational psychology, expert-novice differences, teacher knowledge and thinking, or math instruction.

Lynne Díaz-Rico's case, "From Monocultural to Multicultural Teaching in an Inner-City Middle School," describes the experiences of an excellent and dedicated teacher who encounters problems in one of her history classes. The teacher's genuine efforts to understand how her own biases and beliefs contribute to the problems and her energetic work to improve her teaching will help your students understand the human side of multicultural education. This very rich case can be assigned to accompany topics of cultural diversity and multiculturalism, motivation, individual differences, teacher expectations, classroom management, or teaching strategies.

The third case, "Analysis of Two Middle School Students' Cognitive Strategies, Memory, and Learning," by Paul Pintrich and Allison Young presents interviews with two students who are struggling to understand their science textbook. As these students describe how they try to understand and remember the material, their words provide concrete manifestations of abstract concepts from cognitive learning such as schemata, reconstructive memory, elaboration, and retroactive interference. This case can be assigned to accompany the study of cognitive views of learning, the role of schemata in learning, transfer, learning strategies and study skills, or science instruction.

Margaret Meyer and James Middletown describe and analyze two classroom events that occur in some form or another every day in secondary math classes. Their contribution, "Affect and Motivation in Secondary Mathematics," raises questions about teachers' differential treatment of males and females in math classes and explores the effects of these differences on students' motivation and self-concept. A second segment examines the motivational properties of common tasks in secondary math classes and asks what can be done to improve these tasks. The authors make it clear that the issues they raise are relevant for other subjects in addition to mathematics. This reading can be assigned when your class is studying motivation, gender differences in the classroom, self-concept, or teacher expectations.

The final case, "Motivation in First Grade Literacy," by Julianne Turner examines young students learning about reading and writing. This case contrasts two classes, one with more traditional "closed" tasks and the other with "open" authentic tasks that allow students choice and control. Turner analyzes the different responses of the students in these two classrooms in relation to principles of motivation such as task characteristics, goal setting, dealing with distraction, persistence, interest, difficulty, and social support. This case can be assigned when students consider motivation, teaching strategies, or whole-language approaches to literacy.

I am interested in hearing about how you use these readings and cases in your teaching and about your students' reactions to them. Please send any comments or suggestions to:

Anita E. Woolfolk
Allyn and Bacon
160 Gould Street
Needham, MA 02194

Readings and Cases in Educational Psychology

► Chapter 1

The Obviousness of Social and Educational Research Results

N. L. GAGE

Highly estimable writers have averred that well nigh all of the results of social and educational research are obvious, that is, could have been predicted without doing the research. To examine the justifiability of this allegation, one should examine its accord with actual research results. Thus, is it a "truism" that higher achievement comes about when students spend more time with the subject matter? That smaller groups are easier to control than larger groups? Do judges regard actual results as more obvious and statements of their opposites as nonobvious? Both the century-old research results of Joseph Mayer Rice and recent results throw light on these issues.
—*Educational Researcher, Vol. 20, no. 1, pp. 10–16*

Is what we find out in social and educational research old hat, stale, platitudinous? Are the results of such research mere truisms that any intelligent person might know without going to the trouble of doing social or educational research?

THE IMPORTANCE OF THE OBVIOUSNESS QUESTION

The obviousness question has important ramifications. It can influence the motivation of any person who is thinking about doing social or educational research. Why do research if you are not going to find anything new, anything not already known? Obviousness also relates to the justification of social science departments and schools of education in expecting or requiring their faculties and graduate students to do social and educational research. It also concerns government funding policies, such as those of the National Science Foundation and the

N. L. Gage is at the School of Education, Stanford University, Stanford, California 94305.

National Institute of Mental Health that support social research, and those of the U.S. Department of Education, particularly the Office of Educational Research and Improvement, that support educational research. Foundations, school boards, state legislatures, and Congressional committees need to be convinced, before they put up the money, that social and educational research will produce something that any intelligent adult might not already know.

So, the issue of obviousness, apart from piquing our intellectual curiosity, has tremendous practical importance. Unless social and educational researchers face that issue, they may lack motivation to do research and lose societal support expressed in dollars.

THE CHARGE OF OBVIOUSNESS

Does anyone really hold that social and educational research yields only the obvious? I begin with an old joke attributed to James T. Farrell, the novelist who became famous in the 1930s for *Studs Lonigan.* Farrell was quoted in those days as having defined a sociologist as someone who will spend $10,000 to discover the location of the nearest house of ill fame. He actually used a less polite term, and nowadays he would have said a quarter of a million dollars. I also remember a fellow graduate student who could always get a laugh by referring to the content of some of his textbooks as "unctuous elaborations of the obvious."

Schlesinger's Critique

The first serious piece of writing that I know of that made the same charge appeared in 1949 in *The Partisan Review.* It was in a review by Arthur Schlesinger, Jr., of the two volumes of *The American Soldier,* which had just been published. *The American Soldier* was written by a group led by Samuel A. Stouffer, who later became a professor of sociology at Harvard. It reported on the work done by sociologists and other social scientists in surveying, with questionnaires and interviews, the attitudes of American soldiers during World War II. The first volume, subtitled "Adjustment During Army Life," dealt with soldiers' attitudes during training, and the second, subtitled "Combat and Its Aftermath," dealt with soldiers' attitudes while they were engaged with the enemy and risking their lives. As a young assistant professor, I found the two books impressive for their methodological thoroughness, sophisticated interpretation, and theoretical formulations of such concepts as "relative deprivation."

So I was taken aback after some months when I discovered a review of those two volumes by Arthur Schlesinger, Jr., the distinguished historian. Then a young professor at Harvard University, Schlesinger had just won a Pulitzer Prize for his *Age of Jackson.* Witty and vituperative, Schlesinger's review also denounced what he considered the pretensions of social scientists. Schlesinger wrote:

> *Does this kind of research yield anything new? . . . [T]he answer . . . is easy. Most of the American Soldier is a ponderous demonstration in Newspeak of such facts as these: New recruits do not like noncoms; front-line troops resent rear-echelon troops; combat men manifest a high level of anxiety as compared to other soldiers; married privates are more likely than single privates to worry about their families back home. Indeed, one can find little in the 1,200 pages of text and the innumerable surveys which is not described more vividly and compactly and with far greater psychological insight, in a small book entitled* Up Front *by Bill Mauldin. What Mauldin may have missed will turn up in the pages of Ernie Pyle. (p. 854)*

Lazarsfeld's Examples

At about the same time as Schlesinger, Paul Lazarsfeld, a professor of sociology at Columbia University, also reviewed *The American Soldier.* Lazarsfeld (1949) was dearly aware of the same problem of obviousness. He wrote:

> [I]t is hard to find a form of human behavior that has not already been observed somewhere. Consequently, if a study reports a prevailing regularity, many readers respond to it by thinking "of course, that is the way things are." Thus, from time to time, the argument is advanced that surveys only put into complicated form observations which are already obvious to everyone.
>
> Understanding the origin of this point of view is of importance far beyond the limits of the present discussion. The reader may be helped in recognizing this attitude if he looks over a few statements which are typical of many survey findings and carefully observes his own reaction. A short fist of these, with brief interpretive comments, will be given here in order to bring into sharper focus probable reactions of many readers.
>
> 1. *Better educated men showed more psychoneurotic symptoms than those with less education. (The mental instability of the intellectual as compared to the more impassive psychology of the man-in-the-street has often been commented on.)*
> 2. *Men from rural backgrounds were usually in better spirits during their Army life than soldiers from city backgrounds. (After all, they are more accustomed to hardships.)*
> 3. *Southern soldiers were better able to stand the climate in the hot South Sea Islands than Northern soldiers. (Of course. Southerners are more accustomed to hot weather.)*
> 4. *White privates were more eager to become noncoms than Negroes. ([Because of their*

having been deprived of opportunity for so many years], the lack of ambition among Negroes was [quite understandable].)

5. *Southern Negroes preferred Southern to Northern white officers [because Southerners were much more experienced in having interpersonal interactions with Negroes than Northern officers were].*

6. *As long as the fighting continued, men were more eager to be returned to the States than they were after the Germans surrendered [because during the fighting, soldiers were in danger of getting killed, but after the surrender there was no such danger].* (pp. 379–380)

Keppel's Position

For a later sample of the worry about obviousness, we can turn to an essay by Frank Keppel, titled "The Education of Teachers," which appeared in 1962 in a volume of talks on American education by American scholars that had been broadcast by radio to foreign audiences. Keppel had left the deanship of the Harvard Graduate School of Education to serve as U.S. Commissioner of Education under President Kennedy. As Commissioner he led the movement that resulted in the Elementary and Secondary Education Act of 1965, the first major effort in the U.S. to improve the education of children from low-income families. In his article, Keppel (1962) indicated that some people question the principles that have emerged from psychological studies of teaching and learning. Without committing himself as to whether he agreed, he summed up the critics' arguments this way:

The efforts to use scientific methods to study human behavior seem to them [the critics] ridiculous if not impious. The result is a ponderous, pseudo-scientific language which takes ten pages to explain the obvious or to dilute the wisdom long ago learned in humanistic studies. . . . To build an art of teaching on the basis of the "behavioral sciences," they suggest, is to build on sand. (p. 91)

Conant's Position

The very next year, obviousness was mentioned again, by another prestigious educator, namely, James Bryant Conant, who had been president of Harvard University for 20 years, and then the U.S. High Commissioner (and eventually the U.S. ambassador) in West Germany. During World War II, he had been a member of the highest scientific advisory committees, including the one that led to the production of the atom bomb. When he returned from Germany, he devoted himself almost exclusively to educational problems. In 1963, he published a book titled *The Education of American Teachers*, in which he reported on his studies of teacher education programs and schools—studies made through much interviewing, reading, and visiting. His book gained extremely wide and respectful attention. Yet, when I looked into it, as an educational psychologist, I couldn't help being dismayed by Conant's assertion that educational psychology largely gives us merely common-sense generalizations about human nature—generalizations that are "for the most part highly limited and unsystematized generalizations, which are the stock in trade of every day life for all sane people" (p. 133).

Phillips's Critique

These references to obviousness take us only into the 1960s. Did the attacks disappear after that? Or are there more recent statements on the obviousness of educational and social research results? In 1985, a volume of papers appeared on the subject of instructional time, which had been central in a variety of formulations, such as John B. Carroll's model of school learning, Benjamin Bloom's mastery approach to teaching, and the concept of academic engaged time developed by Charles Fisher and David Berliner. All of these writers seemed to agree that the more time students spent in studying, practicing, and being engaged with the content or skills to be learned, the greater the related learning they achieved. The correlations between academic engaged time and achievement were not perfect, of course, because outside of the laboratory, correlations are never perfect, even in the natural sciences and certainly not in the social and behavioral sciences.

The subject of instructional time thus received a lot of attention in many articles and several books, including the edited volume, *Perspectives on Instructional Time*, to which the philosopher of the social sciences, Denis Phillips (1985), contributed a chapter entitled "The Uses and Abuses of Truisms." Here Phillips first cited Hamlyn, also a philosopher, who had criticized the work of Piaget. Hamlyn had asked his readers to try to imagine a world in which Piaget's main ideas were untrue:

> *a world where children mastered abstract and complex tasks before concrete and simple ones, for example. Such a world would differ crazily from our own, and one gets the sense that many of Piaget's views are unsurprising and necessarily (if not trivially) true. (p. 311)*

Phillips then raised the same kind of question about the research on instructional time: "What sort of world would it be if children learned more the *less* time they spent on a subject? If achievement were not related to the time spent engaged on a topic?" (p. 311). So, just as with Piaget's major findings, "one gets the sense that these findings [about instructional time] are almost necessarily (and perhaps even trivially) true" (p. 311). "Indeed, it suddenly seems strange to dress up these truisms as 'findings' " (p. 312).

Phillips then went on to make a distinction between truisms and statements that are trivially true. "[T]he latter are, in effect, a subgroup of the former. A truism is a statement the truth of which is self-evident or obvious . . . whereas a trivially true statement is one that is true by virtue of the meaning of the terms involved (e.g., 'All colored objects are colored,' or 'All bachelors are unmarried')" (p. 312). He went on to say that " 'It is easier to keep a small group of children working on a task than it is a large group' is a truism, for it is obviously true, but it is not true by virtue of the meanings of the terms involved" (p. 312). Phillips also pointed out that:

> *truisms and statements that are trivially true are not thereby* trivial. *The terms* truism *and* trivially true *refer to the patentness of the truth of statements, whereas* trivial *refers to their degree of value or usefulness. The two do not automatically go together; many a statement the truth of which is far from obvious is of no practical use . . . and many truisms are vitally important and even theoretically significant ("The sky is dark at night" [this truism bears on the theory of the expanding universe]). (p. 313)*

Furthermore,

> *truisms uncovered by researchers, then, are not necessarily trivial. But on the other hand tru-*

isms do not require research in order to be uncovered. *Agencies would be wasting money if they awarded grants to researchers who wanted to determine if all bachelors in the United States were unmarried, or if the sky is dark at night, or if small groups are easier to control than large groups. (p. 313, emphasis added)*

In Short

Let me summarize the argument so far. I have presented a series of opinions quite damaging to the notion that social and educational research yields results that would not already be known to any intelligent and thoughtful citizen. These opinions are hard to ignore. Extremely estimable people—Farrell, Schlesinger, Keppel, Conant, Lazarsfeld, and Phillips—all have made statements that might well give pause to any sensible person considering the pursuit of social and educational research or any organization being asked to part with money to support such research. I have presented these statements in chronological order extending from novelist James T. Farrell in the mid-1930s to philosopher Denis Phillips in the mid-1980s.

EMPIRICAL EXAMINATION OF OBVIOUSNESS

One noteworthy characteristic of all of these criticisms is that they were what might be called nonempirical or, at least, not systematically and formally empirical. Informal and personal, the appraisals were not made with any great specificity, detail, explicitness, or exactitude. Presumably, Schlesinger had not actually compared the statements of results reported in *The American Soldier* with statements made by Bill Mauldin or Ernie Pyle. He did not perform a content analysis of the two kinds of reports about soldiers to show in any literal way that the sociologists' statements of results had been anticipated by the insights of the cartoonist and the journalist. The same point can be made about what was said by Keppel and Conant: They did not go into any detail, or become at all specific, to support their allegations. However, the sociologist Lazarsfeld did go into detail and referred to specific results, namely, soldiers' attitudes of various kinds. Phillips referred to specific findings about instructional time, or time on task, and also findings about size of group or class size.

Rice's Studies

Now I should like to go back and look at some empirical efforts that seem to me to bear upon the whole issue of obviousness. I begin with what may be the first process—outcome study in the history of research on teaching. The results of this investigation were published by Joseph Mayer Rice (1897/1913) under the title "The Futility of the Spelling Grind." Rice reported, after studying tests on 33,000 school children, that there was no correlation worth noticing between amount of time devoted to spelling homework and classwork and competence in spelling.

Rice's evidence is still being cited in support of the argument that spelling competence results from "incidental" learning, rather than from any "systematic" teaching; that is, spelling is "caught" rather than "taught." So far as instructional time or "academic engaged time" is concerned, the issue does not appear to be the open-and-shut case implied by Phillips (1985) when he asked, "What kind of world would it be if achievement were not related to the time spent engaged on a topic?" (p. 311). As Rice (1897/1913) put it, "concerning the amount of time devoted to spelling . . . an increase of time . . . is not rewarded by better results. . . . The results obtained by forty or fifty minutes' daily instruction were not better than those obtained where not more than ten or fifteen minutes had been devoted to the subject" (pp. 86–87).

Apparently, showing a relationship between time on task and achievement was not as easy as falling off a log, as it should have been if the relationship between time-on-task and achievement were necessarily true, that is, a truism. At least in one subject matter, namely, spelling, the relationship between time-on-task and achievement was fragile, perhaps even nonexistent. So perhaps the relationship depended on the subject matter. Perhaps other factors also made a difference. Things may be more complicated than we should expect if the relationship were a truism.

Similarly, if smaller groups were always easier to control, a relationship that Phillips assumed to be a truism, then they should show higher time-on-task and thus higher achievement. However, the trickiness of the relationship between class size and achievement is by now well established. Reducing

class size from 40 to 20 does not improve achievement with any consistency at all. Glass (1987) reported that it required an "exhaustive and quantitative integration of the research" to refute well-nigh unanimous older assessments (e.g., Goodlad, 1960) that class size made no difference in achievement, student attention, and discipline. Even then Glass found that the relationship of class size to achievement appeared only probabilistically (in 111 of 160 instances, or 69%) when classes of approximately 18 and 28 pupils were compared. Moreover, the duration of the instruction made a big difference: the relationship was stronger in studies of pupils taught for more than 100 hours. In addition, the class size had to be reduced dramatically to make a major improvement: "Bringing about even a 10 percentile rank improvement in the average pupil's achievement . . . may entail cutting class size (and, hence, increasing schooling costs) by a third to a half" (p. 544).

Alleging that a relationship (e.g., the size-of-group relationship to the ease of control) is a truism implies that it should always be found and that no exceptions should occur. Thus, all bachelors without exception are unmarried, all colored objects without exception are colored. By the same reasoning, if the group size-controllability relationship were a truism, all smaller groups should be easier to control than all larger groups. If the age-reasoning ability relationship were a truism, all older children should be capable of more abstract and valid reasoning than all younger children. But, of course, the last two examples are untrue. If a truism is "an undoubted or self-evident truth, especially one too obvious or unimportant for mention" (*Webster's New Collegiate Dictionary*, 1979), then these relationships are not truisms because they are not always "undoubted" or "self-evident."

Suppose we change the "truism" to a probabilistic statement (e.g., children *tend* to learn more, the more time they spend on a subject; time on task is positively but *imperfectly* correlated with achievement). Now the research aims to determine the strength of the tendency, or the magnitude of the positive correlation. Does the r equal .05, .25, .45, .65, or .85? It seems to be a truism that the size of the time on task versus achievement correlation depends on many factors: the reliability of the achievement measure, the variabilities of the two variables, perhaps the subject matter, and so on. Is the research to answer these important and specific practical questions still unnecessary?

Here may lie one key to the problem: To enhance the truism with the specifics that make it have value for theory and practice, the research does become necessary. Even if the broad generalization is a truism, the specifics of its actualization in human affairs—to determine the magnitude of the probability and the factors that affect that magnitude—require research. Even if "smaller groups tend to be more easily controlled" were a truism, we would ask, how much difference in group size is needed to produce a given difference in controllability? How do other factors—age and gender of group members, task difficulty, and the like—affect the difference in controllability resulting from changes in group size? Similar questions would apply to all the other seemingly truistic findings. Even if intelligent people could always (without any research) predict the direction (positive or negative) of a relationship between two variables, they could not predict its size and its contingencies without research-based knowledge.

Lazarsfeld's Examples

Let us go back now to Lazarsfeld's examples of obvious results from the World War II studies of *The American Soldier*. Recall his examples of the "obvious" conclusions from that study: better educated men showed more psychoneurotic symptoms; men from rural backgrounds were usually in better spirits than those from cities; Southern soldiers were better able than Northerners to stand the climate in the South Sea Islands; White privates were more eager to become noncoms than Black privates were; Southern Negroes preferred Southern to Northern White officers; and men were more eager to be returned to the States during the fighting than they were after the Germans surrendered.

Lazarsfeld (1949) asked, "Why, since they are so obvious, is so much money given to establish such findings?" However, he then revealed that

> Everyone of these statements is the direct opposite of what was actually found. *Poorly educated soldiers were more neurotic than those with high educations; Southerners showed no greater ability than Northerners to adjust to a tropical climate; Negroes were more eager for promotion than whites, and so on. . . . If we had mentioned the actual results of the investigation*

first, the reader would have labelled these "obvious" also. Obviously something is wrong with the entire argument of obviousness. It should really be turned on its head. Since every kind of human reaction is conceivable, it is of great importance to know which reactions actually occur most frequently and under what conditions . . . (p. 380)

Lazarsfeld's rhetorical ploy has always impressed me as fairly unsettling for those who make the allegations of obviousness, but its force depends on whether we are willing to grant him his assumption that we accepted the first version of the research results as valid, so that he could then startle us with his second presentation, which gave the true findings: the results that were actually obtained. It might be argued that Lazarsfeld's assumption was unwarranted and that most of us would not have believed that first set of statements that he later revealed were spurious.

The Mischels' Study

So I took notice when I heard about investigations that made no assumptions of the kind that Lazarsfeld's exercise required. The first of these (Mischel, 1981; Mischel & Mischel, 1979) consisted of giving fourth- and sixth-grade children ($Ns = 38$ and 49, respectively) items presenting psychological principles stated in both their actual form and the opposite of the actual forms. For example, the first item dealt with the finding by Solomon Asch that college students would respond contrarily to the evidence of their senses about which of three lines had the same length as a comparison line when the students first heard four other students (confederates of the investigator) misidentify the same-length line. The second item concerned Harry Helson's finding that the same water temperature feels cooler on a hot day than on a cool day. In all, there were 17 such items, some of which were presented to only one of the two grade-level groups. The children circled the one of the two to four choices that they thought described what would happen in each situation.

Of the 29 opportunities for either the fourth graders or the sixth graders to select the actual research result to a statistically significant degree, the groups did so on 19, or 66%. One group or the other was wrong to a statistically significant degree on five opportunities, and there was no statistically significant correctness or incorrectness on 5 opportunities. Clearly, the children had substantial success, but far from the perfect record that would support the allegation of almost universal obviousness.

But these were only children. What about college students and adults? And what happens when the research results are presented as flat statements rather than as multiple-choice items requiring the selection of the actual result from two or more alternatives?

Baratz's Study

Baratz (1983) selected 16 social research findings from various studies, and then did an experiment. She manipulated, for each of the findings, whether the statement concerning that finding was the true finding or the opposite of the true finding. She also presented each finding, either the true one or the opposite one, with or without an explanation of the finding. That second manipulation was intended to "explore the possibility that adding explanations to the findings may render the findings more obvious" (p. 20). Thus, each of her subjects—85 male and female undergraduates enrolled in introductory psychology at Stanford University—evaluated 16 findings: four statements with a true finding plus explanation, four statements with the opposite finding plus explanation, four statements with a true finding without explanation, and four statements of an opposite finding without an explanation. Each finding was presented in the same format: first, the question addressed by the study, such as "a study sought to determine whether people spend a larger proportion of their income during *prosperous* times or during a *recession*." And for this study the reported finding was "In prosperous times people spend a larger proportion of their income than during a recession." The statement of the opposite finding differed from that of the true finding only in the order of the critical terms, and half of the findings were followed at the time by a short explanation, which was presented as the "explanation given by our subject."

Here are two sample pairs of the true and opposite findings used by Baratz in her experiment: "People who go to church regularly tend to have more children than people who go to church infrequently" versus "People who go to church infrequently tend to have more children than people who go to church regularly" and "Single women

express more distress over their unmarried status than single men do" versus "Single men express more distress over their unmarried status than single women do."

For each of the 16 findings presented to each student, the students were asked how readily predictable or obvious the finding was and were instructed to choose one of the responses on the following four-point scale:

1. I am *certain* that I would have predicted the result obtained rather than the opposite result.
2. I *think* that I would have predicted the result obtained rather than the opposite result, but I am *not certain*.
3. I *think* that I would have predicted the opposite to the obtained result, but I am *not certain*.
4. I am *certain* that I would have predicted the *opposite to* the obtained result.

The subjects were asked to express their "initial impressions of the relevant findings, i.e., the kind of impression that you might form if you read a brief article about the research in your daily newspaper" (p. 25).

In a summary table, Baratz presented the mean percentage of subjects who marked either "I am *certain* that I would have predicted the reported outcome" or "I *think* I would have predicted the reported outcome" for pairs of opposite findings. When the reported outcome was "A," 80% of her students claimed they would have predicted that outcome. When the reported outcome was "B," 66% of her subjects claimed they would have predicted that outcome. Thus, as Baratz put it, "It is clear that findings that contradict each other were both retrospectively judged 'obvious'. . . . These results show clearly that reading a result made that result appear obvious. No matter which result was presented, the majority of the subjects thought that they would have predicted it" (p. 26).

I considered Baratz's experiment and her findings to be persuasive. They seemed to provide evidence against the argument that social research yields only obvious findings. Her results indicated that intelligent people, namely, Stanford undergraduates, tend to regard any result they read, whether it is the true one or the opposite of the true one, as obvious. This tendency to say results are obvious was, of course, only a tendency; not all of her subjects followed that tendency, but it was a majority tendency.

Wong's Study

Baratz's research on obviousness dealt with results from a fairly wide range of the social sciences, but I had been focusing on research on teaching and particularly on one area within that field: process-outcome research. That kind of research seeks relationships between classroom processes (what teachers and students do or what goes on in the classroom) and outcomes (what students acquire by way of knowledge, understanding, attitude, appreciation, skill, etc.). Would such research results elicit obvious reactions similar to those obtained by Baratz?

A few years ago, Lily Wong, a Stanford graduate student from Singapore, replicated and extended Baratz's experiments, but with findings from process-outcome research on teaching. Wong chose her respondents from four different categories of persons who differed on the dimension of how much they might be expected to know about classroom teaching. At the low end of that dimension were undergraduates in engineering; next, undergraduates majoring in psychology; next, teacher trainees; and at the high end, experienced teachers. Each of these four groups of respondents was sampled both from Singaporeans and from Americans residing either at Stanford University or in the neighboring area. In total, Wong used 862 Singaporeans and 353 Americans. For the research findings, she used 12 statements based on results of process-outcome research carried out in the elementary grades, results that had been cited in the third edition of the *Handbook of Research on Teaching* (Wittrock, 1986) and in textbooks of educational psychology. Her items came from the results of research by Anderson, Evertson, and Brophy; Brophy and Evertson; Good and Grouws; Soar and Soar; and Stallings and Kaskowitz. Here is the first of her 12 items: "When first-grade teachers work on reading with a small group of children, some attend closely to just the children in the small group, whereas others monitor children's activities throughout the classroom. The class's reading achievement is higher *when teachers monitor the entire classroom*" versus "*. . . when teachers attend to just the children in the small group.*" Here is the second item: "When first-grade teachers work on reading with a small group of children, some call on the children in a fixed order, whereas others call on children in a random order. Reading achievement is higher *when children are called on in a fixed order*" versus "*. . . when children are called on in a random order.*"

Wong had five forms of questionnaires: Form A, Forms B_1 and B_2, and Forms C_1 and C_2. Subjects completing Form A had to select in each item the true finding between two options—one stating an actual finding of research on teaching at the primary-grade level and the other stating the opposite of the actual finding. The subject then rated the chosen statement on a 4-point scale from 1, "extremely obvious" to 4, "extremely unobvious."

Subjects completing Forms B_1 or Form B_2 were required to rate the obviousness of each of 12 single statements presented as actual research findings. In fact, 6 were true findings and 6 were the opposite of true findings. Each of the 24 statements from Form A thus appeared in either Form B_1 or Form B_2.

Form C subjects were given the same purported findings as Form B subjects, but in Form C, each statement was accompanied by a possible explanation. Subjects in Form C had to rate not only the obviousness of the findings but also the clarity of the explanations.

Wong's results on Form A showed that her respondents chose both actual findings and opposite findings. On 4 of the 12 items, her subjects chose the actual finding more often (see p. 37), but on the other 8, they chose the false finding more often. The r between percentage choosing a finding and the mean obviousness rating of the finding was .66. The respondents to Forms B and C rated about half of the opposite findings as obvious. Wong concluded that

> *Judging by the smaller proportions of respondents choosing the actual findings as the real findings, and the mean rating of obviousness on the presented (both actual and opposite) finding statements, we can say reasonably that people can not distinguish true findings from their opposites. (p. 86)*

The Singaporeans rated most of the items as more obvious than the American subjects did in all conditions. There were few gender differences in the average responses to the various forms. Teachers were no more accurate, on the average, than the other groups in the selection of true findings: "In the rating of obviousness of items, knowledge and experience [in teaching] were found to have some significant effect on several items. This does not mean that teachers and trainees rated true findings more obvious or opposite findings less obvious than the psychology undergraduates and the engineering undergraduates" (Wong, 1987, p. 87).

Wong concluded that her results "clearly confirmed the idea that knowledge of outcome increases the feeling of obviousness. Thus, when people claim to have known it all along when an event is reported to them, their claim is often not warranted" (p. 88).

WHERE THE ISSUE STANDS

From the work of Baratz and Wong we can conclude that the feeling that a research result is obvious is untrustworthy. People tend to regard as obvious almost any reasonable statement made about human behavior. A recent example comes from the *Arizona Daily Star* of March 8, 1988, in an article about the booklet entitled *What Works*, compiled by the U.S. Department of Education. The booklet contains brief discussions, with references to the research, of 41 research findings considered potentially helpful to schools and teachers. The headline read, "Restating the Obvious."

My most recent example comes from the June 1990 issue of *The Atlantic* (Murphy, 1990): "A recent survey (by me) of recent social-science findings . . . turned up no ideas or conclusions that can't be found in Bartlett's or any other encyclopedia of quotations" (p. 22).

As suggested by an anonymous referee for this article, the results of Baratz and Wong are consistent with the conclusions of Nisbett and Wilson (1977): "[T]here may be little or no direct introspective access to higher order cognitive processes" (p. 231). Thus the cognitive processes that lead one to regard a research result as obvious are probably nonveridical unless, as Ericsson and Simon (1980) argued, the response is based on (a) short-term memory leading to verbalization of information that (b) would have been attended to even without the instructions given. It is questionable whether judging the obviousness of research results always meets these requirements.

The same reviewer also suggested that these results do not belie the fact that most adults' generalizations about human interactions are at least functional. I agree; otherwise human society would be impossible.

Another issue arose in a conversation between Robert D. Hess and me. Upon being apprised of

judges' tendency to regard as obvious both actual research results and their opposites, Hess asked about the frequency with which the results had been confirmed through replications. His question calls for research in which the "obviousness" of research results frequently confirmed with high consistency would be compared with that of research relationships frequently studied with results of only low consistency. Examples of both high-consistency and low-consistency results can be found in the synthesis of results of research on teaching by Walberg (1986). His Table 7.2 (pp. 218–219) contains results whose "percentage positive" across replications ranges from very low (where 50% is completely inconsistent) to very high (where 0% and 100% are completely consistent).

An investigator could administer questionnaires similar to those of Baratz (1983) and Wong (1987), but using items representing both (a) frequently studied with highly consistent results and (b) frequently studied with highly inconsistent results. It would then be possible to determine the difference, if any, in the mean obviousness rating of these two types of research results. It may turn out that only items of Type b would be rated obvious in both their actual and opposite forms. A frequently replicated and highly consistent result—for example, the "result" that auto drivers in England stay to the left side of the road whereas auto drivers in the United States stay to the right side of the road—will almost certainly be rated highly obvious in its actual form and highly nonobvious in its opposite form. Here the requisite knowledge is widely possessed, and the "obvious" reaction will not occur. Much depends on the relationship between the content of the research result and the background knowledge of the judge of the result's obviousness. Both Baratz and Wong may have studied results whose relationship to their judges' background knowledge was tenuous. Even Wong's experienced teachers, who probably had never thought about or encountered the phenomena dealt with in the research results used by Wong, had too little background knowledge to be able to detect the nonobviousness of the opposite-to-actual results.

Thus, the obvious reaction may be hypothesized to occur only when the judge's background knowledge in relation to the judged research result is weak. If the hypothesis is borne out, the question might be raised, How does a representative sample of social and educational research results fare, as to their obviousness in actual and opposite forms, when presented to a representative sample of the persons who might be expected to encounter or be concerned with those results? That is, research on obviousness now needs to be aimed at maximal external validity, or the degree to which the obviousness research is relevant to real life.

The issue joined by Schlesinger when he attacked students of human affairs who use scientific methods has its roots in the old controversy that C.P. Snow (1964) examined later in *The Two Cultures: And a Second Look.* Snow was concerned with the mutual disregard and disrespect of natural scientists and scholars in the humanities. Snow regretted this condition, but it still exists. Schlesinger's denunciation of social research reflected what Karl Popper called the antinaturalist position: the position that the scientific method useful for studying the natural world is inappropriate for the study of human affairs. The response of Paul Lazarsfeld reflects the position, held by Karl Popper and many others, that scientific method is appropriate for the study of human affairs.

Scientific method need not be used, in my opinion, only for the construction of a social science—where such a science is defined as a network of laws that will hold over whole eras and in many different cultural contexts, just as the laws of mechanics hold in different historical periods and in contexts as different as planetary motion and the motion of a pendulum. Rather, scientific method can be used for what Popper called "piecemeal social engineering," a more modest enterprise aimed at improving human affairs by applying scientific methods to the development and evaluation of new "treatments"—in education, in social welfare projects, or in fighting against drugs.

I have speculated (Gage, 1989) that people gravitate toward one or the other of Snow's two cultures—toward science (natural or social) or toward humanistic insight and sensibility—because their upbringing and intellectual experience have inclined them toward one or the other. The wars between the several paradigms in social and educational research may result from temperamentally different (i.e., not entirely rational) intellectual predilections, often developed during the secondary school years. If so, improved education may someday produce scholars and educational researchers who experience no conflict between their scientific and humanistic orientations.

In any case, the allegation of obviousness may now be countered with the research result that people tend to regard even contradictory research results as obvious. Perhaps even that result will henceforth be regarded as obvious.

Note
This article is based in part on the Maycie K. Southall lecture at George Peabody College, Vanderbilt University, on February 27, 1990.

I am grateful to my daughter, Sarah Gage, for calling the Murphy (1990) article to my attention.

REFERENCES

Baratz, D. (1983). How justified is the "obvious" reaction. *Dissertation Abstracts International, 44/02B,* 644B. (University Microfilms No. DA 8314435.)

Conant, J. B. (1963). *The education of American teachers.* New York: McGraw-Hill.

Ericsson, K. A., & Simon, H. A. (1980). Verbal reports as data. *Psychological Review, 87,* 215–251.

Gage, N. L. (1989). The paradigm wars and their aftermath: A "historical" sketch of research on teaching since 1989. *Teachers College Record, 91,* 135–150.

Glass, G. V. (1987). Class size. In M. J. Dunkin (Ed.), *The international encyclopedia of teaching and teacher education* (pp. 540.-545). Oxford: Pergamon.

Goodlad, J. I. (1960). Classroom organization. In C. W. Harris (Ed.), *Encyclopedia of education research* (3rd ed., p. 224). New York: Macmillan.

Keppel, F. (1962). The education of teachers. In H. Chauncey (Ed.), *Talks on American education: A series of broadcasts to foreign audiences by American scholars* (pp. 83–94). New York: Bureau of Publications, Teachers College, Columbia University.

Lazarsfeld, P. F. (1949). *The American soldier—an expository review. Public Opinion Quarterly, 13,* 377–404.

Mischel, W. (1981). Metacognition and the rules of delay. In J. H. Flavell & L. Ross (Eds.), *Social cognitive development: Frontiers and possible futures.* New York: Cambridge University Press.

Mischel, W., & Mischel, H. (1979). *Children's knowledge of psychological principles.* Unpublished manuscript.

Murphy, C. (1990). New findings: Hold on to your hat. *The Atlantic, 265*(6), 22–23.

Nisbett, R. E., & Wilson, T. D. (1977). Telling more than we can know: Verbal reports on mental processes. *Psychological Review, 84,* 231–259.

Phillips, D. C. (1985) The uses and abuses of truisms. In C. W. Fisher & D. C. Berliner (Eds.), *Perspectives on instructional time* (pp. 309–316). New York: Longman.

Rice, J. M. (1913). *Scientific management in education.* New York: Hinds, Noble & Eldredge. (Original work published 1897)

Schlesinger, Jr., A. (1949). The statistical soldier. *Partisan Review, 16,* 852–856.

Snow, C. P. (1964). *The two cultures: And a second look.* New York: Cambridge University Press.

Walberg, H. J. (1986). Syntheses of research on teaching. In M. C. Wittrock (Ed.), *Handbook of research on teaching* (3rd ed., pp. 214–229). New York: Macmillan.

Wittrock, M. C. (Ed.). (1986). *Handbook of research on teaching* (3rd ed.). New York: Macmillan.

Wong, L. (1987). Reaction to research findings: Is the feeling of obviousness warranted? *Dissertation Abstracts International, 48112,* 3709B. (University Microfilms No. DA 8801059.)

A Process for Personal Theory Building

JOELLEN P. KILLION and GUY R. TODNEM

"Reflection has become such a buzzword, Is it the 'in' thing to do, or what?" The teacher's comments sounded like an accusation. She went on, "What's the deal? Doesn't everyone do it?"

But, after she had participated in our workshop, "Inside Out: A Process of Personal Theory Building," this same teacher surprised us when she apologized about her initial comments. She said that, to her, *reflection* had meant a brief mental replay of a series of events and that she did not often reflect deeply. Reflection, she now realized, was a rich source of continued personal and professional growth.

Busy people typically do not engage in reflection. They rarely treat themselves to reflective experiences, unless they are given some time, some structure, and the expectations to do so.

As professionals, we owe ourselves this opportunity for renewal and revival. Reflection is a gift we give ourselves, not passive thought that lolls aimlessly in our minds, but an effort we must approach with rigor, with some purpose in mind, and in some formal way, so as to reveal the wisdom embedded in our experience. Through reflection, we develop context-specific theories that further our own understanding of our work and generate knowledge to inform future practice.

Joellen P. Killion is Staff Development Specialist, Adams 12, Five-Star Schools, Staff Development Training Center, 601 W. 100th Place, Northglenn, CO 80221. Guy R. Todnem is Staff Development Specialist, Du-Page-Cane Educational Service Center, 421 North County Farm Road, Wheaton, IL 60187.

What follows is a description of three types of reflection and the formal process we use to engage workshop participants in reflection.

THREE TYPES OF REFLECTION

Reflection is the practice or act of analyzing our actions, decisions, or products by focusing on our process of achieving them. In his books, *The Reflective Practitioner and Educating the Reflective Practitioner*, Donald Schon describes two types of reflection. *Reflection-on-action* is reflection on practice and on one's actions and thoughts, undertaken after the practice is completed. *Reflection-in-action is* reflection on phenomena and on one's spontaneous ways of thinking and acting in the midst of action.

A third type of reflection, *reflection-for-action*, is the desired outcome of both previous types of reflection. We undertake reflection, not so much to revisit the past or to become aware of the metacognitive process one is experiencing (both noble reasons in themselves), but to guide future action (the more practical purpose). Reflection, then, is a process that encompasses all time designations, past, present, and future simultaneously. Education is not a hard science, so we need to engage in continued knowledge development to further our understanding of classroom events (Cogan 1973, Garman 1986). While examining our past actions and our present actions, we generate knowledge that will inform our future actions, as shown in Figure 1.

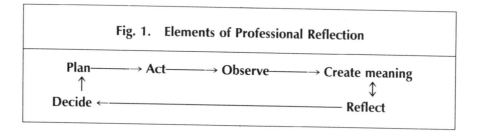

Fig. 1.   **Elements of Professional Reflection**

Plan ──────→ Act ──────→ Observe ──────→ Create meaning

Decide ←──────────────────────────────── Reflect

This model, adapted from Wildman and associates (1987), depicts the steps of knowledge generation for future action. First a teacher plans to act. Then through reflection-in-action, the teacher observes the action as it transpires, almost as if placing herself outside the action itself. From this perspective, the teacher creates meaning, in understanding the dynamics of the cause/effect relationship that occurs between her actions and the students' responses to her behaviors. Engaging in reflection-on-action and reflection-or-action, the teacher analyzes events and draws conclusions that give her insight into future decision points.

It's like this: picture a tank tread that slowly rolls along. To move the tank forward, the tread that carries it continually reverses itself while at the same time the tank makes slow, steady forward progress. This is how reflection works. In order to tap the rich potential of our past to inform our judgment, we move backward, reflect on our experiences, then face each new encounter with a broader repertoire of context-specific information, skills, and techniques.

"PHOTOS" OF OUR WORK

In our 6–10 hour workshops, we provide educators with a structured process for reflection-on-action and reflection-for-action. Drawing on the work of David Hunt (1987), we ask participants to describe their work, develop an understanding of certain patterns in their behaviors, establish cause/effect relationships between their actions and the outcomes they experience, and begin to develop a rationale for their work.

Following the procedure we adapted from Hunt, we ask participants to complete a chart that includes three components: characteristics, outcomes, and strategies (see fig. 2). Asking partici-

Fig. 2.   **"Photo Album" of a Teacher**

CHARACTERISTICS	OUTCOMES	STRATEGIES
Shy, reticent to talk	Protect	Permit student to work alone.
		Allow student to not participate.
Withdrawn, quiet, loner	Protect	Allow student to work independently.

Common themes: Quiet, nonparticipating students.
Common goals: Protect, shelter.
Common tactics: Permit isolation and noninvolvement.
Redirected plan: Engage student in small groups which are self-selected.
Pair student with friend or teacher.
Help student develop appropriate social skills.

pants to describe their clients' characteristics, the outcomes they bring about for those clients, and the strategies they use to achieve those outcomes creates a photo album of their actions. Teachers focus on their students, principals on their staffs, and staff developers on members of their training sessions.

For example, one teacher identified students whose characteristics were *shyness, reticence to talk in class,* and *withdrawn behavior.* In describing the outcome for these students, the teacher realized he wanted to *protect* this type of student. His strategies were to allow these students to be passive and withdrawn, not to ask them to answer questions in front of the class, and to allow them to work independently when the rest of the class gathered in small groups.

In discussing the situation with a colleague, he was able to compare his outcome and strategies with those of the other teacher with a similar student. He discovered that he was actually enabling the shy students *not* to function successfully. Once this picture was developed, the teacher began to ask himself questions about other possible outcomes for these students and other strategies he might try. He then became free to modify, expand, extend, or abandon his actions to achieve a different outcome.

To use another example (see fig. 3), a principal identified the characteristics of *excessive lecturing, poor physical atmosphere in the classroom,* and *no evidence of lesson planning* as characteristics to describe her teacher clients. Her desired outcomes for these teachers' classes were *more student participation, more displays of student work,* and *complete lesson plans and unit outlines.* The strategies she had used to try to achieve these outcomes had been to show the teachers a *videotape* of an effective class, provide a *resource book on bulletin boards,* and send the teachers to a *workshop on effective teaching strategies.*

This principal discovered that she was impatient with the poor instructional and organizational skills of these teachers and that she wanted to make them use the school district's model of effective instruction. Further, she realized that her strategies were impersonal, focused outside the school, and that they placed the burden for change solely on the teachers, and thus were unlikely to produce any real change in teachers' behavior. After talking with other principals and closely examining these pictures in her photo album, the principal reframed her understanding of the problem, realizing she needed to provide support and assistance to guide the teachers through the needed changes.

Fig. 3.   Principal Reflection-for-Action Chart

CHARACTERISTICS	OUTCOMES	STRATEGIES
Excessive lecturing	More student participation	Offer videotape.
Poor physical atmosphere in classroom	More display of of student work	Offer book of bulletin board ideas.
No evidence of planning	Complete lesson plans or unit outcomes	Send to workshop on teaching strategies.

Common themes: Teacher instructional and organizational skills.
Common goals: Use more of the district's model of effective teaching.
Common tactics: Offer ideas outside the school building, school staff, and district resources.

A COMMUNITY OF INQUIRERS

The participants in our program usually gain insights that help them individually and that help their students. As one teacher said, "Reflection offers me a phenomenal self-confidence, unity of purpose, and sense of direction in my teaching role. Now I want my students to become reflective thinkers."

Beyond improving our teaching, reflection can alter our common perspective of education and elevate our work to the status of a profession. We can do that only by accepting the challenge to participate in a community of inquirers and scholars who have the responsibility to contribute to a specialized body of knowledge (Cogan 1953).

REFERENCES

Cogan, M. (1973). *Clinical Supervision.* Boston: Houghton-Mifflin.

Cogan, M. (1953). "Toward a Definition of Profession." *Harvard Educational Review* 23: 33–50.

Garman, N. (Fall, 1986). "Reflection, the Heart of Clinical Supervision: A Modern Rationale for Professional Practice." *Journal of Curriculum and Supervision* 2,1: 1–24.

Hunt, D. (1987). *Beginning with Ourselves.* Cambridge, Mass.: Brookline Books.

Schon, D. (1987). *Educating the Reflective Practitioner.* San Francisco: Jossey-Bass.

Schon, D. (1973). *The Reflective Practitioner.* New York: Basic Books.

Wildman, T., J. Niles, R. McLaughlin, and S. Magliaro. (1987). *Teachers Learning from Teachers: A Mentor's Guide for Supporting Beginning Teachers.* Blacksburg, Va.: College of Education, Virginia Tech.

Synthesis of Research on Teachers' Reflective Thinking

GEORGEA MOHLMAN SPARKS-LANGER and AMY BERSTEIN COLTON

Reflective thinking is not a new idea—Dewey (1933) referred to it in his early works—but only a handful of researchers and practitioners were using the term until Schon (1983, 1987) began to write about reflective practice in education and other professions. Now, those who have always believed in the importance of the critical and analytical thinking of teachers are rallying around the idea.

This shift toward an interest in reflective thinking has come about partly as a reason to the overly technical and simplistic view of teaching that dominated the 1980s. Gradually, however, experts in supervision, staff development, and teacher education have begun to recognize that teaching is a complex, situation-specific, and dilemma-ridden endeavor. Recently they have begun to study teachers' values and philosophies in the face of their everyday dilemmas. Today, professional knowledge is seen as coming both from sources outside the teacher and from the teachers' own interpretations of their everyday experiences.

It is difficult to pin down the exact meaning of the term *reflection*. Most who use the term would probably agree that the opposite of reflective action is the mindless following of unexamined practices or principles. But within that agreement, there is quite a range of opinion regarding what reflection is and what it looks like in action.

Georgea Mohlman Sparks-Langer is Associate Professor of Teacher Education, Eastern Michigan University, College of Education, 234 Boone Hall, Ypsilanti, MI 48197. Amy Berstein Colton is Staff Development Consultant. Ann Arbor Schools Adjunct Faculty, Eastern Michigan University, Ypsilanti. 48197.

This article presents three elements that are important in teachers' reflective thinking. The first is the cognitive element, which describes how teachers process information and make decisions. The second, the critical element, focuses on the substance that drives the thinking—experiences, goals, values, and social implications. The final element of reflection, teachers' narratives, refers to teachers' own interpretations of the events that occur within their particular contexts.

THE COGNITIVE ELEMENT OF REFLECTION

The cognitive part of teacher reflection focuses on how teachers use knowledge in their planning and decision making. Shulman (1987) has described six categories of knowledge: (1) content/subject-matter knowledge; (2) pedagogical methods and theory; (3) curriculum; (4) characteristics of learners; (5) teaching contexts; and (6) educational purposes, ends, and aims. Shulman's idea of "pedagogical content knowledge," which encompasses the first three categories, refers to how teachers portray important ideas specific to their content. These representations (or metaphors) enable the teacher to convey complex ideas in ways that bring meaning to students.

Most cognitive researchers have not delved deeply into how teachers think about the last two categories of the knowledge base: teaching contexts and educational purposes, ends, and aims. They usually stick with what Van Manen (1977) calls the *technical* level of reflection, where the ethical and moral purposes of education remain unexamined.

Another focus of cognitive research is how the knowledge base is organized. One current model depicts information as organized into a network of related facts, concepts, generalizations, and experiences. These organized structures, called *schemata*, constitute the individual's comprehension of the world and allow a large body of information to be stored and accessed very rapidly (Anderson 1984, Berliner 1986). Comparisons of novice and expert teachers' interpretations of classroom events indicate that experts have deeper, richly connected schemata to draw upon when making a decision. In contrast, novices tend to have leaner, less developed schemata, presumably because of lack of experience (Leinhardt and Greeno 1986).

For example, Carter and her colleagues (1988) studied how experts, novices, and aspiring teachers perceive visual information about classrooms. She observed that experts were "better able to weigh the import of one piece of visual information against another, to form connections among pieces of information, and to represent management and instructional situations into meaningful problem units" (p. 25). This ability was attributed to the more elaborate, complex, and interconnected schemata of the experts. These schemata first help determine which events merit attention and, second, trigger other relevant information from memory so the teacher can determine an appropriate response.

A key factor in the thinking of experts appears to be "automaticity." Certain routines (sequences of responses) are automatically stimulated by a situation and put into action with little conscious attention by the teacher. This enables the teacher to perform some behaviors unconsciously while attending to those events that are more novel or important (Carter et al. 1988). These automatic scripts for action are probably stored as schemata.

Borko and Livingston (1989) compared the planning, teaching, and post-lesson reflections of novice and expert teachers in their program at the University of Maryland. During the act of teaching, the novices encountered problems when attempts to be responsive to students led them away from scripted lesson plans. They appeared unable to hook back into their schema for the lesson and had to re-create a meaningful plan on the spot—an unnerving process when more than 20 students are waiting expectantly for the teacher to "get his act together." In contrast to the novices, experts were able to improvise quite naturally from sketchy plans, probably because (1) many of the routines and the content were available in memory as automatic scripts and (2) their rich schemata allowed the experts to quickly consider cues in the environment and access appropriate strategies.

Schemata do not automatically appear in a teacher's mind; they are constructed through experience. Constructivist theory (Greeno et al. 1979) indicates that individuals are constantly creating their own meaning out of what is perceived. This is a dual process of assimilation (fitting the new in with the old) and accommodation (changing the old mental organization to incorporate the new) (Piaget 1978). Therefore, the experiences, values, and beliefs stored in memory certainly have influence on how a new piece of information is perceived and interpreted. Such "culturally based filters" have been investigated by Hollingsworth (1990) and others (Ross 1990), with the result that teacher educators are now giving more attention to how preconceptions about the aims of education can influence what college students do (and do not!) learn from teacher education programs.

Lampert and Clark (1990) believe schema theory may give too little importance to context factors. They refer to "situated cognition," which suggests that knowledge is constructed through interaction between the mind and the context surrounding the problem. Thus, rather than apply a generalized schema (learned rules, principles, or concepts) to a problem, teachers may make a case-by-case response to the particulars of a problem. If this is accurate, then greater opportunities need to be provided for future teachers to "anchor" their knowledge and experience in rich educational contexts.

A third topic investigated by cognitive researchers is teachers' metacognition—self-regulated, purpose-driven behavior. The reflective teacher monitors the effect of an action taken as well as the cognitive processes employed to make decisions. These cognitive processes involve making inferences, or tentative hypotheses. Dewey (1933) observed wisely that it is not our belief in inferences that misleads us, but our belief in *untested* inferences. Upon encountering a novel situation, a teacher attends to it, makes inferences, and then mentally tests them by looking for similarities and differences apparent in this situation and comparing them with events and ideas (schemata) stored in memory. Expert/novice studies by Leinhardt and Greeno (1986) indicate that experts engage in such self-regulated, purpose-driven behavior more than do novices.

Research on Promoting Cognitive Reflection

The studies summarized above contrasted novices with experts. More recent studies purport simply to identify teacher education activities that promote reflective thought. One example is CITE (Collaboration for the Improvement of Teacher Education), part of a four-year undergraduate program at Eastern Michigan University (EMU) (Sparks-Langer et al. 1990). Structured field experiences, micro-teaching, one week of classroom teaching, journals, and writing assignments help prestudent-teachers analyze, question, and reflect on the issues presented in courses. Professors model reflective questioning and discourse through textbook selections,[1] teaching methods, and class assignments.

The evaluations of CITE have produced a framework for assessing the reflective thinking displayed during a short interview about a recent teaching event (Simmons et al. 1989). The framework has seven levels: (1) no description; (2) simple, lay person description; (3) labeling of events with pedagogical concepts; (4) explanation using only tradition or personal preference; (5) explanation using pedagogical principles; (6) explanation using pedagogical principles and context; and (7) explanation with ethical/moral considerations. The progression of levels shows a growing sophistication in teachers' schemata, from technical concepts and rules to contextual and ethical thinking.

In the studies reported below, the research team coded transcripts of all interviews and achieved satisfactory reliability. Of the 16 *average* and *above average* (rating made by professors) CITE students studied at the end of the program, 10 were functioning at level 6, contextual thinking. Of the eight *below average* students, only one was able to function at this level.

In another study of CITE, Grinberg (1989) contrasted a class of CITE students with a similar group not enrolled in CITE. While both groups were initially equal on the reflective thinking scores and other factors the CITE students subsequently achieved significantly higher ratings on their reflective thinking. The courses with guided field experiences apparently promoted greater reflection than did the courses without the field experiences.

In a study of the reflective thinking produced by an inservice program, Pasch and his colleagues (1990) used the CITE framework to evaluate teachers who were studying the ideas of Madeline Hunter. Interviews were conducted before training, after training but before coaching, and after both training *and* coaching. There was no difference between the pre-training and post-training reflective thinking scores; after coaching, however, these scores rose significantly, with a mean score of 5.1 (explanation using pedagogical principles). Thus, coaching may help to promote reflection.

Morine-Dershimer (1989) examined the development of knowledge about teaching associated with a secondary-level methods course that included extensive micro-teaching. At the beginning and the end of the course, students were asked to construct concept maps representing their views of teacher planning. There was a strong increase in the number of main categories used in the maps and a slight increase in the number of levels of subordinate concepts used in the main categories. Thus, the course activities seemed effective in developing richer conceptual networks (schemata), more like those of experts.

Finally, Hollingsworth (1990) conducted a longitudinal study to investigate changes in the knowledge and beliefs of 10 teachers about reading instruction before, during, and after a fifth-year teacher education program. She hoped that the program would help teachers shift attention away from technical concerns with student activities and toward a greater interest in student learning. She found little change until the second or third year of teaching, which, she believes, is when the scripts for the everyday management and activities became automatic, allowing the teachers to focus on student outcomes.

Summary of Research on Cognitive Reflection

One conclusion drawn from the cognitive research is that we should teach novices the schemata of experts. But acting on this conclusion could subvert the lessons learned from constructivism (each of us

---

[1]The textbook, *Teaching as Decision Making*, was written by five faculty in the CITE program at EMU, Pasch, Sparks-Langer, Gardner, Starko, and Moody. It promotes a practical, reflective orientation to methods of teaching and is published by Longman.

must construct our own meaning) and from "situated cognition" (expert teachers probably draw on their own contextually developed knowledge and prior case-experience to develop their own wisdom of practice.) It would also, perhaps, short-circuit the development of professional self-regulated judgement. Research can inform us about how complex and uncertain teaching is, but it "cannot describe the sorts of decisions teachers should be taught to make in any particular situation" (Lampert and Clark 1990, p. 29).

THE CRITICAL ELEMENT OF REFLECTION

While the cognitive element of reflection emphasizes how teachers make decisions, the critical approach stresses the substance that drives the thinking—the experiences, beliefs, sociopolitical values, and goals of teachers. Critical reflection is often contrasted with what Van Manen (1977) refers to as technical reflection, where the teacher considers the best means to reach an unexamined end. For example, a teacher may choose a particular room arrangement to maintain control, without consideration of the other possible effects. In critical reflection, the moral and ethical aspects of social compassion are considered along with the means and the ends. For instance, the teacher may choose a seating arrangement that facilitates cooperative learning in the hope of fostering a more equitable, accepting society.

To understand critical reflection, it is important to look at two orientations to reflective thinking, Schon's concept of reflective action (1983, 1987) and critical theory (McLaren 1989, Tom 1985). Both have highlighted the importance of teachers' thinking about the dilemmas of teaching and the social outcomes of education.

Schon (1983) first analyzed the work of architects and other professionals to see how they reflected on their actions. Surprisingly, he found little emphasis on traditional problem solving. Instead of using a rational process of selecting the best solution for an agreed-upon goal, these professionals engaged in an open debate about the nature of the decisions, the value of the goals, and the ultimate implications of the actions. Schon referred to this reflective dialog as *problem setting*. Among teachers (and others) he also found artistic comfort with ambiguity, no-one-right-answer thinking, and recogni-

tion of the nonlinear, uncertain complexity of professional practice.

Schon (1987) believes that while teachers acquire some professional knowledge from "packaged" educational principles and skills, the bulk of their learning comes through continuous action and reflection on everyday problems. Further, he contends that the information gained from this experience is often tacit and difficult to analyze. Schon does not refer to a cognitive knowledge base for teaching; rather, he refers to an "appreciation system." This system contains the teacher's repertoire of theories, practices, knowledge, and values, which influence how situations are defined, what is noticed, and the kinds of questions and decisions teachers will form about particular actions.

Many who use the term *teacher reflection* (for example, Smyth 1989) think of it in terms of critical theory. McLaren (1989) observed that "critical pedagogy attempts to provide teachers and researchers with a better means of understanding the role that schools actually play within a race-, class-, and gender-divided society" (p. 163). When teacher educators help teachers examine the issues of ethics, morals, and justice in education, they are opening up discourse about the role of schools in a democratic society. Teachers then begin to question common practices such as tracking, ability grouping, competitive grading, and behavioral control. They begin to clarify their own beliefs about the purposes of education and to critically examine teaching methods and materials to look for the hidden lessons about equity and power that might lie therein. We see in critical pedagogy, as in Schon's work, a reaction against an antiseptic, value-free, purely rational view of teaching and learning.

Critical theorists see knowledge as socially constructed, that is, constructed symbolically by the mind through social interaction with others. This knowledge is determined by the surrounding culture, context, customs, and historical era (McLaren 1989). In contrast to cognitive constructivism, this approach places more importance on life values and morals, for example, concepts of justice, ideas about the purpose of the individual in a democracy, ethics related to the treatment of students, and so on. All of these are heavily dependent on the social milieu in which the teacher develops.

What are the thinking processes of a critical reflective practitioner? To (over)simplify, as teachers describe, analyze, and make inferences about classroom events, they are creating their own pedagogical principles. These "short-range theories" (Smyth 1989) help make sense of what is going on and guide further action. Ross (1990) has extended the ideas of Schon, Van Manen, and others into five components of reflective thinking: (1) recognizing an educational dilemma, (2) responding to a dilemma by recognizing both the similarities to other situations and the special qualities of the particular situation, (3) framing and reframing the dilemma, (4) experimenting with the dilemma to discover the consequences and implications of various solutions, (5) examining the intended and unintended consequences of an implemented solution and evaluating the solution by determining whether the consequences are desirable or not (p. 22).

The first three of these items echo Schon's process of problem framing. The fourth and fifth bring us to a key thinking process in critical pedagogy (McLaren 1989)—the examination of the relationship between power and knowledge. Knowledge should be examined "for the way it misrepresents or marginalizes particular views of the world" (p. 183). That is, many accepted explanations are biased in favor of the group in power at the time when the ideas were formed. Teachers, then, need to convey the concept of teaching and learning as a process of inquiry into the problematic by asking questions such as *If we use this process or content, what is the long-term effect on students' values, and thus on society?* Through such questions emerges a "language of hope" for bringing about greater social equity.

Research on Promoting Critical Reflection

Teacher education programs at universities are addressing the goal of critical reflection (only a few will be summarized here). Most program designers have found that it is relatively easy to promote technical and practical reflection and more difficult to achieve critical reflection. Ross (1989) evaluated the effects of a course in Research on Elementary Education as part of a five-year teacher preparation program (PROTEACH). The professor fostered reflection by helping students examine their own socially constructed beliefs about schools and teaching. For example, she required action research projects and 'theory-to-practice' papers from students. She also used research-based teaching techniques and critical discussions of students' learning from those methods.

To assess students' thinking, Ross assigned each of 134 theory-to-practice papers a level of reflection, from 1 (low: description with little analysis of context or multiple perspectives) to 3 (high: multiple perspectives with recognition of pervasive impact of teachers' actions). Most papers were rated 1 or 2. Ross interpreted these findings in a developmental light: "perhaps, even though students demonstrated a low or moderate level of reflection, the development of this knowledge is essential for future reflection" (p. 29).

After several studies of the PROTEACH program, Ross and her colleagues (in press) believe that "change in perspective" is the basis of the development of reflective practice. Future teachers are led to construct their own perspectives by drawing on their past and present personal and professional experiences in schools; theoretical knowledge base; self-image and efficacy; and their interactions with peers, mentors, supervisors, and children in school. Such multidimensional perspectives are probably built gradually through extensive reflective dialogs that help teachers comprehend both the immediate and the long-term ethical and moral aspects of their work.

In the CITE evaluation studies referred to earlier (Sparks-Langer et al. 1990), most students were using principles and contextual clues to make sense of their experiences. Yet, few students displayed level-7 (ethical/moral) thinking, probably because at that point, the program did not have a coherent, critical-theorist orientation in the social foundations courses. (As the critical perspective has been integrated more thoroughly, we are beginning to see more evidence of such thinking in our students.)

At Catholic University, Ciriello, Valli, and Taylor (in press) have designed a teacher preparation program around the concept of critical reflection. The program includes professors' modeling their own thinking processes, students' self-critiques of assignments, action research, and journal writing. Students' responses to questionnaires indicated that action research helped them to value both the context of teaching and systematic thinking about complex phenomena. Further, students expanded their vision of teaching to include moral responsibility and the need to challenge taken-for-granted practices.

Summary of Research on
Critical Reflection

The programs studied have been quite successful in identifying methods that promote technical reflection about methods, principles, outcomes, and contexts for pupil learning. They have had limited success in promoting critical reflection. However, they have contributed much by proposing frameworks that describe types of reflective thinking (for example, Ross 1990, Sparks-Langer et al. 1990) and through providing several techniques for developing reflective thought. These techniques include structured journal writing, critical dialog, examination of multiple perspectives, field experiences, and action research. In spite of this progress, we are not completely clear on how one best promotes or assesses teacher reflection about political, ethical, and moral values, beliefs, and attitudes.

Another difficulty in studying the development of critical reflection arises from the mismatch of research paradigms. Concrete cognitive models have often been used to assess what is essentially a dilemma-ridden, uncertain, changeable thing—teachers' thinking. We at EMU have concluded that our level-7 (ethical/moral) thinking is not necessarily an endpoint on a continuum but rather a separate phenomenon that must be studied with in-depth qualitative and interpretive methods. The next approach to reflection—teachers' narratives—illustrates this view.

TEACHERS' NARRATIVES:
THE THIRD ELEMENT
OF REFLECTION

Cochran-Smith and Lytle (1990), writing about teacher research, contended, "what is missing from the knowledge base of teaching, therefore, are the voices of the teachers themselves, the questions teachers ask, the ways teachers use writing and intentional talk in their work lives, and the interpretive frames teachers use to understand and improve their own classroom practices" (p. 2). This is the essence of the narrative part of reflection. While a teacher's narrative may include cognitive or critical aspects, the emphasis is on the teacher's own interpretations of the *context* in which professional decisions are made. Such narratives can be a powerful

force in heightening teachers' awareness of their own professional reasoning.

Many terms and concepts are joined together in this view of reflection: case studies of the tacit wisdom that guides practice (Shulman 1987), the inclusion of craft knowledge in teacher assessment practices (Leinhardt 1990), the legitimacy of viewing teaching as art (Eisner 1982, Kagan 1988), defining teaching as improvisational performance (Yinger 1987), teacher action research (Cochran-Smith and Lytle 1990), and the appearance of qualitative studies using narrative inquiry (Connelly and Clandinin 1990). The common thread through all these is the emphasis on the validity of teachers' judgments drawn from their own experiences. This view is sympathetic with Schon's notion of "giving reason" because it is the teachers themselves whose voices comprise the story.

Here we describe in greater detail only two of the many ideas listed above: narrative stories and the artistic/aesthetic view of teaching. Connelly and Clandinin (1990) suggest that humans are essentially storytelling organisms. Thus, stories written by and about teachers form the basis of narrative inquiry. The participants in such inquiry construct and reconstruct narrative plots to gain a deeper understanding of their experience. In this view, therefore, the process of reflective thinking is seen is narratives or stories, with settings, plots, and characters.

Kagan (1988), writing from the artistic/aesthetic tradition, concludes that the cognitive-schemata model of teachers' thinking is so patterned, sensitive to environment, and flexible that teaching could be easily viewed as an act of artistic composition. She cites Eisner's (1982) reminder that the term *context* comes from the Latin *contexere*, to weave together. Thus, as a teacher works through the hierarchical planning net, a weaving together of meaning is created. This view of teaching as artistry echoes Yinger's (1987) notion of reaching as improvisational performance. A teacher may begin with broad guidelines for a lesson, but the actual teaching moves are artfully improvised in response to the students and the context.

Research on Promoting
Narrative Reflection

A common theme in the narrative element of reflection is the emphasis on *naturalistic* studies. In contrast to experimental and quantitative studies that manipulate factors in order to produce generalizations, naturalistic studies explore the meanings and interpretations teachers give to their everyday lives. As educational researchers recognize the complexity of teaching and of learning to teach, more and more studies are turning to such qualitative methods.

Action research (Elliott 1985) can be a powerful vehicle for encouraging teachers to tell their own stories. In such research, a teacher identifies questions, plans actions, and collects information about the phenomenon under study. An example of this approach is Lampert's (1990) three-year study of her own teaching of 5th grade math. Her goal was to "make knowing mathematics in the classroom more like knowing mathematics in the discipline" (p. 59). Lampert presented her research "in terms of a story about learning and knowing mathematics in the social setting of the classroom" (p. 33). Her study of her own teaching and her students' learning prompted her to conclude that, though her students met her goals, there was still much to learn.

Another example of action research is provided by Colton and others (1989). As part of the CITE project, a small group of teachers and professors met for six half-days to explore the notion of teacher reflection and to conduct inquiry into their own practice. One teacher's journal (Morris-Curtin 1990) and final reflections provide a vivid story of the benefits:

> *I think the most notable change for me was the ability to start backing away from the need to get an immediate solution to a problem. Instead, by using the problem solving/reflective framing format, I really feel like I'm giving the wealth of knowledge I possess about my profession a chance to come more fully into play. . . . There is something magical and very personal in all of this. Like finally finding just the right word for a poem you've worked on for ages. Teaching, like any other art form, comes from a special place within us (p. 5).*

Using collaborative action research methods (Oja 1989), Canning (1990), engaged student teachers in describing and analyzing their own efforts to become reflective. In addition to writing about the experiences occurring around them, student teachers also considered themselves as objects of reflection. By providing questions, supportive feedback, and affirmations, Canning helped students find their "own voices" as they engaged in open-minded, responsible, and wholehearted reflection on their student teaching experiences.

Summary of Research on Narrative Reflection

Three major benefits are realized from teachers' narratives. First, these studies give us insights into what motivates a teacher's actions and an appreciation for the complexity of teachers' every day lives. Second, teachers' narratives provide us many detailed cases of teaching dilemmas and events (for instance, Shulman and Colbert 1987). Richert (in press) has used such cases successfully to develop reflective thinking in teachers. The third, and most valuable benefit is the insight gained by teachers themselves as a result of this self-inquiry.

In one sense, the emphasis on critical and narrative teacher reflection is a bridge into a new way of thinking about research on teaching. Since many researchers who study the process of learning to teach were trained in the experimental and quantitative research tradition, this can be a tough leap. Yet, as we have seen here, researchers have forged collaborations with teachers and are truly listening and learning from their stories (for example, Huberman 1990).

MUCH TO LEARN

In this review, we have described three aspects of reflection important to teachers' professional thinking. Most researchers in teacher education now recognize the important role of context, case-knowledge, deliberation of educational aims/ends prior beliefs, wisdom-through-action and cognitive complexity reflective thinking.

As we fit together the cognitive, critical, and narrative elements of teachers' reflective thinking, we find that we are moved to "reframe" our images of teacher education and supervision. No longer is direct teaching or "training" necessarily the best mode for professional staff development. University course work and unstructured student teaching experiences are inadequate. Certainly, first-year teachers are woefully without the support that would allow them to move out of novice-like practice. We hope the ideas presented here provide

Highlights of Research on Teachers' Reflective Thinking

Several implications can be derived from this review of research on teachers' reflective thinking:

- Teacher educators can foster growth in cognitive reflection through microteaching with post-teaching reflection journals, teaching with self-analysis of video/audiotapes, action research observation and analysis of selected teaching episodes, coaching, and assessment and discussion of student learning.
- Critical reflection may be promoted through close examination of cases that illustrate particular aspects of context, pedagogy, content, ethical/moral dilemmas, and other elements of teaching and learning that will help teachers develop a rich, flexible repertoire of ideas, attitudes, and skills.
- Teachers need opportunities to construct their own narrative context-based meaning from infor-

mation provided by research, theoretical frameworks, or outside experts.
- A person's preconceptions of teaching, learning, and the purposes of schooling will influence greatly how he or she interprets courses, workshops, and personal teaching experiences. These beliefs must be examined critically from various perspectives to allow for a flexible and thoughtful approach to teaching.
- Future research needs to explore how teachers interpret, give meaning to, and make decisions about their experiences in schools. Teachers themselves will need to be included as co-investigators in such research.

—Georgea Mohlman Sparks-Langer
and Amy Berstein Colton

guideposts that can help us design developmentally appropriate growth experiences for teachers at all levels and that we continue this journey with teachers as co-inquirers into the mysterious process of reflective professional thinking.

REFERENCES

Anderson, R. C. (1984). "Some Reflections on the Acquisition of Knowledge." *Educational Researcher* 13:5–10.

Berliner, D. C. (1986). "In Pursuit of the Expert Pedagogue." *Educational Researcher* 15, 7: 5–13.

Borko, H., and C. Livingston. (1989). "Cognition and Improvisation: Differences in Mathematics Instruction by Expert and Novice Teachers." *American Educational Research Journal* 26, 4: 473–498.

Canning, C. (1990). "Reflection: Out on a Limb. An Intrapersonal Process and the Development of Voice." Paper presented at the annual meeting of the American Educational Research Association, Boston, Mass.

Carter, K., K. Cushing, D. Sabers, P. Stein, and D. Berliner. (1988). "Expert-Novice Differences in Perceiving and Processing Visual Classroom Information." *Journal of Teacher Education* 39, 3: 25–31.

Ciriello, M. J., L. Valli, and N. E. Taylor. (in press). In *Reflective Teacher Education Programs*, edited by L. Valli. New York: Teachers College Press.

Cochran-Smith, M., and S. L. Lytle. (1990). "Research on Teaching and Teacher Research: The issues that Divide." *Educational Researcher* 19, 2: 2–11.

Colton, A. B., G. M. Sparks-Langer, K. Tripp-Opple, and J. M. Simmons. (1989). "Collaborative Inquiry into Developing Reflective Pedagogical Thinking." *Action In Teacher Education* 11, 3: 44–52.

Connelly, F. M., and D. J. Clandinin. (1990). "Stories of Experience and Narrative Inquiry." *Educational Researcher* 19, 4: 2–14.

Dewey, J. (1933). *How We Think: A Restatement of the Relation of Reflective Thinking to the Educative Process.* Chicago, Ill.: D.C. Heath.

Eisner, E. W. (1982). "An Artistic Approach to Supervision." In *Supervision of Teaching* (ASCD 1982 Yearbook, pp. 53–66), edited by T. J. Sergiovanni. Alexandria, Va.: Association for Supervision and Curriculum Development.

Elliott, J. (1985). "Facilitating Action Research in Schools: Some Dilemmas." In *Field Methods in the Study of Education*, edited by R. Burgess. Lewes: Falmer Press.

Greeno, J. G., M. Magone, and D. Chaiklin. (1979). "Theory of Constructions and Set in Problem Solving." *Memory and Cognition* 7, 6: 445–461.

Grinberg, J. G. (1989). "Reflective Pedagogical Thinking in Teacher Education." Master's thesis, Eastern Michigan University, Ypsilanti, Mich.

Hollingsworth, S. (1990). "Teacher Educator as Researcher: An Epistemological Analysis of Learning to Teach Reading." Paper presented at the annual meeting of the American Educational Research Association, Boston, Mass.

Huberman, M. (1990). "Linkage Between Researchers and Practitioners: A Qualitative Study." *American Educational Research Journal* 27, 2: 363–392.

Kagan, D. M. (1988). "Teaching as Critical Problem Solving: A Critical Examination of the Analogy and its Implications." *Review of Educational Research* 58, 4: 482–505.

Lampert, M. and C. M. Clark. (1990). "Expert Knowledge and Expert Thinking in Teaching: A Response to Floden and Klinzing." *Educational Researcher* 19, 4: 21–23.

Leinhardt, G. (1990). "Capturing Craft Knowledge in Teaching." *Educational Researcher* 19, 2: 18–25.

Leinhardt, G., and J. G. Greeno. (1986). "The Cognitive Skill of Teaching." *Journal of Educational Psychology* 78, 2: 75–95.

McLaren, P. (1989). *Life in Schools.* New York: Longman.

Morine-Dershimer, G. (1989). "Preservice Teachers' Conceptions Of Content and Pedagogy: Measuring Growth in Reflective, Pedagogical Decision-Making." *Journal of Teacher Education* 30, 5: 47–52.

Morris-Curtin, K. (1990, Spring). "Teacher Reflection and Empowerment. " *MCSDISI Newsletter 5.*

Oja, S. N. (1989). *Collaborative Action Research: A Developmental Process.* London: Falmer Press.

Pasch, M., T. Arpin, D. Kragt, J. Garcia, J. Harberts, and M. Harberts. (1990). "Evaluating Teachers' Instructional Decision Making." Paper presented at the annual meeting of the Michigan Educational Research Association, Novi, Mich.

Piaget, J. (1978). *Success and Understanding.* Cambridge, Mass: Harvard University Press.

Richert, A. (in press). "Using Teacher Cases to Enhance Reflection." In *Staff Development* (2nd ed.), edited by A. Lieberman. New York: Teachers College Press.

Ross, D. D. (1989). "First Steps in Developing a Reflective Approach." *Journal of Teacher Education* 40, 2: 22–30.

Ross, D. D. (1990). "Programmatic Structures for the Preparation of Reflective Teachers." In *Encouraging Reflective Practice in Education* (pp. 97–118), edited by R. Clift, W.P, Houston, and M.D. Pugach. New York: Teachers College Press.

Ross, D. D., M. Johnson, and W. Smith. (in press). Developing a Professional Teacher at the University of Florida. In *Reflective Teacher Education Programs,* edited by L. Valli. New York: Teachers College Press.

Schon, D. A. (1983). *The Reflective Practitioner.* New York: Basic Books.

Schon, D. A. (February 1987). *Educating the Reflective Practitioner.* San Francisco: Jossey-Bass.

Shulman, L. S. (February 1987). "Knowledge and Teaching: Foundations of the New Reform." *Harvard Educational Review* 57, 1: 31.

Shulman, J., and J. A. Cobert. (1987). *Mentor Teacher Casebook.* San Francisco: Far West Laboratories.

Simmons, J. M., G. M. Sparks, A. Starko, M. Pasch, A. Colton, and J. Grinberg. (1989). "Exploring the Structure of Reflective Pedagogical Thinking in Novice and Expert Teachers: The Birth of a Developmental Taxonomy." Paper presented at the annual conference of the American Educational Research Association, San Francisco, CA.

Smyth, J. (1989). "Developing and Sustaining Critical Reflection in Teacher Education." *Journal of Teacher Education* 40, 2: 2–9.

Sparks-Langer, G. M., J. M. Simmons, M. Pasch, A. Colton, and A. Starko, (1990). "Reflective Pedagogical Thinking: flow Can We Promote It and Measure It?" *Journal of Teacher Education,* November-December.

Tom, A. R. (1985). "Inquiry into Inquiry-Oriented Teacher Education." *Journal of Teacher Education* 36, 5: 35–44.

Van Manen, M. (1977). "Linking Ways of Knowing With Ways of Being Practical." *Curriculum Inquiry* 6, 3: 205–228.

Yinger, R. J. (1987). "By the Seat of Your Pants: An Inquiry into Improvisation and Teaching." Paper presented at the annual meeting of the American Educational Research Association, Washington, DC.

Authors' note: We want to thank Christine Canning, Maureen McCormack, Scott Paris, and Marvin Pasch for their helpful comments on earlier drafts of this article.

▶ Chapter 2

Cognitive Development in Real Children: Levels and Variations*

KURT W. FISCHER and CATHARINE C. KNIGHT

Cognitive developmental theories have often failed to be helpful in educational practice because they have neglected the naturally rich variations in children's behavior. Skill theory is designed to analyze the development of real children—who vary in capacity, motivation, and emotional state and who act in specific contexts. This theory shows how real children can exhibit both stagelike developmental levels and wide variations in performance. Development moves through a series of cognitive levels, which are evident only under optimal performance conditions. However, children rarely function at their optimum under the conditions for assessment in the schools, as shown by research on arithmetic concepts and higher-order thinking skills. Real children also take different developmental pathways while acquiring skills. In mastering early reading skills, for example, children show several distinct pathways; the pathway for children at risk for reading problems shows important limitations in sound-analysis skills.

Analyses of cognitive development have suffered from scholars' tendencies to think too simply about children's behavior. Theory and research have focused on an extremely limited set of characteristics of children's behaviors, and so they have not captured the naturally occurring rich variations that children show. As a result, their concepts have often failed to be helpful in analyzing the behavior of real children—children who are affected by context and experience and who vary from moment to moment in terms of capacity, motivation, and emotional state (Fischer and Bullock 1984).

One group of scholars, epitomized by Piaget (1983) and Kohlberg (1969), has focused on the search for uniform stages by which to characterize the child. As a result, they have neglected the variations in behavior that occur with changes in the environmental context and the child's state. The roles of task, experience, emotion, and other causes of variation have been omitted from this cognitive developmental framework.

The result has been an inaccurate portrait of the child, showing consistent performance at a stage and uniform movement from one stage to another. Even when the facts of variation have been recognized (and labeled as *decalage*), they have not been explained (Colby et al. 1983; Piaget 1971, p. 11). In educational practice the Piagetians have been able to provide global descriptions of how children's understandings change with age, but they have not been able to help teachers deal with the wide range of natural variations in behavior within and among students.

*Preparation of this article was supported by grants from the Spencer Foundation and the MacArthur Foundation. We would like to thank Susan Harter, Karen Kitchener, and Louise Silvern for their contributions to the arguments here.

Another group, epitomized by most information processing approaches to development (e.g., Klahr and Wallace 1976; Siegler 1983), has focused primarily on analyses of tasks, using those analyses to explain changes in behavior. As a result, the consistencies in behavior with development of the child have been neglected. The contribution of the child's general level of understanding has often not even been assessed (e.g., Chi 1978). In educational practice these information processors have been able to provide analyses of behavior on a few specific tasks, but they have not been able to help teachers understand and make use of students' consistencies in behaviors across contexts.

Skill theory is designed to provide a fuller portrait of development, considering the range of behavior across contexts and states. Its central constructs are based on a collaborational or interactive view that child and environment always work together to produce behavior. Children develop skills that they apply specific contexts and that they can transfer from one context to another. Skill theory provides a set of constructs for characterizing the structures of these skills, the transformations that produce change from one skill to another, and the functional mechanisms that induce variations in behavior across contexts and states (Fischer 1980; Fischer and Pipp 1984; Fischer and Lamborn 1989).

Characteristics that have been considered contradictory in the past are integrated in skill theory: children develop through stages, but their development is at the same time continuous. The behavior of individual children varies widely across contexts, but it is also consistent. Different children move along different developmental pathways, but at the same time they also all move through the same general developmental sequence. In real children these "contradictions" do not exist. A theory that begins to characterize the rich variations in children's behavior quickly eliminates such overly simple dichotomies.

OPTIMAL LEVELS AND THE CONDITIONS FOR DETECTING THEM

One of the central hypotheses of skill theory is that variations of behavior are constrained by an upper limit on the complexity of skills, called the *optimal level*. Children's behavior varies widely across contexts and states, but the variations do not exceed a certain level of complexity. It is this optimal level that consistently changes in a stagelike way, whereas most behavior does not show stagelike change. That is how real children can show both stagelike developmental levels and wide variations in performance.

Development moves through a series of hierarchical optimal cognitive levels, each of which emerges abruptly during a specific age period. Table 1 outlines the seven levels that emerge between two and thirty years of age. (Six additional levels emerge in the first two years of life.) During the childhood years, skills involve representations of concrete objects, events, or people. Children gradually construct more and more complex relations between these representations as they move through the first four levels shown in the table. With the attainment of the fourth level, at about ten to twelve years of age, abstractions concerning intangible concepts emerge from the complex relations of these representations. Then students gradually construct more and more complex relations among these abstractions and, thus, move through the fifth to seventh levels shown in the table.

The optimal levels are not simply characteristics of the child, however. They are simultaneously characteristics of a specific set of environmental conditions. Only under optimal performance conditions—with familiar, well-practiced tasks and contextual support for high-level performance, as well as motivated, healthy children—are the levels evident. Under those conditions children demonstrate stagelike development of capacities in a wide range of skills, such as understanding arithmetic concepts and describing their own personalities.

To illustrate this effect, we will focus on abstract mappings—the fifth level in Table 1. At this level, which typically emerges at fourteen to sixteen years of age in middle-class Americans, adolescents can relate one abstraction to another in a simple relation. The integration of the abstractions is crucial for the demonstration of the mapping.

With arithmetic (limited to positive whole numbers), for example, they can relate the abstract concept of addition to the abstract concept of subtraction. Here is an example:

Addition and subtraction are opposites, even though they both involve combining single numbers. With addition, two numbers are put together to make a larger number, like 5 + 7 = 12.

TABLE 1 **Levels of Development in Childhood and Adolescence**

Level	Age of Emergence	Examples of Skills
Rp 1: Single representations	18–24 months	Coordination of action systems to produce concrete representations of actions, objects, of agents: • Pretending that a doll is walking • Saying, "Mommy eat toast."
Rp 2: Representational mappings	3.5–4.5 years	Relations of concrete representations: • Pretending that two dolls are Mommy and Daddy interacting • Understanding that self knows a secret and Daddy does not know it
Rp 3: Representational systems (also called Concrete operations)	6–7 years	Complex relations of subsets of concrete representations: • Pretending that two dolls are Mommy and Daddy as well as a doctor and a teacher simultaneously. • Understanding that when water is poured from one glass to another, the amount of water stays the same.
Rp 4/A 1: Single abstractions (also called Formal operations)	10–12 years	Coordination of concrete representational systems to produce general, intangible concepts: • Understanding the concept of operation of addition • Evaluating how one's parents' behavior demonstrates conformity • Understanding concept of honesty as general quality of interaction.
A 2: Abstract mappings	14–16 years	Relations of intangible concepts: • Understanding that operations of addition and subtraction are opposites • Integrating two social concepts, such as honesty and kindness, in the idea of a social lie
A 3: Abstract systems	18–20 years	Complex relations of subsets of intangible concepts: • Understanding that operations of addition and division are related through how numbers are grouped and how they are combined • Integrating several types of honesty and kindness in the idea of constructive criticism
A 4: Principles*	25 years?	General principles for integrating systems of intangible concepts: • Moral principle of justice • Knowledge principle of reflective judgment • Scientific principle of evolution by natural selection

*This level is hypothesized, but to date there are too few data to test its existence unequivocally.

Note: Table 1 is based on Fischer (1980), Kitchener (1982), and Lamborn (1986). Ages given are modal ages at which a level first appears, based on research with middle-class American or European children. They may differ across cultures and other social groups.

But with subtraction, a smaller number is taken away from a bigger one, like 12 − 5 = 7. So they combine numbers in opposite ways.

In this explanation, the abstract operations of addition and subtraction are related through opposition.

To test the optimal-level hypothesis for abstract mappings, we examined performance on four different types of arithmetic relations—addition and subtraction, addition and multiplication, division and multiplication, and subtraction and division (Fischer, Pipp and Bullock 1984; Fischer and Kenny 1986). Further tasks were also given to assess the two earlier levels of representational systems and single abstractions.

In our research, eight people from each grade from third grade through the sophomore year of college performed two items to test each type of arithmetic mapping. For these eight problems we predicted that there would be a sudden spurt in performance with the emergence of a new optimal level at fourteen to sixteen years of age. But this spurt would be evident only under optimal conditions. Ordinary performance would not evidence a spurt.

To test these predictions, Fischer and Kenny (1986) tested each student individually under four assessment conditions. First, they answered a specific question about an arithmetic relation, such as "How does addition relate to subtraction?" Second, they were provided with environmental support for high-level performance: they were shown a prototypic answer, an explanation of the relation in a few paragraphs. Then the card was taken away, and they were asked to answer the question again, taking into account what they had just read.

After this second condition, they were told that they would be tested again on the same items in two weeks, and they were encouraged to think about the arithmetic relations in the interim. Two weeks later the same procedure was administered again. The student's initial reply to the question constituted the third assessment. The explanation after they had again read the prototypic answer was the fourth assessment.

The condition most like ordinary performance under the most common kinds of assessments was the first one (Session 1, No support), during which the student gave a spontaneous answer to the question. There was no practice, no opportunity to think about the question for awhile, and no demonstra-

tion of a good answer. Here, as shown in Figure 1, performance improved slowly and gradually after ninth grade (fifteen years of age). There was no evidence of a stagelike change. Improvement was continuous and never reached even 40 percent correct.

At the other extreme, the fourth condition (Session 2, Support) showed a dramatic stagelike change. Through ninth grade, no student performed more than one of the eight problems correctly. In tenth grade (sixteen years of age), every student answered all or almost all of them correctly. In the condition that provided optimal conditions—practice and environmental support for a high-level response—there was a true developmental discontinuity, as shown in Figure 1.

The two intermediate conditions showed a gradual transformation from continuous change to discontinuous change. When students were simply shown a prototypic answer in the first session (Session 1, Support), their performance improved dramatically, but it took several years to reach its maximum, and even then it only reached approximately 60 percent correct. When students returned two weeks later and initially answered the questions (Session 2, No support), their performance showed nearly the same discontinuity as the optimal condition.

As these results illustrate, cognitive development is both continuous and discontinuous. Discontinuities take place at certain ages as a new optimal level emerges, but they occur under optimal assessment conditions, not under ordinary, spontaneous conditions.

According to skill theory, these levels reflect a broad change in capacity, not simply a change in one domain. This capacity change produces, for example, a discontinuity not only in arithmetic relations but also in perceived conflict in one's own personality. With the development of abstractions, adolescents can characterize themselves (as well as other people) in terms of abstract personality characteristics, such as outgoing, outspoken, caring, inconsiderate, and depressed. With abstract mappings these abstract characteristics can be related for the first time, and adolescents can detect conflicts or contradictions in their own personalities.

Based on this argument, we predicted that adolescents would experience a spurt in perceived conflict in their own personalities at fourteen to sixteen years of age. Monsour (1985) and Harter (1986)

Figure 1
Development of Arithmetic-Concept Relations
Under Four Conditions

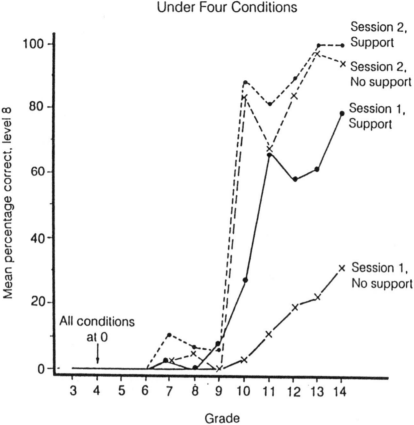

tested this hypothesis with a structured technique designed to support optimal performance. During individual interviews the adolescents were asked what they were like in a variety of specific situations. Each characterization was written on a small piece of paper with glue on the back, and each adolescent then placed the papers on a drawing of three concentric circles to represent her or his personality. The most important characteristics were put on the inner circle and the least important on the outer circle. The interviewer then asked a series of structured questions intended to determine, among other things, what conflicts the adolescent saw among the characteristics.

Students in the predicted age period showed a dramatic spurt in perceived conflict. Between seventh and ninth grades (thirteen and fifteen years of age), the percentage of students reporting some conflict jumped from 34 to 70 percent, and it remained high in eleventh grade.

Other studies, too, indicate that a new cognitive capacity emerges at this time in development (Fischer and Lamborn 1989). The exact age of emergence will vary across assessment conditions, and it might vary across social groups. But at some point in middle adolescence there occurs a cluster of spurts in optimal performance.

According to skill theory, similar spurts occur for each of the levels in Table 1 because of the emergence of the new optimal level. [Of course, other factors can produce spurts, too (Fischer and Bullock 1981)]. Consequently, optimal performance shows a series of clusters of spurts.

Yet ordinary performance under nonoptimal conditions is another matter entirely. Stages occur reliably only in optimal performance, not in ordinary performance. Usually behavior develops gradually and continuously, showing few sudden jumps. A major task for a theory of cognitive development in the real child is to depict the range of variations between optimal level and ordinary performance.

FUNCTIONAL LEVELS AND VARIATIONS IN ORDINARY PERFORMANCE

Most behavior involves variations below optimal level. Our research indicates that students rarely function at their optimum under the kinds of conditions that are used for assessment in the schools. Instead, they function at a level such as that suggested for the initial condition by the graph in Figure 1 (Session 1, No support). Adolescents seventeen or eighteen years of age, for example, failed the tasks requiring abstract mappings, passed some of the tasks for single abstractions, and passed virtually all the tasks for representational systems. Yet under optimal conditions they were clearly capable of abstract mappings. Their level of ordinary functioning was far below their level of optimal performance.

Indeed, our research has demonstrated a fragility in optimal performance in a number of domains. Without environmental support for high-level performance, behavior typically falls to a level far below the optimal. The findings in the arithmetic study were unusual in that students sustained much of their high level of performance in the no-support condition in the second session. By hypothesis, that effect arose from the fact that these students were being taught mathematics regularly in high school, and so it was a highly familiar and practiced domain.

With the removal of support, children's performance levels in most domains plummet in a matter of minutes (Fischer and Elmendorf 1986; Lamborn and Fischer 1988). For example, when students between sixteen and twenty years of age were presented with a series of stories testing their understanding of the relations between intention and responsibility, many of them showed abstract mappings under optimal conditions. Ten minutes later, without the support of having just heard a story embodying a mapping, they were asked to present the best story they could about intention and responsibility. Their performance immediately plummeted. Not one student could sustain the optimal level of performance, even though he or she had done so just minutes before (Fischer, Hand, and Russell 1984).

Instead of performing at optimum, people seem ordinarily to perform at what is called their *functional level,* a limit on their functioning that is typically below what they can do under optimal conditions. Simple manipulations, such as instructing them to do the best they can or giving them the opportunity to practice, do not eliminate this gap between optimal and functional levels. They merely lead people to show their best possible spontaneous performance, their functional level. The only manipulation that seems consistently to reduce or eliminate the gap is reinstituting high environmental support, as was done in the arithmetic study.

One way of interpreting these findings is that people must internalize the high-level structure in order to be able to produce it without support. The high-support conditions show what they can understand when demands of internalization are minimal. The low-support conditions test whether they can produce and organize the complex skill on their own, whether they have internalized it. This process is related to what Vygotsky (1978) referred to as learning in the zone of proximal development.

INDIVIDUAL DIFFERENCES IN DEVELOPMENTAL PATHWAYS

Functional level describes only one way in which people show individual differences in development. According to skill theory, individual differences are the norm in development (Fischer and Elmendorf 1986), even while children also develop through the general levels in Table 1. The specific skills, and therefore the capacities or competencies, vary widely as a function of the children's experiences, their emotions and interests, and their special facilities or disabilities. Whenever possible, assessments of children's developing skills should allow the detection of different developmental sequences. However, many developmental studies are designed so that they cannot detect such individual differences (Fischer and Silvern 1985).

As they master early reading skills, for example, children follow several distinct pathways (Knight 1982; Knight and Fischer 1987). One of the primary tasks of reading is to integrate visual information, captured in writing and print, with sound information, used in normal spoken language. For example, the letters *t, r, e,* and *e* have to be integrated with the sounds in the word *tree.* There are, of course, a number of different potential tasks for assessing this integration. One of the major dimensions along which such tasks vary in our research is degree of environmental support for high-level performance. For example, a recognition task, which allows the child to match the written word with a picture of a tree, provides more support than a production task, which requires the child to produce the spoken word *tree* from the written word without any contextual support.

Figures 2 and 3 show developmental sequences for normal readers and those with sound-analysis deficiency. Each child shows the full sequence in one of the figures. Parallel lines indicate that the skills in the two lines are developing in each child in the order shown but are not related across lines.

In the normative sequence shown in Figure 2, children show separate development of some visual tasks, such as identifying written letters in words, and some sound tasks, such as recognizing rhymes for the same words. As children move down the sequence toward reading production (without environmental support), the visual and sound tasks come to order together because the visual and sound components have been integrated. Rhyming production and reading production thus develop in sequence.

In the sequence for the sound-analysis deficiency, shown in Figure 3, the visual and sound tasks do not come together. Instead, they continue to develop along separate lines in the child. This lack of integration of vision and sound seems to arise from a general deficiency in sound analysis skills (Bradley and Bryant 1983; Pennington et al.

Figure 2
Modal Developmental Sequence for Early Reading

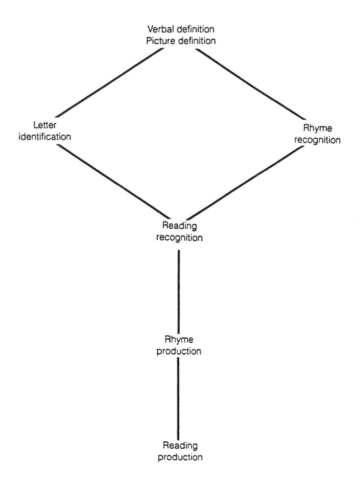

Figure 3
Developmental Sequence for Low Readers
(Read Better Than Rhyme)

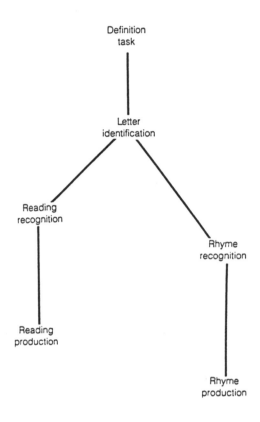

1984). Indeed, most children with specific dyslexia seem to suffer from such sound-analysis problems. Thus dyslexia shows one primary developmental pattern, even though the deficiency appears to arise from diverse sources, ranging from a lack of practice of sound-analysis skills to a specific, genetically based deficiency in sound analysis.

When dyslexic children were tested with a scale designed to provide a direct test of the sequence in Figure 2, they did not merely show low-level performance. Their behavior did not fit the scale but, instead, fit the scale in Figure 3. With most reading assessments there have been no such strict tests of sequence. Without such tests dyslexic children would merely seem to be slow developmentally. Only with the direct test of the sequence has it been possible to determine that, unlike normal readers, these children showed a different developmental pattern.

According to skill theory, children show many such individual differences in developmental se-

quences, but assessment methods often make it impossible to detect these differences. Research that allows such detection should uncover wide variations in developmental patterns.

Application to Assessment of Reflective Judgment

One of the primary lessons from these several research findings is that both developmental sequences and variations should be directly assessed. That is, in any given domain an assessment should include both a range of tasks for assessing different developmental levels and a range of assessment conditions for assessing the developmental range between optimal and functional levels. Using such assessments, researchers can begin to describe both the sequences and the variations in the behavior of real children (Fischer and Canfield 1986). Then their theories of cognitive development will prove to be much more useful in working with real children.

Based on this rationale, several of us have been devising instruments for assessing development in various domains, including arithmetic concepts scales and reading skills scales. With regard to thinking skills, we should also mention a third assessment instrument-reflective judgment scales. A study in progress on these scales illustrates what can be expected in most areas that can be investigated with this sort of methodology.

With Kitchener we have developed a battery of tasks for assessing levels and variations in the development of the kind of higher-order thinking called *reflective judgment.* Kitchener and King (1981) formulated a theory of the development of understanding the bases for knowing that culminates in the conception of reflective judgment. Table 2 reflects the sequence of seven stages in this development, as well as Kitchener's (1982) analysis of how they relate to the levels of skill theory.

In the early stages children show little reflectivity in their conception of knowing, thinking in terms of simple right and wrong. During the intermediate stages they come to understand the uncertainty of knowledge. Gradually at the higher stages they articulate such concepts as viewpoint, justification, and evidence. By the final stage, they understand that knowledge can be fairly certain, provided that it is based on a coherent viewpoint that considers evidence and provides justifications for a conclusion.

Kitchener and King's (1981) first instrument for assessing these stages used an interview based on dilemmas about knowledge (the Reflective Judgment Interview).

TABLE 2 Development of Reflective Judgment

Skill Level	Stages of Reflective Judgment
Rp 1: Single representations	Stage 1: Single category for knowing: To know means to observe directly without evaluation
Rp 2: Representational mappings	Stage 2: Two categories for knowing: People can be right about what they know, or they can be wrong.
Rp 3: Representational systems	Stage 3: Three categories for knowing: People can be right about what they know, or they can be wrong, or knowledge might be incomplete or temporarily unavailable. The status of knowledge might differ in different areas.
Rp 4/A 1: Systems of representational systems, which are single abstractions	Stage 4: Knowledge is uncertain: The fact that knowledge is unknown in several instances leads to an initial understanding of knowledge as an abstract process that is uncertain.
A 2: Abstract mappings	Stage 5: Knowledge is relative to a context or viewpoint; it is subject to interpretation. Thus, it is uncertain in science, history, philosophy, etc. Conclusions must be justified. Abstract systems
A 3: Abstract systems	Stage 6: Although knowledge is uncertain and subject to interpretation, it is possible to abstract some justified conclusions across domains or viewpoint. Knowledge is an outcome of these processes.
A 4: Systems of abstract systems, which are principles	Stage 7: Knowledge occurs probabilistically via inquiry, which unifies concepts of knowledge.

Note: Stages are adapted from Kitchener and King's (1981) Reflective Judgment Scale.

For example, students were asked to consider who built the Egyptian pyramids. Were the ancient Egyptians capable of building the pyramids on their own, or did they require some sort of aid from a more advanced civilization? Using four such dilemmas, Kitchener and King found in a longitudinal study that people did, in fact, move through the seven stages as predicted.

The Reflective Judgment Interview provides little environmental support for high-level performance. Kitchener and Fischer have devised a new instrument, the Prototypic Reflective Judgment Interview, by which people are assessed under high-support conditions. For each dilemma at each stage, they are given a prototypic answer and then asked to explain that answer.

In a study in progress subjects were first assessed with the low-support Reflective Judgment Interview. Second, they were given the high-support Prototypic Reflective Judgment Interview. Then, as in the arithmetic study, they were given two weeks to think about the dilemmas and assessed again.

We are predicting that the results will be more complex than in the arithmetic study because students are not regularly instructed on the bases of knowledge in the same way that they are instructed on arithmetic concepts. Consequently, students will show an optimal-level effect primarily when on their own they show interest in understanding the bases of knowledge. Most students will not reach their optimal level in this domain. Much more instruction would be required for them to attain the optimal performance level (Fischer and Lamborn 1989; Fischer and Farrar 1987).

The high-support assessment will produce an increase in stage, and this increase will consolidate during the second session. That is, students will show an increase in the consistency of their judgments in the second session. Nevertheless, spontaneous performance in the low-support condition will continue to be at a far lower functional level, thus demonstrating once again the gap between high-support and low-support performance. Skills are hard to learn and sustain, and in most domains performance will routinely occur below the optimal level, even with high-support assessments and the opportunity for practice. Movement to the optimal level, the upper limit on performance, requires sustained work at mastering and internalizing the skills.

SUMMARY

Theorists of cognitive development have suffered from tendencies to think dichotomously about children's development. As a result, their concepts have often failed to be helpful in educational practice. For example, one group has typically focused primarily on searching for stages to characterize the children and has neglected the role of task and environment. Another group has focused primarily on analyses of tasks and has neglected the contribution of the child.

Skill theory is designed to analyze the development of real children—children who vary in capacity, motivation, and emotional state and who act in specific contexts. The central constructs of this theory are defined in terms of both child and environmental variables. As a result, skill theory shows how real children can exhibit both stagelike developmental levels and wide variations in performance.

Development moves through a series of hierarchically organized cognitive levels, with seven levels identified between the ages of two and thirty. Each level produces a discontinuous spurt in capacity, but most behaviors do not reflect these spurts because the levels specify the upper limit on performance. These levels are evident only under optimal performance conditions—with familiar, well-practiced tasks; contextual support for high-level performance; and motivated, healthy children. Under those conditions, children demonstrate stagelike development of capacities in, for example, both understanding arithmetic concepts and describing their own personalities.

Most classroom behavior involves variations below the optimal level. Our research indicates that students rarely function at their optimum under the kinds of conditions that are used for assessment in the schools. Instead, as they become familiar with a domain of tasks, they show a functional level—a limit on their functioning that is typically below what they can do under optimal conditions.

Real children also use different approaches to a task and, as a result, move through different developmental pathways. In mastering early reading skills, for example, children show at least two distinct pathways. One pathway may be a much more frequent descriptor of at-risk students.

This theory applies as well as to the development of critical thinking skills. Kitchener and Fischer have developed a battery of tasks for assessing levels and variations in the development of reflective judgment, one kind of critical thinking. In contrast to the arithmetic study, which focused on skills being intensively taught in school, this assessment is expected to produce results more typical of domains that are not yet major targets of school instruction. Even with environmental support for high-level performance, many people will not demonstrate their optimal level because of variations in motivation and background experience. Some students will reach the upper limit in each age group, but others will reach a functional level across tasks that is below their optimum. In addition, the gap between high- support and low-support conditions will remain large for most learners.

REFERENCES

Bradley, L., and Bryant, P. E. 1983. Categorizing sounds and learning to read: A causal connection. *Nature* 301: 419–21.

Chi, M. T. H. 1978. Knowledge structures and memory development. *In Children's thinking. What develops?* ed. R. S. Siegler, 73–96. Hillsdale, N.J.: Lawrence Erlbaum Associates.

Colby, A.; Kohlberg, L.; Gibbs, J.; and Lieberman, M. 1983. *A longitudinal study of moral judgment*. Monographs of the Society for Research in Child Development, vol. 48, no. 1, serial no. 200.

Fischer, K. W. 1980. A theory of cognitive development: The control and construction of hierarchies of skills. *Psychological Review* 87: 477–531.

Fischer, K. W. and Bullock, D. 1981. Patterns of data: Sequence, synchrony, and constraint in cognitive development. In *Cognitive development*, ed. K. W. Fischer, 69–78. New Directions for Child Development, no. 12. San Francisco: Jossey-Bass.

Fischer, K. W. and Bullock, D. 1984. Cognitive development in school-age children: Conclusions and new directions. In *The years from six to twelve: Cognitive development during middle childhood*, ed W. A. Collins, 70–146. Washington, D.C.: National Academy Press.

Fischer, K. W. and Canfield, R. L. 1986. The ambiguity of stage and structure in behavior: Person and environment in the development of psychological structures. In *Stage and structure*, ed. I. Levin, 246–167. New York: Plenum.

Fischer, K. W. and Elmendorf, D. 1986. Becoming a different person: Transformations in personality and social behavior. In *Minnesota symposia on child psychology*. Vol. 18, ed. M. Perlmutter 137–78. Hillsdale, N.J.: Lawrence Erlbaum Associates.

Fischer, K. W. and Farrar, M. J. 1987. Generalizations about generalization: How a theory of skill development explains both generality and specificity. *International Journal of Psychology* 22; 643–77.

Fischer, K. W.; Hand, H. H.; and Russell, S. L. 1984. The development of abstractions in adolescence and adulthood. In *Beyond formal operations*, ed. M. Commons, F. A. Richards, and C. Armon, 43–73. New York: Praeger.

Fischer, K. W. and Kenny, S. L. 1986. The environmental conditions for discontinuities in the development of abstractions. In *Adult cognitive development: methods and models*, ed. R. Mines and K. Kitchener, 57–75. New York: Praeger.

Fischer, K. W. and Lamborn, S. 1989. Sources of variations in developmental levels: Cognitive and emotional transitions during adolescence. In *Mechanisms of transition in cognitive and emotional development*, ed. A. de Ribaupierre. New York: Cambridge University Press.

Fischer, K. W. and Pipp, S. L. 1984. Processes of cognitive development: Optimal level and skill acquisition. In *Mechanisms of cognitive development*, ed. R. J. Sternberg, 45–80. New York: W. H. Freeman & Co.

Fischer, K. W.; Pipp, S. L.; and Bullock, D. 1984. Detecting developmental discontinuities; methods and measurement. In *Continuities and discontinuities in development*, ed. R. Emde and R. Harmon, 9 5–121. New York: Plenum.

Fischer, K. W. and Silvern, L. 1985. Stages and individual differences in cognitive development. *Annual Review of Psychology* 36: 613–48.

Harter, S. 1986. Cognitive-developmental processes in the integration of concepts about emotions and the self. *Social Cognition* 4: 119–51.

Kitchener, K. S. 1982. Human development and the college campus: Sequences and tasks. In *Measuring student development*, ed. G. P, Hanson, 17–45. New Directions for Student Services, no. 20. San Francisco: Jossey-Bass.

Kitchener, K. S., and King, P. M. 1981. Reflective judgment: Concepts of justification and their relation to age and education. *Journal of Applied Developmental Psychology* 2: 8 9–116.

Klahr, D., and Wallace, J. G. 1976. *Cognitive development: An information-processing review*. Hillsdale, N.J.: Lawrence Erlbaum Associates.

Knight, C. C. 1982. Hierarchical relationships among components of reading abilities of beginning readers. Ph.D. diss. Arizona State University, Tempe.

Knight, C. C., and Fischer, K. W. 1987. Learning to read: Patterns of skill development and individual differences. Typescript.

Kohlberg, L. 1969. Stage and sequence: The cognitive developmental approach to socialization. In *Handbook of socialization theory and research*, ed. D. A. Goslin, 347–480. Chicago: Rand McNally.

Lamborn, S. D. 1987. *Relations between social-cognitive knowledge and personal experience. Understanding honesty and kindness in relationships.* Ann Arbor, Mich.: University Microfilms.

Lamborn, S. D., and Fischer, K. W. 1988. Optimal and functional levels in cognitive development: The individual's developmental range. *Newsletter of the International Society for the Study of Behavioral Development* 2 (serial no. 14): 1–4.

Monsour, A. 1985. *The dynamics and structure of adolescent self-concept.* Ann Arbor, Mich.: University Microfilms.

Pennington, G.; Smith, S.; McCabe, L.; Kimberling, W.; and Lubs, H. 1984. Developmental continuities and discontinuities in a form of familial dyslexia. In *Continuities and discontinuities in development*, ed. R. Emde and R. Harmon. New York: Plenum.

Piaget, J. 1971. The theory of stages in cognitive development. In *Measurement and Piaget*, ed. D. R. Green, M. P. Ford, and G. B. Flamer. New York: McGraw-Hill.

Piaget, J. 1983. Piaget's Theory. In *Handbook of child psychology.* 4th ad. ed. P. H. Mussen. Vol. 1, *History, theory, and methods,* ed. W. Kessen, 103–26. New York: John Wiley.

Siegler, R. S. 1983. Information processing approaches to development. In *Handbook of child psychology.* 4th ed., ed. P. H. Mussen. Vol. 1, *History, theory, and methods,* ed. W. Kessen, 129–211. New York: John Wiley.

Vygotsky, L. 1978. *Mind in society: The development of higher psychological processes.* Trans. M. Cole, V. John-Steiner, S. Scribner, and Ellen Souberman. Cambridge, Mass.: Harvard University Press.

How Do Children Learn Words?

"Mrs. Morrow *stimulated* the soup." "Our family *erodes* a lot." Most teachers of older elementary students have run across sentences like these in their students' attempts to use dictionary definitions of new vocabulary words. The student who wrote the first sentence found "stir up" among the definitions for "stimulate," wrote a sentence appropriate for that meaning, and simply substituted the new word. A similar process led the second student to see "erode," "eat away," as a synonym for "eat out."

In the September 1987 issue of *Scientific American*, George A. Miller and Patricia M. Gildea point out that children need to learn 13 new words a day if they are to acquire the 80,000-word vocabulary of the average high school graduate. In trying to understand just how children accomplish this—and how teachers can help them do so—Miller and Gildea investigated the effectiveness of the standard dictionary assignments of the middle elementary years. They concluded that teachers place much too much faith in such assignments.

In one typical exercise the student is given a sentence in which a word is used ambiguously, and sent to the dictionary to decide which sense of the word the author intends. Fourth graders in Miller and Gildea's study performed this task correctly at a rate no better than chance. In another standard assignment, students are given a word and asked to look up its definition and then use the word in a sentence. Here the researchers found many, examples of the "substitution" effect described above. Students seize upon the definition most familiar to them, produce a sentence using the familiar word or phrase, and substitute the new word for it.

Similar mistakes occurred even when students were given model sentences using the word. Here they seemed to focus on only one of the models,

gather a single meaning of the word from its use in that sentence, and then compose other sentences based on that meaning. Thus after reading "The king's brother tried to usurp the throne," some students concluded that "usurp" meant "take" and ended up with new sentences like "Don't try to usurp that tape from the store."

How, then, can teachers help students learn new words? Even though reading remains the best way to facilitate the growth of vocabulary, direct introduction and reinforcement of vocabulary are also crucial. But such reinforcement must go beyond reliance on standard dictionary assignments. In a recent study of reading, Jeanne Chall and Catherine Snow pointed out the importance of providing rich and varied exposure to and practice with vocabulary—from the provision of challenging and varied reading materials in class, to assigned homework in reading, to field trips that expose students to new words (HEL, January 1988).

The value of classroom discussion is confirmed in a recent study of vocabulary learning reported on by Steven Stahl and Charles Clark (*American Educational Research Journal*, Winter 1987). Studying four classes of fifth graders, Stahl and Clark found that students in classrooms where there were discussions of science passages containing new vocabulary words performed better on two measures of concept and vocabulary learning than did those in classes that simply read the passages and took the tests.

To this list of approaches, Miller and Gildea add another possibility: the use of computer programs that couple reading passages with vocabulary assistance. In one such program, children read a text that describes an episode from a movie they have just seen. As the text appears on the screen, certain words are marked for the reader to learn. The children have a choice of asking for definitions, sentences, or pictures depicting the meaning of these words. They thus gain information in a form they want, when they most need it—in the midst of reading. Miller and Gildea found that fifth and sixth graders using this program increased their ability to recognize word meanings and to write acceptable sentences incorporating the new vocabulary.

Implementing Whole Language
Bridging Children and Books

PATRICIA A. ROBBINS

As a child, I hated to read. The task was difficult and I couldn't excel. In 4th grade any hope that I might discover books a source of pleasure was lost. We had returned from our weekly visit to the library, where I had discovered a thin pictorial book on ants. I knew my teacher would not appreciate the book, but I wanted to know more about ants. I concealed the book in my lap and peeked into its contents. The legs of the ant looked like lofty columns holding together a mighty fortress—similar, I thought, to the buildings of ancient Greece. Suddenly my teacher jerked the book from my hands and thrust it high into the air. Proudly she announced that she had "captured an inappropriate book selection—too small in size, too few pages, and too many pictures." I was demoralized. Books were not my friends.

If I were a child today in the Contoocook Valley (ConVal) School District, I would love books. This rural district's eight elementary schools, scattered throughout the shadow of Mt. Monadnock, have achieved wonders with children and books. Every classroom is filled with exciting literature and children's books of all sizes and shapes. Teachers focus on what children *can do* as writers and readers. Children read any and every book that interests them. Whole-language instruction and writing pro-

cesses bridge each child's curiosity and life experiences to language and books.

CHILDREN AS READERS AND WRITERS

From the first day of school, children in ConVal believe themselves to be readers and writers. They read from the books that interest them; they write stories that excite them. On large paper, using crayons and whatever lettering ability they have, children draw and write about a favorite toy or animal or place they have been. As each child reads his or her story out loud, the teacher transcribes it onto a corner of the paper, preserving the story so it can be read again in the future. By the end of 1st grade all students have published at least one book of their own creation. At "authors' teas," students read their books to parents and peers. They always include an explanation about themselves and their reasons for selecting their topic. By the end of 6th grade, students have published as many as a dozen books. Children discover that books preserve their ideas, pictures, and conversations. They learn that authors use written words to express feelings, tell stories, and provide information.

Reading and writing at ConVal are considered integrated processes. Writing generates an enthusiasm for reading, and reading creates the impetus for writing, As children write stories, they organize their thoughts onto paper and analyze them

Patricia A. Robbins is Director of Curriculum and Instruction, ConVal School District, Route 202 North, Peterborough, NH 03458.

during peer conferences. During class sharing and response time, children listen for contextual meaning in stories written by their peers.

Whole-language instruction teaches the value of the writing process during reading activities. While reading "big books" and other children's literature, teachers demonstrate how different authors convey meaning through written language and illustrations. Students talk and write about their perceptions of the author's purpose, meaning, and style of presentation. Sometimes they emulate a favorite author's style as they work to discover their own writing voices.

Children read from "real" books they select according to their own interest and reading levels. Basals and worksheets are not used in any of the district elementary schools.

Ten years ago teachers in the ConVal District began to bridge children and books, first through the writing process and then through whole-language instruction. This movement was generated at the grass roots level by teachers who found a dramatic difference in achievement when students applied the writing process. With support from the superintendent and administration, writing process and whole-language instruction became major district goals. The results include:

- high scores in reading comprehension on the California Achievement Tests;
- an increase in the quantity and quality of books read and written by students;
- a dramatic drop in the number of students identified for special education services;
- recognition by the National Council of Teachers of English as a National Center of Excellence;
- the first ConVal Literacy Conference on Whole Language, which drew 300 educators from six states.

When we reflect over the past decade, it is clear that five distinct, yet interdependent, factors have influenced the widespread integration of writing and reading processes across the district. We believe these are our keys to success.

INNOVATION

At ConVal, innovation is highly valued. Teachers and administrators have created an atmosphere of cooperation, collaboration, and trust, rich in risk-taking and idea sharing. Teachers are encouraged to initiate instructional improvements and curricular adaptations. As Tom Peters (1984) said, "Innovation does not spawn from planning. It sparks from an idea."

And so it happened in ConVal. The writing process began as an idea: to find a way to make written language as meaningful as spoken language. This idea sparked one teacher, Paula Flemming, to integrate the writing process into her remedial reading program for elementary students. The dramatic jump in her students' reading scores gained districtwide attention.

Other teachers initiated instructional innovations connecting writing and reading. Amidst a growing belief that curriculum should be fully integrated and relevant to each child, early risk-takers discarded their basal readers. They developed theme-based, integrated units using trade books and children's literature, creating lessons relevant to the lives of the children in their classes. They gave children time to read and write and the right to choose their books and topics.

Administrators supported these early risk-takers by budgeting for trade books and instructional materials. They provided time for teachers to work together, to share their ideas with other teachers, to attend workshops, and to visit other schools that practice writing process and a whole-language philosophy.

A COMMON MISSION

As writing process and whole language gained wider interest across the district, a common mission emerged: the belief that all students can love to read and write. Love of language is fostered through teacher modeling, by focusing on what students can do as readers and writers, by building skills through relevant and meaningful child-centered experiences, and by connecting skills, concepts, and content through integrated, theme-based learning activities.

In support of this mission, three years ago the district made a commitment to maximize class size at 20 students and to minimize pull-out programs. By lowering class sizes and by keeping children in the classrooms, teachers can focus on creating an atmosphere of excitement about reading and writing that meets the needs of all students, including the handicapped and the academically gifted.

TEACHER SUPPORT

Teacher support is essential to the success of a writing process and whole-language curriculum. Efforts to implement whole language and writing process will fail if teachers do not have consultants readily available to assist them. Teachers simply cannot be expected to implement, on their own after a few workshops, complex instructional processes embedded in an unfamiliar philosophy.

ConVal uses a teacher-consultant model to provide support and inservice training to teachers across the district. The model was piloted seven years ago in one of the elementary schools. For three years Paula Flemming served as full-time writing coordinator to train teachers in the writing process. Once again, her success gained district-wide attention.

The teacher-consultant model created by Flemming has since been implemented across the district. By reallocating staff and redefining job descriptions, ConVal administrators created four language arts teacher consultants who are full-time teacher trainers in writing process and whole-language instruction. They receive the same contract, salary, and benefits as other ConVal teachers.

Just as teachers identify the strengths of individual children in order to create successful reading and writing experiences, the consultants work with the strengths of individual teachers to create successful teaching experiences. Their services to teachers include individual confidential consultation, demonstration and team teaching, group presentations (including faculty meetings), mini-workshops, courses, and grade-level sharing sessions. They conduct response groups where teachers share their own writing, employing the same techniques used with students. The consultants help teachers diagnose and assess student achievement in order to design instructional strategies to meet the needs of each child.

The consultants have credibility with teachers because of their own successes as classroom teachers, their willingness to take risks, and their ability to listen and respond in a confidential manner to the needs of all teachers. As teachers interact with the consultants, trust builds be-

tween them, trust that is the foundation for growth and change.

This spring, two consultants spent three weeks in New Zealand observing and studying whole-language instruction. As a result of this exchange, an "early intervention" paralleling New Zealand's Reading Recovery program was implemented to remedy reading difficulties of first-year 1st grade students (ConVal has no public kindergarten program). In this program, two Chapter I teachers use writing process and whole-language techniques during daily individualized tutoring sessions to help students focus on their reading strengths, not on their deficiencies.

Another new project involves 13 high school teachers who developed a school-within-a-school called the "Pyramid Program." The writing process is the main vehicle for integrating core content areas (English, social studies, math, and science) for a heterogeneous group of 140 students in grades 9 to 12.

Initially the consultants were assigned to specific schools with a predetermined schedule that evenly distributed their time across all 11 schools in the district. This approach was not very effective because the consultant schedules took precedence over the needs of the teachers.

To remedy this situation, the consultants developed a new strategy, which they refer to as "intensified service." Essentially, this means that they flex their schedules to meet the needs and services requested by teachers and administrators. For example, Antrim Elementary's principal and faculty of 10 teachers decided to focus on guided reading as an alternative to traditional reading groups. The principal, the teachers, and a consultant brainstormed different ways to proceed. As a result, three consultants devoted the majority of their time over a six-week period to meet with individual teachers, model specific techniques, and conduct inservice training during faculty meetings.

The consultants make an effort to demonstrate their sensitivity and responsiveness to the needs of teachers through personal gestures. They pick up books at the bookstore and deliver them to teachers, write notes of encouragement, extend personal invitations to attend workshops, and highlight teachers' successes in newsletters. Continuous support of both a personal and a technical nature is essential if teachers are to successfully meet the needs of each student in their classrooms. And student success is the greatest motivator of teacher growth.

STRUCTURE WITHIN THE PHILOSOPHY

In ConVal, both the writing process and whole language are defined as usable frameworks that can be referred to during the stages involved in implementation, assessment, and teacher inservice. This provides a concrete structure and a common language with a philosophy that can appear nebulous without close investigation.

The writing process is defined by these six phases: rehearsal, drafting, revision, editing, publishing, and response. They are described in Figure 1.

As children apply the writing process, the phases are explained and modeled. Publication of books written by students is managed by parent volunteers, who operate publishing houses in each elementary and middle school. Parents type children's stories into book form, laminate the covers, and bind and distribute them to children, classrooms, and school and town libraries.

Teachers draw on *The Elements of Whole Language* (Butler 1987) for a meaningful structure to whole-language instruction. Based on Brian Cambourne's (1987) theories on the conditions of language development, each of 10 elements identifies specific instructional strategies. A brief overview is shown in Figure 2.

To help teachers effectively implement the 10 elements of whole language and the writing pro-

cess, the consultants have developed a teacher handbook that provides definitions, methods for managing a whole-language classroom, time allocation guidelines (see fig. 3), book lists, suggestions for assessment and evaluation, and methods of communicating student achievement to parents. The handbook is intended for use during inservice programs as a reference and resource guide.

Discussions and debates have occurred among the ConVal teachers and administrators regarding the what's and when's of phonics, grammar, and spelling. Although they do not underestimate the importance of these language tools, they agree that they should be integrated within a meaningful context.

Writing and reading are defined into separate instructional processes, but they are considered interrelated and inseparable. Student achievement is strongly affected when reading and writing are taught as integral and connected processes (Flemming 1988). Writing, which creates a personal relationship between the child and the printed word, builds reading skills, and generates enthusiasm for reading and books, cannot be taught well in exclusion of reading.

Perhaps the most important, and yet most difficult, aspect of the writing process and whole-language program is teacher modeling. Teachers must read and write when children read and write; they must share when children share; they must openly experience the process along with their students. Through modeling, teachers not only encourage children to imitate their actions, but they also help their students feel that they are sharing in an interesting process rather than having it imposed on them.

Fig. 1. The Writing Process	
Rehearsal:	sensory experience, thought, reading, writing that is previous to the piece of writing
Drafting:	putting ideas into writing in a tentative form
Revision:	re-seeing the piece and making changes to it
Editing:	fixing the writing mechanics, spelling, grammar, handwriting
Publishing:	presenting the writing to others in its final form
Response:	receiving feedback from others about the piece of writing

---

Fig. 2. Ten Elements of A Whole Language Program

Reading to children—the teacher reads quality literature to children to encourage them to read.

Shared book experience—a cooperative language activity based on the bedtime story tradition; the teacher reads and rereads appealing rhymes, songs, poems, and stories.

Sustained silent reading—everyone, including the teacher, reads for an extended period of time.

Guided reading—the teacher assigns books to groups of 8 to 10 children to read independently followed by reading conferences; books are selected to keep the children on the cutting edge of their reading ability.

Individualized reading—an organized alternative to guided reading; grows out of guided reading; careful monitoring of individual progress is done by both child and teacher.

Language experience—oral language is recorded by a scribe or audio cassette and made available to children in written format; firsthand or vicarious experience is translated into written language.

Children's writing—ConVal uses the writing process described in Fig. 1 (similar to that described by Butler).

Modeled writing—the teacher models writing process and behavior; children see and hear an "expert" writer in action.

Opportunities for sharing—a finished piece is presented to an audience; ConVal uses author's teas and published books as two methods.

Content area reading and writing—students see demonstrations of each type of text (by subject content) and learn about varying reading speed and looking for context clues.

—adapted for use in the ConVal District from Andrea Butler, 1987

Fig. 3. The Ten Elements of Whole Language: Guidelines for Time Allocations

Elements:	Grades 1–2	Grades 3–6	Grades 7–8
Reading to Children	Daily 10–20 min.	Daily 15–30 min.	Daily 15–30 min.
Shared Book Experience	3–5/Week 10–30 min.	only occasionally	
Sustained Silent Reading	Daily 10–20 min.	Daily 15–30 min.	Daily 15–30 min.
Guided Reading or Individualized Reading	Daily 20–45 min.	Daily 20–45 min.	Daily 30–45 min.
Language Experience	3–5/Week 10–20 min.	only occasionally	
Writing Process	Daily 15–30 min.	Daily 30–40 min.	Daily 30–40 min.
Mini-lessons (Modeled Writing)	Daily 5–10 min.	3–5/Week 5–10 min.	3–5/Week 5–10 min.
Opportunities for Sharing	Daily 10–20 min.	Daily 10–20 min.	Daily 10–20 min.
Content Area Reading and Writing	Daily	Daily	Daily
	specified for the specific content		

—constructed by ConVal Language Arts Teacher Consultants, 1988

VOLUNTARY INVOLVEMENT

Teachers are more willing to become involved with new instructional techniques when they feel they have a choice. ConVal teachers have always had this choice, and their participation in district in-service programs on the writing process and whole language has increased dramatically over the past five years. This year the consultants and other Con-Val teachers have scheduled 22 different courses and workshops to enhance instruction in the reading and writing processes. Although teachers do not receive extra pay for their involvement in these programs, which are conducted after school, they can apply inservice hours toward their certification and movement on the salary schedule.

BRIDGING CHILDREN TO BOOKS

Bridging children to books is critical if children are to become literate citizens in the complex world that lies ahead of them. Using whole language and the writing process connects a child's life experiences to the learning activities of the classroom. Teachers are empowered to make curricular decisions in order to address the needs of their children: the curriculum conforms to the child, not the child to the curriculum.

When teachers are empowered, students are empowered. The result in ConVal is a powerful bridge of love for books—one that connects a child's curiosity and life experiences to the world of books and language through the writing process and whole language.

In ConVal, there are no books that are "too small," with "too few pages and too many pictures," like my selection made in 4th grade. But there are many children in our district who have discovered books and who excel at reading and writing.

REFERENCES

Butler, A. (1987). *The Elements of Whole Language.* Crystal Lake, Ill.: Rigby.

Cambourne, B. (1987). *Language, Learning and Literacy.* Crystal Lake, Ill.: Rigby.

Flemming, P. (1988) "The Write Way to Read," in *Understanding Writing,* edited by T. Newkirk and N. Arwell. Portsmouth, N.H.: Heinemann Educational Books.

Peters, T. (1984). "The First Steps to Excellence." Recorded speech from Listen and Learn, Old Greenwich, Conn.

► Chapter 3

Improving Students' Self-Esteem

JACK CANFIELD

Teachers intuitively know that when kids feel better about themselves, they do better in school. The simple fact is, though, that youngsters today are not receiving enough positive, nurturing attention from adults, either at home or at school. The reasons are numerous and complex, but the result is that more and more students have low levels of self-esteem.

To raise the self-esteem of students, you must start with the school staff. The main way students learn is through modeling and imitation. If teachers have low self-esteem, they are likely to pass it on to their students. We must ensure, through preservice and inservice training, that teacher-student interactions are positive, validating, affirming, and encouraging.[1]

The challenge facing schools is great, but there are day-to-day things educators can do to increase children's self-esteem and, in so doing, improve their prospects for success (see "Does Self-Esteem Affect Achievement?"). I use a 10-step model to help students become winners in life.[2]

1. *Assume an aptitude of 100 percent responsibility.* I introduce the following formula: E (events) + R (your response to them) = O (outcomes). When people don't get the outcomes they want, I urge them not to blame external events and other people but to take responsibility for changing *their* responses.

For example, if I ask a class how many of them think it will raise Peter's self-esteem if I tell him he is the biggest idiot I ever met in my whole life, very few of them will raise their hands. I then tell them that it is not what I say to Peter but what Peter says to *himself* afterward that ultimately affects his self-esteem. If Peter says, "Mr. Canfield has only known me for a few days, how did he find out so fast?", his self-esteem will probably go down. But if he says to himself, "Mr. Canfield just picked me out for his example because he knows I can take a little kidding," then his self-esteem will not be damaged.

I also emphasize that we are responsible for our behavioral responses. For example, hit someone who yells at you, and you go to the principal's office. Respond with humor or by ignoring the person, and you stay out of trouble. Surprisingly, most kids don't understand that they have choices, let alone what those different choices are.

2. *Focus on the positive.* In order to feel successful, you have to have experienced success. Many students, because they feel they have never done anything successful, need to be coached. Often this is because they equate "success" with, say, winning a medal or getting rich. I spend a lot of time having students recall, write about, draw, and share their past achievements. With some probing and discussion, students often identify successful aspects of their lives that they have not recognized before.

3. *Learn to monitor your self-talk.* Each of us thinks 50,000 thoughts per day, and many of them are about ourselves. We all need to learn to replace negative thoughts—I can't dance, I'm not smart, I don't like my face—with positive self-talk: I can

---

[1]For more information about raising the self-esteem of faculty in a school, contact the resources listed in the box on p. 70.

[2]The 10-step model is spelled out in greater detail and with many examples in *Self-Esteem in the Classroom: A Curriculum Guide,* which is available from the author at the address given below.

Jack Canfield is President of Self-Esteem Seminars, 6035 Bristol Pkwy., Culver City, CA 90230.

Does Self-Esteem Affect Achievement?

Let's see what happens when a school makes a concerted effort in the area of self-esteem. One of the most detailed studies ever done was conducted by Gail Dusa (current president of the National Council for Self-Esteem) and her associates at Silver Creek High School in San Jose, California. (For more information, contact Gail Dusa, NCSE, 6641, Leyland Park Dr., San Jose, CA 95120.)

She divided the freshman class into three groups. The self-esteem group (93 students) was taught by teachers who adhered to three operating principles.

They (1) treated all students with unconditional positive regard, (2) encouraged all students to be all they could be, and (3) encouraged all students to set and achieve goals. In addition, the group participated in a 40-minute activity to build self-esteem every second Friday throughout their freshman year. The control group (also 93 students) received no treatment but was monitored along with the self-esteem group for four years. The third group was not involved in the study. At the end of four years, Dusa's findings were as follows:

	Self-Esteem Group	*Control Group*
Days of absenteeism per semester	1	16
Percentage of students who completed 90 percent or more of their homeowrk	75%	25%
Percentage of students who participated in 20 or more extracurricular activities	25%	2%
Percentage of class offices held by groups between freshman and senior years	75%	0
Percentage of students who graduated from high school	83%	50%

—Jack Canfield

learn to do anything I want, I am smart, I love and accept myself the way I am. I teach students to say, "Cancel, cancel," when they hear themselves or another person saying something negative about them and to replace the negative remark with a positive one. This technique takes time and practice, but it really makes a difference. Also, whenever others put them down, they are to repeat the following "antidote" sentence: "No matter what you say or do to me, I'm still a worthwhile person."

4. *Use support groups in the classroom.* It's possible for a kid to come to school for a whole day and never once be the center of positive attention. "Sharing dyads" and "support groups" help overcome this alienation. Each day teachers might ask their students to find a partner (preferably a different partner each day) and then give them one or two minutes each of uninterrupted time to talk about a specific topic; for example, *Who is your best friend and why? What is your favorite thing to do on the weekend? If you won a million dollar lottery, what would*

you do with the money? Topics such as these can also be discussed in "buddy groups" of six kids with three sets of buddies. Sometimes youngsters meet with their buddies and sometimes with their whole group. They learn that it is a positive, healing experience to talk about their feelings, and they become bonded to their fellow students.

5. *Identify your strengths and resources.* An important part of expanded self-esteem is the broadened awareness of one's strengths and resources. One technique is to have students in their support groups write down and tell each other what they see as their positive qualities and strengths. Because their assessments need to be realistic as well as positive, it is also important to help students note those areas that need more development if they are to achieve their goals.

6. *Clarify your vision.* Without a clear vision, there is no motivation. Questions such as the following help students clarify their visions: *If you bad only one year left to live, how would you spend your*

Resources for Increasing Students' Self-Esteem

The Alliance for Invitational Education, Room 216, Curry Building, University of North Carolina, Greensboro, NC 27412. The alliance publishes a comprehensive newsletter on self-esteem and invitational education and sponsors one national conference and several regional conferences yearly.

The California Task Force to Promote Self-Esteem and Personal and Social Responsibility, 1130 K St., Suite 300, Sacramento, CA 95814. This 25-member task force was appointed by the California governor and legislature to determine how to raise the self-esteem of at-risk groups in the state. Hawaii, Maryland, and Virginia have also created or begun to create similar task forces. For a copy of California's final report, *Toward a State of Esteem* (January 1990), send $4.50 to the Bureau of Publications, California State Department of Education, P.O. Box 271, Sacramento, CA 95802-0271. A 200-page *Appendix*, which includes an extensive bibliography on self-esteem and personal and social responsibility, is also available for $7.50.

The Center for Self-Esteem, P.O. Box 1532, Santa Cruz, CA 95060; 426-6850. The center sponsors an annual conference; publishes a free newsletter; distributes curriculums, books, and tapes; and provides consultants and workshop leaders.

The Foundation for Self-Esteem, 6035 Bristol Pkwy., Culver City, CA 90230; (213) 568-1505. The foundation has published The GOALS Program, a three-and-a-half hour video training program being used in adult schools, correctional facilities, and with welfare recipients. It also sponsors an annual conference, provides consultants and workshop leaders, and distributes curriculums, books, and tapes.

The National Council for Self-Esteem, c/o Gail Dusa, President, 6641 Leyland Park Dr., San Jose, CA 95120. The council publishes a newsletter and a resource packet and sponsors a national conference and about 20 regional conferences yearly. Write for a free copy of the newsletter and an information packet. Annual dues, $25.

Self-Esteem Seminars, 6035 Bristol Pkwy., Culver City, CA 90230; (213) 3379222. The organization conducts inservice training, offers an intensive Facilitators' Training Course, conducts weekend workshops for personal and professional growth, publishes a free quarterly newsletter, and offers a broad spectrum of books, tapes, and curriculum guides. Write for a free copy of their newsletter/catalogue.

---

time? If a genie granted you three wishes, what would you wish for? If you were guaranteed success in anything you attempted, and money were not a limiting factor, what would you do when you grow up? I also use extended guided visualizations in which students construct, for example, their "perfect life"—complete with their ideal house, job, and marriage partner—and share it with their support groups.

7. *Set goals and objectives.* Until our visions are broken down into specific and measurable goals—with timelines and deadlines—we are not likely to move forward very quickly. I teach students how to set measurable goals and objectives for self, family, school, and community. They then share their goals with the rest of the class, support one another as they work toward them, and celebrate any completed goals.

8. *Use visualization.* The most powerful yet underutilized tool in education is visualization. When we hold a clear vision of our goals as if they were already achieved, the action releases creativ-

ity, increases motivation, and actually alters our perceptions of ourselves and our environments. I ask students to spend five minutes per day visualizing each of their goals ind objectives as if it were already achieved. This can produce radical results very quickly.

9. *Take action.* To be successful, you yourself have to "do the doing." I often cite the following example: you cannot hire someone else to do your push-ups for you and expect to develop your muscles. I constantly work with students to stretch into more and more action steps—doing things they previously did not think possible.

10. *Respond to feedback—and persevere.* I try to inspire students with stories of people like themselves who have gone on to do great things, often by working against the odds; for example, Wilma Rudolph, the great track star who was told as a youth that she would never walk again. I show them how to use mistakes for growth, to employ positive as well as negative feedback to their advan-

tage, and to persevere until they accomplish their goals.

When teachers use these 10 steps in their classrooms, the improvements in students' self-esteem and achievement are rewarding. A comment from a teacher who participated in one of my workshops sums up the dramatic change that can occur in a child's life:

I used to think all I needed to do was to teach mathematics well. Now I teach children, not math. . . . The youngster who really made me understand this was Eddie. When I asked him one day why he thought he was doing so much better than last year, he replied, "It's because I like myself now when I'm with you."

Girls at 11

An Interview with Carol Gilligan

Since the publication of her widely acclaimed book In a Different Voice *(1982), Carol Gilligan, a professor at Harvard University, has conducted and encouraged research on the development of girls. Her new project, "Strengthening Healthy Resistance and Courage in Preadolescent Girls," involves her in interviewing fourth- and sixth-grade girls in public and private schools, observing them in their classrooms, and participating with them in an afterschool club.*

HEL: Girls of 10 and 11 years old have the reputation of being somewhat bossy, or recalcitrant. Is there any contradiction between this and the intriguing title of your new project?

CG: Girls at that age are sometimes called bossy. Based on our studies of development we prefer to think of them as astute observers of the human social world and stalwart resisters of outside pressure to relinquish their own perceptions and judgment.

They seem to carry around a kind of "field guide"—a naturalist's guide to human feelings—not summarized or abstracted, but detailed: how a person feels after this or that event; and of course sequences, narratives of relationships. If so-and-so does something to so-and-so, what happens.

My colleague Lyn Mikel Brown recently analyzed the narratives told by 7-to-16-year-old girls and discovered a key shift just around the age of 11. At this point, girls describe an internal struggle between what they value and what is "good" for them—as defined by their mothers, teachers, or others with greater experience and recognized authority.

In the face of this conflict, girls may begin to feel guilty about attending to their own needs and wants. But 11-year-old girls still value their experiences and knowledge. And they will speak out publicly. If a teacher misinterprets a sixth-grade girl's statement, the girl is likely to insist "That is not what I meant," rather than acquiesce or say "never mind."

HEL: So why does this resistance need strengthening?

CG: Sometime between the ages of 11 and 12, there is a change. I used to ask, "When responsibility to self and others conflicts, how should one choose?" Eleven-year-olds said, "Can you give me an example? That never happens." As one told me, "I am in all my relationships."

Girls a year older would ponder at length over whether it was better to act in terms of yourself or the relationship. In other words, they had begin to separate "self" from relationship—to accept damaging conventions like defining care in terms of self-sacrifice.

In the face of these conventions, it's hard for girls to hold on to their own knowledge about caring and relationships. The clarity and outspokenness disappear. They equivocate, and sometimes even take desperate action to preserve a relationship or meet the expectations of others. They may, for example, risk pregnancy to please a boyfriend or ride in a car with a drunk driver rather than offend a friend.

HEL: What happens to their previous knowledge?

CG: By mid-adolescence, many girls come to question the validity of their own perceptions or feelings and, as a result, become deeply confused about what constitutes truth or trust in relationships. In a sense they withdraw their real selves from their relationships.

Adolescence poses a crisis of connection to a girl coming of age in this culture. What she can say is not what she deeply knows—except when she is in a carefully checked-out, private place. The dilemma is very real, and her solution—I think of it as brilliant, but highly costly—is to take that which she values most and remove it from the situation. It's an incredible price to pay. She loses her voice and connection with others. She is at risk psychologically, in danger of drowning or going underground.

HEL: Isn't adolescence a difficult stage for both boys and girls? Are adolescent girls more at risk?

CG: Adolescent boys come of age in a world "prepared" for them, or "like" them is a very real sense. Conventional norms and values strengthen male voices at adolescence. This is not as true for girls.

Lyn Brown has documented the ways girls struggle over whether to articulate their perceptions. They wonder: "Will I be taken seriously?" Will I damage my relationships? If girls resist the conventions, they must continually struggle to authorize their own voices with very little support from the social system or from institutions like the schools.

I think there may be a greater asymmetry than any of us have ever imagined between girls' and boys' development—in other words, a real difference. I do not mean one is better, one is worse. To understand this you have to put away the usual assumption about child development—that there is a parallel, lockstep progression, with boys and girls marching side by side, stage by stage, toward adulthood.

Adolescence, particularly early adolescence, may be a watershed in girls' development, comparable in some respects to early childhood for boys. There is evidence in the research literature for this theory. For example, Glen Elder and Avshalom Caspi studied families under stress—children of the Great Depression, and families during World War II—and found that the most vulnerable children were boys in early childhood and adolescent girls.

When boys experience psychological difficulties in adolescence, there's usually a history that goes back to childhood. Whereas girls tend to experience these difficulties for the first time in adolescence. They become depressed; by the age of 17 they feel significantly worse about themselves than boys do.

HEL: What implications does this have for educators?

CG: The dilemma of girls' education tends to come to crisis in early adolescence. Girls are encouraged to give up their own experience and tune into the way other people want them to see things. They replace their detailed knowledge of the social world with an idealized, stereotyped notion of relationships and of the type of girl people admire. This nice or perfect girl isn't angry or selfish, and she certainly doesn't disagree in public.

At a faculty meeting in one school we studied, an experienced teacher said. "How can we help the girls to deal with disagreement in public when we can't do it ourselves?" The women then began to talk about how they discussed conflict privately, on the telephone at night, in the bathroom after meetings—but not in public. Girls learn a lot about what is acceptable behavior for women from observing the adults around them.

HEL: It's interesting to think about the role of women teachers. Often girls' problems in high school have been talked about in terms of the insensitivity of male teachers.

CG: Relationships between girls and adult women may be particularly critical during the transition into adolescence. Preadolescents seek out and listen attentively to advice from women; they observe how we treat one another and how we negotiate relationships; they note inconsistencies and discrepancies, and they want to talk about them.

In our studies we have noted that girls often feel abandoned or betrayed by women: they see that mothers on whom they have relied for support can all but disappear in the world. They also become confused about the messages and behaviors of women teachers.

In one school where we did interviews, the younger girls—in the lower school—thought of their teachers as extremely knowledgeable. They could do such essential things as help children learn to read, and you could talk to them about important questions such as "If I have to choose someone for my team and I have two friends, how do I do it without losing a friend?"

But the upper-school teachers did not credit their lower-school colleagues with knowing a great deal. They talked about their colleagues as "nice," or "good with children"—the kinds of things people say about mothers and elementary school teachers. You could predict that girls would have trouble in the middle grades, because their passage to the culture of the upper school was going to involve a kind of betrayal.

HEL: Girls at this age can also betray or be mean to each other. Why are cliques so common?

CG: Last summer Annie Rogers and I started the "Strengthening Healthy Resistance" project with a writing, outings, and theater club. Every time we got on bus, every time we walked, the most important question among the girls was who would be with whom. Everything else paled in intensity.

One way to think about a clique is as an experiment in inclusion and exclusion, a way of gaining information about how it feels to be left out or taken in, and how it feels to include or exclude others. If you take relationships seriously, these are enormously weighty questions. Cliques are an awkward and often extremely painful way in which girls begin to deal with some of these questions.

I also think cliques are a dark mirroring of what girls see in relationships among women. It's not surprising that when cliques start to form, women freeze. We reexperience our own helplessness, and either tell girls they can't act this way or don't engage with them around the issue because it's just too painful. Our selective or ineffective response is part of a tacit agreement that this is how life among women goes.

HEL: Have you found ways to create a different kind of interaction?

CG: The project is premised on our belief that preadolescent girls can benefit from particular kinds of relationships with one another and with adult women. We believe that girls, in order to strengthen their capacities for resistance, courage, and creativity, have to learn to face fears of displeasing others, to feel the genuine risks that are an inevitable part of important relationships, and to sustain their disagreements.

The central activities of the club are journal writing, theater projects, field trips, and group discussion. We want the girls to have opportunities to observe the world and to sort out discrepancies between what they see and what they believe they're supposed to think. The goal is to help them hold on to the veracity of their own perceptions and feelings, even in the face of contradictory norms, and thus to be in real rather than fraudulent relationships with themselves, with others, and with the world.

We also try to provide a safe place for them to explore disagreements. The group discussions become experiments for the girls in speaking publicly about what they know, in being honest with one another and with two adult women.

As the adults, we have to be willing to confront ourselves honestly as well: that is, to consider our own experiences and assumptions about being female in this society at this time and about what it means for women to foster the education and development of girls.

Four Strategies for Fostering Character Development in Children

THOMAS LICKONA

It is a truism that good education, whether for intellect or character, begins by knowing the child. What are children like during their elementary school years? What is their natural stance in the social world? What moral strengths and shortcomings do they present to anyone who would try to foster their character development?

We know that children in elementary school want to be competent—in school subjects, in sports, and in social roles. Furthermore, they want to be recognized as competent—hence their emerging concern with how others view them. Through achievement and the recognition of their achievement by peers, parents, and teachers, elementary school children develop a sense of themselves, a self-concept that is the sum of the things they can do.

By nature, children of this age express themselves through competitiveness. They want to do more things and do them better than the next person. They thus put themselves under a lot of pressure and are often extremely hard on themselves and each other. Quick to say "I'm no good" when they do not succeed at a task, they are easily humil-

Thomas Lickona is a professor of education at the State University of New York, College at Cortland. This article was adapted from a chapter in Character Development in Schools and Beyond (Praeger, 1987), edited by Kevin Ryan and George McClean.

iated by any kind of public failure. At least partly because they are not fully secure about their own competence, they are also notoriously intolerant of incompetence in their peers. Spend time on an elementary school playground, and you will wince at the way children routinely heap scorn ("you stink") on age-mates who have the misfortune to err in a game or otherwise fail to measure up.

Cliques also begin to form during the middle years in elementary school. Membership in one of these peer groups is both a source of approval for competence ("you've made the grade") and a badge of social success ("we like you"). Those within the "inner circle" frequently affirm their coveted status by denigrating those outside it. I heard a fifth-grade teacher say, "The name-calling in my class is constant. Boys who aren't tough or athletic get called 'fags.' The three Japanese children in the class get called 'egg roll' and 'wonton soup'; one Japanese boy was terrified to come to school. Boys also call girls names—'fat,' 'pancake face,' and the like."

Name-calling goes hand in hand with the exclusion of those who are different—from games at recess, from conversation at lunchtime, and from social groups in the classroom. Girls, teachers report, can be even more vicious (though usually more subtle) than boys. Children's reputation for cruelty at this age is well-deserved.

CONTRIBUTIONS OF ENVIRONMENT

Such cruelty, however, is not an inevitable by-product of this developmental period. For better or worse, natural tendencies interact with and are modified by environmental influences. Television violence and snappy put-downs, lack of discipline or love at home, cultural emphasis on self-centered competition, schools that fail to teach caring and cooperation—these factors and more combine to exacerbate the negative developmental tendencies of this age.

But teachers can fashion the school environment, set expectations, and provide moral instruction to channel the natural inclinations of elementary schoolers toward socially constructive ends—and so toward further development. Happily, even in the heyday of the child's callous competition and drive for competence, other developmental forces can be marshaled to check the excesses and to foster the growth of character.

In the cognitive realm, elementary schoolers become increasingly capable of what Piaget calls "decentering"—keeping more than one factor in mind at a time. That means a better ability to consider alternatives and consequences when solving a problem. Robert Selman documents the enormous progress children can make in learning to put themselves in another person's shoes, moving from self-centered egocentrism to a focus on another's viewpoint, to a consideration of two points of view in a dyad, to a mature understanding of the needs of the individual and the group.[1]

In moral judgment, the work of Lawrence Kohlberg shows that, by the end of their elementary school years, children at least begin to apply the Golden Rule. They can understand why trust and mutual helpfulness are essential to human relationships, and they want to be "nice persons" by living up to the expectations of significant others and following the nudge of conscience.[2] Robert Kegan charts the transformation of the strictly autonomous "imperial self" into the more fully integrated

"interpersonal self" as the child negotiates the persistent demands of the surrounding social world.[3]

Thus elementary school children, like their older counterparts, are a constellation of strengths and weaknesses. They are independent and competitive to a fault, overeager to succeed, easily hurt by failure or insult; yet they are often extremely insensitive to the ways in which they hurt others. For all of that, their minds and moral potentials are rapidly unfolding, and the classroom is a logical setting to promote positive social growth.

GOALS OF CHARACTER DEVELOPMENT

Given the nature of elementary students, what are reasonable goals for their moral education? Three stand out:

- to promote development away from egocentrism and excessive individualism and toward cooperative relationships and mutual respect;
- to foster the growth of moral agency—the capacity to think, feel, and act morally; and
- to develop in the classroom and in the school a moral community based on fairness, caring, and participation—such a community being a moral end in itself, as well as a support system for the character development of each individual student.

A classroom dedicated to these broad goals would seek to develop in each child the following specific qualities: 1) self-respect that derives feelings of worth not only from competence but also from positive behavior toward others; 2) social perspective-taking that asks how others think and feel; 3) moral reasoning about the right things to do; 4) such moral values as kindness, courtesy, trustworthiness, and responsibility; 5) the social skills and habits of cooperation; and 6) openness to the positive influence of adults.

To do an adequate job of moral education—one that has a chance of making a real impact on a child's developing character—four processes should be going on in the classroom: 1) building self-esteem and a sense of community, 2) learning to

---

[1]Robert Selman, *The Growth of Interpersonal Understanding* (New York: Academic Press, 1980).

[2]Lawrence Kohlberg, *Essays on Moral Development, Volume 1: The Philosophy of Moral Development* (San Francisco: Harper & Row, 1981).

[3]Robert Kegan, *The Evolving Self* (Cambridge, Mass.: Harvard University Press. 1982).

cooperate and help others, 3) moral reflection, and 4) participatory decision making. Taken together, these four processes embrace both the formal academic curriculum and the "human" curriculum (the rules, roles, and relationships) that make up the life of the classroom. Let us consider each of these processes individually.

Building Self-Esteem and Sense of Community

Building self-esteem in the elementary school years fosters the sense of competence and mastery that is at the core of the child's self-concept. Building self-esteem also teaches children to value themselves as persons, to have the kind of respect for themselves that enables them to stand up for their rights and command the respect of others. To build a sense of community is to create a group that extends to others the respect one has for oneself. More specifically, building a community in the classroom allows students to come to know one another as individuals, to respect and care about one another, and to feel a sense of membership in and accountability to the group.

Self-esteem is important to character development because morality begins with valuing one's own person. Loving your neighbor is easier if you love yourself. A sense of community is important because it contributes to self-esteem, partly by creating a norm of mutual respect that inhibits putdowns and partly by helping children to feel known and positively valued by their peers. A sense of community also supplies a vital affective dimension to moral education, a flow of good feeling that makes it easier for children to be good, easier for them to cross the bridge from knowing what is right to doing it. Teachers who take the trouble to build positive "group feeling" know (at least intuitively) that developing virtue is as much an affair of the emotions as of the mind. Finally, for an increasing number of children, a supportive classroom community provides a surrogate "family" that helps to meet important emotional needs that are not being met at home.

Wise teachers begin to foster self-worth and to develop social bonds on day one of the school year. Two team-teachers of second- and third-graders in Brookline, Massachusetts, greet children when they arrive in September with this message: "All of us will be together for 180 days. It will be much happier for everyone if we get along and are able to cooperate. We don't expect you to *like* everybody, but we do expect you to *respect* each other and to take care not to hurt anyone. During the first several weeks of school, we'll be teaching you the skills you'll need to cooperate and to show respect for others."

Over the ensuing weeks, this orientation is followed by simple activities that enable children to get to know each other: playing games, solving puzzles "with someone you don't know very well," writing down "all the ways you and a new partner are alike and different," and so on. "Through the course of the year," the teachers report, "a sense of trust develops. Children begin to reinforce each other's ideas and abilities; they support one another in difficult times. This doesn't happen overnight. It grows slowly and must be openly encouraged."

A fourth-grade teacher rotates "learning partners." Every three weeks students get new partners with whom they work at least once a day on an assigned task. A fifth-grade teacher finds she can reduce the prevalence of exclusive cliques in her class by holding a seating lottery at the end of every week. Because desks in her room are contiguous in a large rectangle, the drawing means that each week each child is almost sure to have two new neighbors—and a chance to make two new friends.

When others give us their time, their attention, their friendship, we are better able to judge ourselves as individuals worthy of love and respect. Feeling good about ourselves, we have an easier time being good to others. That basic truth underlies this first and most fundamental process of moral education: fostering the self-esteem of the individual in and through human community.

Learning to Cooperate and Help Others

Community experience is thin if students come together only in a class discussion to share thoughts and feelings but spend the rest of the day working individually on academic work. Learning to cooperate and help others requires that students *work* together, as well as talk together. If we want them to develop the skill and spirit of cooperation, we must make cooperation a regular feature of classroom life.

Some elementary teachers use the whole academic curriculum as a vehicle for developing cooperation. For example, fourth-graders in Paula

Barno's parochial school science class worked in pairs to construct and balance mobiles. In art, they drew group murals, and they designed and decorated a quiet "meditation corner" for the classroom. But the crowning achievement came in social studies when the whole class collaborated on a unit on Mexico as their contribution to the school's "Festival of Many Lands." Barno writes:

The children were excited to work on this project. They eagerly settled into their tasks, were able to talk out most disagreements, and objected if one person tried to take over. As they worked on maps, charts, and displays of people, places, and things, it was encouraging for me to hear them discuss new points of view, reconsider their own, and after their first opinions. . . . We all felt a new unity among us that this cooperative experience had made possible.

Cooperation is also made easier when children learn to support each other. A fifth-grade teacher instituted a practice called "appreciation time," a short session at the end of each day when class members describe something that others have done that they appreciate.

For example, at one meeting a pupil said, "I appreciate Julie for lending me some paper when I forgot mine. All I did was say I didn't have any, and she offered me some of hers." A second student said, "I'd like to appreciate Stan for helping me study for my spelling test. That was the first time I ever got 100!"

The teacher reports that appreciation time has become the most popular activity in her classroom. This fact is all the more impressive when we recall that fifth-graders, left to their own devices, typically trade insults rather than compliments.

Many teachers foster helping relationships in the classroom by taking a further step. They use class problem-solving meetings to crystallize feelings of community and interdependence into a clear sense of collective responsibility. Often such meetings address a problem that affects many or all class members: too much noise, people not helping with clean-up, students taking or otherwise abusing others' property, and so on. But collective responsibility means more; it asserts that we are our neighbor's keepers—that even if only one other person has a problem, that problem belongs to everybody. A new classmate who has no friends or who doesn't know how to get around in the school

becomes a classwide concern. The stealing of one person's lunch money is an issue for the entire class.

Social observers often decry "me-first" individualism and lack of concern for the common good among young people. If we wish to strengthen ethical cooperation within society, we should strive to make it a character trait of children, as they live and work in the small society that is the classroom.

Moral Reflection

The third process crucial to moral education in the elementary school years is moral reflection. The word *reflection* refers to a wide range of intellectual activities, including reading, thinking, debating moral questions, listening to explanations by the teacher (e.g., why it is wrong to make fun of a handicapped child), and conducting firsthand investigation to increase children's awareness of the complex social system to which they belong.

Of the four processes of moral education, moral reflection aims most directly at developing the cognitive and rational aspects of moral behavior. At the same time, this self-consciously rational aspect of character development can be nurtured in such a way as to foster a union of cognition and affect, so that children come to feel deeply about what they think and value.

One second-grade teacher. for example, saw an opportunity to merge cognition and affect during a science project in which the class was incubating 20 chicken eggs. She had suggested to the class that they might wish to open one egg each week in order to monitor the embryonic development.

Later that day, in his reading group, 7-year-old Nathaniel confided to his teacher. "Mrs. Williams, I've been thinking about this for a long time. It's just too *cruel* to open an egg and kill the chick inside!"

Mrs. Williams listened without comment and said that she would bring the topic up for discussion with the whole class. When she did, there was some agreement that Nat's point was worth considering. But many children said that they were curious to see what the embryo looked like. Nat replied that being curious wasn't a good enough reason for killing a chick. "How would you like it," he said, "if somebody opened your sac when you were developing because they were curious to see what you looked like?" The library must have pictures of chick embryos, he argued. Wouldn't that be a better way of finding out what an embryo looked like?

Some children countered that they wanted to see a *real* chick. "Is it alive?" one asked. Not until it has hatched, some argued. "It's alive now," countered others, "and it's a chicken!"

Mrs. Williams asked the children to think about the issue overnight. She told them that they would reach a decision as a class the following morning. By that time, a majority of the children had come to feel that Nat's objection should be honored; they did not open the eggs.

The potential for moral learning in this episode was tremendous. The children considered the question of whether all life, even that of a chick embryo, is to be taken seriously. They learned that simply wanting to do something isn't a good enough reason for doing it and that a member of the group who has strong feelings about something has a right to express them. They also learned that others have an obligation to listen and that, if possible, a conflict should be resolved in a way that tries to meet the needs of all parties. The class did, in fact, search out pictures of chick embryos in the library.

This intensive moral reflection resulted from Mrs. Williams' taking the time to allow her students to come to grips with a difficult moral dilemma arising from the real life of the classroom. As a side point, real-life dilemmas such as this one are far more effective in engaging children's thinking and feelings than any "canned" dilemmas from a book or kit.

Moral reflection also helps children realize that, while it is often easy to know the right thing, it is usually harder to do it. Children should talk about why they (and other people) sometimes cheat, lie, put people down, or treat others unfairly, even when they know that such things are wrong. What factors—self-interest, peer pressure, anger, anxiety, low self-esteem—lead them to do such things? What helps them stay on the straight and narrow?

Children need practice both as moral psychologists who understand human weakness and wrongdoing and as moral philosophers who declare what is right. They need to be challenged to develop the self-awareness, self-discipline, and strength of will that can help them hew to the right course.

All of this is clearly a tall order. It should come as no surprise that teachers, even the best ones, usually find guiding moral reflection to be the hardest part of moral education. It involves many sophisticated skills: framing moral issues, using Socratic questioning, paraphrasing responses, mak-

ing connections among the contributions of a variety of students, and drawing out and challenging children's reasoning (rather than settling for mere expression of opinion), to name just a few. Most teachers have rarely seen such skills modeled in their own education and thus will need time, patience, and practice to develop them. But the effort to do so is clearly essential, because moral reflection is at the center of the moral enterprise.

Participatory Decision Making

Based on his work with high schools, University of Notre Dame professor Clark Power observed that it is easy to get students to agree about such moral rules as "don't steal." But it is much harder to develop moral norms that students feel obligated to follow in their behavior.[4] A true norm is an operative moral standard, one to which children will hold themselves and others accountable. Such norms create a support system that helps students live up to their moral standards. Through this process of putting belief into practice, a value becomes a virtue.

Participatory decision making, the fourth process of moral education in the elementary school, provides a motivational push from judgment to action. It does so by requiring children to participate in making rules or solving classroom conflicts; they are then held accountable for these decisions, which eventually become operative group norms.

Piaget was one of the first to argue for such participatory governance in the classroom.[5] He reasoned that, if children are truly to understand that people make rules to help themselves live with one another, they must have a hand in discussing and making classroom rules. Otherwise, rules remain external to the child's mind and have little power over behavior. What is essential, however, is not any specific set of procedures, but rather a *spirit* of participation and shared responsibility for the classroom.

There are many ways to foster responsible participation in classroom decision making. Teachers should begin slowly, using whatever they are comfortable with, and gradually branch out. For exam-

[4]Clark Power, "The Just Community High School," in Kevin Ryan and George McClean, eds., *Character Development in Schools and Beyond* (New York: Praeger. 1987).

[5]Jean Piaget, *The Moral Judgment of the Child* (New York: Free Press, 1932).

ple, giving children a bigger voice in the classroom can start with something as simple as a suggestion box. It can expand to include teacher/student learning contracts, small-group brainstorming sessions as a means of solving a persistent classroom problem, a "Conflict Corner" where two students can go to work out their differences, a teacher-moderated "fairness committee" to propose solutions to classroom problems, written or oral feedback from students on a curriculum unit (What did you learn? How could it have been improved? How can we make the next unit better?), and regular class meetings.

Class meetings can be held weekly or daily, and they can be run by either consensus or by majority rule. Voting can be open (to encourage public stands) or by secret ballot (to minimize peer pressure). Through any of these methods, teachers can send the message to students that they value each child's viewpoint.

Participatory decision-making contributes to character development by helping children apply their moral reasoning to their own behavior and to the society around them. In a democratic society, participatory decision making has a special value in that it teaches democracy through democracy,

training an active citizenry by having children be active citizens in the life of their school.

In summary, not only do these four processes reinforce one another, but each is also necessary for the full success of the others. Discussion of moral issues, especially debate, is very difficult when the sense of community is weak or when students don't know or like their classmates. Debating moral issues is shallow without opportunities for real-life decision making. Class discussion is "all talk" if children never work together on substantive tasks. Cooperative learning fails to realize its full potential if children never plan and evaluate their joint endeavors. And, without the group spirit that is born of cooperative activity, participatory decision making turns into a forum in which students argue for their "rights" with little thought of their obligations or of the community good.

Taken together, these four processes offer elementary school teachers a way to develop the rational, affective, and behavioral aspects of children's character. Many teachers are already practicing this kind of character education with imagination, dedication, and skill. They have shown us that we have the means to bring our children to moral maturity, if only we can muster the will.

► Chapter 4

Making Mainstreaming Work through Prereferral Consultation

ROBERT EVANS

The most significant current development in special education is the growing trend toward prereferral intervention. To better serve low-achieving students and cut the cost of pull-out programs, many school districts are creating programs of consultation to help the teacher maintain students in the classroom before seeking formal evaluation and special education (SPED) service.[1] This effort, often called the Regular Education Initiative, demands significantly broader roles both of teachers and of those staff—usually special educators and school psychologists—who become consultants. The promise of these new roles is compelling: a fuller realization of mainstreaming, a more rapid and collegial response to teachers' concerns, and a better vehicle for enhancing teachers' skills.[2]

But the reality is more complex, the results less encouraging. The conditions vital to effective consultation rarely exist. Regular education has not yet accepted mainstreaming itself, let alone prereferral intervention, and few teachers welcome their enlarged responsibility. Many SPED staff are reluctant to assume the role of consultant. Paradoxically, prereferral efforts often highlight the disparity between mainstreaming's vision and its implementation, raising anew questions about its premises and promises. This article examines the conditions required to make prereferral consultation work in this problematic context.

THE MAINSTREAMING CONTEXT: UNFORESEEN PROBLEMS

At its inception, mainstreaming seemed as valuable for what it would do away with as for what it would do. It sought to end a system that ignored many children with critical needs and warehoused others in residential schools; it sought to expand the rights of these students and their parents; and it sought schools where children would be seen not as better or worse but as different kinds of learners and where teachers would adapt their pedagogy to a wide range of learning styles. Though it has found limited success in these efforts, mainstreaming has been beset by four unforeseen problems.

Oversold, Underfunded

Like many educational innovations, mainstreaming has suffered from inflated promises and inadequate resources. It makes the public school responsible for remediating virtually the entire range of physical, cognitive, and emotional conditions that can

---

[1]Many prereferral efforts also move SPED staff into classrooms as co-teachers. Though this article addresses only consultation, much of it applies equally to co-teaching.

[2]In the literature, it is accepted that the Regular Education Initiative and prereferral consultation will affirm the teacher's ownership of the problem and competence in addressing it. Differences arise on two sets of issues: how comprehensive the effort can be (Braaten et al. 1988, Algozzine et al. 1990, Jenkins et al. 1990, Kauffman et al. 1990, Lieberman 1990); and how to structure consultation that is collaborative (Pugach and Johnson 1989a, 1989b; Graden et al. 1985; Graden 1989).

Robert Evans is Director of the Human Relations Service, 11 Chapel Pl. Wellesley Hills, MA 02181.

affect students. Implicit in this responsibility is a medical model of service: the school is to provide both diagnosis and cure. As tests yield ever more refined assessments of "processing problems" and other conditions, parents assume that successful treatment will follow. This ignores a significant gap between diagnostic technology on the one hand and remedial technology and resources on the other. We are much better able to identify some disabilities than to treat them. And some diagnoses, however elegant, do not offer clear indications for treatment. Others do have remedial implications, but the prognosis, even given ideal resources, is guarded. Special education has proved far more expensive than anyone imagined. Lacking the political clout to obtain adequate funding, schools are often unable to provide the full range of service that would meet all the identified needs.

Overemphasis on Parental Rights

One of the most troubling (but least publicly acknowledged) mainstreaming problems for school staff is dealing with the parents of SPED students. Though, ideally, parent and school are allies, too often their relationship turns adversarial, characterized by mutual disappointment and scapegoating. These problems, to which both sides contribute, are complicated by mainstreaming legislation that is weighted toward parental rights and against professional prerogatives. No one can object to entitling parents to prompt assessments and appropriate programs for their children. But the effect of current law is to swing the pendulum out of balance. Expanded parental awareness of mandated requirements, coupled with the implicit promises noted above, has dramatically increased the number of parents seeking service for their children. Indeed, many students are now receiving more services than they require because parents insist on them, often threatening legal action. "The more we provide, the better our work, the more parents we have demanding services," says one SPED administrator. "It's no longer a matter of what's educationally right for lots of these kids, but of how many legal battles we can afford."

Unrealistically Expanding Roles and Responsibilities

Mainstreaming radically alters the teacher's role and responsibility, making classes more heterogeneous and requiring far more individualization than many teachers are prepared for. Heterogeneous grouping has compelling values of its own, but it complicates instruction and classroom management—particularly when it involves students with behavior problems—and demands smaller teacher-pupil ratios. Because few districts have the resources to reduce ratios, mainstreaming makes teachers' lives more difficult. Compounding this difficulty is mainstreaming's emphasis on individualization: it requires teaching students rather than disciplines. From secondary teachers I have heard endless variations on this theme: "The exceptions I have to make are so extreme that I'm not teaching my subject anymore." Elementary teachers, too, though more accustomed to individualizing and to teaching the "whole child," find the range of approaches required difficult. At both levels, teachers insist that SPED students drain their attention from the majority of the class.

Increasingly Burdened Teachers

Even without mainstreaming, life in schools has grown more onerous. Teachers everywhere report deterioration in the motivation and behavior of students and in the support and responsiveness of families. Many attribute this to high rates of divorce and single-parenting and to rising numbers of two-career families and of children living in poverty. Whatever the causes, children from all walks of life are presenting themselves at school less ready to learn. At the same time, parental expectations continue to rise. Schools are under relentless pressure to upgrade curriculum, teach higher-order thinking skills, accelerate student performance, and meet a growing range of social and emotional needs. "Parents demand more and more service from us, both academic and nonacademic, but do less and less for their own children," says one principal, echoing a common sentiment. Teachers' responses to this dilemma are affected by the fact that they are a veteran, aging group. The average teacher is nearly 50 and a 20-year veteran. Whatever the benefits of age and experience, they do not include flexibility, openness to imposed change, or a wish to have one's job made more demanding (Evans 1989).

These four problems have complicated the delivery of SPED services and the tenor of professional relationships in schools. They have left a large core of teachers unprepared and/or unwilling to adapt to the requirements of mainstreaming. In this context, it is not surprising that an expanded mainstreaming effort based on consultation can provoke resistance among teachers and apprehension among special educators.

COPING: EFFECTIVE PREREFERRAL CONSULTATION

In the face of such problems, implementing a program of prereferral consultation is a complex task. I have had the chance to consult with many districts undertaking such efforts. Those that are succeeding, though their procedures differ, developed a comprehensive plan that includes six elements: (1) selection of consultants; (2) training in consultation techniques for consultants and support for their efforts; (3) administrative sanction; (4) training and support for teachers; (5) parent education; (6) start-up funding.

Selection of Consultants

Most schools designate members of their multidisciplinary team—special educators and psychologists—as consultants. Some adopt variants of the Teacher Assistance Team (Chalfant et al. 1979), in which classroom teachers consult with one another. In the literature there is lively debate about which model is better suited to provide "collaborative" consultation. Because it is so common, I will discuss the former. But I have seen genuinely collaborative help provided by teachers as well as specialists, by individuals as well as teams. The methods outlined below may be learned and applied by all staff. The key is not *who* consults but *how* and whether the necessary conditions obtain to make consultation work.

Training and Support for Consultants

The core requirement for successful consultation is effective training and support for those who are to provide it. Though SPED staff appreciate the rationale for making them consultants, some fear loss of their status as the provider of unique services and eventually of the job itself. Others are intimidated because they imagine the consultant's role to be beyond them. They understand it as the provision of expert opinion by a specialist with superior skill who provides a diagnosis and prescribes a treatment—the medical model of consultation. Applied outside medical settings, this model has two main drawbacks: (1) it does not help the consultee to

develop his own skills but leaves him dependent on the consultant; (2) the consultee rarely implements fully the consultant's remedies, which, after all, are not his own.

Writers on prereferral unanimously reject this approach in favor of a collaborative model of consultation. Since the goal of prereferral is to emphasize teachers' ownership of mainstreaming and ability to meet students' needs—and since teachers have expertise that SPED staff lack—consultation should be an informal, cooperative venture between co-equals who blend their different skills on the basis of parity. Apart from calling for these characteristics, the prereferral literature was scant on the actual how-to of collaborative consultation until recently (Zins et al. 1988). The clearest model is found in the organization development literature, where it is called "process consultation" (Schein 1988). It sees the consultant as catalyst in an effort at joint problem solving. Its premise is that solutions will be more effective and lasting when they are the consultee's own. The consultant's role is to help the consultee make a diagnosis and develop a remedy. While she is glad to provide suggestions where she can, the consultant's main expertise is in collaborative troubleshooting.

Process consultation takes time and experience to learn, but its basic precepts are straightforward. As applied to mainstreaming, they include:

- Consultation depends on mutuality, trust, the consultant's respect for the teacher's skill, and her ability to engage the teacher in problem solving.
- Teaching taxes its practitioners' self-esteem and leaves them periodically vulnerable to loss of perspective and feelings of inadequacy. Consultation must address these issues, not just prescribe new behaviors.
- Each individual has his or her own problem-solving style, with its own strengths and weaknesses. Consultation must respect this style, drawing particularly on the consultee's strengths.

The goals of process consultation are to:

- *expand perspective*—to help the teacher broaden his perspective on the problem, depersonalize it, and see it in the larger context outlined above
- *build skills*—to help the teacher renew and enhance his problem-solving repertoire. This includes helping him recall and draw upon his

existing skill-base and involving him in the design of coping strategies

* *provide support*—to help the teacher restore his self-esteem and commitment. This means helping him to appreciate the successes he has achieved, no matter how small, and is often more important than skill-building.

Throughout the process, the consultant's focus will be: what will work for *this* teacher with *this* student? Her approach does not only help the teacher adjust to the student's learning style; it respects the teacher's own style and seeks to enhance his strengths. Ideally, the consultant provides something concrete—a jointly devised strategy to apply in the classroom—and something felt-conveying to the teacher that he has been heard, that he is not alone with the problem, that his competence is recognized and his efforts to help a student are appreciated.

In addition to training, SPED staff need the necessary logistical support—especially time—to become consultants and collaborators. Most are overtaxed by large caseloads and lengthy paperwork. To function effectively as consultants and as a team overseeing the prereferral process, their schedules must permit them to be available to teachers (both for initial consultations and for follow-up visits) and to confer together. This requires additional staffing to absorb some of their caseload until consultation reduces the population of students referred.

Given good training and logistical support, SPED staff are ready to become consultants. But to succeed in this effort, they need a broader range of support, one which begins with administrators and embraces teachers and parents and which creates conditions that permit consultation to work.

Administrative Sanction

Prereferral consultation is critically dependent on vigorous, sustained top-down advocacy and support. Because mainstreaming depends on classroom teachers but is unwelcome to them, active sanction by those to whom they answer is essential.[3] A clear mission statement to all staff should emphasize the new mainstreaming mandate and outline the consequent changes in structure and roles—an initiative that must start with the super-

intendent and be firmly endorsed by principals. SPED administrators and staff typically have no formal influence over teachers. Lacking status and power, knowing that many teachers haven't "bought into" mainstreaming, they rightly fear resistance ("Teachers don't want me to consult; they want me to take a student out and fix him"). When a special educator announces that he or she will now be consulting with teachers about classroom modifications before any student is referred for a SPED evaluation, teachers have little reason to accept this proclamation. When a principal announces it, there is much more reason for them to do so.

In addition to initial advocacy, administrators must provide continuing support. Acceptance of prereferral's new roles and procedures comes slowly, and sabotage is to be expected. Thus, it is usual to find some teachers seeking to avoid consultation and classroom modifications by suggesting to parents that they exercise their right to demand a formal SPED evaluation. In such cases, only the principal has the standing to insist that procedures be respected. If the principal is known to be out of touch with the prereferral initiative (by not attending meetings of the multidisciplinary team or not confronting resistance), consultation stands little chance of taking hold.

Sanction includes supervisory follow-through. Rather than work with teachers who need to improve their mainstreaming skills, supervisors generally avoid the issue by assigning large numbers of SPED students to teachers who do. Yet if we are serious about mainstreaming, supervisors and evaluators must help teachers recognize the importance of expanding their instructional repertoires and must be prepared to reflect this prominently in teachers' performance appraisals.

Training and Support for Teachers

It is neither fair nor sufficient simply to press teachers to change the patterns of a lifetime: like SPED staff, they deserve appropriate training.[4] To accept their new roles, teachers need inservice that begins

---

[3]Changes in professional roles, relationships, and responsibilities usually provoke uncertainty, suspicion, and resistance. For an excellent review of this key underacknowledged issue, see Zins et al. (1988).

[4]Many approaches are relevant to this task. Some are directly related to special education, such as instruction about learning disabilities. Others have much broader relevance to teaching and to the very structure of scheduling, such as the techniques of cooperative learning and of Theodore Sizer's "essential school." Neither is designed as a mainstreaming remedy, but both emphasize characteristics vital to successful work with SPED students: teacher flexibility; establishment of a cooperative classroom community; and, above all, active, participatory involvement by students.

by enjoining them, not attacking them or condescending to them, and which recognizes that they need encouragement to try new behaviors before they need technical instruction. This is crucial because there is little natural reason for teachers to embrace the changes and complexities mainstreaming requires. Some may respond to the professional challenge of broadening their skills; others may realize that they must accept the inevitable and adapt to it; many may come to appreciate the importance of helping a significant population of students to live fuller lives. But few are likely to respond to inservice training unless it acknowledges frankly the larger context of problems outlined above and the burden that mainstreaming represents.

Inservice must go on to address the concerns that trouble teachers most in their classrooms. These begin not with cognitive or physical handicaps but with motivation and behavior. Endemic problems among SPED students include:

- *attention-seeking behavior*—primary impulse disorders or oppositional, "acting-out" behavior styles;
- *passive refusal*—lethargy, depression, and reluctance to try;
- *variability*—marked fluctuations in attention, concentration, and performance and difficulty sustaining previous gains.

These problems are a daily challenge to teachers' skills, expectations, and self-esteem. Inservice must provide a framework for understanding them so that, for example, teachers can learn to see variability as an intrinsic part of most disabilities and realize that though they prefer a steady, reliable rate of progress, periodic setbacks are predictable.

As part of this framework, training must demystify special education, offer concrete strategies for coping with the above problems, and help teachers adjust their expectations. Many teachers imagine that mainstreaming requires specialized approaches far beyond their ken. Yet much of a special educators do consists of tutoring and small-group instruction, and many methods they employ are easily adopted, including such basic behavioral techniques as emphasizing strengths rather than attacking weaknesses; shortening the wait for rewards; and giving new methods a sustained try (not abandoning them if they don't produce instant results).

Along with useful techniques, inservice must give teachers permission to modify their expecta-

tions for their students—and, most important, for themselves. Everything about mainstreaming, from the term itself to the assertive language of Individual Educational Plans ("Johnny will read on grade level by June 1st") fosters the idea that SPED students can learn in the mainstream like everyone else. Though they need to hear "every student can learn" and need to be inspired to look for the strengths in all students, teachers must not be pressed to fulfill unrealistic promises. Even as it urges them to do their very best, inservice must recognize that coming up short is inevitable. It must encourage teachers to avoid personalizing problems—not to treat misbehavior as a personal attack—and to moderate expectations—to accept the variability noted above and set goals accordingly.

Good training and effective consultation are vital, but not sufficient. Teachers also need tangible support in the form of pupil ratios that enable them to mainstream effectively. Too often, districts imagine that teachers, briefly trained and offered consultation, should be able to integrate most special needs students with no loss of attention to other students. The presence in a classroom of two or three pupils with significant special needs (often, there are five or six) radically complicates a teacher's task, dividing and draining his or her energy and attention.[5] Unless the school is prepared to accept reduced performance, it must be staffed to create manageable, teachable classrooms.

Parent Education

Though much lip service is paid to parental involvement, it is often a source of real ambivalence for school staff, for whom, as noted earlier, parents' mandated rights are a focus of frustration (they often see parents as having too much influence and as being overly critical, in part because of unrealistic expectations). SPED parents rarely need to be sold on the value of more complete mainstreaming. But like teachers and special educators, they need help to bear their own burdens and to improve overall cooperation on students' behalf. They benefit from the same approach recommended above for teacher inservice: presentations that enjoin them, that address the issues that most trouble them at

---

[5]There are two issues here: the number of special needs students and the severity of their conditions. Faced with soaring tuition costs for out-placements, districts are retaining many more very troubled students.

home as well as at school, that demystify learning disabilities and offer concrete coping strategies, and that help them to moderate their expectations.

Start-Up Funding

All of the above elements have costs: trainers, in-service presenters, staff to reduce SPED caseloads and teacher-pupil ratios. Yet, as one superintendent noted, a main impetus behind prereferral initiatives is cost-cutting: "Few of us would be pushing this so hard if we weren't going broke on special ed." Of these costs, all but the last are time-limited. In the corporate world, the need for this kind of initial expense is axiomatic; it is accepted that future savings begin with current costs, that change, even in pursuit of economy, often requires investment. In schools, we too often seek change without expense. Districts that implement effective prereferral programs have pressed successfully for start-up funding. Without this, prereferral cannot fulfill its promise.

BEGINNING

Districts that provide training and support for consultants and teachers, administrative sanction, parent education, and start-up funding are making new models of mainstreaming work—but not easily or quickly. Though prereferral promises to improve mainstreaming and to be more cost-effective than pull-out models, the transition process can be painful. Moreover, it cannot eliminate the need for a broad range of services to students.

Some districts have found that an effective strategy is to begin from strength by starting with a pilot venture, usually in one or two elementary schools that have strong, committed leadership, a good SPED staff, and a core of receptive teachers. As it becomes clear that prereferral does not simply mean more work for teachers, that they do receive effective support and can make significant headway with students, the effort becomes easier to promote throughout the district.

But as they fashion and implement a comprehensive plan, school leaders must remember that they are embarking on a major change in attitudes and behavior and doing so in difficult times. Like the students they seek to serve, and the staff whose roles they seek to change, they need high expecta-

tions to encourage them and a realistic perspective to sustain them.

REFERENCES

Algozzine, B., L. Maheady, K. C. Sacca, L. O'Shea, and D. O'Shea. (1990). "Sometimes Patent Medicine Works: A Reply to Braaten, Kauffman, Braaten, Polsgrove, and Nelson." *Exceptional Children* 56, 6: 552–557.

Braaten, S., J. M. Kauffman, B. Braaten, L Polsgrove, and C. M. Nelson. (1988). "The Regular Education Initiative: Patent Medicine for Behavioral Disorders." *Exceptional Children* 55, 1: 21–28.

Chalfant, J. C., M. V. D. Pysh, and R. Moultrie. (1979). "Teacher Assistance Teams: A Model for Within-Building Problem Solving." *Learning Disability Quarterly* 2: 85–96.

Evans, R. (May 1989). "The Faculty in Mid-career: Implications for School Improvement." *Educational Leadership* 46: 10–15.

Graden, J. (1989). "Redefining 'Prereferral' Intervention as Intervention Assistance: Collaboration Between General and Special Education." *Exceptional Children* 56,3: 227–231.

Graden, J., A. Casey, and S. L. Christenson. (1985). "Implementing a Prereferral Intervention System: Part I. The Model." *Exceptional Children* 51, 5: 377–384.

Jenkins, J. R., C. G. Pious, and M. Jewell. (1990). "Special Education and the Regular Education Initiative: Basic Assumptions." *Exceptional Children* 56, 6: 479492.

Kauffman, J. M., S. Braaten, C. M. Nelson, I.. Polsgrove, and B. Braaten. (1990). "The Regular Education Initiative and Patent Medicine: A Rejoinder to Algozzine, Maheady, Sacca, O'Shea, and O'Shea." *Exceptional Children* 56. 6: 558–560.

Lieberman, L. (1990). "REI: Revisited . . . Again." *Exceptional Children* 56, 6: 561–562.

Pugach, M. C., and L. J. Johnson. (1989a). "Prereferral Interventions: Progress, Problems, and Challenges." *Exceptional Children* 56, 3: 217–226.

Pugach, M.C., and L. J. Johnson. (1989b). "The Challenge of Implementing Collaboration Between General and Special Education." *Exceptional Children* 56, 3: 232–235.

Schein, E. (1988). *Process Consultation.* Reading: Addison-Wesley.

Zins, J. E., M. J. Curtis. J. L. Graden, and C. R. Ponti. (1988). *Helping Students Succeed in the Regular Classroom: A Guide for Developing Intervention Assistance Programs.* San Francisco: Jossey-Bass.

Author's note: I am very grateful to Norman Colb for his conceptual and editorial help.

Multiple Intelligences Go to School

Educational Implications of the Theory of Multiple intelligences

HOWARD GARDNER and THOMAS HATCH

A new approach to the conceptualization and assessment of human intelligences is described. According to Gardner's Theory of Multiple Intelligences, each human being is capable of seven relatively independent forms of information processing, with individuals differing from one another in the specific profile of intelligences that they exhibit. The range of human intelligences is best assessed through contextually based, "intelligence-fair" instruments. Three research projects growing out of the theory are described. Preliminary data secured from Project Spectrum, an application in early childhood, indicate that even 4- and 5-year-old children exhibit distinctive profiles of strength and weakness. Moreover, measures of the various intelligences are largely independent and tap abilities other than those measured by standard intelligence tests.

—*Educational Researcher, Vol. 18, No. 8, pp. 4–10*

Despite swings of the pendulum between theoretical and applied concerns, the concept of intelligence has remained central to the field of psychology. In the wake of the Darwinian revolution, when scientific psychology was just beginning, many scholars became interested in the development of intelligence across species. The late 19th and early 20th centuries were punctuated by volumes that delineated levels of intelligence across species and within the human species (Baldwin, 1895; Hobhouse, 1915; Romanes, 1892). Francis Galton (cousin of Charles Darwin) was perhaps the first psychologically oriented scientist to try to measure the intellect directly. Though Galton (1870) had

Howard Gardner, Professor of Education, Harvard Graduate School of Education, Longfellow Hall, Cambridge, MA 02138, specializes in developmental psychology and neuropsychology.

Thomas Hatch, doctoral candidate, Harvard Graduate School of Education, Longfellow Hall, Cambridge, MA 02138, specializes in human development.

a theoretical interest in the concept of intelligence, his work was by no means unrelated to practical issues. A committed eugenicist, he sought to measure intelligence and hoped, through proper "breeding," to increase the overall intelligence of the population.

During the following half century, many of the most gifted and influential psychologists concerned themselves with the nature of human intelligence. Although a few investigators were interested principally in theoretical issues, most seasoned their concerns with a practical orientation. Thus Binet (Binet & Simon, 1916) and Terman (1916) developed the first general-purpose intelligence tests in their respective countries; Yerkes (Yerkes, Bridges, & Hardwick, 1915) and Wechsler (1939) created their own influential instruments. Even scientists with a strong theoretical bent, like Spearman (1927) and Thurstone (1938), contributed either directly or indirectly to the devising of certain measurement

Rupal Sevak
La clase de espanol 130
Abril 6, 1996

Mujeres al Borde de un Ataque de Nervios--- Segunda Parte

Carlos queda en el apartmento para cuidar para Candela y su novia. Pepa va a la
oficina de Paulina Morales, quien es una abogada feminista. El taxista extrano conduce
Pepa a la oficina. Pepa ve que Paulina va a viajar a Estocolmo. Ivan llama Paulina.
Pepa y Paulina pelean. Carlos llama la policia y revela que los Shittes van a controlar el
vuelto. Pepa decide que ella y Candela van a hacer un viaje. Lucia llama a Pepa, y Pepa
dice que ella no puede visitar. Carlos dice que su madre esta loca y ella odia a el. Ivan
y Lucia no viven en la misma casa cuando el ira joven. El vive con sus abuelos. Ivan
viene al apartmento de Pepa para llevar su maleta, pero tiene miedo de Pepa y no
remove la maleta. Lucia viene al apartmento con la policia y un hombre viene para
arreglar el telefono. La policia piden preguntas sobre los Shittes. Pepa sirve todos
(excepto Lucia) gazpacho, y todos duremen. Lucia tiene una pistola y va con un
hombre con un moto al aeropureto. La novia del hombre y Pepa siguen en el coche del
taxista extrano. Hay un "chase" y ellos entren el aeropuerto. Lucia va a matar Ivan,
pero Pepa dejalo. Pepa sale el aeropuerto, y Ivan siente malo porque sabe que el es un
hombre que no deserva la amor de Pepa.

techniques and the favoring of particular lines of interpretation.

By midcentury, theories of intelligence had become a staple of psychology textbooks, even as intelligence tests were taken for granted in many industrialized countries. Still, it is fair to say that, within scientific psychology, interest in issues of intelligence waned to some extent. Although psychometricians continued to perfect the instruments that purported to measure human intellect and some new tests were introduced (Guilford, 1967), for the most part, the burgeoning interest in cognitive matters bypassed the area of intelligence.

This divorce between mainstream research psychology and the "applied area" of intelligence might have continued indefinitely, but, in fact, by the late 70s, there were signs of a reawakening of interest in theoretical and research aspects of intelligence. With his focus on the information-processing aspects of items in psychological tests, Robert Sternberg (1977, 1982, 1985) was perhaps the most important catalyst for this shift, but researchers from a number of different areas of psychology have joined in this rediscovery of the centrality of intelligence (Baron, 1985; Brown & Campione, 1986; Dehn & Schank, 1982; Hunt, 1986; Jensen, 1986; Laboratory of Comparative Human Cognition, 1982; Scarr & Carter-Salzman, 1982; Snow, 1982).

THE THEORY OF MULTIPLE INTELLIGENCES

A decade ago Gardner found that his own research interests were leading him to a heightened concern with issues of human intelligence. This concern grew out of two disparate factors, one primarily theoretical, the other largely practical.

As a result of his own studies of the development and breakdown of cognitive and symbol-using capacities, Gardner (1975, 1979, 1982) became convinced that the Piagetian (Piaget, 1970) view of intellect was flawed. Whereas Piaget (1962) had conceptualized all aspects of symbol use as part of a single "semiotic function," empirical evidence was accruing that the human mind may be quite modular in design. That is, separate psychological processes appear to be involved in dealing with linguistic, numerical, pictorial, gestural, and other kinds of symbolic systems (Gardner, Howard, & Perkins, 1974; Gardner & Wolf, 1983). Individuals may be precocious with one form of symbol use, without any necessary carryover to other forms. By

the same token, one form of symbol use may become seriously compromised under conditions of brain damage, without correlative depreciation of other symbolic capacities (Wagner & Gardner, 1979). Indeed, different forms of symbol use appear to be subserved by different portions of the cerebral cortex.

On a more practical level, Gardner was disturbed by the nearly exclusive stress in school on two forms of symbol use: linguistic symbolization and logical-mathematical symbolization. Although these two forms are obviously important in a scholastic setting, other varieties of symbol use also figure prominently in human cognitive activity within and especially outside of school. Moreover, the emphasis on linguistic and logical capacities was overwhelming in the construction of items on intelligence, aptitude, and achievement tests. If different kinds of items were used, or different kinds of assessment instruments devised, a quite different view of the human intellect might issue forth.

These and other factors led Gardner to a conceptualization of human intellect that was more capacious. This took into account a wide variety of human cognitive capacities, entailed many kinds of symbol systems, and incorporated as well the skills valued in a variety of cultural and historical settings. Realizing that he was stretching the word *intelligence* beyond its customary application in educational psychology, Gardner proposed the existence of a number of relatively autonomous *human intelligences*. He defined intelligence as the capacity to solve problems or to fashion products that are valued in one or more cultural settings and detailed a set of criteria for what counts as a human intelligence.

Gardner's definition and his criteria deviated significantly from established practices in the field of intelligence (however, see Guilford, 1967; Thurstone, 1938). Most definitions of intelligence focus on the capacities that are important for success in school. Problem solving is recognized as a crucial component, but the ability to fashion a product—to write a symphony, execute a painting, stage a play, build up and manage an organization, carry out an experiment—is not included, presumably because the aforementioned capacities cannot be probed adequately in short-answer tests. Moreover, on the canonical account, intelligence is presumed to be a universal, probably innate, capacity, and so the diverse kinds of roles valued in different cultures are not considered germane to a study of "raw intellect."

For the most part, definitions and tests of intelligence are empirically determined. Investigators search for items that predict who will succeed in school, even as they drop items that fad to predict scholastic success. New tests are determined in part by the degree of correlation with older, already accepted instruments. In sharp contrast, existing psychometric instruments play no role in Gardner's formulation. Rather, a candidate ability emerges as an intelligence to the extent that it has recurred as an identifiable entity in a number of different lines of study of human cognition.

To arrive at his list of intelligences, Gardner and his colleagues examined the literature in several areas: the development of cognitive capacities in normal individuals; the breakdown of cognitive capacities under various kinds of organic pathology; the existence of abilities in "special populations," such as prodigies, autistic individuals, idiots savants, and learning-disabled children; forms of intellect that exist in different species; forms of intellect valued in different cultures; the evolution of cognition across the millennia; and two forms of psychological evidence—the results of factor-analytic studies of human cognitive capacities and the

outcome of studies of transfer and generalization. Candidate capacities that turned up repeatedly in these disparate literatures made up a provisional list of human intelligences, whereas abilities that appeared only once or twice or were reconfigured differently in diverse sources were abandoned from consideration.

The methods and the results of this massive survey are reported in detail in *Frames of Mind* (Gardner, 1983) and summarized in several other publications (Gardner, 1987a, 1987b; Walters & Gardner, 1985). Gardner's provisional list includes seven intelligences, each with its own component processes and subtypes (see Table 1). It is claimed that, as a species, human beings have evolved over the millennia to carry out at least these seven forms of thinking. In a biological metaphor, these may be thought of as different mental "organs" (Chomsky, 1980); in a computational metaphor, these may be construed as separate information-processing devices (Fodor, 1983). Although all humans exhibit the range of intelligences, individuals differ—presumably for both hereditary and environmental reasons—in their current profile of intelligences. Moreover, there is no necessary correlation between

TABLE 1   The Seven Intelligences

Intelligence	End-States	Core Components
Logical-mathematical	Scientist Mathematician	Sensitivity to, and capacity to discern, logical or numerical patterns; ability to handle long chains of reasoning.
Linguistic	Poet Journalist	Sensitivity to the sounds, rhythms, and meanings of words; sensitivity to the different functions of language
Musical	Composer Violinist	Abilities to produce and appreciate rhythm, pitch, and timbre, appreciation of the forms of musical expressiveness
Spatial	Navigator Sculptor	Capacities to perceive the visual-spatial world accurately and to perform transformations on one's initial perceptions.
Bodily-kinesthetic	Dancer Athlete	Abilities to control one's body movements and to handle objects skillfully.
Interpersonal	Therapist Salesman	Capacities to discern and respond appropriately to the moods, temperaments, motivations, and desires of other people
Intrapersonal	Person with detailed, accurate self-knowledge	Access to one's own feelings and the ability to discriminate among them and draw upon them to guide behavior; knowledge of one's own strengths, weaknesses, desires, and intelligences.

any two intelligences, and they may indeed entail quite distinct forms of perception, memory, and other psychological processes.

Although few occupations rely entirely on a single intelligence, different roles typify the "end-states" of each intelligence. For example, the "linguistic" sensitivity to the sounds and construction of language is exemplified by the poet, whereas the interpersonal ability to discern and respond to the moods and motivations of other people is represented in the therapist. Other occupations more clearly, illustrate the need for a blend of intelligences. For instance, surgeons require both the acuity of spatial intelligence to guide the scalpel and the dexterity of the bodily-kinesthetic intelligence to handle it. Similarly, scientists often have to depend on their linguistic intelligence to describe and explain the discoveries made using their logical-mathematic intelligence, and they must employ interpersonal intelligence in interacting with colleagues and in maintaining a productive and smoothly functioning laboratory.

THE EDUCATION AND ASSESSMENT OF INTELLIGENCES

Until this point, we have been reviewing the history of intelligence research, admittedly from the perspective of the Theory of Multiple Intelligences (hereafter MI Theory). Since the publication of *Frames of Mind* (Gardner, 1983), we and our colleagues have been involved in investigating its implications. On the one hand, we seek to determine the scientific adequacy of the theory (for a discussion of some of the scientific questions raised by the theory, see Gardner, 1983, chapter 11, and Walters & Gardner, 1986). On the other hand, in our view, a principal value of the multiple intelligence perspective—be it a theory or a "mere" framework—lies in its potential contributions to educational reform. In both cases, progress seems to revolve around assessment. To demonstrate that the intelligences are relatively independent of one another and that individuals have distinct profiles of intelligences, assessments of each intelligence have to be developed. To take advantage of students' multiple intelligences, there must be some way to identify their strengths and weaknesses reliably.

Yet MI Theory grows out of a conviction that standardized tests, with their almost exclusive stress on linguistic and logical skills, are limited. As a result, the further development of MI Theory requires a fresh approach to assessment, an approach consistent with the view that there are a number of intelligences that are developed—and can best be detected—in culturally meaningful activities (Gardner, in press-a). In the remainder of the paper, we describe our approach to assessment and broadly survey our efforts to assess individual intelligences at different age levels. In addition, we report some preliminary findings from one of our projects and their implications for the confirmation (or disconfirmation) of MI Theory.

If, as argued, each intelligence displays a characteristic set of psychological processes, it is important that these processes be assessed in an "intelligence-fair" manner. In contrast to traditional paper-and-pencil tests, with their inherent bias toward linguistic and logical skills, intelligence-fair measures seek to respect the different modes of thinking and performance that distinguish each intelligence. Although spatial problems can be approached to some degree through linguistic media (like verbal directions or word problems), intelligence-fair methods place a premium on the abilities to perceive and manipulate visual-spatial information in a direct manner. For example, the spatial intelligence of children can be assessed through a mechanical activity in which they are asked to take apart and reassemble a meat grinder. The activity requires them to "puzzle out" the structure of the object and then to discern or remember the spatial information that will allow reassembly of the pieces. Although linguistically inclined children may produce a running report about the actions they are taking, little verbal skill is necessary (or helpful) for successful performance on such a task.

Whereas most standard approaches treat intelligence in isolation from the activities of a particular culture, MI theory takes a sharply contrasting tack. Intelligences are always conceptualized and assessed in terms of their cultural manifestation in specific domains of endeavor and with reference to particular adult "end states." Thus, even at the preschool level, language capacity is not assessed in terms of vocabulary, definitions, or similarities, but rather as manifest in story telling (the novelist) and reporting (the journalist). Instead of attempting to assess spatial skills in isolation, we observe children as they are drawing (the artist) or taking apart and putting together objects (the mechanic).

Ideally, one might wish to assess an intelligence in a culture-independent way, but this goal has proved to be elusive and perhaps impossible to achieve. Cross-cultural research and studies of cognition in the course of ordinary activities (Brown, Collins, & Duguid, 1989; Laboratory of Comparative Human Cognition, 1982; Lave, 1988; Rogoff, 1982; Scribner, 1986) have demonstrated that performances are inevitably dependent on a person's familiarity and experience with the materials and demands of the assessments. In our own work, it rapidly became clear that meaningful assessment of an intelligence was not possible if students had little or no experience with a particular subject matter or type of material. For example, our examination of bodily-kinesthetic abilities in a movement assessment for preschoolers was confounded by the fact that some 4-year-olds had already been to ballet classes, whereas others had never been asked to move their bodies expressively or in rhythm. This recognition reinforced the notion that bodily-kinesthetic intelligence cannot be assessed outside of a specific medium or without reference to a history of prior experiences.

Together, these demands for assessments that are intelligence fair, are based on culturally valued activities, and take place within a familiar context naturally lead to an approach that blurs the distinctions between curriculum and assessment. Drawing information from the regular curriculum ensures that the activities are familiar; introducing activities in a wide range of areas makes it possible to challenge and examine each intelligence in an appropriate manner. Tying the activities to inviting pursuits enables students to discover and develop abilities that in turn increase their chances of experiencing a sense of engagement and of achieving some success in their society.

PUTTING THEORY INTO PRACTICE

In the past 5 years, this approach to assessment has been explored in projects at several different levels of schooling. At the junior and senior high school level, Arts PROPEL, a collaborative project with the Educational Testing Service and the Pittsburgh Public School System, seeks to assess growth and learning in areas like music, imaginative writing, and visual arts, which are neglected by most standard measures (for further details, see Gardner, in press-b; Wolf, 1989; Zessoules, Wolf, & Gardner, 1988). Arts PROPEL has developed a series of modules, or "domain projects," that serve the goals of both curriculum and assessment. These projects

feature sets of exercises and curriculum activities organized around a concept central to a specific artistic domain—such as notation in music, character and dialogue in play writing, and graphic composition in the visual arts. The drafts, sketches, and final products generated by these and other curriculum activities are collected in portfolios (sometimes termed "process-folios"), which serve as a basis for assessment of growth by both the teacher and the student. Although the emphasis thus far has fallen on local classroom assessments, efforts are also under way to develop criteria whereby student accomplishment can be evaluated by external examiners.

At the elementary level, Patricia Bolaños and her colleagues have used MI theory to design an entire public school in downtown Indianapolis (Olson, 1988). Through a variety of special classes (e.g., computing, bodily-kinesthetic activities) and enrichment activities (a "flow" center and apprentice-like "pods"), all children in the Key School are given the opportunity to discover their areas of strength and to develop the full range of intelligences. In addition, over the course of a year, each child executes a number of projects based on schoolwide themes such as "Man and His Environment" or "Changes in Time and Space." These projects are presented and videotaped for subsequent study and analysis. A team of researchers from Harvard Project Zero is now engaged in developing a set of criteria whereby these videotaped projects can be assessed. Among the dimensions under consideration are project conceptualization, effectiveness of presentation, technical quality of project, and originality, as well as evidence for cooperative efforts and distinctive individual features.

A third effort, Project Spectrum, codirected by David Feldman of Tufts University, has developed a number of curriculum activities and assessment options suited to the "child-centered" structure of many preschools and kindergartens (for details, see Hatch & Gardner, 1986; Krechevsky & Gardner, in press; Malkus, Feldman, & Gardner, 1988; Ramos-Ford & Gardner, in press; Wexler-Sherman, Feldman, & Gardner, 1988). At present, there are 15 different activities, each of which taps a particular intelligence or set of intelligences. Throughout the year, a Spectrum classroom is equipped with "intelligence-fair" materials. Miniature replicas and props invite children to deploy linguistic intelligence within the context of story telling; household objects that children can take apart and reassemble challenge children's spatial intelligence in a mechanical task; a "discovery" area including natural objects like rocks, bones, and shells enables children to use their logical abilities to conduct small "experiments," comparisons, and classifications; and group activities such as a biweekly creative movement session can be employed to give children the opportunity to exercise their bodily-kinesthetic intelligence on a regular basis.

Provision of this variety of "high-affordance" materials allows children to gain experiences that engage their several intelligences, even as teachers have the chance unobtrusively to observe and assess children's strengths, interests, and proclivities. More formal assessment of intelligences is also possible. Researchers can administer specific games to children and apply detailed scoring systems that have been developed for research purposes. For instance, in the bus game, children's ability to organize numerical information is scored by noting the extent to which they can keep track of the number of adults and children getting on and off a bus. Adults and children and on and off constitute two different dimensions. Thus, a child can receive one of the following scores: 0—no dimensions recorded; 1—disorganized recording of one dimension (either adults and children or on and off); 2—labeled, accurate recording of one dimension; 3—disorganized recording of two dimensions; 4—disorganized recording of one dimension and labeled, accurate recording of one dimension; or 5—labeled, accurate recording of two dimensions (for further information, see Krechevsky, Feldman, & Gardner, in press).

We have also created a related instrument, the Modified Spectrum Field Inventory, that samples several intelligences in the course of two 1-hour sessions. Although this inventory does not draw directly from the curriculum, it is based on the kinds of materials and activities that are common in many preschools. In addition, related materials from the Spectrum curriculum can be implemented in the classroom to ensure that the children will be familiar with the kinds of tasks and materials used in the inventory.

PRELIMINARY RESULTS FROM PROJECT SPECTRUM

Although none of these programs is in final form, and thus any evaluation must be considered preliminary and tentative, the results so far at the pilot sites seem promising. The value of rich and evoca-

tive materials has been amply documented. In the classrooms in Pittsburgh, Indianapolis, and Boston, teachers report heightened motivation on the part of the students, even as students themselves appreciate the opportunity to reflect on their own growth and development. Moreover, our programs with both older and younger children confirm that a consideration of a broader range of talents brings to the fore individuals who previously had been considered unexceptional or even at risk for school failure.

As for the assessment instruments under development, only those of Project Spectrum have been field tested in classrooms. In 1987–1989, we used these instruments in two different settings to investigate the hypothesis that the intelligences are largely independent of one another. To examine this hypothesis, we sought to determine (a) whether young children exhibit distinct profiles of intellectual strengths and weaknesses and (b) whether or not performances on activities designed to tap different intelligences are significantly correlated. In the 1987–1988 academic year, 20 children from a primarily white upper middle-income population took part in a yearlong Spectrum program. In the 1988–1989 academic year, the Modified Spectrum Field Inventory was piloted with 15 children in a combined kindergarten and first-grade classroom. This classroom was in a public school in a low-to-middle-income school district.

In the preschool study, children were assessed on 10 different activities (story telling, drawing, singing, music perception, creative movement, social analysis, hypothesis testing, assembly, calculation and counting, and number and notational logic) as well as the Stanford-Binet Intelligence Scale, Fourth Edition. To compare children's performances across each of the activities, standard deviations were calculated for each activity. Children who scored one or more standard deviations above the mean were judged to have a strength on that activity; those who scored one or more standard deviations below the mean were considered to have a weakness on that activity. This analysis revealed that these children did not perform at the same level across activities and suggested that they do have distinct intellectual profiles. Of the 20 children, 15 demonstrated a strength on at least one activity, and 12 children showed a weakness on one or more activities. In contrast, only one child was identified as having no strengths or weaknesses, and her scores ranged from −.98 to +.87 standard deviations from the mean.

These results were reinforced by the fact that, for the most part, children's performances on the activities were independent. Using Spearman rank-order correlations, only the number activities, both requiring logical-mathematical intelligence, proved significantly correlated with one another ($r = .78$, $p < .01$). In the other areas, music and science, where there were two assessments, there were no significant correlations. Conceivably, this result can be attributed to the fact that the number activities, both of which involved calculation, shared more features than the music activities (singing and music perception) or the science activities (hypothesis-testing and mechanical skill). Of course, the small sample size also may have contributed to the absence of powerful correlations among measures.

A comparison of the Spectrum and Stanford-Binet assessments revealed a limited relationship between children's performances on these different instruments. Spearman rank-order correlations showed that only performances on the number activities were significantly correlated with IQ (dinosaur game, $r = .69$, $p < .003$; bus game, $r = .51$, $p < .04$). With its concentration on logical-mathematic and linguistic skills, one might have expected a significant correlation with the Spectrum language activity as well. Conceivably, there was no significant correlation because the Stanford-Binet measures children's vocabulary and comprehension, whereas Spectrum measures how children *use* language within a story-telling task.

In the second study, eight kindergartners (four boys and four girls) and seven first graders (five girls and two boys) were assessed on the seven activities of the Modified Spectrum Field Inventory (MSPFI). This inventory, based on the activities developed for the yearlong Spectrum assessments of preschoolers, consists of activities in the areas of language (storyboard), numbers and logic (bus game), mechanics (assembly), art (drawing), music (xylophone games), social analysis (classroom model), and movement (creative movement). These assessments were administered in two 1-hour sessions. Each activity was videotaped, and children were scored by two independent observers. Spearman rank-order correlations between the scores of the two observers ranged from .88 (language) to .97 (art) and demonstrated the interrater reliability of these scores.

As in the first study, strengths and weaknesses were estimated using standard deviations. Unlike the findings from the earlier study, however, these results revealed that some children performed quite well and others performed quite poorly across many of the activities. It appears that the small sample size and wide age ranges may have contributed to this result. Of the five first-grade girls, none demonstrated a weakness in any area; all showed at least one strength, with one girl having strengths in six of the seven areas. The two first-grade boys showed no strengths, and both demonstrated weaknesses in three areas. Of the kindergartners, only two showed any strengths, with all but one of the other children showing at least one weakness. Quite possibly, these results reflect differences in developmental level, and perhaps gender differences as well, that did not obtain in the preschool sample and that may have overpowered certain individual differences. It is also conceivable that a more extended exposure to, and greater familiarity with, the Spectrum materials and activities, as in the yearlong Spectrum program, may have made the individual differences among younger children more visible.

Nonetheless, an examination of children's ranks on each of the activities revealed a more complex picture. Although the first-grade girls dominated the rankings, all but two children in the sample were ranked among the top five on at least one occasion. All but one child also scored in the bottom five on at least one activity. Considered in this way, children did exhibit relative strengths and weaknesses across the seven activities.

To determine whether or not performance on one activity was independent of performance on the other activities, we standardized each of the scores with a mean = 0 and standard deviation = 1 (Sattler, 1988) and performed Spearman rank-order correlations. Because of the superior performance of the first-grade girls, the performances of kindergartners and first graders were computed separately. Consideration of the kindergartners alone revealed only one correlation, between art and social analysis, that approached significance ($r = .66$, $p < .071$). For the sample of first graders, including the "high"-scoring girls, there were a number of significant correlations: language and assembly ($r = .77$, $p < .04$), language and numbers ($r = .81$, $p < .027$), movement and social analysis ($r = .77$, $p < .04$), and assembly and numbers ($r = .79$, $p < .034$).

With the exception of the performance of the first graders in the second study, these results are reasonably consistent with the claims of MI Theory. For younger children, performances on the Spectrum activities were largely independent, relative strengths and weaknesses were uncovered, and there was a significant correlation between preschoolers' performances on the Spectrum activities and the Stanford-Binet in one of the two areas where it would be expected. Further investigations need to be conducted to establish norms, to identify strengths and weaknesses consistently, and to examine fully the effects of age and gender on the Spectrum activities.

CONCLUSION

In this essay, we have sketched the background and the major claims of a new approach to the conceptualization and assessment of human intelligence. Put forth in 1983, the theory of multiple intelligences has inspired a number of research-and-development projects that are taking place in schools ranging from preschool through high school. Until now, our focus has fallen largely on the development of instruments that can assess strengths and weaknesses in an "intelligence-fair" way. This research-and-development process has proved time consuming and costly. The measures must involve materials that are appealing and familiar to children; there is little precedent for developing scoring systems that go beyond linguistic and logical criteria; and materials appropriate for one age group, gender, or social class may not be appropriate for others. Of course, it should be recalled that huge amounts of time and money have already been invested in standard psychometric instruments, whose limitations have become increasingly evident in recent years.

Once adequate materials have been developed, it becomes possible to begin to address some of the theoretical claims that grow out of MI Theory. We have presented here some preliminary findings from one of our current projects. These results give some support to the major claims of the theory, inasmuch as children ranging in age from 3 to 7 do exhibit profiles of relative strength and weakness. At the same time, even these preliminary data indicate that the final story on Multiple Intelligences may turn out to be more complex than we envisioned. Thus, the rather different profile of results obtained with our two young populations indicates that, in future research, we must pay closer attention to three factors: (a) the developmental appropriateness of the materials; (b) the social class background, which may well exert an influence on a child's ability and willingness to engage with di-

verse materials; and (c) the exact deployment of the Spectrum materials and assessment instruments in the classroom.

Some critics have suggested that MI Theory cannot be disconfirmed. The preliminary results presented here indicate some of the ways in which its central claims can indeed be challenged. ff future assessments do not reveal strengths and weaknesses within a population, if performances on different activities prove to be systematically correlated, and if constructs (and instruments) like the IQ explain the preponderance of the variance on activities configured to tap specific intelligences, then MI Theory will have to be revamped. Even so, the goal of detecting distinctive human strengths, and using them as a basis for engagement and learning, may prove to be worthwhile, irrespective of the scientific fate of the theory.

Note

The research described in this article has been generously supported by the Grant Foundation, the Lilly Endowment, the Markle Foundation, the Rockefeller Brothers Fund, the Rockefeller Foundation, the Spencer Foundation, the Bernard Van Leer Foundation, and the Office of Educational Research and Improvement's Center for Technology, in Education at the Bank Street College of Education. We thank our colleagues at the Eliot-Pearson Children's School and in the Somerville Public School system for their collaboration. For comments on in earlier draft of this paper, we are grateful to Robert Glaser, Robert Sternberg, Joseph Walters, and an anonymous reviewer.

REFERENCES

Baldwin, J. M. (1895). *Mental development in the child and the race.* New York: Macmillan.

Baron, J. (1985). *Rationality and intelligence.* New York: Cambridge University Press.

Binet, A., & Simon, T. (1916). *The development of intelligence in children.* Baltimore, MD: Williams & Wilkins.

Brown, A. L., & Campione, J. C. (1986). Academic intelligence and learning potential. In R. J. Sternberg & D. Detterman (Eds.), *What is intelligence?* (pp. 39–49). Hillsdale, NJ: Erlbaum.

Brown, J. S., Collins, A., & Duguid, P. (1989). Situated cognition and the culture of learning. *Educational Researcher, 18*(1), 32–42.

Chomsky, N. (1980). *Rules and representations.* New York: Columbia University Press.

Dehn, N., & Schank, R. C. (1982). Artificial and human intelligence. In R. Sternberg (Ed.), *Handbook of human intelligence* (Vol. 1, pp. 352–391). New York: Cambridge University Press.

Fodor, J. (1983). *The modularity of mind.* Cambridge, MA: MIT Press.

Galton, F. (1870). *Hereditary genius.* New York: Appleton.

Gardner, H. (1975). *The shattered mind.* New York: Knopf.

Gardner, H. (1979). Developmental psychology after Piaget: An approach in terms of symbolization. *Human Development, 15,* 570–580.

Gardner, H. (1982). *Art, mind and brain.* New York: Basic Books.

Gardner, H. (1983). *Frames of Mind.* New York: Basic Books.

Gardner, H. (1987a). Symposium on the theory of multiple intelligences. In D. N. Perkins, J. Lockhead, & J. C. Bishop (Eds.), *Thinking: The second international conference* (pp. 77–101). Hillsdale, NJ: Erlbaum.

Gardner, H. (1987b). Developing the spectrum of human intelligence. *Harvard Education Review, 57,* 187–193.

Gardner, H. (in press-a). Assessment in context: The alternative to standardized testing. In B. Gifford (Ed.), *Report of the commission on testing and public policy.*

Gardner, H. (in press-b). Zero-based arts education: An introduction to Arts PROPEL. *Studies in Art Education.*

Gardner, H., Howard, V., & Perkins, D. (1974). Symbol systems: A philosophical, psychological and educational investigation. In D. Olson (Ed.), *Media and symbols* (pp. 37–55). Chicago: University of Chicago Press.

Gardner, H., & Wolf, D. (1983). Waves and streams of symbolization. In D. R. Rogers & J. A. Sloboda (Eds.), *The acquisition of symbolic skills* (pp. 19–42). London: Plenium.

Guilford, J. P. (1967). *The nature of human intelligence.* New York: McGraw-Hill.

Hatch, T., & Gardner, H. (1986). From testing intelligence to assessing competences: A pluralistic view of intellect. *Roeper Review, 8,* 147–150.

Hobhouse, L. T. (1915). *Mind in evolution.* London: Macmillan.

Hunt, E. (1986). The heffalump of intelligence. In R. J. Sternberg & D. Detterman (Eds), *What is intelligence?* (pp. 101–107). Hillsdale, NJ: Erlbaum.

Jensen, A. R. (1986). Intelligence: "Definition," measurement, and future research. In R. J. Sternberg & D. Detterman (Eds.), *What is intelligence?* (pp. 109–112). Hillsdale, NJ: Erlbaum.

Krechevsky, M., Feldman, D., & Gardner, H. (in press). *The Spectrum handbook.*

Krechevsky, M. & Gardner, H. (in press). The emergence and nurturance of multiple intelligences. In M. J. A. Howe (Ed.), *Encouraging the development of exceptional abilities and talents.*

Laboratory of Comparative Human Cognition. (1982). Culture and intelligence. In R. Sternberg (Ed.), *Handbook of human intelligence* (Vol. 2, pp. 642–722). New York: Cambridge University Press.

Lave, J. (1988). *Cognition in practice.* Cambridge, England: Cambridge University Press.

Malkus, U., Feldman, D. H., & Gardner, H. (1988). Dimensions of mind in early childhood. In A. D. Pellegrini (Ed.), *Psychological bases of early education* (pp. 25–38). New York: Wiley.

Olson, L. (1988). Children flourish here: 8 teachers and a theory changed a school world. *Education Week, 18*(1), 18–19.

Piaget, J. (1962). *Play, dreams and imitation in childhood.* (C. Gattegno & F. M. Hodgson, Trans.). New York: Norton.

Piaget, J. (1970). *Science of education and the psychology of the child* (D. Coltman, Trans.). New York: Orion.

Ramos-Ford, V., & Gardner, H. (in press). Giftedness from a multiple intelligences perspective. In N. Colangelo & G. Davis (Eds.), *The handbook of gifted education.*

Rogoff, B. (1982). Integrating context and cognitive development. In M. Lamb & A. Brown (Eds.), *Advances in developmental psychology* (Vol. 2, pp. 125–169). Hillsdale, NJ: Erlbaum.

Romanes, G. J. (1892). *Animal intelligence.* New York: Appleton.

Sattler, J. M. (1988). *Assessment of children.* San Diego, CA: Author.

Scarr, S., & Carter-Saltzman, L. (1982). Genetics and intelligence. In R. Sternberg (Ed.), *Handbook of human intelligence* (Vol. 2, pp. 792–896). New York: Cambridge University Press.

Scribner, S. (1986). Thinking in action: Some characteristics of practical thought. In R. Sternberg & R. K. Wagner (Eds.), *Practical intelligence: Origins of competence in the everyday world.* New York: Cambridge University Press.

Snow, R. E. (1982). Education and intelligence. In R. Sternberg (Ed.), *Handbook of human intelligence* (Vol. 2, pp. 493–585). New York: Cambridge University Press.

Spearman, C. E. (1927). *The abilities of man: Their nature and measurement.* New York: Macmillan.

Sternberg, R. (1977). *Intelligence, information processing, and analogical reasoning.* Hillsdale, NJ: Erlbaum.

Sternberg, R. J. (Ed.). (1982). *Handbook of human intelligence.* New York: Cambridge University Press.

Sternberg, R. J. (1985). *Beyond IQ.* New York: Cambridge University Press.

Terman, L. M. (1916). *The measurement of intelligence.* Boston: Houghton Mifflin.

Thurstone, L. L. (1938). *Primary mental abilities.* Chicago: University of Chicago Press.

Walters, J., & Gardner, H. (1985). The development and education of intelligences. In F. Link (Ed.), *Essays on the intellect* (pp. 1–21). Washington, DC: Curriculum Development Associates.

Walters, J., & Gardner, H. (1986). The theory of multiple intelligences: Some issues and answers. In R. Sternberg & R. Wagner (Eds.), *Practical intelligence: Origins of competence in the everyday world* (pp. 163–182). New York: Cambridge University Press.

Wapner, W., & Gardner, H. (1979). A study of spelling in aphasia. *Brain and Language, 7*, 363–374.

Wechsler, D. (1939). *The measurement of adult intelligence.* Baltimore, MD: Williams & Wilkins.

Wexler-Sherman, C., Feldman, D., & Gardner, H. (1988). A pluralistic view of intellect: The Project Spectrum approach. *Theory Into Practice, 28*, 77–83.

Wolf, D. P. (1989, April). What's in it?: Examining portfolio assessment. *Educational Leadership.*

Yerkes, R. M., Bridges, J. W., & Hardwick, R. S. (1915). *A point scale for measuring mental ability.* Baltimore, MD: Warwick and York.

Zessoules, R., Wolf, D., & Gardner, H. (1988). A better balance: Arts PROPEL as an alternative to discipline-based art education. In J. Burton, A. Lederman, & P. London (Eds.), *Beyond discipline-based art education.* University Council on Art Education.

Long-Term Effects of Acceleration on the Social-Emotional Adjustment of Mathematically Precocious Youths

TERI M. RICHARDSON and CAMILLA PERSSON BENBOW
Iowa State University

The Study of Mathematically Precocious Youth (SMPY) identified over 2,000 12–14 year-olds who scored as well as a random sample of high school females on the College Board Scholastic Aptitude Test. SMPY encouraged these students to accelerate their education; over 50% did. Their social development at age 18 and at age 23 was then assessed. We investigated the effects of amount and type of educational acceleration (grade skipping and subject matter) on psychosocial indices (self-esteem, locus of control, self-acceptance/identity, and social interaction). No gender differences were significant. Accelerants as well as nonaccelerants reported high self-esteem and internal locus of control. Acceleration did not affect social interactions or self-acceptance/identity and it also did not relate to social and emotional difficulties.

Educational acceleration of intellectually advanced students is often used in American schools. Clear benefits are noted for both short-term and long-term academic performance (e.g., Benbow, 1983; Brody & Benbow, 1987, Daurio, 1979; Feldhusen, 1989; Janos, 1987; Janos & Robinson, 1985b; Kulik & Kulik, 1984; Robinson, 1983). Primarily because of these positive evaluations, acceleration of gifted students is widely endorsed (e.g., Cox, Daniel, & Boston, 1985; Elkind, 1988; Feldhusen, 1989; U.S. Department of Education, 1986). Unfortunately, parents and educators are often skeptical about acceleration because of concerns about the social and emotional development of accelerated youths (Southern, Jones, & Fiscus, 1989). Using data from a 10-year longitudinal study of over 1,200 intellectually talented students who had been encouraged to accelerate their education, we address the validity of these concerns.

The basic premise underlying the use of acceleration is that the pacing of educational programs must be responsive to the capacities and knowledge of individual children (Robinson, 1983); that is, effective teaching involves "the problem of the match"—students should attempt new learning at a level slightly exceeding that already mastered. Acceleration, which involves the adaptation of curricula designed for older students for use with younger gifted students, is one productive and practical means of solving the problem of the match for gifted students (Benbow & Stanley, 1983; Robinson, 1983). In addition, acceleration should enhance gifted students' achievement motivation. Growth in achievement motivation arises out of the challenge and satisfaction gained while mastering tasks that "match" capabilities (Dweck & Elliott, 1983; Heckhausen, 1982).

In spite of strong evidence for the academic benefits of acceleration, educators and psychologists have found its use to be controversial. Resistance to acceleration is often based on preconceived notions (Daurio, 1979). Well-meaning concern about the deleterious effects of acceleration on social and emotional development is repeatedly expressed. This concern is difficult, however, to reconcile with what is known about the social and emotional development of the gifted. Intellectually advanced children exhibit advanced social maturity (for reviews, see Janos & Robinson, 1985a; Schneider, 1987), and they often seek older friends.

Logically, therefore, it would appear that acceleration should be beneficial to gifted students, not only on educational and motivational grounds, but also on social grounds. The existing evidence does suggest that acceleration has at least no detrimental effects on social and emotional development (Brody & Benbow, 1987; Daurio, 1979; Janos, 1987, Pollins, 1983; Robinson & Janos, 1986). Three limitations temper this conclusion, however: (a) Many studies have failed to report the amount and/or type of accelerative method used; (b) there is low consensus among researchers as to what constitutes good social and emotional adjustment; and (c) most studies lack appropriate reference groups, that is, equally gifted nonaccelerants (Pollins, 1983).

The purpose of this study is to provide empirical data on social and emotional development from a 10-year longitudinal study of intellectually talented students, some of whom were accelerated in elementary or secondary school. All students in this study exhibited intellectual abilities at the level of students 4 to 5 years older. They were accelerated by different amounts and in different ways. Some opted for no acceleration. Four generally-agreed upon parameters of social and emotional functioning were evaluated. Our (null) hypothesis was that acceleration, regardless of type and amount, is not related to social and emotional development at age 23. Moreover, it was predicted that most social or emotional difficulties reported at age 18 would be temporary. Because this 10-year longitudinal study involved 1,247 students in a test of our null hypothesis, it has considerable statistical power. It also counters most of the limitations of previous studies.

A further unique aspect of our study is that it evaluates acceleration by examining students both during and near the end of their formal educations. Intellectually talented students were studied at high school graduation and again a year beyond typical college graduation age (i.e., age 23). The latter time point is a minimum of 5 years after any acceleration took place. Because most disadvantages associated with acceleration are usually temporary in nature (Fund for the Advancement of Education, 1957; Pressey, 1967; Terman & Oden, 1947), this is an appropriate time point for an evaluation.

Lastly, our study investigated whether acceleration affected male and female students differently, particularly with respect to psychosocial indices. Although gifted male and female students tend to be alike in self-concept and self-esteem (Brody & Benbow, 1986; Fox, 1977), previous studies have suggested that gender differences may exist. Solano (1987) has reported that gifted boys tended to be better accepted than gifted girls; Kelly and Colangelo (1984) have reported that effects of special program participation differed for gifted boys and girls. Schneider, Clegg, Byrne, Ledingham, and Crombie (1989) obtained slightly different results, however. Yet Fox (1977) reported that female students avoided acceleration because of fears of negative consequences on their peer interactions.

METHOD

Subjects

We investigated students in Cohort 1 of the Study of Mathematically Precocious Youth's (SMPY) longitudinal study (Benbow, 1983). Cohort 1 students had taken part in SMPY's first three talent searches (i.e., in 1972, 1973, or 1974). In those, 7th/8th graders in Maryland were eligible to participate if they had scored in the upper 5% (in 1972) or upper 2% (in 1973 and 1974) nationally on any mathematics achievement subtest. Qualified students took the College Board Scholastic Aptitude Test-Mathematics (SAT-M), and those in 1973 also took the SAT-Verbal (SAT-V). The SAT is designed to measure developed mathematical and verbal reasoning ability of high school 11th and 12th graders. Although the extent to which the SAT is a measure of achievement for high school students has not been established, we have argued that the SAT is a more potent measure of reasoning for 7th/8th graders than for 11th/12th Fraders (Stanley & Benbow, 1986).

Students had to score at least 390 on SAT-M or 370 on SAT-V for entry into Cohort 1 of the study. These SAT criteria selected students who, as 7th or 8th graders, scored as well as the average high school female student. We estimated that Cohort 1 represented the top 1% in ability. Mean 8th-grade SAT scores of Cohort 1 (7th-grade scores had been grade-adjusted) were 556 *(SD* = 73) on SAT-M and 436 *(SD* = 85) on SAT-V for male students and 519 *(SD* = 59) on SATM and 462 *(SD* = 88) for SAT-V for female students.

Participants came from families where parents typically were highly educated and fathers held high-status jobs (Keating, 1974). Participants held positive attitudes toward mathematics, science, and school and had good school performance. SMPY showed these students how to use acceleration to make their educational experiences more appropriate and urged them to accelerate.

After-College Questionnaire

Two questionnaires (an after-high school and an after-college questionnaire) were the sources of data for this study. The after-high school questionnaire is described in Benbow (1983). The 24-page, printed after-college questionnaire, which was the primary source of data, sought information on students' educational and career achievements, decisions, and aspirations; employment history; interests and activities; accomplishments; attitudes and life-style expectations; family encouragement and characteristics; social and emotional development; and evaluation of SMPY. For comparability and validity purposes, and whenever possible, we used items from Project Talent's questionnaires or the sophomore questionnaire of the High School and Beyond National Longitudinal Study (NLS). NLS is conducted by the National Center for Education Statistics. A draft of our questionnaire was critiqued by several experts in the field and was revised accordingly. Then we pilot tested the questionnaire: Graduate students in the mathematical sciences at Johns Hopkins University were paid to complete the survey and to provide comments on the effectiveness of the questionnaire. This led to further revisions.

From this lengthy after-college questionnaire, items that related to self-acceptance/identity, social interaction, self-esteem, and locus of control were selected as indices of social-emotional development (see Appendix). Items from the self-esteem and locus of control measures were the same as those

(with minor modification) used in the NLS questionnaire (Conger, Peng, & Dunteman, 1976; Peng, Fetters, & Kolstad, 1981).

Questions relating to the four psychosocial indices were combined into scales; the Appendix lists the actual questions used and how they were grouped into scales. All four scales were subsequently analyzed for internal reliability by using Cronbach's coefficient alpha. The four-item self-acceptance/identity and social interaction scales were found to have alpha coefficients of .85 and .76, respectively. Alpha coefficients for the six-item self-esteem and six-item locus of control scales were .80 and .59, respectively.

Two acceleration variables also were computed for every student. (Those not accelerating were given a value of zero.) *Grade acceleration* was the number of grades in school skipped, which included early entrance to school, *Subject-matter acceleration* was the number of Advanced Placement (AP)[1] and/or college courses enrolled in while in high school.

Procedure

All students (100%) completed a basic background questionnaire before they took the initial SAT in a talent search. SMPY has now surveyed students in Cohort 1 twice: first at their expected data of high school graduation (91% response rate, Benbow, 1983; Benbow & Stanley, 1982) and then 5 years later at age 23. The second follow-up survey occurred 1 year after expected college graduation date. The procedures were the same as those used in the first follow-up survey (Benbow & Stanley, 1982), except that no monetary incentive was provided in the second follow-up. Initial response rate to the second follow-up was 65%. Because viability of a longitudinal study depends on retaining a large proportion of the original sample, we surveyed nonrespondents by telephone with 20 critical questions. This increased the response rate to over 70%. Our sample included 786 male and 461 female students.[2]

A discriminant analysis was performed by sex to see if nonrespondents differed from respondents on the basis of 8th-grade SAT-M score, high school SAT-M and SAT-V, college attendance, quality of

---

[1]Advanced Placement (AP) courses are geared at the college freshman level but are offered in high school. Depending on test results, students may receive credit and/or advanced standing in college for such work.

[2]Complete data were not available for all subjects.

college attended, parental educational levels, number of siblings, and fathers' occupational status. Respondents and nonrespondents did not differ significantly.

RESULTS

Data on the scales measuring the effects of acceleration on social interaction and self-acceptance/identity were obtained at age 23. Only individuals who had accelerated their education provided responses.[3] The means and standard deviations on the social interaction and self-acceptance/identity variables (O to 4 point scale—from *strongly unfavorable effect* to *strongly favorable effect*) indicated slightly positive effects of acceler-

[3]Grade and subject-matter acceleration related to ability on SAT-M and SAT-V in 7th/8th grade (*r*s ranged from .15 to .41 for male and female students). Grade acceleration was not consistently or even moderately related to any other background or student attitude variable. Subject-matter acceleration did relate modestly to parents' educational and occupational status and students' attitude toward school (*r* < .2). Most of the subject-matter acceleration was in the math/science areas, but there was diffusion (Benbow, 1983; Benbow & Stanley, 1982).

ation on social and emotional development (see Table 1). There were no statistically significant sex differences.

The zero-order correlations among social interaction and self-acceptance/identity scales and amount of grade acceleration or subject-matter acceleration were not statistically significant, except for one (see Table 1). For females, the correlation between subject matter acceleration and social interaction was significant (p .05). The differences in *r*s between male and female students were not significant.

Both accelerants and nonaccelerants responded to the items included in the self-esteem and locus of control scales. Results indicated that the students at age 23 felt good about themselves and felt in control of their lives (Table 1). There were no statistically significant gender differences.

Acceleration of either type, which included no acceleration, did not relate to locus of control, as tested by Pearson *r*s (Table 1). Although not statistically significant except in one case, the relations between self-esteem and grade or subject-matter acceleration were consistently negative. The relations were not substantial, however. Moreover, when only those students who skipped a grade were studied, there was also no relation between amount

TABLE 1 **Descriptive Statistics for the Psychosocial Indices and Their Correlation with Acceleration Measures by Sex**

| | | | | *r* with acceleration | |
| | | | | Grade | Subject matter |
Variable	*N*	*M*	*SD*		
Social interaction					
Male	381	2.28	0.60	−.01	−.02
Female	211	2.44	0.66	.04	−.16
Self-acceptance/identity					
Male	373	2.51	0.73	.06	.05
Female	209	2.62	0.77	−.05	−.01
Self-esteem					
Male	655	3.20	0.62	−.09	−.06
Female	391	3.15	0.68	−.08	−.06
Locus of control					
Male	652	3.03	0.50	.02	.01
Female	398	3.09	0.49	−.03	.02
Grade acceleration					
Male	787	0.22	0.53		.24
Female	461	0.18	0.45		−.02
Subject-matter acceleration					
Male	688	1.42	2.00		
Female	415	0.91	1.36		

Note: See Appendix for coding format of psychosocial variables, which were on a 0- to 4-point scale from negative to positive (2 = neutral).

of acceleration and self-esteem. The relations between acceleration and self-esteem or locus of control did not vary as a function of sex.

Two multivariate analyses of variance (MANOVA) were then calculated between grade and subject-matter acceleration and the psychosocial indices. Scores on the scales measuring the perceived effects of acceleration on self-acceptance/identity and social interaction were available only for individuals who had accelerated. The MANOVA relating these two variables with the two acceleration variables was not significant. The canonical r equaled .11.

Locus of control and self-esteem scores were available for all students regardless of whether they had or had not accelerated. Those scores were related to the two acceleration variables by a MANOVA. The MANOVA was significant, $F(4, 1824) = 3.41$, $p < .01$. The canonical r was .12, which is hardly substantial. Amount of acceleration related negatively to self- esteem only.

We had predicted that there would be gender differences in both the amount and the effects of acceleration. Gender differences were found in subject-matter acceleration, with results favoring male students (50% male vs. 43% female, $p \leq .05$) but not in grade acceleration (17.2% male vs. 16.2% female, *ns;* also see Table 1). Moreover, when we compared female students with male students, twice as many of the rs reported in Table 1 indicated a slightly negative relation between acceleration and the psychosocial indices for female students. That is, for female students, 6 out of the 8 rs were negative, whereas for male students only 3 of the 8 were. This trend in the data was not statistically significant by a sign test. Moreover, all rs were negligible. Thus, these findings indicate that gifted female students as well as gifted male students do not perceive their acceleration to have negative effects on their social and emotional development.

Long-Term Effects of Acceleration

At age 18, a few of the accelerated students (6.4%) had reported detrimental effects from acceleration on their social and emotional development. In comparison, only about one-half (3.3%) of the accelerants reported at age 23 distinctly negative effects of acceleration on self-acceptance/identity or social interaction (i.e., scale scores ≤ 1). This represented a reduction, over time, in the number of accelerants reporting negative effects (termed "negative accelerants").

We also assessed whether negative accelerants at age 18 would evaluate at age 23 the effects of acceleration differently than the other accelerated students. Thus, the scores on the four psychosocial scales were broken down according to the rated effect of acceleration on social and emotional development at age 18 (Table 2). That is, scale scores are reported separately for accelerants who rated at age 18 the social and emotional effects of acceleration: (a) to be negative, (b) to have no effect, or (c) to be positive. Results indicate that for those who at age 18 had reported negative effects from acceleration on social and emotional development, their self-esteem, locus of control, self-acceptance/identity, or social interactions generally were slightly negatively affected at age 23.

We tested these relations with an analysis of variance (ANOVA).[4] Separate ANOVAS were performed on the four scales by gender and by rated effect of acceleration at age 18 (negative, none, or positive). No significant effects were found for the locus of control measure. The main effect for how acceleration was previously rated to affect social and emotional development was statistically significant for self-esteem, $F(2, 701) = 8.23$, $p < .001$; self-acceptance/identity, $F(2, 451) = 17.66$, $p < .001$; and social interaction, $F(2, 455) = 8.80$, $p < .001$. Students who reported no effect or positive effects from their acceleration had higher self-esteem, self-acceptance/identity, and levels of social interaction. The results did not differ as a function of gender, however.

DISCUSSION

We had predicted that amount and/or type of educational acceleration (including no acceleration) of gifted children would not relate to social and emotional development at age 23. Thus, we tested the null hypothesis. Our data, based on 1,247 gifted students, provided support for the null hypothesis. Most students in our sample reported high self-esteem and internal locus of control; the accelerants as well as the nonaccelerants appear to feel good about themselves and feel they have control over their lives. Their sense of self-efficacy was strong.

---

[4]The pattern of unequal Ns in the subgroups resulted in nonorthogonal ANOVAS. Although discarding observations would artificially balance the design, it would also decrease power. Therefore, we followed the four-step procedure outlined by Appelbaum and Cramer (1974) to handle the problems resulting from nonorthogonality.

TABLE 2 **Means and Standard Deviations, at Age 23, Broken Down
by Rated Effect of Acceleration on Social and Emotional Development at Age 18**

Rated effect of acceleration at age 18	Self-esteem			Locus of control			Self-acceptance/ identity			Social interaction		
	M	*SD*	*N*	*M*	*SD*	*N*	*M*	*SD*	*N*	*M*	*SD*	*N*
Negative												
Male	2.89	0.59	34	2.90	0.61	33	1.91	0.65	19	1.93	0.34	20
Female	2.47	0.45	5	3.17	0.53	5	0.50	0.35	2	1.50	0.35	2
None												
Male	3.17	0.69	115	3.00	0.45	117	2.45	0.62	74	2.21	0.51	73
Female	3.11	0.62	68	3.23	0.38	71	2.36	0.81	36	2.22	0.51	34
Positive												
Male	3.25	0.61	306	3.08	0.50	301	2.65	0.73	202	2.36	0.66	207
Female	3.24	0.65	174	3.09	0.49	173	2.66	0.73	119	2.46	0.67	120

Note: See Appendix for coding format of psychosocial variables, which were on a 0- to 4-point scale from negative to positive (2 = neutral).

Moreover, SMPY students who had considered themselves to be educationally accelerated reported no detrimental effects overall from acceleration. In fact, they may have felt that their social and emotional adjustments were positively affected. Greater amounts of acceleration were not related to greater amounts of social and emotional difficulties. This study is therefore consistent with the prevailing view in the literature that concerns about possible social and emotional maladjustment resulting from acceleration are unfounded.

We had predicted that the effects of acceleration on the psychosocial indices would differ as a function of sex. This prediction was not supported by the data. Moreover, Fox (1977) had concluded that female students appeared to be fearful of acceleration because of possible reduced standing within the peer group. Such fears appear to be unfounded. Accelerated gifted female students reported slightly favorable effects of acceleration on their social interactions.

There was one exception to the otherwise consistent set of positive findings. Grade acceleration related weakly but negatively (-.09) to self-esteem. A negative relation has also been reported for participation in segregated (i.e., enrichment) programs for the gifted. Such studies have noted that self-concepts of gifted students tended to decline when the students were placed in special classes for the gifted (Coleman & Fults, 1982, 1985; Kulik & Kulik, 1982; Maddux, Scheiber, & Bass, 1982; Schneider et al., 1989). Thus, the negative relation between acceleration and self-esteem may not be due to acceleration.

Rather, these findings may reflect changes in the social comparisons being made by the accelerants. Being placed in a higher grade with older students or in segregated classes for the gifted may result in gifted students' comparing themselves with other gifted or advanced students. Self-concepts are predicted to decline in such instances (Festinger, 1954).

Although psychosocial adjustment of intellectually talented children is at least comparable to those not so designated, students with extremely high abilities, especially in verbal areas, tend to experience difficulties and these difficulties increase with age (e.g., Brody & Benbow, 1986; Freeman, 1979; Gallagher, 1958; Hollingworth, 1942; Janos & Robinson, 1985a: Schneider, 1987; Terman & Oden, 1947). Because it is also the most extremely talented students who should and do accelerate their education, this may explain why parents and educators believe—despite all evidence to the contrary—that acceleration is detrimental to social and emotional development (Southern et al., 1989). Acceleration may be blamed for psychosocial difficulties that are not associated with acceleration but rather with extreme intellectual talent per se. Ability within our talented group did relate to use of acceleration and to psychosocial indices (except for locus of control). The relations were less than .41 for acceleration and greater than −.20 for the three psychosocial indices. The magnitude of these correlations was greater than those correlations we reported for acceleration and the psychosocial indices (see Table 1).

The number of students who reported negative effects from acceleration decreased by about one-half from age 18 to age 23. Less than 3.5% of the accelerated students reported at age 23 negative effects on self-acceptance/identity or on their social interactions. Possible reasons for this attitudinal change include: (a) viewing negative experiences more positively as one ages: (b) feeling more accepted in college and thus having negative effects diminish; or (c) negative experiences fading with the passage of time. Interestingly, negative effects were rarely reported for social interactions, which is contrary to the widely held belief that students' social interactions suffer from acceleration. Thus, few students who accelerated their educational progress in grades K-12 felt several years later that this acceleration had a distinctly negative effect on their social and emotional development.

This study is limited by reliance on self-report data. Self-report measures seemed appropriate, however, because the subjects' feelings about themselves were the major concern. More lengthy and complex scales would probably have increased the validity of the findings, but, due to the comprehensive nature of the assessment, would have rendered the 24-page questionnaire even more lengthy and thus less likely to be returned. The inclusion of items from other longitudinal studies was intended to increase the validity of the scales and findings. Finally, although we studied amount and type of acceleration, we did not attempt to investigate whether age at acceleration related to psychosocial outcomes. Given the consistent set of null results, this approach did not appear fruitful.

Several important implications of this study can be noted. Acceleration as an educational option for the intellectually precocious is a viable alternative on both academic and psychosocial grounds. The common belief in negative effects of acceleration on psychosocial development may have resulted because those students for whom acceleration is most appropriate are generally those who are also at greater risk for psychosocial problems. Age, not acceleration, exacerbates these problems. It also seems apparent that the female students' fear of acceleration, because of its possible effect on peer interactions, is unwarranted. Almost as many female as male students engaged in grade acceleration; no differential effects of acceleration (grade or subject matter) on social-emotional adjustment were found. This points to the importance of counseling the gifted female student to encourage her to consider acceleration, especially subject-matter acceleration in which gender differences were noted, as a means to provide educational challenge commensurate with her abilities. Finally, the number of students who reported at age 23 negative effects from acceleration had declined from the already low level at age 18, which suggests that perceived benefits of acceleration may increase with the passage of time. SMPI's continued follow-up of these students into their adult years should provide an interesting look at this trend. Meanwhile, this study lends more support to the tenet that appropriate educational acceleration does not result in social or emotional maladjustment, rather, acceleration may even enhance social and emotional adjustment.

REFERENCES

Appelbaum, M. I., & Cramer. E. M. (1974). Some problems in the nonorthogonal analyses of variance. *Psychological Bulletin, 81,* 335–343.

Benbow, C. P. (1983). Adolescence of the mathematically precocious. In C. P. Benbow & J. C. Stanley (eds.) *Academic precocity: Aspects of its development* (p. 9–29). Baltimore, MD: Johns Hopkins University Press.

Benbow, C. P., & Stanley, J. C. (1982). Consequences in high school and college of sex differences in mathematical reasoning ability: A longitudinal perspective, *American Educational research Journal, 19,* 598–622.

Benbow, C. P., & Stanley, J. C. (1983). Opening doors for the gifted. *American Education, 19*(3), 44–46.

Brody, L. E., & Benbow, C. P. (1986). Social and emotional adjustment of adolescents extremely talented in verbal and mathematical reasoning. *Journal of Youth and Adolescence, 15,* 1–18.

Brody, L. E., & Benbow, C. P. (1987). Accelerative strategies: How effective are they for the gifted? *Gifted Child Quarterly, 31,* 105–110.

Coleman, J. M., & Fults, B. A. (1982). Self-concept and the gifted classroom: The role of social comparisons. *Gifted Child Quarterly, 26,* 116–119.

Coleman, J. M., & Fults, B. A. (1985). Special-class placement, level of intelligence, and the self-concepts of gifted children: A social comparison perspective. *Remedial and Special Education, 6,* 7–12.

Conger, A. J., Peng, S. S., & Dunteman, G. H. (1976). *National Longitudinal Study of the high school class of 1972: Group profiles on self-esteem, locus of control, and life goals.* Research Triangle Park, NC: Research Triangle Institute.

Cox, J., Daniel, N., & Boston, B. O. (1985). *Educating able learners: Programs and promising practices.* Austin, TX: University of Texas Press.

Daurio, S. P. (1979). Educational enrichment versus acceleration. In W. C. George, S. J. Cohn, & J. C. Stanley

(Eds.), *Educating the gifted: Acceleration and enrichment* (pp. 13–63). Baltimore, MD: Johns Hopkins University Press.

Dweck, C., & Elliott, E. S. (1983). Achievement motivation. In E. M. Hetherington (Ed.), *Handbook of child psychology: Vol. 4* (4th ed., pp. 643–691). New York: Wiley.

Elkind, D. (1988). Acceleration. *Young Children, 43*(4), 2.

Feldhusen, J. F. (1989). Synthesis of research on gifted youth. *Educational Leadership, 46*, 6–11.

Festinger, L. A. (1954). A theory of social comparison processes. *Human Relations, 7*, 117–140.

Fox, L. H. (1977). Sex differences: Implications for program planning for the academically gifted. In J. C. Stanley, W. C. George. & C. H. Solano (Eds.). *The gifted and the creative: A fifty-year perspective* (pp. 113–138). Baltimore, MD: Johns Hopkins University Press.

Freeman, J. (1979). *Gifted children.* Baltimore, MD: University Park Press.

Fund for the Advancement of Education. (1957). *They went to college early* (Evaluation Rep. No. 2). New York: Ford Foundation.

Gallagher, J. J. (1958). Peer acceptance of highly gifted children in elementary school. *Elementary School Journal, 58*, 465–470.

Heckhausen, H. (1982). The development of achievement motivation. *Review of Child Development Research, 6*, 600–669.

Hollingworth, L. S. (1942). *Children above 180 IQ Stanford-Binet.* Yonkers, NY: World Book.

Janos, P. M. (1987). A Fifty-year follow-up of Terman's youngest college students and IQ-matched agemates. *Gifted Child Quarterly, 31*, 55–58.

Janos, P. M., & Robinson, N. M. (1985a). Psychosocial development in intellectually, gifted children. In F. D. Horowitz & M. O'Brien (Eds.), *The gifted and talented: Developmental perspectives* (pp. 149–196). Washington, DC: American Psychological Association.

Janos, P. M., & Robinson. N. M. (1985b). The performance of students in a program of radical acceleration at the university level. *Gifted Child Quarterly, 29*, 175–180.

Keating, D. P. (1974). The study of mathematically precocious youth. In J. Stanley, D. Keating, & L. Fox (Eds.), *Mathematical talent: Discovery, description. and development* (pp. 23–46). Baltimore, MD: Johns Hopkins University Press.

Kelly, K. R., & Colangelo, N. (1984). Academic and self-concepts of gifted, general, and special students. *Exceptional Children, 50*, 551–554.

Kulik, C. C., & Kuhk, J. A. (1982). Effects of ability grouping on secondary school students. *American Educational Research Journal, 19*, 415–428.

Kulik, J. A., & Kuhk, C. C. (1984). Effects of accelerated instruction on students. *Review of Educational Research, 54*, 409–425.

Maddux, C. D., Scheiber, L. M., & Bass. J. E. (1982). Self-concept and social distance in gifted children. *Gifted Child Quarterly, 26*, 77–81.

Peng, S. S., Fetters, W. B., & Kolstad, A. J. (1981). *High school and beyond.* Washington, DC: National Center for Education Statistics.

Pollins, L. D. (1983). The effects of acceleration on the social and emotional development of gifted students. In C. P. Benbow & J. C. Stanley (Eds.), *Academic precocity: Aspects of its development* (pp. 160–178). Baltimore, MD: Johns Hopkins University Press.

Pressey, S. L. (1967). "Fordling" accelerates ten years after. *Journal Of Counseling Psychology, 14*, 73–80.

Robinson, H. B. (1983). A case for radical acceleration: Programs of the Johns Hopkins University and the University of Washington. In C. P. Renbow & J. C. Stanley (Eds.), *Academic precocity: Aspects of its development* (pp. 139–159). Baltimore, MD: Johns Hopkins University Press.

Robinson, N. M., & Janos, P. M. (1986). The psychological adjustment in a college level program of marked acceleration. *Journal of Youth and Adolescence, 15*, 51–60.

Schneider, B. H. (1987). *The gifted child in peer group perspective,* New York: Springer-Verlag.

Schneider, B. H., Clegg, M. R.. Byrne. B. M., Ledingham, J. E., & Crombie, G. (1989). Social relations of gifted children as a function of age and school program. *Journal of Educational Psychology, 81*, 48–56.

Solano, C. H. (1987). Stereotypes of social isolation and early burnout in the gifted: Do they still exist? *Journal of Youth and Adolescence, 16*, 527–539.

Southern, W. T., Jones. E. D.. & Fiscus. E. D. (1989). Practitioner objections to the academic acceleration of gifted children. *Gifted Child Quarterly, 33*, 29–35.

Stanley, J. C., & Benbow, C. P. (1986). Youths who reason exceptionally well mathematically, In R. J. Stemberg & J. E. Davidson (Eds.), *Conceptions of giftedness* (pp. 361–387). Cambridge, England: Cambridge University Press.

Terman, L. M.. & Oden. M. H. (1947). The gifted child grows up. *Genetics studies of genius: Vol. 4.* Stanford. CA: Stanford University Press.

U.S. Department of Education. (1986). *What works.* Washington, DC: Author.

This research was funded by Grant MDR-8651737 from the National Science Foundation to Camilla Persson Benbow.

We thank Robert M. Benbow, Linda E. Brody, Frederick G. Brown, Keith G. Davis, Jr., Lynn W. Glass, Ann M. Lupkowski, Daniel J. Reschly, and Julian C. Stanley for helpful comments and suggestions and Olga Arjmand for her assistance in the statistical analyses.

Correspondence concerning this article should be addressed to Camilla Persson Benbow, Study of Mathematically Precocious Youth (SMPY), Department of Psychology, Iowa State University, Ames, Iowa 50011-3180.

(Appendix follows)

Appendix: Questions Used in the Study and Their Coding

After-college survey (age 23)

Self-esteem scale[a]

How do you feel about each of the following statements?

4 = Strongly agree   1 = Disagree

3 = Agree   0 = Strongly disagree

2 = No opinion

	4	3	2	1	0
a. I take a positive attitude toward myself.	0	0	0	0	0
b. I feel I am a person of worth, on an equal plane with others.	0	0	0	0	0
c. I am able to do things as well as most other people.	0	0	0	0	0
d. On the whole, I'm satisfied with myself.	0	0	0	0	0
e. At times I think I'm no good at all.	0	0	0	0	0
f. I feel I do not have much to be proud of.	0	0	0	0	0

Locus of control scale

How do you feel about each of the following statements?

4 = Strongly agree   1 = Disagree

3 = Agree   0 = Strongly disagree

2 = No opinion

	4	3	2	1	0
a. Good luck is more important than hard work for success.	0	0	0	0	0
b. Every time I try to get ahead, something or somebody stops me.	0	0	0	0	0
c. Planning only makes a person unhappy, since plans hardly ever work out.	0	0	0	0	0
d. People who accept their condition in life are happier than those who try to change things.	0	0	0	0	0
e. What happens to me is my own doing.	0	0	0	0	0
f. When I make plans, I am almost certain I can make them work.	0	0	0	0	0

Social interaction scale

Indicate the degree to which your total acceleration (kindergarten to present) has affected you overall in each of the following areas. If you did not accelerate, please skip question.

4 = Strongly favorable effect   1 = Moderately unfavorable effect

3 = Moderately favorable effect   0 = Strongly unfavorable effect

2 = No effect

	4	3	2	1	0
a. Ability to get along with age mates	0	0	0	0	0
b. Ability to get along with mental peers	0	0	0	0	0
c. Ability to get along with adults	0	0	0	0	0
d. Social life	0	0	0	0	0

Self-acceptance/identity scale

Indicate the degree to which your total acceleration (kindergarten to present) has affected you overall in each of the following areas. If you did not accelerate, please skip question.

4 = Strongly favorable effect   1 = Moderately unfavorable effect

3 = Moderately favorable effect   0 = Strongly unfavorable effect

2 = No effect

	4	3	2	1	0
a. Acceptance of abilities	0	0	0	0	0
b. Acceptance of self	0	0	0	0	0
c. Self-awareness/sense of identity	0	0	0	0	0
d. Emotional stability	0	0	0	0	0

After-high-school survey (age 18)

If you accelerated, "how do you feel your social/emotional development has been affected by this acceleration? (Check one.)"

—Much for the better	—Negatively
—Positively	—Much for the worse
—No influence	

---

[a]When creating the scales, the numerical coding was reversed for Items e and f in the self-esteem and locus of control scales.

► Chapter 5

New Directions for Educating the Children of Poverty

MICHAEL S. KNAPP, BRENDA J. TURNBULL, and PATRICK M. SHIELDS

More than one in five schoolchildren in the United States come from families in poverty.[1] For educators, policymakers, researchers, and the public, improving these children's schooling is an increasingly urgent concern. Despite extra resources from the federal government and despite recent educational reforms, the children of poverty experience failure disproportionately in their early school years, and they often leave school ill-equipped for adult life.

The predicament of these disadvantaged children is not new. Over the past few decades, scholars and practitioners have invested considerable energy in the search for effective ways of educating such children at the elementary school level. From their efforts, a set of principles and prescriptions has evolved into the conventional wisdom about educating the children of poverty. Stated oversimply, the conventional wisdom focuses on the deficits of disadvantaged learners and sets forth solutions in the form of principles of curriculum organization, instructional approach, classroom management, and instructional grouping.

We do not suggest that this way of thinking must be discarded, although some researchers advocate doing so.[2] Applied skillfully, it may result in good student performance on standardized tests, especially the tests administered in the elementary

Michael S. Knapp is Manager, Education Policy Studies, SRI International, 333 Ravenswood Ave., Menlo Park. CA 94025. Brenda J. Turnbull is Principal, Policy Studies Associates, 1718 Connecticut Ave., N.W., Washington, DC 20009. Patrick M. Shields is Education Policy Analyst, SRI International.

grades, which emphasize basic skills. However, new evidence and recent analysis call into question many of the tenets of this conventional wisdom. Further, this approach may place an unintended ceiling on the learning of disadvantaged students.[3] Our purpose here is to summarize the shortcomings of the conventional wisdom and to suggest alternative approaches for both regular classroom instruction and supplemental programs.

THE CONCEPTION OF THE DISADVANTAGED LEARNER

Conventional Wisdom

A great deal of research and practice has been predicated on the assumptions that disadvantaged students are deficient in their preparation for school and that their families have given them a bad start in life.[4] These assumptions, in effect, locate the problem in the learner and his or her background.

A Critique

These conventional assumptions can be criticized on two general grounds. First, stereotypical ideas about the capabilities of a child who is poor or who belongs to an ethnic minority will detract from an accurate assessment of the child's real educational problems and potential. Second, by focusing on family deficiencies, educators may miss the strengths of the cultures from which many disadvantaged students come. The adverse consequences of these conceptions include (1) low expectations for what these students can accomplish in academic work; (2) failure to examine carefully what the schools do that exacerbates (or facilitates the solution of) these learning problems; and (3) misdiagnosis of the learning problems these students face (e.g., interpreting dialect speech patterns as decoding errors).

An Alternative View
The disadvantaged child may well bring to school speech patterns, cognitive predispositions, and behavior patterns that do not match the way things are done in school. These students must learn the culture of the school while they are also attempting to master academic tasks. While recognizing that there *may* be gaps in disadvantaged students' experience, the educator builds on their experience bases and at the same time challenges the children to expand their repertoires of experiences and skills. This perspective gains support from a decade or more of cognitive research and related theories of learning that portray the learner as an active constructor of knowledge and meaning rather than a passive recipient of information and skills.

The alternative to the common practice suggests that disadvantaged students are better able to meet the academic challenges of school when:

- teachers respect the students' cultural/linguistic backgrounds and communicate this appreciation to them in a personal way;
- the academic program encourages students to draw and build on the experiences they have, at the same time that it exposes them to unfamiliar experiences and ways of thinking;
- the assumptions, expectations, and ways of doing things in school—in short, its culture—are made explicit to these students by teachers who explain and model these dimensions of academic learning.[5]

SEQUENCING AND CHALLENGE IN THE CURRICULUM

Conventional Wisdom
Conventional curriculums, especially for disadvantaged students, are characterized by two basic traits.[6] First, they break up reading, writing, and mathematics into fixed sequences of discrete skills, ordered from the simplest (the basics) to the more complex (higher-order skills). Second, instruction typically emphasizes mastery of these skills by linear progression through the sequence. Children who haven't mastered spelling, for example, are considered not ready to write stories. Or, in mathematics lessons, practical problems involving multiplication are not introduced until the students can do paper-and-pencil multiplication problems, to say nothing of knowing their multiplication tables. Such rigid sequencing appears in curriculums at all elementary grade levels.

From one point of view, this way of building curriculums makes good sense. With basic skills isolated, teachers can identify and teach those assumed to be deficient in the student's repertoire, provide a clear structure for learning, facilitate the charting of students' progress, and have a common vocabulary for diagnosing what low-achieving students need.

A Critique
Despite these advantages, however, there is broad agreement among experts in mathematics and literacy that such curricular assumptions and structures are critically limited in several important respects.[7] They often (1) underestimate students' capabilities; (2) postpone more challenging and interesting work for too long, in some cases forever; (3) fail to provide a context for learning or for meaningfully using the skills that are taught; and (4) even reinforce academic failure over the long term. The students are literally charged with putting the pieces together into an integrated and useful base of knowledge and, more often than not, they don't. In the view of many experts, this approach to curriculum lacks both coherence and intellectual challenge for the students who experience it.

An Alternative
The available evidence suggests that effective curriculums should:

- focus on meaning and understanding from the beginning—for example, by orienting instruction toward comprehending reading passages, communicating important ideas in written text, or understanding the concepts underlying number facts;
- balance routine skill learning with novel and complex tasks from the earliest stages of learning;
- provide a context for skill learning that establishes clear reasons for needing to learn the skills, affords opportunities to apply the skills, and helps students relate one skill to another;

- influence attitudes and beliefs about the academic content areas, as well as skills and knowledge:
- eliminate unnecessary redundancy in the curriculum (e.g., repeated instruction in the same mathematics computation skills year after year).[8]

THE ROLE OF THE TEACHER IN INSTRUCTION

Conventional Wisdom

Since the mid-1970s, the instruction of disadvantaged students has been dominated by a category of teaching approaches known as direct instruction.[9] Although there are variations among them, these approaches typically feature (1) teacher-controlled instruction, with considerable time spent presenting lesson material and directly supervising students' work; (2) extensive opportunities for practice and frequent corrective feedback; (3) careful structuring of academic tasks so that content can be introduced in small, manageable steps; (4) rapid pacing; and (5) whole-group or homogeneous-group formats. Logically, this class of approaches lends itself particularly well to the linear, discrete skills-oriented curriculums discussed earlier. And the research evidence indicates that, for disadvantaged populations, direct instruction does enhance some kinds of academic learning, in particular, those involving discrete basic skills.[10]

A Critique

There is growing dissatisfaction, however, about the ability of direct instruction to convey more integrated and challenging curriculums to students. First, students do not learn to think for themselves when the teacher breaks the learning task into small, manageable steps and explains how to accomplish each step. Second, some important academic learning goals don't lend themselves to small, manageable steps. Third, students can easily become dependent on the teacher to monitor, motivate, and structure all aspects of the work they do.

An Alternative

In this area, current research does not support abandoning the central role of the teacher but instead suggests balancing it with different approaches. A balance of teacher-directed and learner-directed instruction, for example, has much to offer disadvantaged students, especially if the goal is to engage students in activities that are intellectually chal-

lenging.[11] The key is to strike the right balance between teacher direction and student responsibility, so that students understand what they are doing (and why) and that, over time, their capacity for self-regulated learning increases. To achieve an appropriate balance, teachers should:

- teach explicitly the underlying thinking processes along with skills—for example, by modeling the cognitive process involved when interpreting a story problem in mathematics or trying to understand the author's point of view in a piece of literature;
- encourage students to use each other as learning resources and structure their interaction accordingly, as in many cooperative or team learning arrangements;
- and, as students become more accustomed to constructing knowledge and applying strategies on their own, gradually turn over responsibility for their learning to them, within sequences or units of instruction and across the school year.[12]

THE RELATIONSHIP OF CLASSROOM MANAGEMENT TO ACADEMIC WORK

Conventional Wisdom

The conventional wisdom holds that a uniform structure provides students with clear expectations and guidance regarding interactions with teachers and other students. While all classrooms present teachers with the problem of establishing and maintaining order, those that serve large numbers of disadvantaged students confront teachers forcefully with management problems as the year begins, inviting solutions that impose a uniform—sometimes rigid—structure.

To an extent, well-established principles of classroom management have been developed that support this view.[13] These principles combine good prevention, chiefly through tone-setting and the development of routines early in the year, with appropriate remediation as disruptive behavior occurs.

A Critique

However, this way of thinking about classroom management omits a critical element: the relationship between classroom management and the actual academic work that goes on in the room.[14] This relationship is not necessarily problematic or complex when the work itself is routine and oriented toward basic skills instruction. But when more challenging curriculums are introduced, this approach can become unsatisfactory. Conversely, lack of challenge in the curriculum can contribute to classroom disruption, as students get into trouble out of boredom. Project learning in mathematics, for example, may involve simultaneous student groups engaged in projects that, together, increase the level of noise and activity in a room beyond what teachers and principals have come to expect.

An Alternative
A better perspective on classroom management retains two elements of the conventional wisdom: (1) the teacher establishes general ground rules at the beginning of the school year, and (2) the teacher maintains order over time through vigilant monitoring and ongoing problem solving, as he or she anticipates challenges to, or distractions from, learning in the classroom. But this perspective also encourages teachers to find a new basis for order that emanates as much as possible from academics rather than generic rules, incentives, and consequences for misbehavior. In general, then, classroom management should be intimately linked to the nature of the academic work being done. From this perspective, teachers can most effectively manage behavior if they:

- plan a strong "program of action," rooted in interesting and engaging academic activities;
- set expectations for classroom order that are appropriate to the academic work at hand, within broad boundaries established for overall behavior in the room (Students need to be taught explicitly that noise levels, the degree of movement around the classroom, and so on, can vary, and under what circumstances);
- encourage students who initially may resist novel and unfamiliar work that accompanies a more challenging curriculum.[15]

ACCOMMODATING DIFFERENCES IN STUDENT PROFICIENCY

Conventional Wisdom
Several common arrangements for instructing diverse groups place low-achieving children together

and separate them from those who do better. Three are especially pervasive: (1) ability-based reading groups in the primary guides; (2) formal or informal tracking in literacy and mathematics instruction in the upper elementary grades; and (3) group based supplemental services (e.g. Chapter 1 pullout instruction) in both literacy and mathematics. These arrangements appear to solve a fundamental instructional problem—that of matching students with appropriate learning tasks.

A Critique
These differentiated arrangements, however, may create or exacerbate other problems.[16] Most important, low-achieving students often become permanently segregated in these groupings or tracks. To make matters worse, determinations of "low achievement" are not necessarily reliable. Misdiagnoses of students' academic abilities happen all too often when ethnic or linguistic features (e.g., dialect speech or limited-English-proficiency) are interpreted as signs of low ability. In addition, some of these arrangements create groupings of convenience—for example, four to six poor readers in a Chapter 1 reading room drawn from two or three different classrooms—that may not be particularly effective from the students' point of view. Furthermore, segregation in lower-track groups carries a stigma that may lead to certain students' being labeled "dummies," not to mention the more limited curriculums that are sometimes offered such groups.

Still, the research evidence on the efficacy of ability-grouped learning arrangements for low achievers is mixed.[17] Some reviews find positive effects, while others find harmful or inconclusive influences of such arrangements on academic outcomes.

An Alternative
Research evidence does not warrant doing away with ability-based differentiation altogether.[18] However, schools should consider:

- using (1) heterogeneous grouping, such as cooperative and team learning, and (2) more flexible and temporary ability-grouped arrangements;
- integrating supplementary assistance, such as Chapter 1 instruction, as much as possible into mainstream classroom activities and/or pro-

viding supplementary instruction at times when students do not need to be away from their main classrooms;

- maximizing individual help to low-achieving students on an ad hoc basis rather than in long-term group-based arrangements.

PUTTING NEW IDEAS INTO PRACTICE

The preceding discussion suggests alternative conceptions of the learner, the curriculum, and instructional practice that apply across all subject areas in elementary schools. Guiding these conceptions is a conviction that disadvantaged students are capable of much more than is typically expected of them and that schools can organize themselves to demand high academic performance from these students.[19] There is evidence on which to base this conviction—ranging from advances in understanding of student cognition to dramatic demonstrations of results, such as the performance of inner-city youths on advanced-placement calculus tests.[20]

It would be a mistake to take the principles we have presented as new received wisdom about the education of disadvantaged children. These ideas are not a blueprint for change but a call for further experimentation by practitioners and scholars alike, who, as they try these out, will evolve better principles, in addition to discovering altogether different ones. There is much still to be learned about ways to apply them to particular grade levels, mixtures of students, and school settings. We hope that the ideas presented here will lead to the curriculums that disadvantaged students need to participate fully in a complex technological society.

Authors' note about endnotes: Because the argument in this article relies heavily on the commissioned papers and literature review chapters contained in *Better Schooling for the Children of Poverty: Alternative to Conventional Wisdom—Volume II: Commissioned Papers and Literature Review* (M.S. Knapp and P.M. Shields, eds., January 1990, Menlo Park, Calif: SRI International), we refer below simply to the paper or literature review author and "Volume II" to avoid unnecessary repetition in referencing.

1. H. Hodgkinson, (June 1985), *All One System: Demographics of Education, Kindergarten through Graduate School* (Washington, D.C.: Institute for Educational Leadership).

2. For example, see L. Moll's paper, Volume II.

3. See W. Doyle's paper, Volume II.

4. See J. Brophy's paper, Volume II, which makes useful distinctions among common conceptions of the "deficits" many poor children bring to school.

5. See papers by B. Neufeld and L. Moll, Volume II, which summarize evidence related to these principles; see also J. Comer, (1988), "Educating Poor Minority Children," *Scientific American* 259, 5: 42–48.

6. See W. Doyle's paper, Volume II, for an analysis of conventional approaches to organizing curriculum.

7. See papers by A. Porter, R. Allington, and J. Brophy, Volume II.

8. Papers in Volume II review existing evidence regarding the efficacy and desirability of balancing basic skills learning with more challenging curriculums. For example, see papers by A. Porter and C. McKnight regarding mathematics curriculums, by D. Pearson and G. Garcia regarding reading curriculums.

9. By "direct instruction," we mean instructional approaches that emulate the model of the same name that was part of the Follow Through Planned Variation Experiment in the early 1970s. We distinguish direct instruction from what has been described more generically as "active teaching"—that is, instruction in which students spend most of their time being taught or supervised by their teachers rather than working on their own (or emphasize direct teacher control of learning activities in the classroom). However, unlike direct instruction, active teaching does not presuppose any particular type of academic task, pacing, or grouping.

10. For a review of this evidence, see H. McCollum's paper, Volume II.

11. Clear examples can be found in the teaching of reading, for example, the work of Palincsar and Brown with "reciprocal teaching"; see paper by D. Pearson and G. Garcia for a review of this and related work.

12. See papers by D. Pearson and G. Garcia, and J. Brophy, Volume II; see also work by R. Slavin and others on the efficacy of cooperative learning arrangements, as discussed in H. McCollum's review, Volume II.

13. J. Brophy, (1986), "Research Linking Teacher Behavior to Student Achievement: Potential Implications for Chapter 1 Students," in *Designs for Compensatory Education: Conference Proceedings and Papers*, edited by B.I. Williams et al. (Washington, D.C.: Research and Evaluation Associates).

14. See W. Doyle's paper, Volume II.

15. The basis for these principles is best described in W. Doyle's paper and also in H. McCollum's review, Volume II.

16. See H. McCollum's review, Volume II.

17. Consider evidence from research syntheses by Slavin, Hallinan, Persell, and Wilkinson, reviewed in H. McCollum's paper, Volume II.

18. See, for example, R. Slavin, (1986), *Ability Grouping and Student Achievement in Elementary Schools: A Best*

Evidence Synthesis (Baltimore, Md.: Center for Research on Elementary and Middle Schools, Johns Hopkins University).

19. The point is persuasively argued by R. Calfee, (1986), "Curriculum and Instruction in Reading," in *Designs for Compensatory Education: Conference Proceedings and Papers,* edited by B. I. Williams et al. (Washington. D.C.: Research and Evaluation Associates).

20. J. Mathews, (1988), *Escalante: The Best Teacher in America* (New York: Holt, Rinehart).

Authors' note: This paper is a condensed version of the first report (summary volume) to emerge from the Study of Academic Instruction for Disadvantaged Students. The summary volume, entitled *Better Schooling for the Children of Poverty: Alternatives to Conventional Wisdom,* synthesizes ideas contained in a companion volume (see endnotes). We wish to acknowledge the contributions of other study team members and scholars who wrote commissioned papers and literature review chapters in the companion volume: R. Allington, J. Brophy, W. Doyle, G. Garcia, H. McCollum, C. McKnight, L. Moll, M. Needels, B. Neufeld, D. Pearson, A. Porter, W. Secada, and A. Zucker.

Kids Who Speak Spanish: Schools That Help Them Learn

Americans tend to be intolerant of people who do not have a firm command of the English language. Too often in our schools this translates into an assumption that children who do not have good English skills are lacking in intelligence—a belief that appears to be even stronger when the children are Latino students who are not fully literate in either Spanish or English.

This assumption is not supported by research. In fact, a number of recent studies conclude that Latino students have greater linguistic and intellectual competence than they demonstrate in a typical classroom and that they think at more complex levels than their usual class performance would suggest. The challenge for teachers is how to tap into that potential.

IGNACIO'S STORY

Ignacio is doing very poorly in fifth grade. He still uses a second-grade text; his writing is peppered with misspellings. He usually says as little as possible during discussions, in either Spanish or English. Recently he was suspended for three days for swearing at the gym teacher.

Ignacio is one of four students profiled by Nancy Commins and Ofelia Miramontes. Selecting two new bilingual programs in a southwestern urban school district, they set out to analyze the language abilities of four of the lowest-achieving fifth and sixth graders: Ignacio, Marta, Reina, and Jose. All of these students are native Spanish-speakers who have been in school in the United States since kindergarten. All are at high risk of failing in school and eventually dropping out.

Commins and Miramontes spent more than two hundred hours observing in the classroom and interviewing past and current teachers. They also engaged students in individual and group tasks designed to illuminate their thinking and reasoning skills. In addition, they went on outings with the students and spent more than fifty hours with them and their families.

All four students were considerably more fluent in one or both languages when they were outside the usual whole-group instructional context. Marta, for example, often stumbled over words and repeated herself in class. But she conversed easily in English with her friends and was a successful advocate for her family with the phone company.

Even at school-like tasks, students seemed more competent when away from the classroom setting. For example, a gravity experiment conducted by the researchers elicited an articulate answer from Reina, who rarely spoke in class. After watching two clay balls hit the ground simultaneously, she explained: "They're like parallel lines and they go at the same distance and the same amount." The language is imprecise, but Reina was able to transfer a lesson about parallelism from math class to this new situation.

Perhaps the biggest surprise was Ignacio. Although he was shy or sullen in class, in a small group with Spanish-speaking peers he became outgoing and relaxed. Working on a reasoning task presented by the research team, Ignacio made suggestions for action, defended his choices, and even corrected Jose's Spanish grammar and pronunciation.

Responding to a passage about dogs read aloud by a researcher, Ignacio's answers (in Spanish) were among the strongest of any of the four students. When asked what all dogs have in common, Ignacio did not simply say "tails" or "paws": he was the only one to explain that dogs are part of an animal "family." His knowledge of scientific concepts was evident again when the researchers dropped two balls of clay to the floor. Ignacio asked: "What is this all about, gravity?"

WHAT GOES WRONG

The discourse of all four students showed evidence of sophisticated thought. They were able to analyze and synthesize information and make predictions or deductions.

Why, then, did these students seem so slow and hesitant in class? Why didn't any of them demonstrate their real levels of conceptual understanding or linguistic fluency? Commins and Miramontes point to two factors they observed about life in the classroom.

Although the students were in a bilingual program, Spanish was not treated as a legitimate language for academic work. During thirty days of observation, the researchers never heard a sustained period of discourse in Spanish. Students might use Spanish to tease the teacher or an aide, but they rarely used the language to converse about an English text or a math concept.

Furthermore, lessons consisted mainly of whole-group lessons and skill-building activities designed to prepare the class for district-mandated competency exams. Thus students read aloud from low-level basal readers, memorized spelling lists and word definitions, and filled in worksheets.

Failing to do well at such basic tasks, children were almost never given the opportunity to read or discuss real books or to write their own stories. Rather than seeing the need for a more language-rich environment, the teachers came to believe that their students lacked underlying thinking abilities and needed more drill.

USING SPANISH

In nearly a decade of research in San Diego and Tucson classrooms, Luis Moll and Stephen Diaz have found similar patterns of low-level instruction and low achievement. But they have also found ways to accelerate the learning of Latino students.

In a case study of reading instruction, Moll and Diaz looked at third- and fourth-grade classes in a bilingual program. They found that students who were good readers in Spanish were treated as low-level readers in English because they "never quite sounded right to their monolingual teachers." Lessons proceeded at a slow pace, with frequent interruptions by teachers to correct pronunciation or define an unfamiliar word.

Collaborating with the teachers, Moll and Diaz tried an experiment. Immediately after a teacher led a lesson with the lowest reading group, a researcher asked the children questions in Spanish about what they had just read in English. The children's answers demonstrated a much fuller understanding of the text than they could display in English.

The question was how to use children's Spanish language skills to enhance their performance in English. Setting aside the low-level texts, the researchers began to teach lessons from regular grade-level English texts. The explicit goal of each lesson was comprehension; the researcher and students could switch to Spanish as needed to clarify the meaning.

In the first two lessons, a researcher read a story aloud to the students, then probed to find out how much they understood. By the third lesson the children did the reading on their own and were able, with bilingual assistance, to answer comprehension questions required of monolingual English readers at grade level.

The level of lessons, Moll and Diaz conclude, need not be reduced to accommodate students' limited proficiency in English. Students can comprehend grade-level texts if the teacher provides what the researchers term "bilingual communicative support."

CALLING ON PARENTS

Ina A. felt frustrated by how difficult it was to get her bilingual class of sixth graders to write anything. She thought it might help to enlist support from their parents, but the parents too seemed to feel somewhat alienated from the school, even though Ina A., like them, was a native of Mexico.

So far, Ina A.'s story is typical of what many teachers experience. But she had access to an unusual source of support and information. At an afterschool lab initiated by Moll and his colleagues, she had the opportunity to meet with other teachers and researchers interested in creating

Schools Where Speaking Spanish is an Asset

- Spanish-speaking students continue to take Spanish all the way up to an advanced placement course that helps them gain college credit for skills in their native language.
- Students in the bilingual program no longer take remedial classes. The program now includes the full range from basic courses to college preparatory courses such as algebra. Tutorial assistance is available.
- Counselors, who are fluent in Spanish, actively encourage bilingual students and their parents to plan for college.
- Teachers learn Spanish and make a special effort to use the language inside and outside their classrooms.
- As one of many extracurricular options, students write and produce a monthly Spanish newspaper.

These are among the exemplary practices identified by a team of researchers who studied six high schools serving large populations of Latino students in California and Arizona. Each of these schools had previously received recognition for excellence at the local, state, or federal level.

Underlying these practices are features of school organization and ethos that set these schools apart. First and foremost, all six place great value on the students' native language and culture. The ability to speak Spanish is treated as an advantage, not a liability—so much so that a number of teachers have learned to speak Spanish and use the language both in the classroom and out.

These schools do not confuse language with culture; they acknowledge that Latino students come from many different countries. The schools also take into account the diversity of students' educational backgrounds, interests, and abilities.

The schools recognize that a student's limitations in English should not prevent progress in other subject areas. To help students in their academic efforts, they provide a range of support services—from tutorials and extended learning time before or after school to counselling, mentoring, and advocacy.

A high level of staff commitment is evidenced by the extra time teachers give to tutor students, sponsor activities in school, and become advocates for students and their families. Many also participate in regular workshops designed to help them better serve bilingual students as well as monolingual students who are low achievers.

Finally, several features are similar to those identified in other effective schools—high expectations, strong school leadership, and parental involvement. The administration and teachers in these schools have found concrete ways to communicate their expectations to bilingual students and to exercise their leadership on behalf of this group. In addition, these schools encourage parental involvement by sponsoring everything from breakfasts to ESL classes for adults and by assigning kids to bilingual counselors.

The need for new educational approaches is apparent in the data about the school failures of Latino youth—high dropout rates, low test scores, poor attendance, and low college-going rates. One of the central implications of this study for high schools serving Latino students is that improving students' English language skills, while critical, is not enough.

The exemplary schools also made it a priority to give students access to higher levels of content knowledge and opportunities to develop their Spanish language skills. In short, they offered students a range of courses, as well as academic and personal support.

See T. Lucas, R. Henze, and R. Donato, "Promoting the Success of Latino Language-Minority Students: An Exploratory Study of Six High Schools," *Harvard Educational Review*, August 1990.

---

new ways to develop the literacy skills of Spanish-dominant students.

In one of these sessions, she heard researchers talk about community field studies in which they had discovered what Moll calls "households funds of knowledge." Learning that many people in the community were knowledgeable about building construction, she hatched the idea for a new thematic unit.

Students would read books and magazines—from how-to manuals to histories of various dwellings—and use this information to build a model structure and to write brief essays describing what

they did. In addition, parents and other community members would come in to share their considerable knowledge about various aspects of construction.

The visits proved to be far more successful than Ina A.—or the visitors—expected. Students not only learned a great deal of new information but also began to see that their parents could contribute substantively to their schooling. As a result of these visits, students read more books, interviewed community members, and worked collaboratively on building a model of a town—sharing what they were learning in both written and oral accounts.

Moll sees Ina A.'s class as an excellent example of what can occur when a teacher mobilizes the knowledge that exists beyond the classroom. Students begin to see themselves, and their families, as people who can make an intellectual contribution.

FINDING OUT

Children with limited proficiency in English can also make unexpected progress by learning to use their peers as resources. Since 1979, Elizabeth Cohen has studied and worked with classrooms using Finding Out/ Descubrimiento—a bilingual, hands-on curriculum designed to foster the development of math and science concepts and thinking skills.

The curriculum materials consist of activity cards presented in English, in Spanish, and in pictures. Students go to learning centers where they read these cards, carry out the activities suggested on the cards, and answer questions about what happened and why.

Studies have consistently shown that students with limited language skills in English or in both Spanish and English make significant gains on tests of oral proficiency after participating in this program. In addition, on the California Test of Basic Skills (CTBS), students make striking gains in math concepts, applications, and computation, and in reading comprehension.

These results seem directly connected to experiences in the classroom. The more frequently the dominantly Spanish-speaking students talk about a task, the larger their gains in English, even if they talk in Spanish. Students who talk and work together more also show higher average gains on the math concepts and problem-solving sections of the CTBS. When teachers move away from the learning-center approach, or stop delegating as much authority to the groups, the gains rapidly diminish. As Cohen concludes, success depends upon teachers' learning a new classroom management system and new roles.

It is intriguing that both oral language skills and reading skills are enhanced by a curriculum focusing on science concepts. Cohen attributes this to the fact that children are exposed to a rich language experience: they work in small groups where English is spoken, and the new vocabulary on the activity cards is reinforced by contextual and nonverbal cues.

FINDING HELP

None of the studies reported on here provide a blueprint for what schools can do. But they do challenge the watered-down curriculum and lowered expectations confronting the many Ignacios in our schools. And they raise provocative questions for educators who want to change such practices.

How can we provide intellectual challenges that inspire children to call upon all of their language resources? How can we create classroom environments in which students will talk more, interact freely, and take academic risks? How can we use the social and intellectual resources of the community to support classroom learning?

Finding answers to these questions will not be easy. Moll points out an interesting irony: schools, like most households, need more resources than they have to address the needs of young people. But while many households are part of larger social networks, teachers often function in isolation.

As a first step we need more settings—like the afterschool study group in Tucson—in which teachers and researchers can share ideas, discuss field and classroom studies, and develop innovations. Only by overcoming their isolation will teachers be able to make fuller use of social and intellectual resources in both the school and the community.

FOR FURTHER INFORMATION

E. Cohen. *Designing Groupwork: Strategies for the Heterogeneous Classroom*, pp. 135–143. New York: Teachers College Press, 1986.

N. Commins and O. Miramontes. "Perceived and Actual Linguistic Competence: A Descriptive Study of Four Low-Achieving Hispanic Bilingual Students." *American Educational Research Journal* 26, no. 4 (Winter 1989): 443–472.

J. A. Langer et al. "Meaning Construction in School Literacy Tasks: A Study of Bilingual Students." *American Educational Research Journal* 27, no. 3 (Fall 1990): 427–471.

L. Moll. *Community Knowledge and Classroom Practice.* Technical Report, Innovative Approaches Research Project. Arlington, VA: Development Associates, Inc., 1990.

L. Moll and S. Diaz. "Change as the Goal of Educational Research." *Anthropology and Education Quarterly* 18 (1987): 300–311.

Dick and Jane in 1989

PIPER PURCELL and LARA STEWART
Southwestern University

This study is a replication of the 1972 study Dick and Jane as Victims *done by Women on Words and Images. The original study exampled 134 children's readers, and found sex stereotyping in both number of times males and females appeared, and the activities in which they were shown. The replication is a content analysis of 62 children's readers in use in 1989 to determine if males and females were still shown in sex-stereotyped roles. It was found that although there are still differences in the rate of portrayal for males and females, and in the variety of roles assigned to each, the differences are not as pronounced as they were in 1972.*

How our children learn to perceive themselves is in many ways dependent on the role models they are given. In our society many of these role models are given by official sanction in school materials. Because obsolete or too narrow role models can make it difficult for children to grow into happy and productive adults (Association of Women Psychologists, 1970), it is important to make sure the role models children are presented with coincide with social realities, and are not based on outdated stereotypes.

In 1972 Women on Words and Images did a content analysis of 134 elementary readers from 13 publishers in use in 3 cities in New Jersey to determine if females and males were portrayed in stereotyped roles. This study, *Dick and Jane as Victims,* found that males were portrayed more often, in more roles, and as being more active than females, who were often shown in passive or domestic roles (Women on Words and Images, 1975). A study of 84 additional readers done by the same group in 1975 found similar results (Women, 1975).

In the 14 years since 1975, many things have changed in this country. In 1975 legislation was passed making it illegal for schools to show bias toward male sports at the expense of female sports (Women, 1975). The majority of women, even married women with children, are out in the work place (Lott, 1987). In keeping with these trends, textbook manufacturers have set more stringent standards for the portrayals of men and women. Publishers who promised that their new books would be more egalitarian after the 1975 study have had these new books on the market for years (Women, 1975). In this light we decided to replicate the studies done by Women on Words and Images in order to determine what changes have occurred in sex-roles as portrayed in elementary readers since 1975.

LITERATURE REVIEW

The idea that what children read can affect the way they perceive themselves is based on four assumptions.

1. Sex roles are learned behavior and are not solely biologically defined.
2. Sex role definitions can be learned from role models including people presented in media such as picture books, storybooks, and films.

3. Role definitions that are too narrow or rigid can be harmful to a child's development,
4. Such narrowly defined sex-role definitions have been found by prior research in children's literature.

A review of the literature supported these four assumptions.

The literature indicated that the concept that each sex should fill a different role is developed, and that children understand this concept by age 3 (Flerx, Fidler, & Rogers, 1976; Michel, 1986; Wilson, Epstein, Fechey, & Wilson, 1966). As children get older, their definitions of "proper" behavior for their sex become narrower, and their inhibitions against breaking out of these defined roles become stronger (Brown, 1958; Wilson et al., 1966). One of the ways in which a child learns to define these roles is through the imitation of role models including those from media such as picture books, storybooks, readers, and television (Astron, 1983; Bandura & Walters, 1963; Flerx et al., 1976; Michel, 1986; Saario, Jacklin, & Tittle, 1973; Weitzman, 1975; Child Study Association, 1960).

Although role models help a child develop, it is important that they are not too rigid or too narrowly defined. These types of sex roles may hinder a child's development (Child Study, 1960; Ellis & Betler, 1973; Flerx et al., 1976; Michel, 1986; Saario et al., 1973; Sadker & Sadker, 1982; Weitzman, 1975; Women, 1975). Ellis and Betler (1973) found that "A significant amount of the literature suggests that traditional sex-determined role standards are not only nonfunctional but perhaps dysfunctional." Flerx et al. (1976) said, "sex-role stereotyping has restrictive, dysfunctional consequences for both sexes, the deleterious effects are more pronounced for females. . . . " Males, too, suffer from restrictive roles. Boys who score high on sex-appropriate behavior scales have also been found to score high on anxiety scales (Sadker & Sadker, 1982).

After establishing that sex role concepts could be developed from role models and that narrow role definition could be harmful, it was necessary to try to find out if narrow and rigid sex role stereotypes had previously been found in children's literature. A number of studies have been done on the existence of sexism and stereotyped sex roles present in children's readers as well as other forms of children's media. A review of selected studies shows that there is cause for concern about the role options children's literature presents.

In a 1979 study of children's magazines, Sylvia-Lee Tibbetts found that the magazines showed dif-

ferences by sex in areas such as social role, economic dependency, and attitude towards others. A study comparing readers in the 1960s and 1970s found that the books had not changed their role models to keep pace with the changing social and political climate (Prida & Ribner, 1974). Even factual matter is not free from stereotypes. A study of eight children's dictionaries found that in sentences used to illustrate definitions, males were given a more active role than females (Schram, 1974a).

The studies done by Women on Words and Images showed quite clearly the differences in the way men and women are portrayed in children's literature. The 1972 study found that the ratio of boy-centered stories to girl-centered stories was 5:2, and the ratio of adult male main characters to adult female main characters was 3:1. Animal stories were closer in the incidence of portrayal of male and female characters with a ratio of 2 to 1, while male characters dominated folktales with a ratio of 4 to 1. After studying a variety of children's books, Carol Jacklin concluded that there was some level of sex bias in all children's books (Saario et al., 1973).

METHOD

Our study followed the original study as far as possible in method. We included 62 readers in use in 3 Texas cities. Several pre-primers were not included in the study as they contained only object pictures and single works. Only 4 publishers were represented as these are the only publishers approved for use by the Texas Approved Textbook List (1987). A short summary of each story was written, and it was classified by type of story (child, animal, adult, or folktale) and by whether it was male-centered, female-centered, mixed, or neutral. A list was kept of all occupations attributed to men and to women, either in writing or in pictures, and a list of biographies was kept. (These lists are available from the authors.) Illustrations were characterized using hair, clothing, and body shape as male or female, and the number of each was counted.

The stories were also analyzed by the presence of certain traits, such as bravery, cleverness, and ingenuity in boys' or girls' actions. Each story in which one of these traits was attributed to a boy or girl was counted only once, regardless of the number of times the trait appeared, or the number of children in which it was shown. It was possible for one story to contain several different traits. Intercoder reliability on these measures was calculated from the analysis of two books from series not included in the study.

RESULTS

The 62 readers surveyed contained 1883 stories. Intercoder reliability on story types was 95%. These readers showed more females in almost every category than the readers surveyed in 1972 and 1975 (Tables I and II). There were not only more stories about women, but they were shown doing more things. A change in the types of stories can also be seen. There was a larger percentage of informational and gender neutral stories. Many animal stories used gender-neutral names and used no pronouns. That a higher percentage of the stories are gender-neutral should be considered when looking at the male to female story type ratios. Even though males still appear more than females in several categories, there are significantly more stories that are not gender specific. Thus, the readers in this study are less male focused than those of 1972.

In 1972 the ratio of male-focused child stories to female-focused child stories was found to be 7:1. In our sample the ratio of male to female child stories was almost 1:1 with 210 male child stories and 215 female child stories. Four of the series had more female-child stories than male-child, one had an equal number, and line, Macmillan Odyssey, had twice as many male-focused child stories as female. Although girls in the readers were sometimes still shown in traditional roles, they were also shown saving lives and solving mysteries, while a boy might be seen babysitting or helping out around the house. In several cases an identical story appeared in more than one reader. However, in one series the main character was a boy and in another a girl. It appears that in order to increase the number of female characters the publishers had simply substituted a female name and pronoun for a male name. One common theme still found in female stories

was that of rescue. A number of stories showed girls being rescued by a pet or wild animal, while boys almost never had to depend on animals to get them out of trouble.

There were more male adult-centered stories than female centered, but not by nearly the same margin as in 1972. While the earlier study found a male to female ratio of 3 to 1 (35, 26) current data indicates the ratio is 4:3. Four of the series had more male than female adult stories, while the other two contained a majority of women. In the 1972 study only one series had more women than men, while two contained equal numbers of malecentered and female-centered stories. There were more biographies of females than of males with 56 females and 48 males. One of the biggest concerns reported by the original study was that there were 169 male biographies and only 27 female biographies, thus providing few role models for young girls. While the newer books contain fewer biographies overall, there is more even representation of men and women.

In the category of animal stories there were substantially more male-centered stories than female-centered stories. There were 62 male-centered animal stories but only 17 that were female-centered, which at 78% to 22% represents a lower percentage of female stories than the 30% found in 1972. Although it appears as if little progress has been made in the portrayal of animals, it should be remembered that the number of mixed or gender-neutral animal stories has increased. Whereas the 1972 study found only a small percentage of mixed animal stories, more than half of the animal stories in 1989 placed emphasis on characters of both sexes. Even though there are more stories based on male characters than female characters, only 42% of the stories display a gender bias. While one would hope that there would be equal representation of men and women, the inclusion of more mixed-gender stories is a positive step.

Folktales, too, still had a much higher percentage of males than females. Seventy percent of folktales were male focused and only 30% were female

TABLE I. **Story-Type Comparison**

| | Child (%) | | Adult (%) | | Biography (%) | | Animal (%) | |
Year	M	F	M	F	M	F	M	F
1972	72%	28%	76%	24%	86%	14%	70%	30%
1989	49%	51%	57%	43%	46%	54%	78%	22%

TABLE II. **Story Type by Publisher**[a]

Type	1	2	3	4	5	6
Male child	44	34	39	33	29	28
Female child	57	37	43	34	29	14
Mixed child	37	5	19	15	25	6
Adult male	10	2	8	5	9	1
Adult female	12	1	5	1	5	2
Male biography	5	2	8	11	8	14
Female biography	8	1	10	12	9	16
Male animal	14	11	11	9	7	10
Female animal	3	2	3	4	1	4
Mxied animal	19	12	10	96	11	8
Male folktale	14	9	12	13	5	2
Female folktale	5	4	5	4	45	5
Mixed folktale	5	4	1	4	5	7
Family	19	10	10	4	5	7
Informative	173	127	105	146	116	166
Male illustration	1612	1495	1782	1474	1514	1236
Female illustration	1420	1239	1272	1031	1189	820

[a] 1: Scott Foresman, 2: Houghton Mifflin Basal, 3: Macmillan—Connections, 4: Harcourt—Basal, 5: Macmillan—Reading Express, 6: Harcourt—Odyssey.

focused. This is only slight improvement from the 1972 study when 79% of the folktales were male focused and 21% were female focused. It has been argued that folktales are different than the other categories of stories in that they are often many centuries old, and do not change as easily as more modern works. Proponents of this position say that to demand equal representation in folktales would be to destroy parts of our culture ("Race, Sex and Class," 1980). Still, the lack of representation of women is not in folktales as a group, but in the folktales that are chosen for children's readers. It certainly seems possible to include more folktales about women without changing those about men.

Even though there were more females in these books than in the previous years, they were still not pictured as often as males. There were 9191 illustrations of men and only 7053 of women, a 4 to 3 ratio compared to the 2 to 1 ratio in 1975 (Table III). Girls were pictured in more active roles than previously.

TABLE III. **Ratio of Illustrations**

Year	Male	Female
1975	2	1
1989	4	3

In addition to being shown in traditional activities, girls were shown climbing trees, running, and playing baseball. Boys, however, were still seldom shown in any form of domestic activity.

Although more women were in these readers, they were still not shown in as wide a range of careers as men. There were 80 careers mentioned for women and 136 for men. In 1972 there were 262 occupations for men and only 75 for women. While women were shown in what were once primarily male fields, only men were shown in the more adventurous areas. A woman doctor was now common, but women explorers and big-game hunters were still few and far between.

Although we did analyze story content by themes, we were not comfortable with this method of analysis. Several articles in our literature review criticized this type of analysis as being too subjective ("Race, Sex, and Class," 1980; Reeder, 1974). For example, one article discussed how Pippi Longstocking books are considered antifeminist from one perspective, and ultrafeminist from another (Reeder, 1974). It was also problematic that the original study contained no information on intercoder reliability, and did not fully define the categories. As our own intercoder reliability was only 70%, we do not feel we can draw any firm conclusions about

TABLE IV.

		Boys		Girls	
		1972	1989	1972	1989
Active themes					
1. Ingenuity, cleverness		131	27	33	28
2. Industry, problem solving ability		169	34	47	34
3. Strength, bravery, heroism		143	29	36	23
4. Routine helplessness, elective or creative helpfulness		107	21	87	22
5. Apprenticeship, acquisition of skills, coming of age		151	30	53	38
6. Earning, acquisition, unearned rewards		87	33	53	38
7. Adventure, exploration, and imaginative play		216	56	68	31
Passive themes					
8. Passivity and dependence		19	8	119	8
9. Altruism		55	9	22	12
10. Goal constriction and rehearsal for domesticity		50	2	166	4
11. Goal constriction and rehearsal for domesticity		51	22	60	22
12. Victimization and humiliation by the opposite sex		7	0	68	0

these measures. Our results are included, but should be read with the above considerations in mind (Table IV).

DISCUSSION

Overall, our sample of readers is much more egalitarian than those sampled in 1972 and 1975. This may be in part influenced by the smaller sample size and the representation of fewer publishers. Girls appear just as often as boys as this sample, and are pictured in a wider range of activities than previously. Women appear more often than in the previous study, but still not as often as men, or in as wide a range of occupations, even though women biographies outnumber those of men. It appears that the portrayal of females in textbooks has mirrored the changes in real life. Advancements have been made, but some concerns still remain. Even though girls are now shown in active roles, they are still shown as needing rescue in many more instances than are boys. Girls are shown as being very brave while waiting for rescue, but they still cannot help themselves out of trouble. Although stories do show boys babysitting and crying over a bruise, boys are still portrayed many times as being forced to deny their feelings to show their manhood. Perhaps the most important concern is that of women and occupations. Girls need a wider variety of working role models. Women have been allowed into mundane "male" fields; they should be allowed to be adventurous too.

While there have been great strides made in the portrayal of sex roles in children's readers, it is important that this continue to go forward. Girls should be more active and women should be shown in a wider variety of occupations. Boys should be allowed to show their emotions, and more men should show off their cooking. Readers should explore the vast body of women's folklore in addition to that of men. Most importantly, publishers, educators, parents, and researchers should continue to focus their attention on the content of children's readers. Constant attention will assure that the quality of these textbooks continues to increase, and that standards are not allowed to lapse. By improving the quality of role models, we improve the quality of children's lives, and we improve the quality of tomorrow.

REFERENCES

Astron, E. (1983). Measures of play behavior: The influence of sex-role stereotyped children's books. *Sex Roles, 9,* 43–47.

Association of Women Psychologists. (1970, September). Statement, resolutions and motions. Presented to the American Psychological Association.

Bandura, A., & Walters, R. (1963). The role of imitation. *Social Learning and Personality Development.* New York: Holt, Rinehart and Winston.

Brown, D. (1958). Sex role development in a changing culture. *Psychological Bulletin, 55,* 232–242.

Child Study Association. (1960). *List of Recommendation Books.* New York.

Ellis, L. V., & Betler, P. M. (1973). Traditional sex-determined role standards and sex-stereotypes. *Journal of Personality and Social Psychology, 25*, 28–34.

Flerx, V. Fidler, D. & Regers. S. (1976). Sex-role stereotypes: Developmental aspects and early intervention. *Child Development, 47*, 998–1007.

Lott, B. (1987). *Women's lives: Themes and variation in gender learning.* Monterey, CA: Brooks/Cole Publishing.

Michel, A. (1986). *Down with stereotypes! Eliminating sexism from children's literature and school textbooks.* UNESCO.

Mischel, W. (1966). A social learning view of sex differences in behavior. In E. Maccoby (Ed.) *The development of sex differences.* Stanford, CA: Stanford University Press.

Race, sex, and class in children's books: 2, 3, 4, and 6. (1980). *New Statesman, 100*, Nov. 21, 28, Dec. 4, 19/26.

Reeder, K. (1974). Pippi Longstocking—Feminist or anti-feminist? *Interracial Books for Children.* New York: Roman.

Saario, T., Jacklin, C. N., & Tittle, C. K. (1973). Sex role stereotyping in public schools. *Harvard Educational Review, 43*, 386A 16.

Sadker, P., & Sadker, D. M. (1982). Cost of sex bias in the schools: The report card. In *Sex Equity Handbook for Schools.* New York: Longman.

Schram, B. (1974a). *D is for dictionary, S is for stereotyping.* New York: Interracial Books for Children.

Schram, B. (1974b). *Misgivings About the Giving Tree.* New York: Interracial Books for Children.

Stacey, J., Bereaud, S., & Daniels, J. (1974). *Jill came tumbling after.* New York: Dell Publishing Company.

Tibbetts, S. L. (1979). Sexism in children's magazines. Doctoral Thesis, University of Pennsylvania. Ann Arbor, MI: University Microfilms (microfiche).

Weitzman, L. J. (1975). Sex-role socialization. In *Women: A feminist perspective.* Mayfield Publishing Company.

Women on Words and Images. (1975). *Dick and Jane as Victims: Sex Stereotyping in Children's Readers.* Princeton, NJ.

▶ Chapter 6

Assertive Discipline—
More Than Names on the Board
and Marbles in a Jar

[handwritten annotation: Assertive Discipline uses positive reinforcement]

LEE CANTER

About a year ago I was on an airline flight, seated next to a university professor. When he found out that I had developed the Assertive Discipline program, he said, "Oh, that's where all you do is write the kids' names on the board when they're bad and drop marbles in the jar when they're good."

The university professor's response disturbed me. For some time I've been concerned about a small percentage of educators—this professor apparently among them—who have interpreted my program in a way that makes behavior management sound simplistic. More important, I'm concerned with their misguided emphasis on providing only negative consequences when students misbehave. The key to dealing effectively with student behavior is not negative—but positive—consequences. To clarify my views for *Kappan* readers, I would like to explain the background of the program and address some of the issues that are often raised about Assertive Discipline.

I developed the program about 14 years ago, when I first became aware that teachers were not trained to deal with student behavior. Teachers were taught such concepts as "Don't smile until Christmas" or "If your curriculum is good enough, you will have no behavior problems." Those concepts were out of step with the reality of student behavior in the 1970s.

Lee Canter is president of Lee Canter & Associates, Santa Monica, Calif. He is the author of many books on behavior management and is the developer of the Assertive Discipline program.

When I discovered this lack of training, I began to study how effective teachers dealt with student behavior. I found that, above all, the master teachers were assertive; that is, they *taught* students how to behave. They established clear rules for the classroom, they communicated those rules to the students, and they taught the students how to follow them. These effective teachers had also mastered skills in positive reinforcement, and they praised every student at least once a day. Finally, when students chose to break the rules, these teachers used firm and consistent negative consequences—but only as a last resort.

It troubles me to find my work interpreted as suggesting that teachers need only provide negative consequences—check marks or demerits—when students misbehave. That interpretation is wrong. The key to Assertive Discipline is catching students being good: recognizing and supporting them when they behave appropriately and letting them know you like it, day in and day out.

THE DISCIPLINE PLAN

It is vital for classroom teachers to have a systematic discipline plan that explains exactly what will happen when students choose to misbehave. By telling the students at the beginning of the school year what the consequences will be, teachers insure that all students know what to expect in the class-

DISCIPLINE PLAN IS NEEDED

room. Without a plan, teachers must choose an appropriate consequence at the moment when a student misbehaves. They must stop the lesson, talk to the misbehaving student, and do whatever else the situation requires, while 25 to 30 students look on. That is not an effective way to teach—or to deal with misbehavior.

Most important, without a plan teachers tend to be inconsistent. One day they may ignore students who are talking, yelling, or disrupting the class. The next day they may severely discipline students for the same behaviors. In addition, teachers may respond differently to students from different socioeconomic, ethnic, or racial backgrounds.

An effective discipline plan is applied fairly to all students. Every student who willfully disrupts the classroom and stops the teacher from teaching suffers the same consequence. And a written plan can be sent home to parents, who then know beforehand what the teacher's standards are and what will be done when students choose to misbehave. When a teacher calls a parent, there should be no surprises.

MISBEHAVIOR AND CONSEQUENCES

I suggest that a discipline plan include a maximum of five consequences for misbehavior, but teachers must choose consequences with which they are comfortable. For example, the first time a student breaks a rule, the student is warned. The second infraction brings a 10-minute timeout; the third infraction, a 15-minute timeout. The fourth time a student breaks a rule, the teacher calls the parents; the fifth time, the student goes to the principal.

No teacher should have a plan that is not appropriate for his or her needs and that is not in the best interests of the students. Most important, the consequences should never be psychologically or physically harmful to the students. Students should never be made to stand in front of the class as objects of ridicule or be degraded in any other way. Nor should they be given consequences that are inappropriate for their grade levels. I also feel strongly that corporal punishment should *never* be administered. There are more effective ways of dealing with students than hitting them.

Names and checks on the board are sometimes said to be essential to an Assertive Discipline program, but they are not. I originally suggested this particular practice because I had seen teachers interrupt their lessons to make such negative comments to misbehaving students as, "You talked out again. I've had it. You're impossible. That's 20 minutes after school." I wanted to eliminate the need to stop the lesson and issue reprimands. Writing a student's name on the board would warn the student in a calm, non-degrading manner. It would also provide a record-keeping system for the teacher.

Unfortunately, some parents have misinterpreted the use of names and checks on the board as a way of humiliating students. I now suggest that teachers instead write an offending student's name on a clipboard or in the roll book and say to the student, "You talked out, you disrupted the class, you broke a rule. That's a warning. That's a check."

In addition to parents, some teachers have misinterpreted elements of the Assertive Discipline program. The vast majority of teachers—my staff and I have probably trained close to 750,000 teachers—have used the program to dramatically increase their reliance on positive reinforcement and verbal praise. But a small percentage of teachers have interpreted the program in a negative manner.

There are several reasons for this. First, Assertive Discipline has become a generic term, like Xerox or Kleenex. A number of educators are now conducting training in what they call Assertive Discipline without teaching all the competencies essential to my program. For example, I have heard reports of teachers who were taught that they had only to stand in front of their students, tell them that there were rules and consequences, display a chart listing those rules and consequences, and write the names of misbehaving students on the board. That was it. Those teachers were never introduced to the concept that positive reinforcement is the key to dealing with students. Such programs are not in the best interests of students.

Negative interpretations have also come from burned-out, overwhelmed teachers who feel they do not get the support that they need from parents or administrators and who take out their frustrations on students. Assertive Discipline is not a negative program, but it can be misused by negative teachers. The answer is not to change the program, but to change the teachers. We need to train administrators, mentor teachers, and staff developers to coach negative teachers in the use of positive reinforcement. If these teachers cannot become more positive, they should not be teaching.

POSITIVE DISCIPLINE

I recommend a three-step cycle of behavior management to establish a positive discipline system.

First, whenever teachers want students to follow certain directions, they must *teach* the specific behaviors. Teachers too often assume that students know how they are expected to behave. Teachers first need to establish specific directions for each activity during the day—lectures, small-group work, transitions between activities, and so forth. For each situation, teachers must determine the *exact* behaviors they expect from the students.

For example, teachers may want students to stay in their seats during a lecture, focusing their eyes on the lecturer, clearing their desks of all materials except paper and pencil, raising their hands when they have questions or comments, and waiting to be called on before speaking. Once teachers have determined the specific behaviors for each situation, they must teach the students how to follow the directions. They must first state the directions and, with younger students, write the behaviors on the board or on a flip chart. Then they must model the behaviors, ask the students to *restate* the directions, question the students to make sure they understand the directions, and immediately engage the students in the activity to make sure that they understand the directions.

Second, after teaching the specific directions, teachers—especially at the elementary level—must use *positive repetition* to reinforce the students when they follow the directions. Typically, teachers give directions to the students and then focus attention only on those students who do *not* obey. ("Bobby, you didn't go back to your seat. Teddy, what's wrong with you? Get back to work.") Instead, teachers should focus on those students who do follow the directions, rephrasing the original directions as a positive comment. For example, "Jason went back to his seat and got right to work."

Third, if a student is still misbehaving after a teacher has taught specific directions and has used positive repetition, only then should the teacher use the negative consequences outlined in his or her Assertive Discipline plan. As a general rule, a teacher shouldn't administer a disciplinary consequence to a student until the teacher has reinforced at least two students for the appropriate behavior. Effective teachers are always positive first. Focusing on negative behavior teaches students that negative behavior gets attention, that the teacher is a negative person, and that the classroom is a negative place.

An effective behavior management program must be built on choice. Students must know beforehand what is expected of them in the classroom, what will happen if they choose to behave, and what will happen if they choose not to behave. Students learn self-discipline and responsible behavior by being given clear, consistent choices. They learn that their actions have an impact and that they themselves control the consequences.

I wish teachers did not need to use negative consequences at all. I wish all students came to school motivated to learn. I wish all parents supported teachers and administrators. But that's not the reality today. Many children do not come to school intrinsically motivated to behave. Their parents have never taken the time or don't have the knowledge or skills to teach them how to behave. Given these circumstances, teachers need to set firm and consistent limits in their classrooms. However, those limits must be fair, and the consequences must be seen as outcomes of behaviors that students have *chosen*.

Students need teachers who can create classroom environments in which teaching and learning can take place. Every student has the right to a learning environment that is free from disruption. Students also need teachers who help them learn how to behave appropriately in school. Many students who are categorized as behavior problems would not be so labeled if their teachers had taught them how to behave appropriately in the classroom and had raised their self-esteem.

WHY ASSERTIVE DISCIPLINE?

The average teacher never receives in-depth, competency-based training in managing the behavior of 30 students. No one teaches teachers how to keep students in their seats long enough for teachers to make good use of the skills they learned in their education classes. In most instances, behavior management is taught through a smorgasbord approach—a little bit of William Glasser, a little bit of Thomas Gordon, a little bit of Rudolf Dreikurs, a little bit of Lee Canter. The teachers are told to find an approach that works for them.

Such an approach to training teachers in behavior management is analogous to a swimming class in which nonswimmers are briefly introduced—

without practice—to the crawl stroke, the breast stroke, the back stroke, and the side stroke; then they are rowed to the middle of a lake, tossed overboard, and told to swim to shore, using whatever stroke works for them. In effect, we're telling teachers to sink or swim, and too many teachers are sinking.

The lack of ability to manage student behavior is one of the key reasons why beginning teachers drop out of teaching. Teachers must be trained thoroughly in classroom management skills. It is not sufficient for them to know how to teach content. They will never get to the content unless they know how to create a positive environment in which students know how to behave.

Assertive Discipline is not a cure-all. It is a starting point. Every teacher should also know how to use counseling skills, how to use group process skills, and how to help students with behavioral deficits learn appropriate classroom behaviors. in addition, classroom management must be part of an educator's continuing professional development. Teachers routinely attend workshops, enroll in college courses, receive feedback from administrators, and take part in regular in-service training to refine their teaching skills. Classroom management skills deserve the same attention. Unfortunately, some educators view training in Assertive Discipline as a one-shot process; they attend a one-day workshop, and that's supposed to take care of their training needs for the rest of their careers.

One day is not enough. It takes a great deal of effort and continuing training for a teacher to master the skills of classroom management. A teacher also needs support from the building administrator. Without an administrator backing a teacher's efforts to improve behavior management, without an administrator to coach and clinically supervise a teacher's behavior management skills, that teacher is not going to receive the necessary feedback and assistance to master those skills.

Parental support for teachers' disciplinary efforts is equally important. Many teachers become frustrated and give up when they don't receive such support. We must train teachers to guarantee the support of parents by teaching teachers how to communicate effectively with parents. In teacher training programs, participants are led to believe that today's parents will act as parents did in the past and give absolute support to the school. That is rarely the case. Today's teachers call parents and are told, "He's your problem at school. You handle it. You're the professional. You take care of him. I don't know what to do. Leave me alone."

RESEARCH AND ASSERTIVE DISCIPLINE

Over the last several years, a number of dissertations, master's theses, and research projects have dealt with Assertive Discipline. The results have consistently shown that teachers dramatically improve student behavior when they use the skills as prescribed. Teachers who use Assertive Discipline reduce the frequency of disruptive behavior in their classrooms, greatly reduce the number of students they refer to administrators, and dramatically increase their students time-on-task.[1] Other research has demonstrated that student teachers trained in Assertive Discipline are evaluated by their master teachers as more effective in classroom management.[2] Research conducted in school districts in California, Oregon, Ohio, and Arizona has shown that an overwhelming majority of teachers believe that Assertive Discipline helps to improve the climate in the schools and the behavior of students.[3]

No one should be surprised that research has verified the success of the program when teachers use the skills properly. Numerous research studies have shown that teachers need to teach students the specific behaviors that they expect from them. Research also shows that student behavior improves when teachers use positive reinforcement effectively and that the pairing of positive reinforcement with consistent disciplinary consequences effectively motivates students to behave appropriately.[4]

Any behavior management program that is taught to teachers today must have a solid foundation in research. Many so-called "experts" advocate programs that are based solely on their own opinions regarding what constitutes a proper classroom environment. When pressed, many of these experts have no research validating their opinions or perceptions, and many of their programs have never been validated for effectiveness in classrooms. We can't afford to train educators in programs based only on whim or untested theory. We have an obligation to insure that any training program in behavior management be based solidly on techniques that have been validated by research and that have been shown to work in the classroom.

Research has demonstrated that Assertive Discipline works and that it isn't just a quick-fix solution. In school districts in Lennox, California, and

Troy, Ohio, teachers who were trained 10 years ago still use the program effectively.[5] The program works because it is based on practices that effective teachers have followed instinctively for a long time. It's not new to have rules in a classroom. It's not new to use positive reinforcement. It's not new to have disciplinary consequences.

Teachers who are effective year after year take the basic Assertive Discipline competencies and mold them to their individual teaching styles. They may stop using certain techniques, such as putting marbles in a jar or writing names on the board. That's fine. I don't want the legacy of Assertive Discipline to be—and I don't want teachers to believe they have to use—names and checks on the board or marbles in a jar. I want teachers to learn that they have to take charge, explain their expectations, be positive with students, and consistently employ both positive reinforcement and negative consequences. These are the skills that form the basis of Assertive Discipline and of any effective program of classroom management.

1. Linda H. Mandlebaum et al., "Assertive Discipline: An Effective Behavior Management Program," *Behavioral Disorders Journal*, vol. 8, 1983, pp. 258–64; Carl L. Fereira, "A Positive Approach to Assertive Discipline," Martinez (Calif.) Unified School District, ERIC ED 240 058, 1983; and Sammie McCormack, "Students' Off-Task Behavior and Assertive Discipline" (Doctoral dissertation, University of Oregon, 1985).

2. Susan Smith, "The Effects of Assertive Discipline Training on Student Teachers' Self Concept and Classroom Management Skills" (Doctoral dissertation, University of South Carolina, 1983).

3. Kenneth L. Moffett et al., "Assertive Discipline," *California School Board Journal*, June/July/August 1982, pp. 24–27; Mark Y. Swanson, "Assessment of the Assertive Discipline Program," Compton (Calif.) Unified School District, Spring 1994; "Discipline Report," Cartwright (Ariz.) Elementary School District, 10 February 1982; and Confederation of Oregon School Administrators, personal letter, 28 April 1980.

4. Helen Hair et al., "Development of Internal Structure in Elementary Students: A System of Classroom Management and Class Control," ERIC ED 189 067, 1980; Edmund Emmer and Carolyn Everston, "Effective Management: At the Beginning of the School Year in Junior High Classes," Research and Development Center for Teacher Education, University of Texas, Austin, 1980; Marcia Broden et al., "Effect of Teacher Attention on Attending Behavior of Two Boys at Adjacent Desks," *Journal of Applied Behavior Analysis*, vol. 3, 1970, pp. 205–11; Hill Walker et al., "The Use of Normative Peer Data as a Standard for Evaluating Treatment Effects," *Journal of Applied Behavior Analysis*, vol. 37, 1976, pp. 145–55; Jere Brophy, "Classroom Organization and Management," *Elementary School Journal*, vol. 83, 1983, pp. 265–85; Hill Walker et al., "Experiments with Response Cost in Playground and Classroom Settings," Center for Research in Behavioral Education of the Handicapped, University of Oregon, Eugene, 1977; Thomas McLaughlin and John Malaby, "Reducing and Measuring Inappropriate Verbalizations," *Journal of Applied Behavior Analysis*, vol. 5, 1972, pp. 329–33; Charles Madsen et al., "Roles, Praise, and Ignoring: Elements of Elementary Classroom Control," *Journal of Applied Behavior Analysis*, vol. 1, 1968, pp. 139–50; Charles Greenwood et al., "Group Contingencies for Group Consequences in Classroom Management: A Further Analysis," *Journal of Applied Behavior Analysis*, vol. 7, 1974, pp. 413–25; and K. Daniel O'Leary et al., "A Token Reinforcement Program in a Public School: A Replication and Systematic Analysis," *Journal of Applied Behavior Analysis*, vol. 2, 1969, pp. 3–13.

5. Kenneth L. Moffett et al., "Training and Coaching Beginning Teachers: An Antidote to Reality Shock," *Educational Leadership*, February 1987, pp, 34–46; and Bob Murphy, "Troy High School: An Assertive Model," *Miami Valley Sunday News*, Troy, Ohio, 12 March 1989, p. 1.

Developing Self-Regulated Learners
The Role of Private Speech and Self-Instructions

KAREN R. HARRIS
Department of Special Education
University of Maryland

The theoretical and research bases for the belief that private speech performs a cognitive self-guidance function and that verbally mediated control of behavior is an integral component of self-regulation are explored in this article. Major perspectives on the role of self-verbalizations are presented, and the role of self-speech in multicomponent interventions is discussed. Finally, the need to establish intervention integrity is discussed, and research regarding confirmation of mediating variables in multicomponent interventions is reviewed. Although the empirical basis to date is positive, we cannot yet make precise and experimentally verifiable claims as to either the unique and nontransferable role of private speech in the development of self-regulation or the role of self-instructions in multicomponent interventions.

This article explores the theoretical and research bases for the belief that private speech performs a cognitive self-guidance function and that verbally mediated control of behavior is an integral component of self-regulation. Although private speech is typically thought of as self-verbalizations that perform a self-regulatory function, both definitions and functions of private speech have varied depending on the perspective of the theorist or researcher. The role of self-verbalizations in the development of self-control has been investigated from at least three major perspectives: that of the Soviet researchers, including Vygotsky and Luria; the mediational perspective; and the behavioral perspective (Kohlberg, Yaeger, & Hjertholm, 1968; Pressley, 1979). These three perspectives, as well as Piaget's (1923/1955) conceptualization of *egocentric speech,* are presented in the first part of this article in order to help clarify what researchers consider to be private speech and to provide a historical and theoretical framework for the importance of this phenomena. The evolution and nature of self-instructional interventions and current issues in self-instructional research are also discussed.

PERSPECTIVES ON SELF-VERBALIZATION

Piaget (1923/1955) and Vygotsky (1934/1962) were among the first researchers to address children's self-verbalizations. Their views of such speech, however, differed in important ways indicative of the underlying differences in their understandings of intellectual development.

Requests for reprints should be sent to Karen R. Harris, Department of Special Education, University of Maryland, College Park, MD 20742.

PIAGET → BELIEVES SPEECH SHOULD BE INTERNALIZED

Piaget: Egocentric Speech

Piaget (1923/1955) described egocentric speech as presocial and noncommunicative speech carried on alone or in the presence of others; such speech is not adapted to the point of view of the listener and does not invite dialogue and exchange of ideas. He noted that, by the age of 6 or 7, children have developed socialized speech and are aware that it is considered inappropriate to talk out loud to oneself in the company of others. In short, Piaget did not assign cognitive-developmental functions to egocentric speech, and he did not speculate on the possibility of covert self-speech; rather, he saw such speech as an indication of the "unsocialized" state of the child (Zivin, 1979).

It would be inaccurate to say that Piaget failed to ascribe any positive functions to egocentric speech. Meichenbaum and Goodman (1979) identified three positive functions stated or implied in Piaget's analysis of egocentric speech. Egocentric speech could perform as (a) a self-command or a stimulus to excite or accelerate an action, (b) a reinforcer for an action or an accompanying task, or (c) an aid in marking the rhythm of an action. It should be noted that Kohlberg et al. (1968) conducted a series of studies and presented a developmental hierarchy that integrated both Piaget and Vygotsky's forms of self-speech. Although this work has been critiqued for several reasons (cf. Zivin, 1979), the integrative concept of Kohlberg et al. deserves further attention from researchers.

Vygotsky: Regulatory Self-Speech

Piaget's position elicited a strong response from Vygotsky. The two authors differed in their views of social functioning, language, and mind. When Vygotsky's (1934/1962) book, *Thought and Language,* was published, he severely criticized Piaget's conception of egocentric speech. Although Vygotsky also used the term *egocentric speech,* he focused on language and the social origin of each child's experience as critical components in the development of thought and intellect. Piaget did not consider the development of covert self-speech central to the understanding of intellectual development; rather, he saw mature operations of the mind as acting on abstract representations of propositions developed through the internalization of nonverbal action (Zivin, 1979; also see Piaget, 1934/1962). Vygotsky (1934/1962), on the other hand, presented a theory of the development of human intellect and thought in which the development and internalization of private speech played a central role. He emphasized the self-regulatory, planning function of private speech and saw such speech as serving the cognitive functions of orienting, organizing, and structuring behavior. To Vygotsky, children come to use private speech to consciously understand or focus on a problem or situation and to overcome difficulties.

Vygotsky saw all speech, including the infant's earliest cries, gestures, and babbling, as socialized, adaptive communication (as an infant, such communication promotes survival). As the child grows and develops, social interactions with capable others eventually enable the child to function as an independent, self-regulated problem solver. Vygotsky saw the child-adult dyad functioning as an integrated social system, with the adult initially responsible for planning, implementing, and monitoring the strategies and behaviors necessary for reaching a goal. Working in the "zone of proximal development," or the area between what a learner can do independently and what can be accomplished with the assistance of a competent other, the adult facilitates the gradual transfer of self-regulated performance to the child. In terms popular today, social interaction provides the origins of metacognition.

To Vygotsky, language and self-speech were critical to this gradual development of self-regulation. The most primitive form of self-regulation occurred in the child's early egocentric speech, which Vygotsky saw as accompanying activity and as capable of accidently capturing or regulating behavior (Zivin, 1979). The child then becomes able to use self-verbalizations for emotional release; these verbalizations occur during action and continue to be primarily involuntary. Finally, the child develops the capability for socioemotional expression—the use of self-verbalizations before an action in order to regulate performance.

Thus, Vygotsky theorized that overt self-speech represented the transitional stage between external speech (initial ability to pronounce words, name objects, etc.) and internal speech. Inner speech was seen as the third step in a four-step process of the development of pure thought. Pure thinking is the fourth step, where, in Vygotsky's (1934/1962) terms, "words die as they bring forth thought" (p. 149). To support this four-step process, Vygotsky theorized that there would be differences in both the structure and content of self-verbalizations at each step. As the transition to inner speech begins, the child's egocentric speech becomes increasingly inaudible, condensed, and incomprehensible, accompanied by changes in its semantic, structural, and grammatical form. Vygotsky presented a series of experiments validating these changes in the child's overt self-speech; he reported evidence of a curvilinear developmental pattern with self-speech increasing until the age of 6 or 7, then declining and virtually disappearing by 8 to 10 years of age. He also reported finding a positive relationship between amount of self-speech and task difficulty (Vygotsky, 1934/1962; Vygotsky & Luria, 1930). After his premature death, others continued the work he had begun.

Luria: Intraindividual, Stimulation Functions of Self-Speech

Although space precludes a thorough discussion of the work of other Soviet researchers (for thorough discussion, see A. Harris, 1979; Wertsch, 1979), Luria's work is briefly described here because it has been instrumental in the Western development of self-instructional interventions. Although Luria, who was Vygotsky's student, believed that verbal self-regulation played an important role in human development, his theory and research took a different focus and direction. Vygotsky focused on the semantic aspect of self-verbalizations, and Luria emphasized the activational, impulse, and semantic aspects of such speech. Luria (1959, 1961) approached self-regulation primarily as an intraindividual process due to neurophysiological/central nervous system processing, while Vygotsky conceived of self-regulation as an interindividual process dependent on socialization. Further, Vygotsky theorized about and studied naturally occurring, spontaneous speech and then made inferences to inner speech, whereas Luria primarily studied induced, experimenter-directed speech in laboratory settings (Zivin, 1979).

Based on a series of studies, Luria (1961) described the three stages in the development of verbal self-regulation that have become the backbone of self-instructional approaches: (a) the speech of others controls and directs the child's behavior; (b) the child's own overt speech begins to regulate her or his behavior (such speech can initiate but not inhibit behavior); and (c) the content/meaning of the child's overt or covert speech effectively regulates behavior. Luria (1959, 1961) further hypothesized that the self-regulatory function of private speech could intervene when behavioral problems

were due to processes that were immature, damaged, or dysfunctional, and conducted promising interventions with children with a syndrome similar to hyperactivity and with adults with Parkinson's disease.

Soviet Research: Problems of Replication

Although the Soviet theories regarding the development of self-regulation have been widely influential, the empirical basis for these theories has been criticized by other researchers. Differences in Soviet and American approaches to empirical research have made it difficult to assess and replicate Soviet work (A. Harris, 1979). Soviet researchers investigating self-verbalizations have tended to present case studies, individual protocols, and raw data rather than summary statistics, and have frequently failed to discuss features of the experimental design. Translation problems have also contributed to uncertainty regarding the experimental validity of the work. Several attempted replications of Luria's studies failed to repeat his results (cf. Beiswenger, 1968; Jarvis, 1968; Miller, Shelton, & Flavell, 1970; Wilder, 1968). Wozniak (1972), however, critiqued non-Soviet attempts at replication, noting significant differences between Soviet and American researchers in terms of directions given to subjects, and the tendency among American researchers to use overly complex directions, inappropriate warm-up procedures, and low statistical power. Wozniak's criticisms resulted in new attempts among American researchers; Rondal (1976), for example, attempted to correct these problems and reported results generally consistent with those of Luria.

Western Mediational Perspective

The mediational deficiency hypothesis contends that there is a stage in human development when verbal responses are available to the child but fail to mediate between external stimuli and overt responses (Kendler, Kendler, & Wells, 1960). The Western concept of mediational deficiency can be traced at least as far back as 1946, when Kuenne reported that possession of a concept of the relation between stimuli in a discrimination task did not facilitate transposition for younger preschool children to the extent that it did for older preschool children. Although he did not use the term *mediational deficiency*, Kuenne suggested two developmental stages in terms of the relation of verbal responses to overt choice behavior. In the first stage, the child is able to make relevant, overt verbalizations, but these verbalizations do not control or influence choice behavior; in the second stage, such verbalizations come to gain control and dominate choice behavior. It was not until 1960 that Kendler et al. proposed the mediational deficiency hypothesis and noted the similarities between their conclusions and those of Luria. In 1962, Reese reviewed research which, while not conducted under the rubric of mediational deficiency, provided support for the concept. In this important article, Reese reasoned that instructions to use verbal mediators would vary in effect depending on the task, the age of the individual, and the individual's level of concept attainment. Even though Reese did not use the term *private-speech,* his suggestions had an important influence on subsequent private speech research.

Flavell: Production Deficiency

Flavell, Beach, and Chinsky (1966) followed Maccoby's (1964) lead regarding an ambiguity in the mediation deficiency hypothesis and developed the production deficiency hypothesis. Production deficiency referred to the younger child's tendency not to produce the relevant words when needed; thus, the nonmediated nature of overt task behavior was seen as failure to produce the relevant verbalizations rather than failure of the verbalizations to mediate behavior. The work of both Luria and Vygotsky was cited and related to the concept of production deficiency. In subsequent studies, Flavell and his colleagues found evidence for the existence of both mediational and production deficiencies, although they believed production deficiencies to be more significant, and noted that a child's mediational deficiency is likely to disappear before her or his production deficiency does (Corsini, Pick, & Flavell, 1968; Keeney, Cannizzo, & Flavell, 1967).

Flavell and his colleagues (Flavell et al., 1966; Miller et al., 1970) characterized Luria as investigating the mediational hypothesis and questioned Luria's previous results. Zivin (1979), however, challenged Miller et al.'s conclusions, noting that they failed to distinguish between Vygotsky's spontaneous speech and Luria's induced speech. She also noted that whereas previous research had focused on the role of self-speech in fostering general activation and goal-oriented self-guidance, Flavell and his colleagues introduced a new function for private speech—aiding recall. Further, Zivin described

the experimental tasks used by Flavell as having little parallel in daily intellectual life.

Behavioral Perspective

Behavioral studies have made a significant contribution to our knowledge of self-control. Rather than view self-control as a generalized trait, behaviorists have attempted to identify "conditions under which self-controlling responses occur and the processes by which they influence the actions to be controlled" (Coates & Thoresen, 1979, p. 6). Thus, behaviorists have studied primarily the ways in which self-speech can facilitate self-control; in other words, their focus has been similar to Luria's concern with induced self-speech rather than Vygotsky's emphasis on spontaneous self-speech. The role of induced self-speech (i.e., self-instructions) in the implementation of self-regulation processes (self-monitoring, self-evaluation, self-determined consequences) is emphasized. Behavioral researchers have described self-speech as a verbal chaining process and have theorized that it provides discriminative stimuli and conditioned reinforcers (Blackwood, 1972). Self-instructions may provide cues that guide behavior and may prompt, direct, or maintain behavior. Self-speech, therefore, can be viewed as part of a complex cognitive-symbolic process that mediates and maintains behaviors when consequences are either delayed or not evident (Mahoney & Thoresen, 1974).

Two major reviews of behavioral research in self-regulation were published in 1979. In their review, O'Leary and Dubey (1979) characterized self-instructions as behavioral antecedents, and concluded that self-instructions are effective self-control agents when children are required to implement them, have been reinforced for adhering to them in the past, and are capable of the behavior that the self-instructions are meant to influence. Although Rosenbaum and Drabman (1979) were more cautious regarding the applied significance of self-instructional procedures, they concluded, as did O'Leary and Dubey, that more research was clearly warranted. In addition, the authors of both reviews acknowledged the importance of developmental-level and task-type and task difficulty in interpreting results; these remain important issues to date. Rosenbaum and Drabman further voiced a concern that has been repeatedly noted in the past 10 years—the need for well-controlled components analyses of multicomponent self-instructional interventions. The nature of such multicomponent self-instructional interventions and progress made in components analyses research are discussed next.

SELF-INSTRUCTIONAL INTERVENTIONS

Self-instructional interventions represent a cognitive-behaviorally based approach to the development of self-regulated learners (Meichenbaum, 1977). Cognitive-behavioral approaches are somewhat misleadingly named, as they actually represent an integration of affective, behavioral, cognitive, social, and developmental theories and research (K. R. Harris, 1982). Meichenbaum (Meichenbaum & Goodman, 1979), citing his 10 years of research in this area, phrased the question that has shaped this area of research, "But can't we teach talking to ourselves over and above its natural amount, content, and timing initially to guide and later to train behavior that causes us (or a client) problems?" (p. 350).

Meichenbaum (1976) proposed that self-instructions perform five functions, allowing an individual to (a) direct attention to relevant events, (b) interrupt an automatic response to environmental stimuli, (c) search for and select alternative courses of action, (d) use rules and principles to guide behavior (i.e., self-instructions stipulate criteria for success, aid in the recall of certain actions, and focus thinking along relevant dimensions), and (e) maintain a sequence of actions in short-term memory so they can be enacted. Meichenbaum and Asarnow (1979) elaborated on these functions and discussed ways in which self-instructions can facilitate behavior or behavior change in the classroom. Particularly relevant here, they noted the motivational aspects of self-instructions: They can enhance positive task orientation, elicit an achievement set, reinforce and help maintain task-relevant behaviors, and provide ways of coping with failure and self-reinforcing success. The theorized functions of self-instructions and cognitive-behavioral interventions gave rise to hope of greater maintenance and generalization of intervention effects. Although this hope has yet to be fully realized, recent reviewers have found that sound strategy interventions conducted from a cognitive-behavioral vantage point (i.e., involving self-instructions, active learning, strategy mastery, etc.) frequently do result in some degree of maintenance and generalization (cf. K. R.

Harris, Graham, & Pressley, in press; Reeve & Brown, 1985; Wong, 1985).

Although the focus on self-instructions and the functions claimed are intuitively appealing and exciting, empirical evidence is still needed to substantiate both the critical role of self-instructions and their functions. Researchers have found evidence of the importance of self-instructions (for reviews, see Pressley, 1979; Schunk, 1986), yet they have also found that other powerful variables may interact with or affect the efficacy of self-instructions. These variables include important student characteristics such as chronological and mental age; cognitive capacity and capabilities; developmental status; language development; initial knowledge state; currently produced strategies; learning style; nature of the child's disorder or learning problem (e.g., Kendall, 1985, provided a discussion of the implications of cognitive deficiency vs. cognitive distortion); and aspects of motivation, including attributions and presence or absence of a mastery orientation (cf. Copeland, 1981; K. R. Harris, 1982; K. R. Harris et al., in press; Kendall, 1977; Kendall & Cummings, 1988; Meichenbaum, 1977; Meyers, Cohen, & Schieser, 1989). Aspects of the task and environmental contexts can also affect the efficacy of self-instructions (Schunk, 1986). Finally, the nature and content of self-instructions can be critical; the impact of self-statements may depend on their patterns, functions, focus (task-specific vs. metacognitive), personal meanings, and the individual's degree of belief in them (K. R. Harris, 1985; Kendall & Hollon, 1981; Schunk, 1986).

A Multicomponent Approach

To complicate things further, Meichenbaum's (1977) self-instructional training is actually a multicomponent intervention of which self-instructions are only one part. In addition to self-instructions, Meichenbaum (1977) emphasized interactive learning between teachers and students, and suggested modeling, dialogue, and guided discovery as vehicles for development of self-regulated learners. He also stressed the need for cognitive-functional assessment to inform instruction; the importance of affective variables, including motivation; and the importance of conducting instruction within the zone of proximal development. In Meichenbaum's self-instructional approach, students progress from modeled, induced use of strategic, task-relevant private speech to the use of covert private speech in order to reach a goal (K. R. Harris, 1986). Graduated difficulty, prompts, feedback, and social reinforcement are used to help the child achieve self-regulation.

The child is not passive, however, during the gradual transfer of strategy control in Meichenbaum's self-instructional approach, but rather plays an active, collaborative role in the design, implementation, and evaluation of the strategy(s) used. Dialogue and guided discovery are incorporated during the intervention as the teacher and student determine together the purpose of the task, a strategy likely to facilitate performance, and how the strategy can be executed most effectively (K. R. Harris & Pressley, in press; Meichenbaum, 1977). Unfortunately, some researchers have failed to attend to the detailed guidelines and principles provided by Meichenbaum (1977), and self-instructional interventions have occasionally resembled the imposition of static routines on passive learners (K. R. Harris, 1985; K. R. Harris & Pressley, in press).

Intervention Integrity

Although self-instructional training involves multiple components, many researchers continue to believe self-instructions to be one of its most critical components (cf. Kendall, 1977; Meichenbaum & Genest, 1980; Schunk, 1986). Only a handful of studies, however, have been done to confirm the mediational effects of self-instructional intervention components (i.e., to differentiate between therapeutic procedures and therapeutic processes); to determine the active, necessary, and sufficient components with particular learners engaged in particular tasks; or to determine cost-benefit relationships among components (Graham & K. R. Harris, 1989; K. R. Harris, 1985; Kendall & Hollon, 1981). Thus, establishing intervention integrity has become a critical issue in self-instructional intervention research.

K. R. Harris (1988) and K. R. Harris et al. (in press) introduced the concept of intervention integrity to expand on and subsume the treatment integrity concept in ways particularly relevant to multicomponent interventions. Paralleling treatment integrity, intervention integrity first requires that each and every component of a strategy/self-instructional intervention is both delivered and carried out as intended and recommended based on available empirical literature. Unfortunately, this has not clearly been established in some of the self-

regulation literature. Intervention integrity expands the concept of treatment integrity by further requiring *assessment of the processes of change as related to both intentions and outcomes.* Specification and assessment of intervention processes (i.e., establishing intervention integrity) is necessary to determine whether or not cognitive-behavioral interventions, including self-instructional training, work for the reasons they are hypothesized to work (K. R. Harris et al., in press). Establishing intervention integrity can therefore both test and expand the cognitive-behavioral model/theoretical base.

Encouragingly, researchers have begun to attend to confirmation of mediating variables and components analyses. For example, Kendall and Finch (1979) investigated the effects of self-instructional training on private speech among impulsive, emotionally disturbed children. The self-instructional intervention resulted in significant increases in task-relevant verbalizations, as well as significant improvement on the Matching Familiar Figures Test. K. R. Harris (1986) provided confirmation of self-instructional intervention effects on rate and content of self-statements, as well as on task performance, among learning-disabled and normally achieving children working on a problem-solving task. Differences in rate and content of private speech and in task performance were also found between learning-disabled and normally achieving children in a nontreatment, naturalistic condition.

Components Analyses

Components analyses studies involving sound self-instructional interventions have also begun, and illustrative studies are noted. Elliott-Faust and Pressley (1986) found that teaching third-grade students to self-instruct deployment of a comprehension strategy and to self-monitor strategy use promoted durable use of the strategy and was superior to simply teaching the children the task strategy directly. Although Schunk and Coxe's (1986) study did not involve full-fledged, self-instructional training, they found that continuous verbalization of subtraction with regrouping operations led to higher self-efficacy and skillful performance than did discontinued and no-verbalization conditions among 11- to 16-year-old students with learning disabilities. Schunk and Cox concluded that self-verbalization is important in teaching students to systematically use a task strategy. Manning (1988) combined self-instructional training with cueing (cue cards were employed as prompts during training and during immediate follow-up) and compared this condition to a control condition where self-instructions were not used; the control condition was equated for modeling (by peers and an adult), practice, and cueing. First- and third-grade students who had been exhibiting inappropriate classroom behaviors served as subjects. The self-instructional group performed significantly better on the dependent measures (teacher ratings, on-task behavior, and locus of control) on both immediate and delayed posttests. Manning concluded that children can be taught to produce self-instructional mediators that promote regulation of behavior.

Finally, Graham and K. R. Harris have completed two studies in a series of components analyses. In the first study (Graham & K. R. Harris, 1989), they investigated the theoretically proposed, incremental effects of explicit, self-regulation procedures (including proximal goal setting, self-assessment, and self-recording) over and above self-instructional strategy training combined with instruction in the significance of the strategies, among fifth- and sixth-grade students with learning disabilities. Although self-instructional strategy training produced meaningful and lasting effects on several composition measures and on self-efficacy, explicit self-regulation did not produce augmental effects on any of the measures. Graham and K. R. Harris pointed out that the situation may be even more complex than previously realized; future research might profitably focus on the characteristics as well as the components of training. Important characteristics of their intervention included interactive learning, instruction in the school setting, and criterion-based rather than time-based instruction. Sawyer, Graham, and K. R. Harris's (1989) study involved three groups of learning-disabled students who received: direct instruction on the composition strategy, self-instructional strategy training, or self-instructional strategy training plus explicit self-regulation training. A practice control group was also included. The group that received explicit self-regulation training performed significantly better than the control group and the direct-instruction group on both posttest and generalization composition measures. Differences between the self-instructional training only and self-regulation groups were not significant, thus replicating the previous study's results. Only the self-regulation training, however, resulted in non-significant differences between the learning-dis-

abled students and normally achieving peers on story-quality ratings.

These studies provide a great deal of insight and illustrate the promising nature of components analyses research. However, it must be noted that none of these studies represent an analysis fine grained enough to determine the contributions of self-instructions alone across affective, behavioral, and cognitive systems. The challenges involved in "decomposing" self-instructional interventions and the related challenges in assessment and methodology promise to occupy researchers for some time to come (cf. K. R. Harris, 1985; Kendall & Hollon, 1981).

CONCLUSION

Despite the early interest in private speech and recognition of its importance in self-regulation, research in this area has not progressed as far as might have been hoped. The significant assessment and methodology difficulties encountered by researchers in this area, particularly in attempting naturalistic studies in children's homes, communities, and schools, provide a partial explanation. Emphasis on private-speech-based interventions, rather than on descriptive, developmental studies, is also a factor (K. R. Harris, 1985; Kendall & Hollon, 1981). We do not have a clear developmental picture as to whether or not (and if so, how), in specific situations or on specific tasks, private speech comes to allow planning and self-regulation of goal-directed behavior. As can be seen in this special issue of *Educational Psychologist*, self-regulation can be achieved through a variety of mechanisms; the Soviet position that the directive and planning functions of private speech are unique and nontransferable (A. Harris, 1979) remains to be validated.

Similarly, we cannot yet make precise and experimentally verifiable claims as to the role of self-instructions in multicomponent interventions. Furthermore, as Meichenbaum and Goodman (1979) noted, the fact that private speech can play a role in altering behavior does not prove that private speech plays a critical role in the natural development of self-regulation. The empirical basis to date, however, is positive and encouraging regarding both private speech and self-instructions. Our ability to explain, predict, and develop self-regulatory behavior in children and adults cannot help but profit from further research in these areas.

REFERENCES

Beiswenger, H. (1968). Luria's model of the verbal control of behavior. *Merrill-Palmer Quarterly, 14*, 267–284.

Blackwood, R. (1972). *Mediated self-control: An operant model of rational behavior.* Akron, OH: Exordium.

Coates, T. J., & Thoresen, C. E. (1979). Behavioral self-control and educational practice: Or do we really need self-control? In D. C. Bertiner (Ed.), *Review of research in education* (Vol. 7, pp. 345). New York: Guilford.

Corsini, D. A., Pick, A. D., & Flavell, J. H. (1968). Production deficiency of non-verbal mediators in young children. *Child Development, 39*, 53–58.

Copeland, A. P. (1981). The relevance of subject variables in cognitive self-instructional programs for impulsive children. *Behavior Therapy, 12*, 520–529.

Elliott-Faust, D. J., & Pressley, M. (1986). How to teach comparison processing to increase children's short- and long-term listening comprehension monitoring. *Journal of Educational Psychology, 78*, 27–33.

Flavell, J. H., Beach, D. R., & Chinsky, J. M. (1966). Spontaneous verbal rehearsal in a memory task as a function of age. *Child Development, 37*, 283–299.

Graham, S., & Harris, K. R. (1989). A components analysis of cognitive strategy instruction: Effects on learning disabled students' compositions and self-efficacy. *Journal of Educational Psychology, 81*, 353–361.

Harris, A. (1979). Historical development of the Soviet theory of self-regulation. In G. Zivin (Ed.), *The development of self-regulation through private speech* (pp. 51–78). New York: Wiley.

Harris, K. R. (1982). Cognitive-behavior modification: Application with exceptional children. *Focus on Exceptional Children, 15*(2), 1–16.

Harris, K. R. (1985). Conceptual, methodological, and clinical issues in cognitive-behavioral assessment. *Journal of Abnormal Child Psychology, 13*, 373–390.

Harris, K. R. (1986). The effects of cognitive-behavior modification on private speech and task performance during problem solving among learning disabled and normally achieving children. *Journal of Abnormal Child Psychology, 14*, 63–77.

Harris, K. R. (April, 1988). *What's wrong with strategy intervention research: Intervention integrity.* Paper presented at the annual meeting of the American Educational Research Association, New Orleans.

Harris, K. R., Graham, S., & Pressley, M. (in press). Cognitive strategies in reading and written language. In N. Singh & I. Beale (Eds.), *Current perspectives in learning disabilities: Nature, theory, and treatment.* New York: Springer-Verlag.

Harris, K. R., & Pressley, M. (in press). The nature of cognitive strategy instruction: Interactive strategy construction. *Exceptional Children.*

Jarvis, P. E. (1968). Verbal control of sensory-motor performance: A test of Luria's hypothesis. *Human Development, 11*, 172–183.

Keeney, T. J., Cannizzo, S. R., & Flavell, J. H. (1967). Spontaneous and induced verbal rehearsal in a recall task. *Child Development, 38*, 953–966.

Kendall, P. C. (1977). On the efficacious use of verbal self-instruction procedures with children. *Cognitive Therapy and Research, 1*, 331–341.

Kendall, P. C. (1985). Toward a cognitive-behavioral model of child psychopathology and a critique of related interventions. *Journal of Abnormal Child Psychology, 13*, 357–372.

Kendall, P. C., & Cummings, L. (1988). Thought and action in educational interventions: Cognitive-behavioral approaches. In J. C. Witt, S. N. Eliott, & F. N. Gresham (Eds.), *Handbook of behavioral therapy in education* (pp. 403–418). New York: Plenum.

Kendall, P. C., & Finch, A. J. (1979). Analyses of changes in verbal behavior following a cognitive-behavioral treatment for impulsivity. *Journal of Abnormal Child Psychology, 7*, 455–463.

Kendall, P. C., & Hollon, S. D. (Eds.). (1981). *Assessment strategies for cognitive-behavioral interventions.* New York: Academic.

Kendler, T. S., Kendler, H. H., & Wells, D. (1960). Reversal and nonreversal shifts in nursery school children. *Journal of Comparative and Physiological Psychology, 53*, 83–88.

Kohlberg, L., Yeager, J., & Hjertholm, E. (1968). Private speech: Four studies and a review of theories. *Child Development, 39*, 691–736.

Kuenne, M. K. (1946). Experimental investigation of the relation of language to transposition behavior in young children. *Journal of Experimental Psychology, 36*, 471–490.

Luria, A. R. (1959). The directive function of speech in development and dissolution. *Word, 16*, 341–352.

Luria, A. R. (1961). *The role of speech in the regulation of normal and abnormal behavior* (J. Tizard, Trans.). New York: Liveright.

Maccoby, E. E. (1964). Developmental psychology. *Annual Review of Psychology, 15*, 203–250.

Mahoney, M. J., & Thoresen, C. E. (1974). *Self-control: Power to the person.* Monterey, CA: Brooks/Cole.

Manning, B. H. (1988). Application of cognitive behavior modification: First and third graders' self-management of classroom behaviors. *American Educational Research Journal, 25*, 193–212.

Meichenbaum, D. (1976). Cognitive-functional approach to cognitive factors as determinants of learning disabilities. In R. M. Knights & D. J. Bakker (Eds.), *The neuropsychology of learning disorders: Theoretical approaches* (pp. 423–442). Baltimore: University Park Press.

Meichenbaum, D. (1977). *Cognitive-behavior modification: An integrative approach.* New York: Plenum.

Meichenbaum, D., & Asarnow, J. (1979). Cognitive-behavioral modification and metacognitive development: Implications for the classroom. In P. C. Kendall & S. D. Hollon (Eds.), *Cognitive-behavioral interventions: Theory, research, and procedures.* New York: Academic.

Meichenbaum, D., & Genest, M. (1980). Cognitive-behavior modification: An integration of cognitive and behavioral methods. In F. H. Kanfer & A. P. Goldstein (Eds.), *Helping people change: A textbook of methods* (2nd ed., pp. 40–56). New York: Pergamon.

Meichenbaum, D., & Goodman, S. (1979). Clinical use of private speech and critical questions about its study in natural settings. In G. Zivin (Ed.), *The development of self-regulation through private speech* (pp. 325–360). New York: Wiley.

Meyers, A. W., Cohen, R., & Schleser, R. (1989). A cognitive-behavioral approach to education: Adopting a broad-based perspective. In J. Hughes & R. Hall (Eds.), *Cognitive behavioral psychology in the schools: A comprehensive handbook* (pp. 62–86). New York: Guilford.

Miller, S. A., Shelton, J., & Flavell, J. H. (1970). A test of Luria's hypothesis concerning the development of verbal self-regulation. *Child Development, 41,* 651–665.

O'Leary, S. G., & Dubey, D. R. (1979). Applications of self-control procedures by children: A review. *Journal of Applied Behavior Analysis, 12,* 449–465.

Piaget, J. (1955). *The language and thought of the child* (M. Gabain, Trans.). New York: Meridian. (Original work published 1923)

Piaget, J. (1962). *Comments on Vygotsky's critical remarks* (A. Parsons, Trans.). Cambridge, MA: MIT Press. (Original work published 1934)

Pressley, M. (1979). Increasing children's self-control through cognitive interventions. *Review of Educational Research, 49,* 319–370.

Reese, H. W. (1962). Verbal mediation as a function of age level. *Psychological Bulletin, 59,* 502–509.

Reeve, R. A., & Brown, A. L. (1985). Metacognition reconsidered: implications for intervention research. *Journal of Abnormal Child Psychology, 13,* 343–356.

Rondal, J. A. (1976). Investigation of the regulatory power of the impulsive and meaningful aspects of speech. *Genetic Psychology Monographs, 94,* 3–33.

Rosenbaum, M. S., & Drabman, R. S. (1979). Self-control training in the classroom: A review and critique. *Journal of Applied Behavior Analysis, 12,* 467–485.

Sawyer, R. J., Graham, S., & Harris, K. R. (1989). [Improving learning disabled students' composition skills with story grammar strategy training: A components analysis]. Unpublished raw data.

Schunk, D. H. (1986). Verbalization and children's self-regulated learning. *Contemporary Educational Psychology, 11,* 347–369.

Schunk, D. H., & Cox, P. D. (1986). Strategy training and attributional feedback with learning disabled students. *Journal of Educational Psychology, 78,* 201–209.

Vygotsky, L. S. (1962). *Thought and language.* Cambridge, MA: MIT Press. (Original work published 1934)

Vygotsky, L. S., & Luria, A. R. (1930). The function and fate of egocentric speech. *Proceedings of the Ninth International Congress of Psychology.* Princeton: Psychology Review.

Wertsch, J. V. (1979). The regulation of human action and the given-new organization of private speech. In G. Zivin (Ed.), *The development of self-regulation through private speech* (pp. 79–98). New York: Wiley.

Wilder, L. N. (1968). The role of speech and other feedback signals in the regulation of the sensorimotor behavior of three and five-year-old children (Doctoral dissertation, Pennsylvania State University, 1968). *Dissertation Abstracts International, 30,* 1262A.

Wong, B. Y. L. (1985). Issues in cognitive-behavioral interventions in academic skill areas. *Journal of Abnormal Child Psychology, 13,* 425–442.

Wozniak, R. I. (1972). Verbal regulation of motor behavior: Soviet research and non-Soviet replications. *Human Development, 15,* 13–57.

Zivin, G. (Ed.). (1979). *The development of self-regulation through private speech.* New York: Wiley.

► # Chapter 7

Putting Learning Strategies to Work

SHARON J. DERRY

Recent research in cognitive and educational psychology has led to substantial improvements in our knowledge about learning. Researchers have identified certain mental processing techniques—learning strategies—that can be taught by teachers and used by students to improve the quality of school learning. Let me illustrate.

As a professor of educational and cognitive psychology, I often begin the semester with a simulation exercise designed to illustrate major principles about the role of learning strategies in classroom instruction. For example, recently I presented my students with the following scenario:

You are a high school student who has arrived at school 20 minutes early. You discover that your first-period teacher is planning to give a test covering Chapter 5. Unfortunately, you have prepared the wrong chapter, and there is no one around to help you out. Skipping class is not the solution, since this results in an automatic "F," and you would never dream of cheating. So you open your book and use the next 15 minutes as wisely as you can.

I gave my students 15 minutes to study. They then took a quiz with eight main idea questions and two application questions. At the end of the quiz, I asked them to write in detail exactly what they did when they studied. Quizzes (without names) were collected and then distributed randomly to the class for scoring and for analyzing the study strategies reported in them.

Sharon J. Derry is Associate Professor and Chair, Cognitive and Behavioral Sciences, Department of Psychology, Florida State University, Tallahassee, FL 32306-1051.

Few people performed well on this test. A student who did wrote the following:

There wasn't enough time for details. So I looked at the chapter summary first. Then I skimmed through the chapter and tried to understand the topic paragraphs and the summary paragraphs for each section. I also noticed what the headings said, to get the organization, and I noticed certain names that went with each heading, figuring they did something related to each topic, a study or something. I started to do some memory work on the headings, but time was up before I finished.

By comparison, most students answered only two or three of the main idea questions, reporting a study strategy something like the following.

Panic. There was not enough time! I started going over the chapter and got as far as I could, but it was hopeless. I assume you do not plan to grade this quiz, because that would be unfair!

As illustrated in these two examples, the differences between successful and unsuccessful learning strategies often are clear and striking. Whereas the successful learners assessed the learning situation and calmly developed a workable plan for dealing with it, the less successful learners were occupied with fruitless worries and vague strategies but little planning effort.

Such an exercise serves to introduce the following important principles about self-directed learning:

1. The plan that one uses for accomplishing a learning goal is a person's learning strategy. Learning strategies may be simple or complex, specific or vague, intelligent or unwise. Obviously, some learning strategies work better than others.

2. Learning strategies require knowledge of specific learning skills, or "tactics" (e.g., Dern, and Murphy 1986), such as skimming, attending to chapter structure, and memorization techniques. The ability to devise appropriate learning strategies also requires knowledge about when and when not to use particular types of learning tactics.

3. Learning is a form of problem solving that involves analyzing a learning task and devising a strategy appropriate for that particular situation. Different learning situations may call for different strategies.

Further, I asked my students to determine whether any reported learning strategy had produced useful knowledge. Alas, no participant had applied the knowledge acquired in the 15-minute study session to the two application questions on the quiz. Even when learning strategies are apparently successful according to one form of measurement, the resultant learning is not necessarily usable later in problem solving. Thus, we added a fourth principle to our list:

4. In most school learning situations, strategies should be devised with the aim of creating usable, rather than inert, knowledge. Clearly, not all learning strategies will lead to the formation of usable knowledge structures.

Next I will elaborate these principles in greater detail, suggesting how they can influence classroom practice.

STRATEGIES AS LEARNING PLANS

There is much confusion about the term *learning strategy*. The term is used to refer to (1) specific learning tactics such as rehearsal, imaging, and outlining (e.g., Cook and Mayer 1983, Levin 1986); (2) more general types of self-management activities such as planning and comprehension monitoring (e.g., Pressley et al. in press a); and (3) complex plans that combine several specific techniques (e.g., Derry and Murphy 1986, Snowman and McCown 1984).

To clarify the uses of the term, I distinguish between the specific tactics and the learning strate-

gies that combine them. Thus, a learning strategy is a complete plan one formulates for accomplishing a learning goal; and a learning tactic is any individual processing technique one uses in service of the plan (Derry and Murphy 1986, Snowman and Mc-Cown 1984). That is, a learning strategy is the application of one or more specific learning tactics to a learning problem. Within this definition, the plethora of learning techniques (popularly called "strategies") being promoted by various researchers and practitioners can be viewed as potentially useful learning tactics that can be applied in various combinations to accomplish different learning jobs.

This definition points to the need for two distinct types of strategies instruction: specific tactics training and training in methods for selecting and combining tactics into workable learning plans. Teachers can incorporate both types of training into regular classroom instruction by thoughtfully combining different study tactics—outlining plus positive self-talk, for example—and assigning them along with regular homework.

LEARNING STRATEGIES EMPLOY SPECIFIC LEARNING TACTICS

In this section I discuss tactics in three major categories: (1) tactics for acquiring verbal knowledge, that is, ideas and facts fundamental to disciplines such as science, literature, and history; (2) tactics for acquiring procedural skills such as reading, using language, and solving problems that underlie various curriculum disciplines; and (3) support tactics for self-motivation, which are applicable to all types of learning situations. (For a more thorough treatment of these topics, see the reviews by Derry and Murphy 1986, Weinstein and Mayer 1985, Levin 1986, and Pressley et al. in press b.)

Verbal Learning Tactics

Strategies aimed at improving comprehension and retention of verbal information should build upon tactics that enhance these mental processes: (1) focusing attention on important ideas, (2) schema building, and (3) idea elaboration (see fig. 1).

Attentional Focusing
Two types of attention-focusing tactics are simple focusing and structured focusing. In the simple focusing category, highlighting and underlining are

Category	Examples	Some Conditions of Use	Strengths or Weaknesses
Attentional Focusing			
Simple focusing	Highlighting. Underlining.	Structured, easy materials. Good readers.	No emphasis on importance or conceptual relations of ideas.
Structured focusing	Looking for headings, topic sentences. Teacher-directed signaling.	Poor readers. Difficult but considerate materials.	Efficient, but may not promote active elaboration, deep thinking.
Schema Building	Use of story grammars, theory schemas. Networking.	Poor text structure. Goal is to encourage active comprehension.	Inefficient, but develops higher-order thinking skills.
Idea Elaboration	Some types of self-questioning. Imagery.	Goal is to comprehend and remember specific ideas.	Powerful, easy to combine. Difficult for some students unassisted. Will not ensure focus on what is important.

FIGURE 1.   **Tactics for Learning Verbal Information**

common examples. Unfortunately, the use of simple focusing procedures does not necessarily ensure identification of important information. I have often confirmed this point by requesting to see the textbooks of students who are having academic problems. Frequently I find almost every word in their texts highlighted.

Students, weaker ones in particular, should be taught to combine simple focusing with structured focusing, whereby the learner directs primary attention to headings, topic sentences, or other signals provided by the instructional presentation. The teaching of structured focusing is a well- established practice in English classes, and it can profitably be reinforced in other courses to help students identify information they need to learn. However, the success of structured focusing depends heavily on well-structured, considerate instructional presentations (as well as on considerate teachers who test for the main ideas). And the use of these tactics does not ensure that the ideas identified will actually be remembered.

Schema Building

A more powerful type of verbal-learning tactic is schema building, which encourages active analysis of an instructional presentation and formation of a synthesizing framework. One well-known form of schema building is networking (Dansereau 1985, Dansereau et al. 1979), whereby a student draws a node-link map representing the important ideas in a text and the interrelationships among them. This technique is powerful, but it is difficult to teach and time-consuming to apply (McKeachie 1984). Simpler forms of schema building include the use of teacher-suggested schemas, such as the well-known tactic of requiring students to analyze stories in English literature by identifying the theme, setting, plot, resolution, and so on. Similar assignments can facilitate verbal learning in other courses of study. For example, Dansereau (1985) improved students' performance on science tests by teaching them to use a theory schema as a study aid for scientific text.

Schema building encourages in-depth analysis and is particularly useful if instruction is inconsiderate or unclear. Schema-building strategies are generally employed as comprehension aids; however, they also aid memory through the organization and elaboration of ideas.

Idea Elaboration

Idea elaboration is a memory-enhancing process whereby students link each important new idea with prior knowledge so as to connect them. These linkages can be based on an image, a logical inference, or on anything else that serves to connect new ideas to prior knowledge (Gagne 1985).

Many elaboration tactics capitalize on imagery, a powerful memory-enhancing technique. For example, the key-word method for acquiring foreign vocabulary involves creating a mental image (prior knowledge) representing the sound of a foreign word (new information), and relating that image to another image (prior knowledge) representing the meaning of the word's English equivalent. Many types of elaboration tactics facilitate memorization (e.g., Bransford and Stein 1984), and these can be employed to great advantage in many courses.

Procedural Learning Tactics

Most learning strategies research has examined tactics for acquiring verbal information. However, some strategy researchers are developing techniques for acquiring procedural skills. Procedural learning has three aspects (Anderson 1983, Gagne 1985): (1) learning how to carry out basic actions such as performing long division or executing a tennis lob; (2) learning to recognize the conceptual patterns that indicate when it is appropriate to perform particular actions (such as recognizing that a word problem is a division situation or that a tennis lob is required); and (3) learning to combine many pattern-action pairs into a smooth overall system of response. Consider, for example, the complex combining of subskills that underlies the actual playing of a tennis match.

Based on this view, Figure 2 presents three categories of mental tactics for procedural learning: (1) tactics for learning conceptual patterns that cue applicability of associated actions; (2) tactics for acquiring the component actions (performance subskills) themselves; and (3) tactics for perfecting and tuning complex overall performance.

Category	Examples	Some Conditions of Use	Strengths or Weaknesses
Pattern Learning			
Hypothesizing	Student reasons and guesses why particular pattern is or isn't example of concept.	Goal is to learn attributes of concepts and patterns.	Inefficient unless feedback given. Encourages independent thinking.
Seeking reasons for actions	Student seeks explanations why particular actions are or are not appropriate.	Goal is to determine which procedures are required in which situations.	Develops meta-cognitive knowledge. Inefficient if not guided. If too guided, might not promote thinking skills.
Reflective Self-Instruction	Student compares reification of own performance to expert model.	Goal is to tune, improve complex skill.	Develops understanding of quality performance. May increase self-consciousness, reduce automaticity.
Practice			
Part practice	Student drills on one specific aspect of performance.	A few specific aspects of a performance need attention.	Develops subskill automaticity. Doesn't encourage subskill integration.
Whole practice	Student practices full performance without attention to subskills.	Goal is to maintain or improve skill already acquired or to integrate subskills.	May consolidate poorly executed subskills. Helps develop smooth whole performance.

FIGURE 2. **Tactics for Learning Procedural Knowledge**

Pattern-Recognition Tactics

Pattern recognition plays an important role in the development of procedural performance; however, students are probably not aware of this. Thus, developing students' procedural learning abilities includes both conveying the important function of pattern recognition and helping students develop tactics for acquiring performance-related patterns.

Examples of tactics in the patterns-acquisition category include hypothesizing and seeking reasons for actions. in applying these tactics, the learner attempts to discover the identifying features of a pattern or concept through guesswork, reasoning, and investigation. For example, while watching a tennis pro at work, the student might hypothesize about the features of play that cause the pro to execute a lob or a groundstroke. Hypotheses are confirmed or altered through continued observation, until the pattern features are known. Alternatively, the student might seek reasons by consulting the tennis pro directly. Seeking information overcomes the major weakness of the hypothesizing tactic, inefficiency. However, the virtue of hypothesizing is that it can be used in situations where expert advice is not available.

Practice Tactics

Other aspects of procedural learning include the acquisition of basic component actions (subskills) and, ultimately, the development of smooth complex performances that combine those subskills. There are learning tactics that can help students derive maximum benefit from their practice sessions. One example is part practice, whereby the student attempts to improve a complex performance by perfecting and automating an important subcomponent of that performance. For example, a student might greatly improve performance on mathematics tests by memorizing and practicing square-root tables. Or performance in tennis might be improved by concentrating practice on service and smashes. Part practice should be alternated with whole practice (Schneider 1985), whereby the student practices the full complex performance with little attention to individual subskills.

Reflective Self-Instruction

Another class of procedural learning tactics is reflective self-instruction, whereby the student attempts to improve personal performance by studying an expert model. For example, a student might videotape her tennis swing and compare that to a tape of an expert's swing. Or the student might critically compare her homework solution for a geometry proof to the teacher's expert solution presented on the board. Reflective self-instruction can concentrate either on specific component subskills or on whole complex performances. One key to successful self-instruction is the availability of adequate performance models. By providing models of expert performance and guiding students in how to benefit from those models while learning, teachers can provide training in the valuable technique of reflective self-instruction.

Mental Support Tactics

Acquiring useful knowledge in school is a lengthy and difficult process demanding a great investment of time and effort on the part of the student. Thus, tactics are needed for helping learners maintain a positive attitude and a high state of motivation during learning and practice. Researchers (e.g., Dansereau et al. 1979, 1985; Meichenbaum 1980; McCombs 1981–82) recommend several types of support tactics: (1) behavioral self-management, (2) mood management, and (3) self-monitoring (see fig. 3).

The behavioral self-management category includes such tactics as breaking a complex learning chore into subgoals, developing a schedule for meeting subgoals, devising a reporting procedure for charting progress, and devising a self-reward system for completing major subgoals. Mood management tactics include concentration and relaxation techniques (useful for combating test anxiety); and positive self-talk, used to establish and maintain a positive frame of mind before and during learning and performance (e.g., Meichenbaum 1980). Finally, an example of self-monitoring is the technique of stopping periodically during learning and practice to check and, if necessary, readjust strategy, concentration, and mood.

Frequently used by professional athletes, mental support tactics can also be used by students to increase academic performance and motivation and to decrease tension associated with evaluation. They are applicable to all types of learning situations and can be combined with both verbal and procedural learning tactics in study assignments. For example, to study for a history test, a student might devise a learning strategy that orchestrates several specific tactics, such as positive self-talk with self-checking (to maintain motivation), net-

Category	Examples	Some Conditions of Use	Strengths or Weaknesses
Behavioral Self-Management	Student breaks task into sub-goals, creates goal-attainment plan, rewards.	Complex, lengthy task; low motivated students.	Promotes extrinsic, rather than intrinsic, motivation. Very powerful.
Mood Management			
Positive self-talk	Student analyzes, avoids negative self-statements, creates positive self-statements.	Preparation for competitive or difficult performance; presence of negative ideas.	Good intrinsic motivator; requires conscious attention during performance.
Relaxation techniques	Student uses deep breathing, counting, other clinical relaxation methods.	Text anxiety; highly anxious students.	Techniques controversial in some districts.
Self-Monitoring	Student stops self during performance to consciously check mood, progress, etc.	Goal is to increase conscious awareness and control of thinking process.	May interrupt concentration.

FIGURE 3.   **Tactics for Developing Motivation**

working (to help organize facts in a meaningful way), and use of imagery or mnemonics (to help with memorization).

STRATEGY-BUILDING AS PROBLEM SOLVING

The ultimate aim of tactics training is to provide students with tools that will enable them, as autonomous learners, to devise their own strategies. Unfortunately, a persistent problem in strategy training has been students' failure to apply tactics in situations outside the class in which they were learned originally.

However, several training techniques can alleviate these problems. A large number of researchers (e.g., Baron 1981, Bransford and Stein 1984) suggest teaching students to respond to all learning tasks using a general problem-solving model. For example, Derry, Jacobs, and Murphy (1987) taught soldiers to use the "4C's" to develop plans for study reading. The 4C's stood for: clarify learning situation, construct a learning strategy, carry out the strategy, and check results.

One presumed advantage of such plans is that they remind students to stop and think reflectively about each learning situation prior to proceeding with the task (Baron 1981). Also, such plans may

serve as mnemonic devices that help students recall previously learned tactics associated with each step. There is some empirical support for the idea that problem-solving models enhance tactics transfer (Belmont et al. 1982).

Another procedure for inducing tactics transfer is informed training (Campione et al. 1982, Pressley et al. 1984). This procedure enhances direct tactics instruction with explicit information regarding the effectiveness of various tactics, including how and when they should be used. As Levin (1986) points out, there are different learning tools for different learning jobs. With informed training, students learn that tactics selection is always influenced by the nature of the instructional material as well as the nature of the learning goal. For example, if a text is not highly structured and the primary aim of study is to comprehend and remember important ideas, a strategy that combines networking with idea elaboration would be appropriate. However, if the aim is primarily comprehension rather than retention, a schema-building technique alone would suffice. Informed training is superior to "blind training" in producing transfer and sustained use of specific learning tactics (Pressley et al. 1984, Campione et al. 1982).

Previously I suggested that teachers can help develop students' learning skills by devising, assigning, and explaining learning strategies and by providing feedback on strategy use. Such established classroom practices are excellent vehicles for informed training.

LEARNING STRATEGIES SHOULD PRODUCE USEFUL KNOWLEDGE

Cognitive psychology has taught us much about the nature and structure of usable knowledge. Verbal information is likely to be called into service only if it is understood when learned and only if it is stored in memory within well-structured, well-elaborated networks of meaningfully related ideas. Procedural skills, on the other hand, are likely to be accessed and accurately executed only if they have been developed through extensive practice and only if the environmental patterns that indicate their applicability are well learned. If the primary aim of schooling is the creation of useful knowledge, then strategy application should result in the deliberate creation of a well-structured knowledge base, whether verbal, procedural, or both.

It is unlikely that reliance on any single learning tactic alone will ensure the creation of well-constructed knowledge. Rather, multiple tactics are usually required. For example, if an elaboration technique is applied for the purpose of enhancing individual ideas, another schema-building tactic may be needed to tie related ideas together. Or if practice is used to perfect a specific aspect of procedural performance, a pattern-learning tactic may still be needed to ensure that the skill is executed only when appropriate. Thus, useful knowledge is most likely to evolve through a dynamic process requiring, first, an informed analysis of each learning problem, then selection and combining of all the learning tactics needed to produce a well-formed mental structure.

Not every learning strategy produces useful knowledge. Some strategies lead to isolated, unstructured bits of learning that will remain forever inert. For this reason, both teachers and students should be aware of the nature and form of useful knowledge and of learning strategies that are likely to facilitate its creation.

STRATEGY TRAINING FOR LIFELONG LEARNING

Students who receive good strategy training during their years in school can acquire a form of knowl-edge especially useful in coping with the wide variety of learning situations they will encounter throughout their lives. Given the amount of time that people spend in school, in job-related training, and in acquiring knowledge associated with their interests and hobbies, the ability to find good solutions to learning problems may be the most important thinking skill of all.

REFERENCES

Anderson, J. R. (1983). *The Architecture of Cognition.* Cambridge, Mass.: Harvard University Press.

Baron, J. (1981). "Reflective Thinking as a Goal of Education." *Intelligence* 5: 291–309.

Belmont, J. M., E. C. Butterfield, and R. P. Ferretti. (1982). "To Secure Transfer of Training instruct Self-Management Skills." In *How and How Much Can Intelligence Be Increased,* edited by D. K. Detterman and R. J. Sternberg, pp. 147–154. Norwood, N.J.: ABLEX.

Bransford, J. D., and B. S. Stein. (1984). *The Ideal Problem Solver: A Guide For Improving Thinking, Learning, and Creativity.* New York: Freeman.

Campione, J. C., A. L. Brown, and R.A. Ferrara. (1982). "Mental Retardation and Intelligence." In *Cognitive Strategy Research: Educational Applications,* edited by P. J. Sternberg, pp. 87–126. New York: Springer-Verlag.

Cook, L. K., and R. E. Mayer. (1983). "Reading Strategies Training for Meaningful Learning from Prose." In *Cognitive Strategy Research: Educational Applications,* edited by M. Pressley and J. R. Levin, pp. 87–126. New York: Springer-Verlag.

Dansereau, D. F. (1985). "Learning Strategy Research." in *Thinking and Learning Skills,* edited by J. W. Segal, S. F. Chipman, and R. Glaser, vol. 1, pp. 209–240. Hillsdale, N.J.: Erlbaum.

Dansereau, D. F., K. W. Collins, B. A. McDonald, C. D. Holley, J. C. Garland, G. M. Diekhoff, and S. H. Evans. (1979). "Development and Evaluation of an Effective Learning Strategy Program." *Journal of Educational Psychology* 79: 64–73.

Derry, S. J., J. Jacobs, and D. A. Murphy. (1987). "The JSEP Learning Skills Training System." *Journal of Educational Technology Systems* 15, 4: 273–284.

Derry, S. J. and D. A. Murphy. (1986). "Designing Systems That Train Learning Ability: From Theory to Practice." *Review of Educational Research* 56, 1: 1–39.

Gagne, E. D. (1985). *The Cognitive Psychology of School Learning.* Boston: Little, Brown and Company.

Levin, J. R. (1986). "Four Cognitive Principles of Learning-Strategy Instruction." *Educational Psychologist* 21, 1 and 2: 3–17.

McCombs, B. L. (1981–82). "Transitioning Learning Strategies Research in Practice: Focus on the Student in Technical Training." *Journal of Instructional Development* 5: 10–17.

McKeachie, W. J. (1984). "Spatial Strategies: Critique and Educational Implications." *In Spatial Learning Strategies: Techniques, Applications, and Related Issues,* edited by C. D. Holley and D. F. Dansereau, pp. 301–312. Orlando, Fla.: Academic Press.

Meichenbaum, D. H. (1980). "A Cognitive-Behavioral Perspective on Intelligence." *Intelligence* 4: 271–283.

Pressley, M., J. G. Borkowski, and J. T. O'Sullivan. (1984). "Memory Strategy Instruction Is Made of This: Metamemory and Durable Strategy Use." *Educational Psychologist* 19: 94–107.

Pressley, M., J. G. Borkowski, and W. Schneider. (In press a). "Cognitive Strategies: Good Strategy Users Coordinate Metacognition and Knowledge." In *Annals of Child Development*, edited by R. Vasta and G. Whitehurst, vol. 4. Greenwich, Conn.: JAI Press.

Pressley, M., F. Goodchild, J. Fleet, R. Zajchowski, and E. D. Evans. (in press b). "The Challenges of Classroom Strategy Instruction." In *The Elementary School Journal.*

Schneider, W. (1985). "Training High-Performance Skills: Fallacies and Guidelines." *Human Factors* 27: 285–300.

Snowman, J., and R. McCown. (April 1984). "Cognitive Processes In Learning: A Model for Investigating Strategies and Tactics." Paper presented at the annual meeting of the American Educational Research Association, New Orleans.

Weinstein, C. E., and F. E. Mayer. (1985). "The Teaching of Learning Strategies." *In Handbook of Research on Teaching*, 3rd ed., edited by M. C. Wittrock. New York: Macmillan.

What We Really Know about Strategy Instruction

MICHAEL PRESSLEY and KAREN R. HARRIS

On a Monday morning last spring, a 2nd grade teacher taught a class of bright underachievers at Benchmark School near Philadelphia how to summarize an excerpt from their social studies text. This teacher believed his students' comprehension would be improved if they could sum up what they had been reading. That same morning, a 1st grade teacher in Madison, Wisconsin, taught her class to subtract by counting down from the larger number to the smaller. She felt this strategy would improve her pupils' understanding of subtraction. Later in the day, a group of 3rd grade students in East Lansing, Michigan, watched their teacher "think aloud" as he read a story to the class: when he did not understand the text, he reread it, looking for clues to its meaning.

All these teachers were teaching *strategies:* procedures for accomplishing academic tasks. Strategies can enhance student performance in reading, composing, computation, and problem solving.

We realize now that many students do not learn strategies automatically. This assertion may be startling, especially to those who know the "classic" literature on children's use of simple memory strategies. For instance, preschool children typically do not rehearse when asked to learn lists of items (e.g., *apple, car, dog, grass, bottle*)—that is, they do not say the words over and over in order. In contrast, 11

and 12-year-olds do. Thus, many commentators have concluded that autonomous use of strategies develops between 4 and 12 years of age. But even in adults, the development of some strategies is observed infrequently, for example, the use of self-questioning to learn facts (Pressley et al. 1988b). So we've found that our earlier assumptions were not accurate.

And we've also learned a partial explanation for the dearth of strategy use: many people do not know strategies because their teachers, unlike those in the opening paragraph, don't teach them in school. Researchers find little strategy instruction in classrooms (see Pressley et al. 1989a). Information about strategies is rarely included in textbooks either, despite the growing database on strategies applicable to school tasks.

THE STATUS OF STRATEGY INSTRUCTION

Is cognitive strategy instruction really developed well enough to distribute to schools? The answer is complicated. Some school tasks and academic strategies have been studied much more thoroughly than others. On one end of the continuum is reading comprehension, which has been the concern of many reading researchers and educational psychologists. Quite a few reading comprehension strategies have been evaluated in true experiments, and about half a dozen have been found to improve memory and comprehension, at least for some chil-

Michael Pressley is Professor of Human Development, EDHD Benjamin Building, and Karen R. Harris is Associate Professor of Special Education, EDSP Benjamin Building, University of Maryland, College of Education, College Park. MD 20742.

dren. These include summarization, imagery, story grammar, prior knowledge activation, self-questioning, and question-answering strategies (Pressley et al. 1989b) (see fig. 1).

Today's researchers are energetically investigating the matter of essay—construction strategies, aimed at affecting the entire planning, translating, and revising cycle that constitutes skilled writing (Harris et al. in press a). Englert, Raphael, and their colleagues at Michigan State are completing the evaluation of a strategy-instructional package that fosters the development of mature composition skills in elementary school children. Karen Harris, Steve Graham, and their associates at the University of Maryland have validated both a self-instructional strategy training approach and a set of strategies that promote effective writing (cf., Harris and Graham 1985; Graham and Harris 1989a, 1989b). For example, Graham and his associates (1989) produced striking improvements in the compositions of 11- to 13-year-old learning-disabled students. They taught these children a particular method for setting writing goals, generating and organizing notes in anticipation of writing, continued planning as writing proceeds, and evaluation of goal attainment.

So, some powerful strategies appropriate to particular academic goals and populations have been developed. However, much more research is required before a full panorama of well-validated strategies will be available.

Although this may come as a surprise to teachers, many strategies endorsed by curriculum and instruction publications represent only conventional wisdom about the nature of teaching and learning and have never demonstrated their worth in objective experimental evaluations. Take, for example, the presumed benefits of semantic-context strategies for acquisition of vocabulary-definition associations. Teachers are typically advised to teach students to use new words in context, that is, to construct meaningful sentences containing new vo-cabulary, to generate synonyms, or to practice semantic mapping of a word, including specification of related terms and opposites. These methods of vocabulary acquisition share one problem, however: They do not work. Quite a few experiments conducted during the last 15 years compared these methods to that of simply giving students words and their meanings to study. None of the semantic-context procedures produced better learning of vocabulary-meaning associations than the no-strategy control procedures (see Pressley et al. 1987). Many strategies that have traditionally been recommended simply lack research support.

METHODS OF TEACHING STRATEGIES

It is very difficult, based on the available research, to make definitive statements about how to teach strategies, but some guidelines can be stated. Ideally, most researchers agree, cognitive strategies should be taught in conjunction with content and in response to learner needs and capabilities.[1] Thus, before they begin strategy instruction, teachers should take affective, behavioral, and cognitive assessments of learners as they attempt the target task (Harris 1982, Harris et al. in press, Graham and Harris 1989b, Wang and Palincsar 1989). Once a task-appropriate strategy that matches a student's abilities has been selected, the teacher and the student should establish the potential benefits of that strategy, the goals of strategy instruction, and how and when to use the strategy (e.g., Brown et al. 1981, Pressley et al. 1984b, 1985).

[1]A set of procedures, components, and characteristics common to effective strategy instruction can be seen in the work of such researchers as Donald Deshler, Jean Schumaker, and their associates at the University of Kansas; Laura Roehler, Gerald Duffy, and their colleagues at Michigan State University; Karen Harris, Steve Graham, and their coworkers at the University of Maryland; Michael Pressley at the University of Maryland; John Borkowski of Notre Dame; and Wolfgang Schneider at the Max Planck Institute.

Fig. 1.   Tried and True Reading Comprehension Strategies

The following half-dozen strategies have been found to improve children's memory and comprehension:

Summarization: Creating a representation of gist.
Imagery: Constructing an internal visual representation of text content.
Story grammar: Identifying the setting, problem, goal, action, and outcome in a narrative.

Prior knowledge activation: Relating what one already knows to the content of text.
Self-questioning: Generating questions that integrate across different parts of a text.
Question-answering: Teaching students to analyze questions as a part of trying to respond to them.

Teacher modeling and self-regulated use of the procedure lie at the heart of good instruction. The teacher demonstrates the use of the strategy in the context of meaningful academic tasks and introduces strategies one or a very few at a time (that is, teaches one or two strategies over the course of several weeks or months). At first students may not "get it," at least not completely, but they will be able to start trying the procedure. The teacher guides their initial attempts, providing many prompts at this point about what to do and when to do it and tailoring feedback and re-explanations of the strategies to individual student needs.

Gradually the teacher transfers control of strategy performance to the student; the student assumes responsibility for recruiting, applying, monitoring, and evaluating the strategy over a number of sessions, with the teacher ready to intervene with additional instruction if difficulties arise. Throughout the instructional sequence, the teacher fades input at a pace permitting competent performance by the student. Strategy instruction is "scaffolded" (Wood et al. 1976), to use a term that is popular today. Student progression is criterion-based rather than time-based (Graham and Harris 1989a), with teaching and interactive practice continuing until the student understands the strategy and can carry it out.

Good strategy instruction is interactive: students should collaborate in determining the goals of instruction as well as in the implementation, evaluation, and modification of the strategy and strategy acquisition procedures (Harris and Pressley in press). In short, the teacher helps students to understand what they are learning and why they are learning it.

TEACHING FOR TRANSFER

Once a student can carry out a strategy independently with instructional tasks, the challenge is to teach him or her to use the technique consistently for appropriate tasks. One way to do this is to have students apply strategies across the curriculum. Thus, the students can use variations of summarization strategies taught in reading lessons to increase comprehension and recall of science and social studies texts; similarly, students can apply planning-translation-revision writing strategies (like the one being investigated by Graham and Harris 1989a, 1989b; Graham et al. 1989) whenever they are required to write a multiple-paragraph essay.

Throughout instruction, students need to see evidence that the strategies they are learning really do lead to improved performance. Nothing motivates students to use a strategy like seeing that the strategy increases competent completion of an important task (Pressley et al. 1984a, 1984c, 1988a).

But simply being motivated to use a strategy is not enough. Students must learn where and when a strategy can be deployed profitably (e.g., O'Sullivan and Pressley 1984). Such information can often be provided by teachers or peers, although students sometimes discover this type of metacognitive information about strategies on their own (Pressley et al. 1984b, 1985). Teachers should do everything possible to encourage the development of this knowledge. They can prompt students to apply strategies or provide assistance to students in adjusting the strategy. Use of the strategy throughout the school day and across the curriculum can be encouraged by cueing strategy use, by re-explaining strategic techniques, and through additional teacher modeling of strategy use; in other words, by "coaching" (Schon 1987).

WHAT'S NEXT?

Although we have learned a great deal about how to teach strategies, we are on the verge of new discoveries. Teachers like the ones we mentioned in Pennsylvania, Wisconsin, and Michigan are providing new information about which strategies are really useful to students, how students master particular strategies, and how misunderstandings can be corrected when they occur. Many more specific recommendations will follow as research on strategies proceeds.[2] But we know enough now to begin to offer students these profitable and helpful avenues to learning.

REFERENCES

Brown, A. L., J. C. Campione, and J. D. Day. (1981). "Learning to Learn: On Training Students to Learn from Texts." *Educational Researcher* 10: 14–21.

Deshler, D. D., and J. B. Schumaker. (1986). "Learning Strategies: An Instructional Alternative for Low-Achieving Adolescents." *Exceptional Children* 52: 583–590.

[2]See Pressley et al. (in press) for an example of such research as well as further discussion about how such inquiries can affect future instruction.

Graham, S., and K. R. Harris. (1989a). "A Components Analysis of Cognitive Strategy Instruction: Effects on Learning Disabled Students' Compositions and Self-Efficacy." *Journal of Educational Psychology* 81: 353–361.

Graham, S., and K. R. Harris. (1989b). "Cognitive Training: Implications for Written Language." In *Cognitive-Behavioral Psychology in the Schools: A Comprehensive Handbook,* edited by J. Hughes and P. Hall. New York: Guilford Press.

Graham, S., C. MacArthur, S. Schwartz, and V. Voth. (1989). *Improving LD Students' Compositions Using a Strategy Involving Product and Process Goal Setting.* Technical Report. College Park, Md.: University of Maryland, Department of Special Education.

Harris, K. R. (1982). "Cognitive-Behavior Modification: Applications with Exceptional Students." *Focus on Exceptional Children* 15: 1–16.

Harris, K. R., and S. Graham. (1985). "Improving Learning Disabled Students' Composition Skills: Self-Control Strategy Training." *Learning Disability Quarterly* 8: 27–36.

Harris, K. R., S. Graham, and M. Pressley. (In press a). "Cognitive-Behavioral Approaches in Reading and Written language: Developing Self-Regulated Learners." In *Current Perspectives in Learning Disabilities: Nature, Theory, and Treatment,* edited by N. N. Singh and I. L. Beale. New York: Springer-Verlag.

Harris, K. R., and M. Pressley. (In press). "The Nature of Cognitive Strategy Instruction: Interactive Strategy Construction." *Exceptional Children.*

O'Sullivan, J. T., and M. Pressley. (1984). "Completeness of Instruction and Strategy Transfer." *Journal of Experimental Child Psychology* 38: 275–288.

Pressley, M., J. R. Levin, and S. L. Bryant. (1983). "Memory Strategy Instruction During Adolescence: When Is Explicit Instruction Needed?" In *Cognitive Strategy Research: Psychological Foundations,* edited by M. Pressley and J. R. Levin. New York: Springer-Verlag.

Pressley, M., J. R. Levin, and E. S. Ghatala. (1984a). "Memory Strategy Monitoring in Adults and Children." *Journal of Verbal Learning and Verbal Behavior* 23: 270–288.

Pressley, M., J. G. Borkowski, and J. T. O'Sullivan. (1984b). "Memory Strategy Instruction Is Made of This: Metamemory and Durable Strategy Use." *Educational Psychologist* 19: 94–107.

Pressley, M., K. A. Ross, I. R. Levin, and E. S. Ghatala. (1984c). "The Role of Strategy Utility Knowledge in Children's Decision Making." *Journal of Experimental Child Psychology* 38: 491–504.

Pressley, M., J. G. Borkowski, and J. T. O'Sullivan. (1985). "Children's Metamemory and the Teaching of Memory Strategies." In *Metacognition, Cognition, and Human Performance,* edited by D. L. Forrest-Pressley, G. E. MacKinnon, and T. G. Waller. Orlando, Fla.: Academic.

Pressley, M., J. R. Levin, and M. A. McDaniel. (1987). "Remembering Versus Inferring What a Word Means: Mnemonic and Contextual Approaches." In *The Nature of Vocabulary Acquisition,* edited by M. McGeown and M. E. Curtis. Hillsdale, N.J.: Erlbaum.

Pressley, M., J. R. Levin, and E. S. Ghatala. (1988a). "Strategy-Comparison Opportunities Promote Long-Term Strategy Use." *Contemporary Educational Psychology* 13: 157–168.

Pressley, M., S. Symons, M. A. McDaniel, B. L. Snyder, and J. E. Turnure. (1988b). "Elaborative Interrogation Facilitates Acquisition of Confusing Facts." *Journal of Educational Psychology* 80: 268–278.

Pressley, M., F. Goodchild, J. Fleet, R. Zajchowski, and E. D. Evans. (1989a). "The Challenges of Classroom Strategy Instruction." *Elementary School Journal* 89: 301–342.

Pressley, M., C. J. Johnson, S. Symons, J. A. McGoldrick, and J. Kurita. (1989b). "Strategies That Improve Children's Memory and Comprehension of Text." *Elementary School Journal* 90: 3–32.

Pressley, M., I. W. Gaskins, E. A. Cunicelli, N. A. Burdick, M. Schaub-Matt, D. S. Lee, and N. Powell. (In press). "Perceptions of Benchmark School's Experienced Strategy Teachers and Perceptions of Strategy Researchers About the Nature of Long-term Strategy Instruction." *Learning Disability Quarterly.*

Schon, D. A. (1987). *Educating the Reflective Practitioner Toward a New Design for Teaching and Learning in the Professions.* San Francisco: Jossey-Bass.

Wang, M. C., and A. S. Palincsar. (1989). "Teaching Students to Assume an Active Role in Their Learning." In *Knowledge Base for the Beginning Teacher,* edited by M. C. Reynolds. New York: Pergamon Press.

Wood, D. J., J. S. Bruner, and G. Ross. (1976). "The Role of Tutoring in Problem Solving." *Journal of Child Psychology and Psychiatry,* 17: 89–100.

► Chapter 8

Solving the Arithmetic Problem

The last ten years of research on children's problem solving suggest that elementary schoolers learn more mathematics when teachers connect their students' everyday knowledge about numbers with the written procedures and formal rules of school math. The research also suggests some imaginative ways to build these bridges.

WHAT CHILDREN LEARN ON THEIR OWN

Young children are immersed in numbers—two eyes, ten fingers, three candies apiece. By the time they enter kindergarten, most can count, and they first understand arithmetic facts in relation to their counting. Thomas Carpenter of the University of Wisconsin and his colleagues have found that most children invent problem-solving strategies themselves before they have classroom instruction. They start doing simple addition and subtraction problems by making sets of concrete objects and counting the total or the difference between them. Gradually, they begin to count in their heads and to substitute their fingers or marks on a paper for objects. After a while, they no longer need to count every item in every set: to add, they adopt the more efficient strategy of starting with the first or—better yet—the larger number and counting on from there. To subtract, they modify their addition strategy, counting up from the smaller number to the larger to find the difference between the two.

Eventually, children learn to add and subtract as adults do, recalling number facts automatically, and borrowing or carrying to solve multiple-column problems. Nevertheless, many youngsters rely on counting strategies at least occasionally throughout elementary school. Some devise transitional methods, using facts they *can* recall to figure out

those they cannot: stumped by the problem 6 + 8, for example, a child might say to himself "6 and 6 is 12, and 2 more makes 14."

Mismatches with School Math

Most children encounter formal mathematical symbols, terms, and notation only in the classroom, where they spend 90 percent of their time practicing written computation. Carpenter thinks this early emphasis on computation is out of phase with children's natural approach to math. He advocates using simple word problems as the context for introducing computation, rather than teaching addition and subtraction as detached skills that are later "applied" to practical problems.

The British researcher Martin Hughes has also found young children confused about the purpose of formal language and symbols. When he presented 5-year-olds with some simple addition problems—"If one child is inside a shop and two more go in after him. How many children are in the shop?"—most youngsters solved them easily. They looked bewildered, though, when he asked "What does two and two make?" or "How much is it if you have two and add one more?" Hughes argues that the children failed not because the second problems were more abstract but because they, were couched in the formal language of "adding" and "2 and 2 makes 4." Other researchers have also found that formal language can make a problem opaque: when Tom Hudson asked kindergarteners and first graders how many more birds than worms there were in a picture, the youngsters stared blankly. But when told that each bird wanted to eat a worm and asked how many birds would have to go hungry, most children answered readily.

Separating informal knowledge from the learning of symbols and rules can also lead students to learn and practice incorrect methods. When the psychologist Herbert Ginsburg observed 8-year-old Jennifer doing long division, he noticed that she got the same quotient, 61, for two different problems—$8 \div 488$ and $8 \div 4808$—and defended her answer on the grounds that "zero doesn't count for anything." She stuck firmly to her faulty rule and applied it consistently in other problems until her teacher steered the conversation toward children's ages and asked her to think about the numbers "1" and "10" in that context. Jennifer's misconception about zero quickly collided with what she knew about 1-year-olds and 10-year-olds—and her face lit up with a new understanding of place value.

Fourth graders in Babylon, New York, remembered most of the steps they had learned the year before to solve problems like 19×21: "first we X's one times nine. Next we X's the one by the one. Then we go down a line and put a zero under the nine. Next we Xs the two by the nine . . . " But when asked why, they changed lines or why they put a zero on the second line, most responded, "That's the rule." They seemed to have stopped expecting their work to make sense: asked why their answers to the problem 47×23 were reasonable, most said they had followed the rules or worked carefully, only a few gave explanations like "23 is almost 20, and 47 is almost 50, and my answer is about 50×20, or 1000."

Once students put their faith in procedures and give up on sense, they ignore the concrete materials that could help them. When Hughes asked students to do two-column subtraction problems, he gave them blocks and rods, but most struggled along without them. To his surprise, children saw no relationship between the written problems and the concrete materials.

Are Cognitive Skills Context-Bound?

D. N. PERKINS
GAVRIEL SALOMON

Effective problem solving, sound decision making, insightful invention—do such aspects of good thinking depend more on deep expertise in a specialty than on reflective awareness and general strategies? Over the past thirty years, considerable research and controversy have surrounded this issue. An historical sketch of the arguments for the strong specialist position and the strong generalist position suggests that each camp, in its own way, has oversimplified the interaction between general strategic knowledge and specialized domain knowledge. We suggest a synthesis: General and specialized knowledge function in close partnership. We explore the nature of this partnership and consider its implications for educational practice.

Once upon a time, an astute and beneficent leader in a remote country anticipated increasing aggression from a territory-hungry neighbor nation. Recognizing that the neighbor had more military might, the leader concluded that his people would have to out-think, rather than overpower, the enemy. Undistinguished in its military armament and leadership, the country did have one remarkable resource: the reigning world chess master, undefeated for over twenty years. "Aha," the leader said to himself, "we will recruit this keen intellect, honed so long on the whetstone of chess, teach him some politics and military theory and then outmaneuver the enemy with the help of his genius."

A fanciful tale, to be sure, but consider the leader's plan for a moment: Is it disastrously naive, possibly helpful, or a pretty good bet? In fact, the tale has no definite conclusion. Rather, it is the be-

David Perkins is at the Harvard University Graduate School of Education, Cambridge, Massachusetts 02138. Gavriel Salomon is at the Department of Communication, University of Arizona, Tucson, Arizona 85721.

ginning of another tale, a tale about psychology and the human intellect that research is gradually spinning. Questions like that of the chess master's political and military potential stand in the center of one of the most puzzling and important issues that cognitive psychology has addressed: the roles of general and of context-specific knowledge in thinking.

Within the discipline of psychology and across three decades, very different voices might be heard sizing up the chances of the chess master. One says, "Basically, the chess master plays chess well because he knows the moves of the game well. There's no reason at all why that knowledge should carry over powerfully to political or military matters." Another voice counters: "Well, there are analogies to be mined between chess and matters of political and military strategy. Control of the center, for example—that's a principle important in chess, but also in politics and war." Still another voice emphasizes not the transferrable aspects of chess skill but general problem solving abilities: "Above all, a chess player is a problem solver, needing to plan ahead, explore alternatives, size up strategic options, just as a politician or military tactician does. So we might expect a lot from the chess master."

Which of these voices speaks with most authority? Or do we need to listen for another voice altogether, stating some more complicated opinion? On this question has hung a good deal of psychological research, as psychologists have sought to understand the factors that underlie cognitive skills in domains like chess play, problem solving in mathematics and physics, medical diagnosis, musical composition, and more. Let us see how that story has unfolded and, at the end, appraise the chess master's chances.

THE HEART OF THE ISSUE

Some sharpening of the problem is needed at the outset. At issue is the generality of cognitive skill. Is skillful thought-demanding performance relatively context-bound, or does it principally reflect use of general abilities of some sort?

There can be little doubt that some aspects of cognitive skill are quite general: IQ and *g* for general intelligence measure a side of human intellectual functioning that correlates with effective performance over a wide range of academic and nonacademic tasks. For this aspect of cognitive skill, the answer is in, and favors generality. By way of qualification, however, arguments can be made that giftedness in particular domains, such as music, reflects neurologically based, relatively inborn aspects of intelligence (Gardner, 1983). These arguments have been somewhat controversial but certainly have a considerable following.

At any rate, neither *g* nor any more specialized aspect of giftedness speaks directly to the role of *knowledge* in intellectual functioning. And it's obvious that knowledge counts for a lot. Without considerable experience, the most gifted individual cannot play chess, repair a car, play the violin, or prove theorems. Indeed, recent research on *g* argues that it wields its influence on performance *by way of* knowledge: People with high *g* tend to perform well because they have a rich knowledge base, the direct determinant of performance (Hunter, 1986). And people with a lower *g* but more knowledge than those with high *g* will usually perform better—it's the knowledge that counts, rather than *g*.

The question is, which kind of knowledge counts most—general knowledge of how to think

well, or specific knowledge about the detailed ins and outs of a field? General knowledge includes widely applicable strategies for problem solving, inventive thinking, decision making, learning, and good mental management, sometimes called *autocontrol, autoregulation* or *metacognition.* In chess, for example, very specific knowledge (often called local knowledge) includes the rules of the game as well as lore about how to handle innumerable specific situations, such as different openings and ways of achieving checkmate. Of intermediate generality are strategic concepts, like *control of the center,* that are somewhat specific to chess but that also invite far-reaching application by analogy.

There is an obvious partial answer to the question, "what counts most?" It's plain that some local knowledge is necessary; one can't play chess without knowing the rules of the game, after all. But that partial resolution misses the real issue—*where is the bottleneck in attaining mastery?* Does it lie in acquiring a deep and detailed knowledge of chess, whereas anyone can learn whatever general thinking strategies are needed? Or does it lie in becoming reflective and cultivating the general thinking strategies, whereas anyone can learn the relevant particulars of the game?

These different theories write different endings to the chess master's story. If he is masterful in virtue of his general savvy about the use of his mind, the chess master might carry it over to the political and military realms. At the opposite extreme, if his mastery depends on richly developed local knowledge of chess, the chances seem slender.

Such enigmas arise in every domain and bring with them fundamental questions about educational design. Should we teach entirely for richly developed local knowledge, subject matter by subject matter? Or should we invest a significant portion of educational resources in developing general skills of problem solving, self-management, and so on? Or, indeed, does this dichotomy obscure some important factors? To work toward an answer, let us examine the controversy, adopting a broad-stroke historical perspective without pretense of reconstructing events in detail.

BEFORE THE FALL: THE GOLDEN AGE OF GENERAL HEURISTICS

Thirty years ago, it was widely thought that good problem solving and other intellectual performances reflected general strategies (supported by *g*) operating on whatever database of knowledge happened to be needed. True ability resided in the general strategies, with the database an incidental necessity.

One source of this perspective was the mathematician Gyorgy Polya's analysis of mathematical problem solving (Polya, 1954, 1957). Polya argued that the formalities of mathematical proof and derivation had little to do with the real work of problem solving in mathematics. Although such formalities were the evening dress of journal publication, success in finding solutions depended on a repertoire of *heuristics,* general strategies for attacking a problem that did not guarantee a solution, but often helped. Polya discussed such heuristics as breaking a problem into subproblems, solving simpler problems that reflected some aspect of the main problem, using diagrams to represent a problem in different ways, and examining special cases to get a feel for a problem. Polya spoke to mathematical problem solving specifically, but many of the heuristics he emphasized were plainly applicable to problems of all sorts, which encouraged the notion that problem solving could be achieved as a general ability and mathematical problem solving simply a special case.

Another source of encouragement was early work on Artificial Intelligence (AI), the design of computer programs to carry out processes such as chess playing or theorem proving that, in a human being, would be considered intelligent. The "General Problem Solver" was one outstanding example (Ernst & Newell, 1969; Newell & Simon, 1972). Developed around 1957 by Alan Newell, J. P. Shaw, and Herbert Simon, this program relied on a flexible heuristic called *means-end analysis.* Input to the program included information about a beginning state, an end state (the goal) and allowable operations on states, all in a compact notation. Many simple puzzles and problems in logic could be cast into this form. The program pursued a chain of operations for transforming the beginning state into the end state. It did so by comparing and contrasting the beginning with the end state and seeking an operation that would reduce the contrast—a means that would bring the beginning state closer to the end state. After executing that operation, the program would seek another operation to reduce the contrast yet further, and so on. If it encountered a cul-de-sac that forbade further progress, the program would back up and try another path. There were other sophisticated features as well. Here

again, as in the perspective of Polya, it appeared that problem solving power lay in some rather general principles, systematically applied to whatever the relevant database of knowledge happened to be.

A host of factors—its generating interesting data; its accord with intuitions about the value of analytic ability; its economy, elegance, and availability to testing in computer models—reinforced the position that good thinking depended in considerable part on a repertoire of rather general heuristic knowledge. Many such heuristics were identified, heuristics for problem solving, memorizing, inventive thinking, decision making, general mental management, and so on (cf. Nickerson, Perkins, & Smith, 1985). As to local knowledge, the part of knowledge specific to a domain like chess or mathematics, it was thought not very important. Of course, one had to have it. But there really wasn't much to it beyond a few rules in the case of chess, a few axioms in the case of a mathematical system, and so on. There didn't seem to be *enough to know* about such databases to make them central to thinking ability.

THE POWER OF THE PARTICULAR

The golden age could not last. Even then, certain results in the literature gave warning that all was not well with this picture of general heuristics driving intellectual performance. In the years to come, a wave of compelling findings would cast profound doubt on the centrality of general ability in human thinking, particularly ability based on heuristics. The gathering force of contrary findings falls neatly into three parts: the argument from expertise, the argument from weak methods, and the argument from transfer.

The Argument from Expertise

Investigators even during the golden age were discovering that the seeming smallness of the database demanded by chess, symbolic logic, and other favorite areas of research was deceptive. To be sure, chess, for example, looked like a game of general reasoning applied to a few specific rules. It seemed that all a player needed to do was to know the rules and reason well about options and consequences: "If I move there, my opponent might move there, but then I could . . . , but then my opponent could

...," and so on. But close observation showed that there was much more to it.

Research on the games of grand master chess players showed that their tactics depended on an enormous knowledge base of important patterns of chess pieces—not only the standard patterns such as pins, forks, and rooks on open files, but far more, with a diversity and complexity not recognized by the chess masters themselves. Expert chess players reasoned about the game using these chunk-like configurations, rather than thinking about one piece at a time, and so had much more power to think ahead and devise strategies than a simple command of the rules would afford.

The classic experiments demonstrating this began with examinations of the reputed ability of grand master players to memorize the layout of pieces on a chess board at a glance (Chase & Simon, 1973; de Groot, 1965). The experiments showed that experts could indeed do this-but only if the chess pieces' positions had emerged in the natural course of play, not if the same pieces were arranged randomly on the board. Beginning players did just as well as the grand masters in recalling random layouts and, significantly, their recall did *not* improve on the layouts that emerged in the course of a game. These results showed that the grand masters knew something very powerful, but *very specific to chess*, else they would have done well on the random layouts too. Chase and Simon (1973) used certain approximations to estimate the grand master chess player's repertoire of something like fifty thousand chess-specific configurations, or *schemata*, as they are usually called, that provide the "chunks" that the grand master thinks with.

The experiments in chess inspired similar studies in a number of areas, with parallel findings. A general profile of expertise began to emerge (cf. Glaser, 1984; Rabinowitz & Glaser, 1985): Expert performance entailed (a) a large knowledge base of domain-specific patterns (for example, typical configurations of pieces in chess, typical uses of conservation laws in physics); (b) rapid recognition of situations where these patterns apply; and (c) reasoning that moves from such recognition directly toward a solution by working with the patterns, often called *forward reasoning*.

In contrast, novices tended not to see the relevant patterns, because they did not know them or lacked rapid recognition-like access to them. Novices often based their reasoning on superficial problem content, for instance treating inclined plane problems similarly when different physics princi-

ples applied. Novices often solved problems by focussing first on the unknown and seeking equations or rules that bridged back from the unknown toward the givens. If they found equations or rules, then they plugged in the givens to determine the unknown. This *backward reasoning* ran opposite to experts' forward reasoning from givens toward the unknown. These contrasts between experts' and novices' performances emerged in such domains as physics problem solving (e.g. Chi, Feltovich, & Glaser, 1981; Larkin, 1982; Larkin, McDermott, Simon, & Simon, 1980a; Larkin, McDermott, Simon, & Simon, 1980b), mathematical problem solving (Schoenfeld & Herrmann, 1982), computer programming (Ehrlich & Soloway, 1984), and medicine (Elstein, Shulman, & Sprafka, 1978; Patel & Groen, 1986). The investigations came to be known as research on expertise, because the account of proficient performances was so compelling.

These studies of expertise revealed the naivete in a key premise of the golden age. To be sure, chess, symbolic logic, Newtonian physics, and so on, each involved a fairly parsimonious foundation of basic rules or axioms. Nonetheless, experts depended on a much richer database, an elaborate superstructure of ramifications erected on top of the parsimonious foundation. General heuristics appeared to be no substitute for the rich database of ramifications, stored, in memory, accessed by recognition processes, and ready to go. Indeed, the broad heuristic structure of expert as contrasted to novice problem solving—the reasoning forward rather than reasoning backward—seemed attributable not to any heuristic sophistication on the part of the experts, but to the driving influence of the experts' rich database. General heuristics no longer looked as central or as powerful.

The Argument from Weak Methods

Work in AI, although it initially supported the idea that general heuristics drive skillful problem solving, also began to take a different turn. To be sure, programs like the General Problem Solver could solve some rather simple formal problems, such as those in elementary symbolic logic. But these generic programs seemed quite helpless in complex problem solving domains such as chess play, integrating mathematical expressions, or medical diagnosis. In contrast, programs designed specifically for those knowledge domains scored significant successes (Boden, 1977; Rich, 1983). In the late 1960s and early 1970s, the AI community became increasingly aware of these successes, and many investigators began to lay their bets differently as they tried to construct powerful artificial intelligence systems (Gardner, 1985, pp. 160–161).

Investigators in the AI community came to refer to general heuristics such as means-end analysis as *weak methods* (see Rich, 1983, section 3.6). When new to a domain, all a computer or a human could do was deploy weak methods that turned out weak results. Real power in problem solving emerged over time, as application of weak methods created the opportunity to learn and store up the ramifications of particular moves in the domain and build the rich database. This database would become the real power behind good problem solving, leaving the weak methods behind. Investigators spoke of the "power-generality tradeoff," the more general the method, the weaker the method. Seeking to make the best of the situation and taking a cue from the work of psychologists on expertise, many AI researchers turned to developing *expert systems*, which sought to simulate the intelligence of an expert in a domain through manipulating a massive domain-specific knowledge base in areas such as medical diagnosis (cf. Rich, 1983; Wenger, 1987).

Although the argument from weak methods derived principally from AI, little happened in the psychological community to make a countercase. In particular, a number of investigators sought to teach Polya's heuristics for mathematical problem solving with little success. Students exhibited just exactly the difficulties expected, given the results of the research on expertise: They didn't know *what to do* with the heuristics. They understood the heuristics in broad terms but didn't seem to understand the mathematics well enough to apply them in the rather complex and context sensitive ways required. Local knowledge, more than general problem-solving heuristics, appeared to be the bottleneck (Schoenfeld, 1985, pp. 71–74).

The Argument from Transfer

A third line of argument seemed to drive the last nail in the coffin of general cognitive skills. According to the premise of the "golden age," much of the knowledge acquired in a particular domain is inherently general, at least implicitly, and should lead to transfer to other areas. Thus, learning the logic imbedded in mathematics or in Latin should, for example, yield improved scores on standard IQ tests or better learning in other seemingly unrelated

fields. Similarly, learning to program computers in a powerful language such as LOGO should improve students' reasoning and planning abilities.

A variety of studies, initiated as far back as the turn of the century, generally failed to uphold these predictions. E. L. Thorndike (e.g., 1923) and Thorndike and Woodworth (1901) reported experiments, some on a large scale, showing that training in such fields as Latin and math has no measurable influence on other cognitive functions, thus dispelling a then prevalent belief in the training of the mind's "faculties."

More recent studies have yielded similar findings. Such studies suggest, for example, that training on one version of a logical problem has little if any effect on solving an isomorphic version, differently represented (Hayes & Simon, 1977); that becoming literate with no schooling does not improve mastery of general cognitive skills (Scribner & Cole, 1981); or that teaching children to use general, context-independent cognitive strategies has no clear benefits outside the specific domains in which they are taught (for a summary, see Pressley, Snyder, and Cariglia-Bull, 1987). Findings from research on the cognitive effects of programming have generally been negative (Pea & Kurland, 1984; Salomon & Perkins, 1987).

Overall, research on transfer suggests the same conclusion as the arguments from expertise and weak methods: Thinking at its most effective depends on specific, contextbound skills and units of knowledge that have little application to other domains. To the extent that transfer does take place, it is highly specific and must be cued, primed, and guided; it seldom occurs spontaneously. The case for generalizable, context-independent skills and strategies that can be trained in one context and transferred to other domains has proven to be more a matter of wishful thinking than hard empirical evidence (Pressley et al., 1987).

THE SKELETON
OF A SYNTHESIS

We said that the argument from transfer might be the last nail in the coffin of general cognitive skills. But the skeleton is restless. Some people seem generally smart—not just knowledgeable, but insightful no matter the subject.

For instance, if you have mixed some with academic philosophers, you may have noticed that they have an unsettling habit: You mention some casual claim, and they often smack you with a counterexample. Moreover, the discussion does not have to deal with a topic in academic philosophy. You may be discussing politics, family life, the dangers of nuclear power plants, or the latest bestseller. It almost seems as though the philosophers have a general cognitive skill: the strategy of looking for counterexamples to test claims.

Is this a general cognitive skill? Recalling the arguments from expertise, weak methods, and transfer, you might object this way: "What has the appearance of a general reasoning strategy in these philosophers' remarks is really a highly contextualized strategy. The philosophers can only construct counterexamples in domains where they have a good knowledge base."

"More than that," your objection might continue, "certain domains bring with them special criteria for what counts as a counterexample. A counterexample to a mathematical claim would have to be constructed appropriately from the premises of the mathematical system; a counterexample to a legal claim would have to be the result of prior due process. This is a special case of a point that Toulmin (1958), among others, has emphasized: Different domains share many structures of argument, but bring with them somewhat different criteria for evidence."

These points ought to be granted at once. Yet there is something disturbing about casting them as an objection: They treat *general* and *contextualized* as though they were exclusive of one another. The heart of the synthesis we would like to suggest challenges this dichotomy. There are general cognitive skills; but they always function in contextualized ways, along the lines articulated in considering the philosophers' habit of mind (cf. Perkins & Simmons, 1987; Perkins, Schwartz, & Simmons, in press).

Granting the need for contextualization through a knowledge base, what argues that the philosophers' move of seeking counterexamples is nonetheless a general, learnable, and worthwhile cognitive skill? First of all, seeking counterexamples is a strategy for which philosophers show *seeming use:* That is, it certainly looks as though they are applying a general strategy, although perhaps their thinking is entirely contextualized and only appears to be general. Second, the seeking of counterexamples itself appears to play an *important role* in the philosophers' reasoning: It allows them to detect the flaws in claims that otherwise might be missed. Third, the seeking of counterexamples

seems to be *transferrable:* Apparently, philosophers pick it up from their philosophical studies and apply it widely to other domains. Fourth, the move of seeking counterexamples is *commonly absent:* Everyday experience suggests that most people do not reflexively seek counterexamples. Moreover, research on everyday reasoning shows that seeking any sort of evidence on the other side of the case is a relatively rare move, even in educated populations (Perkins, 1985; Perkins, in press).

Of course, this is only one case, informally argued through everyday observation, and subject to several objections. Its real purpose is not to mount a compelling argument for general cognitive skills but to illustrate what a general cognitive skill might look like—and rattle the skeleton that met an early and unceremonious end. To flesh out that skeleton, we would have to find patterns of information processing that (a) show seeming use, (b) play an important role, (c) are demonstrably transferrable, and (d) are commonly absent. It would be reasonable to call a pattern of information processing that satisfies those conditions a general cognitive skill.

GENERALITY ON THE REBOUND

Throughout the period of "the fall," considerable interest, in some quarters, continued to focus on the nature of general cognitive skills and the potentials of teaching such skills. In recent years, results have begun to emerge that challenge the picture of expert performance as driven primarily by a rich knowledge base of highly context-specific schemata. One by one, the arguments from expertise, weak methods, and transfer have begun to show cracks.

We take those arguments up again, reexamining each in light of new findings. In doing so, we enter the region of recent history and contemporary work, where results are scattered, and replications are few. Nonetheless, from our perspective, a new outline is emerging.

When Experts Face Unfamiliar Problems

Most of the research on expertise has examined experts addressing standard problems in a domain—typical chess positions, physics problems, programming problems, and so on. In these circumstances, the experts' behavior appears to be strongly driven by local knowledge. But this picture could be misleading. What happens when experts tackle atypical problems—not problems outside the domain, but problems less "textbookish?" Might more general kinds of knowledge play a more prominent role?

One response to this question would be to dismiss it from the outset. What does it matter how experts respond to atypical problems? Expertise certainly should be assessed and examined with problems typical of the domain. But such a response takes a narrow view of expertise. Presumably, in many domains, people become experts not to function as technicians solving new variants of the classic problems but to open the field further. From this standpoint, atypical problems are just the right test of truly flexible expertise.

John Clement, working at the University of Massachusetts, Amherst, has examined experts' responses to atypical problems. The results are provocative (Clement, 1982, in press; see also Johnson, Ahlgren, Blount, & Petit, 1980). As in other work on expertise, the experts addressing such problems certainly use their rich physics knowledge base, trying to see the deep structure of the problem and deploying principles like conservation of energy. But, because these unusual problems do not yield to the most straightforward approaches, the experts also apply many general strategies.

For example, the experts faced with an unfamiliar problem will often: (a) resort to analogies with systems they understand better; (b) search for potential misanalogies in the analogy; (c) refer to intuitive mental models based on visual and kinesthetic intuition to try to understand how the target system would behave; (d) investigate the target system with "extreme case" arguments, probing how it would work if various parameters were pushed to zero or infinity; (e) construct a simpler problem of the same sort, in hopes of solving that and importing the solution to the original problem.

There are just a few of the Polya-like strategies that seem to appear in Clement's protocols; no doubt others could be identified as well. Such results suggest that a number of general heuristics not apparent when experts face typical problems play a prominent role when experts face atypical problems.

How does Clement's evidence speak to the four conditions needed for the synthesis: seeming use, important role, transferrable, and common absence? These studies give distinct evidence of seeming use of heuristics. They also give clear evidence

of an important role: In the protocols, the heuristics often constitute crucial steps along a subject's path to a solution.

However, Clement's studies offer no evidence of transfer. Although it may seem plausible that a problem solver acquainted with, let us say, extreme case arguments from physics would sometimes carry them over to chemistry or mathematics problems, that remains to be shown. Also, Clement's studies give no direct evidence of common absence. It's plausible that many weaker students of physics fail to pick up the "extreme case" pattern of argument simply from normal learning in the domain, but, again, that remains to be shown. (These points are not criticisms of Clement's studies, which were designed to address other issues.)

It's notable that the general heuristics seemingly used by Clement's subjects certainly do not substitute for domain knowledge. On the contrary, the general heuristics operate in a highly contextualized way, accessing, and wielding sophisticated domain knowledge. In particular, conservation of energy, conservation of momentum, and other deep structure principles of physics are brought to bear, held in the pincers, so to speak, of these general heuristics.

When Weak Methods Work

Recall that the argument from weak methods complained that general heuristics appeared not to work very well, either in instructional experiments or in AI. The years have brought changes in that appraisal. Mathematician and educator Alan Schoenfeld, in extensive work on teaching mathematical problem solving, has demonstrated that heuristic instruction can yield dramatic gains in college students' mathematical problem solving (Schoenfeld, 1982; Schoenfeld & Herrmann, 1982). Schoenfeld emphasizes that this success requires teaching many of the heuristics in a very contextualized way, so the heuristics make good contact with students' knowledge base in the domain (Schoenfeld, 1985, Chapter 3). At the same time, an important thrust of Schoenfled's approach is fostering a seeming quite general level of control or problem management. Students learn to monitor and direct their own progress, asking questions such as, "What am I doing now," "Is it getting me anywhere," "What else could I be doing instead?" This general metacognitive level helps students to avoid perseverating in unproductive approaches, to remember to check candidate answers, and so on.

Again, it's worth asking how Schoenfeld's work speaks to the four elements of the synthesis position. His research gives evidence of students' use of Polya-like heuristics (Schoenfeld, 1985), and Schoenfeld's experiments demonstrated that students indeed acquired the use of these heuristics (Schoenfeld, 1982; Schoenfeld & Herrmann, 1982). Regarding the heuristics' important role, Schoenfeld's studies also demonstrated that the better performance of the students on posttesting directly depended on their active use of the heuristics. Protocol analysis disclosed that those students who used the heuristics performed better, whereas those who did not failed to show gains. Regarding common absence, the impressive gains students exhibited showed that they did not already possess the heuristics they acquired.

However, Schoenfeld's studies offer no evidence of transfer. To be sure, many of the Polya-like heuristics seem straightforwardly applicable to chemistry and physics, and the general problem management strategy seems even more widely relevant. However, such observations do not make the empirical case that these skills can be decontextualized and applied more broadly.

Another recent effort has focussed on teaching general reading skills to poor readers. Palincsar and Brown (1984) developed and evaluated a method called *Reciprocal Teaching* that through a process of modeling, guiding, and group participation, has helped young poor readers learn to monitor and direct their reading. The intervention encourages and refines four key cognitive activities: *questioning* about the main points of a paragraph, *clarifying* to try to resolve difficulties of understanding, *summarizing* to capture the essence of a text, and *predicting*, to forecast what might happen next in the text. Palincsar and Brown's approach yielded dramatic gains in the students' reading comprehension, transfer to in-class reading in science and social studies, and long-term retention.

The direct cultivation of these reading strategies and the resultant gains give evidence of seeming use, important role, and common absence (in the poor reader population). The matter of transfer can be looked at in two ways: One might say that transfer across domains was demonstrated, because students showed reading gains *in situ* in school subject-matters. Or, one might say that transfer across domains was not addressed, because students were taught and tested on reading performance specifically. The two perspectives seem equally defensible because reading is what

might be called a "tool domain," like writing or arithmetic: We learn reading, writing, and arithmetic in order to apply them to various content domains, such as literature, history, or biology.

It's worth noting that the very existence of tool domains that enhance thinking and learning in content domains, in itself, constitutes evidence for general cognitive skills of a sort. Reading *is* a general cognitive skill, which people routinely transfer to new subject matters, beginning to read in a domain with their general vocabulary and reading tactics and, as they go along, acquiring new domain-specific words, concepts, and reading tactics. However, reading as a general cognitive skill does not much resemble those skills that have been at issue over the past thirty years—such strategy-like skills as Polya's heuristics, for instance.

There have been several other seemingly successful efforts to teach cognitive skills of some generality in recent years, for example, the development and testing of Project Intelligence, a general course to teach skills of problem solving, decision making, inventive thinking, and other sorts (Herrnstein, Nickerson, Sanchez, & Swets, 1986) and the *guided design* perspective developed by Wales and his colleagues (Wales & Nardi, 1984; Wales & Stager, 1978). A general resource reviewing many such programs is Nickerson et al. (1985). The collection edited by Segal, Chipman, and Glaser (1985) offers somewhat earlier assessments of several programs. Resnick (1987) has authored a monograph appraising the promise of work in this area, with cautiously optimistic conclusions. Likewise, there is considerable evidence from more basic investigations that learning in human beings depends on the deployment of general learning strategies (e.g., recent findings by Bereiter & Tinker, 1988; Chan & Burtis, 1988; Ng, 1988; Ogilvie & Steinbach, 1988).

In artificial intelligence, although work has continued on expert systems, investigators have also returned to the challenge of producing more general models of mind. Two systems in particular, ACT* (Anderson, 1983) and SOAR (Laird, Rosenbloom, & Newell, 1984) have been developed as general models of cognitive processing. Both are learning systems that learn by trying to solve problems. Given a new class of problems, they commence by applying week methods. As they work, they search for and store shortcuts in the solution process and so gradually build up a repertoire of domain-specific chunks, much as human beings do, through extended experience in a domain.

Moreover, the functioning of SOAR, for example, is in some ways not unlike the functioning of Clement's physicists facing an unfamiliar kind of physics problem. SOAR tries the specific moves compiled into its library through experience. But, if SOAR encounters an "impasse," as it is called, in which the specialized techniques it has compiled do not work, it resorts to more general methods.

Important instructional applications are being built that continue this AI tradition. An example is GUIDON 2 (Clancey, 1986, 1987), a medical diagnostic expert system that combines specific medical expertise with more general reasoning strategies. The latter teach tactics for the management of diagnostic hypotheses whereby cases can be grouped and then differentiated into finer categories. The heuristics used are quite general and applicable to other domains of problem solving requiring heuristic classification. It is expected that through interaction with the program, students might become better problem solvers in medicine as well as in other domains.

ACT*, SOAR, and GUIDON 2 represent a provocative reengagement with issues concerning the interaction between general and local knowledge.

When Transfer Happens

During the fall, negative findings on transfer generally were interpreted as showing that skill depends mostly on local knowledge and that we have little ability to decontextualize knowledge and apply it in different domains. However, a more careful examination of the research discloses that the findings that support these conclusions allow other explanations altogether. These other explanations accord general knowledge more potency, without challenging the idea that local knowledge has great importance.

A casual look at the research on transfer might suggest that our cognitive apparatus simply does not incline very much to transfer. But this would be a misapprehension. On the contrary, when faced with novel situations, people routinely try to apply knowledge, skills, and specific strategies from other, more familiar domains. In fact, people commonly ignore the novelty in a situation, assimilating it into well-rehearsed schemata and mindlessly bringing to bear inappropriate knowledge and skill, yielding negative transfer (Langer, in press). In other cases, although people fail to apply purely logical, abstract, or syntactical rules to formally presented problems (e.g., Wason,

1966), they clearly do employ analogous inferential rules to more everyday versions of such problems (e.g. Cheng & Holyoak, 1985).

Moreover, recent research shows that, when general principles of reasoning are taught together with self-monitoring practices and potential applications in varied contexts, transfer often *is* obtained (e.g. Nickerson, et al., 1985; Palincsar & Brown, 1984; Schoenfeld, 1978, 1982; Schoenfeld & Herrmann, 1982). Relatedly, Lehman, Lempert, and Nisbett (1988) have recently demonstrated that graduate students in such fields as psychology and medicine show clear transfer of probabilistic and methodological reasoning to everyday problems.

Brown and her associates (e.g., Brown & Kane, 1988; Brown, Kane, & Long, in press; Brown & Palincsar, in press) have recently shown in a series of laboratory and classroom studies that transfer to new problems does take place, even among three- and four-year-olds, when (a) learners are shown how problems resemble each other; (b) when learners' attention is directed to the underlying goal structure of comparable problems; (c) when the learners are familiar with the problem domains; (d) when examples are accompanied with rules, particularly when the latter are formulated by the learners themselves; and perhaps most importantly, (e) when learning takes place in a social context (e.g., reciprocal teaching), whereby justifications, principles, and explanations are socially fostered, generated, and contrasted. It becomes evident from this research, as it does from that of others (e.g., Gick & Holyoak, 1987), that transfer is possible, that it is very much a matter of how the knowledge and skill are acquired and how the individual, now facing a new situation, goes about trying to handle it. Given appropriate conditions, such as cueing, practicing, generating abstract rules, socially developing explanations and principles, conjuring up analogies (e.g. Strauss, 1987), and the like, transfer from one problem domain to another can be obtained. General skills and bits of knowledge taught within a specific context can become transferable.

Specifically, we have proposed two different mechanisms by which transfer of specific skill and knowledge takes place (Perkins & Salomon, 1987; Salomon & Perkins, in press). One mechanism, called the "low road" to transfer, depends on extensive and varied practice of a skill to near automaticity (see also Anderson, 1983, on automaticity). A skill so practiced in a large variety of instances becomes applied to perceptually similar situations by way of response or stimulus generalization. For example, having driven different cars under a variety of conditions allows us to shift to driving a truck fairly easily. Unfortunately, learning in many natural settings and in many laboratory experiments does not meet the conditions for low road transfer: *much* practice, in *a large variety* of situations, leading to a *high level of mastery and near-automaticity.* For example, these conditions were not met by the Vai literates studied by Scribner and Cole (1981), or the young programmers studied by Pea and Kurland (1984).

The second mechanism, called the "high road," depends on learners' deliberate mindful abstraction of a principle. People sometimes abstract principles in advance, keeping them in mind in anticipation of appropriate opportunities for application, or, in a new situation, reach back to prior experiences and abstract from them principles that might be relevant. For an example of the latter, in a recent partial replication of Gick and Holyoak's (1987) analogy studies, Salomon and Globerson (1987) showed that college students who were urged to formulate an abstract principle from two problems did not show more transfer to a new, analogous problem than students who were given the principle ready-made. However, the former (but not the latter) showed impressive transfer when urged to search their memories for an appropriate principle that they may have encountered before.

Likewise, the expert chess player mobilized to save his country in our opening story would be expected to mine the context of chess for chess-bound principles such as "get hold of the board's center," decontextualize them, and apply them in forms like "let's capture or destroy the enemy's command centers." Unfortunately, in many real-world situations and many laboratory experiments on transfer, there is nothing to provoke the active decontextualization of knowledge, so the high-road mechanism does not operate.

But it can be activated. The transfer findings of Lehman and his colleagues (1988) are a case in point. In the treatment employed, graduate students did not just absorb statistical principles and practice them to near automaticity; they were urged to comprehend the logic behind them and mindfully generate abstractions, applying them in a variety of learning situations. Similarly, Salomon, Globerson, and Guterman (Salomon, 1988) have found that children can acquire reading strategies involving self-monitoring from a computerized Reading Aid and apply them a month later to essay writing, a clear case of high-road transfer of a generalized ability (see also Brown & Palincsar, 1988).

In summary, recent research and theorizing concerning transfer put the negative findings cited earlier in a different light. These findings do not imply either that people have little ability to accomplish transfer or that skill is almost entirely context bound. Rather, the negative results reflect the fact that transfer occurs only under specific conditions, which often are not met in everyday life or laboratory experiments (Brown, Kane, & Long, in press). When the conditions are met, useful transfer from one context to another often occurs.

SO ARE COGNITIVE SKILLS CONTEXT-BOUND?

As the psychological tale has unfolded, the answer to the question looks to be, "Yes and no." The tale is one of neglected complexities. Early advocacy of general cognitive skills overlooked the importance of a rich knowledge base, took it for granted that general heuristics would make ready contact with a person's knowledge base, and had few worries about transfer, which was supposed to happen more or less spontaneously. Mistakes all three, these oversights led to considerable skepticism about general cognitive skills, the view that cognitive skills in the main were context bound, and interesting developments in the psychology of expertise as well as artificial intelligence work on expert systems.

But more recent results suggest that this trend had its blind spots too, in neglecting how general heuristics help when experts face atypical problems in a domain, how general heuristics function in contextualized ways to access and deploy domain specific knowledge, and how lack of conditions needed for transfer, rather than domain specificity, is to blame for many cases of failure of transfer. These more recent results point toward the synthesis that we now think might be fleshed out.

What General Cognitive Skills Are Like

In the synthesis, general cognitive skills do not function by somehow taking the place of domain-specific knowledge, nor by operating exactly the same way from domain to domain. Rather, cognitive skills are general tools in much the way the human hand is. Your hands alone are not enough;

you need objects to grasp. Moreover, as you reach for an object, whether a pen or a ball, you shape your hand to assure a good grip. And you need to learn to handle different objects appropriately—you don't pick up a baby in the same way you pick up a basket of laundry.

Likewise, general cognitive skills can be thought of as general gripping devices for retrieving and wielding domain-specific knowledge, as hands that need pieces of knowledge to grip and wield and that need to configure to the kind of knowledge in question. Remember, for instance, the case of thinking of counterexamples. As you learn a new subject matter, trying to think of counterexamples to claims surely is a good critical posture to maintain. But you have to accumulate knowledge in the domain with which to find or build counterexamples. And you have to develop a sense of what *counts* as a counterexample in the domain. Similarly, in applying to this new domain a reading strategy that asks you to summarize, you have to develop a sense of what counts as relevant. Or, in applying an extreme case heuristic to the new domain, you have to find out what dimensions are significant, so that you will know how to push a proposition to an extreme meaningful in that domain.

Of course, none of this need to learn and to adjust implies that the cognitive gripper you using lacks generality. All specific applications of anything general need to configure to the context. This approach acknowledges the importance of domain-specific adjustments, which indeed often are challenging, while maintaining the reality and power of general cognitive skills.

Completing the Case

It should be acknowledged that the findings supporting this synthesis paint a partial and scattered picture. Indeed, the four conditions for generality mentioned earlier—seeming use, important role, transferable, and common absence—offer a map of the kinds of empirical work needed to test the matter further.

Regarding *seeming use*, more protocol studies are needed that examine experts addressing atypical problems within their domain of expertise, to check for seeming use of general strategies. Also, more experiments in teaching heuristics are needed that test whether gains in problem solving can be attributed directly to the use of the heuristics. Both sorts of studies would also address the ques-

tion of *important role*, because they can show general strategies figuring crucially in finding solutions. Teaching experiments can also address *common absence*, by documenting that students lack certain strategies before intervention and gain from their use after intervention.

Supposing that positive results accrue on seeming use, important role, and common absence, then the issue of generality hangs on the question of transfer, where considerably more work is needed. Transfer can prove more or less robust, even the least robust case providing some evidence of generality. In the strongest case, a person mastering a general method by contextualizing it to a domain would spontaneously transfer it to other domains. Lacking spontaneous transfer, the person might show transfer if a teacher or other source alerted the learner to its relevance in the new domain. If even that failed, it might still be so that instruction systematically helping the learner to contextualize the method in the new domain would go more quickly because of prior experience in the original domain. As mentioned in the section on transfer, some contemporary results show one or another of these patterns. But much careful systematic work on the question has yet to be done.

EDUCATING MEMORIES VERSUS EDUCATING MINDS

We are fairly confident in the synthesis position outlined here, not only because it makes sense of both the negative and positive findings so far, but also because it makes sense of everyday observations—such as the philosophers' wont to pick apart claims with counterexamples. But what is its import for education?

Despite many efforts to refashion educational practices to cultivate more thoughtful learning within and across domains, the fact of the matter is that most educational practice remains doggedly committed to imparting facts and algorithms. Regrettably, E. D. Hirsch (1987) and other educators have even taken the negative arguments from expertise, weak methods, and transfer as reasons to eschew attention to higher order skills so that more time is given to building students' factual knowledge base in a domain.

This seems particularly unfortunate. To be sure, general heuristics that fail to make contact with a rich domain-specific knowledge base are *weak*. But when a domain-specific knowledge base operates without general heuristics, it is brittle—it serves mostly in handling formulaic problems. Although we don't want the weak results of the kind of attention to general heuristics that neglects knowledge base, we also don't want the brittle competency forged by exclusive attention to particularized knowledge! We would hope for more from education. And, according to the synthesis theory, we can get more.

As noted earlier, several contemporary experiments in the direct teaching of cognitive skills have yielded very positive results. Moreover, guidelines are available for classroom practices that can foster the transfer of knowledge and skills (Perkins & Salomon, 1987, 1988). The fact remains, however, that most efforts to cultivate general cognitive skills have not focussed on bringing together context-specific knowledge with general strategic knowledge. Rather, they have taken the form of courses or minicourses segregated from the conventional subject matters and make little effort to link up to subject matter or to nonacademic applications (cf. Nickerson et al., 1985; Segal et al., 1985).

In contrast, the approach that now seems warranted calls for the intimate intermingling of generality and context-specificity in instruction. A few methodologies and educational experiments have addressed exactly that agenda (e.g. Mirman & Tishman, 1988; Palincsar & Brown, 1984; Perkins, 1986; Schoenfeld, 1985; Wales & Stager, 1978). We believe that this direction in education is promising and provocative: It gets beyond educating memories to educating minds, which is what education should be about.

THE CHESS MASTER'S CHANCES

It's high time to return to the chess master's chances of becoming an insightful political and military counsel. In the golden age of general cognitive skills, many might have said, "Give it a try!" albeit with some caveats. After the fall, most would have said, "No way!" Now, what should we say?

The right response seems to be that we should first gather more information about this chess master. Does he already have some general principles ("control the center—any center") rather than entirely contextualized principles ("control the middle squares of the chess board")? How metacognitive is his thinking about his chess play and other life activities? Does he tend to do what

high-road transfer calls for: mindfully decontextualizeprinciples? Or, in contrast, is he a gifted intuitive player of chess, with an enormous fund of experience but little predilection to reflect and generalize? Depending on the answers to such questions, we might forecast his chances as ranging from "No way!" to "There's some hope." Although recognizing the great importance of years of experience in a domain, the latter would be far from a sure bet.

If there is a sure bet to be had, it is that, with the polarized debate about general as opposed to local knowledge quieting down, we are open to learning much more about how general and local knowledge interact in human cognition. And, of course, we can put that understanding to use in educational contexts. We forecast that wider scale efforts to join subject-matter instruction and the teaching of thinking will be one of the exciting stories of the next decade of research and educational innovation.

REFERENCES

Anderson, J. R. (1983). *The architecture of cognition.* Cambridge, MA: Harvard University Press.

Bereiter, C., & Tinker, G. (1988, April). *Consistency of constructive learning effort across domains of high and low cultural familiarity.* Paper presented at the annual meeting of the American Educational Research Association, New Orleans, LA.

Boden, M. (1977). *Artificial intelligence and natural man.* New York: Basic Books.

Brown, A. L., & Kane, M. J. (1988, April). *Cognitive flexibility in young children: The case for transfer.* Symposium paper presented at the Annual Meeting of the American Educational Research Association, New Orleans, LA.

Brown, A. L., Kane, M. J., & Long, C. (in press). Analogical transfer in young children: Analogies as tools for communication and exposition. *Applied Cognitive Psychology.*

Brown, A. L., & Palincsar, A. S. (in press). Guided, cooperative learning and individual knowledge acquisition. In L. Resnick (Ed.), *Knowing and Learning: Essays in honor of Robert Glaser.* Hillsdale, NJ: Erlbaum.

Chan, C., & Burtis, J. (1988). *Level of constructive effort, prior knowledge, and learning.* Paper presented at the annual meeting of the American Educational Research Association. New Orleans, LA.

Chase, W. C., & Simon, H. A. (1973). Perception in chess. *Cognitive Psychology, 4,* 55–81.

Cheng, P. W., & Holyoak, K. J. (1985). Pragmatic reasoning schemas. *Cognitive Psychology, 17,* 391–416.

Chi, M. T. H., Feltovich, P., & Glaser, R. (1981). Categorization and representation of physics problems by experts and novices. *Cognitive Science, 5,* 121–152.

Clancey, W. J. (1986). From GUIDON to NEOMYCIN and HERACLES in twenty short lessons. ONR Final Report, 1979–1985. *AI Magazine, 7,* 40–60.

Clancey, W. J. (1987). *The knowledge engineer as student: Metacognitive bases for asking good questions* (Technical Report STAN-CS-87-1183). Stanford, CA: Department of Computer Science, Stanford University.

Clement, J. (1982). Analogical reasoning patterns in expert problem solving. *Proceedings of the Fourth Annual Conference of the Cognitive Science Society.* Ann Arbor, MI: University of Michigan.

Clement, J. (1982). Students' preconceptions in introductory mechanics. *American Journal of Physics, 50,* 66–71.

Clement, J. (in press). Nonformal reasoning in physics: The use of analogies and extreme cases. In J. Voss, D. N. Perkins, & J. Segal (Eds.), *Informal reasoning.* Hillsdale, NJ: Lawrence Erlbaum Associates.

de Groot, A. D. (1965). *Thought and choice in chess.* The Hague: Mouton.

Ehrlich, K., & Soloway, E. (1984). An empirical investigation of the tacit plan knowledge in programming. In J. Thomas & M. L. Schneider (Eds.), *Human Factors in Computer Systems.* Norwood, NJ: Ablex.

Elstein, A. S., Shulman, L. S., & Sprafka, S. A. (1978). *Medical problem solving: An analysis of clinical reasoning.* Cambridge, MA: Harvard University Press.

Ernst, G. W., & Newell, A. (1969). *GPS: A case study in generality and problem solving.* New York: Academic Press.

Gardner, H. (1983). *Frames of mind.* New York: Basic Books.

Gardner, H. (1985). *The mind's new science.* New York: Basic Books.

Gick, M. L., & Holyoak, K. J. (1987). The cognitive basis for knowledge transfer. In S. M. Cormier & J. D. Hagman (Eds.), *Transfer of learning* (pp. 81–120). New York: Academic.

Glaser, R. (1984). Education and thinking: The role of knowledge. *American Psychologist, 39,* 93–104.

Hayes, J. R., & Simon, H. A. (1977). Psychological differences among problem isomorphs. In N. J. Castellan, Jr., D. B. Pisone, & G. R. Potts (Eds.), *Cognitive theory* (pp. 21–41). Hillsdale, NJ: Erlbaum.

Herrnstein, R. J., Nickerson, R. S., Sanchez, M., & Swets, J. A. (1986). Teaching thinking skills. *American Psychologist, 41,* 1279–1289.

Hirsch, E. D. (1987). *Cultural literacy: What every American needs to know.* Boston, MA: Houghton-Mifflin.

Hunter, J. E. (1986). Cognitive ability, cognitive aptitudes, job knowledge, and job performance. *Journal of Vocational Behavior, 29,* 340–362.

Johnson, P. E., Ahlgren, A., Blount, J. P., & Petit, N. J. (1980). Scientific reasoning: Garden paths and blind alleys. In J. Robinson (Ed.), *Research in science education: New questions, new directions.* Colorado Springs, CO: Biological Sciences Curriculum Study.

Laird, J. E., Rosenbloom, P. S., & Newell, A. (1984). Towards chunking as a general learning mechanism. In *Proceedings of the National Conference on Artificial Intelligence,* (pp. 188–192). Los Altos, CA: W. Kaufman, Inc.

Langer, E. (in press). *Mindfulness.* Reading, MA: Addison-Wesley.

Larkin, J. H. (1982). The cognition of learning physics. *American Journal of Physics, 49,* 534–541.

Larkin, J. H., McDermott, J., Simon, D P., & Simon, H. A. (1980a). Expert and novice performance in solving physics problems. *Science, 208,* 1335–1342.

Larkin, J. H., McDermott, J., Simon, D. P., & Simon, H. A. (1980b). Modes of competence in solving physics problems. *Cognitive Science, 4,* 317–345.

Lehman, D. R., Lempert, R. O., & Nisbett, R. E. (1988). The effects of graduate training on reasoning: Formal discipline and thinking about everyday-life problems. *American Psychologist, 43,* 431–442.

Mirman, J., & Tishman, S. (1988). Infusing thinking through "Connections." *Educational Leadership, 45(7),* 64–65.

Newell, A., & Simon, H. (1972). *Human problem solving.* Englewood Cliffs, NJ: Prentice-Hall.

Ng, E. (1988, April). *Three levels of goal-directedness in learning.* Paper presented at the annual meeting of the American Educational Research Association, New Orleans, LA.

Nickerson, R., Perkins, D. N., & Smith, E. (1985). *The teaching of thinking.* Hillsdale, NJ: Lawrence Erlbaum Associates.

Ogilvie, M., & Steinbach, R. (1988, April). *The development of skill across domains: The role of learning strategies.* Paper presented at the annual meeting of the American Educational Research Association, New Orleans, LA.

Palincsar, A. S., & Brown, A. L. (1984). Reciprocal teaching of comprehension- fostering and comprehension-monitoring activities. *Cognition and Instruction, 1,* 117–175.

Patel, V. L., & Groen, G. J. (1986). Knowledge-based solution strategies in medical reasoning. *Cognitive Science, 10,* 91–116.

Pea, R. D., & Kurland, D. M. (1984). On the cognitive effects of learning computer programming. *New Ideas In Psychology, 2,* 137–168.

Perkins, D. N. (1985). Postprimary education has little impact on informal reasoning. *Journal of Educational Psychology, 77(5),* 562–571.

Perkins, D. N. (1986). *Knowledge as design.* Hillsdale, NJ: Lawrence Erlbaum Associates.

Perkins, D. N. (in press). Reasoning as it is and could be. In D. Topping, D. Crowell, & V. Kobayashi (Eds.), *Thinking: The third international conference.* Hillsdale, NJ: Lawrence Erlbaum Associates.

Perkins, D., & Salomon, G. (1987). Transfer and teaching thinking. In D. N. Perkins, J. Lochhead, & J. Bishop (Eds.), *Thinking: The second international conference* (pp. 285–303). Hillsdale, NJ: Lawrence Erlbaum Associates.

Perkins, D. N. & Salomon, G. (1988). Teaching for transfer. *Educational Leadership, 46*(1), 22–32.

Perkins, D. N., Schwartz, S., & Simmons, R. (in press). Toward a unified theory of problem solving: A view from computer programming. In M. Smith (Ed.), *Toward a unified theory of problem solving*. Hillsdale, NJ: Erlbaum.

Perkins, D. N., & Simmons, R. (1987). Patterns of misunderstanding: An integrative model of misconceptions in science, mathematics, and programming. In J. D. Novak (Ed.), *Proceedings of the second international seminar on misconceptions and educational strategies in science and mathematics* (Vol. 1, pp. 381–395). Ithaca, NY: Cornell University.

Polya, G. (1954). *Mathematics and plausible reasoning* (2 vols.). Princeton, NJ: Princeton University Press.

Polya, G. (1957). *How to solve it: A new aspect of mathematical method* (2nd ed.). Garden City, NY: Doubleday.

Pressley, M., Snyder, B. L., & Cariglia-Bull, T. (1987). How can good strategy use be taught to children? Evaluation of six alternative approaches. In S. M. Cormier & J. D. Hagman (Eds.), *Transfer of learning* (pp. 81–120). New York: Academic.

Rabinowitz, M., & Glaser, R. (1985). Cognitive structure and process in highly competent performance. In F. D. Horowitz & M. O'Brien (Eds.), *The gifted and talented: Developmental perspectives* (pp. 75–98). Washington, DC: American Psychological Association.

Resnick, L. B. (1987). *Education and learning to think.* Washington, DC: National Academy Press.

Rich, E. (1983). *Artificial intelligence.* New York: McGraw-Hill.

Salomon, G. (1988). AI in reverse: Computer tools that turn cognitive. *Journal of Educational Computing Research, 4,* 123–139.

Salomon, G., & Globerson, T. (1987, October). Rocky roads to transfer. *The second Annual Report to the Spencer Foundation.* Israel: Tel-Aviv University.

Salomon, G., & Perkins, D. N. (1987). Transfer of cognitive skills from programming: When and how? *Journal of Educational Computing Research, 3,* 149–169.

Salomon, G., & Perkins, D. N. (in press). Rocky roads to transfer: Rethinking mechanisms of a neglected phenomenon. *Educational Psychologist.*

Schoenfeld, A. H. (1978). Presenting a strategy for indefinite integration. *American Mathematical Monthly, 85,* 673–678.

Schoenfeld, A. H. (1982). Measures of problem-solving performance and of problem-solving instruction. *Journal for Research in Mathematics Education, 13*(1), 31–49.

Schoenfeld, A. H. (1985). *Mathematical problem solving.* New York: Academic Press.

Schoenfeld, A. H., & Herrmann, D. J. (1982). Problem perception and knowledge structure in expert and novice mathematical problem solvers. *Journal of Experimental Psychology: Learning, Memory, and Cognition, 8,* 484–494.

Scribner, S., & Cole, M. (1981). *The psychology of literacy.* Cambridge, MA: Harvard University Press.

Segal, J. W., Chipman, S. F., & Glaser, R. (Eds.). (1985). *Thinking and learning skills, Volume 1: Relating instruction to research.* Hillsdale, NJ: Lawrence Erlbaum Associates.

Strauss, S. (1987). Educational-development psychology and school learning. In L. S. Liben (Ed.), *Development and learning: Conflict or congruence?* (pp. 133–158). Hillsdale, NJ: Erlbaum.

Thorndike, E. L. (1923). The influence of first year Latin upon the ability to read English. *School Sociology, 17,* 165–168.

Thorndike, E. L., & Woodworth, R. S. (1901). The influence of improvement in one mental function upon the efficiency of other functions. *Psychological Review, 8,* 247–261.

Toulmin, S. E. (1958). *The uses of argument.* Cambridge, England: Cambridge University Press.

Wales, C. E., & Nardi, A. (1984). *Successful decision-making.* Morgantown, WV: West Virginia University, Center for Guided Design.

Wales, C. E., & Stager, R. A. (1978). *The guided design approach.* Englewood Cliffs, NJ: Educational Technology Publications.

Wason, P. C. (1966). Reasoning. In B. M. Foss (Ed.), *New horizons in psychology.* Harmondsworth, England: Penguin.

Wenger, E. (1987). *Artificial intelligence and tutoring systems: Computational and cognitive approaches to the communication of knowledge.* Los Altos, CA: Morgan Kaufmann Publishers.

Acknowledgements: The writing of this paper was partially supported by a grant given jointly to Gavriel Salomon and to the late Tamar Globerson by the Spencer Foundation.

► Chapter 9

Sorting Out the Self-Esteem Controversy

JAMES A. BEANE

The idea of enhancing self-esteem seems innocent enough to most people. Common sense suggests that those who have positive self-esteem are likely to lead satisfying lives while those who do not are just as likely to find life dissatisfying and unhappy. Yet, like so many other seemingly common-sensical things, the idea of self-esteem has become a source of considerable controversy and contention in the school context. So it is that, as we enter the 1990s, another "great debate" is emerging. This one is about whether schools ought to try to enhance self-esteem and, if so, how, on what grounds, and to what extent?

That the school might play a role in the development of self-esteem is not a recent idea. it has been part of educational thinking for most of this century, particularly since the 1960s, when many educators came to realize that affect in general and self-esteem specifically loom large in school life.[1] But it was in the 1980s that self-esteem was catapulted into educational policy thinking. It became linked not only to academic achievement but also to substance abuse, antisocial acts, adolescent pregnancy, suicide, and other self-destructive behaviors. The theory was this: people, including the young, will not hurt themselves if they like themselves. Moreover, if they have self-confidence, they are more likely to do well at whatever they might try to do.

James A. Beane is a Professor in the National College of Education at National-Louis University, Evanston, Ill. He can be reached at 928 West Shore Dr., Madison, WI 53715.

This theory has driven many states and school districts to add development of self-esteem to their list of goals. It also served as the underlying theme of the notorious California self-esteem project that simultaneously appealed to the most humane impulses of some while offending the Puritan streak of self-denial that still runs deep in the values of others.[2] Meanwhile, in the schools, the terrain is cluttered with conflicting and contradictory theories about self-esteem and ways to enhance it. The purpose of this article is to sort out this "mess" and to make some sense out of the idea of enhancing self-esteem in schools.

WHY ENHANCE SELF-ESTEEM?

The argument for enhancing self-esteem in schools follows three lines of reasoning. The first speaks to the school's role as a social agency that is meant to contribute to the general health and well-being of young people. We are living in very complex times. This is the age of discontinuity and disbelief, of ambiguity and ambivalence. As difficult as it is for so many adults to find anything to hang on to, we can only imagine what this age looks like through the eyes of young people who typically lack the resources that are available to most adults. The litany of statistics about self-destructive tendencies such as substance abuse, crime, and suicide must surely be seen as a signal from young people that many do not find much about themselves to like. The idea of enhancing self-esteem becomes a moral imperative for schools, especially in a time when other social institutions and agencies seem unwilling or unable to provide support and encouragement in the process of rowing up.

The second line of reasoning is found within the school itself. When we look at the rowing collection of studies on self-esteem, we find a persistent correlation between it and such school concerns as participation, completion, self-direction, and various types of achievement.[3] This last correlation, between self-esteem and achievement, is a driving force in the growing interest in self-esteem. Nonetheless, it is widely misunderstood. The correlation is relatively weak when global self-esteem is involved but strong when self-esteem is situation-specific, as in the case, for example, of self-esteem in mathematics, reading, physical education, or some other area.[4] This link between self-esteem and school concerns ought to persuade those who have trouble with the moral argument that they, too, have a vested interest in enhancing self-esteem.

The third line of reasoning is less often used, yet more powerful. It extends the idea of personal development beyond coping with problems and into personal efficacy or power, which, in turn, may lead toward action.[5] Only the most ignorant or arrogant could fail to see that we face increasing problems with inequitable distribution of wealth, power, and justice. Conditions like racism, sexism, poverty, and homelessness detract from human dignity and for that reason debilitate one of its central features, self-esteem. The resolution of these issues will depend less on rhetoric and more on action, but action is not likely unless people believe they can make a difference.

When looked at this way, enhancing self-esteem helps build the personal and collective efficacy that helps us out of the morass of inequity that plagues us. Needless to say, the hint of social reconstructionism in this line of reasoning may account for its absence in most of the rhetoric of the self-esteem movement. Nevertheless it is a powerful argument for the schools, which have a responsibility to extend democracy, human dignity, and cultural diversity throughout the larger society.

VERSIONS OF SELF-ESTEEM IN SCHOOL

Over the past few decades, the idea of enhancing self-esteem in schools has become increasingly popular. True, many school officials have questioned the idea by contending they have enough on their hands, with the deluge of mandates coming down from state legislatures, without having to take on issues that ought to be addressed by the home and other "socializing" agencies. Certainly not all of these people are uncaring toward young people; often they speak out of frustration over multiplying demands placed upon the school and taking the flack for any lack of progress on these demands. Even so, such protests have diminished as the evidence linking self-esteem and school success has grown.

Now the issue is not *whether* the schools should try to enhance the self-esteem of young people, but *how*. It is here that we encounter the cluttered terrain of conflicting and contradictory methods for enhancing self-esteem. There are three main approaches that account for most efforts in this area.

The first approach follows from personal development activities, such as sensitivity training, that enjoyed some popularity in the late 1960s and early 1970s. To envision how this approach is practiced, we might picture a teacher and a group of students sitting in a circle talking about how much they like themselves and everyone else for 20 minutes on a Wednesday afternoon. Such activities are like parlor games of pop psychology and, no doubt, have about the same momentary effects in real life. Saying "I like myself and others" in front of a group is not necessarily the same as actually feeling that way, especially if I am only doing it because I am supposed to. Being nice has a place in enhancing self-esteem, but it is not enough.

The second approach involves putting young people through a self-esteem program or course offered in a set-aside time slot during the school day. Here the teacher comes armed with more than good feelings, namely a self-esteem "curriculum," locally prepared or commercially purchased, assuring that students who go through the program will have better self-esteem and thus be immune to self-destructive behaviors and school failure. In 1970 Weinstein and Fantini estimated that there were at least 350 such programs with about 3,000 "affective exercises and techniques."[6] The number may be greater now, although I estimate that about 30 are widely known and used.[7] That schools would buy a package to enhance self-esteem is not surprising when we remember that the commodification of the self was an idea promoted in the 1980s. If "we are what we buy," then perhaps we can also buy our way into self-esteem.

The "self-esteem program" approach suffers from two problems, one practical and the other conceptual. Hartshorne and May, in the late 1920s, showed that direct instruction in courselike settings does not produce lasting or strong effects in the affective domain.[8] While their research focused on character education, similar conclusions were drawn more recently by Lockwood and others in reviewing studies on values clarification and moral development.[9] Aside from glowing testimonials by participants (which cannot be completely disregarded) after self-esteem programs, there is scant evidence to warrant claims made by program developers.

Current research suggests that one area in which packaged programs evidence little short-term gain is "self in school."[10] This may seem hard to believe when we remember that such programs are sponsored and taught in schools by school personnel. Yet why would we expect otherwise if there is no guarantee that anyone in any other place in the school will care much about newfound self-esteem, personal goals, or decision-making skills?

Beyond that, self-esteem programs suffer from a conceptual problem that they share with most personal development programs. Their underlying theory is that to enhance self-esteem we must go inside individuals and encourage them to push ahead with confidence, even in the face of difficult odds. Such an inside-out approach ignores the fact that in the balance of interactions between the individual and the environment out of which self-esteem grows, the environment is almost inevitably more powerful. If we want to enhance self-esteem, we must first check to see whether the social environment is safe for the individual. A debilitating environment is likely to squash fledgling self-confidence no matter how much we exhort the individual to persist. We may all know individuals who have defied this rule, but the fact that we can name them suggests they are the exception rather than the rule.

Since the environment powerfully informs their self-perceptions, insisting that young people are responsible for their own self-esteem is blatantly unjust. Moreover, suggesting that self-esteem can be preserved by developing "coping skills" endorses the status quo and, in so doing, ignores the fact that having positive self-esteem is almost impossible for many young people, given the deplorable conditions under which they are forced to live by the inequities in our society.

The third approach to enhancing self-esteem in school recognizes the power of the environment and searches for possibilities across the whole institution.[11] Every nook and cranny in the school has the potential to enhance or debilitate self-esteem. For example, a school that enhances self-esteem could be characterized by a humanistic and democratic climate, student participation in governance, heterogeneous grouping, and positive expectations. In the areas of curriculum and teaching, a premium would be placed upon collaborative teacher-student planning, cooperative learning, thematic units that emphasize personal and social meanings, student self-evaluation, multicultural content, community service projects, and activities that involve making, creating, and "doing." This approach also emphasizes the need to enhance adults' self-esteem, particularly teachers', since it is unlikely they can contribute to positive self-esteem in young people if their own is negative.

Proponents of this third approach recognize that even our most salutary efforts in the area of self-esteem are threatened by poor conditions outside the school. To what extent can we expect progress within the school to stand up in the face of poverty, homelessness, racism, sexism, and ageism? Hence, we must place the larger community and society under the same scrutiny as the school, so that we may see what work is needed there.

THE GREAT SELF-ESTEEM DEBATE

Recently the argument over which approach to use in enhancing self-esteem has been overshadowed by a much larger debate concerning the assumption that positive self-esteem is necessary for school achievement. Three factors fuel this debate. First, it seems that while young people in South Korea and Japan score higher than those in the United States on international comparison tests in mathematics, the U.S. students come out on top in measures of self-esteem.[12] Second, there has been considerable backlash against the California task force report on self-esteem, which is seen by many people as an unsupported statement of New Age, pop psychology "fluff."[13] Third, the present Conservative Restoration in education and elsewhere rings with the rhetoric of self-denial that those of the New Right believe is necessary for "repairing" the "frayed" moral fabric of society.[14] Put together, these factors make a superficially convincing argument against the usual view of enhancing self-esteem, yet one that can be packaged in neat slogans like the title of a *Time* magazine commentary, "Education: Doing Bad and Feeling Good."[15]

However, when this rhetoric is examined, its transparency is revealed. For example, I asked some South Korean, Japanese, and Chinese educators to explain how they might account for the inverse correlation between self-esteem and mathematics scores reported from the international comparisons of achievement. Their uncomplicated answer was this: "In our cultures it is impolite to say one can do well, even if one thinks so." While this is not evidence to end the argument, it at least raises the question of whether United States' students are arrogant incompetents or victims of criticism based upon culturally embedded differences in educational findings.[16]

As for the other two factors, we might easily write off the first as an interpretation of a report (that of the California Task Force) that represents a sometimes unclear vision of enhancing self-esteem[17] and the second as another piece of the belt-tightening rhetoric of 1980s educational "reform." We might further ask when and how young people were excluded from the right to be happy. And one might facetiously suggest that the international tests indicate that we who value self-esteem are doing a good job with it while those enamored with academic achievement are not pulling their weight. These criticisms should not be taken so lightly, however, because they have deeper implications.

First, by focusing only on the pop psychology school of enhancing self-esteem, these criticisms ignore other versions which are quite different from it. In so doing, the very idea of self-esteem enhancement is threatened by the same red-flag mentality that fails to differentiate between the cross-curriculum values clarification theory and the collections of cute activities, like the venerable "lifeboat" simulation, that ruined its reputation.

Even more dangerous is the kind of statement made by critic Mike Schmoker: "Self-esteem, as it is now used, isn't something earned, but given."[18] "The fact is that it is neither. In its practical form, self-esteem is personally constructed out of interactions with the environment; in other words, it is learned. At a conceptual level self-esteem is a central feature in human dignity and thus an inalienable human entitlement.[19] As such, schools and other agencies have a moral obligation to help build it and avoid debilitating it. The "no pain, no gain"

metaphor may be justified in the weight room, but it is dangerous in human development, especially when pain is already inequitably distributed and gain so inequitably accessible. The failure to recognize the obligation to enhance self-esteem works harshly against all young people, but particularly so against those in our society who are least privileged.

So that I do not seem to be imagining this last point, another illustration from the self-esteem critics might be helpful. One of the more obvious ways to contribute to clear self-concept and positive self-esteem is to expand curriculum content in ways that include the stories of diverse cultures so that more young people can see themselves as part of what is valued in the school's curriculum. Yet Krauthammer, for example, extends his concern about self-esteem enhancement into an attack on multicultural inclusion in the curriculum. Among other things, he claims "there is little to be said . . . about the contribution of women to the Bill of Rights."[20] Perhaps so, but there is much to be said about why; and young people, especially women, should not be denied the opportunity to find out. Nor should all young people, especially Native Americans, be left ignorant of the influence of the "Great Law of the Iroquois" on early documents of white, United States democracy like the Articles of Confederation and the Bill of Rights.[21] Criticism of multicultural education and its connection to self-esteem is a thinly veiled version of the Eurocentric arrogance that has marred schools and is unbecoming in a culturally diverse society.

I believe that the "Great Debate" over self-esteem at this level should be seen for exactly what it is: a part of the tug-of-war between the long line of progressive efforts to create humane schools and the new Conservative Restoration that grew up in the 1980s. The latter is not a unidimensional movement. It is a package that involves interrelated interests of economic utilitarianism, classical Eurocentric humanism, and old-line "get tough" pedagogy. There is little room for the idea of enhancing self-esteem beyond its relation to individual achievement, especially as it is broadly defined in the context of personal efficacy and the resolution of large social inequities. This package marginalizes the same nonprivileged young people upon whom the schools have always worked most harshly and continues the unjust status they have historically been assigned.

In saying this, I do not mean to glorify or over-romanticize the self- esteem "movement." Many of those involved in it still fail to differentiate between self-concept (the description of self) and self-esteem (the evaluation of self) or to understand the intricate role played by values in self-esteem judgments.[22] Efforts to improve self-perceptions must contribute to the quality of all three dimensions. For example, multicultural education and cooperative learning have as much to do with expanding the concept of self and promoting the value of interdependence as they do with self-esteem. Critics such as those cited above apparently do not understand this, but their analyses seem all the more accurate when people inside the schools also do not.

Moreover, as I have pointed out, the self-esteem movement is still full of the kind of fluff and radical individualism that is as threatening to authentic progressivism as the conservative restoration. In fact, the overly individualistic tendencies of many self-esteem programs and projects play right into the hands of that restoration by focusing on self-protection mechanisms rather than the environment that creates their need. This is, of course, "privatizing" at its extreme. It is a theory of alienation that pits the individual against the world.

BEYOND THE "MESS"

In retrospect, it may seem ironic that the idea of enhancing self-esteem would become a buzzword amidst the hardening of academic categories in the 1980s. As we have seen, however, this should not be surprising since that idea has many different meanings, some of which fit rather well with the Horatio Alger reform notions in the last decade. The important question now focuses on what we will do to find our way out of the confusion and contradiction that has arisen.

I suggest that we stop seeing self-esteem only in individualistic terms and move instead toward an integrated view of self and social relations. This transition would involve at least three main parts. First, the construction of personal meanings should be understood as emerging from interactions with the environment. Self-perceptions are a central feature of human personality from which flow many social manifestations, but environment powerfully informs self-perceptions. Moreover, it is clear that people do not learn about themselves either apart from or prior to learning about their world. Rather, they learn about both simultaneously and in light of their interdependence.

Second, self-esteem is properly seen as one dimension of the larger concept of affect that also involves values, morals, ethics, character, and the like, and is connected to cognition. By itself, self-esteem addresses only part of what Dewey called the "affective-ideational" connection that underlies social relations.[23] When we make self-esteem decisions, we do so on the basis of our values.[24] Moreover, such decisions involve thinking; they may be more or less thoughtful, but they are not empty of thought.[25] Thus, if schooling for self-esteem does not simultaneously address other aspects of affect as well as cognition, it is incomplete and artificial.

Third, self-esteem alone is an incomplete definition of the concept of human dignity upon which work on self-esteem is partly justified. It is not enough that young people like themselves. They must also have a sense that what they say, and think, and do counts for something. In other words, self-esteem must be accompanied by a sense of personal efficacy. But even that is not enough. Individuals do not live in isolation, and to imply such is dangerous. Personal efficacy must be connected to collective efficacy so that individuals see themselves as part of groups that can and do have meaning and power. In making this point, I am connecting the idea of enhancing self-esteem to the broader themes of democracy, human dignity, and cultural diversity—themes that ostensibly permeate the lives of those in our society.[26]

What does this mean for schools' role in enhancing self-esteem? It means they must place a premium on authentic participation, collaborative action, a problem-centered curriculum, and interdependent diversity. Likewise, they should work to remove policies and practices that can debilitate self-esteem like tracking, autocratic procedures, unicultural curriculum, and competition.

This kind of effort is not without controversy. After all, it suggests that people not only feel good about themselves, but also come to believe they can change things. Perhaps it is here that the gatekeepers of the school as well as the advocates of the conservative restoration sense the real problem with self-esteem. Perhaps it is here, too, that we may understand the individualistic "coping strategies" of packaged programs as something of a failure of nerve. Work with self-esteem that promotes integration of self and social interests and personal and social efficacy offers the possibility that young people will challenge the status quo, not simply accept it. Besides, the very idea of packaged programs seems largely inappropriate for any genuine work with self-esteem.

In the end we are faced with some very serious challenges. Finding our way out of the self-esteem "mess" must begin with several understandings. First, being nice is surely a part of this effort, but it is not enough. Second, there is a place for some direct instruction regarding affective matters, but this is not enough either. Self-esteem and affect are not simply another school subject to be placed in set-aside time slots. Third, the negative affect of "get tough" policies is not a promising route to self-esteem and efficacy. This simply blames young people for problems that are largely not of their own making. Fourth, since self-perceptions are powerfully informed by culture, comparing self-esteem across cultures without clarifying cultural differences is distracting and unproductive.

Authentic work in the area of self-esteem is more complex than most people, including participants in the great debate, have been willing to admit. It involves broadening our understanding of the reasons behind such work, extending the definition of self-esteem into a larger concept of affect that integrates self and social interests, extending self-enhancement efforts across the entire school, and relating the work of the school with the larger world of conditions that detract from human dignity. Self-esteem is not just a psychological construct. It also has meaning for creating and understanding the philosophical and sociological themes that permeate our lives. Clearly, enhancing self-esteem is not the soft or simple work that so many people believe it to be.

1. See, for example, A. W. Combs, ed., (1962), *Perceiving, Behaving Becoming: A New Focus for Education*, (Washington, D.C.: Association for Supervision and Curriculum Development).

2. California Task Force to Promote Self-Esteem and Personal and Social Responsibility, (1990), *Toward a State of Esteem*, (Sacramento: State of California). The report was supplemented by a larger volume: A. M. Mecca, N. S. Smelser, and J. Vasconellos, (1989), *The Social importance of Self-Esteem*, (Berkeley: University of California Press).

3. See, for example, W. W. Purkey, (1970), *Self-Concept and School Achievement*, (Englewood Cliffs, N.J.: Prentice-Hall); M. Rosenberg, (1979), *Conceiving the Self* (New York: Basic Books); and J. A. Beane and R. P. Lipka, (1986), *Self-Concept, Self-Esteem and the Curriculum*, (New York: Teachers College Press).

4. B. M. Byrne, (1984), "The General/Academic Self-Concept Nomological Network: A Review of Construct Validation Research," *Review of Educational Research* 54: 427–456.

5. J. A. Beane, (1990), *Affect in the Curriculum: Toward Democracy, Dignity and Diversity* (New York: Teachers College Press).

6. G. Weinstein and M. D. Fantini, (1970), *Toward Humanistic Education: A Curriculum of Affect*, (New York: Praeger).

7. A content analysis of many of theses is included in A. M. Kaiser-Carlso, (1986), *A Program Description and Analysis of Self-Esteem Programs for the Junior High School*, (Santa Clara, Calif: Educational Development Center).

8. H. Hartshorne and M. A. May, (1928, 1929, 1930, respectively), *Studies in the Nature of Character: Volume I: Studies in Deceit, Volume II: Studies in Service and Self-Control, Volume III* (with F. K. Shuttleworth): *Studies in the Organization of Character*, (New York: Macmillan.)

9. See, for example, A. L. Lockwood, (1978), "The Effects of Values Clarification and Moral Development Curricula on School-Age Subjects: A Critical Review of Research," *Review of Educational Research* 48: 325–64; J. S. Leming, (1981), "Curricular Effectiveness in Value/Moral Education," *Journal of Moral Education* 10: 147–64.

10. See, for example, P. E. Crisci, (1986). "The Quest National Center: A Focus on Prevention of Alienation," *Phi Delta Kappan* 67: 440–42.

11. See, for example, Beane and Lipka, op. cit.

12. C. Krauthammer, (February 5, 1990), "Education: Doing Bad and Feeling Good," *Time*, p. 78.

13. See, for example, J. Leo, (April 2. 1990), "The Trouble With Self-Esteem," U.S. *News and World Report*, p. 16. The California report was also a target, on these same grounds, of *Doonesbury* cartoonist Gary Trudeau.

14. See B. Ehrenreich, (1989), *Fear of Falling: The Inner Life of the Middle Class*, (New York: Random House). Ehrenreich argues that self-denial is a persistent theme in the rhetoric, if not the real lives, of the professional/managerial middle class.

15. Krauthammer, op. cit.

16. This same critique might be aimed at most of the reactive instruments typically used to "measure" self-esteem since the statements that make up the instruments reflect the values of their developer(s) and not necessarily those of the young people who are subjected to them.

17. In what may have been anticipation of this criticism, the California Task Force expanded its work to include the connection of self-esteem to personal and social responsibility.

18. M. Schmoker, (January-February 1990). "Self-Esteem Is Earned, Not Learned," newsletter of the Thomas Jefferson Center, pp. 1 ff.

19. Beane, op. cit.

20. Krauthammer, op. cit.

21. D. Grinde, (1988), "It Is Time to Take Away the Veil," *Northeast Indian Quarterly* 4 and 5: 28–34. Two Iroquois ideas that the framers of the white documents of democracy "forgot" were equality of women and the prohibition of slavery.

22. J. A. Beane and R. P. Lipka, "Self-Concept and Self-Esteem: A Construct Differentiation," *Child Study Journal* 10: 1–6.

23. J. Dewey, (1939), *Theory of Valuation*, (Chicago: University of Chicago Press).

24. Beane and Lipka, op. cit.

25. Beane, op. cit.

26. For further discussion of these ideas, see Beane, op. cit.

Students Need Challenge, Not Easy Success

MARGARET M. CLIFFORD

Hundreds of thousands of apathetic students abandon their schools each year to begin lives of unemployment, poverty, crime, and psychological distress. According to Hahn (1987), "Dropout rates ranging from 40 to 60 percent in Boston, Chicago, Los Angeles, Detroit, and other major cities point to a situation of crisis proportions." The term *dropout* may not be adequate to convey the disastrous consequences of the abandonment of school by children and adolescents; *educational suicide* may be a far more appropriate label.

School abandonment is not confined to a small percentage of minority students, or low ability children, or mentally lazy kids. It is a systemic failure affecting the most gifted and knowledgeable as well as the disadvantaged, and it is threatening the social, economical, intellectual, industrial, cultural, moral, and psychological well-being of our country. Equally disturbing are students who sever themselves from the flow of knowledge while they occupy desks, like mummies.

Student apathy, indifference, and underachievement are typical precursors of school abandonment. But what causes these symptoms? Is there a remedy? What will it take to stop the waste of our intellectual and creative resources?

To address these questions, we must acknowledge that educational suicide is primarily a motivational problem—not a physical, intellectual, financial, technological, cultural, or staffing problem. Thus, we must turn to motivational theories and research as a foundation for examining this problem and for identifying solutions.

Curiously enough, modern theoretical principles of motivation do not support certain widespread practices in education. I will discuss four such discrepancies and offer suggestions for resolving them.

MODERATE SUCCESS PROBABILITY IS ESSENTIAL TO MOTIVATION

The maxim, "Nothing succeeds like success," has driven educational practice for several decades. Absolute success for students has become the means *and* the end of education: It has been given higher priority than learning, and it has obstructed learning.

A major principle of current motivation theory is that tasks associated with a moderate probability of success (50 percent) provide maximum satisfaction (Atkinson 1964). Moderate probability of success is also an essential ingredient of intrinsic motivation (Lepper and Greene 1978, Csikszentmihalyi 1975, 1978). We attribute the success we experience on easy tasks task ease; we attribute the success we experience on extremely difficult tasks to luck. Neither type of success does much to enhance self-image. It is only success at moderately difficult or truly challenging tasks that we explain in terms of personal effort, well-chosen

Margaret M. Clifford is Professor of Educational Psychology, University of Iowa, College of Education, Iowa City, IA 52242.

strategies, and ability; and these explanations give rise to feelings of pride, competence, determination, satisfaction, persistence, and personal control. Even very young children show a preference for tasks that are just a bit beyond their ability (Danner and Lonky 1981).

Consistent with these motivational findings, learning theorists have repeatedly demonstrated that moderately difficult tasks are a prerequisite for maximizing intellectual development (Fischer 1980). But despite the fact that moderate challenge (implying considerable error-making) is essential for maximizing learning and optimizing motivation, many educators attempt to create error-proof learning environments. They set minimum criteria and standards in hopes of ensuring success for all students. They often reduce task difficulty, overlook errors, de-emphasize failed attempts, ignore faulty performances, display "perfect papers," minimize testing, and reward error-free performance.

It is time for educators to replace easy success with challenge. We must encourage students to reach beyond their intellectual grasp and allow them the privilege of learning from mistakes. There must be a tolerance for error-making in every classroom, and gradual success rather than continual success must become the yardstick by which learning is judged. Such transformations in educational practices will not guarantee the elimination of educational suicide, but they are sure to be one giant step in that direction.

EXTERNAL CONSTRAINTS ERODE MOTIVATION AND PERFORMANCE

Intrinsic motivation and performance determine when external constraints such as surveillance, evaluation by others, deadlines, threats, bribes, and rewards are accentuated. Yes, even rewards are a form of constraint! The reward giver is the General who dictates rules and issues orders; rewards are used to keep the troops in line.

Means-end contingencies, as exemplified in the statement, "If you complete your homework, you may watch TV" (with homework being the means and TV the end), are another form of external constraint. Such contingencies decrease interest in the first task (homework, the means) and increase interest in the second task (TV, the end) (Boggiano and Main 1986).

Externally imposed constraints, including material rewards, decrease task interest, reduce creativity, hinder performance, and encourage passivity on the part of students—even preschoolers (Lepper and Hodell 1989)! Imposed constraints also prompt individuals to use the "minimax strategy"—to exert the minimum amount of effort needed to obtain the maximum amount of reward (Kruglanski et al. 1977). Supportive of these findings are studies showing that autonomous behavior—that which is self-determined, freely chosen, and personally controlled—elicits high risk interest, creativity, cognitive flexibility, positive emotion, and persistence (Deci and Ryan 1987).

Unfortunately, constraint and lack of student autonomy are trademarks of most schools. Federal and local governments, as well as teachers, legislate academic requirements; impose guidelines, create rewards systems; mandate behavioral contracts; serve warnings of expulsion, and use rules, threats, and punishments as routine problem-solving strategies. We can legislate school attendance and the conditions for obtaining a diploma, but we cannot legislate the development of intelligence, talent, creativity, and intrinsic motivation—resources this country desperately needs.

It is time for educators to replace coercive, constraint-laden techniques with autonomy-supportive techniques. We must redesign instructional and evaluation materials and procedures so that every assignment, quiz, test, project, and discussion activity not only allows for, but routinely *requires*, carefully calculated decision making on the part of students. Instead of minimum criteria, we must define multiple criteria (levels of minimum, marginal, average, good, superior, and excellent achievement), and we must free students to choose criteria that provide optimum challenge. Constraint gives a person the desire to escape; freedom gives a person the desire to explore, expand, and create.

PROMPT, SPECIFIC FEEDBACK ENHANCES LEARNING

A third psychological principle is that specific and prompt feedback enhances learning, performance, and motivation (Ilgen et al. 1979, Larson 1984). Informational feedback (that which reveals correct responses) increases learning (Ilgen and Moore 1987) and also promotes a feeling of increased competency (Sansone 1986). Feedback that can be used to improve future performance has powerful motivational value.

Sadly, however, the proportion of student assignments or activities that are promptly returned with informational feedback tends to be low. Students typically complete an assignment and then wait one, two, or three days (sometimes weeks) for its return. The feedback they do get often consists of a number or letter grade accompanied by ambiguous comments such as "Is this your best?" or "Keep up the good work." Precisely what is good or what needs improving is seldom communicated.

But, even if we could convince teachers of the value of giving students immediate, specific, informational feedback, our feedback problem would still be far from solved. How can one teacher provide 25 or more students immediate feedback on their tasks? Some educators argue that the solution to the feedback problem lies in having a tutor or teacher aide for every couple of students. Others argue that adequate student feedback will require an increased use of computer technology. However, there are less expensive alternatives. First, answer keys for students should be more plentiful. Resource books containing review and study activities should be available in every subject area, and each should be accompanied by a key that is available to students.

Second, quizzes and other instructional activities, especially those that supplement basic textbooks, should be prepared with "latent image" processing. With latent image paper and pens, a student who marks a response to an item can watch a hidden symbol emerge. The symbol signals either a correct or incorrect response, and in some instances a clue or explanation for the response is revealed. Trivia and puzzle books equipped with this latent image, immediate feedback process are currently being marketed at the price of comic books.

Of course, immediate informational feedback is more difficult to provide for composition work, long-term projects, and field assignments. But this does not justify the absence of immediate feedback on the learning activities and practice exercises that are aimed at teaching concepts, relationships, and basic skills. The mere availability of answer keys and latent image materials would probably elicit an amazing amount of self-regulated learning on the part of many students.

MODERATE RISK TAKING IS A TONIC FOR ACHIEVEMENT

A fourth motivational research finding is that moderate risk taking increases performance, persistence, perceived competence, self-knowledge, pride, and satisfaction (Deci and Porac 1978, Harter 1978, Trope 1979). Moderate risk taking implies a well-considered choice of an optimally challenging task, willingness to accept a moderate probability of success, and the anticipation of an outcome. It is this combination of events (which includes moderate success, self-regulated learning, and feedback) that captivates the attention, interest, and energy of card players, athletes, financial investors, lottery players, and even juvenile video arcade addicts.

Risk takers continually and freely face the probability of failing to attain the pleasure of succeeding under specified odds. From every risk-taking endeavor—whether it ends in failure or success—risk takers learn something about their skill and choice of strategy, and what they learn usually prompts them to seek another risk-taking opportunity. Risk taking—especially moderate risk taking—is a mind-engaging activity that simultaneously consumes and generates energy. It is a habit that feeds itself and thus requires an unlimited supply of risk-taking opportunities.

Moderate risk taking is likely to occur under the following conditions.

- The success probability for each alternative is clear and unambiguous.
- Imposed external constraints are minimized.
- Variable payoff (the value of success increases as risk increases) in contrast to fixed payoff is available.
- The benefits of risk taking can be anticipated.

My own recent research on academic risk taking with grade school, high school, and college students generally supports these conclusions. Students do, in fact, freely choose more difficult problems (a) when the number of points offered increases with the difficulty level of problems, (b) when the risk-taking task is presented within a game or practice situation (i.e., imposed constraint or threat is minimized), and (c) when additional opportunities for risk taking are anticipated (relatively high risk taking will occur on a practice exercise when students know they will be able to apply the information learned to an upcoming test). In the absence of these conditions we have seen students choose tasks that are as much as one-and-a-half years below their achievement level (Clifford, 1988). Finally, students who take moderately high risks express high task interest even though they experience considerable error making.

In summary, risk-taking opportunities for students should be (a) plentiful, (b) readily available, (c) accompanied by explicit information about success probabilities, (d) accompanied by immediate feedback that communicates competency and error information, (e) associated with payoffs that vary with task difficulty, (f) relatively free from externally imposed evaluation, and (g) presented in relaxing and nonthreatening environments.

In today's educational world, however, there are few opportunities for students to engage in academic risk taking and no incentives to do so. Choices are seldom provided within tests or assignments, and rarely are variable payoffs made available. Once again, motivational theory, which identifies risk taking as a powerful source of knowledge, motivation, and skill development, conflicts with educational practice, which seeks to minimize academic risk at all costs.

We must restructure materials and procedures to encourage moderate academic risk taking on the part of students. I predict that if we fill our classrooms with optional academic risk-taking materials and opportunities so that all students have access to moderate risks, we will not only lower our educational suicide rate, but we will raise our level of academic achievement. If we give students the license to take risks and make errors, they will likely experience genuine success and the satisfaction that accompanies it.

USING RISK CAN ENSURE SUCCESS

Both theory and research evidence lead to the prediction that academic risk-taking activities are a powerful means of increasing the success of our educational efforts. But how do we get students to take risks on school-related activities? Students will choose risk over certainty when the consequences of the former are more satisfying and informative. Three basic conditions are needed to ensure such outcomes.

- First, students must be allowed to freely select from materials and activities that vary in difficulty and probability of success.

- Second, as task difficulty increases, so too must the payoffs for success.
- Third, an environment tolerant of error making and supportive of error correction must be guaranteed.

The first two conditions can be met rather easily. For example, on a 10-point quiz, composed of six 1-point items and four 2-point items, students might be asked to select and work only 6 items. The highest possible score for such quizzes is 10 and can be obtained only by correctly answering the four 2-point items and any two 1-point items. Choice and variable payoff are easily built into quizzes and many instructional and evaluation activities.

The third condition, creating an environment tolerant of error making and supportive of error correction, is more difficult to ensure. But here are six specific suggestions.

First, teachers must make a clear distinction between formative evaluation activities (tasks, that guide instruction during the learning process) and summative evaluation activities (tasks used to judge one's level of achievement and to determine one's grade at the completion of the learning activity). Practice exercises, quizzes, and skill-building activities aimed at acquiring and strengthening knowledge and skills exemplify formative evaluation. These activities promote learning and skill development. They should be scored in a manner that excludes ability judgments, emphasizes error detection and correction, and encourages a search for better learning strategies. Formative evaluation activities should generally provide immediate feedback and be scored by students. It is on these activities that moderate risk taking is to be encouraged and is likely to prove beneficial.

Major examinations (unit exams and comprehensive final exams) exemplify summative evaluation; these activities are used to determine course grades. Relatively low risk taking is to be expected on such tasks, and immediate feedback may or may not be desirable.

Secondly, formative evaluation activities should be far more plentiful than summative. If, in fact, learning rather than grading is the primary objective of the school, the percentage of time spent on summative evaluation should be small in comparison to that spent on formative evaluation (perhaps about 1:4). There should be enough formative evaluation activities presented as risk-taking opportunities to satisfy the most enthusiastic and adventuresome learner. The more plentiful these activities are, the less anxiety-producing and aversive summative activities are likely to be.

Third, formative evaluation activities should be presented as optional; students should be enticed, not mandated, to complete these activities. Enticement might be achieved by (a) ensuring that these activities are course-relevant and varied (e.g., scrambled outlines, incomplete matrices and graphs, exercises that require error detection and correction, quizzes); (b) giving students the option of working together; (c) presenting risk-taking activities in the context of games to be played individually, with competitors, or with partners; (d) providing immediate, informational, nonthreatening feedback; and (e) defining success primarily in terms of improvement over previous performance or the amount of learning that occurs during the risk-taking activity.

Fourth, for every instructional and evaluation activity there should be at least a modest percentage of content (10 percent to 20 percent) that poses a challenge to even the best students completing the activity. Maximum development of a country's talent requires that all individuals (a) find challenge in tasks they attempt, (b) develop tolerance for error making, and (c) learn to adjust strategies when faced with failure. To deprive the most talented students of these opportunities is perhaps the greatest resource- development crime a country can commit.

Fifth, summative evaluation procedures should include "retake exams." Second chances will not only encourage risk taking but will provide good reasons for students to study their incorrect responses made on previous risk-taking tasks. Every error made on an initial exam and subsequently corrected on a second chance represents real learning.

Sixth, we must reinforce moderate academic risk taking instead of error-free performance or excessively high or low risk taking. Improvement scores, voluntary correction of errors, completion of optional risk-taking activities—these are behaviors that teachers should recognize and encourage.

TOWARD A NEW DEFINITION OF SUCCESS

We face the grim reality that our extraordinary efforts to produce "schools without failure" have not yielded the well-adjusted, enthusiastic, self-confident scholars we anticipated. Our efforts to mass-produce success for every individual in every educational situation have left us with cheap reproductions of success that do not even faintly represent the real thing. This overdose of synthetic success is a primary cause of the student apathy and school abandonment plaguing our country.

To turn the trend around, we must emphasize error tolerance, not error-free learning; reward error condition, not error avoidance; ensure challenge, not easy success. Eventual success on challenging tasks, tolerance for error making, and constructive responses to failure are motivational fare that school systems should be serving up to all students. I suggest that we engage the skills of researchers, textbook authors, publishers, and educators across the country to ensure the development and marketing of attractive and effective academic risk-taking materials and procedures. If we convince these experts of the need to employ their creative efforts toward this end, we will not only stem the tide of educational suicide, but we will enhance the quality of educational success. We will witness self-regulated student success and satisfaction that will ensure the intellectual, creative, and motivational well-being of our country.

REFERENCES

Atkinson, J. W. (1964). *An Introduction to Motivation*, Princeton, N.J.: Van Nostrand.

Boggiano, A. K. and D. S. Main. (1986). "Enhancing Children's Interest in Activities Used as Rewards: The Bonus Effect." *Journal of Personality and Social Psychology* 51: 1116–1126.

Clifford, M. M. (1988). "Failure Tolerance and Academic Risk Taking in Ten- to Twelve-Year-Old Students." *British Journal of Educational Psychology* 58: 15–27.

Csikszentmihalyi, M. (1975). *Beyond Boredom and Anxiety.* San Francisco: Jossey-Bass.

Csikszentmihalyi, M. (1978). "Intrinsic Rewards and Emergent Motivation." In *The Hidden Costs of Reward*, edited by M. R. Lepper and D. Greene. N.J.: Lawrence Erlbaum Associates.

Danner, F. W., and D. Lonky. (1981). "A Cognitive-Developmental Approach to the Effects of Rewards on Intrinsic Motivation." *Child Development* 52: 1043–1052.

Deci, E. L., and J. Porac. (1978). "Cognitive Evaluation Theory and the Study of Human Motivation." In *The Hidden Costs of Reward*, edited by M. R. Lepper and D. Greene. Hillsdale, N.J.: Lawrence Erlbaum Associates.

Deci, E. L., and R. M. Ryan. (1987). "The Support of Autonomy and the Control of Behavior." *Journal of Personality and Social Psychology* 53: 1024–1037.

Fischer, K. W. (1980). "Learning as the Development of Organized Behavior." *Journal of Structural Learning* 3: 253–267.

Hahn, A. (1987). "Reaching Out to America's Dropouts: What to Do?" *Phi Delta Kappan* 69: 256–263.

Harter, S. (1978). "Effectance Motivation Reconsidered; Toward a Developmental Model." *Human Development* 1: 34–64.

Ilgen, D. P., and C. F. Moore. (1987). "Types and Choices of Performance Feedback." *Journal of Applied Psychology* 72: 401–406.

Ilgen, D. P., C. D. Fischer, and M. S. Taylor. (1979). "Consequences of Individual Feedback on Behavior in Organizations." *Journal of Applied Psychology* 64: 349–371.

Kruglanski, A., C. Stein, and A. Riter. (1977). "Contingencies of Exogenous Reward and Task Performance: On the 'Minimax' Strategy in Instrumental Behavior." *Journal of Applied Social Psychology*, 2: 141–148.

Larson, J. P., Jr. (1984). "The Performance Feedback Process: A Preliminary Model." *Organizational Behavior and Human Performance* 33: 42–76.

Lepper, M. R., and D. Greene. (1978). *The Human Costs of Reward*. Hillsdale, N.J.: Lawrence Erlbaum Associates.

Lepper, M. R., and M. Hodell. (1989). "Intrinsic Motivation in the Classroom." In *Motivation in Education, Vol. 3*, edited by C. Ames and R. Ames. N.Y.: Academic Press.

Sansone, C. (1986). "A Question of Competence: The Effects of Competence and Task Feedback on Intrinsic Motivation." *Journal of Personality and Social Psychology* 51: 918–931.

Trope, Y. (1979). "Uncertainty Reducing Properties of Achievement Tasks:" *Journal of Personality and Social Psychology* 37: 1505–1518.

History of Motivational Research in Education

BERNARD WEINER
University of California, Los Angeles

The history of motivational research in education is traced through chapters on motivation in the Encyclopedia of Educational Research *from 1941 to 1990. Discussion of the drive concept, the motivation-learning distinction, the role of individual differences, and the emergence of cognitive concerns and the self are examined. Great shifts are documented, and current as well as future trends are discussed.*

The 10th anniversary of the founding of the Motivation in Education Special Interest Group of the American Educational Research Association provided the occasion for me to look back on the field of motivation and ask where we have been and where we are going. There are many possible strategies to take in reaching a retrospective summary. One might count and catalog past articles, solicit and synthesize opinions of the major figures in the field, and so forth. The material for my analysis of the state of motivational psychology is provided by the *Encyclopedia of Educational Research,* which is perhaps a compromise between personal cataloging and soliciting the opinions of others. This volume has been published each decade starting in 1941; thus five articles exist and a sixth is forthcom-

This article was an invited address given to the Motivation in Education Special Interest Group at the convention of the American Educational Research Association, April 1990, Boston, Massachusetts.

Thanks are extended to Russell Ames and Jaana Juvonen for their roles in initiating this project. Correspondence concerning this article should be addressed to Bernard Weiner, Department of Psychology, University of California, 405 Hilgard Avenue, Los Angeles, California 90024-1563.

ing which summarize the research conducted between 1930 and 1990. I have been asked to write the chapter for the 1990 edition. This will be my second review, for I also wrote the chapter 20 years earlier for the 1970 publication. Hence, not only am I able to examine the contents of the field over a 60-year time span, but I also can overcome the confounding involved in comparing the writings and biases of different authors by considering differences within the same author (myself) over a 20-year time span (making the questionable assumption that my own biases remained constant over this period).

In this article, I will use the contents of the *Encyclopedia of Educational Research* articles as a scaffold for discussing the history of our field, the emergence and disappearance of central issues in motivation, the progress that has and has not been made, the problems that exist, current directions, and a potpourri of related topics.

I view this field with a schizophrenic reaction. On the one hand, I feel some despair. The question that teachers and parents ask of us is how to motivate their students and children, and we are not very adept at providing answers. The lofty place that motivation once occupied in the research enterprise of psychology is no longer held. At one time, motivation was the dominant field of study; certainly this is no longer true. During the decades between 1950 and 1970, the *Nebraska Symposium on Motivation* was one of the most prestigious publications and commanded a great deal of attention; that is no longer the case. In one year, Clark Hull, the pivotal figure in the growth of drive theory and the experimental approach to motivation, was cited in almost 70% of the published experimental articles; we have no contemporary figure of such dominance.

At the other pole of my schizophrenic reaction, I feel optimistic. There are now well more than 150 active members of the Motivation in Education Special Interest Group, many with their own students and research groups. Interest in and articles about motivation are increasing in a number of journals (see Ball, 1984); there is a recent three-volume set edited by R. Ames and C. Ames (1984) and C. Ames and R. Ames (1985, 1989) on motivation in education; and for the first time in nearly 20 years, there is going to be a *Nebraska Symposium* volume that is actually devoted to motivation (Dienstbier, 1990). The future therefore looks promising for the general field of motivation and for motivational research related to education.

Having shared my deeply mixed emotions, let me turn my thoughts to history. This will allow further opportunity for expression of these conflicting personal opinions.

MOTIVATION AS REPRESENTED 1940-1960

The first two motivation chapters in the *Encyclopedia of Educational Research* were written by Paul Thomas Young (1941, 1950). Young, who was at the University of Illinois, was known for his hedonic theory of motivation and his examination of the intrinsic emotional and motivational properties of substances such as saccharin. He was a prolific writer, producing some of the very early books that outlined an experimental approach to the study of motivation. Young wrote both the 1941 and 1950 chapters, following the same outline in each publication.

The contents of his chapters are shown in Table 1. It can be seen in Table 1 that the major research topics in the field were activity level, appetites and aversions, homeostasis, chemical controls, and neural structures, as well as incentives, defense mecha-

nisms, and the degree of motivation (the Yerkes-Dodson law of optimal motivational level). Some specific concerns for educators were discussed, including praise and reproof, success and failure, knowledge of results (feedback), cooperation and competition, and law and punishment. The educational topics not only overlap but also appear more contemporary and familiar than his outline of general motivational research.

These fields of study, popular just 40 years ago between 1930 and 1950, are readily understandable, given the roots of motivational psychology. Initially, the experimental study of motivation (the Latin root of *motive* means to move) was linked with the search for the motors of behavior and was associated with concepts such as instinct, drive, arousal, need, and energization. Motivational psychologists were concerned with what moved a resting organism to a state of activity. Accordingly, hungry rats were deprived of food, and even curious monkeys were placed in rooms without visual stimulation. It was believed that a discrepancy between an ideal "off" state and a less-than-ideal "on" state (i.e., the presence of a need) would be detected by the organism and would initiate activity until this disequilibrium was redlined to zero. Hence, the effects of a variety of need states on a variety of indexes of motivation, including speed of learning and choice behavior, were examined. Borrowing concepts such as energy systems from the physical sciences and using machine-based metaphors such as overflowing energy and drainage from a container of fixed capacity constituted one strategy used to gain scientific respectability for this uncertain field.

The concept of a deprived organism living in an environment of limited resources gave a functionalistic, Darwinian flavor to the field of motivation, which in the decades between 1930 and 1950 was dominated by the tribal leaders of Hull and Spence and by the less expansionistic Tolman. It also gave rise to taxonomies of instincts and basic need states, as exemplified in the writings of William McDougall (1923) and Henry Murray (1938), and to other issues related to the dynamics of behavior and the instrumental value of action. For example, motivational psychologists examined conflict resolution under circumstances in which a positive goal is located in a shocked region, what behavior follows when an anticipated goal is not attained, and whether psychological equilibrium requires reduction in need state to a zero level of internal stimulation (as opposed to an optimal level greater than

TABLE 1 Contents of the Chapters on Motivation in the Encyclopedia of Educational Research, 1941–1990

Descriptor	1941 and 1950	1960	1969	1982	1990
Author	P. T. Young	M. Marx	B. Weiner	S. Ball	B. Weiner
Contents	Need and activity level Appetite and aversion Equilibrium and homeostasis Chemical controls Neural structures Incentives Defense mechanisms Degree of motivation Education Applications Praise and reproof Success and failure Knowledge of results Cooperation and competition Reward and punishment	Theories Techniques Drive and learning Drive and frustration Activation of drives and motives Reward Knowledge of results Fear and anxiety Arousal	Theories Associative Drive Cognitive Psychoanalytic Topics Curiosity (exploratory behavior) Affiliation Imbalance (dissonance) Frustration Aggression Relation to Processes Learning Perception Memory	Attribution theory Achievement motivation Anxiety Self-esteem Curiosity Minor areas Level of aspiration Affiliation Biochemical correlates Reinforcement theory	Cognitions Causal attributions Self-efficacy Learned helplessness Individual differences Need for achievement Anxiety about failure Locus of control Attributional style Environmental determinants Cooperation versus competition (goal structure) Intrinsic versus extrinsic rewards Praise

zero). The reader is directed to Atkinson (1964), Brown (1961), Mook (1987), Petri (1986), and Weiner (1972, 1980) for historical overviews of earlier research activities. It is evident, then, that Young captured the mainstream preoccupations in motivation through his coverage of need and activity, approach and avoidance tendencies, homeostasis, and underlying motivational mechanisms.

The topics linked with educational psychologists were quite divorced from the mainstream of the study of motivation. Basic research in motivation was associated with subhuman behavior, for example, the maze or straight-alley actions of hungry or thirsty rats. Human behavior was considered too complex to study directly and not subject to experimental manipulation, which meant deprivation because the basic motivational model embraced viscerogenic needs and homeostasis.

Forty years after 1950, the problem of being out of the mainstream no longer applies to educational psychologists, as is discussed in the following paragraphs. However, another problem that in 1941 was considered to have been solved has remained a serious burr in our saddles. The dilemma involves the motivation-learning or performance-acquisition distinction. A key juncture in the field of motivation occurred in the 1930s when it separated from the field of learning. Hullians had argued that in order for learning to occur, there must be response reinforcement and drive reduction. That is, a response must be followed by an incentive for there to be a change in habit strength and a subsequent increase in strength of motivation. But Tolman (1932), in his acclaimed research on latent learning, demonstrated that there can be learning without reward and drive reduction; incentives, which were introduced into the goal box after an animal had an opportunity to explore the maze, were shown to affect performance, or the utilization of structure, rather than learning, or the change in structure. Motivational psychologists at that time argued that the study of motivation is therefore separable from the study of learning; motivation examines the use, but not the development, of knowledge.

However, for the educational psychologist, the prime issue always has been how to motivate people to engage in new learning, not how to get people to use what they already know, which is a more appropriate issue for industrial psychologists. The study of motivation for the educational researcher thus has been confounded with the field of learning; indeed, motivation often is inferred from learning, and learning usually is the indicator of

motivation for the educational psychologist. This lack of separation, or confounding, between motivation and learning has vexed those interested in motivational processed in education, in part because learning is influenced by a multiplicity of factors including native intelligence. This confounding problem can even be seen in the outline of Young, because he included knowledge of results, for example, among the determinants of motivation, yet it surely influences the degree of learning.

I will mention only briefly the ensuing *Encyclopedia of Educational Research* article because it continued in the tradition set forth by Young. The chapter was written by Melvin Marx (1960) of the University of Missouri (see Table 1). Marx also linked motivation with energy and drive level. The main topics he examined (after a lengthy discussion of types of drive theories and methods of study) were drive and learning, drive and frustration, activation of drive, rewards, knowledge of results, fear and anxiety (which were considered learned drives) and arousal. Hence, Marx remained in the tradition of Hull, Spence, Mowrer, N. Miller, and others of the Yale and Iowa schools who were guided by the machine metaphor of motivation. The center of motivational research still had little connection with or relevance for educational psychologists.

MOTIVATION AS REPRESENTED IN 1969

I was responsible for the next *Encyclopedia of Educational Research* chapter, which summarized the research in the 1960s (Weiner, 1969). The topics covered are in Table 1. First, I reviewed the four most dominant theoretical approaches: associationistic theory (John Watson), drive theory (Hull and Spence), cognitive theory (Kurt Kewin and John Atkinson), and psychoanalytic theory (Freud). In addition, the specific research areas reviewed included exploratory behavior, affiliation, balance (dissonance), frustration, and aggression. Furthermore, motivation was related to other process areas including learning, perception, and memory. It is quite evident that although Hull and Spence were represented, there was relatively little discussion of drive, energy, arousal, homeostasis, and other mainstays of drive theory.

One can attribute this rather dramatic shift to the writer, but as a chronicler (i.e., a historian without a philosophy) I deserve neither the credit nor the blame. Major changes had occurred, some starting before Marx (1960) wrote his chapter on motivation and others flowering in the 1960s. First, there was the more general shift in psychology away from mechanism and toward cognition. For example, in the psychology of Edward Thomdike, which was entirely incorporated by Hull, proponents believed that a reward would automatically increase the probability of the immediately prior response, thus augmenting later motivation when in that environment. However, it was gradually learned that if reward is perceived as controlling, then it undermines future effort, whereas reward perceived as positive feedback is motivating (Deci, 1975). Furthermore, reward for successful completion of an easy task is a cue to the receiver of this feedback that he or she is low in ability, a belief that inhibits activity, whereas reward for successful completion of a difficult task indicates that hard work was expended in conjunction with high ability, a belief that augments motivation. In addition, reward in a competitive setting is based on social comparison information, signaling that one has high ability and is better than others, whereas reward in a cooperative context signals that one has bettered oneself and has tried hard. Hence, it became recognized that reward has quite a variety of meanings and that each connotation can have different motivational implications. For the field of motivation, this ultimately signaled that the "winner" of the Hull-Tolman debate was Tolman, the cognitivist, rather than Hull, the mechanist. The broader Tolman cognitive camp included, or was preceded by, Lewin, who at times teamed with Tolman at Berkeley, and John Atkinson, as well as Julian Rotter, who was unfortunately and unfairly overlooked in my 1969 chapter.

The cognitivists had, in general, a different research agenda than did the mechanists. For example, one of Lewin's main research interests was level of aspiration, or the goal for which one is striving. In a similar manner, Atkinson devoted his attention to the choice between achievement-related tasks differing in level of difficulty. Thus, when cognitive approaches to motivation carried the day, this resulted not only in a different theoretical orientation but also in a new empirical outlook. That is, it was not "business as usual" with Tolman's cognitive maps merely replacing Hull's habit strengths. Rather, researchers began to concentrate on human rather than on infrahuman behavior. It became just as respectable to generalize from human to nonhuman behavior as vice versa.

So, just as Hull speculated about human motivation from studies of rats, Lewin speculated about the behavior of rats from the study of humans! Furthermore, of the many possible topics for human research, issues associated with success and failure and achievement strivings formed the heart of the empirical study of motivation. This was in part because of the manifest importance of achievement strivings in our lives. In addition, success and failure could be readily manipulated in the laboratory and their effects on subsequent performance determined. This was perhaps no more difficult than depriving or not depriving lower organisms of food and testing the effects of deprivation on performance. Finally, there were many naturally occurring instances of achievement outcomes that could be subject to field research, including the classroom. There was an open door for educational research.

In sum, motivational research became almost synonymous with achievement motivation research. Educational psychology thus shifted into the spotlight, away from the periphery where it was, properly, first identified in the reviews of Young (1941, 1950) and Marx (1960) shown in Table 1. Of course, other uniquely human concerns were captured in the 1960s, including affiliative behavior and cognitive balance. But these pale in comparison to the attention given to achievement strivings.

However, in the 1960s motivational psychologists were not totally transformed by the general shift from mechanism to cognition. For example, research concerned with cognitive balance and dissonance made use of drive theory concepts, particularly drive reduction and homeostasis (e.g., cognitive dissonance, or an imbalance among cognitive beliefs, was considered to be a drive, and humans were believed to be driven to bring themselves back to a state of equilibrium, or cognitive consonance, in which all beliefs "fit"). In addition, theorists in the 1960s primarily (but not quite exclusively) embraced the concept of subjective expectancy of success, albeit little else from the vast array of relevant motivational thoughts. Thus, there was some contentment merely in eliminating the term *drive* and replacing the notion of *habit* with that of *expectancy*.

In addition, the cognitive motivational theorists remained wedded to the "grand formal theory" approach of Hull and Tolman, setting as their task the isolation of the determinants of behavior and the specification of the mathematical relation among these factors. This is illustrated in the very dominant Motive × Probability × Incentive formula of Atkinson (1957, 1964) and the very closely related (and prior) theories of Lewin (1935) and Rotter (1954). All of these were known as expectancy–value theories—motivation was determined by what one expected to get and the likelihood of getting it. The cognitive approach also embraced the "slice in time" construal advocated by Lewin. An ahistorical construal of motivation lent itself to analysis of variance as the appropriate statistical methodology, so that variables typically were manipulated in 2 × 2 designs (or what might be called "Noah's Arc" experiments). Finally, it became accepted that organisms always are active, and as a result, the key dependent variables in motivation became choice and persistence, indicators of the direction of behavior.

With the waning of "mechanism," of machine metaphors, drive and homeostasis as motivational constructs, and research with lower organisms, along with the advent of cognitivism, rational person metaphors, human motivational research, and achievement strivings as the center of motivational thought, there also came another important research direction. Attention began to be focused on individual differences, with persons characterized as high or low in achievement needs, high or low in anxiety, high or low in internal control, and so forth (following the Noah's Arc paradigm). For the educational psychologist, so interested in those individuals not performing well in the classroom, this was an important and a compatible shift that could not have come about with a psychology based on nonhumans.

The main individual differences that were studied were not derived from broad concerns about personality structure. Rather, an individual difference variable was selected on the basis of motivational theory; a measure of that variable was created; and then this measure was added to other factors within a more encompassing research design that included individual differences as one variable. How this structure related to or fit with other personality structures was not of concern, and researchers often paid little attention to the measure in comparison with the measures developed by assessment psychologists. When Spence was asked what he would do if a measure of anxiety did not result in the predictions made by drive theorists, he quickly said that he would throw out the assessment instrument!

The dominant individual differences that were studied and their linked assessment instruments—need for achievement and the Thematic Appercep-

tion Test, anxiety about failure and the Test Anxiety Questionnaire or the Manifest Anxiety Scale, and locus of control and the Internal-External Scale—share a common process of development. First it was demonstrated within a well-articulated theoretical framework that a particular situational manipulation had a motivational effect. Then it was documented that individuals could be selected who differed in ways that mirrored the environmental effect. For example, achievement theory specified that when achievement concerns are aroused by means of test instructions or failure, achievement strivings are augmented as compared with a neutral or nonarousing manipulation (see Atkinson, 1964). It was then contended that some individuals act as if they are more aroused than others when both groups are in the identical environment. That is, some individuals are more sensitized to achievement cues than are others and thus exhibit augmented achievement strivings, as though the two groups actually were in differentially arousing environments. In sum, the creation of the individual difference measure followed the successful manipulation of a situational variable that captured a particular motivational phenomenon.

In a similar manner, drive theorists had demonstrated that conditioning is more rapid when individuals are exposed to a large aversive stimulus, such as an intense shock, than when subject to a less severe shock. It was then reasoned that some individuals might be more emotionally aroused in the same aversive environment than are others, and thus would condition faster. Such people were labeled as high in drive or high in anxiety (Spence, 1958). Subsequent demonstrations showing that individuals who scored high on the Manifest Anxiety Scale did condition faster than those who scored low not only validated the individual difference measure but also lent supporting evidence to drive theory.

Finally, social learning theorists had documented that expectancy shifts are more typical (increments after success, decrements after failure) when individuals' perform on skill rather than chance tasks. Social learning theorists then reasoned that some individuals would perceive events in the world as skill determined and therefore subject to personal control, whereas others would construe events as chance determined and therefore not amenable to personal control. Thus, in the identical neutral context, individuals in the former group would exhibit more typical expectancy shifts than luck-oriented individuals (Rotter, 1966).

To summarize, individual difference measures for achievement needs, anxiety, and locus of control were devised to identify persons thought to differ in motivationally significant ways. In their early stages of development, these measures and their corresponding predictions were closely tied to the theories that spawned them and generated a vast amount of research, which I touched upon in the 1969 *Encyclopedia of Educational Research* article.

MOTIVATION AS DEPICTED IN 1982

The next motivation chapter in the *Encyclopedia of Educational Research* appeared in 1982 and was written by Samuel Ball. Ball is in part known to us because of his service as editor of the *Journal of Educational Psychology*. In that capacity, he very much encouraged the submission of motivation articles, and publications in motivation flourished under his editorship.

The topics covered by Ball (1982) included attribution theory, achievement motivation, anxiety, self-esteem, curiosity and, to a much lesser extent, level of aspiration, affiliation, biochemical correlates of motivation, and reinforcement (see Table 1). Thus, there clearly is a continuation of the trends observed in the 1960s. That is, there is even greater focus on human behavior, particularly achievement strivings; there is an increasing range of cognitions documented as having motivational significance, such as causal ascriptions; and there is enduring interest in individual differences in achievement needs, anxiety about failure, and perceptions of control. In addition, we see the beginnings of attention paid to the self, as illustrated in self versus other causal ascriptions for success and failure, strategies that maintain personal beliefs in high ability, self-efficacy (Bandura, 1977), and so forth. During the 1970s, the study of infrahuman motivation (excluding the physiological mechanisms) and the associated drive concept had virtually vanished, indeed not that many years after the heyday of Hull and Spence.

MOTIVATION TODAY

Finally, we come to the 1990 motivation chapter (Weiner, in press). The outline is shown in Table 1. The topics include the cognitions of causal attribu-

tions, self-efficacy, and learned helplessness; the individual differences of need for achievement, anxiety about failure, locus of control, and attributional style; and the environmental variables of competitive versus cooperative contexts, intrinsic versus extrinsic rewards, and praise. It is of interest to note that the category of environmental determinants includes topics similar to those contained in the outlines of Young (1941, 1950). The remaining topics, however, were not existent in his earlier articles. This indicates not only the emergence of new areas of research but also the ascendance of issues relevant to educational psychologists.

Let me expand somewhat on the chapter contents and link this material with the larger historical framework that has been outlined.

1. The grand formal theories that composed the first part of my 1969 chapter—drive, psychoanalytic, cognitive, and associationistic conceptions—have for the most part faded away. After all, Freud's emphasis on the unconscious, sexual motivation, and conflict and Hull's emphasis on drive and drive reduction, seem to have little relevance in classroom contexts. What remain are varieties of cognitive approaches to motivation; the main theories today are based on the interrelated cognitions of causal ascriptions, efficacy and control beliefs, helplessness, and thoughts about the goals for which one is striving.

There is some loss with the fading of larger theories, because this is exactly what a number of central ideas and concepts in motivational psychology need. For example, the differentiation of intrinsic and extrinsic motivation, which was of central importance in the history of the cognitive emergence, is not developed in the sense of being included within a system of interrelated concepts. Thus, its relation to other concepts such as origin-pawn, internal-external control, the flow of experience, and so forth, is unclear. The lack of theoretical elaboration reduces both the generality and the precision of these intertwined approaches.

2. Achievement strivings remain at the center of the study of motivation. There are major pockets of research on power motivation, affiliation, exploratory behavior and curiosity, altruism, aggression, and so on. But these are circumscribed areas in which researchers focus on domain-specific content rather than on the development of general theory. I regard this narrowing as a major shortcoming of the field, one that greatly limits the generality of our laws as well as the likelihood of discovering new regularities. On the other hand, for those solely interested in classroom achievement strivings, the lack of theoretical generality may not be of great concern.

Within the achievement field, a somewhat new approach is vying for a dominant role with the need for achievement and causal ascriptions. This approach, sometimes called "goal theory," embraces the linked concepts of ego-involvement, competitive reward structure, social comparison as the indicator of success and ability attributions (as contrasted with task-involvement, cooperative structure, self-comparison as the indicator of success and effort attributions; Ames, 1984; Covington, 1984; Nicholls, 1984). I regard this as a major new direction, one pulling together different aspects of achievement research.

3. As intimated previously, there is increasing incorporation of a variety of cognitive variables, as exemplified in the triad of causal cognitions, efficacy beliefs, and helplessness, as well as in the source of information (self or others) that is used to determine subjective success or failure. However, the main new cognitive direction is the inclusion of the self. Indeed, even the aforementioned cognitions all concern perceptions about the self as a determinant of prior or future success and failure. Add to these the constructs of self-actualization, self-concept, self-determination, self-esteem, self-focus, self-handicapping, and the remainder of the self-alphabet, and it is evident that the self is on the verge of dominating motivation.

4. The review of the individual difference variables conveyed that this direction of motivational research is rapidly diminishing, if it has not already been abandoned. The difficulty with motivational (as opposed to cognitive) trait concepts, which was pointed out by Mischel (1968), is the lack of cross-situational generality. This has created a tremendous barrier for the motivational psychologist. For example, if an individual has high achievement strivings in sports but not academics, and this individual is classified as high in achievement needs, then predictions will be upheld in one situation but disconfirmed in the other. A second major problem is that the individual difference variables took on lives of their own and became more popular and focal than their founding theories; these monsters consumed their masters so that, for example, locus of control was related to a huge number of variables but not to expectancy of success, which was the one variable that it was linked with theoretically.

I do not mourn the passing of this stage, but I do mourn the loss of activity that the motivational trait approach spawned. One reason for the current void in research on individual differences is the lack of larger theoretical frameworks that provide the context for the identification and growth of pertinent individual difference variables. The importance of theory for individual difference research has been recently documented in the creation of attributional style questionnaires, which developed from learned helplessness and attribution theory (Seligman, 1975; Weiner, 1986).

5. There is growing interest in emotion, which is touched upon in the forthcoming *Encyclopedia of Educational Research* motivation chapter (see Clark & Fiske, 1982). When Hull argued for the centrality of drive and Tolman argued for the centrality of cognition, they both neglected emotion (save for the acceptance of the very general pleasure-pain principle). In addition, other investigators considered only in a cursory manner affects such as pride (Atkinson, 1964) or frustration (Lewin, 1935). However, the neglect of emotion is now being redressed. The central cognitions of causal ascriptions and helplessness perceptions are linked with emotional reactions. In a similar manner, focus on the self has promoted interest in self-directed emotions including pride, shame, and guilt. I feel quite certain that emotions will be examined at great length in the *Encyclopedia of Educational Research* motivation article written for the year 2000. At that time, there will be some mapping between the structure of thought, discrete emotional experiences, and the motivational messages of these experiences.

MOTIVATION IN THE FUTURE

In addition to the research agendas implied in the prior paragraphs, there are two others that I believe or hope will become manifest. First, there should be a greater number of motivational investigations that are not linked with learning. There is an abundance of evidence that motivation influences a vast array of other variables, including affective experience, self-esteem, and so forth. Educational psychologists must broaden their nets to capture the richness of motivational impact.

My second hoped-for agenda stems from the current dominance of issues related to the self self-directed emotions. and what may be called a psychology of the individual. I view this narrow focus with mixed emotions and some trepidation. To explain this reaction, let me return to some basics about motivation and what this concept means to teachers and parents. When teachers and parents say that a child is "not motivated," they may refer to a behavioral observation (e.g., the child is not working with intensity or persistence at homework), to inferences about intrinsic interest (e.g., the child is studying only because of extrinsic bribes), or to engagement in activities that are antithetical to the goals of teachers and parents (e.g., the child is engaged in sports). Thus, for example, if someone is playing baseball whenever possible and spending time thinking about baseball rather than school-related concerns, then that person is considered by teachers and parents as "not motivated." However, if this same behavior characterized a professional baseball player, then that person would be described as highly motivated. He or she would be admired and praised. Motivation therefore is a work-related rather than a play-related concept and must be considered within the context of social values and the goals of the superordinate culture.

When the study of motivation shifted from animal to human research, there indeed was an increase in the accepted importance of cognitions as determinants of behavior and in the centrality of achievement strivings as opposed to deprivation-related activity. But there is another overlooked aspect of this research shift, namely, achievement behavior influences and affects others, who have behavioral expectations. Rats are engaged in a zero-sum game; if they do not strive to get food, the other rats are not necessarily unhappy about this and Darwinian principles are likely to prevail. However, learning need not be divided and shared and school motivation requires the development and the incorporation of the values of others. Hence, we have to consider frameworks larger than the self, and older motivational constructs, such as "belongingness," must be brought into play when examining school motivation. This has been implicitly part of the trend toward cooperative learning, but it must be explicitly recognized and studied. In sum, school motivation cannot be divorced from the social fabric in which it is embedded, which is one reason that claims made upon motivational psychologists to produce achievement change must be modest. There will be no "person-in-space" for the field of classroom motivation unless there is corresponding social change.

A CONCLUDING NOTE

Tracing the history of our field through the motivation chapters of the *Encyclopedia of Educational Research* reveals great vigor and movement. In just 60 years there have been major upheavals in the field, metaphors replaced, important new areas uncovered, and essential new concepts introduced. We now have a broad array of cognitions and emotions to work with, the self to consider, thoughts about goals, and so forth. In addition, we still have many uncharted areas to incorporate. In sum, we are in a fine position.

REFERENCES

Ames, C. (1984). Competitive, cooperative, and individualistic goal structures: A cognitive-motivational analysis. In R. Ames & C. Ames (Eds.), *Research on motivation in education: Vol. 1. Student motivation.* (pp. 177–207). San Diego, CA: Academic Press.

Ames, C., & Ames, R. (Eds.). (1985). *Research on motivation in education: Vol. 2. The classroom milieu.* San Diego, CA: Academic Press.

Ames, C., & Ames, R. (Eds.). (1989). *Research on motivation in education: Vol 3. Goals and cognitions.* San Diego, CA: Academic Press.

Ames, R., & Ames, C. (Eds.). (1984). *Research on motivation in education: Vol. 1. Student motivation.* San Diego, CA: Academic Press.

Atkinson, J. W. (1957). Motivational determinants of risk-taking behavior. *Psychological Review, 64,* 359–372.

Atkinson, J. W. (1964). *An introduction to motivation.* Princeton, NJ: Van Nostrand.

Ball, S. (1982). Motivation. In H. E. Mitzel (Ed.), *Encyclopedia of educational research,* (5th ed., pp. 1256–1263). New York: Macmillan.

Ball, S. (1984). Educational psychology as an academic chameleon: An editorial assessment. *Journal of Educational Psychology, 76,* 993–999.

Bandura, A. (1977). Self-efficacy: Toward a unifying theory of behavioral change. *Psychological Review, 84,* 191–215.

Brown, J. S. (1961). *The motivation of behavior.* New York: McGraw-Hill.

Clark, M. S., & Fiske, S. T. (Eds.). (1982). *Affect and cognition: The 17th annual Carnegie symposium on cognition.* Hillsdale, NJ:

Covington, M. (1984). The motive for self-worth. In R. Ames & C. Ames (Eds.), *Research on motivation in education: Vol. 1. Student motivation.* (pp. 77–112). San Diego, CA: Academic Press.

Deci, E. L. (1975). *Intrinsic motivation.* New York: Plenum Press.

Dienstbier, R. A. (Ed.). (1990). *Nebraska Symposium on Motivation: Vol. 38. Perspectives on motivation.* Lincoln, NE: University of Nebraska Press.

Lewin, K. (1935). *A dynamic theory of personality.* New York: McGraw-Hill.

Marx, M. (1960). Motivation. In L. W. Harris (Ed.), *Encyclopedia of educational research,* (3rd ed., pp. 888–901). New York: Macmillan.

McDougall, W. (1923). *Outline of psychology.* New York: Scribner.

Mischel, W. (1968). *Personality and assessment.* New York: Wiley.

Mook, D. G. (1987). *Motivation.* New York: Norton.

Murray, H. A. (1938). *Explorations in personality.* New York: Oxford University Press.

Nicholls. J. G. (1984). Conceptions of ability and achievement motivation. In R. Ames & C. Ames (Eds.), *Research on motivation in education: Vol. 1. Student motivation* (pp. 39–73). San Diego, CA: Academic Press.

Petri, H. L. (1986). *Motivation.* Belmont, CA: Wadsworth.

Rotter, J. B. (1954). *Social learning and clinical psychology.* Englewood Cliffs, NJ: Prentice-Hall.

Rotter, J. B. (1966). Generalized expectancies for internal versus external control of reinforcements. *Psychological monographs, 80,* 1–28.

Seligman, M. E. P. (1975). *Helplessness: On depression, development, and death.* San Francisco: Freeman.

Spence, K. W. (1958). A theory of emotionally based drive (D) and its relation to performance in simple learning situations. *American Psychologist, 13,* 131–141.

Tolman, E. C. (1932). *Purposive behavior in animals and man.* New York: Appleton-Century-Crofts.

Weiner, B. (1969). Motivation. In R. L. Ebel (Ed.) *Encyclopedia of educational research,* (4th ed., pp. 878–888). New York: Macmillan.

Weiner, B. (1972). *Theories of motivation.* Chicago: Rand McNally.

Weiner, B. (1980). *Human motivation.* New York: Holt, Rinehart, & Winston.

Weiner, B. (1986). *An attributional theory of motivation an demotion.* New York: Springer-Verlag.

Weiner, B. (in press). Motivation. In M. C. Alkin (Ed.), *Encyclopedia of educational research, 6th ed.* New York: Macmillan.

Young, P. T. (1941). Motivation. In W. S. Monroe (Ed.), *Encyclopedia of educational research* (pp. 735–742). New York: Macmillan.

Young, P. T. (1950). Motivation. In W. S. Monroe (Ed.), *Encyclopedia of educational research,* (Rev. ed., pp. 755–761). New York: Macmillan.

▶ Chapter 10

Creating a Vision of the Future

JEANNETTE ABI-NADER

Scene 1: "Okay, what school are we going to be today?" the teacher asks his class, and the students call out, "Harvard . . . Georgetown . . . UCLA . . . Princeton." The teacher says, "Okay, today we are at Princeton, and I am the professor. I'm going to lecture, and you are going to take notes." As he reads a passage from the workbook, the students write so furiously that they wind up shaking their wrists in agony. "Talking college, folks," he says. "This is what it's going to be like."

Scene 2: A student is at his after-school job cleaning stairs in a hospital. At each landing, he takes out index cards and reads sentences with highlighted vocabulary words. He checks the definitions at the bottom of the cards and then goes on to the next set of stairs.

Scene 3: A student at home after school interviews her uncle about his memories of the assassination of President Kennedy. After interviewing other family members and neighbors, she draws conclusions about people's reactions to this event and prepares a written report for an oral presentation.

The students in each of these scenes are Hispanics who attend an inner-city public high school and are enrolled in a college-preparatory program called PLAN (Program: Learning According to Needs). They are not gifted or talented. Most of them are on welfare and come from single-parent homes. But they want to go to college, and PLAN is designed to get them there.

Jeannette Abi-Nader (Spokane Area Washington Chapter) is a professor of teacher education at Gonzaga University, Spokane.

PLAN grew out of a Title VII project that was begun in 1975 to help Hispanics succeed in college. The designers of the project believed that the fear of communicating in English was a greater barrier to academic success than was limited proficiency in English. To overcome this obstacle, they devised a three-year sequence of courses in reading, writing, and public speaking that was intended not just to train students but to *motivate them* to communicate. The program, which begins in the students' sophomore year, incorporates workbooks, magazines, TV scripts, communication games, and videos to enliven skill-building exercises and stimulate creative activities. Students in PLAN do not contribute to the approximately 70% dropout rate among Hispanic students. Not only do they graduate, but most of them earn full-tuition scholarships to colleges and universities.

To determine why these students are motivated to learn and what strategies enhance their sense of well-being in school, I spent six months observing and participating in the PLAN program at Heritage High School.[1] I taped hours of teacher/student interaction in the classroom and interviewed students, alumni, parents, teachers, administrators, and community members. A complete description of my findings is available in my doctoral dissertation, "A House for My Mother."[2] For this article, I have chosen to focus on one of the implicit goals of instruction that characterizes this program, to analyze teacher talk to reveal strategies for motivating students, and to outline some principles for staff development that can help teachers generate their own successful strategies.

HELPING HISPANIC STUDENTS CREATE A VISION OF THE FUTURE

The PLAN approach addresses the fact that many inner-city minority students believe that they have no control over their lives and are therefore powerless to shape their future.[3] They lack motivation, are unable to set goals, and are indifferent about school. Pedro, a junior in PLAN, summed up this attitude: "Hispanic girls and guys don't like to think about the future. They just like to live life one day at a time." In PLAN, one of the implicit goals of instruction is to help students create a vision of the future. Consequently, strategies for teaching study skills and academic content go beyond the surface structures of exercises and learning activities to counteract the "dead-end" attitude of so many of the students.

I witnessed an example of this approach during the first week I spent in a PLAN class. The seniors had read "The Monkey's Paw," by William Jacobs, which tells the story of a family who used the magic of a mysterious monkey's paw to get their wishes—with unfortunate results. As a follow-up assignment, the students were to present three-minute speeches about their dreams and wishes. Bypassing the Faustian theme of the story, the teacher asked the students to imagine their future and to talk about their dreams and how they would achieve them. In shaping this assignment, the teacher was applying a PLAN technique to focus students' attention on their future and to help them develop confidence and skills in planning and goal setting. PLAN uses three major strategies to accomplish these objectives: a mentor program, the oral tradition of PLAN, and future-oriented classroom talk.

MODELS AND MENTORS

The mentor program assumes that, although inner-city minority students may be intellectually capable of pursuing academic studies, life on a college campus is completely foreign to them. These students need role models—first, to show them that it is possible for someone from their background to go to college, and second, to give them some understanding of what college is about. In the mentor program, Hispanic college students, many of them PLAN graduates, serve that function, visiting classes to talk about budgeting time and money, choosing courses, taking notes, and being accepted by Anglo professors and classmates. During my six months with the PLAN program, five groups of college students addressed the seniors. Besides warning them against cutting classes and becoming too involved in social life, the mentors told of personal successes that they attributed to skills they had learned in PLAN.

The comments of two seniors attest to the effectiveness of the mentor program:

> It is a good idea. . . . When I see all the Hispanics going to college, I know that, if they can, I can.

> I think it helps [the students] because they're like, "Wow! She's from Honduras, you know, and she's not a rich person. She has the same background that I have—she comes from a big family, and things like that." And it's like, "If she can go to a private institution, well, so can I."

The mentor program also demands reciprocity. The students are expected not only to meet—and even exceed—the record of PLAN graduates but also to become mentors themselves once they have gone on to college. The mentors find that returning to share their stories with high school students is an enriching experience. One graduate said, "I was trembling during my presentation. But I like talking about college life because I think that's helped me a lot also."

STORYTELLING PROVIDES ROLE MODELS

Many Hispanic students are the first members of their families to finish high school or even to think about college. Their family histories do not include visual or oral records of relatives who graduated from school. There is no family tradition of expectations of academic success. PLAN compensates for this lack by creating its own oral tradition. Between visits from graduates, the teacher keeps the vision of the future alive by recounting stories about the academic and social achievements of students, past and present. Storytelling provides PLAN students with an oral scrapbook of role models. Stories encourage students to emulate graduates who held elective offices, were valedictorians, or distinguished themselves as student leaders. Stories tell of success in college based on the skills in reading, writing, and public speaking that the PLAN curriculum emphasizes. Letters from graduates who praise the program are read and posted on the bulletin board. Copies of term papers written by former students are displayed as models of form and content and are accompanied by stories about the authors' success in writing papers in college.

For students who cannot identify easily with the success stories, the teacher tells the story of Frank. For three years Frank earned only D's in PLAN, but he wanted to stay in the program with his friends. He went to college and was soon put on academic probation. At some point in his sophomore year, Frank made a breakthrough. He decided to turn his record around, to work harder, to do assignments, and to pass tests. He eventually earned a degree in engineering. Frank inspired the teacher's motto—"I never give up on them"—and Frank's story is used to inspire others.

FUTURE-ORIENTED CLASSROOM TALK

One of the first patterns to emerge from my field notes on classroom talk was the frequency of references to the future—both to college and to a future in the professions. These references were generally associated with four types of classroom activities: 1) preparation, such as learning how to fill out a financial aid form or planning a visit to a local university; 2) descriptions of situations likely to be encountered in college, such as following a syllabus, resolving racial confrontations, or deciding not to go to a party; 3) storytelling about PLAN graduates and their successes in college; and 4) providing a rationale for PLAN's skill-building exercises. Out of a total of 20 class sessions for seniors that I transcribed and analyzed for future-oriented classroom talk, seven entire classes were spent in preparation activities. The remaining 13 classes contained 57 instances of description, storytelling, or providing a rationale for building skills.

It is important to note that references to the future are most often expressed in the indicative rather than in the conditional mood. For example, the teacher says *"when* you go to college" rather than "if you go to college"—or perhaps, "You are the reporters doing a profile of Kennedy." The students pick up this attitude and sometimes correct

the teacher when an "if" or a "might" slips by. In assigning roles for a simulation, for example, the teacher gives Andy the part of a policeman, "because he's interested and might be on the police force someday." "Might?" Andy repeats indignantly. "You mean will!" And the students around him applaud.

The teacher talks about characteristics needed for future success. "Okay, what kind of person do you want working for you? You want the task-oriented person who meets deadlines." Or "You're at a parents' meeting. You want a good education for your children. You are the ones who must speak up. That's why it's important to learn public-speaking skills." Such future-oriented classroom talk distinguishes PLAN classes from other classes at the school, in which the teachers and students rarely mention college—let alone the possibility that inner-city Hispanic students could be future employers, managers, professionals, or community leaders.

DOES IT WORK?

What evidence is there that the instructional strategies described here actually work? Do PLAN students gain the desire and commitment to succeed in school and develop a vision of the future? First, PLAN's success is demonstrated in the number of college acceptances and scholarships recorded over the program's history. Typically, 60% to 65% of PLAN students attend college, compared to 40% of all seniors at the school who declare an intention of going to college. Many PLAN students attend private four-year colleges and universities and study law, nursing, computers, medicine, political science, or engineering.

Second, observations and interviews reveal that students use the problem-solving processes they learn in PLAN to reflect on and shape their future, to make decisions, and to set goals. The students described in the three scenes at the beginning of this article demonstrated their ability to carry out assigned tasks. They are typical of PLAN students who learn how to carefully plot a sequence of activities that culminate in completing their education, in getting a job or a scholarship, or in buying a microwave. They connect their goals to concrete needs in the community and to their own interests: "I want to go back to Puerto Rico and help my people."

Finally, the power of these strategies is demonstrated when students credit PLAN with giving them motivation and confidence about the future. "Every time my teacher talks about college, I get more confidence in myself about going to college," said one student. "The only thing that brought me back to school after dropping out was the time the teacher said, 'You can do it if you wish to do it,' " said another. "I knew myself that I could do it. I know of my ability. But the teacher's words were like a tape that reminded me of that."

IMPLICATIONS FOR STAFF DEVELOPMENT

Clearly, helping minority students create a vision of the future is only one way to avoid or reverse the cycle of failure. The aim of staff development should be to search continually for culturally responsive strategies that will motivate and inspire students. These approaches emerge from a pedagogy of empowerment that is based on the following propositions: 1) that the context of education is shaped by cultural forces that are sometimes beyond our control, but not beyond our awareness; 2) that awareness is essential to an effective pedagogy that respects the students' cultures; and 3) that a priority for staff development is to increase awareness of the cultural differences that affect the context of the school.[4] Awareness is a profoundly personal experience, like insight or conversion. It cannot be mandated but must be cultivated through study, reflection, and action.

Study need not be totally academic, although research on cultural differences in learning and cognition is an important part of the knowledge base for effective teaching.[5] Study must also include direct experience of the home communities in which the students live. In addition, teachers need time and a setting in which to reflect on, analyze, and share with colleagues their experiences in multicultural classrooms and in the students' communities.[6]

Moreover, teachers need freedom to explore ways in which their own experiences can help shape instruction and especially to collaborate in the development of instructional materials. Collaboration between teachers will emphasize the "wisdom of practice" that is essential for solid instruction.[7] Collaboration between teachers and researchers will ensure that instructional materials

and activities are theory-driven and effective.[8] Collaboration between teachers and members of the minority community will help clarify "local meanings" so that the significance of language and action in a neighborhood or ethnic group is understood.[9]

Finally, it is not only students who need to create a vision of the future. Being aware of the effects of culture on teaching and learning will radically shift the vision of the future that teachers hold for their students and for themselves as educators. The strategies that emerge from such a vision can empower minority students—as well as their teachers to achieve a successful and fulfilling future.

1. All names in this article are fictitious.
2. Jeannette Abi-Nader, "A House for My Mother: An Ethnography of Motivational Strategies in a Successful College Preparatory Program for Hispanic High School Students" (Doctoral dissertation, Georgia State University, 1987).
3. Thomas P. Carter, "Mexican-Americans in School: A History of Educational Neglect," in Jarries C. Stone and Donald P. DeNevi, eds., *Teaching Multi-Cultural Populations: Five Heritages* (New York: Van Nostrand Reinhold, 1971), pp. 197–246.
4. Jim Cummins, "Empowering Minority Students: A Framework for Intervention," *Harvard Educational Review*, vol. 56, 1986, pp. 18–36.
5. Stephen Diáz, Luis C. Moll, and Hugh Mehan, "Sociocultural Resources in Instruction: A Context-Specific Approach," in *Beyond Language: Social and Cultural Factors in Schooling Language Minority Students* (Los Angeles: Evaluation, Dissemination, and Assessment Center, California State University, 1986), pp. 187–220; D. Scott Enright, "Use Everything You Have to Teach English: Providing Useful Input to Young Language Learners," in Pat Rigg and D. Scott Enright, eds., *Children and ESL: Integrating Perspectives* (Washington, D.C.: Teachers of English to Speakers of Other Languages, 1986), pp. 115–62; Shirley Brice Heath, *Ways with Words: Language, Life, and Work Communities and Classroom* (New York: Cambridge University Press, 1983); idem, "Sociocultural Contexts of Language Development," in *Beyond Language . . .*, pp. 143–86; Henry Truba, ed., *Culture and the Bilingual Classroom Studies in Classroom Ethnography* (Urbana: University of Illinois Press, 1981); and Virginia, Zanger, "The Social Context of Second Language Learning: An Examination of Barriers to Integration in Five Case Studies" (Doctoral dissertation Boston University, 1987).
6. Linda Lambert, "Staff Development Redesigned," *Phi Delta Kappan*, May 1988, pp. 665–617.
7. Lee S. Shulman, "The Wisdom of Practice: Managing Complexity in Medicine and Teaching," in David Berliner and Barak Rosenshine, eds., *Talks to Teachers: A Festschrift for N. L. Gage* (New York: Random House, 1987), pp. 369–86.

8. Ann L. Brown, Annemarie S. Palincsar, and Linda Purcell, "Poor Readers: Teach, Don't Label," in Ulric Neisser, ed., *The School Achievement of Minority Children: New Perspectives* (Hillsdale, N.J.: Lawrence Erlbaum Associates, 1986), pp. 105–43.

9. Frederick Erickson, "Qualitative Research on Teaching," in Merlin C. Wittrock, ed., *Handbook of Research on Teaching*, 3rd ed. (New York: Macmillan, 1986), pp. 119–61.

"Some Third Graders Are Passing Because I Work with Them"

In San Antonio, Texas, more than half of Mexican-American students drop out of school before graduation. In an effort to improve these statistics, the schools, together with Coca Cola and the Intercultural Development Research Association, in 1985 created the Valued Youth Partnership Dropout Prevention program. In each of four high schools and middle schools, counselors choose twenty-five students who seem to be on the brink of dropping out and invite them to tutor elementary school students. All tutors work at least eight hours a week and earn the minimum wage.

Although it is too soon to judge the overall effectiveness of the program, some students testify eloquently on its behalf. Socorro Salinas gave up on school in ninth grade:

> When I dropped out I wasn't going to come back . . . I was always into trouble, fighting and skipping school alot.

When Socorro returned to give school another try she heard about the tutoring program and asked her counselor if she could sign up. Today she sees everything differently, and she traces some of the changes to tutoring:

See Aurelio Montemayor, *Valued Youth Speak* (San Antonio: Intercultural Development Research Association, 1986).

> Right now I feel very good about school and would give it an eight out of ten, but when I was a freshman I would have given it a one.
>
> To tell you the truth, what I really like about the program is the kids. I took care of my little brothers since they were small, one is four and the other is six. I just like them, the way they talk and work. It makes me feel good, proud of myself. I'm working with third graders and some of them are passing because I worked with them.
>
> This has helped me because I used to be real impatient with kids. They would ask me for something, and I would say "Get away!" Now, they ask me for something, and I'm there to help them. Even my mom got surprised. She told me I had changed. "What happened to you?" And this has been a result of working with the kids.
>
> As a tutor, I got to deal more with the teachers . . . I worked with Mrs. Aleman and got real close to her and I got to understand teachers better. I was like a teacher and I know what the teacher goes through and so I don't give them so many problems.
>
> Now I go to school every day, and when I'm absent I really miss it . . .
>
> I'm so excited about graduating . . . My godmother is going to take me to several business colleges so that I can sign up. For right now I want to be a legal secretary . . . And I want all of my brothers to finish school also.

Synthesis of Research on Cooperative Learning

ROBERT E. SLAVIN

There was once a time when it was taken for granted that a quiet class was a learning class, when principals walked down the hall expecting to be able to hear a pin drop. Today, however, many schools are using programs that foster the hum of voices in classrooms. These programs, called *cooperative learning*, encourage students to discuss, debate, disagree, and ultimately to teach one another.

Cooperative learning has been suggested as the solution for an astonishing array of educational problems: it is often cited as a means of emphasizing thinking skills and increasing higher-order learning; as an alternative to ability grouping, remediation, or special education; as a means of improving race relations and acceptance of mainstreamed students; and as a way to prepare students for an increasingly collaborative work force. How many of these claims are justified? What effects do the various cooperative learning methods have on student achievement and other outcomes? Which forms of cooperative learning are most effective, and what components must be in place for cooperative learning to work?

To answer these questions, I've synthesized in this article the findings of studies of cooperative learning in elementary and secondary schools that have compared cooperative learning to traditionally taught control groups studying the same objectives over a period of at least four weeks (and up to

Robert E. Slavin is Director of the Elementary, School Program, Center for Research on Effective Schooling for Disadvantaged Students, The Johns Hopkins University, 3505 N. Charles Street Baltimore, MD 21218.

a full school year or more). Here I present a brief summary of the effects of cooperative learning on achievement and noncognitive outcomes; for a more extensive review, see *Cooperative Learning: Theory, Research, and Practice* (Slavin 1990).

COOPERATIVE LEARNING METHODS

There are many quite different forms of cooperative learning, but all of them involve having students work in small groups or teams to help one another learn academic material. Cooperative learning usually supplements the teacher's instruction by giving students an opportunity to discuss information or practice skills originally presented by the teacher; sometimes cooperative methods require students to find or discover information on their own. Cooperative learning has been used—and investigated—in every imaginable subject in grades 2–12, and is increasingly used in college.

Small-scale laboratory research on cooperation dates back to the 1920s (see Deutsch 1949; Slavin 1977a); research on specific applications of cooperative learning to the classroom began in the early 1970s. At that time, four research groups, one in Israel and three in the U.S., began independently to develop and study cooperative learning methods in classroom settings.

Now researchers all over the world are studying practical applications of cooperative learning principles, and many cooperative learning methods

---

Highlights of Research on Cooperative Learning

In cooperative learning, students work in small groups to help one another master academic material. There are many quite different forms of cooperative learning and the effectiveness of cooperative learning (particularly for achievement outcomes) depends on the particular approach used.

- For enhancing student achievement, the most successful approaches have incorporated two key elements: group goals and individual accountability. That is, groups are rewarded based on the individual learning of all group members.
- When group goals and individual accountability are used, achievement effects of cooperative learning are consistently positive; 37 of 44 experi-

mental/control comparisons of at least four weeks' duration have found significantly positive effects, and none have favored traditional methods.

- Achievement effects of cooperative learning have been found to about the same degree at all grade levels (2–12), in all major subjects, and in urban, rural, and suburban schools. Effects are equally positive for high, average, and low achievers.
- Positive effects of cooperative learning have been consistently found on such diverse outcomes as self-esteem, intergroup relations, acceptance of academically handicapped students, attitudes toward school, and ability to work cooperatively.

—Robert E. Slavin

---

have been evaluated in one or more experimental/control comparisons. The best evaluated of the cooperative models are described below (adapted from Slavin 1990). These include four Student Team Learning variations, Jigsaw, Learning Together, and Group Investigation.

Student Team Learning

Student Team Learning (STL) techniques were developed and researched at Johns Hopkins University. More than half of all experimental studies of practical cooperative learning methods involve STL methods.

All cooperative learning methods share the idea that students work together to learn and are responsible for one another's learning as well as their own. STL methods, in addition to this idea, emphasize the use of team goals and team success, which can only be achieved if all members of the team learn the objectives being taught. That is, in Student Team Learning the students' tasks are not to *do* something as a team but to *learn* something as a team.

Three concepts are central to all Student Team Learning methods: *team rewards, individual accountability,* and *equal opportunities for success.* Using STL techniques, teams earn certificates or other team rewards if they achieve above a designated criterion. The teams are not in competition to earn scarce rewards; all (or none) of the teams may achieve the criterion in a given week. *Individual accountability* means that the team's success depends

on the individual learning of all team members. This focuses the activity of the team members on explaining concepts to one another and making sure that everyone on the team is ready for a quiz or other that they will take without teammate help. *Equal opportunities for success* means that students contribute to their teams by improving over their own past performances. This ensures that high, average, and low achievers are equally challenged to do their best and that the contributions of all team members will be valued.

The findings of these experimental studies (summarized in this section) indicate that team rewards and individual accountability are essential elements for producing basic skills achievement (Slavin 1983a, 1983b, 1990). It is not enough to simply tell students to work together. They must have a reason to take one another's achievement seriously. Further, if students are rewarded for doing better than they have in the past, they will be more motivated to achieve than if they are rewarded based on their performance in comparison to others, because rewards for improvement make success neither too difficult nor too easy for students to achieve (Slavin 1980).

Four principal Student Team Learning methods have been extensively developed and researched. Two are general cooperative learning methods adaptable to most subjects and grade levels: Student Teams-Achievement Divisions (STAD) and Teams-Games-Tournament (TGI). The remaining two are comprehensive curriculums designed for use in particular subjects at particular grade levels:

Team Assisted Individualization (TAI) for mathematics in grades 3–6 and Cooperative Integrated Reading and Composition (CIRC) for reading and writing instruction in grades 3–5.

Student Tests-Achievement Divisions (STAD)

In STAD (Slavin 1978, 1986), students are assigned to four-member learning teams mixed in performance level, sex, and ethnicity. The teacher presents a lesson, and then students work within their teams to make sure that all team members have mastered the lesson. Finally, all students take individual quizzes on the material, at which time they may *not* help one another.

Students' quiz scores are compared to their own past averages, and points are awarded based on the degree to which students can meet or exceed their own earlier performances. These points are then summed to form team scores, and teams that meet certain criteria earn certificates or other rewards. The whole cycle of activities, from teacher presentation to team practice to quiz, usually takes three to five class periods.

STAD has been used in a wide variety of subjects, from mathematics to language arts and social studies. It has been used from grade 2 through college. STAD is most appropriate for teaching well-defined objectives with single right answers, such as mathematical computations and applications, language usage and mechanics, geography and map skills, and science facts and concepts.

Teams-Games-Tournament (TGT)

Teams-Games-Tournament (DeVries and Slavin 1978; Slavin 1986) was the first of the Johns Hopkins cooperative learning methods. it uses the same teacher presentations and teamwork as in STAD, but replaces the quizzes with weekly tournaments. In these, students compete with members of other teams to contribute points to their team scores. Students compete at three-person "tournament tables" against others with similar past records in mathematics. A "bumping" procedure changes table assignments to keep the competition fair. The winner at each tournament table brings the same number of points to his or her team, regardless of which table it is; this means that low achievers (competing with other low achievers) and high achievers (competing high achievers) have equal opportunities for success. As in STAD, high-performing teams earn certificates or other forms of team rewards. TGT is appropriate for the same types of objectives as STAD.

Team Assisted Individualization (TAI)

Team Assisted Individualization (TAI; Slavin et al. 1986) shares with STAD and TGT the use of four-member mixed ability learning teams and certificates for high-performing teams. But where STAD and TGT use a single pace of instruction for the class, TAI combines cooperative learning with individualized instruction. Also, where STAD and TGT apply to most subjects and grade levels, TAI is specifically designed to teach mathematics to students in grades 3–6 (or older students not ready for a full algebra course).

In TAI, students enter an individualized sequence according to a placement test and then proceed at their own rates. In general, team members work on different units. Teammates check each others' work against answer sheets and help one another with any problems. Final unit tests are taken without teammate help and are scored by student monitors. Each week, teachers total the number of units completed by all team members and give certificates or other team rewards to teams that exceed a criterion score based on the number of final tests passed, with extra points for perfect papers and completed homework.

Because students take responsibility for checking each others' work and managing the flow of materials, the teacher can spend most of the class time presenting lessons to small groups of students drawn from the various teams who are working at the same point in the mathematics sequence. For example, the teacher might call up a decimals group, present a lesson, and then send the students back to their teams to work on problems. Then the teacher might call the fractions group, and so on.

Cooperative Integrated Reading and Composition (CIRC)

The newest of the Student Team learning methods is a comprehensive program for teaching reading and writing in the upper elementary grades called Cooperative Integrated Reading and Composition (CIRC) (Stevens et al. 1987). In CIRC, teachers use basal or literature-based readers and reading groups, much as in traditional reading programs. However, all students are assigned to teams composed of two pairs from two different reading groups. For example, a team might have two "Bluebirds" and two "Redbirds." While the teacher is working with one reading group, the paired students in the other groups are working on a series of cognitively engaging activities, including reading to one another, making predictions about how narrative stories will come out, summarizing stories to one another, writing responses to stories, and practicing spelling, decoding, and vocabulary. If the reading class is not divided into homogeneous reading groups, all students in the teams work with one another. Students work as a total team to master "main idea" and other comprehension skills. During language arts periods, students engage in writing drafts, revising and editing one another's work, and preparing for "publication" of team books.

In most CIRC activities, students follow a sequence of teacher instruction, team practice, team pre-assessments, and quizzes. That is, students do not take the quiz until their teammates have determined that they are ready. Certificates are given to teams based on the average perform team members on all reading and writing activities.

Other Cooperative Learning Methods

Jigsaw

Jigsaw was originally designed by Elliot Aronson and his colleagues (1978). In Aronson's Jigsaw method, students are assigned to six-member teams to work on academic material that has been broken down into sections. For example, a biography might be divided into early life, first accomplishments, major setbacks, later life, and impact on history. Each team member reads his or her section. Next, members of different teams who have studied the same sections meet in "expert groups" to discuss their sections. Then the students return to their teams and take turns teaching their teammates about their sections. Since the only way students can learn sections other than their own is to listen carefully to their teammates, they are motivated to support and show interest in one another's work.

Slavin (1986) developed a modification of Jigsaw at Johns Hopkins University and then incorporated it in the Student Team Learning program. In this method, called Jigsaw II, students work in four or five-member teams as in TGT and STAD. Instead of each student's being assigned a particular section of text, all students read a common narrative, such as a book chapter, a short story, or a biography. However, each student receives a topic (such as "climate" in a unit on France) on which to become an expert. Students with the same topics meet in expert groups to discuss them, after which they return to their teams to teach what they have learned to their teammates. Then students take individual quizzes, which result in team scores based on the improvement score system of STAD. Teams that meet preset standards earn certificates. Jigsaw is primarily used in social studies and other subjects where learning from text is important.

Learning Together

David Johnson and Roger Johnson at the University of Minnesota developed the Learning Together models of cooperative learning (Johnson and Johnson 1987). The methods they have researched involve students working on assignment sheets in four or five-member heterogeneous groups. The groups hand in a single sheet and receive praise and rewards based on the group product. Their methods emphasize team-building activities before students begin working together and regular discussions within groups about how well they are working together.

Group Investigation

Group Investigation, developed by Shlomo Sharan and Yael Sharan at the University of Tel-Aviv, is a general classroom organization plan in which students work in small groups using cooperative inquiry, group discussion, and cooperative planning and projects (Sharan and Sharan 1976). In this method, students form their own two- to six-member groups. After choosing subtopics from a unit being studied by the entire class, the groups further break their subtopics into individual tasks and carry out the activities necessary to prepare group reports. Each group then makes a presentation or display to communicate its findings to the entire class.

RESEARCH ON COOPERATIVE LEARNING

Cooperative learning methods are among the most extensively evaluated alternatives to traditional instruction in use today. Outcome evaluations include:

- academic achievement,
- intergroup relations,
- mainstreaming,
- self-esteem,
- others.

Academic Achievement

More than 70 high-quality studies have evaluated various cooperative learning methods over periods of at least four weeks in regular elementary and secondary schools; 67 of these have measured effects on student achievement (see Slavin 1990). All these studies compared the effects of cooperative learning to those of traditionally caught control groups on measures of the same objectives pursued in all classes. Teachers and classes were either randomly assigned to cooperative or control conditions or matched on pretest achievement level and other factors.

Overall, of 67 studies of the achievement effects of cooperative learning, 41 (61 percent) found significantly greater achievement in cooperative than in control classes. Twenty-five (37 percent) found no differences, and in only one study did the control group outperform the experimental group. However, the effects of cooperative learning vary considerably according to the particular methods used. As noted earlier, two elements must be present if cooperative learning is to be effective: *group goals* and *individual accountability* (Slavin 1983a, 1983b, 1990). That is, groups must be working to achieve some goal or to earn rewards or recognition, and the success of the group must depend on the individual learning of every group member.

In studies of methods such as STAD, TGT, TAI, and CIRC, effects on achievement have been consistently positive; 37 out of 44 such studies (84 percent) found significant positive achievement effects. In contrast, only 4 of 23 studies (17 percent) lacking group goals and individual accountability found positive effects on student achievement. Two of these positive effects were found in studies of Group Investigation in Israel (Sharan et al. 1984; Sharan and Shachar 1988). In Group Investigation, students in each group are responsible for one unique part of the group's overall task, ensuring individual accountability. Then the group's overall performance is evaluated. Even though there are no specific group rewards, the group evaluation probably serves the same purpose.

Why are group goals and individual accountability so important? To understand this, consider the alternatives. In some forms of cooperative learning, students work together to complete a single worksheet or to solve one problem together. In such methods, there is little reason for more able students to take time to explain what is going on to their less able groupmates or to ask their opinions. When the group task is to do something, rather

than to *learn* something, the participation of less able students may be seen as interference rather than help. It may be easier in this circumstance for students to give each other answers than to explain concepts or skills to one another.

In contrast, when the group's task is to ensure that every group member learns something, it is in the interests of every group member to spend time explaining concepts to his or her groupmates. Studies of students' behaviors within cooperative groups have consistently found that the students who gain most from cooperative work are those who give and receive elaborated explanations (Webb 1985). In contrast, Webb found that giving and receiving answers without explanations were *negatively* related to achievement gain. What group goals and individual accountability do is to motivate students to give explanations and to take one another's learning seriously, instead of simply giving answers.

Cooperative learning methods generally work equally well for all types of students. While occasional studies find particular advantages for high or low achievers, boys or girls, and so on, the great majority find equal benefits for all types of students. Sometimes teachers or parents worry that cooperative learning will hold back high achievers. The research provides absolutely no support for this claim; high achievers gain from cooperative learning (relative to high achievers in traditional classes) just as much as do low and average achievers (see Slavin, this issue, p. 63).

Research on the achievement effects of cooperative learning has more often taken place in grades 3–9 than 10–12. Studies at the senior high school level are about as positive as those at earlier grade levels, but there is a need for more research at that level. Cooperative learning methods have been equally successful in urban, rural, and suburban schools and with students of different ethnic groups (although a few studies have found particularly positive effects for black students; see Slavin and Oickle 1981).

Among the cooperative learning methods, the Student Team Learning programs have been most extensively researched and most often found instructionally effective. Of 14 studies of STAD and closely related methods, 11 found significantly higher achievement for this method than for traditional instruction, and two found no differences. For example, Slavin and Karweit (1984) evaluated STAD over an entire school year in innercity Philadelphia 9th grade mathematics classes. Student performance on a standardized mathematics test increased significantly more than in either a mastery learning group or a control group using the same materials. Substantial differences favoring STAD have been found in such diverse subjects as social studies (e.g., Allen and Van Sickle 1984), language arts (Slavin and Karweit 1981), reading comprehension (Stevens, Slavin, Farnish, and Madden 1988), mathematics (Sherman and Thomas 1986), and science (Okebukola 1985). Nine of 11 studies of TGT found similar results (DeVries and Slavin 1978).

The largest effects of Student Team Learning methods have been found in studies of TAI. Five of six studies found substantially greater learning of mathematics computations in TAI than in control classes, while one study found no differences (see Slavin 1985b). Experimental control differences were still substantial (though smaller) a year after the students were in TAI (Slavin and Karweit 1985). In mathematics concepts and applications, one of three studies (Slavin et al. 1984) found significantly greater gains in TAI than control methods, while two found no significant differences (Slavin and Karweit 1985).

In comparison with traditional control groups, three experimental studies of CIRC have found substantial positive effects on scores from standardized tests of reading comprehension, reading vocabulary, language expression, language mechanics, and spelling (Madden et al. 1986, Stevens et al. 1987, Stevens et al. 1990). Significantly greater achievement on writing samples was also found favoring the CIRC students in the two studies which assessed writing.

Other than STL methods, the most consistently successful model for increasing student achievement is Group Investigation (Sharan and Sharan 1976). One study of this method (Sharan et al. 1984) found that it increased the learning of English as a foreign language, while Sharan and Shachar (1988) found positive effects of Group Investigation on the learning of history and geography. A third study of only three weeks' duration (Sharan et al. 1980) also found positive effects on social studies achievement, particularly on higher-level concepts. The Learning Together methods (Johnson and Johnson 1987) have been found instructionally effective when they include the assignment of group grades based on the average of group members' individual quiz scores (e.g., Humphreys et al. 1982, Yager et al. 1985). Studies of the original Jigsaw method have not generally supported this approach (e.g., Mos-

kowitz et al. 1983); but studies of Jigsaw II, which uses group goals and individual accountability, have shown positive effects (Mattingly and VanSickle 1990, Ziegler 1981).

Intergroup Relations

In the laboratory research on cooperation, one of the earliest and strongest findings was that people who cooperate learn to like one another (Slavin 1977b). Not surprisingly, the cooperative learning classroom studies have found quite consistently that students express greater liking for their classmates in general as a result of participating in a cooperative learning method (see Slavin 1983a, 1990). This is important in itself and even more important when the students have different ethnic backgrounds. After all, there is substantial evidence that, left alone, ethnic separateness in schools does not naturally diminish over time (Gerard and Miller 1975).

Social scientists have long advocated inter-ethnic cooperation as a means of ensuring positive intergroup relations in desegregated settings. Contact Theory (Allport 1954), which is in the U.S. the dominant theory of intergroup relations, predicted that positive intergroup relations would arise from school desegregation if and only if students participated in cooperative, equal-status interaction sanctioned by the school. Research on cooperative learning methods has borne out the predictions of Contact Theory. These techniques emphasize cooperative, equal-status interaction between students of different ethnic backgrounds sanctioned by the school (Slavin 1985a).

In most of the research on intergroup relations, students were asked to list their best friends at the beginning of the study and again at the end. The number of friendship choices students made outside their own ethnic groups was the measure of intergroup relations.

Positive effects on intergroup relations have been found for STAD, TGT, TAI, Jigsaw, Learning Together, and Group Investigation models (Slavin 1985b). Two of these studies, one on STAD (Slavin 1979) and one on Jigsaw II (Ziegler 1981), included follow-ups of intergroup friendships several months after the end of the studies. Both found that students who had been in cooperative learning classes still named significantly more friends outside their own ethnic groups than did students who had been in control classes. Two studies of Group Investigation (Sharan et al. 1981, Sharan and Shachar 1988) found that students' improved attitudes and behaviors toward classmates of different ethnic backgrounds extended to classmates who had never been in the same groups, and a study of TAI (Oishi 1983) found positive effects of this method on cross-ethnic interactions outside as well as in class. The U.S. studies of cooperative learning and intergroup relations involved black, white, and (in a few cases) Mexican-American students. A study of Jigsaw II by Ziegler (1981) took place in Toronto, where the major ethnic groups were Anglo-Canadians and children of recent European immigrants. The Sharan (Sharan et al. 1984, Sharan and Shachar 1988) studies of Group Investigation took place in Israel and involved friendships between Jews of both European and Middle Eastern backgrounds.

Mainstreaming
Although ethnicity is a major barrier to friendship, it is not so large as the one between physically or mentally handicapped children and their normal-progress peers. Mainstreaming, an unprecedented opportunity for handicapped children to take their place in the school and society, has created enormous practical problems for classroom teachers, and it often leads to social rejection of the handicapped children. Because cooperative learning methods have been successful in improving relationships across the ethnicity barrier—which somewhat resembles the barrier between mainstreamed and normal progress students—these methods have also been applied to increase the acceptance of the mainstreamed student.

The research on cooperative learning and mainstreaming has focused on the academically handicapped child. In one study, STAD was used to attempt to integrate students performing two years or more below the level of their peers into the social structure of the classroom. The use of STAD significantly reduced the degree to which the normal-progress students rejected their mainstreamed classmates and increased the academic achievement and self-esteem as well as normal-progress (Madden and Slavin 1983). Similar effects have been found for TAI (Slavin et al. 1984), and other research using cooperative teams has also shown significant improvements in relationships between mainstreamed academically handicapped students and their normal-progress peers (Ballard et al. 1977, Cooper et al. 1980).

In addition, one study in a self-contained school for emotionally disturbed adolescents found that the use of TGT increased positive interactions and friendships among students (Slavin 1977a).

Five months after the study ended, these positive interactions were still found more often in the former TGT classes than in the control classes. In a study in a similar setting, Janke (1978) found that the emotionally disturbed students were more on-task, were better behaved, and had better attendance in TGT classes than in control classes.

Self-Esteem
One of the most important aspects of a child's personality is his or her self-esteem. Several researchers working on cooperative learning techniques have found that these methods do increase students' self-esteem. These improvements in self-esteem have been found for TGT and STAD (Slavin 1990), for Jigsaw (Blaney et al. 1977), and for the three methods combined (Slavin and Karweit 1981). Improvements in student self-concepts have also been found for TAI (Slavin et al. 1984).

Other Outcomes
In addition to effects on achievement, positive intergroup relations, greater acceptance of mainstreamed students, and self-esteem, effects of cooperative learning have been found on a variety of other important educational outcomes. These include liking school, development of peer norms in favor of doing well academically, feelings of individual control over the student's own fate in school, and cooperativeness and altruism (see Slavin 1983a, 1990). TGT (DeVries and Slavin 1978) and STAD (Slavin 1978, Janke 1978) have been found to have positive effects on students' time-on-task. One study found that lower socioeconomic status students at risk of becoming delinquent who worked in cooperative groups in 6th grade had better attendance, fewer contacts with the police, and higher behavioral ratings for teachers in grades 7–11 than did control students (Hartley 1976). Another study implemented forms of cooperative learning beginning in kindergarten and continuing through the 4th grade (Solomon et al. 1990). This study found that the students who had been taught cooperatively were significantly higher than control students on measures of supportive, friendly, and prosocial behavior; were better at resolving conflicts; and expressed more support for democratic values.

USEFUL STRATEGIES

Returning to the questions at the beginning of this article, we now see the usefulness of cooperative learning strategies for improving such diverse outcomes as student achievement at a variety of grade levels and in many subjects, intergroup relations, relationships between mainstreamed and normal-progress students, and student self-esteem. Further, their widespread and growing use demonstrates that cooperative learning methods are practical and attractive to teachers. The history of the development, evaluation, and dissemination of cooperative learning is an outstanding example of the use of educational research to create programs that have improved the educational experience of thousands of students and will continue to affect thousands more.

REFERENCES

Allen, W. H., and R. L. Van Sickle. (1984). "Learning Teams and Low Achievers." *Social Education:* 60–64.

Allport, G. (1954). *The Nature of Prejudice.* Cambridge, Mass.: Addison-Wesley.

Aronson, E., N. Blaney, C. Stephan, J. Sikes, and M. Snapp. (1978). *The Jigsaw Classroom.* Beverly Hills, Calif: Sage.

Ballard, M., L. Dorman, J. Gottlieb, and M. Kauffman. (1977). "Improving the Social Status of Mainstreamed Retarded Children." *Journal of Educational Psychology* 69: 605–611.

Blaney, N. T., S. Stephan, D. Rosenfeld, E. Aronson, and J. Sikes. (1977). "Interdependence in the Classroom: A Field Study." Journal *of Educational Psychology* 69: 121–128.

Cooper, L., D. W. Johnson, R. Johnson, and F. Wilderson. (1980). "Effects of Cooperative, Competitive, and Individualistic Experiences on Interpersonal Attraction Among Heterogeneous Peers." *Journal of Social Psychology* 111: 243–252.

Deutsch, M. (1949). "A Theory of Cooperation and Competition." *Human Relations* 2: 129–152.

DeVries, D. L., and R. E. Slavin. (1978). "Teams-Games-Tournament (TGT): Review of Ten Classroom Experiments." *Journal of Research and Development in Education* 12: 28–38.

Gerard, H. B., and N. Miller. (1975). *School Desegregation: A Long-Range Study.* New York: Plenum.

Hartley, W. (1976). *Prevention Outcomes of Small Group Education with School Children: An Epidemiologic Follow-Up of the Kansas City School Behavior Project.* Kansas City: University of Kansas Medical Center.

Humphreys, B., R. Johnson, and D. W. Johnson. (1982). "Effects of Cooperative, Competitive, and Individualistic Learning on Students' Achievement in Science Class." *Journal of Research in Science Teaching* 19: 351–356.

Janke, R. (April 1978). "The Teams-Games-Tournament (TGT) Method and the Behavioral Adjustment and

Academic Achievement of Emotionally impaired Adolescents." Paper presented at the annual convention of the American Educational Research Association, Toronto.

Johnson, D. W., and R. T. Johnson. (1987). *Learning Together and Alone.* 2nd ed. Englewood Cliffs, N.J.: Prentice-Hall.

Madden, N. A., and R. E. Slavin. (1983). "Cooperative Learning and Social Acceptance of Mainstreamed Academically Handicapped Students." *Journal of Special Education* 17: 171–182.

Madden, N. A., R. J. Stevens, and R. E. Slavin. (1986). *A Comprehensive Cooperative Learning Approach to Elementary Reading and Writing: Effects on Student Achievement.* Report No. 2. Baltimore, Md.: Center for Research on Elementary and Middle Schools, Johns Hopkins University.

Mattingly, R. M., and R. L. VanSickle. (1990). *Jigsaw II in Secondary Social Studies: An Experiment.* Athens, Ga.: University of Georgia.

Moskowitz, J. M., J. H. Malvin, G. A. Schaeffer, and E. Schaps. (1983). "Evaluation of a Cooperative Learning Strategy." *American Educational Research Journal* 20: 687–696.

Oishi, S. (1983). "Effects of Team-Assisted Individualization in Mathematics on Cross-Race Interactions of Elementary School Children." Doctoral diss., University of Maryland.

Okebukola, P. A. (1985). "The Relative Effectiveness of Cooperative and Competitive Interaction Techniques in Strengthening Students' Performance in Science Classes." *Science Education* 69: 501–509.

Sharan, S., and C. Shachar. (1988). *Language and Learning in the Cooperative Classroom.* New York: Springer.

Sharan, S., and Y. Sharan. (1976). *Small-group Teaching.* Englewood Cliffs, N.J.: Educational Technology Publications.

Sharan, S., R. Hertz-Lazarowitz, and Z. Ackerman. (1980). "Academic Achievement of Elementary School Children in Small group vs. Whole Class Instruction." *Journal of Experimental Education* 48: 125–129.

Sharan, S., P. Kussell, R. Hertz-Lazarowitz, Y. Bejarano, S. Raviv, and Y. Sharan. (1984). *Cooperative Learning in the Classroom: Research in Desegregated Schools.* Hillsdale, N.J.: Erlbaum.

Sherman, L. W., and M. Thomas. (1986). "Mathematics Achievement in Cooperative Versus Individualistic Goal-structured High School Classrooms." *Journal of Educational Research* 79: 169–172.

Slavin, R. E. (1977a). "A Student Team Approach to Teaching Adolescents with Special Emotional and Behavioral Needs." *Psychology in The Schools* 14: 77–84.

Slavin, R. E. (1977b). "Classroom Reward Structure: An Analytical and Practical Review." *Review of Educational Research* 47:633–650.

Slavin, R. E. (1978). "Student Teams and Achievement Divisions." *Journal of Research and Development in Education* 12: 39–49.

Slavin, R. E. (1979). "Effects of Biracial Learning Teams on Cross-Racial Friendships." *Journal of Educational Psychology* 71: 381–387.

Slavin, R. E. (1983a). *Cooperative Learning.* New York: Longman.

Slavin, R. E. (1983b). "When Does Cooperative Learning Increase Student Achievement?" *Psychological Bulletin* 94: 429–445.

Slavin, R. E. (March 1985a). "Cooperative Learning: Applying Contact Theory in Desegregated Schools." *Journal of Social Issues* 41: 45–62.

Slavin, R. E. (1985b). "Team Assisted Individualization: A Cooperative Learning Solution for Adaptive Instruction in Mathematics." In *Adapting Instruction to Individual Differences*, edited by M. Wang and H. Walberg. Berkeley, Calif.: McCutchan.

Slavin, R. E. (1986). *Using Student Team Learning.* 3rd ed. Baltimore, Md.: Center for Research on Elementary and Middle Schools, Johns Hopkins University.

Slavin, R. E. (1990). *Cooperative Learning: Theory, Research, and Practice.* Englewood Cliffs, N.J.: Prentice-Hall.

Slavin, R. E. (February 1991). "Are Cooperative Learning and 'Untracking' Harmful to the Gifted?" *Educational Leadership* 48: 63–74.

Slavin, R. E., and N. Karweit. (1981). "Cognitive and Affective Outcomes of an Intensive Student Team Learning Experience." *Journal of Experimental Education* 50: 29–35.

Slavin, R. E., and N. Karweit. "Mastery Learning and Student Teams: A Factorial Experiment in Urban General Mathematics Classes." *American Educational Research Journal* 21: 725–736.

Slavin, R. E., and N. L. Karweit. (1985). "Effects of Whole-Class, Ability Grouped, and Individualized Instruction on Mathematics Achievement." *American Educational Research Journal* 22: 351–367.

Slavin, R. E., M. Leavey, and N. A. Madden. (1984). "Combining Cooperative Learning and Individualized Instruction: Effects on Student Mathematics Achievement Attitudes and Behaviors." *Elementary School Journal* 84: 409–422.

Slavin, R. E., M. B. Leavey, and N. A. Madden. (1986). *Team Accelerated Instruction Mathematics.* Watertown, Mass.; Mastery Education Corporation.

Slavin, R. E., N. A. Madden, and M. B. Leavey. (1984). "Effects of Team Assisted Individualization on the Mathematics Achievement of Academically Handicapped and Nonhandicapped Students." *Journal of Educational Psychology* 76: 813–819.

Slavin, R. E., and E. Oickle. (1981). "Effects of Cooperative Learning Teams on Student Achievement and Race Relations: Treatment × Race Interactions." *Sociology of Education* 54: 174–180.

Solomon, D., M. Watson, E. Schaps, V. Battistich, and J. Solomon. (1990). "Cooperative Learning as Part of a Comprehensive Classroom Program Designed to Promote Prosocial Development." In *Current Research on Cooperative Learning*, edited by S. Sharan, New York: Praeger.

Stevens, R. J., N. A. Madden, R. E. Slavin, and A. M. Farnish. (1987). "Cooperative Integrated Reading and Composition: Two Field Experiments." *Reading Research Quarterly* 22: 433–454.

Stevens, R. J., R. E. Slavin, and A. M. Farnish. (April 1990). "A Cooperative Learning Approach to Elementary Reading and Writing Instruction: Long-Term Effects." Paper presented at the annual convention of the American Educational Research Association, Boston.

Stevens, R. J., R. E. Slavin, A. M. Farnish, and N. A. Madden. (April 1988). "The Effects of Cooperative learning and Direct Instruction in Reading Comprehension Strategies on Main Idea Identification." Paper presented at the annual Convention of the American Educational Research Association. New Orleans.

Webb, N. (1985). "Student Interaction and Learning in Small Groups: A Research Summary." in *Learning to Cooperate, Cooperating to Learn*, edited by R. Slavin, S. Sharan, S. Kagan, R. Herts-Lazarowitz, C. Webb, and R. Schmuck. New York; Plenum.

Yager, S., D. W. Johnson. and R. T. Johnson. (1985). "Oral Discussion, Group-to-Individual Transfer, and Achievement in Cooperative Learning Groups." *Journal of Educational Psychology* 77: 60–66.

Ziegler, S. (1981). "The Effectiveness of Cooperative Learning Teams for Increasing Cross-Ethnic Friendship: Additional Evidence." *Human Organization* 40: 264–268.

Author's note. This article was written under funding from the Office of Educational Research and Improvement, U.S. Department of Education (Grant No. OERI-R117-R90002). However, any opinions expressed are mine and do not represent OERI positions or policy.

▶ Chapter 11

Managing Disruptive Students

RAY PETTY

What should a school system do with its most disruptive students? In 1978, the Hartford Public School System was faced with the problem of providing education for its students with serious behavioral disorders ("BD students"). Out-of-district tuition was increasing rapidly, P.L. 94-142 required more local programming, the number of identified BD students was rising, and schools were having to accept students expelled from out-of-district placements.

Hartford responded by creating the Special Education Learning Center (SELC), a specialized therapeutic school for students with violent behavior. Starting with five students, one teacher, a teacher's aide, and an administrator, the SELC now serves a student population of 185 (K-12) with a staff of 50. This review of SELC's first decade may help your school district address the problem of programming for those students who are too disruptive to remain in regular schools.

THE BEHAVIORAL CURRICULUM

In developing a program students, it is important to remember that traditional school programs have not worked for them. In fact, traditional schools often contribute to BD students' behavioral problems. Therefore, alternative programming must not be merely a smaller version of "business as usual."

Program developers must give careful attention to teaching a behavioral curriculum. While we are

Ray Petty is Principal, Special Education Learning Center, Hartford Public Schools, 249 High St., Hartford, CT 06103.

all aware of the need for subject-area curriculums, we often forget that a curriculum in the *behavioral* area is equally important. What are our behavioral expectations? How do we expect students to progress in behavioral skill development? What are our reinforcers and punishments? How do we deal with advanced students and students requiring remediation? A behavioral curriculum addresses these issues.

Subject-area curriculums in the SELC parallel the curriculums in the rest of the school system. But this academic curriculum is secondary to our behavioral curriculum. Regular classroom teachers often continue their lessons despite minor behavioral infractions; SELC teachers, who are in the business of teaching behavioral basics, always stop class to deal with inappropriate behavior. Consequently, students realize that inappropriate behaviors will be dealt with quickly.

One might expect this practice to have a negative effect on academic growth. Yet we have found just the opposite to be true. When teachers stop class immediately to deal with behavioral problems, more time-on-task is ultimately devoted to academic lessons. It is not surprising, therefore, that in addition to behavioral growth, our students make important academic gains. For example, their year-for-year growth in math and reading is normal.

EXPECTATIONS AND REWARDS

Teachers of BD students should hold high expectations for appropriate behavior—despite students' behavioral histories. Specialized programming must also provide a structure that enables students to develop more appropriate behaviors while eliminating inappropriate ones.

Within the SELC, teachers give students brief report cards *at the end of each period.* Teachers rate each student on conduct and academic work: two points for meeting behavioral expectations, only one if a small problem developed, and none if there was a major problem requiring discipline. Academic performance is rated similarly. Once a month, students with the highest points get a special treat: a movie, lunch out, or some other recognition. This point system provides students with reinforcement and feedback.

PUNISHMENTS

Teachers must choose punishments carefully to ensure that students perceive them as negative. In our school, *boredom* is a major punishment. When a student has misbehaved, he or she has to stand rigid in the corner, facing the wall, for 10 minutes. For more serious behavioral problems, we use a special room for Controlled Time-Out. When the time is up, the student returns to his or her desk and continues work. No need for a teacher's lecture—the students know what they have done wrong. Further, if you warn a child at the end of punishment about repeating an act, you are setting an expectation for such repetition.

SETTING AND SUPPLIES

Those developing a specialized school for the behaviorally disordered must give careful attention to its design. Physical space must be attractive, compact, and functional. Since BD students tend to wander and become "lost," the school should have as little unsupervised space as possible.

One of our buildings has a large central open space, used for breaks, program meetings, and the like, surrounded by 10 small classrooms. Classrooms and bathrooms all open onto this central space. There are no corridors, stairs, or corners where students can go for unsupervised activity. We simply don't give behavioral problems a place to begin.

Because staff in a program for BD students need to spend maximum time planning, they need a wide variety of educational materials, books, and supplies. Our teachers receive over $1,000 in start-up costs when they join the staff and $400-$500 a year after that to replenish used items. (These figures do not take into account normal classroom furnishings and supplies.) With only, 5-10 students in a class, this represents considerable funding per teacher. But with such a challenging student population, teachers need to spend their time developing behavioral plans and interventions rather than academic materials.

COLLEGIAL SUPPORT

Given the manipulative skills of BD students, teachers need to coordinate their efforts and provide collegial support. In the SELC, we operate a four-hour school day for students and a six and one-half hour workday for staff. This gives staff a half hour before students arrive and two hours after they leave for this important team function. After a difficult day, staff members can review the and learn from their experiences.

To work effectively, teams must be kept to reasonable numbers. Though there are 50 staff members at the SELC, they are divided into 5 separate teams, with fewer than 10 members in each. While the number of students assigned to a team may vary according to their degree of violent behavior, each team consists of five teachers, several aides, and a therapist (social worker). This grouping enhances the team's ability to get to know their students.

PHYSICAL INTERVENTION

One of the most controversial elements of an effective program for BD students is physical intervention. This is *not* the use of corporal punishment. Physical intervention is the use of reasonable physical force to ensure student compliance with appropriate staff direction. If a BD student is allowed to win a confrontation because an adult cannot take appropriate physical action, the student assumes the position of control, and the program will eventually collapse.

Let me give an example. Ms. Smith asks Harry to step to the board. Harry refuses. She asks a second time. He sits defiantly in his chair. Ms. Smith approaches Harry, takes him gently by the arm, and pulls him toward the board. He gives an exasperated sigh, rises to his feet, and goes to the board.

Ms. Smith used a gentle physical nudge when words were ineffective.

In another case, John jumps to his feet screaming profanities and begins swinging at Mark. Ms. Smith calls for help in physically separating John and Mark. The team quickly arrives. Because John is still struggling wildly, four staff members each hold a limb, Ms. Smith his head, and another teacher his torso, as John is lowered to the floor and restrained. Once they have John under physical control, the staff members begin a planned and practiced "talk-down" procedure. As John calms down, they slowly release him from restraint—limb by limb.

Of course, safeguards must be built into any system that allows physical intervention. The staff must not abuse their ability to physically control students. Proper teaming provides such safeguards, as team members observe one another's behavior and then discuss differences of opinion at team meetings.

Since one-on-one physical interventions, except in a mild case like Ms. Smith and Harry, can result in staff or student injury, we *always* use a team approach in physical restraint. In addition to preventing injury, this practice guarantees that other staff members are present during restraint in case one becomes overly emotional and loses control. On the rare occasions when this occurs, the understood code words "I'll take over now" give that staff member a nondebatable order to leave the area and regain control. When his or her control returns, so can the staff member. Teachers are human; they need to plan for the occasional instance when emotion overcomes professional skill.

DEMONSTRATED SUCCESS

For over 10 years, the SELC has demonstrated that it is possible to provide a program for severely BD students within the public school setting. Moreover, the SELC saves the district money, complies with P.L. 94-142, allows Hartford to set its own placement priorities for disruptive students, and provides a model for other districts. And each year, one third of our student population moves to a less restrictive environment.

What Research Really Shows about Assertive Discipline

GARY F. RENDER, JE NELL M. PADILLA, and H. MARK KRANK

In the October 1988 issue of *Educational Leadership*, Lee Canter ("Let the Educator Beware: A Response to Curwin and Mendler") cited studies that he believes provide strong support for the effectiveness of Assertive Discipline. He has also stated that Assertive Discipline is based on research and will produce an 80 percent reduction in student misbehavior (Canter and Associates 1987). Canter has made this statement repeatedly (Canter 1979a, 1979b, 1983) but has provided no evidence to support it.

A SMALL DATABASE

We believed that a program in existence for 12 years and so widely used (reports suggest that 500,000 people have been trained in Assertive Discipline) would have generated an extensive database (Canter and Associates 1987). We therefore reviewed the literature (Render et al. in press, Render et al. 1987) and reported only studies in which information was gathered in some systematic way and in which results were presented. We found only 16 studies (10 dissertations, 3 journal articles, and 3 other reports) meeting our criteria. Equally surprising is the nature of the studies. Not one

Gary F. Render is Professor of Educational Psychology, University of Wyoming, College of Education, Department of Educational Foundations and Instructional Technology, Box 3374, Laramie, WY 82071. Je Nell M. Padilla and H. Mark Krank both are Ph.D. candidates in Educational Psychology, Department of Educational Foundations and Instructional Technology, University of Wyoming.

study systematically investigated the program's effectiveness compared with any other specific approach. The studies of Assertive Discipline have been generated primarily by beginning researchers, and no strongly generalizable data have resulted. The research is sparse and unsophisticated.

Figure 1 presents a brief description of the existing studies of Assertive Discipline. We have presented the information as it was reported without any interpretations of the data.

LIMITED EVIDENCE

The claims made by Canter (1988) and also made in Barrett's (1987) review are simply not supported by the existing and available literature. We would agree that Assertive Discipline could be helpful in severe cases where students are behaving inappropriately more than 96 percent of the time, as in the study of Mandelbaum and colleagues (1983). We would also argue that teachers such as the one in that study would benefit from *any* intervention. However, we can find no evidence that Assertive Discipline is an effective approach deserving school-wide and districtwide adoption.

Canter has also stated that teachers have no need for educational literature; they need "answers" (1988, p. 73). We believe teachers deserve answers based on more than limited studies that suffer from a lack of generalizability to various settings, teachers, subject areas, and grade levels. (We suggest that readers form their conclusions regard-

FIGURE 1 **Studies of Assertive Discipline (AD)**

Authors	Subjects	Variables	Findings
1. Ersavas (1981)	Teachers, administrators, and 5th grade students.	Perceptions of AD implementation.	The school with the highest California assessment program achievement results experienced the least growth from AD. Students who perceived themselves as reading better than their peers experienced the least growth from AD.
2. Bauer (1982)	Grade 9 students drawn from high school using AD. Comparison from high school not using AD (no N reported).	Reduction of discipline problems. Increasing student satisfaction. Improving student attitude.	AD effective in discipline areas related to social skills. Problems related to learning not affected. Teachers reported greater satisfaction. No increase in student morale or attitudes (no data reported).
3. Henderson (1982)	Elementary teachers (no N reported).	Locus of control, pupil control ideology, self-concept, assertive teacher characteristics.	Teachers trained in AD were significantly different from controls on all measures. No study was made of behavior of these teachers' students.
4. Moffett, Jerenka, and Kovan (1982)	67% of district teachers (N = 94)	Teachers' perceptions of AD.	21% perceived student behavior as somewhat improved; 48% as improved in an observable degree; 30% as totally improved. Authors claim that AD "virtually eliminated classroom disruptions."
5. Crawley (1983)	Teachers (N = 52) and students (N = 580)	Perceptions of teachers trained or not trained in AD. Perceptions of students of teachers trained or not trained in AD.	"... There are no benefits measured by this study derived from Assertive Discipline training."
6. Mandelbaum, Russell, Krouse, and Gonter (1983)	One 3rd grade classroom (N = 31) and the teacher.	Student out-of-seat behavior (OB). Student inappropriate talking (IT) measured in percent of time.	Before After Remove Reinstate AD AD AD AD OB 96% 45% 87% 42% IT 99% 54% 91% 65% Never did out-of-seat behavior occur less than 35% of the time.
7. Fereira (1983)	Elementary students in one school of 356 students (1979–80) and 365 students (1982–83).	Number of students referred to office for disciplinary reasons.	During 1979–80 school year 350 students referred to office. During 1982–83 school year 247 students referred. Referrals changed from interpersonal problems to on-task behavior problems. No indication of what actually happened in classrooms.
8. Ward (1984)	Not reported.	Classroom disruptions.	Before AD—17.09 disruptions/100 students/day. After AD—10.44 disruptions/100 students/day. Seven other variables were significantly related to the results.

(Continued)

FIGURE 1 *(Continued)*

Authors	Subjects	Variables	Findings
9. Allen (1984)	7th, 8th, and 9th grade students (N = 353).	Disciplinary referrals.	There was a 31.8% (*p* < .05) decrease in referrals from 3,646/year to 2,492/year. A survey of the staff indicated that AD was effective. The number of referrals after AD suggests the school still had a severe discipline problem.
10. Smith (1984)	Student teachers trained in AD (no N reported).	Student teachers' assertiveness.	Student teachers trained in AD rated themselves more assertive than controls. Supervising teachers agreed. No report on student behavior in these student teachers' classrooms.
11. Webb (1984)	Teachers K–12 (N = 129), principals (N = 12).	Perceptions of teachers and principals regarding effectiveness of AD.	86% liked AD; 82% perceived improved student behavior; 77% perceived improved control of student behavior; 43% perceived improvement in student behavior to be lasting.
12. Braun, Render, and Moon (1984)	Elementary and junior high students (N = 1,087), teachers (N = 86), and parents (N = 446).	Involvement of students in the establishment of classroom rules and consequences of misbehavior.	71% of students said they rarely or never were given an opportunity for input in establishing classroom rules or consequences for misbehavior.
13. McCormack (1985)	36 3rd grade classes; 18 using AD, 18 not. N = 687.	Off-task behavior during reading instruction.	Students in classes without AD off-task 13% of time. Students with AD were off-task 5% less. AD was said to account for 9% of the variance in off-task behavior.
14. Parker (1985)	Administrators, secondary teachers, students, and parents (no N reported).	Perceptions of AD.	AD favored by administrators. Teachers preferred their own discipline styles. Parents generally approved but did not expect or desire to see AD used with their own children.
15. Barrett and Curtis (1986)	Student teachers trained in AD (N = 248) 1981–82; student teachers not trained in AD (N = 288) 1982–83; supervisors (N = 396) rated student teachers not trained in AD in 1981–82. Supervisors (N = 307) rated student teachers trained in AD in 1982–83.	Perceptions of student teachers regarding their ability to use appropriate discipline techniques. Perceptions of supervisors regarding student teachers' use of techniques.	Student teachers trained in AD perceived significantly (*p* < .05) better preparation in use of techniques. Supervisors rated student teachers trained in AD significantly (*p* < .05) better at using appropriate techniques. Appropriate techniques were not defined. The use of assertive discipline techniques was not a focus of the study. The study does not support or fail to support the use of AD. The *use* of AD techniques was not studied.

FIGURE 1 *(Continued)*

Authors	Subjects	Variables	Findings
16. Barrett (1987)	A review of literature on AD, all of which is included here.	The same variables lited above. Findings are drawn from several of the studies listed here— no others than listed here.	"Based upon research conducted at this early stage [AD] has proven to be effective." "It [AD] has been proven beneficial in both decreasing the number of referrals and as an effective means to increase on-task behavior of students." "[AD] also has proven significantly effective in reducing student disruptions."

ing Assertive Discipline by evaluating the existing literature.)

WHERE ARE THE FACTS?

Canter and Assertive Discipline advocates suggest that the program is "proven" effective. Even after years of investigation and numerous studies and replications, no reputable scholar would state that "the research *proves*" any particular educational approach. Ten dissertations, three journal articles, and three other reports is certainly limited evidence to support *any* educational strategy. We agree with Canter that "facts are hard to dispute" (1988, p. 71); however, facts result from systematic, scientific investigations, replications, and evaluations by scholars, not from hopeful claims and promotions.

REFERENCES

Allen, R. D. (1984). "The Effect of Assertive Discipline on the Number of Junior High School Disciplinary Referrals." *Dissertation Abstracts International* 44: 2299A–2300A.

Barrett, E. R. (1987). "Assertive Discipline and Research." Unpublished manuscript available from Canter and Associates, P.O. Box 2113, Santa Monica, CA 90406.

Barrett, E. R., and K. F. Curtis. (Spring/Summer 1986). "The Effect of Assertive Discipline Training on Student Teachers." *Teacher Education and Practice*: 53–56.

Bauer, R. L. (1982). "A Quasi-Experimental Study of the Effects of Assertive Discipline." *Dissertation Abstracts International* 43: 25A.

Braun, J. A., G. F. Render, and C. E. Moon. (1984). "Assertive Discipline: A Report of Student, Teacher, and Parent Perceptions." *Journal of the Association for the Study of Perception* 19, 1: 18–25.

Canter and Associates. (1987). "Abstracts of Research Validating Effectiveness of Assertive Discipline." Unpublished manuscript available from Canter and Associates, P.O. Box 2113, Santa Monica, CA 90406.

Canter, L. (1979a). "Competency-Based Approach to Discipline—It's Assertive." *Thrust for Educational Leadership* 8:11–13.

Canter, L. (1979b). "Taking Charge of Student Behavior." *National Elementary Principal* 58, 4:33–36, 41.

Canter, L. (October 1983). "Assertive Discipline: A Proven Approach." *Today's Catholic Teacher*: 36–37.

Canter, L. (October 1988). "Let the Education Beware: A Response to Curwin and Mendler." *Educational Leadership* 46, 2: 71–73.

Crawley, K. E. (1983). "Teacher and Student Perceptions with Regard to Classroom Behavior Conditions, Procedures, and Student Behavior in Classes of Teachers Trained in Assertive Discipline Methods." *Dissertation Abstracts International* 43: 2840A.

Ersavas, C. M. (1981). "A Study of the Effect of Assertive Discipline at Four Elementary Schools." *Dissertation Abstracts International* 42: 473A.

Fereira, C. L. (1983). *A Positive Approach to Assertive Discipline.* Martinez, Calif.: Martinez Unified School District. (ERIC Document Reproduction Service No. ED 240 058).

Henderson, C. B. (1982). "An Analysis of Assertive Discipline Training and Implementation on Inservice Elementary Teachers' Self-Concept. Locus of Control, Pupil Control Ideology, and Assertive Personality Characteristics." *Dissertation Abstracts International* 42: 4797A.

Mandelbaum, L. H., S. C. Russell, J. Krouse, and M. Gonter. (1983). "Assertive Discipline: An Effective Classwide Behavior Management Program." *Behavior Disorders* 8, 4: 258–264.

McCormack, S. L. (1985). "Students' Off-Task Behavior and Assertive Discipline." (Doctoral diss., University of Oregon.) *Dissertation Abstracts International* 46: 1880A.

Moffett, K. L., D. J. Jurenka, and J. Kovan. (June/July/August 1982). "Assertive Discipline." *California School Boards:* 24–27.

Parker, P. R. (1985). "Effects of Secondary-Level Assertive Discipline in a Central Texas School District and Guidelines to Successful Assertion and Reward Strategies." *Dissertation Abstracts International* 45:3504A.

Render, G. F., J. M. Padilla, and H. M. Krank. (October 1987). "Assertive Discipline: A Critical Review and Analysis." Paper presented at the annual meeting of the Northern Rocky Mountain Educational Research Association, Park City, Utah.

Render, G. F., J. M. Padilla, and H. M. Krank. (In press). "Assertive Discipline: A Critical Review and Analysis." *Teachers College Record.*

Smith, S. J. (1984). "The Effects of Assertive Discipline Training on Student Teachers' Self-Perceptions and Classroom Management Skills." *Dissertation Abstracts International* 44: 2690A.

Ward, L. R. (1984). "The Effectiveness of 'Assertive Discipline' as a Means to Reduce Classroom Disruptions." *Dissertation Abstracts International* 44: 2323A–2324A.

Webb, M. M. (1984). "An Evaluation of Assertive Discipline and Its Degree of Effectiveness as Perceived by the Professional Staff in Selected School Corporations." *Dissertation Abstracts International* 44: 2324A–2325A.

Response to Render, Padilla, and Krank: But Practitioners Say It Works!

SAMMIE McCORMACK

Remember the six blind men of Indostan who went to see the elephant? They argued that it "is very like a wall . . . is very like a spear . . . is very like a snake . . . is very like a tree . . . is very like a rope." In his fable, John B. Saxe concluded that the men were "Each in his own opinion, Exceedingly stiff and strong. Though each was partly in the right, And all were in the wrong" (Saxe, "The Blind Men and the Elephant," Boston, 1852).

So also can it be said of authors who criticize the programs of others without basis. Like the blind men, Render, Padilla, and Krank are both partly the right and partly in the wrong.

PARTLY RIGHT

I too am surprised that so little research about Assertive Discipline is available. That concern, however, is not limited to the study of Assertive Discipline; in fact, no other copyrighted classroom management program is better researched. Render, Padilla, and Krank are correct in chastising the research community for failure to compare the program's effects with other approaches to classroom management. Is that an indictment of Assertive Discipline? Does the absence of that comparison mean

Sammie McCormack is Coordinator, High Performance Schools, San Diego County Office of Education, 6401 Linda Vista Rd., San Diego, CA 92111-7399.

Assertive Discipline lacks a support base? To both questions, the answer is "no."

Other studies, beyond those examined by Render, Padilla, and Krank, indicate that from a "practitioner's perspective," Assertive Discipline achieves the outcomes that Canter and Associates promote (1976). The sample findings in Figure 1 come from school districts and state organizations; the publications cited are reports to their constituencies.

PARTLY WRONG

Render, Padilla, and Krank are also partially wrong in their findings. I do not choose to challenge their chart of studies, item by item. However, the information they present appears to come from a reading of abstracts rather than the complete research. I uncovered enough discrepancies to cast doubt on their conclusions. For example:

- Ersavas (1981) studied four schools. Render, Padilla, and Krank report "the school."
- Bauer (1982) studied 315 students and 23 teachers at a high school where Assertive Discipline was used, and 255 students and 45 teachers at a different high school where Assertive Discipline was not used. Render, Padilla, and Krank state "no N reported."
- Henderson (1982) studied 25 teachers with Assertive Discipline training and 25 teachers with-

FIGURE 1   **Findings from School Districts and State Organizations about Assertive Discipline**

Location/Author	Subjects	Variables	Findings
1. Cartwright School District Phoenix, Ariz. (1982)	445 teachers All district records of behavior referrals	Tardiness Bus referrals Weapons referrals Theft Classroom management techniques	Down 54% in the district Down 71% in the district Down 71% in the district Down 88% in the district 86% of teachers felt student behavior improved
2. Compton, Calif., School District Swanson (1984)	30 principals 241 teachers 258 parents 72 secondary students	The need for Assertive Discipline Implementation time Teaching time Program effectiveness	66% felt the program was needed. 85% felt outcomes justified the administrative implementation time. 83% of teachers felt it freed more time for instruction. Conclusion: "Program is perceived as a success. The goals and objectives of this program have been achieved to a significant extent."
3. Lennox School District Inglewood, Calif. Moffett, Jurenka, and Kovan (1982)	94 K–12 teachers (67% of district)	Student behavior	78% felt that student behavior was observably or totally improved.
4. Troy City Schools Troy, Ohio Becker (1980)	100 elementary teachers 33 teachers of grades 7–8 40 teachers of grades 9–12	Student behavior Teaching time	91% of elementary teachers, 99% of teachers of grade 7–8, and 95% of teachers of grades 9–12 felt that student behavior was observably or totally improved. 86% of elementary teachers, 99% of teachers of grades 7–8, and 90% of teachers of grades 9–12 felt more time was spent on educational experiences and less time on disruptive behavior.
5. State of Oregon Confederation of Oregon School Administrators (1980)	Random sample from over 7,800 teachers and administrators trained in Assertive Discipline (workshops sponsored by COSA) (N = not reported)	Student behavior	81% felt schoolwide student behavior was improved. 79% felt there was a decrease in classroom management problems.

out. Render, Padilla, and Krank state "no N reported."
- Crawley (1983), in summarizing his own research, states, "The research may not have been properly designed to avoid contamination from variables not controlled."

There are others. But the errors, omissions, and even value judgments that understandably result from attempting to reduce a 100-plus page research document to one or two sentences are not as important as the conclusions that Render, Padilla, and Krank draw.

AS AN ADMINISTRATOR

Would I as a site administrator let these findings guide me in the decision to train my staff in Assertive Discipline techniques? I would be interested, but my decision would be influenced by many other factors. Professional educators, unlike professional researchers, use a variety of sources from which to draw conclusions. These sources include the network of local administrators and professional organizations. I've even made phone calls to officials in districts, for example, like Irving, Texas (C. Green, personal communication, August 19, 1988), where they have just completed their eighth annual districtwide new teacher training in Assertive Discipline. Lennox School District, which is cited both in the findings of Render and his colleagues and here, also continues to report the success of its program. Assertive Discipline is now a regular part of the district's new teacher training (Moffett et al. 1987).

AS A PRINCIPAL

As a principal, did I want to know if it worked before we began the program? Certainly. My information, however, came from practitioners who told me "it works," from my observations of schools that used the program, and from the personal commitment of my faculty to employ a discipline program that would encourage students to be self-managers. I found that teachers who did not use positive recognition as part of their management system did not use Assertive Discipline (McCormack 1981). It is not necessary for research to support, as Render, Padilla, and Krank imply, that "any particular educational approach" works before an administrator makes a program decision.

NO BASIS FOR CRITICISM

My point is, if their findings supported the position that the approach did *not* work—and Render, Padilla, and Krank do *not* come to that conclusion—there would be a reasonable reason for rejection. The findings they cite, on the other hand—improved student self-perceptions, greater teacher satisfaction, improved student behavior, fewer office referrals, reduction of classroom disruptions,

improved time-on-task, better student teacher preparation, and appreciation of the program by students and staff—support the benefits of Assertive Discipline. The researchers "doth protest too much, methinks."

Author's note: I reviewed all of the following references to check Render, Padilla, and Krank's research. Not all of these references are cited in the above text.

REFERENCES

Barrett, E. R. (1987). "Assertive Discipline and Research." Unpublished manuscript.

Bauer, R. L. (1982). "A Quasi-Experimental Study of the Effects of Assertive Discipline." *Dissertation Abstracts International* 43: 25a. (University Microfilms No. 82–14316).

Becker, R. G., ed. (March 1980). *Troy Reporter.* Available from Troy Schools, 500 N. Market St., Troy, OH 45373.

Canter, L., and Associates. (1976). *Assertive Discipline: A Take-Charge Approach for Today's Educator.* Los Angeles: Canter and Associates.

Cartwright School District. (February 10, 1982). *Discipline Report,* Available from Cartwright School District, 3401 N. 67th Ave., Phoenix, AZ 85033.

Confederation of Oregon School Administrators. (April 29, 1980). Personal letter to Lee Canter.

Crawley, K. E. (1983). "Teacher and Student Perceptions with Regard to Classroom Conditions, Procedures, and Student Behavior in Classes of Teachers Trained in Assertive Discipline Methods." *Dissertation Abstracts International* 43: 2840A. (University Microfilms No. 83–01140).

Ersavas, C. M. (1981). "A Study of the Effect of Assertive Discipline at Four Elementary Schools." *Dissertation Abstracts International* 42: 0473A. (University Microfilms No. 82–09893).

Henderson. C. B. (1982) "An Analysis of Assertive Discipline Training and Implementation on Inservice Elementary Teachers' Self-Concept. Locus of Control, Pupil Control Ideology and Assertive Personality Characteristics" *Dissertation Abstracts International* 42: 4797A. (University Microfilms No. 82–09893).

Lennox School District, (1980). *Evaluation of District Assertive Discipline Program.* Available from Lennox School District. 10319 S. Firmona Ave., Inglewood. CA 90304.

Mandlebaum, L. H., S. E. Russell, J. Krouse, and M. Gonter. (1983). "Assertive Discipline: An Effective Classroom Behavior Management Program." *Behavior Disorders Journal* 8, 4: 258–264.

McCormack, S. L, (November 1981). "To Make Discipline Work, Turn Kids into Self-Managers." *Executive Educator:* 26–27.

McCormack, S. L. (1985). "Students' Off-Task Behavior and Assertive Discipline." Doctoral diss., University of Oregon. 1986. *Dissertation Abstracts International* 46: 1880A.

McCormack, S. L. (March 1988). "Assertive Discipline: What Do We Really Know?" *Resources in Education* (ERIC Document Reproduction Service No. ED 286 618).

Moffett, K. L., D. Jurenka, and J. Kovan. (June/July/August 1982). "Assertive Discipline." *California School Board:* 24–27.

Moffett, K. L., J. St. John, and J. Isken. (February 1987). "Training and Coaching Beginning Teachers: An Antidote to Reality Shock." *Educational Leadership* 44: 34–46.

Swanson, M. Y. (Spring 1984). *Assessment of the Assertive Discipline Program.* (Available from Compton Unified School District, Compton, Calif.)

Ward, L. R. (1983). "The Effectiveness of Assertive Discipline as a Means to Reduce Classroom Disruptions." *Dissertation Abstracts International* 44: 2324A (University Microfilms No. 83–28411).

Webb, M. M. (1983). "An Evaluation of Assertive Discipline and Its Degree of Effectiveness as Perceived by the Professional Staff in Selected School Corporations." *Dissertation Abstracts International* 44: 2324A. (University Microfilms No. 83-28107).

▶ Chapter 12

Four Stories about National Goals for American Education

LARRY CUBAN

Historians invent the past. I do not mean that historians invent facts, although they frequently discover new ones; I mean that historians ask questions of the past, analyze the available sources and evidence, and filter the data through their experiences, values, and expertise to create their own versions of what happened. Because historians are products of their times and differ one from the other, histories of the same event, era, or institution will vary. As vividly demonstrated in the classic film *Rashomon,* in which the story of an attack on medieval nobles is told from different points of view, history is woven out of multiple interpretations of what happened.[1]

Does this mean that the facts seldom speak for themselves, since historians select and array those facts? Does this mean that there is no one true version of the past? Does this mean that histories get revised by each generation of historians? The answer to these questions is yes. Does this mean that knowing about the past is immaterial, since truth is elusive and history only an interpretation? The answer is no. It is no because interpretations of the past matter. It is no because policy makers, practitioners, and scholars who are not historians also create their own versions of the past.[2]

I introduce this special section in this manner because there are at least four histories recounting

Larry Cuban is a professor of education at Stanford University, Stanford, Calif., and a member of the *Kappan* Board of Editorial Consultants.

the movement to create national goals and standards for American education. Each one is plausible; each contains facts that historians informed about state and federal roles would generally accept. Yet each story creates a different meaning for the swift, swelling consensus among state and federal policy makers that burst forth in 1989 when President George Bush met with the 50 governors to discuss national goals.

Federal and state policy makers use the different meanings generated by these stories as support for various policy proposals. Each history suggests a different way of framing policy problems. For example, some reform-minded policy makers, researchers, and practitioners view the history of American public schools as a steady, century-long growth in centralized bureaucracies. Because they value schools that are responsive to their clients, these reformers believe that district and state bureaucracies strangle parents and teachers's will to improve schools. Thus they favor solutions that increase parental choice or that dismantle bureaucracies.

To the degree that multiple historical interpretations of the federal role and national interest in public schooling give rise to multiple ways of framing policy issues and directions for action, the four stories matter. They may broaden the current debate about national goals and standards and their consequences for public schooling in general and—of far greater importance—for what happens in classrooms. Here are the four histories.

1. CREEPING STATE AND FEDERAL CENTRALIZATION

With the enactment of the Northwest Ordinance in 1787 the federal government established a national interest in nourishing public education. The Ordinance allowed federal land to be sold and the monies acquired to be used by the states for education. Since the Constitution, adopted in the same year, and the Bill of Rights, adopted later, contain no mention of education, the control of public education came to reside in the states. Since the late 18th century, then, the establishment and spread of public schooling has been largely a state enterprise, making occasional use of federal funds. The states, in turn, have delegated to local districts the operation of schools.[3]

The tradition of local control of schools is anchored in the states' delegation to individual school districts of the power to use funds derived from a combination of state and district revenues. Throughout the late 19th and early 20th centuries, the repeated defeat of bills in Congress recommending general federal aid to schools confirmed the strength of this tradition. Local control of schools, under the light touch of state authorities and without federal interference, became a sacred belief in the folklore of school governance.[4]

Even with this tripartite, decentralized system of school governance, the federal government played a peripheral but important role in maintaining a national interest in education throughout the 19th century. During the Civil War, the Morrill Act established land-grant colleges. After the Civil War federal agencies actually ran schools for former slaves and Indians, and in 1867 a federal agency was established to collect information on public education. However, no federal money, beyond funds generated from land sales, was allocated to the states for education.[5]

Beginning in the closing decades of the 19th century, when social movements to reduce urban blight, to minimize the excesses of industrial growth, and to clean up political corruption spurred state and local efforts to improve schools, the offices of state superintendents and their departments of education expanded. State legislatures mandated that schools teach the perils of alcohol and tobacco use. States required physical education, vocational courses, and instruction in American history. State departments of education took over the certification and supervision of teachers and administrators. These departments grew from an average of just two civil servants in 1890 to an average of more than 100 employees half a century later.[6]

By 1900 the nation also turned its attention to industrial education as a way of producing skilled workers to compete with Germany and Great Britain. Gaining momentum from the support of President Theodore Roosevelt in the first decade of the new century and from astute lobbying at the state and national levels, the movement culminated in the passage of the Smith-Hughes Act in 1917. By this act Congress set aside funds for states to implement certain vocational curricula, and a National Vocational Board was established to approve state plans for using the funds; federal officials monitored the early years of implementation in the 1920s. Successive renewals of the legislation throughout the pre-World War II years and passage of the tradition-breaking Vocational Education Act in 1963 established an informal national policy of manpower development through the public schools. Even in this area, however, the federal role was to establish the direction, appropriate the funds, and let the states implement the programs designed to achieve a national goal.[7]

In the 1950s, when the Cold War prompted growing public concern about Soviet scientific leadership in military and space ventures, the federal government continued its pattern of setting informal national goals, funding particular school programs, and letting states carry out the tasks. Under President Dwight Eisenhower, Congress passed the National Defense Education Act (NDEA) in 1958 to help raise academic standards. Federal funds flowed through an enlarged U.S. Office of Education directly to states and districts in a massive effort to expand the number of graduates in math and science. Other federal agencies, such as the National Science Foundation, allocated funds for curriculum development and sponsored fellowships for public school teachers of math and science.[8]

Increased federal involvement in education also marked the 1960s, although the focus shifted from national defense to desegregation, as the civil rights movement mobilized the public and the federal government. As the spreading social movement fought for full black participation in American life, its agenda broadened to include the elimination of poverty. The federal government had already acknowledged a link between the economy and education when it passed the Smith-Hughes Act and subsequent vocational education laws. In

1965 that link was further strengthened in the Elementary and Secondary Education Act (ESEA), which became a primary weapon in President Lyndon Johnson's War on Poverty.[9]

More federal funds flowed to the states. Bureaucracies expanded, and the rhetoric of local control, while still heard, became muffled in the search for additional federal funds. By 1972 federal dollars accounted for 9% of total school expenditures—the highest level ever. Regulations governing the spending of these funds also mushroomed in the 1970s.[10]

The establishment of the U.S. Department of Education as a Cabinet-level post in the Administration of President Jimmy Carter was further acknowledgment of a broader national interest in public education. Not until Carter's successor, President Ronald Reagan, took office was there a questioning of the federal role (but not of the national interest). President Reagan reduced regulations and consolidated funds for many federal programs. States were given more discretion and urged to take on more responsibilities. Federal funding dipped to 6.1% of the total education expenditures by 1985, its lowest level in almost two decades. Ironically, it was Reagan and his first two secretaries of education, anxious to reduce federal involvement while shunting more responsibility for the improvement of public schools onto the states, who helped make education a national concern.[11]

A major expansion of the states' role, underwritten by federal funds (Title V of the ESEA), had occurred in the mid-1960s and had continued in the 1970s with the proliferation of programs targeted at minorities, the disadvantaged, the disabled, and other groups. But the 1980s virtually exploded with state-driven reforms of schooling led by both governors and legislatures. The impetus this time came less from federal funds than from increases in state revenues from income and sales taxes, combined with the Reagan Administration's ideology of federal deregulation. Both were married to a growing state awareness of improved schooling as an instrument of economic growth.[12]

State mandates and directives on matters that had usually been left to the discretion of local school boards and superintendents flowed to the districts in an ever-broadening stream. Curriculum, testing, textbook selection, evaluation, and dozens of other areas were now detailed and aligned to district goals as a major strategy of school improvement. The growing percentage of state funding in district budgets in the 1980s marked further gains in state control over schooling and the relentless shrinking of local influence.[13]

By 1989, then, when the 50 governors and the President gathered at Charlottesville, Virginia, for an unprecedented summit on education, the pattern of creeping centralization of authority at the state level, combined with the clear recognition of an expanded national interest in improved schooling had two centuries of irregular but steady growth behind it. "The time has come," the President and the governors declared, "to establish clear, national performance goals, goals that will make us internationally competitive."[14]

Such developments still fell far short of the levels of centralization of public schools common throughout the rest of the world, especially in Europe, Asia, and the developing nations, where national ministries operate schools. Nonetheless, the pattern of increasing centralization and bureaucratization inched the U.S. closer to other countries with national systems of education.

2. FRAGMENTED CENTRALIZATION

Yes, over the last century public school governance in the U.S. has grown large and complicated. Yes, state and federal roles in governing public schools have expanded. Yes, there are large bureaucracies in big-city districts, in state departments of education, and in the federal government.

But if there is more centralization, there is also more fragmentation. If there is a multilayered complexity about public schooling that would shock mid-19th-century reformers, there is also a lack of direction that those same reformers would find familiar. "Educational governance," one writer put it, "more closely resembles many busy colonies of Lilliputians, working in many different ways toward many different ends, than a single clumsy giant doggedly pursuing its own selfish purposes at the expense of its clients."[15]

The system of school governance in the United States may appear centralized, but three features keep it disjointed.[16] First, there are multiple units: about 80,000 public schools, some 15,000 districts, the 50 states, and the federal government (including diverse departments dealing with education). Decisions about schools and classrooms are made at every level. In effect, authority to operate schools is divided.

Second, both the pace and the scope of decision making at each level have increased. In the 20th century—and especially since World War II—schools, districts, states, and the federal government have assumed some of the responsibilities of other social institutions, so that they now find themselves concerned with matters of health, employment, educating the disadvantaged and the handicapped, dealing with pregnant teenagers, and so on. Because political groups and coalitions have entered the arena of schooling seeking solutions to social problems, school governance at each level has become busier and more political during the last half-century than ever before. Policies spill out from districts, states, and the federal government.

Third, each of these busy and political sites possesses considerable autonomy. There are, of course, some constraints (e.g., money) imposed on each layer of this multilevel system of school governance. Still, schools within a district operate with a large measure of discretion, districts have considerable independence from the state in many areas, and states have wide latitude insofar as the federal government is concerned. The independence that characterizes each level in our decentralized system derives from tradition and law as much as from the difficulty of inspecting what happens and enforcing compliance with regulations. That units usually submit reports on their activities rather than being monitored more directly also permits a great deal of discretion and covert autonomy.

Thus the apparent centralization of public schooling that has proceeded irregularly but steadily over the last century hides the divided authority, the policy clutter, and the inability to enforce mandates and regulations. The difficulties of getting teachers to attend to principals' directions, principals to superintendents', and so on through state departments of education, governors, and legislatures suggest the extent to which authority over the nation's schools is splintered.

Such fragmentation dissuades the national leadership from setting long-term goals. Such fragmentation cultivates contradictory policies across levels, encouraging partial rather than comprehensive reforms. Such fragmentation seldom allows programs to improve teaching to be linked to efforts to improve curriculum, further dividing professionals from concerted action. Such fragmentation produces little accountability. In short, such fragmentation is a recipe for educational mediocrity.

By the 1989 Charlottesville summit, the country needed a unified purpose, strengthened by national standards, that would eliminate the disarray of fragmented authority and would harmonize the discordant, autonomous units of a system that had little direction.

3. SOLVING NATIONAL PROBLEMS THROUGH SCHOOLS

American faith in schooling has been pronounced, persistent, and historic. The founders of the nation were firm believers in the notion that there are essential links between an informed citizenry and democracy. The Northwest Ordinance expressed that fundamental belief.

The common school movement that swept through New England and the Midwest in the early decades of the 19th century saw public schooling in political, social, and economic terms. Horace Mann and other mid-19th-century reformers viewed the spread of common schools in cities and rural areas as a way of binding the nation together to eliminate growing distinctions between social classes and to counter the emergence of urban crime and poverty.

At the turn of the century a later generation of reformers, also deeply concerned about the excesses of industrialization and about the effects of mushrooming immigration on the cities, wanted the schools to remake immigrants into Americans as a way of easing the distress caused by slums, deepening poverty, and child neglect. Moreover, by the end of the 19th century and the beginning of the 20th, growing economic competition with Germany and Great Britain convinced business leaders that schools should produce skilled workers in order to advance the country's international economic interests. Political, social, and economic aims—grounded in a potent faith in the power of schooling to erase the nation's ills while sustaining its economic growth—fueled the expansion of rural and urban public school systems throughout the 19th and early 20th centuries.[17]

What made schooling appealing to families and individuals was the promise of self-improvement. In the 19th century, the belief that schooling could provide an avenue for personal success grew, and the belief that ethnic groups could rise from a lowly status became pervasive as each wave of immigrants used education to climb the socioeconomic ladder.[18]

The fabric of beliefs shared by the American public and its officials—that public schooling could improve not just individuals and groups but the entire nation politically, socially, and economically—has been labeled by some observers as a civic religion. The British political scientist Denis Brogan referred to the public schools as "the formally established national church of the United States."[19] Signs of this faith can be seen in the willingness of citizens to tax themselves to support schools, to serve without salary on district boards, and to send their children to school every day. The faith is also evident in the readiness of public officials to turn to the schools to solve current social and economic problems.

The growth of state and federal authority in school matters during the last two centuries, then, has been an expression of a deep faith in public schooling as an instrument for solving national problems—whether it is an effective one or not. Since the late 19th century, federal, state, and local crusades have reflected these beliefs in the curative powers of public schooling. If alcohol and tobacco abuse inflict harm on individuals and families, then teach children the evils of these habits. If sexually transmitted diseases are on the rise, then require the schools to offer sex education. If poverty is the enemy, then enlist teachers and schools to fight it by expanding children's knowledge and building marketable skills. If foreign economic competition threatens the country, then promote vocational education as another line of national defense.[20]

Although there is some evidence that this faith is eroding—negative attitudes surfacing in public opinion polls, defeats of tax referenda, fewer citizens willing to serve on district school boards—the overall strength of the country's beliefs in the political, social, economic, and individual benefits of supporting public schooling persists.

Thus when the governors and the President gathered at the Charlottesville summit, they sought to link improved schooling to a reversal of the deteriorating position of the U.S. in the global economy. The meeting was just the most recent demonstration of a durable faith in the power of public schooling to resolve national problems.

4. THE WATERSHED YEARS

America's first century saw the steady growth of a decentralized system of schooling that permitted a great deal of discretion to schools, districts, states, and the federal government. This system of multilayered federalism was largely successful through the time of the Civil War because it was roughly in sync with a nation that was geographically insulated from other continents that were torn by warfare, economic strife, and religious turbulence.

Between the Civil War and the turn of the century, however, the U.S. matured into a world power. With the end of World War I, the nation emerged as a creditor to many war-scarred, debt-ridden countries. By the end of World War II, no nation was economically and militarily stronger. The Cold War, for all its domestic and international economic and political consequences, still produced almost half a century of world peace, albeit a peace punctuated by regional wars.

By the time the U.S. had become a world power, the world had changed significantly. In the decades following World War II, a global economy emerged in which international corporations and money markets were intimately linked. Components of a product could be made in four separate countries, assembled in a fifth, and marketed worldwide. The inventions of television, the transistor, microchips, and magnetic recordings made possible telecommunications, computers, and the electronic mass media. The capability for instant exchanges of information shrank the industrialized world. Developed nations shifted from heavy manufacturing to increasingly high-skilled service industries.

These economic and technological changes have fundamentally altered the usual ways of viewing the world. With a global economy and instant communication, national boundaries and identities have bluffed. The pace of change has accelerated. Speed and mobility are of the essence. Flexibility and adaptability in individuals have become valued characteristics.[21]

In the last two decades even these economic, social, and political changes have been exceeded. In 1970 the U.S. was almost self-sufficient; it produced the most products and had the largest trade surplus of any nation. The American dollar was prized among world currencies. By 1990 the U.S. had become a debtor nation. Mounting budget deficits from a combination of reduced revenues and high defense expenditures forced the nation to borrow from international investors. The country's imports exceeded its exports.

Our onetime enemies, Japan and Germany, have now outstripped the U.S. on economic indicators and simple measures of wealth. The dollar has been devalued, and the yen and the mark are now prized currencies. With a devalued dollar, Japanese, European, and Middle Eastern investors have purchased major American corporations and property. More businesses and real estate are now owned by non-Americans than at any time in the history of the nation.[22]

Finally, the political and economic changes launched by Mikhail Gorbachev in 1985 have begun to transform the Soviet government, society, and economy. The effects have spilled over the Soviet borders into Europe, Asia, and the U.S. *Perestroika* and *glasnost* have penetrated Eastern Europe. A series of stunning political changes in 1988-89 ended the Cold War. With Soviet consent, Poland, East Germany, Hungary, Czechoslovakia, Rumania, and Bulgaria dismantled one-party rule and state-planned economies. The Warsaw Pact collapsed. and the removal of Soviet troops has begun. The former satellite nations are moving toward the formation of multiparty states in which they will adopt some form of democratic socialism.

And how have the schools changed in light of the century's fundamental economic and political shifts? The U.S. continues to be admired for its commitment to universal schooling and for its success in getting three out of every four students to complete high school. Higher percentages of American youth attend college than youth in other economically developed nations. Broadened access to schooling for minorities, handicapped students, and females has been achieved and is admired internationally. The decline in scores on the Scholastic Aptitude Test and on standardized achievement tests charted in the 1970s has leveled off. Higher academic standards are in place.

But these improvements have not kept pace with the revolutionary economic, social, and political changes in the world. To corporate leaders and public officials who see public schools as engines of national economic progress, shortages of college graduates in science and engineering are a consequence of how poorly public schools teach math and science. That increasing numbers of high school graduates fail tests for entry-level jobs in telephone and insurance companies and in technology-based industries raises serious questions about the worth of the schooling they receive. When students with limited exposure to the newer technologies enter the computerized workplace, it becomes apparent that the schools are producing graduates armed with insufficient knowledge, inadequate basic skills, and poor work habits.

Changing demographics portend a shrinking labor pool in the early decades of the 21st century, and educational researchers predict that large numbers of low-income minority students will drop out of school. Studies of U.S. public schools show that traditional forms of teaching, organizing the curriculum, and scheduling the school day still prevail. Moreover, the state-driven reforms of the mid-1980s appear to have failed to produce the predicted gains. With schools being viewed as a first line of economic defense in the battle to remain internationally competitive, national and state leaders have become increasingly impatient with such shortcomings in school performance.[23]

Thus when the 50 governors and the President met at the Charlottesville summit, they saw a world dramatically different from the one that their parents and grandparents had seen. Fundamental changes in American schools had to be made—and made soon. No longer was business as usual acceptable. The nation needed extraordinary measures to cope with extraordinary political, social, and economic changes. A sharp departure from the past—such as the establishment of national goals, even national standards based on national tests—was needed.[24]

DIFFERENT HISTORIES MEAN DIFFERENT PROBLEMS

These four versions of the past, of course, do not exhaust the possibilities. Any informed reader could blend two or more of these stories into additional interpretations. The point is that each version contains within it a different way of framing national policy for schools.

The first story focused on the persistent but irregular growth of federal influence and state authority in directing schools. Implied in this story is the notion that the tradition of local control has become an obstacle blocking national progress. If we adopt this view of the problem, then a solution is for top federal and state officials to set national goals and standards; such a solution is an inevitable next step in further centralizing authority in order to tie schooling more closely to national economic and political interests.

The second story cast the problem as one of too much autonomy and policy clutter in a multilayered, decentralized system of school governance. Order can be imposed on this divided authority by constructing some national guidance for a decentralized system of schooling.

The third story viewed the setting of national goals as another instance of American faith that schooling can solve national ills. The problem implied by this interpretation is how to get the nation to focus on the crisis of inadequate schooling and its link to the nation's economic health. The President's and governors' setting of goals and standards was another crusade to mobilize the nation to deal with a serious issue. Whether or not such a campaign would influence how districts and schools operated was less important than focusing public attention on a crisis.

The last version emphasized cascading national and international changes to which the U.S. responded with extraordinary reforms. The problem was cast in terms of the U.S. becoming a post-industrial society and being left behind economically and politically by the collapse of the Soviet empire, the end of the Cold War, and the swift erosion of America's international economic position. Massive changes in schools had to occur, and these changes needed to be guided nationally through the goal-setting of the President and the governors.

These four versions of the past, then, produce different ways of framing problems to be solved. The stories and their variations nest within the minds of policy makers, practitioners, and researchers. Often unacknowledged, they shape how all of us view problems.

Yet note that, as diverse as these histories are, as varied as their definitions of problems are, I have had each one of them arrive at the same solution— national goals and standards. Do the stories matter, then, if the solution appears to be the same for all four? Yes, for two reasons. First, policy makers, practitioners, and researchers are divided over the appropriateness of this solution. Those opposed to the steady growth in centralization, for example, may prefer to see vouchers or some mechanism of parental choice as a more fitting solution than larger, more powerful state and federal bureaucracies. Thus the same four stories could yield a variety of solutions. Second, I believe that stories matter because it is important to examine the fit of the problem to the solution.

The soundness of that fit relies on the answers to two seldom-asked but critical questions: To what degree will these national goals and performance standards reverse, alleviate, or worsen the present conditions in big-city school systems? And in what ways will national goals and performance standards reshape current subject matter and teaching practices?[25] As the solution of national goals and standards is converted into structures to assess district performance, we need to ask and answer these questions explicitly.

1. Edward Hallett Carr, *What Is History?* (New York: Vintage Books, 1967), p. 26.

2. Carl Becker, *Everyman His Own Historian* (Chicago: Quadrangle Books, 1966).

3. David Tyack, Thomas James, and Aaron Benavot, *Law and the Shaping of Public Education, 1785–1954* (Madison: University of Wisconsin Press, 1987), pp. 13–42.

4. Carl Kaestle and Marshall Smith, "The Federal Role in Elementary and Secondary Education, 1940–1980," *Harvard Educational Review*, vol. 52, 1982, pp. 384–87.

5. Ibid.; and Tyack et al., op. cit.

6. David Tyack and Elisabeth Hansot, *Managers of Virtue* (New York: Basic Books, 1982), p. 18; and "Statistics of State School Systems, 1945–1946," in *Biennial Survey of Education in the United States, 1944–1946* (Washington, D.C.: Federal Security Agency, 1949), p. 33.

7. Larry Cuban, "Enduring Resiliency: Enacting and Implementing Federal Vocational Education Legislation," in Harvey Kantor and David Tyack, eds., *Work, Youth, and Schooling: Historical Perspectives on Vocationalism in American Education* (Stanford, Calif.: Stanford University Press, 1982), pp. 48–51.

8. Diane Ravitch, *The Troubled Crusade* (New York: Basic Books, 1983), pp. 228–33.

9. Richard Jung and Michael Kirst, "Beyond Mutual Adaptation, into the Bully Pulpit: Recent Research on the Federal Role in Education," *Educational Administration Quarterly*, vol. 22, 1986, pp. 80–109.

10. Frederick Wirt and Michael Kirst, *Schools in Conflict* (Berkeley, Calif.: McCutchan, 1989), p. 381.

11. Ibid., pp. 355, 372–76.

12. James Guthrie and Julia Koppich, "Exploring the Political Economy of National Education Reform," in William Boyd and Charles Kerchner, eds., *The Politics of Excellence and Choice in Education* (Philadelphia: Falmer Press, 1987), pp. 29–33; and David Clark and Terry Astuto, "The Significance and Permanence of Changes in Federal Educational Policy," Policy Studies Center of the University Council for Educational Administration, Occasional Paper, Arizona State University, 1986, pp. 1–16.

13. William Firestone, Susan Fuhrman, and Michael Kirst, *The Progress of Reform: An Appraisal of State Education Initiatives* (New Brunswick, N.J.: Center for Policy Research in Education, Eagleton Institute of Policy Studies, Rutgers University, 1989), pp. 7–14.

14. National Governors' Association, "Report Adopted by Members of the National Governors' Association," 25 February 1990, p. 1.

15. David Cohen, "Governance and Instruction: The Promise of Decentralization and Choice," paper presented at a conference sponsored by the LaFollette Institute of Public Policy at the University of Wisconsin, Madison, May 1989, p. 3. I first noted the phrase "fragmented centralization" in a report by John Meyer, W.

Richard Scott, and David Strang, *Centralization, Fragmentation, and School District Complexity* (Stanford, Calif.: Stanford Education Policy Institute, School of Education, Stanford University, 1986).

16. The three features described here are drawn from Cohen, op. cit.

17. Henry J. Perkinson, *The Imperfect Panacea: American Faith in Education, 1865–1965* (New York: Random House, 1968), pp. 62–93.

18. Gunnar Myrdal, *An American Dilemma: The Negro Problem and Modern Democracy*, vol. 1 (New York: Harper & Brothers, 1944), pp. 3–8.

19. Denis W. Brogan, *The American Character* (New York: Time Inc. Paperback, 1962), p, 137.

20. This argument comes from a variety of sources. See, for example, Murray Edelman, *Politics as Symbolic Action* (New York: Academic Press. 1971); Joseph Gusfield, *Symbolic Crusade* (Urbana: University of Illinois Press, 1963); and John Meyer, "The Politics of Educational Crises in the United States," in William Cummings et al., eds., *Educational Policies in Crisis* (New York: Praeger, 1986). For a specific article applying the idea of identifying a national problem and responding to it through the schools, see Herbert Kliebard, "Vocational Education as Symbolic Action: Connecting Schooling with the Workplace," *American Educational Research Journal*, Spring 1990, 19–26.

21. Alvin Toffler, *Future Shock* (New York: Bantam Books, 1970), pp. 19.

22. Kevin Phillips, *The Politics of Rich and Poor: Wealth and the American Electorate in the Reagan Aftermath* (New York: Random House, 1990), 116–42.

23. William Clune, Paula White, and Janice Patterson, *The Implementation and Effects of High School Graduation Requirements: First Steps Toward Curriculum Reform* (New Brunswick, N.J.: Center for Policy Research in Education, Eagleton Institute of Policy Studies, Rutgers University, 1989), 47; and John I. Goodlad, *A Place Called School* (New York: McGraw-Hill 1984).

24. I thank Jane David for suggesting this fourth story.

25. Few recent studies examine what occurs in classrooms as a consequence of state reform policies. Most researchers interview policy makers, administrators, and teachers and collect their opinions. Some count course titles establish that students are indeed taking more academic courses. Rare is the scholar who observes classroom teachers, stays in schools for more than a week, and asks why things are happening as they do. Two recent efforts have rejected the usual superficial approaches and have begun to assess how state policies affect what teachers do in their classrooms. They are David Cohen and Penelope Peterson, *Effects of State-Level Reform of Elementary School Mathematics Curriculum on Classroom Practice* (East Lansing: Center for Learning and Teaching of Elementary Subjects, College of Education, Michigan State University, 1990); and Beverly Carter, "The Limits of Control: Case Studies of High School Science Teachers' Responses to State Curriculum Reform" (Doctoral dissertation, Stanford University, 1990). These studies show wide variation in how teachers take mandates, directives, formal curriculum, textbooks, and materials and filter them through their beliefs and expertise as they apply them in classrooms.

IBM's Writing to Read: Is It Right for Reading?

ROBERT E. SLAVIN

By most measures, Mississippi is the poorest state in the U.S. It has the lowest per-capita income, the largest percentage of children in poverty, and the second-lowest per-pupil expenditure of all states. Yet last year Mississippi began implementing a plan to place IBM Writing to Read computer laboratories in every elementary school in the state. Across the country, school districts are pouring millions of dollars into this program. Many of the districts adopting it are, like those in Mississippi, the ones that seem least able to afford expensive programs: Atlanta, Baltimore, Tulsa, Nashville, Dallas, Fort Worth, and Washington, D.C.

The principal purpose of Writing to Read is to improve the reading and writing performance of students in kindergarten and first grade. Students in the program rotate among five workstations, two of which involve computers. At one of the computer workstations, students work with computers to learn phonics skills; at the other, they type stories on computers (or electric typewriters). A third learning station provides students with tape-recorded stories that they can follow in books. A fourth gives students the opportunity to write stories using paper and pencil, and a fifth provides additional practice with letter sounds.[1]

Robert E. Slavin is co-director of the Early and Elementary Education Program at the Center for Research on Effective Schooling for Disadvantaged Students, Johns Hopkins University, Baltimore. The research for this article was funded by a grant from the Office of Educational Research and Improvement (OERI-R-117-R90002) of the U. S. Department of Education, but the opinions expressed are the author's own.

Writing to Read is an expensive program. IBM lists a first-year cost of between $20,000 and $24,000 per lab, but a recent Baltimore installation in 43 elementary schools cost as much as $65,000 per school. Such figures do not include the cost of one or more instructional aides or teachers to manage the lab or the costs for maintenance, security, insurance, consumable materials, and so on. The program takes up a lot of time as well. The hour per day used for Writing to Read is usually in addition to other time spent teaching reading and language arts, and this reduces the time available for other activities.

Writing to Read has been particularly popular in school districts serving large numbers of disadvantaged students. These districts hope that the program will give their students a "leg up" on reading. In such school districts, many children fail to learn to read well, and early in their school careers they begin a downward spiral that leads through remedial programs, retentions, and special education to truancy, delinquency, and dropping out. If Writing to Read could in fact prevent reading failure and set students on the road to success in reading, it would be well worth its costs in money, time, and effort.

DOES IT WORK?

IBM has advertised huge reading gains for Writing to Read, and school districts have bought the program largely on the basis of these claims. But are the claims justified?

In order to find out, I obtained every evaluation report I could locate that compared reading outcomes of Writing to Read with those of traditional programs in kindergarten and first grade.[2] I found a total of 29 separate evaluations in 22 school districts. Thirteen of these were part of an evaluation conducted by the Educational Testing Service under contract to IBM.[3]

The difference between Writing to Read and control groups in the 29 evaluations can best be understood in terms of "effect sizes." An effect size is the difference between the experimental and control groups divided by the control group's standard deviation, adjusted for any pretest differences.[4] In general, an effect size of +.25 or more is considered educationally significant.

The median effect size for studies of Writing to Read in kindergarten is +.23. However, in first-grade studies the positive effect sizes in some studies were canceled out by equally large negative effect sizes in others. Thus the median effect size for the first-grade studies is zero.

The most important studies are the multi-year studies. Two two-year studies of Writing to Read in kindergarten *and* first grade found no positive effects. Four follow-up studies found no differences in reading performance by second grade between Writing to Read and control groups.

From these data, one might conclude that, although Writing to Read has no effects on first-graders and no lasting effects on children at any level, it is at least temporarily effective in kindergarten. The median effect size of +.23 may not be impressive, but it is a respectable difference. However, even this figure is probably seriously inflated. The problem is that the traditional kindergartens with which Writing to Read is compared are often nonacademic programs that do not teach reading. For example, consider this description of the intentions of the Tulsa (Oklahoma) Public Schools in implementing Writing to Read, written by the superintendent and the district's director of testing.

> *Historically, the kindergarten instructional program in Tulsa Public Schools has been a* traditional *program. Socialization, language, and emotional development were emphasized. Formal instruction in reading and math were not endorsed. All 65 elementary schools in the district followed this traditional approach in 1983-84.*

> *In 1984–85, 25 kindergartens began the Writing to Read program. This instructional approach emphasizes intentional, systematic, sequential writing skills development based on a phonemic approach. It is a sharp departure from the traditional approach.*[5]

Many early childhood experts oppose the teaching of reading in kindergarten,[6] but that is not the issue here. What is important is the likelihood that, in many evaluations of Writing to Read (such as the one in Tulsa), academic kindergartens were being compared to nonacademic kindergartens on measures of reading. Obviously, students of any age who are *taught* to read will perform better on a reading test than students who are *not taught* to read, at least in the short run.

So far, I've discussed *reading* outcomes only. I should point out that Writing to Read does unquestionably have positive effects on *writing* for kindergartners and first-graders.[7] However, here again, the effects on writing are largely explained by the fact that, until recently, writing was not taught in kindergarten and first grade, so evaluations of Writing to Read are really comparisons of writing instruction and no writing instruction, rather than of one form of writing instruction and another. As increasing numbers of schools are teaching writing in kindergarten and first grade, comparisons of Writing to Read and early-writing programs that use paper and pencil have become possible. But meaningful comparisons have not yet been made.

An advocate of Writing to Read might argue with considerable justification that group-administered standardized reading tests in the early grades are nearly meaningless and that the program may have important effects on reading that are not measured by these tests. Such tests are indeed of very limited value, yet no other reading measures have been used in the evaluations. Until they are, the best that can be said about the reading effects of Writing to Read is that they remain unknown.

One interesting sidelight to the story of Writing to Read is the widespread adoption of such an expensive means of improving kindergarten reading scores when much less expensive alternatives exist. Recall that across 21 kindergarten studies the median effect size for Writing to Read was +.23. Nancy Karweit identified five kindergarten reading programs that produced effect sizes (in comparison to control groups) ranging from +.25 to +.89 on standardized reading tests.[8] These programs (Alphaphonics, MECCA, TALK, MARC, and

INSTRUCT) are all part of the U.S. Department of Education's National Diffusion Network and involve costs on the order of $100 to $150 per class, plus training.

Given its modest and short-lived impact on reading, its expense, and the ready availability of much cheaper and more effective alternatives, one must wonder why Writing to Read has been so widely adopted. I offer a few speculations. First, the program appeared at a fortunate moment. Kindergartens were shifting toward a focus on reading instruction, and writing that used invented spelling was expanding in kindergartens and first grades. In addition, there is a growing acceptance of the need for early intervention for disadvantaged students, which can be seen in the movement to expand preschools and full-day kindergartens for such children. Writing to Read has certainly benefited from riding these currents.

Another major factor in the commercial success of Writing to Read must be the allure of computers themselves. It is very impressive to see young children, particularly disadvantaged minority children, happily typing out stories on powerful computers. Moreover, children do seem to enjoy the computers, and Writing to Read is very popular with parents, who like the idea that their children are becoming "computer literate."

However, I think there is also a darker reason for the prevalence of Writing to Read (and other computer-assisted instruction programs) in schools serving large numbers of disadvantaged students. Writing to Read may benefit from a lack of faith in teachers and schools—a belief that, since schools have failed so many students, we should give large and successful corporations a chance to show what they can do. I have heard school board members, businesspeople, and others despair of the quality of teaching—particularly that available to poor children—and express the belief that, if only IBM or some other successful corporation could be put in charge of the schools, it would turn them around. Along with this sentiment often goes the belief that teachers should in essence be replaced by the products of these corporations or that their jobs should be "McDonaldized"—made to serve an efficient system of knowledge distribution.

In fact, in the case of Writing to Read, IBM has demonstrated precisely the capabilities that have made it the most successful computer company in the world. It produced an attractive and timely product to meet a substantial demand and then aggressively marketed it. The corporation has be-

haved more responsibly than most in encouraging evaluations of Writing to Read; it has even distributed a guide to doing so.[9] How many textbook publishers commission studies of the effectiveness of their products?

However, the evaluations that have been done to date simply do not support the effectiveness of Writing to Read as a means of improving the reading achievement of young children.[10] The most optimistic reading of the research would suggest that Writing to Read is an expensive means of moderately improving the reading achievement of kindergarten children, with no known long-term effects. A less optimistic reading would question even the kindergarten effects. Schools might be justified in choosing the program as a means of introducing writing in their kindergartens and first grades, but there are certainly less expensive and less elaborate ways of doing this.

I do not believe that there are any real villains in the disappointing story of IBM's Writing to Read program. I am sure that IBM believes in its products, and many school districts have shared this belief. The long-term studies of Writing to Read, which really provide the most damning evidence related to reading outcomes, have only recently been published. I hope that IBM uses the evidence now available as an indication that it is time to carefully study Writing to Read with an eye toward restructuring the program to make it achieve the goals for which it was originally designed.

1. For a more detailed description, see John Henry Martin, *Writing to Read Teacher's Manual*, 2nd ed. (Boca Raton, Fla.: IBM, 1986).

2. A detailed report of the methods, findings. and citations for the evaluations is presented in Robert E. Slavin, "Reading Effects of IBM's 'Writing to Read' Program: A Review of Evaluations," *Educational Evaluation and Policy Analysis*, in press.

3. Richard T. Murphy and Lola Rhea Appel, *Education of the Writing to Read Instructional System, 1982–1984* (Princeton, N.J.: Educational Testing Service, 1984).

4. Readers who wish to know more about the specific studies, their design, and their findings or about my analysis that is summarized in this article should see Slavin, op. cit.

5. Larry L. Zenke and Mary Joe Keatley, "Progress Toward Excellence: Tulsa's Kindergarten Program," *ERS Spectrum*, vol. 3, 1985, p. 4.

6. See, for example, David Elkind, "Developmentally Appropriate Practice: Philosophical and Practical Implications," *Phi Delta Kappan*, October 1989, pp. 113–17.

7. Murphy and Appel, op. cit.

8. Nancy L. Karweit, "Effective Kindergarten Programs and Practices for Students at Risk," in Robert E. Slavin et al., eds., *Effective Programs for Students at Risk* (Boston: Allyn and Bacon, 1989).

9. *Writing to Read: Evaluation Guidelines* (Atlanta, Ga.: IBM, 1986).

10. Other reviewers of Writing to Read evaluations have also concluded that the reading effects are small or zero. See Pamela Freyd and James Lytle, "Corporate Approach to the 2 R's: A Critique of IBM's Writing to Read," *Educational Leadership*, vol. 47, 1990, pp. 83–89; Kathy A. Krendl and Russell B. Williams, "The Importance of Being Rigorous: Research on Writing to Read," *Journal of Computer-Based Instruction*, in press; Walter E. Hathaway, *A Critique of the ETS 'Evaluation of the Writing to Read Instructional System, 1982–1984'* (Portland, Ore.: Portland Public Schools, 1985); and Joyce Clark Newman, "Teaching Initial Writing and Reading by Computer: An Evaluation of Writing to Read" (Master's thesis, University of Delaware, 1988).

Chapter 13

Hunter Lesson Design: The Wrong One for Science Teaching

CRAIG A. BERG and MICHAEL CLOUGH

The "Madeline Hunter Teacher Effectiveness Training Program" has been marketed to numerous school districts with claims of improved instruction, increased student achievement, and an "all-purpose lesson plan" appropriate for every lesson in all disciplines. However, we contend that Hunter's lesson design model is not consistent with many goals of science education, it is not appropriate for every lesson in science, and it contradicts important principles of science teaching. In fact, this model supports only the teaching of low-level facts that require only the recall of information and low-level skills such as titrating, handling microscopes, and cutting glass tubing.

The complete Hunter program involves a variety of topics, but this discussion will focus on lesson design because teachers, when asked about the Hunter program, usually talk about the "seven steps of a lesson" (Moore 1988, Wolfe 1987). Hunter and her colleagues claim this model was never intended to be strictly linear in nature or contain all seven components in every lesson; nevertheless, they do suggest teachers and administrators consider using these seven elements when teaching any lesson. Many schools require daily lesson plans in the seven-step format. Teachers *use* it this way, especially when they are being observed by an ad-

Craig A. Berg is Assistant Professor of Science Education, 379 Enderis Hall, The University of Wisconsin-Milwaukee, Milwaukee, WI 53211. Michael Clough is a Science Teacher, Memorial High School, 2225 Keith St., Eau Claire, WI 54701.

ministrator or Hunter program facilitator (Garman and Hazi 1988).

Why do administrators and teachers believe effective teaching should result from the Hunter lesson plan? Freer and Dawson (1987) suggest that it provides a clear model and a common language for administrators and teachers, while Wolfe (1987) sees it as a generic lesson plan for overworked teachers. Common language in itself, however, does not make a model effective. We contend that exemplary science teaching strategies *do not follow* from the Hunter generic lesson design.

PROPOSITIONS DO NOT EQUAL PROCEDURES

To Hunter's credit, she clearly identifies the dilemma involved in any attempt to improve teaching:

> *Propositions are easy to learn; artistic performance procedures are much more difficult to attain . . . [The Hunter] model is deceptively simple in conceptualization. incredibly complex in application. There is a quantum leap from knowing propositions to creating artistic procedures. (Hunter 1985)*

However, although she recognizes the problem, Hunter's model also fails in its attempt to translate propositions into procedures.

First, too many propositions in the Hunter scheme are *not* translated into procedures. The propositions described are often general and vague—they fail to delineate appropriate teaching behaviors and strategies. For example, Hunter (1985) writes, "Teaching decisions may be delegated to the learner," and Wolf (1987) states, "As teachers prepare to instruct, they need to consider many factors: the content, their students' previous knowledge. . . . "

But the Hunter literature and videotapes don't show us what delegating teaching decisions might look like in active science inquiry or what the teacher should consider about content to help students learn. Too often, teaching behaviors and strategies—the translation of propositions into the procedures that directly impact learning—appropriate for science instruction goals are simply not addressed.

Second, several Hunter propositions and a number of teaching behaviors and strategies for translating the propositions into procedures contradict many important goals of science education and many principles of effective science content instruction. Lawson and associates (1989) call Hunter's methods (and the methods of currently popular mastery learning/outcome-based education) "naive," and they go on to say that these methods "quickly degenerate into teaching of only the simplest, most useless facts."

STUDENTS, NOT
TABULAE RASAE

Thus, Hunter's teaching suggestions contrast sharply with research on effective science teaching. For example, her statements in *Mastery Teaching* (1982a) and in *Mastery Teaching Video Cassette Tapes* (1982b), provide glaring contrast to the science education literature:

Lesson Element—Anticipatory Set: *At the beginning of class, use an activity or statement that focuses student attention. The set provides a brief practice and/or develops a readiness for instruction that will follow.*

Hunter suggests the teacher ask review questions. For example [emphasis is ours]:

. . . call on a student who you think will give the right answer. [In this way] correction of un-

voiced misunderstandings or erroneous answers can be accomplished without visibility or embarrassment . . . Ask the students to write something (e.g. definitions in their own words, the solution to a problem, a short summary of yesterday's, or this week's content) . . . Always, however, tell students the key ideas that they should have included so they have the opportunity to immediately verify or correct their knowledge (Mastery Teaching, pp. 27–28).

But students cannot "immediately verify or correct their knowledge," and are not just *tabulae rasae* on which the teacher need only write new knowledge and meaning (Osborne and Freyberg 1985, Piaget 1964). Students hold views of the world and meaning for words which significantly affect the outcome of instruction, or are influenced in unanticipated ways (Osborne and Freyberg 1985).

Although Hunter does suggest that teachers ask questions for diagnostic purposes, the methods she suggests (short answer and lower-level questions, thumbs up/down, and similar procedures) are very different from those suggested by research. According to Osborne and Freyberg, for example, teachers looking for necessary beginning points for instruction must:

- Find what logical structures of thought the child is capable of, and match the logical demands of the curriculum to them (Shayer and Adey 1981);
- Find the alternative viewpoints possessed by the child, and provide material in such a way so as to encourage the child to reconsider or modify these viewpoints (Driver 1980);
- Find the meanings and concepts that the learner has generated from his or her background, attitudes, abilities and experiences, and determine ways in which the learner will generate new meanings and concepts (Wittrock 1974).

What are science teachers to do with students' extensive ideas about the natural world? Hunter (1985) seems to he aware of Wittrock's generative theory of cognition, but what is observed in the Hunter literature and videotapes bears little resemblance to science educators' best use of "generative learning" when designing instructional strategies.

Lesson Element—Objective: *A time when the teacher informs the students what they will be able to do at the end of instruction (purpose) and how the lesson is relevant.*

Hunter contends, "In most (not all) cases you will find it facilitating to tell students today's objective and the purpose or reason for that learning" (p. 29). This practice of informing the students what the expected learning is before instruction again implies *tabulae rasae,* unless one is teaching isolated facts and concepts or performance skills that follow invariable explicit steps. But Lawson and associates (1989) write:

> [Hunter] argues correctly that good instruction includes a few essential elements but she incorrectly concludes that these elements are things such as teaching one objective at a time and telling the students beforehand precisely what they are supposed to learn . . . Further, telling students precisely what they are supposed to learn robs the lesson of its inquiry nature and, therefore, eliminates curiosity, the most powerful source of motivation in science that we know. The Hunter approach also appears to directly contradict the notion that the child actively constructs his/her knowledge, which is a basic tenet of the learning cycle method (p. 87).

WHAT IS RELEVANCE?

Hunter attempts to make science relevant by saying things like "We're going to learn the classification system of plants so you will be able to correctly categorize each one in the final exam" (p. 30), And she does this in other areas besides science: regarding English instruction Hunter states, "Analyzing poems for meaning is important in itself, but even more so if it's going to help you on the final" (Tape 4). These examples demonstrate lack of relevance; they do not suggest that students have intrinsic motivation for learning.

Even more disturbing, the Hunter approach doesn't help teachers give a rationale for learning science. Students are often told, "You're going to need this some day," and that "some day" is test day. But the National Assessment of Educational Progress (1978) data reveal that only 22 percent of young adults believe what they studied in school science will be useful in the future (Yager and Penick 1984). Stressing learning just for a test

reinforces poor attitudes about the usefulness of science.

Hunter emphasizes that teachers should be good at conveying information: "Information is the foundation of all learning. You can't think without it. Once you have that information, you can build concepts, generalizations . . . and proceed to do higher thinking" (Tape 5).

> Lesson Element—Instructional input (Providing Information): *A time when the teacher provides information that is needed by the student to perform a skill or complete a process. Input may be facts, generalizations, steps in a process, or critical attributes.*

Here is one of her suggestions for presenting information to students:

> *Energy comes from the sun. That energy is absorbed by plants and enables them to use elements from the soil to manufacture food. This process is called photosynthesis. Animals eat plants and, with oxygen from the air, are able to convert them to energy. This process is called cellular respiration.* (Mastery Teaching)

Hunter then goes on to suggest, "Once students have perceived the basic relationships inherent in photosynthesis and respiration, they are able to add more complex information."

This "basic information" consists of several extremely difficult concepts, each requiring student-generated understanding. An ability to simply regurgitate this information is not, in our view, indicative of learning. Too often "understanding" is assumed to be commensurate with pronunciation of terminology. Students who have been exposed to this same "basic information" have later been observed to think plants somehow mechanically "make their own food" in much the same way as one "makes" a salad or hamburger (Osborne and Freyberg 1985). Thus, when facts are presented as unconnected to students' prior knowledge, they, too, lose their relevance to further learning.

THE LECTURE ROUTINE

Hunter acknowledges that this generic lesson model is more suited to lecture (1982b), and this is demonstrated throughout her videotapes. She rationalizes the emphasis on lecturing with statements such as, "You see lots of it, most teachers lecture, so let's make them more effective lecturers" (Hunter 1982a).

Most teachers do lecture a great deal (Yager 1981; Yager and Stodghill 1979; Stake and Easley 1978; Goodlad 1982, 1984; Weiss 1984), but most educators lament this problem—they, don't try to train teachers to lecture better and then call it effective teaching.

A multitude of research studies suggest that directive teacher behaviors and strategies are detrimental to children. For example, Flanders (1951) and Cogan (1956) claim that directive teacher behaviors produce anxieties in students and reduce the learning of new concepts. Shymansky and Matthews (1974) found that the more directive the teacher behaviors (such as evaluating students' ideas, telling students what to do and how to do it), the less productive and involved the students were in science. Shymansky and Penick's (1981) study showed that teacher-structured classrooms resulted in teacher dependency, less creative problem solving, and more disruptive behavior. Brophy (1981) indicated that direct, teacher oriented, instruction is effective only when basic skill mastery is the primary goal.

TEACHER AS MODEL

> Lesson Element—Modeling the Information: *When the students see examples of an acceptable finished product or process. Critical elements of the example must be labeled.*

Hunter suggests that the teacher, when helping students work toward an acceptable finished product, should identify the critical attributes, label the similarities, and present an example and exceptions. In addition, when helping students work toward an acceptable process, Hunter also suggests success will be greater if the teacher will "show the students exactly what they're supposed to do" (Tape 7).

These may be helpful strategies, but only when the goal of instruction is knowledge or imitation (the lowest level of Bloom's Taxonomy). In addition, modeling information for a class of students presupposes that students possess the exact same levels of cognitive development, when in reality any group of students possesses a wide range of cognitive development and abilities. Imagine a doctor who walks into a waiting room with patients of

every ailment imaginable and prescribes aspirin to everyone. The doctor would be seen as incompetent, yet the Hunter model prescribes treatment en masse. While we do not deny the value of modeling in facilitating certain student goals, the examples of modeling provided in the Hunter literature and videotapes are largely inappropriate.

Proponents of the Hunter lesson design may charge that we have misrepresented lesson elements *Instructional Input* and *Modeling of Information.* They will maintain that student exploration, experimentation, and discovery may constitute the input and modeling for a lesson. What the Hunter lesson design is in theory, however, is irrelevant to how it is portrayed in the Hunter literature and videotapes and how it is perceived by administrators, teachers, and especially students. Moreover, those who suggest that better examples would rectify this problem miss the critical argument that although exemplary teaching may be reconstructed to fit the Hunter lesson design after the fact, the lesson design does not lead to exemplary science teaching. In this respect the Hunter lesson design is much like astrology: all experiences can be reconstructed to fit a horoscope, but the horoscope doesn't accurately predict or facilitate the experiences.

ANYBODY IN THERE?

> Lesson Element—Checking for Understanding: *When the teacher checks for students' possession of essential information and skills necessary to achieve the instructional objective.*

Hunter suggests that teachers should avoid dysfunctional questioning methods (*Okay?, You all understand?, Any questions?*), but she then goes on to suggest methods that are only slightly less dysfunctional (calling on the more able students to get correct answers, choral responses, and similar methods). In Tape 9, the science example shows a teacher asking a student to list the lab procedure sequence that he had just explained to the class. This element would more accurately be labeled "a check for memory."

The examples of questioning provided in her literature and videotapes suggest that Hunter's interpretation of good questioning invariably involves recall of information. But these checks may or may not coincide with students' true understanding of the material. Inadequate checks for understanding often result in unexpected outcomes such as those described in Osborne and Freyberg's (1985) *Learning in Science.*

AN EMPHASIS ON CONTENT ACQUISITION

Lesson Element—Guided Practice: *Students' first attempts with learning are guided by the teacher so they are accurate and successful. The teacher circulates to see that instruction has taken.*

Lesson Element—Independent Practice: *Students perform the skill or process without major errors and are ready to develop fluency by practicing without the availability of the teacher.*

The two elements above deal simply with performance skills, procedures, and rules—a very small component of scientific literacy. Clearly, the premise of Hunter's model is that learning is the acquisition of information. One facilitator of the Hunter model states that the lesson design is "most effective when students are engaged al the lower level of Bloom's Taxonomy—specifically at the knowledge and comprehension levels, when the teacher's objective is to teach performance skills or mastery of a body of knowledge" (Ceroni 1987). But again, this is a very small component of scientific literacy; it falls far short of "learning" in science as defined by Phillips (1986):

Learning is not acquiring knowledge, The essence of intelligence is the mental structures used to relate, interpret, synthesize, classify, order, predict, and make inferences and hypotheses about the data or facts.

Furthermore, these student-developed thinking abilities (sometimes called "process skills") cannot be acquired vicariously (Novak and Gowin 1984, Osborne and Wittrock 1983, Phillips 1986, Piaget 1964).

Content acquisition is only one goal among many noble goals in science education. Traditionally, content acquisition has been emphasized at the expense of other student goals (Harms 1978). Unfortunately, the Hunter model conveys this same kind of tunnel vision.

FOLLOW THE LEADER

The role of the teacher in the Hunter model is essentially that of organizer and presenter of information, whereas the role of the student consists mainly of passively following directions and regurgitating information. In Goodlad's (1984) and Cunningham's (1971) observations of classrooms, these roles, although typical, were seen as indicative of the crisis in education.

The general view of the Hunter teaching model as "research-based" seems tenuous at best (Gibboney 1987). Conspicuously missing in this model is attention to:

- Use of wait-time (Rowe 1969, 1974a, and 1974b);
- Appropriate/inappropriate use of praise (Brophy 1981, Deci 1975, Treffinger 1978, Rowe 1974a and 1974b, Lewin 1935);
- Evaluation (Treffinger 1978, Marchall 1960);
- Effective diagnostic strategies (Piaget 1964, Phillips 1986, Osborne and Freyberg 1985, Novak and Gowin 1984);
- Questioning and responding strategies (McGlathery 1978);
- Facilitating creativity (Flanders 1960, Payne 1958, Torrance 1963 and 1965, Torrance and Meyers 1970, MacKinnon 1960, Treffinger 1978);
- Constructivism: How students construct their own knowledge and what teaching strategies foster this (Osborne and Freyberg 1985).

Finally, there is no existing research showing that students learn more or faster as a result of having been instructed via the Hunter lesson design (Slavin 1989a and 1989b). The popularity of the Hunter model, as Wolf (1987) and Freer and Dawson (1987) suggest, seems to comes from its generic nature and common language—not from empirical evidence.

NOT THE ANSWER FOR SCIENCE

Hunter's emphasis on student acquisition of information distorts the nature of science by making science appear to be merely an enormous body of facts and rules about the natural world. Many scientists and science educators well versed in the history and philosophy of science have criticized this overemphasis on information acquisition in school science (Einstein 1936/1954, Szent-Gyorgy 1964, Feynman 1966, Klopfer 1969, Rachelson 1977).

Instructional strategies designed to facilitate authentic science inquiry simply do not follow from the Hunter lesson design regardless of the number of elements left out or how the elements are arranged. Active science inquiry is too complex to set down a predetermined step-by-step procedure (Einstein 1933/1960, Feyerabend 1975, Margetson 1982, Hodson 1988).

The use of teacher directive models and behaviors in teaching science has been of great concern to science educators (Penick and Yager 1986), precisely because of the issues we have raised here. Although educators may find Hunter's suggestion easy to use, the potential damage of her approach lies in the diversion of energy, resources, and attention away from critical problems and issues in science education when they implement her model. Indiscriminate use and promotion of the Hunter model will only serve to exacerbate the problems that currently plague science education.

REFERENCES

Ausubel, D. (1968). *Educational Psychology*. New York: Holt, Rinehart and Winston.

Brophy, J. (1981). "Teacher Praise: A Functional Analysis." *Review, of Educational Research* 51,1: 5–32.

Ceroni, K. M. (April 1987). *The Madeline Hunter Phenomenon: Questions Bothering a Trainer*, paper presented at American Educational Research Association. Washington, D.C.

Charron, E. H. and H. Tuan. (March 1987). *Constructivism in Elementary Science Teacher Education: A Course Description*. Paper presented at annual meeting of AETS, Washington, D.C.

Cogan, M. L. (1956). "Theory and Design of a Study of Teacher-Pupil Interaction." *Harvard Educational Review*, 26.4: 315–342.

Cunningham, R. T. (1971). *Developing Teacher Competencies*. Prentice-Hall, Inc.

Deci, E. (1975). *Intrinsic Motivation*. New York: Plenum.

Driver, R. H. (1980). "A Response to a Paper by Michael Shayer." In *Cognitive Development Research in Science and Mathematics*, edited by W.F. Archenhold et al. University of Leeds: Leeds. pp. 80–86.

Einstein, A. (1936/1954). "On Education." In *Ideas and Opinions*. New York: Crown Publishers.

Einstein, A. (1933/1960) "The Method of Science," In *The Structure of Scientific Thought*, edited by E. H. Madden. Boston: Houghton Mifflin Company. p. 80.

Feynman, R. (April 1966). *What is Science?* Paper presented at the 15th Annual Meeting of the National Science Teachers Association, New York, N.Y.

Feyerabend, P. (1975). *Against Method. An Outline of an Anarchistic Theory of Knowledge*. London: New Left Books.

Flanders, N. A. (1951). "Personal-Social Anxieties as a Factor in Experimental Learning Structures." *Journal of Educational Research* 45,2: 100–110.

Flanders, N. (1960). "Teacher Effectiveness." In *Encyclopedia of Educational Research*, 4th edition, edited by R.L. Ebell. New York: Macmillan. pp. 1423–1436.

Freer, M., and J. Dawson. (1987). "The Pudding's the Proof" *Educational Leadership*, 44,5: 67–68.

Gagne, R. M., and R. T. White. (1978). "Memory Structures and Learning Outcomes." *Review of Educational Research* 48,2: 187–222.

Garman, N. B., and H. M. Hazi. (1988). "Teachers Ask: Is There Life After Madeline Hunter?" *Educational Leadership* 69,9: 669–672.

Gibboney, R. A. (1987). "A Critique of Madeline Hunter's Teaching Model From Dewey's Perspective." *Educational Leadership* 44,5: 46–50.

Goodlad, J. I. (1982). "What Some Schools and Classrooms Teach." *Educational Leadership* 40,7: 8–19.

Goodlad, J. I. (1984). *A Place Called School*. New York: McGraw-Hill.

Harms, N. (1978). "Project Synthesis: Summary and Implications For Teachers." In *What Research Says to the Science Teacher*, Volume 3, edited by N. C. Harms and R. E. Yager. Washington, D.C.: National Science Teachers Association.

Hunter, M. (1982a). *Mastery Teaching*. El Segundo, Calif: TIP Publications.

Hunter, M. (1982b). *Mastery Teaching Tapes*. Pacific Palisades, Calif: Instructional Dynamics Inc.

Hunter, M. (1985). "What's Wrong With Madeline Hunter?" *Educational Leadership* 42,5: 57–60.

Klopfer, L. (1969). "The Teaching of Science and the History of Science." *Journal of Research in Science Teaching* 6,1: 87–95.

Lawson, A. E., M. R. Abraham, and J. W. Renner. (1989). "A Theory of Instruction: Using the Learning Cycle to Teach Science Concepts and Thinking Skills." *National Association of Research in Science Teaching Monograph*, Number One.

Lewin, D. (1935). *Dynamic Theory of Personality*. New York: McGraw-Hill.

MacKinnon, D. W. (1960). "The Highly Effective Individual." *Teachers College Record* 61,7: 367–78.

Marchall, M. (1960). "Self-Evaluation in Seventh Grade." *Elementary School Journal* 60,5: 249–252.

Margetson, D. (1982). "Some Educational Implications of the Uncertain Identity of Science." *European Journal of Science Education* 4,4: 357–365.

McGathery, G. (1978). "Analyzing the Questioning Behaviors of Science Teachers." In *What Research Says to the Science Teacher*, Vol. 1, edited by M. B. Rowe. Washington, D.C.: National Association of Science Teachers.

Moore, L. (1988). Personal Communication. Madeline Hunter Facilitator, Grantwood Area Education Association, Cedar Rapids, Iowa.

National Assessment of Educational Progress (1978). *The Third Assessment of Science, 1976–1977*. Released Exercise Set. Denver, Colo.: Educational Commission of the States.

Novak, J. D., and D. B. Gowin (1984). *Learning How To Learn*. New York: Cambridge University Press.

Osborne, R. J., and M. C. Wittrock. (1983). "Learning Science: A Generative Process." *Science Education* 67,4: 489–508.

Osborne, R. J., and P. Freyberg. (1985). *Learning in Science*. Portsmouth, N.H.: Heinemann Publishers.

Payne, J. N. (1958). "Teaching Mathematics to Bright Pupils." *University of Michigan School of Education Bulletin* 29: 97–102.

Penick, J. E., and R. E. Yager. (1986). "Science Education: New Concerns and Issues." *Science Education* 70,4: 427–431.

Phillips, D.G. (1986). *Towards Logical Thinking*. Iowa City: The University of Iowa.

Piaget, J. (1964). "Development and Learning, Part 1 of Cognitive Development in Children." *Journal of Research in Science Teaching* 2,3: 176–186.

Rachelson, S. (1977). "A Question of Balance: A Wholistic View of Scientific Inquiry." *Science Education*, 61,1: 109–117.

Rowe, M. B. (1969). "Science, Silence, and Sanctions." *Science and Children* 6,6: 11–13.

Rowe, M. B. (1974a). "Wait-Time and Rewards as Instructional Variables, Their Influence on Language Logic, and Fate Control: Part I—Wait-Time." *Journal of Research in Science Teaching* 11,2: 81–94.

Rowe, M. B. (1974b). "Relation of Wait-Time and Rewards to the Development of Language, Logic and Fate-Control: Part II—Rewards." *Journal of Research in Science Teaching* 11,4: 291–308.

Shayer, M., and P. Adey. (1981). *Toward a Science of Science Teaching*. London: Heinemann Publishers.

Shymansky, J. A., and C. C. Mathews. (1974). "A Comparative Laboratory Study of the Effects of Two Teaching Patterns on Certain Aspects of the Behavior of Students in Fifth Grade Science." *Journal of Research in Science Teaching* 11,2: 157–168.

Shymansky, J. A., and J. E. Penick. (1981). "Teacher Behavior Does Make A Difference In Hands-on Science Classrooms." *School Science and Mathematics* 81,5: 412–422.

Slavin, R. E. (1989a). "On Mastery Learning and Mastery Teaching." *Educational Leadership* 46,7: 77–79.

Slavin, R. E. (1989b). "PET and the Pendulum: Faddism in Education and How to Stop It." *Phi Delta Kappan* 70,10: 752–758.

Stake, R. E., and J. A. Easley. (1978). *Case Studies in Science Education*. Urbana, Ill.: University of Illinois.

Szent-Gyorgy, A. (1964). "What is Science: Decisions-Decisions-Decisions." *Science* 146, 36–49: 1278–1279.

Torrance, E. P. (1963). "Toward the More Humane Education of Gifted Children." *Gifted Child Quarterly* 7,4: 135–145.

Torrance, E. P. (1965). *Regarding Creative Behavior*. Englewood Cliffs, NJ.: Prentice Hall, Inc.

Torrance, E. P., and R. E. Meyers. (1970). *Creative Learning and Teaching*. New York: Dodd, Mead and Co.

Treffinger, D. (1978). "Guidelines For Encouraging Independence and Self-Direction Among Gifted Students." *Journal of Creative Behavior* 12,1: 14–20.

Weiss, I. R. (1978). *Report of the 1977 National Survey of Science, Mathematics, and Social Studies Education*. Research Triangle Park, N.C.: Center for Educational Research and Education.

Wittrock, M. C. (1974). "Learning as a Generative Process." *Educational Psychologist* 11,2: 87–95.

Wolfe, P. (1987). "What the 'Seven-Step Lesson Plan' Isn't!" *Educational Leadership* 44,5: 70–71.

Yager, R. E. (September 1981). "Science Education." *ASCD Curriculum Update*.

Yager, R. E., and R. Stodghill. (1979). "School Science in an Age of Science." *Educational Leadership* 35,6: 439–445.

Yager, R. E., and J. E. Penick. (1984). "What Students Say About Science Teaching and Science Teachers." *Science Education*, 68(2), 143–152.

Cognitive Approaches to Teaching Advanced Skills to Educationally Disadvantaged Students

BARBARA MEANS and MICHAEL S. KNAPP

Once again, we are in a period of widespread concern about the education of the students regarded as least likely to succeed in school. Variously labeled "at risk," "disadvantaged," or "educationally deprived," these students come disproportionately from poor families and from ethnic and linguistic minority backgrounds.

In decades past, various diagnoses of school failure for these students focused on what they lacked—exposure to print outside of school, family support for education, and so on. Based on these diagnoses, the most widely accepted prescriptions for compensatory education sought to remedy the students' deficiencies by teaching "the basics" through curricula organized around discrete skills taught in a linear sequence—much like the academic program these students had previously encountered in their regular classrooms.

New evidence, however, suggests that more "advanced" skills can—and should—be taught to those who are at a disadvantage in today's schools. From this perspective, the sources of disadvantage and school failure lie as much with what schools do

Barbara Means is director of education and human services research at SRI International, Menlo Park, Calif. Michael S. Knapp, formerly program manager of the Education Policy Studies Program at SRI International, is an associate professor of education leadership and policy studies at the University of Washington, Seattle. This article is adapted, with permission, from Barbara Means, Carol Chelemer, and Michael S. Knapp, eds., Teaching Advanced Skills to At-Risk Students: Views from Research and Practice. © 1991, Jossey-Bass Inc.

as with what the children bring to the schoolhouse door. By reconceiving what is taught to disadvantaged youngsters and by rethinking how it is taught, schools stand a better chance of engaging students from impoverished and minority backgrounds in an education that will be of use to them in their lives outside school.

A fundamental assumption underlying much of the curriculum in America's schools is that certain skills are "basic" and so must be mastered before students are given instruction in more "advanced" skills, such as reading comprehension, written composition, and mathematical reasoning. For many students, particularly those most at risk of school failure, one consequence of adherence to this assumption is that instruction focuses on these so-called basics (such as phonetic decoding and arithmetic operations) to the exclusion of reasoning activities, of reading for meaning, or of communicating in written form. Demonstrated success on basic skills measures becomes a hurdle that must be overcome before the student receives instruction in comprehension, reasoning, or composition.

The findings of research in cognitive science question this assumption and lead to quite a different view of the way children learn. By discarding assumptions about skill hierarchies and by attempting to understand children's competencies as constructed and evolving both within and outside of school, researchers are developing models of intervention that start with what children know and expose them to explicit applications of what has traditionally been thought of as higher-order thinking.

The research on which these models are based has provided a critical mass of evidence that students regarded as educationally disadvantaged can profit from instruction in comprehension, composition, and mathematical reasoning from the very beginning of their education. In what follows, we highlight a set of instructional principles that have evolved from this research and provide some concrete examples of the kinds of instruction that have been developed as a result.[1] To provide a context for this discussion, we first offer a brief description of the kind of teaching that most educationally disadvantaged students are receiving today.[2]

CONVENTIONAL APPROACHES

Classroom studies document the fact that disadvantaged students receive less instruction in higher-order skills than do their more advantaged peers.[3] Their curriculum is less challenging and more repetitive. Their teachers are typically more directive, breaking each task down into smaller pieces, walking the students through procedures step by step, and leaving them with less opportunity to engage in higher-order thinking. As a consequence, disadvantaged students receive less exposure to problem-solving tasks in which there is more than one possible answer and in which they have to structure problems for themselves.[4]

The majority of efforts to provide at-risk students with compensatory education have tended to increase the differences between the kinds of instruction provided to the "haves" and to the "have nots." Children who score lower than their peers on standardized tests of reading and on teacher evaluations of their reading abilities—many of them from poor backgrounds and/or from cultural or linguistic minorities—are given special practice in reading, most often in a special pullout room, sometimes in the regular classroom.[5] In these settings, children in compensatory programs typically receive drill on phonics, vocabulary, and word decoding. Each of these is taught as a separate skill, with little or no integration. Often there is little or no coordination between the compensatory and regular classroom teachers and no congruence between the content of the two classes.

Similarly, compensatory programs in mathematics tend to have students practice basic arithmetic operations using workbooks or dittos. On the assumption that they cannot be expected to do even simple math-related problem solving until they have mastered the basics of computation, students are drilled on the same numerical operations year after year.

The results of state and national testing programs suggest that this kind of instruction has had some positive (though not dramatic) effects on student scores on measures of basic skills, especially in the early years of elementary school. What has been disheartening, however, is the fact that comparable gains have not been seen on measures of more advanced skills. In fact, despite years of back-to-basics curricula, minimum competency testing, and compensatory education, the majority of educationally disadvantaged children appear to fall ever farther behind their more advantaged peers as they progress through school and as the emphasis increases on advanced skills in comprehension, problem solving, and reasoning.

For too long, there has been a tendency to blame this situation on the students. Tacitly or explicitly, it was assumed that they lacked the capability to perform complex academic tasks. Recently, however, there has been a reexamination of the premises underlying the instruction provided to educationally disadvantaged students. Critics have pointed out that we have decried these students' failure to demonstrate advanced skills even as we have failed to provide them with instruction designed to instill those skills.[6] There is a growing understanding that the failures lie both in the dominant approaches to compensatory education and in the regular classrooms in which educationally disadvantaged students receive the rest of their instruction.

A recent summary of critiques of conventional approaches to teaching academic skills to at-risk students, offered by a group of national experts in reading, writing, and mathematics education, concluded that such approaches tend to:

- underestimate what students are capable of doing;
- postpone more challenging and interesting work for too long—in some cases, forever; and
- deprive students of a meaningful or motivating context for learning or for employing the skills that are taught.[7]

THE ALTERNATIVE VIEW

Cognitive psychologists who study learning and the process of instruction point out that we have been too accepting of the assumption that learning certain skills must take place before learning others. In particular, they single out the assumption that mastery of those skills traditionally designated as "basic" is an absolute prerequisite for learning the skills that we regard as "advanced."

Consider the case of reading comprehension. Cognitive research on comprehension processes has shown the importance of trying to relate what you read to what you already know, of checking to see that your understanding of new information fits with what you have already read, and of setting up expectations for what is to follow and seeing whether those expectations are fulfilled.[8] Research on the reciprocal teaching approach demonstrates clearly that students can acquire comprehension skills—which we have traditionally called advanced—well before they are good decoders of the printed word.[9] Children can learn to reason about new information, to relate information from different sources, to ask questions, and to summarize by using orally presented text before they have mastered all the so-called basics.

Similarly, recent research on children's understanding of math concepts shows that, using modeling and counting, first-graders can solve a wide variety of math problems before they have memorized the computational algorithms that are traditionally regarded as prerequisites.[10] Likewise, Robert Calfee quotes two young children as an illustration of the fact that children can perform sophisticated composition tasks before they have acquired the mechanics of writing.

What you have to do with a story is, you analyze it, you break it into parts. You figure out the characters, how they're the same and different. And the plot, how it begins with a problem and goes on until it is solved. Then you understand the story better, and you can even write your own.—First-Grader, Los Angeles

We started out the play by finding a theme, something really important to us personally. A lot of us come from broken homes, so we made the play about that. We did a web [a semantic map] on home; that gave us lots of ideas. Then we talked about how things are now and how we

would like them to be. It's pretty lonely when you don't have a daddy, or maybe not even a mommy. So the play began with nothing on the stage, and one of us came out, sat down, and said, "My life is broke." We thought that would get the theme across. It worked pretty good.— Second-Grader, Los Angeles[11]

In the early school years, children's achievement is typically measured in terms of their ability to perform basic skills in an academic context. The skills are formally assessed, and children are asked to perform independently and to execute the skills for their own sake, not as part of any task they're trying to accomplish. Children from impoverished and linguistic-minority backgrounds often perform poorly on these assessments. Their performance leads many educators to conclude that they are severely deficient academically, a conclusion predicated on the assumption that the skills being tested are the necessary foundation for all later learning.

Ironically, the decontextualized measures of discrete skills that we've come to regard as basic offer less opportunity for connecting with anything children know from their past experiences than would more complex exercises emphasizing the skills we regard as advanced. To prepare them for writing, children from different linguistic backgrounds are drilled on the conventions of standard written English. These will be harder for them than for other children because the conventions often conflict with the children's spoken language.[12] On the other hand, a task that focuses on higher-level issues of communication—e.g., formulating a message that will be persuasive to other people—is perfectly consistent with many of these children's out-of-school experiences. At the level of language mechanics and communication formats, there are many inconsistencies between the backgrounds of many disadvantaged children and the conventions of the schoolhouse, but at the level of the goals of communication, there is much more common ground.

A similar argument can be made about reading instruction. Young readers deemed at risk of school failure are subjected to more drill and tighter standards regarding correct pronunciation in oral reading.[13] These children must struggle with a pronunciation system that often differs from that of their spoken language or dialect at the same time that they're trying to master basic reading.

Cognitively Guided Instruction

While most of the children in this first-grade class are solving word problems independently or in small groups, Ms. J. is sitting at a table with three students, Raja, Erik, and Ernestine (Ern). Each child has plastic cubes that can be connected together, a pencil, and a big sheet of paper on which are written the same word problems.

Ms. J.: Okay. Who wants to read the first one?

All: Me!

Ms. J.: Well, let's read them together.

All: [Reading] Raja made 18 clay dinosaurs. Ernestine has nine clay dinosaurs. How many more clay dinosaurs does Raja have than Ernestine?

Ms. J.: Okay. [Reads the problem again as the students listen.]

The students work on the problem in different ways. Raja puts together 18 cubes. She removes nine of them and counts the rest. She gets 11. She writes the answer down, then looks up at the teacher for confirmation. Ms. J. looks at the answer, looks back at the problem, and then says, "You're real close." As Raja re-counts the cubes, Ms. J. watches her closely. This time Raja counts nine.

Ernestine also connects 18 cubes. Then she counts nine and breaks them off. She counts what she has left. Ernestine exclaims, "I've got it!" Ms. J. looks at Ernestine's answer and says, "No, you're real close." Ernestine does the same procedure over again.

Erik connects nine cubes, and in a separate group he connects 18. He places them next to each other and matches them up, counting across each row to make sure there are nine matches. Then Erik breaks off the unmatched cubes and counts them. "I've got it!" he announces. Erik writes down his answer. He says to Ms. J., "Got it. Want me to tell you?" Ms. J. nods "Yes." Erik goes to Ms. J. and whispers his answer in her ear. Ms. J. nods "Yes" in reply. Turning to the group, she queries, "Okay now, how did you get your answers? Remember, that's what's the important thing: How did you get it? Let's see if we can come up with different ways this time. [Erik has his hand raised.] Erik, what did you do?"

Erik: I had nine cubes, and then I had and then I put 18 cubes and then I put them together. And the 18 cubes . . . I took away some of the 18 cubes.

Ms. J.: Okay, let's see if we can understand what Erik did. Okay, you got—show me 18 cubes.

Erik: Okay. [He puts together two of the three sets of nine he has lined up in front of him.]

Ms. J.: Okay, so you have 18 cubes. Then you had nine.

Erik: [He takes nine cubes in his other hand and puts them side by side.] Yeah.

Ms. J.: Then you compared.

Erik: [Simultaneously with Ms. J.] Then I put them together.

Ms. J.: Then you put them together.

Erik: Then I took . . .

Ms. J.: Nine away.

Erik: Nine away, and I counted them [the ones left], and there were nine.

Ms. J.: Okay. So that's one way to do it. Nice job, Erik. Which way did you do it, Raja?

Ms. J. discusses their solution methods with Raja and Ernestine.

Ms. J.: So we had—how many different ways did we do that problem? Erik, you did it one way, right? Raja, was your way different from Erik's? [Raja nods "Yes."] Was your way different from Ernestine's? [Raja nods "Yes."] So that was two ways. Ernestine, was your way different from Raja?

Ern: Yes.

Ms. J.: Was your way different from Erik?

Ern: Yes.

Ms. J.: So we did the problem in three different ways. Let's read the next problem.

In a CGI [Cognitively Guided Instruction] classroom, the teacher poses problems that each child can solve at his or her level of mathematics knowledge and understanding. The teacher encourages each child to solve mathematical problems using ways that make sense to the child. Ms. J. encourages each child to tell her how he or she solved the problems and uses what the child tells her to make instructional decisions. Children are aware that their thinking is as important as the answer and are not only comfortable, but determined that Ms. J. understand how they have solved each problem.

This excerpt comes from Barbara Means, Carol Chelemer, and Michael S. Knapp, eds., *Teaching Advanced Skills to At-Risk Students* (San Francisco: Jossey-Bass, 1991), pp. 80–83.

When it comes to comprehension skills, however, we have every indication that disadvantaged children can make use of their past experiences to help them understand a story. Annemarie Palincsar and Laura Klenk provide examples of how young children regarded as academically "at risk" apply their background knowledge to make inferences about text.[14] They show how a first-grade girl uses her prior knowledge about seasons to make inferences while listening to a story about a baby bear who played too roughly with his sister and fell from a tree into the water: "You know, it kind of told you what time of year it was because it told you it went 'splash,' because if it was this time of year [February], I don't think he'd splash in the water, I think he'd crack." This inference making is exactly the kind of comprehension-enhancing strategy that we regard as advanced. Real-life experiences and skills are relevant to these higher-level academic skills. Instruction in advanced skills offers opportunities for children to use what they already know in the process of developing and refining academic skills.

Educators and psychologists have been developing and studying new models, based on cognitive theory and research, that enable them to teach educationally disadvantaged students advanced skills in mathematics reasoning, reading comprehension, problem solving, and composition. These models represent a new attitude toward learners who have been labeled "at risk" and lead to a fundamental rethinking of the content of the curriculum. They have also made it possible to develop instructional strategies that allow the children to be active learners and that do not require them to work in isolation. Although the research encompasses a wide range of academic content and involves different grade levels, we can extract a set of major themes and principles from this work.

A NEW ATTITUDE TOWARD DISADVANTAGED LEARNERS

The instructional models coming out of cognitive psychology reflect a new attitude toward educationally disadvantaged learners. These researchers do not start with a list of academic skills, administer formal assessments, and catalogue children's deficits. Instead, they start with the conviction—bolstered by years of research in cognitive psychology and linguistics—that children from all kinds of backgrounds come to school with an impressive set of intellectual accomplishments. When we analyze what it means to understand numbers, what it takes to master the grammar of a language, what is required to be able to categorize and recategorize objects, we can appreciate the magnitude of young children's intellectual accomplishments. When we look closely at how these kinds of understandings are achieved, we begin to understand that concepts are not "given" to the child by the environment but rather are constructed by the child through interactions with the environment.

Children from impoverished and affluent backgrounds alike come to school with important skills and knowledge. They have mastered the receptive and expressive skills of their native language. (The particular language or dialect the children have acquired may or may not match that of the classroom, but the intellectual feat is equivalent in any case.) They have learned basic facts about quantity—e.g., the fact that rearranging objects does not change their number. They have learned much about social expectations, such as the need to take turns talking when participating in a conversation. Moreover, they have a vast collection of knowledge about the world: grocery stores are places where you pay money for food; new flowers bloom in the spring; nighttime is for sleeping.

Instead of taking a deficit view of the educationally disadvantaged learner, cognitive researchers developing alternative models of instruction focus on the knowledge, skills, and abilities that the children possess. Early accomplishments, attained before coming to school, demonstrate that disadvantaged children can do serious intellectual work. What we need to do is design curricula and instructional methods that will build on that prior learning and complement rather than contradict the child's experiences outside of school.

RESHAPING THE CURRICULUM

Once the conventional assumption about a necessary hierarchy of skills has been abandoned, a new set of curricular principles follows.

Focus on Complex, Meaningful Problems
The dominant curricular approach over the last two decades has broken academic content down into small skills, with the idea that each piece would be easy to acquire. An unfortunate side effect is that, by the time we break something down into its

smallest parts, the vision of the whole is often totally obscured. Children drill themselves on the spellings and definitions of long lists of words, often without understanding what the words mean or without any motivation to use them. High school students practice computations involving logarithms, but most of them leave school with no idea of what the purpose of logarithms is or how they might aid in solving practical problems.[15]

The alterative is to keep tasks at a level high enough that the purpose of the task is apparent and makes sense to students. Thus children might write to their city council in support of a public playground. In the course of the exercise, they might need to acquire new vocabulary (*alderman, welfare, and community*), but each word would be acquired in a context that gave it meaning. At the same time, children would be attending to higher-level skills. What are the arguments in favor of a good playground? Which of these arguments would be most persuasive to a politician? What counter-arguments can be expected? How can these be refuted?

Allan Collins, Jan Hawkins, and Sharon Carver describe a math and science curriculum organized around the problem of understanding motion.[16] Students engage in extended investigations of such topics as the physical principles of motion underlying an amusement park ride of their own design or a foul shot in basketball. The Instructional Technology Group at Vanderbilt University has been developing programs that use interactive video to present students with complex problem situations, such as moving a wounded eagle to a distant veterinarian by the safest and fastest route. A whole series of rate, fuel consumption, and distance problems must be identified and solved in the process of devising a plan.[17]

Certainly these tasks are more complex than performing simple computations or phonics exercises, but there are instructional techniques that can lessen the burden on any individual student. Moreover, as we argued above, these more complex tasks build on things that students already know.

Embed Basic Skills Instruction in the Context of More Global Tasks

Teaching advanced skills from the beginning of a child's education does not mean failing to teach those skills traditionally called basic. Instead, these alternative approaches advocate using a complex, meaningful task as the context for instruction in both advanced and basic skills. In place of constant drill on basic addition and subtraction, these skills are practiced in the context of trying to solve real problems. Penelope Peterson, Elizabeth Fennema, and Thomas Carpenter have described the pedagogical use of problems stemming from daily classroom activities—for example, figuring out how many hot lunches and how many cold lunches are ordered each day.[18] Children can practice addition, subtraction, record-keeping, and the use of fractions in the course of this authentic classroom activity.

There are multiple advantages to this approach. First, the more global task provides a motivation for acquiring the knowledge and skills needed to accomplish it. The conventions of written English are worth learning if that will enable you to communicate with a distant friend. Word decoding is much more palatable if the words are part of a message you care about.

Second, embedding basic skills in more complex contexts means that students receive practice in executing a given skill in conjunction with other skills. One of the findings of cognitive research on learning is that it is possible to be able to perform all the subskills of a task without being able to coordinate them in any type of coherent performance. Cognitive psychologists call this the problem of orchestration. The ability to orchestrate discrete skills into the performance of a complex task is critical. After all, the desired outcome of schooling is not students who can perform arithmetic calculations on an arithmetic test but students who can use these skills to complete real-world tasks, and this requires that the calculations be performed in conjunction with the higher-level skills of problem recognition and formulation.

Finally, teaching basic skills in the context of meaningful tasks will increase the probability that the skills will transfer to real-world situations. The decontextualized academic exercises within which many basic skills have been taught are so different from what any of us encounter in the everyday world that it is little wonder that students question the relevance of much of what they learn in school. Some students come to accept the idea of performing academic exercises for their own sake; others reject the whole enterprise. Neither group could be expected to use what they have learned in school when they encounter problems in their everyday lives.

Moreover, much classroom instruction focuses on how to execute a skill without giving adequate attention to when to execute it. Students learn how to make three different kinds of graphs, but they receive no instruction or practice in deciding which kind of graph is most useful for a specific purpose. The matter of deciding which skill to apply and when doesn't come up when skills are taught in isolation; it is unavoidable when skills are taught in a complex, meaningful context.

Make Connections with Students' Out-of-School Experience and Culture

Implicit in the argument above is the notion that in-school instruction will be more effective if it both builds on what children have already learned out of school and makes connections to situations outside of school. Lauren Resnick and her colleagues have found positive effects for a program in which disadvantaged elementary children are not only given realistic problems to solve with arithmetic in class, but are also encouraged to bring in their own real-life problems for their classmates to solve.[19]

At the same time, it is important to recognize that the great cultural diversity in the U.S. means that many children in compensatory education come from homes with languages, practices, and beliefs that are at variance with some of those assumed in "mainstream" classrooms. Luis Moll argues that the strengths of a child's culture should be recognized, and instruction should capitalize on them.[20] He describes an intricate network for sharing practical knowledge and supporting the acquisition of English skills in a Hispanic community. This cultural practice of knowledge sharing can become an effective model for cooperative learning and problem solving in classrooms.

In addition, curriculum materials can be adapted to children's cultures. Thus typical mathematics problems involving figuring out how to obtain five liters of liquid, given only a three-liter and a seven-liter container, were converted to a Haitian story involving children using calabashes to obtain water from a spring.[21] This technique encouraged participation from the Haitian students in a culturally mixed classroom.

Peg Griffin and Michael Cole describe another example. They had black students compose rap lyrics in collaborative sessions using computers.[22] Although rap songs are not a form of literature found in many standard textbooks, they are no different from the sonnet in terms of having a structure and a set of conventions. When working with this form, which was both relevant to their culture and motivating, black students from low-income homes demonstrated a high degree of sophistication in their composition and revision skills.

NEW INSTRUCTIONAL STRATEGIES

The rethinking of the curriculum described above must be matched by a change in the methods that are employed to impart that curriculum. The approaches reviewed here stress teaching methods that are quite different from the structured drill and practice that typify most compensatory education.

Model Powerful Thinking Strategies

Research in cognitive psychology has long been concerned with making the thinking of expert performers manifest. A key goal of this effort has been to understand the processes that expert performers use in addressing complex tasks and solving novel problems and to model these processes explicitly for novice learners. Great strides have been made in understanding the strategies that accomplished readers use to monitor and enhance their understanding, that mathematicians use when faced with novel problems, and that skilled writers employ. The research on instructional approaches that provide models of expert thinking confirms the instructional value of making these strategies explicit for learners.

Cognitive psychologists recommend that teachers explicitly and repeatedly model the higher-order intellectual processes that they are trying to instill. This means thinking aloud while reading a text and trying to understand how the information in it fits with previously known facts; it means externalizing the thought processes that go into an effort to solve a mathematical puzzle; it means demonstrating the planning and revision processes involved in composition. For too long we have shown students the product that they are supposed to achieve (e.g., the right answer to a math problem or a polished essay) without demonstrating the critical processes required to achieve it.

Encourage Multiple Approaches to Academic Tasks

The alternative programs differ from the instruction conventionally provided in most classrooms in their encouragement of teaching multiple strategies for solving problems. Rather than try to teach the one right way to solve a problem, these programs seek to foster students' ability to invent strategies for solving problems.

In some cases, this kind of thinking is elicited by providing students with open-ended questions to which there is no single right answer. For example, given the assignment to develop a description of one's city that would entice other people to live there, students are free to follow very different paths and to produce different kinds of solutions. In other cases, such as elementary mathematics, problems do have one correct solution. Still, there may well be more than one way to reach that solution, and one of the clearest demonstrations of real understanding of mathematical concepts is the ability to use those concepts to invent solution strategies on one's own.

To support the development of this essential component of problem solving, innovative programs are inviting students to think of their own ways to address a problem. In the classroom described in the box on pages 342–343, titled "Cognitively Guided Instruction," individuals or small groups of students are given mathematics problems to solve. As each child finds an answer, the teacher asks him or her to describe how the solution was reached. When all students have finished, the students' different paths to the answer are compared and discussed so that students can see alternative approaches modeled and come to realize that there is no single right way to find the answer.

Provide Scaffolding to Enable Students to Accomplish Complex Tasks
On reading our recommendation that disadvantaged students be presented with authentic, complex tasks from the outset of their education, a reader's natural reaction might be concern about how the students will handle the demands of such tasks. We need to be sensitive to the fact that many of the components of the task will be difficult and will require mental resources. How is the disadvantaged student, particularly the young student, to handle all of this?

A key instructional concept is that of scaffolding—enabling the learner to handle a complex task by taking on parts of the task. For example, the instructor can perform all the computations required when first introducing students to algebra problems, or the instructor can use cue cards to remind novice writers to do things such as consider alternative arguments.[23] The reciprocal teaching approach alluded to above uses many kinds of scaffolding.[24] In the early stages of teaching, the teacher cues the student to employ various comprehension-enhancing strategies, leaving students free to concentrate on executing those strategies. A more extensive form of scaffolding can be provided for students who have yet to master decoding skills: the teacher reads the text orally, allowing students

to practice comprehension strategies before they have fully mastered word decoding.

Like the physical scaffolding that permits a worker to reach higher places than would otherwise be possible, instructional scaffolding makes it possible for students to accomplish tasks with special materials or with assistance from the teacher or other students. The ultimate goal, of course, is for the student to be able to accomplish the task without assistance. This requires the judicious removal of the support as the student gains more skill.

Make Dialogue the Central Medium for Teaching and Learning
In conventional modes of instruction, the key form of communication is transmission: the teacher has the knowledge and transmits it to the students. Just as a television viewer cannot change the content of a program transmitted to his or her home, the student is a passive recipient of the message the teacher chooses to deliver. The student can pay attention or not, but the message will be the same.

A dialogue is a very different form of communication. It is an interchange in which two parties are full-fledged participants, both with significant influence on the nature of the exchange. This concept of dialogue is central to the cognitive approaches to instruction. Reciprocal teaching occurs through dialogue initially between the teacher and a small group of students, later among the students themselves.

The specifics of the instructional content emerge in the back-and-forth interchange. In their description of an innovative math/science program in a Harlem secondary school, Allan Collins, Jan Hawkins, and Sharon Carver provide an example of the value of student-to-student dialogue: students who had developed hypermedia information displays found that students from another school were bored by the work they had regarded as exemplary.[25] This experience led the student developers to look at their work from an audience's perspective and to undertake design changes to make their product better.

The instructional principles described here show that much more can be done in teaching comprehension, composition, and mathematical reasoning to educationally disadvantaged students than has generally been attempted—whether in compensatory programs or in regular classrooms. It is time to rethink our assumptions about the relationship between basic and advanced skills and to examine critically the content and teaching methods that we bring to the classroom.

The models described here were inspired by research in cognitive psychology, and they focus on teaching the kind of content generally regarded as "conceptual," "higher order," or "advanced." The curricular emphases of these models have long been accepted as appropriate for teaching gifted children, older students, or those from educationally advantaged backgrounds. What has not been adequately appreciated is the value of these models for all learners—young and old, advantaged and disadvantaged alike.

1. This article is based on a set of papers commissioned as part of a project sponsored by the U.S. Department of Education. The complete set of papers has been published in Barbara Means, Carol Chelemer, and Michael S. Knapp, eds., *Teaching Advanced Skills to At-Risk Students: Views from Theory and Practice* (San Francisco: Jossey-Bass, 1991).

2. For a description of a nationwide sample of such programs, see Michael S. Knapp et al., *What is Taught, and How, to the Children of Poverty* (Washington, D.C.: Office of Planning, Budget, and Evaluation, U.S. Department of Education, 1991).

3. Richard L. Allington and Anne McGill-Franzen, "School Response to Reading Failure: Chapter 1 and Special Education Students in Grades 2, 4, and 8," *Elementary School Journal*, vol. 89, 1989, pp. 529–42; and Jeannie Oakes, "Tracking, Inequality, and the Rhetoric of School Reform: Why Schools Don't Change," *Journal of Education*, vol. 168, 1986, pp. 61–80.

4. Jean Anyon, "Social Class and the Hidden Curriculum of Work," *Journal of Education*, vol. 162, 1980, pp. 67–92.

5. Beatrice F. Birman et al., *The Current Operation of the Chapter 1 Program: Final Report from the National Assessment of Chapter 1* (Washington, D.C.: U.S. Government Printing Office, 1987).

6. Michael Cole and Peg Griffin, eds., *Contextual Factors in Education: Improving Science and Math Education for Minorities and Women* (Madison: Wisconsin Center for Education Research, University of Wisconsin, 1987).

7. Michael S. Knapp and Patrick M. Shields, "Reconceiving Academic Instruction for the Children of Poverty," *Phi Delta Kappan*, June 1990, pp. 753–58.

8. Ann L. Brown, Bonnie B. Armbruster, and Linda Baker, "The Role of Metacognition in Reading and Studying," in Judith Orasanu, ed., *Reading and Comprehension* (Hillsdale, N.J.: Lawrence Erlbaum, 1986).

9. Annemarie S. Palincsar and Ann L. Brown, "Reciprocal Teaching of Comprehension-Fostering and Comprehension-Monitoring Activities," *Cognition and Instruction*, Vol. 1, 1984, pp. 117–75.

10. Thomas P. Carpenter, "Learning to Add and Subtract: An Exercise in Problem Solving," in Edward A. Silver, ed., *Teaching and Learning Mathematical Problem Solving: Multiple Research Perspectives* (Hillsdale, N.J.: Lawrence Erlbaum, 1987); and Herbert A. Ginsberg, *The Development of Mathematical Thinking* (New York: Academic Press, 1983).

11. Robert Calfee, "What Schools Can Do to Improve Literacy Instruction," in Means, Chelemer, and Knapp, p. 178; and Mary Bryson and Marlene Scardamalia, "Teaching Writing to Students at Risk for Academic Failure," in Means, Chelemer, and Knapp, pp. 141–75.

12. Jerie Cobb Scott, "Nonmainstream Groups: Questions and Research Directions," in Jane L. Davidson, ed., *Counterpoint and Beyond* (Urbana, Ill.: National Council of Teachers of English, 1988).

13. Richard Allington, "Teacher Interruption Behavior During Primary-Grade Oral Reading," *Journal of Educational Psychology*, vol. 72, 1980, pp. 371–77; and Jere E. Brophy and Thomas L. Good, *Teacher-Student Relationships: Causes and Consequences* (New York: Holt, Rinehart & Winston, 1974).

14. Annemarie S. Palincsar and Laura J. Klenk, "Learning Dialogues to Promote Text Comprehension," in Means, Chelemer, and Knapp, pp. 112–40.

15. Robert D. Sherwood et al., "Macro-contexts for Learning," *Journal of Applied Cognition*, Vol. 1, 1987, pp. 93–108.

16. Allan Collins, Jan Hawkins, and Sharon M. Carver, "A Cognitive Apprentices for Disadvantaged Students," in Means, Chelemer, and Knapp, pp. 216–54.

17. Nancy Vye et al., "Commentary," in Mean Chelemer, and Knapp, pp. 54–67.

18. Penelope Peterson, Elizabeth Fennema, and Thomas Carpenter, "Using Children's Mathematical Knowledge," in Means, Chelemer, and Knapp, pp. 68–111.

19. Lauren Resnick et al., "Thinking in Arithmetic Class," in Means, Chelemer, and Knapp, pp. 27–67.

20. Luis Moll, "Social and Instructional Issues Educating 'Disadvantaged' Students," in Michael S. Knapp and Patrick M. Shields, eds., *Better Schooling for the Children of Poverty: Alternatives to Conventional Wisdom—Vol. II: Commissioned Paper and Literature Review* (Washington, D.C.: Office of Planning, Budget, and Evaluation, U.S. Department of Education, 1990).

21. Judith J. Richards, "Commentary," in Means, Chelemer, and Knapp, pp. 102–11.

22. Peg Griffin and Michael Cole, "New Technologies, Basic Skills, and the Underside of Education: What's to Be Done?" in Judith A. Langer, ed., *Language, Literacy, and Culture: Issues of Society and Schooling* (Norwood, N.J.: Ablex, 1987), pp. 199–231.

23. Bryson and Scardamalia, pp. 141–75.

24. Palincsar and Brown, pp. 117–75.

25. Collins, Hawkins, and Carver, pp. 216–54.

The Use of Scaffolds for Teaching Higher-Level Cognitive Strategies

BARAK ROSENSHINE and CARLA MEISTER

The teaching of higher-level thinking operations is a topic that interests many of today's educators. These operations include comprehension and interpretation of text, scientific processes, and mathematical problem solving. While much has been written on the need for students to perform higher-level thinking operations in all subject areas, the teaching of these operations often fails, not because the idea is poor, but because the instruction is inadequate.

How does one help students perform higher-level operations? One solution that researchers have developed is to teach students cognitive strategies (Pressley et al. 1990; Perkins et al. 1989; Weinstein 1979). A strategy is not a direct procedure; it is not an algorithm. Rather a strategy is a heuristic that supports or facilitates the learner as he or she learns to perform the higher-level operations.

For example, to facilitate reading comprehension, students may be taught to use cognition strategies such as generating questions about their reading. To generate questions, students need to search the text and combine information, which in turn helps them comprehend what they read. To help students in the writing process, they may be taught how to organize their writing and how

Barak Rosenshine is Professor of Educational Psychology and Carla Meister is a Teacher in School District #129, Aurora, Illinois, and a doctoral student in educational psychology at the University of Illinois. They can be reached at the University of Illinois, Bureau of Educational Research, 230 Education Building, 1310 S. Sixth St., Champaign, IL 61820-699.

to use self-talk prompts to facilitate the revision process. These cognitive strategies are more like supports or suggestions than actual step-by-step directives.

But how does one teach cognitive strategies? Our review of about 50 studies in which students ranging from 3rd grade through college were taught cognitive strategies showed that successful teachers of such strategies frequently used instructional procedures called *scaffolds* (Palincsar and Brown 1984; Paris et al. 1986, Wood et al. 1976). Scaffolds are forms of support provided by the teacher (or another student) to help students bridge the gap between their current abilities and the intended goal. Scaffolds may be tools, such as cue cards, or techniques, such as teacher modeling. Although scaffolds can be applied to the teaching of all skills, they are particularly useful, and often indispensable, for teaching higher-level cognitive strategies, where many of the steps or procedures necessary to carry out these strategies cannot be specified. Instead of providing explicit steps, one supports, or scaffolds, the students as they learn the skill.

The support that scaffolds provide is both temporary (Tobias 1982) and adjustable, allowing learners "to participate at an ever-increasing level of competence" (Palincsar and Brown 1984, p. 122). Scaffolding gradually decreases as the learning process unfolds and students become proficient.

Before using scaffolds, it is important to determine whether students have sufficient background ability to learn a new cognitive strategy. Researchers (particularly Palincsar and Brown 1984) note that scaffolds are only useful within the student's "zone of proximal development" (Vygotsky 1978), that is, the area where the student cannot proceed alone, but can proceed when guided by a teacher using scaffolds. When Palincsar and Brown (1984) taught strategies designed to foster reading comprehension, they selected students whose decoding skills were near grade level, but whose comprehension was below grade level. They did not select students with poor decoding skills, because such students did not have sufficient background skills to profit from this instruction. Similarly, scaffolds cannot help students read a physics text or history text for which they do not have the necessary background knowledge.

PRESENTING A NEW COGNITIVE STRATEGY

In the studies we reviewed, teachers typically began teaching a cognitive strategy by introducing and explaining a concrete prompt. Concrete prompts, also called procedural facilitators (Scardamalia et al. 1984), are scaffolds specific to the strategy being taught, yet general enough to allow application to a variety of different contexts. For example, to help students learn the strategy of generating questions, some teachers first gave students "question words"—*who, what, when, where, why, how*—and taught them to use these words as prompts. These six simple question words were the concrete prompts. In the study by King (1989), students used a list of general question stems that could be used to form questions about a particular passage:

> *How are ____ and ____ alike?*
> *What is the main idea of ____?*
> *What do you think would happen if ____?*
> *What are the strengths and weaknesses of
>   ____?*
> *In what way is ____ related to ____?*
> *How does ____ affect ____?*
> *Compare ____ and ____ with regard to
>   ____.*
> *What do you think causes ____ ?*
> *How does ____ tie in with what we have
>   learned before?*
> *Which one is the best ____ and why?*

> *What are some possible solutions for the prob-
>   lem of ____?*
> *Do you agree or disagree with this statement:
>   ____? Support your answer.*
> *What do I (you) still not understand about
>   ____?*

Several different concrete prompts have also been developed for teaching the strategy of summarizing. Baumann (1984) and Taylor (1985) used the following prompt:

> *Identify the topic.*
> *Write two or three words that reflect the topic.*
> *Use these words as a prompt to help figure
>   out the main idea of the paragraph.*
> *Select two details that elaborate on the main
>   idea and are important to remember.*
> *Write two or three sentences that best incorpo-
>   rate these important ideas.*

Palincsar (1987) used a different prompt for teaching summarizing:

> *Step 1: Identify the topic sentence.*
> *Step 2: If there is not a topic sentence, identify
>   the topic and the most important informa-
>   tion about that topic.*
> *Rule 1: Leave out unimportant information.*
> *Rule 2: Give steps or lists a title.*
> *Rule 3: Cross out information that is redun-
>   dant/repeated.*

To assist students during the writing process, Scardamalia, Bereiter, and Steinbach (1984) offered students cues to stimulate their thinking about the planning of compositions. These cues took the form of introductory phrases and were grouped according to the function they served: planning a new idea, improving, elaborating, goal setting, and putting it all together. Students first determined the type of cue needed, then chose a particular cue to incorporate into a silent planning monologue (see box page 29, for cues for opinion essays).

Other investigators developed specific prompts to help students improve their writing. For example, Englert, Raphael, Anderson. Anthony, and Stevens (1991) provided Plan Think-Sheets that cued students to consider their audience ("Who am I writing for?" "Why am I writing this?"), and Orga-

---

How to Teach Higher-Order Cognitive Strategies

1. Present the new cognitive strategies.
   (a) Introduce the concrete prompt.
   (b) Model the skill.
   (c) Think aloud as choices are made.

2. Regulate difficulty during guided practice.
   (a) Start with simplified material and gradually increase the complexity of the task.
   (b) Complete part of the task for the student.
   (c) Provide cue cards.
   (d) Present the material in small steps.
   (e) Anticipate student errors and difficult areas.

3. Provide varying contexts for student practice.
   (a) Provide teacher-led practice.
   (b) Engage in reciprocal teaching
   (c) Have students work in small groups.

4. Provide feedback.
   (a) Offer teacher-led feedback.
   (b) Provide checklists.
   (c) Provide models of expert work.

5. Increase student responsibility.
   (a) Diminish prompts and models.
   (b) Gradually increase complexity and difficulty of the material.
   (c) Diminish student support.
   (d) Practice putting all the steps together (consolidation).
   (e) Check for student mastery.

6. Provide independent practice.
   (a) Provide extensive practice.
   (b) Facilitate application to new examples.

---

nize Think-Sheets to help students sort their ideas into categories ("What is being explained?" "What are the steps?").

After presenting the concrete prompt, the teacher modeled its application as the students observed. Thus, when teaching students to generate questions, the teacher modeled how to use the cues to think of questions related to a particular passage. When teaching students to write a summary, the teacher identified the details of a paragraph or passage, used the details to form a main idea, and stated the details in the summary. In writing an explanation paper, the teacher used the planning cues in a self-talk (monologue) style. The teacher modeled how to use the Plan Think-Sheet to record ideas and thoughts about the topic.

Modeling of the process by the teacher gradually diminished as students began to take on more of the responsibility for completing the task. The teacher continued to model only the part(s) of the process that students were unable to complete at a particular time. Often during the transitional stage, when the students were ready to take on another part of the task, the teacher continued to model, but requested hints or suggestions from the students on how to complete the next step in the task. Several studies also relied on more capable students to provide the modeling.

Another scaffold, similar to modeling, is "thinking aloud." For example, when teaching students to generate questions, the teacher describes the thought processes that occur as a question word

is selected and integrated with text information to form a question.

Anderson (1991) provides illustrations of think-alouds for several cognitive strategies in reading:

For clarifying difficult statements or concepts: *I don't get this. It says that things that are dark look smaller. I know that a white dog looks smaller than a black elephant, so this rule must only work for things that are about the same size. Maybe black shoes would make your feet look smaller than white ones would.*

For summarizing important information: *I'll summarize this part of the article. So far, it tells where the Spanish started in North America and what parts they explored. Since the title is "The Spanish in California," the part about California must be important. I'd sum up by saying that Spanish explorers from Mexico discovered California. They didn't stay in California, but lived in other parts of America. These are the most important ideas so far.*

For thinking ahead: *So far this has told me that Columbus is poor, the trip will be expensive, and everyone's laughing at his plan. I'd predict that Columbus will have trouble getting the money he needs for his exploration.*

In a mathematics study by Schoenfeld (1985), the teacher thought aloud as he went through the steps in solving mathematical problems. He also identified and labeled the problem-solving procedures he was using (for example, making diagrams, breaking the problem into parts). Thus, as Schoenfeld points out, thinking aloud may also provide labels that students can use to call up the same processes in their own thinking.

When teaching mathematical problem solving, Schoenfeld (1985) asked the college students in his class to provide him with particularly difficult problems. Each class began with his attempt to solve one of the problems. Through modeling and thinking aloud, he applied problem-solving procedures and revealed his reasoning about the problems he encountered. Students saw the flexibility of the strategies as they were applied to a range of problems and observed that the use of a strategy did not guarantee success.

The following excerpt is an example of Schoenfeld modeling his thinking process as he gets a feel for a problem:

What do you do when you face a problem like this? I have no general procedure for finding the roots of a polynomial, much less for comparing the roots of two of them. Probably the best thing to do for the time being is to look at some simple examples and hope I can develop some intuition from them. Instead of looking at a pair of arbitrary polynomials, maybe I should look at a pair of quadratics: at least I can solve those. Now, what happens if . . .

As individual students accepted more responsibility in the completion of a task, they often modeled and thought aloud for their less capable classmates. Not only did student modeling and think-alouds involve the students actively in the process, but it allowed the teacher to better assess student progress in the use of the strategy. Thinking aloud by the teacher and more capable students provided novice learners with a way to observe "expert thinking" usually hidden from the student.

REGULATING DIFFICULTY DURING GUIDED PRACTICE

In order to help the learner, many teachers began with simpler exercises and then gradually in-

creased the difficulty of the task. This allowed the learner to begin participating very early in the process. For example, in a study by Palincsar (1987). an early task consisted of generating questions about a *single sentence.* The teacher first modeled how to generate questions, and this was followed by student practice. Then the complexity was increased to generating questions after reading a *paragraph*, followed by more student practice. Finally, the teacher modeled and the class practiced generating questions after reading an entire *passage.*

When learning the strategy of summarizing, students in the study by Dermody (1988) first learned how to write summary statements on single paragraphs. After students received guided practice on this task, teachers showed them how to combine several summary statements to produce a single summary for a longer passage and had them practice this more difficult task.

In many of the studies, instruction on the cognitive strategy began with the teacher completing most or all of the task through modeling and thinking aloud. The teacher continued to carry out the parts of the task not yet introduced to the students or those parts students were unable to complete at the time. Additional components were added to the students' responsibilities as they became more skillful. Sometimes, their participation began at a very simple level. For example, as the teacher modeled the strategy, the students were asked to provide the label. Or students were requested to state the next step in the process the teacher needed to model. As student involvement increased, teacher involvement was withdrawn. Teachers provided hints, prompts, suggestions, and feedback when students encountered difficulty in their attempts to complete part of the task. Sometimes these difficulties required the temporary increase of teacher involvement until students were able to overcome the difficulty.

In some studies, students received cue cards containing the concrete prompts they had been taught. Having a cue card allows the student to put more effort into *applying* the prompt, rather than *remembering* it. For example, in the study by Billingsley and Wildman (1984), the students were provided with a card containing the list of question words (*who, what, why*) they could use to generate questions. Singer and Donlon (1982) taught students to use the elements of story grammar (for example, leading character, goal, obstacles, outcomes, and theme) as a prompt to generate questions and gave them lists of these story elements for reference. Wong and Jones (1982) provided students with cue cards printed with a concrete prompt to use as they generated questions on the main idea of a passage. Eventually the cue cards were removed, and students were asked to formulate questions or write summaries without them. Below is a Self-Questioning Cue Card:

(a) *Why are you studying this passage? (So you can answer some questions you will be given later.)*

(b) *Find the main idea/ideas in the paragraph and underline it/ them.*

(c) *Think of a question about the main idea you have underlined. Remember what a good question should be like.*

(d) *Learn the answer to your question.*

(e) *Always look back at the questions and answers to see how each successive question and answer provides you with more information.*

When presenting a prompt that has several steps, the difficulty can be regulated by "teaching in small steps," that is, first teaching one step and providing for student practice before teaching the next step. In this way, students deal with manageable, yet meaningful, bits. In a study (Blaha 1979) in which students were taught a strategy for summarizing paragraphs, the teacher explained and modeled the first step, identifying the topic of a paragraph, and provided for student practice on new paragraphs. Then she taught the concept of main idea, and students practiced both finding the topic and locating the main idea. Following this, she taught students to identify the supporting details, and the students practiced that part of the task. Finally, the students practiced doing all three steps of the strategy.

Another way to regulate the difficulty of learning a new cognitive strategy is to anticipate and discuss potential student errors. For example, in one study the teacher anticipated errors in summarizing by presenting a summary with a poorly written topic sentence and asking students to identify the problem. In a questioning study, the teacher showed questions that were inappropriate because they were about a minor detail and then asked students to state why they were inappropriate. The students then used these hints and suggestions as they generated their questions.

Another example of anticipating errors occurs in the study conducted by Brady (1990). The investigator noticed that students had a tendency to produce summary statements that were too broad, often providing only the general topic of the passage (for example, "This paragraph was about toads.") To help students avoid this error, Brady developed a simple yet successful concrete prompt; he suggested students begin their summary statements with the phrase "This paragraph tells us that

---

Planning Cues Used for Opinion Essays

New Idea
An even better idea is . . .
An important point I haven't considered yet is . . .
A better argument would be . . .
A whole new way to think of this topic is . . .
No one will have thought of . . .

Improve
I'm not being very clear about what I just said
    so . . .
A criticism I should deal with in my paper is . . .
I really think this isn't necessary because . . .

Putting it Together
If I want to start off with my strongest idea, I'll . . .
I can tie this together by . . .
My main point is . . .

Elaborate
An example of this . . .
This is true, but it's not sufficient so . . .
My own feelings about this are . . .
I'll change this a little by . . .
The reason I think so . . .
Another reason that's good . . .
I could develop this idea by adding . . .
Another way to put it would be . . .
A good point on the other side of the argument
    is . . .

Goals
A goal I think I could write is . . .
My purpose is . . .

_____." This prompt significantly improved the quality of summary statements.

VARYING THE CONTEXT FOR PRACTICE

Students in most studies practiced the application of cognitive strategies in one or more of three different contexts: teacher-guided practice, reciprocal teaching, and work in small groups. When teaching cognitive strategies, the teachers guided students by providing hints, reminders of the concrete prompts, reminders of what was overlooked, and suggestions on how something could be improved. Students participated by giving answers and deciding upon the correctness of other students' answers. Where appropriate, students were asked to justify their procedures by explaining their thinking. Through this process, students' "oversimplified and naive conceptions are revealed" (Brown and Campione 1986). Such dialogue may also aid in understanding. As Brown and Campione (1986) write, "Understanding is more likely to occur when a student is required to explain, elaborate, or defend his or her position to others; the burden of explanation is often the push needed to make him or her evaluate, integrate, and elaborate knowledge in new ways."

In some studies, guided practice took place in the context of a dialogue among teacher and students—reciprocal teaching (Palincsar and Brown 1984)—with students and teacher rotating the role of teacher. This allowed for shifting of responsibility to the students and gradual internalization of the cognitive strategies. As the student took on the role of the teacher in the process of applying the strategies to a text, the teacher was able to evaluate the student's progress and provide feedback or assistance (see box, page 30, for an example of a dialogue).

Collaborative social dialogue was also emphasized in Englert and colleagues' (1991) Cognitive Strategy Instruction in Writing. During guided practice, students were invited to participate in a dialogue about a class writing project. Students and teacher worked collaboratively to generate self-questions, apply the new cognitive strategies, and carry on the dialogue to complete a class paper. The students progressively took on more responsibility for completing the writing task. The investigators contend that as students accept more responsibility in the exchange that takes place during the instructional dialogues, they begin to internalize the dialogue. The investigators suggest that this inner dialogue allows students to (1) talk to themselves about their own writing, (2) hear what their own writing has to say, and (3) talk to others about their writing.

In some studies, notably those conducted with high school and college students, the students practiced the task in small groups without the teacher. For example, King (1989) reported that after hearing a lecture, students met in small groups and practiced generating questions about the lecture. Students in Schoenfeld's (1985) study had opportunities to participate in small group mathematical problem solving. Schoenfeld suggests small group work facilitates the learning process in four ways. First, it provides an opportunity for the teacher to assess students, to provide support and assistance as students actively engage in problem solving. Second, group decision making facilitates the articulation of knowledge and reasoning as students justify to group members their reasons for choosing alternative solutions. Third, students receive practice in collaboration, a skill required in real-life problem solving. Fourth, students who are insecure about their abilities to solve problems have the opportunity to see more capable peers struggle over difficult problems.

PROVIDING FEEDBACK

Feedback is important in teaching cognitive strategies as it is for all forms of learning. Traditional feedback from teachers and other students on the correctness of response took place throughout the lessons on cognitive strategies.

In several studies the teacher provided self-checking procedures to increase student independence. For example, as part of their instruction in teaching students to summarize a passage, Rinehart, Stahl, and Erickson (1986) had students use the following list of questions to check their summaries:

> *Have I found the overall idea that the passage is about?*
> *Have I found the most important information that tells me more about the overall idea?*

*Have I used any information that is not di-
rectly about the main idea?*
Have I used any information more than once?

Checklists for writing programs ranged from
checklists on punctuation ("Does every sentence
start with a capital letter?") to checklists on style
elements. For example, students being taught to
write explanations were taught to ask, "Did I tell
what materials you need?" "Did I make the steps
clear?" (Englert et al. 1991). Teachers usually presented these checklists at the end of guided practice. The teacher modeled the use of the checklist
and provided students with guidance as they began
to use the checklists.

In some studies, students were provided with
expert models to compare their work to. For example, where students were taught to generate questions, they could compare their questions with
those generated by the teacher. Similarly, when
learning to write summaries, students could compare their summaries on a passage with those generated by an expert.

INCREASING STUDENT RESPONSIBILITY

Just as it is important to simplify material and provide support for students in the initial stages of
learning a cognitive strategy, it is also important to
reduce the number of prompts and provide students with practice using more complex material.
Thus, the responsibility for learning shifts from the
teacher to the student. This gradual decrease in
supports and gradual increase in student responsibility has been described as a shift in the teacher's
role from that of coach to that of supportive and
sympathetic audience (Palincsar and Brown 1984).

After the students in the study by Wong and
Jones (1982) had used cue cards to develop fluency
in writing a summary, the cue cards were removed
and students wrote summaries without these
prompts. In the studies by King (1989), in which
students used half-completed sentences as references when generating questions, the teacher with-
drew the supports after the guided practice, and
students were left to generate questions on their
own.

Increasing the complexity of material was evident in the study by Palincsar (1987), in which stu-

dents learning to generate questions began by
working on a single sentence, then a paragraph,
and finally, an entire passage. Schoenfeld (1985) se-
quenced the problems he presented to his students
when teaching mathematical problem solving. He
first gave students problems they were incapable of
solving on their own; this provided the motivation
for learning the strategy he planned to introduce.
After presenting the strategy, he provided problems
that were easily solved when the strategy was applied. As students became skilled at applying the
strategy, he introduced a new strategy. Interspersed
among these new problems were several problems
requiring the application of previously taught problem-solving strategies, forcing students to dis-
criminately apply the strategies learned to the type
of problems encountered. As the course progressed,
students were expected to combine strategies to
solve complex problems.

In some studies, the support that students received from other students was also diminished as
work progressed. For example, in the study by
Nolte and Singer (1985), the students first spent
three days working in groups of five or six and then
three days working in pairs before working alone
on the task.

In the study by Englert and colleagues (1991),
in which students were taught cognitive strategies
in writing, students first participated in a collaborative dialogue that centered on the application of the
newly learned strategies to a whole-class writing
project. Students then chose their own topic, applying the same strategies used in the group writing.
Students were encouraged to collaborate with a
peer or peers by sharing ideas, discussing each
other's writing, asking questions, getting feedback,
reporting progress, or asking advice. The teacher
provided additional support by finding examples
of strategy use or problems found in the students'
writing, displaying them on the overhead. The
teacher initiated a class dialogue on the student
examples, focusing the discussion on the strategies
used, the problems encountered by the students,
and possible solutions. After the students completed this piece of writing, the teacher asked them
to independently write another paper for publication in a class book.

When series of steps have been taught and
practiced separately, as in some summarizing and
writing strategies, one of the final tasks during
guided practice is having the students practice putting the component parts of the strategy together. A

teacher can then assess student implementation of the complete strategy, correct errors, and determine whether additional teaching or practice is necessary. Such assessment is important before students begin independent practice.

PROVIDING INDEPENDENT PRACTICE

The goal of independent practice is to develop *unitization* of the strategy, that is, the blending of elements of the strategy into a single, unified whole. The extensive practice, and practice with a *variety* of material—alone, in groups, or in pairs—also *decontextualizes* the learning. That is, the strategies become free of their original "bindings" and can now be applied, easily and unconsciously, to various situations (Collins et al. 1990). Cognitive Strategy Instruction in Writing (the program implemented in the Englert et al. 1991 study) provided students with several opportunities to apply the strategies they had been taught, first in a whole-group setting, then individually with peer and teacher assistance, and then a third time independently.

TOWARD A BROADER APPLICATION?

Scaffolds and the procedures for using them provide us with many ways to think about how to help students learn cognitive strategies (see box, page 27). Such concepts as modeling, thinking aloud, using cue cards, anticipating errors, and providing expert models can also be applied to the teaching of well-structured skills. This suggests that instead of a dichotomy, there is a continuum from well-structured explicit skills to cognitive strategies. At all points in the continuum, some instructional processes, such as presenting information in small steps and providing guided practice, are important. Yet, as one moves from well-structured skills to cognitive strategies, the value of providing students with scaffolds—models, concrete prompts, think-alouds, simplified problems, suggestions, and hints—increases.

The tools and techniques we refer to as scaffolds are at a middle level of specificity. That is, they provide support for the student, but they do not specify each and every step to be taken. There is

something appealing about this middle level. It lies somewhere between the specificity of behavioral objectives that seemed overly demanding to some, and the lack of instruction that many criticized in discovery learning settings. Perhaps it is the beginning of a synthesis.

REFERENCES

Anderson, V. (April 1991). "Training Teachers to Foster Active Reading Strategies in Reading-Disabled Adolescents." Paper presented at the annual meeting of the American Educational Research Association, Chicago.

Baumann, J. F. (1984). "The Effectiveness of a Direct Instruction Paradigm for Teaching Main Idea Comprehension." *Reading Research Quarterly* 20: 93–115.

Billingsley, B. S., and T. M. Wildman. (1984). "Question Generation and Reading Comprehension." *Learning Disability Research* 4: 36–44.

Blaha, B. A. (1979). "The Effects of Answering Self-Generated Questions on Reading." Unpublished doctoral diss., Boston University School of Education.

Brady, P. L. (1990). "Improving the Reading Comprehension of Middle School Students Through Reciprocal Teaching and Semantic Mapping Strategies." Unpublished doctoral diss., University of Oregon.

Brown, A. L., and J. C. Campione. (1986). "Psychological Theory and the Study of Learning Disabilities." *American Psychologist* 41: 1059–1068.

Collins, A., J. S. Brown, and S. E. Newman. (1990). "Cognitive Apprenticeship: Teaching the Crafts of Reading, Writing, and Mathematics." In *Knowing, Learning, and Instruction: Essays in Honor of Robert Glaser*, edited by L. Resnick. Hillsdale, N.J.: Erlbaum Associates.

Dermody, M. M. (1988). "Effects of Metacognitive Strategy Training on Fourth Graders' Reading Comprehension." Unpublished doctoral diss., University of New Orleans.

Englert, C. S., T. E. Raphael, L. M. Anderson, H. Anthony, and D. D. Stevens. (1991). "Making Strategies and Self-Talk Visible: Writing, Instruction in Regular and Special Education Classrooms." *American Educational Research Journal* 28: 337–372.

King, A. (April 1989). "Improving Lecture Comprehension: Effects of a Metacognitive Strategy." Paper presented at the annual meeting of the American Educational Research Association, San Francisco.

Nolte, R. Y., and H. Singer. (1985). "Active Comprehension: Teaching a Process of Reading Comprehension and Its Effects on Reading Achievement." *The Reading Teacher* 39: 24–31.

Palincsar, A. S. (April 1987). "Collaborating for Collaborative Learning of Text Comprehension." Paper presented at the annual meeting of the American Educational Research Association, Washington, D.C.

Palincsar, A. M., and A. L. Brown. (1984). "Reciprocal Teaching of Comprehension-Fostering and Comprehension-Monitoring Activities." *Cognition and Instruction* 2: 117–175.

Palinscar, A. S. (1986). "The Role of Dialogue in Providing Scaffolded Instruction." *Educational Psychologist* 21: 73–98.

Paris, S. G., K. K. Wixson, and A. S. Palincsar. (1986). "Instructional Approaches to Reading Comprehension." *In Review of Research in Education*, edited by E. Z. Rothkof. Washington, D.C.: American Educational Research Association.

Perkins, D. N., R. Simmons, and S. Tishman. (March 1989). "Teaching Cognitive and Metacognitive Strategies." Paper presented at the annual meeting of the American Educational Research Association, San Francisco.

Pressley, M., J. Burkell, T. Cariglia-Bull, L. Lysynchuk, J. A. McGoldrick, B. Schneider, S. Symons, and V. E. Woloshyn. (1990). *Cognitive Strategy Instruction.* Cambridge, Mass.: Brookline Books.

Rinehart, S. D., S. A. Stahl, and L. G. Erickson. (1986). "Some Effects of Summarization Training on Reading and Studying." *Reading Research Quarterly* 21: 422–437.

Scardamalia, M., C. Bereiter, and R. Steinbach. (1984). "Teachability of Reflective Processes in Written Composition." *Cognitive Science* 8: 173–190.

Schoenfeld, A. H. (1985). *Mathematical Problem Solving.* New York: Academic Press.

Singer, H., and D. Donlan. (1982). "Active Comprehension: Problem-Solving Schema with Question Generation of Complex Short Stories." *Reading Research Quarterly* 17: 166–186.

Taylor, B. M. (1985). "Improving Middle-Grade Students' Reading and Writing of Expository Text." *Journal of Educational Research* 79: 119–125.

Tobias, S. (1982). "When Do Instructional Methods Make a Difference?" *Educational Researcher* 11: 4–10.

Vygotsky, L. S. (1978). *Mind in Society: The Development of Higher Psychological Processes*, edited and translated by M. Cole, V. John Steiner, S. Schribner and E. Souberman. Cambridge, Mass.: Harvard University Press.

Wong, Y. L., and W. Jones. (1982). "Increasing Metacomprehension in Learning Disabled and Normally Achieving Students Through Self-Questioning Training." *Learning Disability Quarterly* 5: 228–239.

Wood, D. J., J. S. Bruner, and G. Ross. (1976). "The Role of Tutoring in Problem Solving." *Journal of Child Psychology and Psychiatry* 17: 89–100.

Authors' note: We hope that the ideas presented here can serve as a heuristic for teachers to support their classroom instruction in cognitive strategies. The teaching of cognitive strategies is a higher-level operation itself; there is no specific, predetermined, or guaranteed path of instructional procedures to follow. Rather, there are sets of procedures, suggestions and scaffolds that a teacher selects, develops, presents, attempts, modifies, and even abandons in order to help students learn the cognitive strategy.

This research was supported by the Bureau of Educational Research, College of Education, University of Illinois.

► Chapter 14

Interview on Assessment Issues with Lorrie Shepard

The News and Comment section will feature a number of formats for examining research issues. This is the first use of the interview format for eliciting opinions about controversial areas. The *ER* interviewer is News and Comment editor, Michael Kirst of Stanford University. He first talks with Lorrie Shepard, who is professor at the School of Education at the University of Colorado, Boulder, and then with James Popham, who is professor in the UCLA Graduate School of Education and director of IOX Assessment Associates.

ER: What are the reasons for the movement towards authentic testing and what does this concept mean to you?

Shepard: Use of the *authentic assessment* is intended to convey that the assessment tasks themselves are real instances of extended criterion performances, rather than proxies or estimators of actual learning goals. Other synonyms are *direct* or *performance assessments*. The intense interest we are seeing in these alternative measures is a response to some of the deadly effects of multiple-choice tests, which are, in turn, the result of the inordinate weight given to traditional standardized tests in the past decade as a key feature of educational reform. Under pressure to raise test scores, the known limitations of multiple-choice tests have become greatly exaggerated. They become less valid indicators of what students know (because scores can go up without a commensurate gain in achievement); and more seriously, when multiple-choice tests become the focus of instructional effort, they have a negative effect on teaching and learning.

ER: What are your concerns about using multiple-choice tests to drive classroom instruction?

Shepard: When important standardized tests become the curriculum guides in a school or classroom, the quality of instruction is reduced in several respects. First, as many critics warned in advance, the curriculum is narrowed to only those topics that are tested. This often means that writing, social studies, and science are driven out of the instructional day, as well as "frills" such as art and music.

In addition to the predicted distortion of curricular frameworks, we now have evidence of unanticipated effects on the way that even basic skills subjects are taught. For example, in many cases teachers teach reading and math using worksheets and practice materials that closely resemble test materials. The behavioristic decomposability and decontextualization assumptions—which the Resnicks identified as the faulty learning-theory assumptions underlying standardized tests—then shape the daily mode of instruction, leading to repeated drill on isolated skills. Even if well-crafted multiple-choice tests can assess higher order thinking skills, measurement specialists should recognize that the classroom tests created by teachers to mimic accountability tests are much more likely to elicit rote learning. Emphasis on raising test scores above all else reinforces other behaviorist principles widely held in schools, like the idea that thinking and reasoning should be postponed until after basic skills have been mastered. Instead of instruction being improved as intended, poor test performers get more drill, while only high scorers are provided with instruction aimed at teaching comprehension and problem solving.

Lastly, conceiving of instruction in the format of tests also affects children's attitudes and the inferences they draw about the purpose of learning. They learn, for example, that there is one right answer to every question, that the right answer resides in the head of the teacher or test maker, and that their job is to get that answer by guessing if necessary—hardly a perspective consistent with the goal of having children construct their own understandings.

ER: How would authentic assessments help with the problem of postponing instruction that teaches thinking?

Shepard: The tasks and problems used in authentic assessments are complex, integrated, and challenging instructional tasks. They require children to think to be able to arrive at answers or explanations. Thus performance assessments mirror good instruction, which engages children in thinking from the very beginning. For example, in first grade good teaching would not sort children into readers and nonreaders, letting readers do comprehension work because they had passed the decoding threshold while denying to nonreaders a chance to think about comprehension from text. Instruction aimed at thinking and the construction of meaning would instead focus on listening comprehension and ask all of the children to do some of the things to understand a story line and remember some of the important elements of the story, whether or not they were decoding. These expectations would then situate decoding instruction properly in the context of why we do it, which is to be able to read and get meaning from texts.

Authentic assessment supports good teaching by not requiring teachers to redirect attention away from important concepts, in-depth projects, and the like. To the extent that performance assessments merely replace standardized tests as a different external demand, then at least when classroom instruction imitates these types of tasks and gives children practice with solving these kinds of problems, the focus is more likely to be on thinking rather than eliminating wrong answers.

ER: What are some of the problems with implementing authentic assessment in the next two years or so?

Shepard: My answer to that question depends on the purpose of the intended assessment. If the idea is to provide better classroom assessments in support of instruction and learning, then the problem is inadequate education of teachers, and the remedy is to extend to a wider group of professionals the insights that the best teachers have about how to

construct their own assessment tasks and conduct systematic observations to inform instruction.

If the purpose is, however, to conduct a large-scale survey for accountability purposes, then the technical problems to produce reliable and representative scores are potentially much greater. We have many admirable examples of authentic assessments, but they are invariably judge or observer intensive compared to paper-and-pencil devices run through optical scanning machines. Therefore cost is a big factor, both for development and scoring. It is possible to have sufficient funds to conduct authentic assessments well without raising the total price-tag, at the state level for example, if legislators could be convinced to test less. Rather than testing every pupil in every grade in every subject, policymakers should be willing to invest in a few exemplary assessments in key subject areas by using a sampling of students and grade levels. The trade-off between quantity and quality of data should seem worthwhile once one recognizes both the corruptibility of standardized tests as indicators and their distorting effect on the teaching of challenging content.

ER: Now in the sampling procedure, would authentic assessment be similar to current procedures where we gather teachers to judge writing samples? You get a consensus among two or three judges as to what the score is. Is that part of it?

Shepard: Yes, current writing assessments and the College Board's Advanced Placement (AP) exams are examples of performance assessments. Although there are quarrels about the content of some AP exams (breadth over depth) and some writing assessments as currently administered, these examples demonstrate that we know how to solve problems of scoring standards and inter-judge reliability. The general strategies for ensuring reliable and valid scores from subjective judgments can be applied whether judges are asked to evaluate written products, video-tapes of performances, oral interviews, or observations during science experiments.

ER: Do you see this likely to happen in major ways at the local or state level in the next three to five years? Jim Popham, whom I interviewed earlier, was somewhat skeptical that this was going to happen very soon.

Shepard: I don't think you'll see the 35 states now using norm-referenced tests all chucking them in the next three years and replacing them with authentic assessment. But I think you'll be surprised at the enthusiasm for these ideas. Some legislators are still absolutely convinced that holding schools accountable with mandatory basic-skills tests will make education better; I submit that they reside disproportionately in states that have just recently instituted such tests. In states that began high-stakes testing in 1984, however, proponents are now not so sure. As negative evidence accumulates—such as poor performance on higher order tasks on National Assessments of reading and mathematics—policymakers are becoming increasingly interested in alternatives to standardized tests.

ER: States are sometimes going in one direction on testing towards authentic and performance testing but the local districts still use standardized norm-referenced tests like Iowa, Stanford, Metropolitan, or the California to test basic skills, which don't really have the same concept as the state assessment. What will happen if we have these two different concepts implemented, one at the state level and another at the local level?

Shepard: Well, making a prediction about that really depends on which of the tests has the greatest power. When OERI (Office of Educational Research and Improvement) commissioned CRESST (Center for Research on Evaluation, Standards, and Student Testing) to do a follow-up study of Cannell's report (that all 50 states are above average), we interviewed a nationally representative sample of 50 local testing directors, as well as an 50 state testing directors. Based on those data, we know that there is variation from state to state as to whether the state or district tests have the greatest political clout. We also learned that the states associated with a given test are based as much on the public visibility of test scores as on important decisions or sanctions that follow from test results. The test that leads to ranking of schools in the local paper is the one that is more likely to drive instruction. Therefore, it is possible that multiple-choice tests will continue to have a deadly effect if districtized tests receive the greatest media attention.

There is even the danger that the advice I gave earlier about using sampling to make performance assessments feasible will unwittingly yield greater power to local standardized tests because they will the only ones that continue to produce rankings of schools. While I think this problem has to be thought through, I remain convinced that impressively different authentic assessments can help to redirect effort toward important learning goals. In the case of science and social studies, for example,

a state-level assessment would not be upstaged by local standardized test scores. To command attention for more ambitious assessments of reading and mathematics, it might be effective to extend the state-level sampling to provide district comparisons, as an external check on local claims made on the basis of standardized tests.

ER: Let's shift to another subject now. You have been concerned about the effects of testing on various public policies. Let's start with your impression on where we are on readiness testing for kindergartners and first graders in terms of holding them back or starting them late. What has been the recent policy trend in terms of using tests? Now some policymakers seem to be removing them. Why is this?

Shepard: I agree that at the state level readiness testing has been mandated and then withdrawn or greatly modified—the most infamous example being the Georgia kindergarten exit test. Policymakers were simply embarrassed by the public outcry. Whatever the public's understanding is about the fallibility and potential bias of tests, it's just much more believable that asking a 5-year-old or 6-year-old to take a test may lead to invalid results.

However, I do not think that there has been a diminution in the local use of readiness testing where it remains largely unscrutinized by the public. In a recent survey sponsored by the National Research Council, only three states did not report the use of readiness tests, at the state or district level, to delay school entry, to deny entrance to first grade, or to make special placements such as developmental kindergarten or pre-first grade. Recently we have begun to see a new use of screening and readiness tests which is to place "at-risk" children into kindergarten classes tracked by ability.

ER: Your view is that the technology and validity and reliability of these preschool and first-grade tests are not adequate to do the job they're intended and that the locals want them to do?

Shepard: The reliabilities of these instruments typically do not meet the standards of accuracy expected when making important life decisions for individual children, and their construct validity is questionable. Anne Stallman and David Pearson have done an illuminating analysis of academic readiness tests. They look pretty much like the first reading readiness tests given in the 1930s and are wholly incompatible with recent research on emergent literacy. And screening measures, often used as readiness measures, are basically short IQ tests.

The more serious problem, however, is that the treatments that follow as a consequence of the tests are themselves inadequate, even harmful.

ER: You mean the educational program that follows low test results?

Shepard: That's right. It is acceptable to give a treatment based on a fallible diagnosis if the treatment is unambiguously a benefit and has no side effects. But in this case, the treatments in the form of various two-year kindergarten programs are demonstrably ineffective based on controlled studies. And kindergarten retention and transitional grades often have negative emotional consequences for children. Therefore, the tests lack validity for these types of placements because the placements themselves are invalid.

ER: Let me shift now to tests which are being used by localities or states for promotion purposes to hold kids back from grade to grade, and your view of both the validity and reliability of those tests, plus the impact of the educational prescriptions and treatments that come from nonpromotion.

Shepard: Once again, I think the issue should be the efficacy of the treatments that follow from low test scores, not just the reliability coefficient associated with the test instrument. The research on retention is overwhelmingly negative. Out of 63 controlled studies identified by C. Thomas Holmes at Georgia, only 9 showed positive effects for retention. The average effect size was quite negative and did not improve when only the studies with the most extensive controls were aggregated. What's more, in the years following retention, retained children were further behind promoted controls on achievement measures than on self-esteem measures, which contradicts popular wisdom about the benefits of retention.

ER: Do you have concerns about the large amount of testing used for placing special education pupils in special programs?

Shepard: Yes. In the case of testing to identify children in mildly handicapped categories the costs of assessment and staffing procedures use up half of the extra per-pupil resources available without any evidence that pro forma administration of tests adds to the scientific integrity of placement decisions. In research that Mary Lee Smith and I have done, and in other studies, there is a very high correspondence between initial teacher referrals and final placement decisions, with all of the testing in between serving to justify placement. At least half of the children labeled by schools as learning disabled (LD), by far the largest category of handicap, are misidentified. Rather than fitting the original clinical definition of LD, they are more aptly described as slow learners, linguistically different children, misbehaving boys, children who are absent or whose families move too frequently, or as average learners in above-average contexts. And again, in the case of special education placement for these children, there is no evidence that pull-out programs they receive are certain to be a beneficial treatment.

ER: Your view is that you're concerned equally about both the quality of testing and the quality of the educational intervention; it's the two together, not just one or the other.

Shepard: That's right, if you had an unambiguously wonderful treatment, people would be clamoring to get into it. They'd be clamoring for retention; they'd be clamoring for special education placement. It would be reasonable to use a fallible measuring device, on the grounds that some information is better than none, and err in the direction of giving special treatment.

But time and again we have seen the parallels among special educational treatments that are not benign: tracking, special education placement for mildly affected learners, extra-year programs before first grade, and grade retention. So it's really the harm of the treatment that is more worrisome than the fallibility of the measure.

ER: What are your views about the merits of measurement-driven instruction?

Shepard: Measurement-driven instruction comes from the behavioristic test-teach-test learning model. It assumes that all of the constituent elements important insights and understanding can be broken down and taught one by one. As I indicated earlier, this learning theory is seriously flawed and has a deadening effect on instruction, especially because it postpones attention to thinking and problem solving.

Very recently we are seeing a new version of measurement-driven instruction from advocates of authentic and performance assessments. Although I generally concur that more admirable assessments will have a more salutary effect on instruction and learning, I have two reservations about using assessments (however impressive) to leverage educational reform. (a) Under great pressure, the weaknesses of any assessment will be exaggerated. Therefore, you are always in danger of encouraging teaching to the assessed version of the learning goals rather than the original goals. (b) Forcing modes of instruction via external high-stakes assessments detracts from the professional role of teachers. It trades making the worst 10% of teachers better by fiat against empowering the other 90%. Both of these concerns can be alleviated, of course, if the assessments are sufficiently broad so that tasks are not prespecified and taught to, and there are multiple paths to successful performance. But in litigious environments these features are often negotiated out of testing programs because there is safety in specificity. These problems have yet to be worked out and should be resolved before powerful assessment programs are installed.

Interview on Assessment Issues with James Popham

ER: Jim, you've been actively involved in the testing field for many years. Why do you think there is so much testing going on now, particularly at the state level?

Popham: Heightened demands for testing are, in my view, a function of public incredulity regarding the quality of public schooling. The test-focused accountability movement of the seventies that initially manifested itself in the establishment of high-school graduation tests was clearly triggered by taxpayers' doubts regarding the caliber of the nation's educational system. If our citizenry had really believed that the public schools were doing a dandy job, I'm confident that today's testing demands would be tiny.

ER: Have you seen a steady increase in tests since the minimum competency test movement in the seventies, and then the educational excellence movement in the eighties? What would be the fits and starts of this?

Popham: The big push for state minimum competency testing came in the mid-seventies and continued for a full decade or so. Currently, relatively few states do not have some sort of minimum competency assessment statute on their books. Most of the competency testing activity in the seventies started out on the East and West Coasts and then shifted to the South. Only in recent years have substantial pressures to establish competency testing programs reached the Midwest. The educational excellence era to which you refer has, in fact, caused a shift in some state-level testing programs. We now find a number of states moving well beyond minima in their statewide assessments.

ER: How would you distinguish the requests that you currently see for testing work between states who want basically minimal bask skills testing as against so-called higher order skills testing? Are you seeing any demand by states to really do higher order testing or is this just a lot of rhetoric?

Popham: It's far more than rhetoric. The distinguishing feature of many of the early minimum competency programs was that they really focused on the most minimum imaginable competencies. Many early minimum-competency testing programs, unfortunately, attempted to assess genuinely trivial sorts of skills.

What the legislators who established the early test-based accountability systems failed to realize was just how crafty educators could be once they recognized that they were going to be held accountable on the basis of students' test performances. Because educators typically controlled or influenced the content of those early tests, those educators often made sure the tests were relatively simple so that almost all students looked good, and as a consequence, so did educators. Sadly, many educators were more concerned with presenting an image of successfulness than they were with determining whether students had mastered truly defensible skills. Now, however, as legislators have become more insightful regarding the possibility that some self-serving educators may subvert legislative intentions, one sees the enactments of legislative requirements that explicitly stipulate the need to assess higher order thinking skills. In 1989, for example, South Carolina legislators installed a legislative requirement so that both their state-developed tests and nationally normed tests must include assessment of higher order thinking skills. Assessment officials in a good many states are currently in the process of revising their earlier minimal competency programs so that those assessments will deal with more demanding sorts of student attainments.

ER: Is your test-development company completely revising its approaches to these new higher order thinking skills tests, or are these just a souped-up version of what you were doing during the minimum competency testing era?

Popham: That's a really interesting question. When a state adopted a criterion-referenced test in the early days of competency testing, one of the distinguishing features of that test was that it clearly defined the nature of the skill being assessed. The strength of such a test was that it provided teachers with a clear depiction of what it was that they should be pursuing instructionally in their classes. But, as in most aspects of life, one's strength is almost always one's weakness. What happened over the years was that the very clarity that abetted instructional-design decisions also led to a kind of fragmented skills-focused approach that, in the end, may have been harmful to a number of students. Because the early competency tests promoted a clear understanding of what was to be taught, many teachers became preoccupied with a "skill and drill" approach to teaching.

Now the pendulum seems to be swinging decisively away from specificity. We appear to be moving toward the assessment of more generalizable kinds of concepts and higher order thinking skills. There's less of a quest for clarity these days in criterion-referenced test specifications. As a consequence, there's an emphasis on measuring more holistic kinds of outcomes. The problem, however, is that this shift toward more generalizable assessment targets does not yield the clarity of targets for classroom instruction that we previously had. In education assessment, as in most aspects of life, we must constantly make trade offs.

ER: So there are strengths and weaknesses to the two different kinds of approaches rather than just a constant progress towards the higher level attainment.

Popham: Unfortunately, there's no way to carry out this sort of high-stakes educational assessment so that one retains one's cake while simultaneously consuming it. You asked whether our organization was busy developing the same kinds of tests that we had in the early 1980s or whether we were creating something dramatically different. Although we still develop criterion-referenced tests, in some ways these newer tests look very different from their predecessors. For example, the kinds of test-item specifications that we are preparing today are much less explicit and deal with much more global content than was the case 10 years ago. Frankly, 10 years ago, had we produced a set of test-item specifications that we currently create, I would have castigated the developers because the specifications would simply not have been sufficiently precise.

Now, however, state officials are moving in the direction of more comprehensive, holistic assessment targets. As a consequence, rather than completely explicating one particular type of test item, we find that state-level policymakers want to measure a particular competency with various kinds of test items. One creates, therefore, a criterion-referenced assessment device that focuses on multiple assessment tactics rather than only one. Thus, the student will be more apt to possess the competency in a manner than can be generalized to various sorts of tasks. I think that this shift is sensible.

ER: What states would you identify as moving in this new direction?

Popham: I think that South Carolina has been at the vanguard of a movement toward more "instructionally defensible" state-level assessment. South Carolina is in the process of revising its decade-old student program by moving toward a more challenging assessment program that is in tune with current curriculum knowledge.

It's fascinating to see what's occurring, in the advisory committees of South Carolina educators that have been established to help revise the testing program. In all basic-skills fields—that is, reading, writing, and mathematics—the advisory committees are moving away from the advocacy of highly skill-focused assessment. Instead they're moving toward more comprehensive assessment targets. They're also advocating the inclusion of affective assessment instruments to find out what youngsters' attitudes are regarding a subject. Finally, South Carolina educators are attempting to measure students' *progress* with respect to the assessment targets, not merely students' end-of-year status via an end-of-year test. South Carolina officials are planning to accomplish this by means of a series of informal state-provided assessment instruments that are administered periodically to students at the teacher's discretion. So we do see very significant shifts in states that are trying to improve their student assessment programs. In my view, these shifts are very exciting.

ER: What are the problems with comparing results over time when states like South Carolina make this shift in testing? States are under pressure from legislators and other politicians to show that there's progress over a five- to six-year period, and if you change your statewide testing concepts in the middle of that period, where does that leave you?

Popham: In the first place, most states don't really change their student assessment programs all that rapidly. The South Carolina assessment alterations, for example, will be made after a full decade. Over the years, what educational policymakers in many states saw was that improved and more targeted instruction led to rising scores on basic skills tests. Although the rise in test scores was very encouraging, in many states there were decisive ceding effects, that is, tests on which too many students were attaining perfect or near-perfect scores. In such settings, state educators apparently did awfully well with respect to the prior assessment targets, but now must adopt more demanding assessment goals. I think that states where this happens will find that their citizens approve the idea of heading towards more challenging assessment targets.

ER: Let's shift subjects to another level. We've been reading in the newspapers about kindergarten readiness tests and first-grade readiness tests. Some states moved into this sort of assessment and are now withdrawing. What is the situation as you see it with respect to kindergarten tests?

Popham: There are legislative accountability pressures at the kindergarten level, just as there are accountability pressures in the later grades. As I mentioned before, legislative assessment mandates usually arise from a disbelief on the part of legislators that educators are doing their job well. That is no less true at the kindergarten level. Some state legislators think that kindergarten involves too much "play-time" and that kindergarten children aren't learning as much as they should. Thus, there are states in which laws have been enacted that require kindergarten youngsters to be tested in order to indicate that they are "ready" for the first grade. Distressingly, some state officials have unthinkingly applied the same kinds of group-administered lock-step tests to those youngsters that were administered at a higher grade level. This

has caused some major difficulties. As a consequence, a number of states have dramatically revised their kindergarten assessment programs or eliminated them altogether.

ER: Did legislators feel that they weren't getting the information they wanted?

Popham: The nature of early childhood education is something that people who have not studied it don't generally understand. I certainly put myself prominently in the nonexpert group, because until the last year or two, I really hadn't kept up with what was happening in early childhood education.

The current thrust in early childhood education is towards what is known as "developmentally appropriate practice." Developmentally appropriate practice focuses on instruction that is not only *age-appropriate* for children but also *individually appropriate*. Thus, you try to provide instruction for a child at that particular child's level of development. This kind of approach to instruction leads to a good deal more individualization. Moreover, developmentally appropriate practice attempts to get children to become positive both about themselves and about learning. The individualized *instructional* approach at the kindergarten level does not lend itself to group-administered testing.

In Georgia, for example, group-administered kindergarten tests were thoroughly repudiated throughout the state. But Georgia officials have now moved towards development of an *individualized* assessment program for kindergarten youngsters in which teachers decide *when* to administer assessment activities to a particular child. This assessment takes place throughout the entire year and is administered in the context of instruction. Thus, most youngsters will not even know they have been assessed. If legislatively established requirements for kindergarten testing do exist, then Georgia's new approach makes the most instructional sense.

ER: How widespread in the nation's schools are entirely new conceptions of testing such as the ideas of Ted Sizer, the use of portfolios, and dispensing with the traditional pencil-and-paper type test?

Popham: I'm not all that optimistic about certain of these innovative approaches to assessment. I believe there is potential virtue in some of them, but a substantial amount of energy is characteristically required to make newer forms of assessment work effectively. For example, in some cases portfolio assessments have recently been employed for high-stakes tests, that is, tests linked to important decisions. One such application of portfolio-based assessment occurred in Tennessee when that state was attempting a few years ago to build a career-ladder assessment system for its educators. Those educators who were being examined demanded that the criteria to be used in judging the portfolios be made public so that examinees could become familiar with the criteria by which they were being judged. It was not an unreasonable request. Immediately thereafter, however, one found portfolio-preoccupied teachers and the creation of portfolio-generation companies. Once the criteria became public, examinees prepared portfolios that assiduously adhered to the criteria. As a consequence, inferences regarding examinees' capabilities based on the portfolios were typically invalid.

It takes a good deal of effort to install some of these newer assessment approaches. In a limited number of settings have seen some successful attempts to create innovative kinds of testing, but there's often more talk than genuinely innovative test development. Innovative assessment programs are far less prevalent than one would think, given the amount of attention such programs receive in education journals.

ER: Let's shift the assessment focus to testing of experienced teachers in states such as Texas and Arkansas. I know you worked in both states. What's the story regarding relicensure testing?

Popham: I think the motive guiding the legislators who installed those kinds of educator relicensure tests was, as noted earlier, doubts regarding whether or not educators were competent. In both Texas and Arkansas there were reported instances of teachers who could not read and/or write at a level sufficient to teach students. Although such teachers were few in number, it was impossible to deny that there were at least some teachers in those states who were, in fact, illiterate.

When we first received the request for proposals to develop the Arkansas relicensure tests, it was clear that a teacher relicensure test was, in fact, going to be administered in Arkansas. If such a test were to be given, we thought we could devise the fairest, most psychometrically defensible test for that purpose. As it turned out, we ended up developing the educator relicensure tests for both Arkansas and Texas.

In Arkansas and Texas, a meaningful number of incumbent teachers did, in fact, display an inability to pass very low-level basic skills tests. Such teach-

ers were unable to read or write at a satisfactory level of proficiency.

I was pleased to be associated with those two test-development activities. Through the use of those two tests, a number of genuinely illiterate teachers were eliminated from the teaching ranks. It was regrettable that in some settings these tests had a disparate impact on minorities. But in Arkansas, as a consequence of the kind of criterion-referenced test that we developed, after several years there was literally no significant difference in the White and Black pass-rates. This result dissuaded the National Education Association and the Arkansas Education Association from taking the test to court because there was literally no disparate racial impact.

ER: Did we essentially get the illiterate teachers out of the system in those states? Is educator relicensure testing still going on?

Popham: No, the shift is toward requiring beginning teachers to demonstrate literacy and mastery of subject matter. I think most states have adopted the position that there is too much difficulty in trying to weed out a relatively small number of incumbent teachers. There is certainly the likelihood of political strife whenever a relicensure tests for teachers is installed. The focus now is on assessment devices for incoming teachers.

ER: So Texas and Arkansas don't test experienced teachers any more. They figured that they got rid of the bad apples, and so they don't need to keep repeating such tests. And other states have not picked this up?

Popham: No, in Georgia there was also a test of incumbent teachers, but I know of no other state in which experienced teachers have been administered relicensure tests.

ER: What have been the changes in the last 5 to 10 years in the types of requests and style of specifications for teacher licensing tests in the states that are asking various test-development agencies like yours to prepare assessment instruments?

Popham: The request for licensure tests is quite substantial. Currently, state officials who wish to verify that their state's teachers know the necessary subject matter and possess basic knowledge about teaching have few choices. First, there's the National Teachers Examination Program administered by the Educational Testing Service. There are also somewhat customized examinations available through test-development firms that have previously created such teacher licensure tests. Then there's the possibility of a state's budding its own tests from scratch, but that's at a very substantial cost because states have to cover so many licensure areas.

There are very few assessment options these days open to state officials who want to be assured that their state's teachers possess mastery of their subject matters, basic skills, or pedagogy. I'm hoping that there will soon be more competition for this assessment market because, quite frankly, what is available at the moment is not all that wonderful. In many cases, the tests were developed for a different purpose than for the initial licensing of teachers. In many instances, the available tests were not subjected to any solid psychometric analyses. Many states are even required to verify locally the psychometric quality of the tests that they select because there has been no national psychometric appraisal of the tests. So, in spite of the fact that over 80% of our states require some kind of teacher licensing tests, the currently available assessment instruments are far from satisfactory.

ER: The expense is quite high, then, of developing such tests on your own. And there aren't that many competitors in the field, So the chances for getting more competition here—do they look good to you?

Popham: We need to find some assessment agencies that are willing to invest the resources necessary to develop first-rate assessment alternatives for prospective teachers. Educational Testing Service (ETS) is currently creating a battery of tests for beginning teachers that they promise will be a substantial improvement over the tests currently available in the NTE program. The new ETS tests are scheduled to be available in a few years.

It is an eminently reasonable expectation to want a history teacher to know history, and a mathematics teacher to know mathematics. We also want our teachers to be fundamentally literate. Finally, if possible, we want beginning teachers to know something about instructional principles. Thus, I think it is highly appropriate to have incoming teachers demonstrate their skills via some kind of testing program. At the moment, however, we don't have an adequate number of high-quality tests from which to choose.

ER: We've covered a fair number of test-related topics today. Given your responses, I suspect you'll agree that the assessment world is not exactly static.

Popham: Years ago, as an undergraduate philosophy major, I learned that it was the view of Heraclitus that everything was always in a state of flux. It's certainly true that the educational assessment world is currently in an almost frenzied state of flux. And flux, as we know, is an F-word with four letters.

Innovation or Enervation?

Performance Assessment in Perspective

GREGORY J. CIZEK

The first recorded performance assessment was literally a bloodbath. The interesting narrative of that event describes a truly "high stakes" examination, in which the Gilead guards "tested" fugitives from the tribe of Ephraim who tried to cross the Jordan River:

> "Are you a member of the tribe of Ephraim?" they asked. If the man replied that he was not, then they demanded, "Say Shibboleth." But if he couldn't pronounce the "H," and said "Sibboleth" instead of "Shibboleth," he was dragged away and killed. So forty-two thousand people of Ephraim died there at that time.[1]

Well, performance assessment is back. It is surely possible to overstate the parallels between the current calls for increased reliance on performance assessments and the Biblical example. Undoubtedly, the stakes involved in existing examination programs are not as momentous as those in the story. But there are similarities, not the least of which is the almost religious zealotry of some proponents of performance assessment.

Before fully embracing the doctrine of performance assessment, however, professional educators would do well to scrutinize the movement's claims, costs, and characteristics. Indeed, such scrutiny is a professional responsibility. Addressing a related testing controversy over a decade ago, Robert Glaser and Lloyd Bond reminded us of that responsibility:

> In the heat of the current controversy, it is especially necessary to be our own sternest critics. It is not possible to attend to every criticism, especially those that are ill-founded and well beyond the state of the knowledge of human behavior. However, it is necessary to examine the point and counterpoint in public and professional debate in order to move forward with research and development in human assessment and with analysis of institutional policy and test use. The examination should be conducted in a way that is open not only to the members of our own discipline but also the larger public that is affected by and must make decisions about tests.[2]

PERFORMANCE ASSESSMENT IN PERSPECTIVE

Performance assessment might be the answer to many social and educational problems, or so say its advocates. The recent report of the National Commission on Testing and Public Policy enthusiastically argues that this new kind of assessment must be pursued in order to halt the undermining of vital social policies and to promote greater development of the talents of all people.[3] Certainly these are wor-

Gregory J. Cizek is a program associate in the Professional Assessment Services Division of American College Testing, Iowa City, Ia.

thy goals. But is performance assessment the answer? The purposes of this article are to define what is currently called *performance assessment*, to examine the goals of the advocates of performance assessment, and to offer practical and technical cautions to the makers and consumers of performance assessments.

WHAT IS PERFORMANCE ASSESSMENT?

Educational tests are, fundamentally, attempts to gauge what students know or can do. An *indirect* measure of, for example, a student's woodworking ability might be obtained through a paper-and-pencil test that asks the student to state the uses of different lathe chisels, to recognize grain patterns of different species of wood, or to identify the proper way to feed stock into a planer. Another way to gauge the student's woodworking ability would be to use a more *direct* measure. Such a test might consist of presenting the student with a block of wood and the appropriate tools and requiring the student to turn a bowl. This more direct way of assessing woodworking ability could be called a performance assessment.

Of course, this kind of direct assessment has been going on for quite some time and is not particularly new. Elementary students still solve problems in math classes, middle-schoolers go to spelling bees, high school students give speeches, education majors do their student teaching, and dentists-in-training are evaluated on their ability to fill cavities. Indeed, Walter Haney and George Madaus of the Center for the Study of Testing, Evaluation, and Educational Policy at Boston College have reminded us that performance assessment per se is not innovative: "A point worth noting about evaluation alternatives that have been suggested over the last 20 years is that many of them are not at all new. Evaluation tools such as live performances, products, teacher judgment, and school grades have a long history in education."[4]

Elsewhere, Haney recounted three trends in educational measurement that were apparent *in the 1930s:*

1. *A growing emphasis upon validity and a consequent decreasing emphasis upon reliability as the criterion for evaluating measuring instruments;*

2. *a decline of the faith in indirect measurement and an increasing emphasis upon direct measurement as a means of attaining satisfactory validity; and*

3. *a growing respect for essay examinations as instruments for measuring certain outcomes of education.*[5]

IF NOT NEW, THEN WHAT?

The three trends identified in the 1930s must certainly sound familiar to policy makers in the 1990s. They bear a remarkable resemblance to what the proponents of performance assessment are currently urging. But if the idea itself is not new, then what is original about the movement? Unfortunately, perhaps all we have up to this point is a new *name* for these activities—performance assessments. And there may not even be consensus on the name, with such aliases as genuine assessment, authentic evaluation, and practical testing—to list just a few enjoying wide circulation. But performance assessment by any other name is the same, and its advocates have yet to spell out how the current version is substantially different from its relatives.

Whatever the name, one thing is certain: performance assessment is chic. Many educational leaders, directors of state-level assessment projects, and administrators of large-scale testing programs are seriously contemplating increased reliance on performance assessment. But the push for this type of assessment should be judged on more than its current popularity. In a courageous article on educational faddism, Robert Slavin states that "education resembles such fields as fashion and design, in which change mirrors shifts in taste and social climate and is not usually thought of as true progress."[6] Slavin's article was intended to document how educational innovations are often funded and implemented before research on their effectiveness has taken place. The same insight should guide us in current policy considerations involving performance assessment. It is my contention that we have not yet been offered a well-conceived rationale for action, when such a rationale should be a sine qua non for widespread change and the investment of resources.[7] By my reckoning, performance assessment is flourishing somewhere between the "gee whiz" and the "hot topic" stages in Slavin's schematization of the 12 characteristic phases of the swinging education pendulum.

WHO ARE THESE PEOPLE AND WHAT DO THEY WANT?

The performance assessment bandwagon is evidently big enough to accommodate quite a crowd. Although proponents of performance assessment may not be totally sure of what they want, they know what they don't want: standardized, multiple-choice tests.

The National Education Association has encouraged the elimination of group standardized intelligence, aptitude, and achievement tests."[8] David Owen, author of a critique of the Scholastic Aptitude Test (SAT), thinks that the answer might be to "abolish the Educational Testing Service."[9] Another article accuses standardized testing of being "harmful to educational health."[10] The final report of the California Education Summit goes even farther, recommending that "all multiple-choice tests should be eliminated."[11] The recent report of the National Commission on Testing and Public Policy is more moderate, suggesting that "testing programs should be redirected from overreliance on multiple-choice tests."[12] Gerald Bracey, the director of research and evaluation for a Colorado school district, waxed philosophical about what needs to be done: "As a sociologist pointed out some years back, to make the world safe for democracy, it is not sufficient to destroy totalitarian regimes. You have to eliminate the *mentality* that produces totalitarianism. It will not be sufficient, similarly, to eliminate tests.[13]

But those touting performance assessment definitely want your money. It is highly surprising that a common complaint of testing prohibitionists is that testing is expensive. Bracey has assailed the SAT as "the $150 million redundancy."[14] The National Commission on Testing and Public Policy lodged a similar complaint, noting that "reported sales [of elementary and secondary tests and testing services] rose to over $100 million by 1986."[15] The proponents of performance assessment typically cite these figures and point out that the money could be better spent on programs for the disadvantaged, Head Start, or teachers' salaries. Certainly, education policy makers should be concerned about how limited resources are allocated. The irony is that, despite their advocates' apparent concern about cost, the vaguely defined alternative assessments will surely be costlier. For example, the National Board for Professional Teaching Standards recently requested proposals for the development of a prototype credentialing program for

"early adolescence/English language arts teachers" involving performance assessment. The estimated amount of the award for this *one* specialized program exceeds $1.4 million.[16] Another $1.4 million is expected to be awarded for the development of an "early adolescence/generalist" assessment.[17] These figures are for development only and *do not* include any printing, administrative, scoring, or reporting costs. If other performance assessments are as expensive—and surely large-scale assessments will be even more costly—the tab will be staggering.

The hidden price of increased reliance on performance assessments may be even more invidious than the actual monetary costs. For example, performance assessment advocate Ruth Mitchell of the Council for Basic Education noted in a recent interview that there is "no reliable way to compare the costs" of traditional tests and the proposed alternatives. Further, Mitchell asserts that "alternative assessment yields dividends for professional development and curriculum development. Such assessment efforts can, therefore, legitimately absorb other parts of a school district's budget."[18]

Whether such "absorption" is truly legitimate is—or should be—debatable. At minimum, Mitchell's observations should serve as a portent of future educational turf warfare if the high cost of the new assessments is balanced on the backs of other important budgetary considerations.

And what will be purchased in the rush to invest in this latest innovation? Proponents of performance assessments have offered only vague descriptions of what the new instruments will look like. For example, Mitchell has proffered that alternative assessments "can take as many forms as the imagination will allow."[19] In essence, educators are being asked to purchase this amorphous product sight unseen.

Neither is it clear that the new instruments will actually measure something different from more traditional forms of testing. Bracey, a proponent of performance assessment, contends that the new assessments will measure abilities that "are hard, if not impossible, to measure with standardized, multiple-choice tests." He goes on to say that what *should* be measured is "higher-order thinking," which is "nonalgorithmic" and "complex," "yields multiple solutions," and involves "nuanced judgment," "uncertainty," and "imposing meaning."[20] Zowie! Such fantastic claims have led education policy analyst Chester Finn to note that performance assessment is "like 'Star Wars': the idea remains to be demonstrated as feasible."[21] Certainly,

Bracey's descriptors *sound* good, but essential questions about what is actually to be measured and how these goals will be accomplished remain unanswered.

WILL PERFORMANCE ASSESSMENTS BE ANY GOOD?

I really don't mean to be a naysayer about innovation, but I do think that serious discussion about improving evaluation should not be muddied by the current euphoria surrounding performance assessment. Performance assessment advocates have built a straw person to knock down in the form of standardized, multiple-choice tests. This expenditure of energy could have been better invested elsewhere.

For example, no one claims that multiple-choice tests can solve all educational problems or that different types of measures shouldn't be matched with particular purposes. Even performance assessment zealots want whatever new measures are developed to be standardized in terms of administration and scoring. To fuss and fixate on format is to miss the point. Similarly, to intimate, as some proponents of performance assessment do, that testing may be the cause of "a palpable decrease in the quality of education" is to further obscure a troubling and enduring issue.[22]

Advocates of the new kinds of tests also frequently criticize current tests in general for being culturally biased or unfair. In bygone days it was newsworthy to discover a vocabulary test with the word *polo* or a reading selection using the word *quiche*. But real test-makers don't use *quiche*—anymore. Certainly, performance assessment enthusiasts would admit that impressive progress has been made toward the elimination of ethnic, gender, and socioeconomic bias. So it's difficult to comprehend why the proponents of performance assessment would now call for—I'm not kidding—more culturally biased tests. As one example, the National Commission on Testing and Public Policy reports favorably on efforts to "establish and maintain a program of research and development to provide accurate and *culturally specific* instruments" (emphasis added).[23] Educators would do well to consider seriously whether these culturally specific assessments represent a welcome advance or a misguided regression in fair testing policy.

WHAT MATTERS?

What really matters—ignoring cost for the time being—is whether performance assessment will actually be "fairer" or "better" by any reasonably rigorous and widely accepted standards. The early polls are in on this question, and the results are discouraging. It is my opinion that test-makers can develop performance assessments that rival multiple-choice tests in terms of reliability; many quite reliable performance assessments exist now. It is disconcerting, however, that standards for the new instruments are rarely discussed. One person who is concerned about the issue is Edward Haertel, who has recognized the obstacles to reliable, judgment-based measurement and who has suggested several factors to consider.[24] But such caution is not the rule. References to benchmarks such as the *Standards for Educational and Psychological Testing* or the *Code of Fair Testing Practices in Education*[25] are conspicuously absent from the discussion. What should especially trouble policy makers, educators, and testing professionals is that disciples of the performance assessment movement generally tend to ignore the question of validity.

In the first course I took on educational measurement, I recall discussing what was called "face validity." Anne Anastasi commented on the concept of face validity some time ago:

> *Face validity . . . is not validity in the technical sense; it refers, not to what the test actually measures, but to what it appears superficially to measure. Face validity pertains to whether the test "looks valid" to the subjects who take it, the administrative personnel who decide upon its use, and other technically untrained observers. Fundamentally, the question of face validity concerns rapport and public relations.*[26]

By the time I was in Robert Ebel's measurement class at Michigan State University, the professor had already penned his frequently cited sentences on validity: "Validity has long been one of the major deities in the pantheon of the psychometrician. It is universally praised, but the good works done in its name are remarkably few." Indeed, Ebel was seriously concerned about test validity, reminding test-makers that it is "the quality we have said is more important than any other."[27]

So, whither validity? In the current press for more genuine assessment, the only talk about validity that one hears—if one even hears such talk—is about face validity. My fear is that we have begun a search for genuine-*looking,* authentic-*looking,* real-*looking* assessments and have eschewed more rigorous standards of validity. It would certainly be tragic if face validity were to become the reigning deity in the psychometrician's pantheon. Bracey has gone so far as to say, "Validity, to me, is a nonissue. . . . For the new assessments, if we agree that this is what children should know or be good at, *and* we agree that the assessment strategy used represents this well, then Q.E.D., the test is valid."[28] Similarly, Dale Carlson, director of the California Assessment Program, has labeled concerns about validity "a red herring."[29] One hopes that this kind of enthusiasm represents the far point of the pendulum's arc.

CONCLUSION

By the time the pendulum completes its downswing, the current calls for more performance assessment will surely have yielded benefits. A heightened awareness of the importance of examining the match between assessment and instruction has already developed. We are—however grudgingly—acknowledging the role that social policy and ideology play in putatively objective assessment practice. When appropriate, direct assessment of certain skills and abilities will receive renewed support and resources.

But the future of performance assessment is uncertain. As sure as testing generally is not the answer to the multifaceted and complex problems facing contemporary American education, performance assessment is not the panacea either. The euphoria of its proponents should give us pause. The lowered psychometric standards to which it is currently held should cause alarm. Its cost should cause us to hide the silver under the mattress.

Slavin comments that, "as each innovation swings up and down through the arc of the pendulum, we do learn something that may be of use now or in the future."[30] While we should possibly hesitate to put all our hopes in the promise of performance assessment, it would be useful now to embark on a careful analysis of its potential, so that this innovation does not fall by the educational wayside, another cast-off quick fix in the larger school reform effort.

1. Judg. 12:5–6, quoted in William A. Mehrens and Irvin J. Lehmann, *Measurement and Evaluation in Education and Psychology,* 3rd ed. (New York: Holt, Rinehart and Winston, 1984), p. 575.

2. Robert Glaser and Lloyd Bond, "Testing: Concepts, Policy, Practice, and Research," *American Psychologist,* October 1981, p. 997.

3. *From Gatekeeper to Gateway: Transforming Testing in America* (Chestnut Hill, Mass.: National Commission on Testing and Public Policy, 1990).

4. Walter Haney and George Madaus, "Searching for Alternatives to Standardized Tests: Whys, Whats, and Whithers," *Phi Delta Kappan,* May 1989, p. 685.

5. Walter Haney, "Validity, Vaudeville, and Values," *American Psychologist,* October 1981, p. 1023.

6. Robert E. Slavin, "PET and the Pendulum: Faddism in Education and How to Stop It," *Phi Delta Kappan,* June 1989, p. 752.

7. Gregory J. Cizek, "The 'Sloppy' Logic of Test Abolitionists," *Education Week,* 4 April 1990, p. 64.

8. Frances Quinta and Bernard McKenna, *Alternatives to Standardized Testing* (Washington, D.C.: National Education Association, 1977), p. 7.

9. David Owen, *None of the Above: Behind the Myth of Scholastic Aptitude* (Boston: Houghton Mifflin, 1985), p. 285.

10. D. Monty Neill and Noe J. Medina, "Standardized Testing: Harmful to Educational Health," *Phi Delta Kappan,* May 1989, pp. 688–97.

11. *California Education Summit Report: Meeting the Challenge* (Sacramento: California State Department of Education, 1989).

12. *From Gatekeeper to Gateway . . . ,* p. 26.

13. Gerald W. Bracey, "Measurement-Integrated Instruction and Instruction-Integrated Measurement: Two of a Kind," paper presented at the Academy for the Colorado Association of School Executives, Denver, April 1990.

14. Gerald W. Bracey, "The $150 Million Redundancy," *Phi Delta Kappan,* May 1989, pp. 698–702.

15. *From Gatekeeper to Gateway . . . ,* p. 16.

16. *Request for Proposals: Early Adolescence/English Language Arts* (Washington, D.C.: National Board for Professional Teaching Standards, 1990).

17. *Request for Proposals: Early Adolescence/Generalist* (Washington, D.C.: National Board for Professional Teaching Standards, 1990).

18. Scott Willis, "Transforming the Test: Experts Press for New Focus on Student Assessment," *ASCD Update,* September 1990, p. 5.

19. Ibid., p. 4.

20. Gerald W. Bracey, "Advocates of Basic Skills 'Know What Ain't So,'" *Education Week,* 5 April 1989, p. 36.

21. Chester E. Finn, Jr., quoted in Robert Rothman, "New Tests Based on Performances Raise Questions," *Education Week,* 12 September 1990, p. 1.

22. Grant Wiggins, "Reconsidering Standards and Assessment," *Education Week,* 24 January 1990, p. 36.

23. *From Gatekeeper to Gateway . . . ,* p. 33.

24. Edward H. Haertel, "From Expert Opinions to Reliable Scores: Psychometrics for Judgment Based Teacher Assessment," paper presented at the annual meeting of the American Educational Research Association, Boston, April 1990.

25. American Educational Research Association, American Psychological Association, and the National Council on Measurement in Education, *Standards for Educational and Psychological Testing* (Washington, D.C.: American Psychological Association, 1985); and *Code of Fair Testing Practices in Education* (Washington, D.C.: Joint Committee on Testing Practices, 1988).

26. Anne Anastasi, *Psychological Testing*, 2nd ed. (New York: Macmillan, 1961), p. 138.

27. Robert L. Ebel. "Must All Tests Be Valid?," *American Psychologist*, May 1961, pp. 640, 646.

28. Bracey, "Measurement-Integrated Instruction . . . ," p. 21.

29. Dale Carlson, quoted in Rothman, p. 12.

30. Slavin, p. 757.

A Response to Cizek

GRANT WIGGINS

Methinks that Gregory Cizek doth protest disingenuously. How else can we explain his view that performance assessment is nothing more than a voguish fad—"chic"—situated somewhere near the margin of sound assessment principles and practice? Why does he not cite the many performance assessments long in place in this country or the extensive and long-established body of writing calling for the need to get beyond proxy tests?

Let us note, for example, a test publisher's introductory comments to a proposed performance assessment:

> The acquisition of specific facts and concepts is important, but not the only important outcome. . . . At least equally important is the acquisition of the ability to apply specific facts and concepts in work, family, and community roles. . . . Since the outcomes described stress the application of knowledge in real life rather than merely recalling it or engaging in mental exercises, [our test] emphasizes a variety of measurement techniques and procedures other than the usual multiple-choice tests.
>
> [The test] is a series of fifteen simulation activities based on realistic materials drawn from the adult public domain, in six outcome areas: Communicating, Solving Problems, Clarifying Values, Functioning Within Social Institutions, Using Science and Technology, and Using the Arts. . . . Student responses are judged by faculty raters using standardized rating scales.

Is this a description of a naive, unvalidated assessment from an unknown vendor trying to cash in on the latest trend? No. I am quoting from a technical report produced a decade ago *by Cizek's own employer, American College Testing.* The excerpt summarizes the rationale behind the development of COMP, the College Outcome Measures Project, a battery of assessments that have been used for 10 years to evaluate the results of a liberal arts education. The tasks it requires range from preparing a report on the appropriateness of a piece of artwork for a public space to giving an oral presentation that will demonstrate speaking effectiveness.

Technical soundness? Contained in the COMP report are summaries of technical studies that conclude that the performance tests are both valid and reliable and that the objective "proxies"—their word—are not adequate replacements since the "performance tests measure certain abilities not tested by the multiple-choice format."[1]

Surely something more than trendiness is at work in the current push for assessment reform. Has Cizek failed to note the soul-searching that has gone on for years throughout the measurement community—as evidenced by the insightful criticism of conventional testing provided years ago by Norm Frederiksen of the Educational Testing Ser-

---

Grant Wiggins is director of research and development for Consultants on Learning, Assessment, and School Structure (CLASS), Rochester, N.Y.

[1] Aubrey Forrest and Joe Steele, *Defining and Measuring General Education Knowledge and Skills* (Iowa City, Ia.: American College Testing, College Outcome Measures Project, Technical Report No. 1976–81, 1982).

vice (ETS) and David McClelland of Harvard?[2] Why would test companies be willing to develop performance measures, at the seeming expense of their other products, if there were not a need? For example, ETS, in its publication highlighting the results of the hands-on science test it developed and implemented for the National Assessment of Educational Progress (NAEP), states:

> *We should recognize that schools teach what is tested. In conjunction with improving science and mathematics curricula, we must provide for both instruction [in] and assessment of higher-order thinking skills. The use of hands-on assessment techniques will guide instruction in more beneficial directions as well as provide better information about students' understandings of the concepts underlying science and mathematics.*[3]

Note the subtle criticism here of multiple-choice measures, including, presumably, those produced by ETS: higher-order understandings are implicitly not well-assessed by conventional tests.

Chic? The simple fact is that state departments of education, test companies, and ministries of education in other countries have been using direct, nonproxy measures of academic performance for years, even decades. The following list represents just a sample of state and national activity:

- Advanced Placement exams, including not only essays in most subjects but 15 years of experience with the Art Portfolio;
- ACTFL (American Council on the Teaching of Foreign Languages) foreign language proficiency exams;
- statewide writing assessments in over two dozen states;
- hands-on assessment in vocational programs in most states;
- NAEP performance assessments in science, writing, history, and reading;
- New York Regents Examinations;

- High School International Baccalaureate;
- Assessment of Performance Unit (APU) national studies in Great Britain (performance assessments in science, mathematics, reading, speaking, listening, and writing); and
- GCSE (General Certificate for Secondary Education) exams in Great Britain (and their equivalents in Australia and New Zealand).

Of course, most of the world has long been assessing student performance directly—even in high-stakes settings. Alas, as Daniel Resnick and Lauren Resnick put it years ago, American students remain the most tested but least examined in the world.[4] The Canadians, British, Australians, French, Italians, Germans, Russians, and Dutch (to name a few) all routinely demand of their students the production of high-quality documents and oral performances—even in mathematics, as Tom Romberg and Lynn Steen have recently pointed out.[5]

Cizek conveniently ignores a vast literature on direct assessment. Where is mention of the work of Ronald Berk, George Madaus, Richard Shavelson, Howard Gardner, and Edward Chittenden? What about the 10 years that went into researching and implementing the British APU? What about the ETS work in portfolios and performance assessment, the competency-based work at the college level, and the judgment-based instruments and studies available in professional fields such as medicine and music? When citing me, Cizek chose to ignore half a dozen published articles, focusing instead on one sentence taken out of context from an *Education Week* "Commentary." (It was hardly my aim to "further obscure" the issue of the relation between education and testing. I began a discussion of local quality control by posing a few rhetorical questions, one of which asked, "Is it too cranky to suggest that the decline of educational performance coincides with a massive increase in testing?" This hardly obscures the issue, since there is such a correlation, and the implication is plausible.)

Ah, but then we are taken to task for reinventing the testing wheel. Cizek cannot have it both ways, at one moment decrying the trendiness of

[2]Norm Frederiksen, "The Real Test Bias: Influences of Testing on Teaching and Learning," *American Psychologist*, March 1984, pp. 193–202; and David McClelland, "Testing for Competence Rather Than for 'Intelligence,'" *American Psychologist*, January 1973, pp. 1–14.

[3]*Learning by Doing: A Manual for Teaching and Assessing Higher-Order Thinking in Science and Mathematics* (Princeton, N.J.: Educational Testing Service, 1987), p. 31.

[4]Daniel P. Resnick and Lauren B. Resnick, "Standards, Curriculum, and Performance: A Historical and Comparative Perspective," *Educational Researcher*, April 1985, pp. 5–21.

[5]Tom Romberg, "Problematic Features of the School Mathematics Curriculum," in Philip Jackson, ed., *Handbook of Research on Curriculum* (New York: Macmillan, forthcoming); and Lynn Arthur Steen, "Mathematics in the Soviet Union," *Educational Leadership*, February 1991, pp. 26–27.

this idea and at another reminding us that the idea has a lineage that runs back at least through the Thirties.[6] Whoever claimed that this idea was new? Certainly not any of us who have written on the subject. Our point is the opposite: we bemoan the repeated rejection of *established* common sense when fundamental pedagogical and policy decisions are based on superficial, proxy, norm-referenced data.

The essential question, then, is not, "But if the idea is not new, then what is original about the movement?"—a question Cizek begs, by the way—but rather, "Why has education been driven by indirect measures that cannot provide, in principle, direct feedback for improving local schools?" Why have local and state policy makers consistently resisted using direct instead of proxy measures? Is it cost? A mistrust of teachers? An "audience" for such data that consists of boards and legislators—not practitioners with different needs but no clout? (Is Cizek really unconcerned about the dangers to quality and integrity implied by the Lake Wobegon effect of recent years?)

Instead of trying to explore *why* at this time in our history a clearly commonsensical old idea has resurfaced, we are given a glib, somewhat slyly ad hominem proposition: "By my reckoning, performance assessment is flourishing somewhere between the "gee whiz" and "hot topic" stages. . . . Although proponents of performance assessment may not be totally sure of what they want, they know what they don't want: standardized, multiple-choice tests."

Enough obstructionism. Let's quickly remind ourselves why assessment reform is essential, why spending less than a penny per student on the "objective" scoring of student work via Scantrons is a profound mistake—if our aim is to exemplify, measure, *and* evoke high-quality performance. Conventional forms of standardized testing, in Cizek's own words, offer only "indirect" ways of measuring performance. Instead of setting standards for quality performance, they merely audit those abilities in an indirect, superficial way.

As Cizek notes, direct assessment is typically found in use at the classroom level. What he conveniently fails to mention, however, is that, until recently, direct forms of assessment have rarely been used on a large scale at either the school, the district, or the state level. We have had a long and unfortunate tradition in public schooling in America of testing cheaply what can easily be scored "objectively" and quickly, not of testing rigorously what we value as intellectual accomplishment—a very different approach from that used by other countries at the K–12 level and by all our colleges and professions.

Are typical tests being criticized as "invalid"? Not in any technical sense. But predictive or correlative validity for large samples-of students should never be the *essential* aim of any testing program. At stake is feedback to local educators and students—genuinely insightful, useful information. Cizek apparently feels little responsibility for the impact of traditional forms of testing on teaching, learning, policy making, and expenditures what has recently been called "systemic validity."[7] Why should we not finally begin to assess the assessments in terms of their benefit to schooling? Consider the obvious drawbacks of steady doses of multiple-choice tests, apparent to anyone who spends time in schools:

- The generic nature of the test cannot possibly align with all the instructional aims of a given school or district.
- The simplistic and "closed" nature of the questions ensures that students never have adequate access to more realistic, ill-structured tasks and questions.
- Students receive the anti-intellectual message that a "test" involves choosing the sanctioned, orthodox answer instead of being challenged and allowed to justify one's answers.
- One-shot, end-of-year testing that yields only norm-referenced data can have no direct impact on teaching and learning; the feedback is not useful.
- Tests that require students merely to point to answers can never tell us whether students are capable of using knowledge to fashion high-quality products or performances.

---

[6]Cizek's view of history seems limited: the reform urge in the Thirties was spearheaded by the Progressives in the Eight-Year Study, with performance measures developed by a young Ralph Tyler and his staff. This was in response to the dreadful excesses of the I.Q., "efficiency scales," and Army standardized testing, which led to a highly reductionist view of teaching, learning, and testing in schools—from which we still suffer.

[7]John Frederiksen and Allan Collins, "A Systems Approach to Educational Testing," *Educational Researcher*, December 1989, pp. 27–32.

- The "security" required for ensuring the validity of such tests disempowers both teachers and students, making it impossible for three essential elements of real-world learning to occur: appropriate rehearsal, intelligent use of available resources, and increased self-assessment.
- The routine reliance on outside assessors ensures that both the quality of and the faith in local assessment will decrease—despite the fact that it is local assessment that will ultimately determine whether students are held to high standards.
- Finally, the tests have a debilitating effect on students who are below the norm and will likely remain so, given the nature of test design and norming processes that deliberately exaggerate differences.

Neither I nor anyone else has proposed that validity and reliability are not central to assessment design and execution. (To intimate that Dale Carlson, the head of California's Assessment Program, does not care about validity is outrageous, given his job and distinguished record in assessment.) What we who have criticized current policy in testing have insistently claimed is that the failure to demand "authenticity" or better "systemic validity" from our large-scale testing has impoverished instruction and lowered local standard-setting. "Teaching to the test" is inevitably impoverishing when the multiple-choice test is, by design, a simplistic proxy.

Nor is reliability in direct assessment the overwhelming problem that critics of performance assessment make it out to be. Yes, we must be vigilant about making sure it does not fall below a *tolerable* minimum. But recent technical reports from the NAEP note that interrater reliability is 90% or better on the scoring of essays now used in various NAEP subject-area tests. Similar data exist for the writing assessments required by some states and for those used in other countries. It is worth noting an irony about reliability, however: such established and well-regarded tests as the New York Regents Examinations admit of far less reliability than test and policy makers claim is required for accountability (since the tests are scored by each classroom teacher, and only small samples are audited by the state). Yet these exams retain their reputation and integrity.

Yes, to ensure fairness, we must have reliability; on that we all agree. The best way to ensure fairness, however, is to demystify testing and to have oversight and audit practices—"sunshine" laws. The current proprietary and validity-required secrecy of the design and administration of tests makes fairness far less likely; local students and teachers are routinely prevented from fully grasping their de facto obligations (or challenging the test design or answer key).

Cizek thus misses the point about the need for greater face validity. Does he seriously believe that the form of the assessment (think of the simplistic tasks students repeatedly encounter) has no impact on local instruction and assessment—on our view as to what intellectual challenges are about? Can he be serious in suggesting that face validity is of little importance to students and teachers? Does he seriously believe that a third grade reading test that bores the student and angers the teacher by its dopey questions is in any vital sense of the term "valid"?

The aim is not the *semblance* of realism but the educative and motivational power that comes from tests built out of exemplary and vital challenges and from the model performances from which we learn and are inspired.

The word *performance* in performance assessment is thus not idly used. How would pilots, musicians, engineers, or athletes learn to perform adequately if they were tested only through multiple-choice tests? Are we to believe that the constant essay, oral, and hands-on tests I have seen regularly used in other countries are not likely to lead to better local learning, instruction, and assessment? If Cizek demands an "original" perspective on direct assessment, let it be this one: it is time that test designers gave up the medieval view implied in their work and realized that "knowledge that" something is the case is *not* a prerequisite for or indicator of masterly "knowhow." While not very original for anyone with a knowledge of learning theory or of the history of ideas, this notion appears truly novel when one does an item analysis of conventional tests that purport to meet acceptable standards of construct and content validity.

The result of the ubiquity of multiple-choice tests is, sadly, writ large all over America's classrooms: a school "test" in this country is, de facto, a secret, simplistic instrument for "objectively" scoring student answers on a curve. No matter that a curve is indefensible on such a small scale; no matter that validity is assumed, not proven; no matter that unending secrecy and one-shot testing in assessment are counterproductive to mastery even if they work for audit accountability—*our teachers have internalized the form of standardized testing because it is the only, sanctioned kind of assessment mandated in their districts and in the education courses they once took.* Another way to look at the effects of the form of the assessment is to consider the positive trends: California's first-class writing assessment and New York's hands-on science assessment for fourth graders have had just the result we would hope for: an increase in more focused instruction on (and thus performances of) writing and experimenting.

We are in a vicious cycle: the more we have relied on externally designed multiple-choice tests for accountability, the more local assessment practices have deteriorated; the more they deteriorate, the more the public and school officials do not trust teachers to bear the primary burden for assessing students. Yet we know from the experience of other countries that adequate reliability is eminently possible in local assessment when proper procedures are followed for administration and oversight (as in the British moderation process or as in our state-wide writing assessments). More to the point, school reform built on the entrepreneurial efforts of local educators is impossible without reliable, usable data from the measures and standards by which we agree to abide.[8] At issue is not some quaint view of "face validity" but the proper de-

mand for credible, rich, direct measures that admit of no excuses when the results are poor.

For those of us concerned with school improvement, that last point is vital. We will not improve schools until local teachers and administrators have complete faith that the assessment system will adequately represent their students' (and thus, indirectly, their own) achievements. Such a view is not merely commonsensical; it is the only moral position we can take. Does Cizek want his salary tied to a "secure" proxy test imposed on him by his employer—when he has no say in or adequate prior knowledge of that test's content? Are hypocritical policy makers prepared to be held accountable for measures and standards of which they know little or nothing in advance—as they expect teachers to be?

So please, Gregory Cizek, give up the coy and disingenuous rhetoric about the "faddishness" of direct assessment. Yes, we have to be sure that the performances assessed do justice to the whole knowledge domain; yes, we have to ensure a lack of bias, drift, and other sources of error in judgment-based assessing. Let us then have a more constructive debate about the pressing issues of costs versus benefits, about the place of face validity in assessment design, about the differing needs in reporting of assessment data, and about what kinds of assessment and standard setting actually *improve* schools (as opposed to merely auditing, in a simplistic way, their current performance). We must begin at last to assess our assessments from a "performance-based" point of view: to judge them by their measurable *effect* on teaching and learning.

---

[8]Grant Wiggins, "Standards, Not Standardization: Evoking Quality Student Work," *Educational Leadership*, February 1991, pp. 18–25.

► Chapter 15

Synthesis of Research on Reviews and Tests

FRANK N. DEMPSTER

"Practice makes perfect" in itself is hardly a reliable guide to successful learning. Mere repetition over the course of days or even weeks is no guarantee of long-term learning. How many Americans, despite weeks of concentrated practice, can recall more than the opening phrase of the preamble to *The Constitution*, which has just 52 words? Yet most of us can still remember the "Pledge of Allegiance" or an evening prayer we once recited daily for years.

When, then, is practice most effective? Answers from learning research show that the effectiveness of repetition depends on a number of factors, including the time interval between repetitions, the frequency of repetitions, and even the form of the repetition, that is, whether it is in the form of a review or a test. The effects of these factors are currently being explained in terms of *constructive* processing. My purpose here is to review research and theory relating to effective practice and to suggest implications for classrooms.

RESEARCH ON REVIEWS

Several findings concerning the effects of reviews deserve special attention. First, with total study time constant, two or more opportunities to study the same material are more effective than a single opportunity. or example, in a study conducted early

in the century, Edwards (1917) had one group of elementary school children study a history or arithmetic lesson for six-and-one-half minutes continuously and another group for four minutes on one occasion and for two-and-one-half minutes several days later. Overall, the group given the opportunity to study the material twice performed about 30 percent better on the achievement measure than the group that did not receive a review.

More recent research has found that an opportunity to review previously presented material may affect not only the quantity of what is learned but also the quality. For example, Mayer (1983) found that repeated presentations of a science passage resulted in a hefty increase in recall of conceptual principles but did little to promote the recall of technical details. Thus, reviews may do more than simply increase the amount learned; they may shift the learner's attention away from the verbatim details of the material being studied to its deeper conceptual structure.

Another important finding about reviews is that the amount of learning following two reviews that occur close together in time (massed) often is only slightly better than that following a single study opportunity. Thus, massed reviews, such as reviews that occur just a few hours apart, may be entirely uneconomical when evaluated in terms of additional learning. Much more effective are reviews that are spread out or distributed over lengthier periods of time. This phenomenon—known as the "spacing effect"—is one of the most robust and dependable phenomena yet

Frank N. Dempster is Professor, University of Nevada, Las Vegas, Department of Educational Psychology, 4505 Maryland Pkwy., Las Vegas, NV 89154–3003.

documented by psychologists (Dempster 1988, Hintzman 1974, Melton 1970). In fact, two spaced presentations are often about twice as effective as two massed presentations, and this advantage tends to increase as the frequency of review increases. In a recent study of vocabulary learning, for example, a surprise retention test was administered to 35 adults who had studied Spanish vocabulary words at 30-day intervals, 24-hour intervals, or all in one day, in an experiment conducted eight years earlier (Bahrick and Phelps 1987). At the end of the experiment, each of the subjects had achieved a high level of initial learning. On the retention test, however, only the subjects who had received reviews at 30-day intervals remembered a respectable number of definitions. For subjects in the other spacing conditions, even words reviewed seven times or more were almost always forgotten eight years later.

The spacing effect also is remarkable in the scope of its application: with students of all ages and ability levels, in all sorts of situations, and with a wide variety of materials and procedures. Spacing effects have been found in a variety of instructional modes, including learning from text (for example, Dempster 1986, English et al. 1934), lecture presentations (Glover and Corkill 1987), and computer-assisted instruction (Gay 1973). Subject matter has included historical facts (Edwards 1917), arithmetical rules (Gay 1973), addition facts (Pyle 1913), science concepts (Reynolds and Glaser 1964), and vocabulary (Bahrick and Phelps 1987, Dempster 1987).

RESEARCH ON TESTS

One of the complexities of research is that the act of measurement often has an effect on what is measured. In physics, for example, procedures designed to pinpoint the location of a single quantum of light may actually alter its behavior. Memory is no exception; it is affected not only by additional study opportunities but also by tests—even though they may be designed simply to assess the individual's state of knowledge about a subject. As Lachman and Laughery (1968) put it, "Test[s] . . . though they be designed to measure changes in the state of the human memory system have profound and perhaps residual effects on the state of that system" (p. 40).

Research on learning—specifically research on the effectiveness of tests—has found consistently that tests do more than simply test; they also promote learning (for example, Jones 1923–24, Nungester and Duchastel 1982, Rea and Modigliani 1985, Slamecka and Katsaiti 1988). In many cases, the effect has been strong. For example, Jones (1923–24) found that the retention test scores of previously tested students were twice that of untested students. In other words, taking a test can confer substantial benefits on the retention of the same material tested at a later date, even when no corrective feedback is provided and when there are no further study opportunities. Moreover, testing may be more productive than an additional review, especially if the student has achieved a high level of initial learning (Nungester and Duchastel 1982).

As with reviews, however, the most effective tests are those that come at spaced intervals, especially if the intervals are of an expanding nature (Landauer and Bjork 1978, Rea and Modigliani 1985). This means that three or more tests covering the same educational objectives are likely to result in more learning if there is a progressive increase in the interval between each of the successive tests (for example, 1 day, 3 days, 6 days), than if the interval between the tests is the same.

Research on testing has revealed a number of other conditions that either lengthen or diminish the effects of tests, whether massed or spaced. First, tests are most effective if the material to be learned is first tested relatively soon after its presentation. The importance of early testing is nicely illustrated in a study by Spitzer (1939), who tested the entire 6th grade population of 91 elementary schools in Iowa. Each child read a highly factual article and was then tested one or more times at various intervals. An especially noteworthy outcome was that students whose initial test occurred either 1 day or 7 days after reading scored 15 to 30 percent higher on a final test two weeks later than did students whose initial test occurred either 14 or 21 days following reading.

Second, information tested but not remembered at the first opportunity is not as likely to be remembered later as is information that was successfully negotiated on the first test (for example, Jones 1923–24, Modigliani 1976, Runquist 1986). Thus, the facilitating effect of tests applies mainly to questions with successful outcomes. Third, the effects of testing are greater for repeated questions than for new items (Anderson and Biddle 1975, Nungester and Duchastel 1982, Runquist 1986, Sones and Stroud 1940). For example, Rothkopf (1966) had students study a lengthy selection from a book on marine biology, followed by a quiz on the passage. On a later test, these students performed substantially better than a control group on repeated items and modestly better on new items (an indirect effect), even though knowing the answer to one question should not have given the answer to another. However, as Anderson and Biddle (1975) noted, the aggregate indirect benefit is likely to be greater than the direct benefit: "Only the points of information about which . . . questions are asked could be directly affected, whereas presumably every point in the text could be indirectly influenced" (p. 92).

Finally, research has demonstrated that frequent cumulative tests result in higher levels of achievement than do infrequent tests or tests related only to content since the last test. For example, Fitch et al. (1951) found that students who received weekly quizzes followed by cumulative monthly quizzes had significantly higher final exam scores than did students who had only the monthly quizzes. Similarly, 5th graders tested daily performed better on cumulative weekly spelling tests than did students who received only the weekly tests (Reith et al. 1974). However, even quizzes that contain just one or two questions covering previously tested material can be helpful, so long as the quizzes are frequent (Burns 1970, MacDonald 1984).

SPACED VS. MASSED REPETITIONS

Psychologists have attempted to understand the relation between practice and learning for nearly a century. Yet for many years, the theoretical picture surrounding spacing effects was confused and uncertain, despite numerous attempts at clarification. Recently, however, the "reconstruction" or "accessibility" hypothesis has emerged as the single most compelling explanation of spacing effects (for example, Dempster 1988, Rea and Modigliani 1987).

The basic idea is that when an individual is confronted with a repetition, he or she makes an attempt to remember, that is, to "retrieve" or "access" the previous experience with the repeated information. If the spacing between occurrences is relatively short, memory of the previous encounter will be more accessible than if the spacing between repetitions is relatively lengthy. Thus, the individual will need to devote more attention or processing effort to spaced repetitions than to massed repetitions. In general terms, the assumption is that

repetitions are effective to the extent that they engender successful retrieval of the results of earlier processing and that the effort involved in a successful retrieval operation, and thus the additional learning, increases with spacing.

One bit of evidence favoring the reconstruction hypothesis is that spaced reviews and tests have been found to be more attention-grabbing than similar massed events (Dempster 1986, Magliero 1983, Zechmeister and Shaughnessy 1980). Massed repetitions, because there is not much time between them, tend to inspire a false sense of knowing or confidence (Zechmeister and Shaughnessy 1980). Thus, they receive relatively little attention ("Since I remember it so well, why pay much more attention to it?"). In short, massed repetitions are likely to encourage superficial rote processing. Spaced repetitions, on the other hand, are likely to encourage exactly the kinds of constructive mental processes, founded on effort and concentration, that teachers hope to foster.

Another finding congruent with the reconstructive hypothesis is that research subjects have consistently reported that spaced repetitions are more interesting and enjoyable than either massed repetitions or single presentations (for example, Burns 1970, Dempster 1986, Elmes et al. 1983). Massed repetitions, in fact, are perceived as "boring" and unnecessarily repetitive (Dempster 1986).

THE USE OF REVIEWS AND TESTS IN CLASSROOMS

Reviews and tests are currently underutilized in terms of their potential for improving classroom learning. First, we'll look at teachers' use of reviews. In a study of the effectiveness of an experimental mathematics teaching program, the teachers summarized the previous day's lessons only about 25 percent of the time, and homework was checked or reviewed only about 50 percent of the time (Good and Grouws 1979). Many topics are presented just once (for example, Armbruster and Anderson 1984). In their synthesis of research on classroom instruction, Rosenshine and Stevens (1986) noted that review is a teaching function that could be done more frequently in most classrooms. Unfortunately, textbooks do not help much. In surveys of mathematics texts, for example, the use of a distributed method of presentation, with frequent use of spaced review, is clearly the exception rather than the rule (Saxon 1982, Stigler et al. 1986).

Clearly, review—and certainly *spaced* review—is not a common practice in the classroom.

As to the use of tests in the classroom, many, if not most, courses of instruction offer far less than optimal testing patterns. For example, tests are rarely as frequent as they could be. They do not appear to be an integral part of teachers' regular instruction at the elementary level, even though a particular subject may be taught three to five times a week. In one survey, 4th and 6th grade mathematics teachers reported having administered an average of about 18 curriculum-embedded tests per year, or approximately one test every two weeks (Burry et al. 1982). Research also suggests that teachers test more frequently in mathematics than in reading and that grade level and amount of testing are inversely related (Yeh 1978).

There appear to be two primary reasons for this state of affairs. First, there is no evidence of any serious effort to disseminate the results of research on reviews and tests to the educational community. In a recent sampling of practitioner-oriented textbooks suitable for use in teacher education programs (for example, Good and Brophy 1986, Kim and Kellough 1987, Maver 1987, Slavin 1988, Woolfolk 1987), I found very little mention of spacing effects and no mention of the relation between testing and learning. Tests are regarded as instruments for making decisions about grading and pacing, not as vehicles for promoting learning (Kuhs et al. 1985).

Second, spacing effects are not intuitively obvious. Students tend to be more confident they will remember material presented under massed conditions than under spaced conditions (Zechmeister and Shaughnessy 1980). Thus, it is not surprising that cramming—"a heavy burst of studying immediately before an exam following a long period of neglect"—is the rule rather than the exception among students (Sommer 1968). Even experienced educators, when judging the instructional effectiveness of text passages, tend to rate prose in which the repetition of information is massed as better than prose in which it is spaced (Rothkopf 1963).

IMPLICATIONS FOR EDUCATORS

With relatively little difficulty, teachers can incorporate spaced reviews and tests into a variety of their existing instructional activities. For example, they can ask questions about concepts and skills taught in previous lessons, assign and check homework, and provide feedback (a form of review) on quizzes covering material from previous lessons. Discussion, too, can be an occasion for spaced review. DiVesta and Smith (1979), for example, showed that spaced discussions of a topic interspersed during a lecture facilitated learning more than did massed discussions.

Teachers can organize lessons by setting aside a brief period of time each day for reviewing the main points of the previous day's lessons. Once or twice a month, they can set aside a longer period of time for a more comprehensive review covering the main points of all previously presented material. To make the most efficient use of these review sessions, teachers can interweave related new material with old material expressed in paraphrased form. To be effective, reviews need not consist of verbatim repetitions of previously presented material (for example, Rothkopf and Coke 1966).

Saxon (1982) demonstrated that textbooks also can be designed to make use of spaced practice. In his algebra text, each lesson contains a set of problems in much the same fashion as most other mathematics texts. However, of the two dozen or so problems contained within each problem set, only a few deal with the most recently-presented topic; the remaining problems are review questions containing elements of all previously presented topics. Notably, this text has fared very well in comparisons with standard algebra texts in terms of achievement gains, at least when the students have been of low and average ability (Johnson and Smith 1987, Klingele and Reed 1984, Saxon 1982).

Ideally, tests should be cumulative and administered according to a pattern of increasing intervals between successive tests. A test administered soon after the material is introduced is likely to have a successful outcome, engender feelings of success and accomplishment, and strengthen the information in memory sufficiently to survive a somewhat longer interval. A recent example of this sort of application has been provided by Siegel and Misselt (1984), who conducted a study in which students were taught foreign language vocabulary using a computer-assisted instruction program. When a student made an error, he or she received corrective feedback, and the missed word was programmed to reappear according to an expanded ratio practice schedule. For example, the first retesting of a missed word might occur after an interval

---

Highlights of Research on Reviews and Tests

- With total study time equated, two or more opportunities to study the same material are much more effective than a single opportunity.
- Achievement following two massed study opportunities often is only slightly higher than that following a single study opportunity.
- Spaced reviews yield significantly better learning than do massed reviews.
- The effectiveness of spaced review, relative to massed review, tends to increase as the frequency of review increases.

- Tests promote learning, especially if the material to be learned is first tested relatively soon after its introduction.
- Spaced tests are more effective than massed tests, especially if the inter-test intervals are of an expanding nature.
- Frequent spaced testing results in higher levels of achievement the relatively infrequent testing.
- The use of cumulative questions on tests is one of the keys to effective learning.

—Frank N. Dempster

---

of three intervening items; if that test had a successful outcome, the third test would occur after an interval of six intervening items, and so forth. Clearly this technique could be expanded to guide instruction in a variety of areas, including spelling, arithmetic, history, English, and science.

In addition, tests, as well as informal recitation questions, should be frequent. Process-outcome research (reviewed in Brophy and Good 1985) indicates a positive relationship between frequency of academic questions addressed to students and size of gain in student achievement. Moreover, the largest gains are seen in classes where most, perhaps 75 percent, of the teachers' questions are answered correctly (Brophy and Evertson 1976), just as the results of research on testing would predict.

THE BENEFITS OF FREQUENT SPACED PRACTICE

To summarize, more frequent use of properly spaced reviews and tests in the classroom can dramatically improve classroom learning and retention. In addition, research suggests that spaced repetitions can foster time-on-task and help students develop and sustain positive attitudes toward school and learning.

Another potential benefit hinges on recent theoretical developments (that is, the reconstruction hypothesis), which suggest that spaced repetitions encourage highly constructive thinking. Exactly how this works is still a mystery, but there is reason to believe that spaced repetitions result in a richer,

more elaborate understanding of the topic (McDaniel and Masson 1985). The point is that spaced repetitions require the student to engage in active, conscious processing, whereas a massed repetition or a single presentation tends to evoke shallow, effortless processing—which, though it involves "no pain," results in little or "no gain."

Obviously, frequent spaced practice requires a precious classroom resource—namely, time, which otherwise could be devoted to the presentation of new material. However, schools are already exposing students to too many topics, a high percentage of which are taught only briefly and thus superficially (see, for example, Armbruster and Anderson 1984, Porter 1989). The alternative is to expose students to relatively few, but important, ideas (Porter 1989) and—with the aid of principles of distributed practice—attempt to teach them thoroughly.

REFERENCES

Anderson, R. C., and W. B. Biddle (1975). "On Asking People Questions about What They Are Reading." In *The Psychology of Learning and Motivation*, Vol. 9, pp. 90–132, edited by G. H. Bower. New York: Academic Press.

Armbruster, B. B., and T. H. Anderson. (1984). "Structures of Explanation in History Textbooks, or So What If Governor Stanford Missed the Spike and Hit the Rail?" *Journal of Curriculum Studies* 16: 181–194.

Bahrick, H. P., and E. Phelps. (1987). "Retention of Spanish Vocabulary over Eight Years." *Journal of Experimental Psychology: Learning, Memory, and Cognition* 13: 344–349.

Brophy, J., and C. Evertson. (1976). *Learning from Teaching: A Developmental Perspective.* Boston: Allyn and Bacon.

Brophy, J., and T. Good (1985). "Teacher Effects." In *Handbook of Research on Teaching*, 3rd ed., p. 372, edited by M. C. Wittrock. New York: Macmillan.

Burns, P. C. (1970). "Intensive Review as a Procedure in Teaching Arithmetic." *Elementary School Journal* 60: 205–211.

Burry, J., J. Catteral, B. Choppin, and D. Dorr-Bremme. (1982). *Testing in the Nation's Schools and Districts. How Much? What Kinds? To What Ends? At What Costs?* (CSE Report No. 194). Los Angeles: Center for the Study of Evaluation, University of California.

Dempster, F. N. (1986). "Spacing Effects in Text Recall: An Extrapolation from the Laboratory to the Classroom." Manuscript submitted for publication.

Dempster, F. N. (1987). "Effects of Variable Encoding and Spaced Presentations on Vocabulary Learning." *Journal of Educational Psychology* 79: 162–170.

Dempster, F. N. (1988). "The Spacing Effect: A Case Study in the Failure to Apply the Results of Psychological Research." *American Psychologist* 43: 627–634.

DiVesta, F. J., and D. A. Smith. (1979). "The Pausing Principle: Increasing the Efficiency of Memory for Ongoing Events." *Contemporary Educational Psychology* 4: 288–296.

Edwards, A. S. (1917). "The Distribution of Time in Learning Small Amounts of Material." In *Studies in Psychology: Titchener Commemorative Volume*, pp. 209–213. Worcester, Mass.: Wilson.

Elmes, D. G., C. J. Dye, and N. J. Herdelin. (1983). "What Is the Role of Affect in the Spacing Effect?" *Memory and Cognition* 11: 144–151.

English, H. B., E. L. Wellborn, and C. D. Killian. (1934). "Studies in Substance Memorization." *Journal of General Psychology* 11: 233–260.

Fitch, M. L., A. J. Drucker, and J. A. Norton, Jr. (1951). "Frequent Testing as a Motivating Factor in Large Lecture Courses," *Journal of Educational Psychology* 42: 1–20.

Gay, L. R. (1973). "Temporal Position of Reviews and Its Effect on the Retention of Mathematical Rules." *Journal of Educational Psychology* 64: 171–182.

Glover, J. A., and A. J. Corkill. (1987). "Influence of Paraphrased Repetitions on the Spacing Effect." *Journal of Educational Psychology* 79: 198–199.

Good, T. L., and J. E. Brophy. (1986). *Educational Psychology*, 3rd ed. New York: Longman.

Good, T. L., and D. A. Grouws. (1979). "The Missouri Mathematics Effectiveness Project: An Experimental Study in Fourth-Grade Classrooms." *Journal of Educational Psychology* 71: 355–362.

Hintzman, D. L. (1974). "Theoretical Implications of the Spacing Effect." In *Theories in Cognitive Psychology: The Loyola Symposium*, pp. 77–99, edited by R. L. Solso. Potomac, Md.: Erlbaum.

Johnson, D. M., and B. Smith (1987). "An Evaluation of Saxon's Algebra Text." *Journal of Educational Research* 81: 97–102.

Jones, H. E. (1923–24). "The Effects of Examination on Permanence of Learning." *Archives of Psychology* 10: 21–70.

Kim, E. C., and R. D. Kellough. (1987). *A Resource Guide for Secondary School Teaching.* 4th ed. New York: Macmillan.

Klingele, W. E., and B. W. Reed. (1984). "An Examination of an Incremental Approach to Mathematics." *Phi Delta Kappan* 65: 712–713.

Kuhs, T., A. Porter, R. Floden, D. Freeman, W. Schmidt, and J. Schwille. (1985). "Differences among Teachers in Their Use of Curriculum-Embedded Tests." *The Elementary School Journal* 86: 141–153.

Lachman, R., and R. R. Laughery. (1968). "Is a Test Trial a Training Trial in Free Recall Learning?" *Journal of Experimental Psychology* 76: 40–50.

Landauer, T., and R. Bjork. (1978). "Optimum Rehearsal Patterns and Name Learning." In *Practical Aspects of Memory*, pp. 625–632, edited by M. M. Gruneberg, P. E. Morris, and R. N. Sykes. New York: Academic Press.

MacDonald, C. J., II. (1984). "A Comparison of Three Methods of Utilizing Homework in a Precalculus College Algebra Course." Doctoral diss., Ohio State University, 1984. *Dissertation Abstracts International* 45: 1674-A.

Magliero, A. (1983). "Pupil Dilations Following Pairs of Identical Words and Related To-Be-Remembered Words." *Memory and Cognition* 11: 609–615.

Mayer, R. E. (1983). "Can You Repeat That? Qualitative Effects of Repetition and Advanced Organizers on Learning from Science Prose." *Journal of Educational Psychology* 75: 40–49.

Mayer, R. E. (1987). *Educational Psychology: A Cognitive Approach.* Boston: Little, Brown.

McDaniel, M. A., and M. E. J. Masson. (1985). "Altering Memory Representations through Retrieval." *Journal of Experimental Psychology: Learning, Memory, and Cognition* 11: 371–385.

Melton, A. W. (1970). "The Situation with Respect to the Spacing of Repetitions and Memory." *Journal of Verbal Learning and Verbal Behavior* 9: 596–606.

Modigliani, V. (1976). "Effects on a Later Recall by Delaying Initial Recall." *Journal of Experimental Psychology: Human Learning and Memory* 2: 609–622.

Nungester, R. J., and P. C. Duchastel. (1982). "Testing Versus Review: Effects on Retention." *Journal of Educational Psychology* 74: 18–22.

Porter, A. (1989). "A Curriculum Out of Balance: The Case of Elementary School Mathematics." *Educational Researcher* 18: 9–15.

Pyle, W. H. (1913). "Economical Learning." *Journal of Educational Psychology* 3: 148–158.

Rea, C. P., and V. Modigliani. (1985). "The Effect of Expanded Versus Massed Practice on the Retention of

Multiplication Facts and Spelling Lists." *Human Learning* 4: 11–18.

Rea, C. P., and V. Modigliani. (1987). "The Spacing Effect in 4- to 9-Year-Old Children." *Memory and Cognition* 15: 436–443.

Reith, H., S. Axelrod, R. Anderson, F. Hathaway, K. Wood, and C. Fitzgerald. (1974). "Influence of Distributed Practice and Daily Testing on Weekly Spelling Tests." *Journal of Educational Research* 68: 73–77.

Reynolds, J. H., and R. Glaser. (1964). "Effects of Repetition and Spaced Review upon Retention of a Complex Learning Task." *Journal of Educational Psychology* 55: 297–308.

Rosenshine, B., and R. Stevens. (1986). "Teaching Functions." In *Handbook of Research on Teaching*, 3rd ed., pp. 376–391, edited by M. C. Wittrock. New York: Macmillan.

Rothkopf, E. Z. (1963). "Some Observations on Predicting Instructional Effectiveness by Simple Inspection." *Journal of Programmed Instruction* 3: 19–20.

Rothkopf, E. Z. (1966). "Learning from Written Instructive Materials: An Exploration of the Control of Inspection Behavior by Test-Like Events." *American Educational Research Journal* 3: 241–249.

Rothkopf, E. Z., and E. V. Coke. (1966). "Variations in Phrasing and Repetition Interval and the Recall of Sentence Materials." *Journal of Verbal Learning and Verbal Behavior* 5: 86–91.

Runquist, W. N. (1986). "The Effect of Testing on the Forgetting of Related and Unrelated Associates." *Canadian Journal of Psychology* 40: 65–76.

Saxon, J. (1982). "Incremental Development: A Breakthrough in Mathematics." *Phi Delta Kappan* 63: 482–484.

Siegel, M. A., and A. L. Misselt. (1984). "Adaptive Feedback and Review Paradigm for Computer-Based Drills." *Journal of Educational Psychology* 76: 310–317.

Slamecka, N. J., and L. T. Katsaiti. (1988). "Normal Forgetting of Verbal Lists as a Function of Prior Testing." *Journal of Experimental Psychology: Learning, Memory, and Cognition* 14: 716–727.

Slavin, R. E. (1988). *Educational Psychology: Theory into Practice*. 2nd ed. Englewood Cliffs, N.J.: Prentice-Hall.

Sommer, R. (1968). "The Social Psychology of Cramming." *Personnel and Guidance Journal* 9: 104–109.

Sones, A. M., and J. B. Stroud. (1940). "Review with Special Reference to Temporal Position." *Journal of Educational Psychology* 31: 665–676.

Spitzer, J. F. (1939). "Studies in Retention." *Journal of Educational Psychology* 30: 641–656.

Stigler, J. W., K. C. Fuson, M. Ham, and M. S. Kim. (1986). "An Analysis of Addition and Subtraction Word Problems in American and Soviet Elementary Mathematics Textbooks." *Cognition and Instruction* 3: 153–171.

Woolfolk, A. E. (1987). *Educational Psychology*. 3rd ed. Englewood Cliffs, N.J.: Prentice-Hall.

Yeh, J. P. (1978). *Test Use in Schools*. Washington, D.C.: National Institute of Education, U.S. Department of Health, Education, and Welfare.

Zachmeister, E. B., and J. J. Schaughnessy. (1980). "When You Know That You Know and When You Think That You Know But You Don't." *Bulletin of the Psychonomic Society* 15: 41–44.

Retention: Can We Stop Failing Kids?

In May, Jimmy still seems surprised by the classroom routines. When other third-graders move smoothly into reading or math groups, Jimmy wanders—apparently confused about where he should be or what to bring with him. When Mrs. Jones calls on him to read, he can make out most words, but he needs help finding the passage and seems to have little sense of the meaning. Even on the playground Jimmy seems less self-sufficient and socially adept than his peers.

As report card time approaches, Mrs. Jones feels very uneasy about sending Jimmy on to the fourth grade, where the academic and social demands will be greater. She shares her concerns with his mother, reminding her that this standardized test scores place him in the bottom quarter of his class. They agree that it would be best for Jimmy to spend another year in third grade.

HELP THAT HURTS

Teachers do not like to hold children back. But many see no pressing reason to reexamine this practice. After all, in their own classrooms, flunking is a relatively rare occurrence. Most children go on to the next grade. Furthermore, teachers do not feel right about promoting a child with very marginal skills. To do so would be counter-intuitive.

In the last two decades, grade retention has become a common "treatment" for low achievers. This practice appears to be as prevalent today as it was at the turn of the century before social promotion became the norm. Lorrie Shepard and Mary Lee Smith, researchers who recently edited a book on retention called *Flunking Grades*, estimate that by ninth grade nearly half of all students in the United States have flunked at least one grade and/or are no longer in school.

The assumption in many schools today is that although repeating a grade may be a bitter pill for kids to swallow, it can help low achievers "catch up" to the expected level of skill mastery and avoid failure later. Yet, despite the good intentions and optimism surrounding grade retention, a large body of research reveals almost no evidence of lasting beneficial effects (see *HEL*, March 1986).

In a recent synthesis of the evidence, C. Thomas Holmes of the University of Georgia reviewed 63 controlled studies in which students who had repeated a grade were compared with equally low-achieving peers who had been promoted. Fifty-four of the studies found retention to be detrimental.

The most negative results emerged in studies comparing retained and promoted children who were the same age but in different grades. Thus, for example, if children were kept back in first grade, these studies compared their test scores at the end of their repeated first-grade year with the performance of a matched group of promoted peers who were completing second grade.

In this type of comparison, children at the end of their repeated year performed significantly worse than the promoted control group. This difference increased with each subsequent year.

In other studies, researchers waited a year, until the repeating children had finished second grade. They then compared their scores to those attained by the promoted group the year before, when *they* had completed second grade. The two groups were thus compared in the same grade but at different ages.

At first glance, this group of studies appeared to suggest positive effects of retention. For example, at the end of second grade, children who had repeated first grade did somewhat better on achievement tests than their promoted peers had done the year before. But, when he examined the achievement data for succeeding years, Holmes found that this positive effect did not last. By the fourth grade, repeaters were not scoring better, despite having spent an extra year in school.

In another analysis of the data, Holmes looked at the effects of retention by grade level. Being held back in the upper elementary grades had a more negative effect on achievement than did retention in earlier grades. But even in the primary grades his analysis revealed "harm rather than benefit" from retention.

Holmes turned up nine studies that showed positive effects on achievement. All these studies focused on suburban schools, where retained students received extra help through individualized approaches and smaller classes. Furthermore, most of these students, even before they were kept back, did not have severe academic deficiencies. Although they did not perform well enough to make the grade in their own schools, their test scores showed them to be of average I.Q. and already performing near the national norm for their grade level.

A FATE WORSE THAN . . .

Critics of retention often quote Kaoru Yamamoto's 1980 study of stress in childhood, in which children listed only two life events as more stressful than being retained: going blind and losing a parent.

More recently, Deborah Byrnes interviewed 71 retained children and found similar feelings about flunking. The vast majority used words like "sad," "bad," "upset," or "embarrassed" to describe how being retained made (or "would make") them feel. Even though all of these children had repeated a grade, a surprising number—especially of the girls—did not name themselves when answering whether they or any of their classmates had ever been asked to spend another year in the same grade.

Nearly 50 of the studies Holmes reviewed included social or emotional outcomes as well as achievement. These studies confirm what Yamamoto and Byrnes found. On average, retained students do less well than their matched peers on a variety of followup measures, including social adjustment and attitude toward school.

PAY NOW, PAY LATER

Not surprisingly, many students who flunk a grade in elementary school experience continuing problems in school. According to a recent Boston City Hospital study, students who become truant in middle school are very likely to have repeated a grade earlier in their schooling. In the group studied, nearly 80 percent of the student with serious attendance problems were at least one year behind their age-appropriate grade level.

Numerous studies have identified a similar relationship between flunking and dropping out of school. Dropouts are five times more likely to have repeated a grade than are high school graduates. Students who repeat two grades have a probability of dropping out of nearly 100 percent.

Of course, such statistics do not tell us how much retention affects a student's decision to become truant or to drop out. It is certainly possible that the academic deficiencies that keep a student from being promoted also explain why the student starts skipping school and later drops out.

But recent studies suggest that repeating a grade has its own negative effect on a student's academic career. James Grissom and Lorrie Shepard looked at the school records of thousands of African-American males in Austin, Texas. They found that those with below-average achievement have a 45 percent chance of dropping out of school, while those with identical achievement scores who have repeated a year have a 75 percent chance.

Grissom and Shepard conducted two other large-scale studies, one of which focused on a large affluent suburban school district with a low overall dropout rate. The same pattern held. They conclude that students who repeat a grade are 20 to 30 percent more likely to drop out of school than their peers with equally poor achievement who are not retained.

COMPARED TO WHAT?

Giving out a review of such research to all the members of a faculty might raise some eyebrows and spark some discussions, but it would not be likely to change what teachers do. Experienced teachers tend to rely on their own source of evidence—what they see year after year in their classrooms—and this tells them a different story.

After all, most children who are retained do perform better their second time through the curriculum. By the end of the repeated year, they probably no longer stand out as particularly lost or behind. Their teachers feel okay about passing them along to the next grade, and justified in having asked them to spend an extra year.

Unfortunately, teachers have no way of knowing how well retained students would have performed if they had been promoted: whether, for example, their achievement scores at the end of fourth grade would have been as high or higher than their scores at the end of a second year in third grade.

Furthermore, teachers do not usually have the opportunity to follow a retained child's progress over time, or to monitor how the child fares compared to a similar peer who never repeated a grade. And they almost certainly will not know whether the retained student later becomes truant in middle school or drops out of high school.

TEACHER RESEARCH

As long as teachers are isolated from their colleagues at other grade levels, they win see little reason to question school policy regarding grade retention. Teachers need a more complete picture of the prevalence of this practice in the school as a whole and among particular populations of students. They also need a sense of retention's cumulative effects over a student's entire academic career.

One way to develop such a picture would be for groups of teachers across grade levels to conduct their own research, starting with questions like the following: What is the annual retention rate for the school? By the time a cohort of students graduate from the school, what percentage of the entering group has been left behind? How do these rates compare to those of other schools? Does the likelihood of being retained differ by race, ethnicity, or gender?

In many cases, the answers to such questions would surprise teachers and lead them to question other assumptions about the beneficial effects of retention. Eventually their research could extend to a consideration of the longer-term effects of retention on a child's academic progress. How well are retained children performing three or more years after repeating a grade?

Whether or not a school or district supports teachers' engagement in this type of inquiry, the district itself should be held responsible for monitoring the effects of retention. This is a lesson that Ernest House drew from overseeing the evaluation of New York City's Promotional Gates Program. Under this program nearly a quarter of all fourth- and seventh-graders were held back each year after failing to achieve the cut-off score on standardized math and reading tests.

Research revealed that the policy failed to help these students academically. "If districts were required to study and provide special assistance to retained students for a number of years," notes House, "they would be less arbitrary and casual in holding students back and in assuming good effects from doing so."

CREATING ALTERNATIVES

It would, of course, be better for everyone involved if retention could be replaced by better ways to help low-achieving students. Most parents and teachers are all too aware of how empty the promise of remedial services can be. In a time of tight budgets, you simply cannot count on the survival of after-school programs, summer school, special aides, or tutors.

Nevertheless, it is not fair to ask our most vulnerable students to pay the price of retention in lowered self-esteem and extra years in school. Given the overwhelming evidence that retention does not usually work as intended, teachers should be encouraged to promote low-achieving students, working closely with parents and next-grade teachers to see to it that these students' strengths are recognized and their weaknesses addressed.

In the concluding chapter of *Flunking Grades*, Shepard and Smith draw an intriguing analogy. The trend in programs for gifted students, they point out, is to avoid separating children from their social peers. Instead, gifted children are placed in their normal grade with formally agreed upon enrichment activities and educational approaches. Why not give poorly performing students the same consideration given to gifted ones? Instead of retaining students, schools could keep them with their grade, providing them and their teachers with added support and resources.

FOR FURTHER INFORMATION

L. A. Shepard and M. L. Smith. *Flunking Grades: Research and Policies on Retention.* London: Falmer, 1989. See especially chapters by D. Byrnes, J. B. Grissom and L. A. Shepard, C. T. Holmes, and E. House.

Center for Policy Research in Education. Rutgers University. "Repeating Grades in School: Current Practice and Research Evidence." *CPRE Policy Briefs* (January 1990).

Massachusetts Board of Education. *Structuring Schools for Student Success: A Focus on Grade Retention.* Quincy, MA, April 1990.

K. Yamamoto. "Children Under Stress: The Causes and Cures." *Family Week, Ogden Standard Examiner,* 6–8 (September 1980).

What Makes a Portfolio a Portfolio?

F. LEON PAULSON, PEARL R. PAULSON, and CAROL A. MEYER

"I used all my writing skill to make this persuade. Word choice was very important to me." Tony attached these words to a paper in his writing portfolio to explain why the paper was significant to him. His self-reflective statements help illustrate a key value associated with student portfolios and a rationale for using them: portfolios permit instruction and assessment woven together in a way that more traditional approaches do not.

This article explores the question, "What makes a portfolio a portfolio?" Let's begin with a definition that we helped formulate while working with a group of educators from seven states under the auspices of the Northwest Evaluation Association[1]:

A portfolio is a purposeful collection of student work that exhibits the student's efforts, progress, and achievements in one or more areas. The collection must include student participation in selecting contents, the criteria for selection, the criteria for judging merit, and evidence of student self-reflection.

The writing portfolios used in Tony's class are in many ways similar to the portfolios artists assemble in order to gain entrance into an art school or to secure a commission. For example, the Pacific Northwest College of Art[2] gives the following rationale for portfolios:

An application portfolio is a visual representation of who you are as an artist, your history as well as what you are currently doing. . . . It is representing you when you're not present. . . . Part of the evaluation of a portfolio is based on the personal choices [you] make when picking pieces for the portfolio. It tells the school something about [your] current values; that's why you will rarely get a school to be very specific about what they look for in a portfolio. [You] should not be afraid to make choices.

THE PORTFOLIO: A POWERFUL CONCEPT

Portfolios have the potential a lot about their creators. They can become a window into the students' heads, a means for both staff and students to understand the educational process at the level of the individual learner. They can be powerful educational tools for encouraging students to take charge of their own learning.

[1]This working definition grew out of discussions at a conference on "Aggregating Portfolio Data" held at Union, Washington, in August 1990. For more information, see: *White Paper on Aggregating Portfolio Data*, rev. ed., (1990), by C. Meyer and S. Schuman, which is available from the Northwest Evaluation Association, 5 Centerpointe Dr., Lake Oswego, OR 97035.

F. Leon Paulson is Program Assessment Specialist at Multnomah Education Service District in Portland, Oregon. He may be contacted at 6800 S.W. Gable Pkwy., Portland, OR 97225. Pearl R. Paulson is Student Services Coordinator and Carol A. Meyer is Evaluation Specialist, both with Beaverton School District, P.O. Box 200, Beaverton, OR 97075.

[2]Pacific Northwest College of Art, (1985), *Preparing your Application Portfolio*, (pamphlet); available from the college at 1219 S.W. Park, Portland OR 97205.

> *Please read this. It is persuasive. I used all my writing skills to make this paper persuade. Word choice was very important to me.*

Portfolios allow students to assume ownership in ways that few other instructional approaches allow. Portfolio assessment requires students to collect and reflect on examples of their work, providing both an instructional component to the curriculum and offering the opportunity for authentic assessments. If carefully assembled, portfolios become an intersection of instruction and assessment: they are not just instruction or just assessment but, rather, both. Together, instruction and assessment give more than either gives separately.

GUIDELINES FOR REALIZING THAT POWER

Fulfilling the potential of portfolios as an intersection of instruction and assessment is neither simple nor straightforward. We must find new ways for

> *The Ways I've Grown in Writing*
>
> *I have learned that you can use other words that give more detail and more elaboration. Such as, from bad to grim, and from big to enormous. It has been really fun comparing stories. and finding out in many ways how I've grown.*

```
To Whom it May Concern:

        In the pages that follow in this portfolio, you will
find the work that I feel represents my strengths in my
written work from my junior year at Hillsboro High School.
In order that you may see the overall picture, I have
included expository, informative, and creative pieces
in this portfolio.  All six samples were constructed in
an atmosphere that provided ample time for revision and
peer reviewing.  Each sample represents skills that I
have found to enhance the quality of my writing.
```

the two processes to work together. Doing so involves answering a question that has no simple answer: "What makes a portfolio a portfolio?" The portfolio is a concept that can be realized in many ways. Portfolios are as varied as the children who create them and as the classrooms in which they are found. However, to preserve those aspects of the portfolio that give the concept its power, we offer this list of guidelines[3]:

1. Developing a portfolio offers the student an opportunity to learn about learning. Therefore, the end product must contain information that shows that a student has engaged in self-reflection.

2. The portfolio is something that is done *by* the student, not *to* the student. Portfolio assessment offers a concrete way for students to learn to value their own work and, by extension, to value themselves as learners. Therefore, the student must be involved in selecting the pieces to be included.

3. The portfolio is separate and different from the student's cumulative folder. Scores and other cumulative folder information that are held in central depositories should be included in a portfolio only if they take on new meaning within the context of the other exhibits found there.

4. The portfolio must convey explicitly or implicitly the student's activities; for example, the ra-

tionale (purpose for forming the portfolio), intents (its goals), contents (the actual displays), standards (what is good and not-so-good performance), and judgments (what the contents tell us).[4]

5. The portfolio may serve a different purpose during the year from the purpose it serves at the end. Some material may be kept because it is instructional, for example, partially finished work on problem areas. At the end of the year, however, the portfolio may contain only material that the student is willing to make public.

6. A portfolio may have multiple purposes, but these must not conflict. A student's personal goals and interests are reflected in his or her selection of materials, but information included may also reflect the interests of teachers, parents, or the district. One purpose that is almost universal in student portfolios is showing progress on the goals represented in the instructional program.

7. The portfolio should contain information that illustrates growth. There are many ways to demonstrate growth. The most obvious is by including a series of examples of actual school performance that show how the student's skills have improved. Changes observed on interest inventories, records of outside activities such as reading, or on attitude measures are other ways to illustrate a student's growth.

8. Finally, many of the skills and techniques that are involved in producing effective portfolios

---

[3]This list draws on discussions on metacognition (thinking about thinking) held at Northwest Evaluation Association conferences on portfolio assessment in December 1989 and August 1990. Participants were from seven states and included teachers, curriculum and assessment specialists, administrators, and representatives of state departments of education. We would like to acknowledge the contributions of the 57 people who participated.

[4]See F. L. Paulson and P. R. Paulson, "How Do Portfolios Measure Up?: A Cognitive Model for Assessing Portfolios," paper presented at the conference of the Northwest Evaluation Association on "Aggregating Portfolio Data," Union, Washington, August 1990 (available from the authors at the addresses given below and also through ERIC).

5-11-90

BIBLE: ,

At the beginning of the year,
I havit been yoosng periods
and I amnow.
At the beginning of theyear,
I havit been yoosng sentence
and I am now. ,
At the beginning of the year,
I havit been yoosnge laboration
and I'am nowthEnd

2

Today I looked at all my
stories in my writing folder.
I read some of my writing since
September. I noticed that IVe
impooved some stuff. Now I edit my
stories, and revise. Now I use periods,
quotation mark. Some times my stories
are longer I used to mis spell my
words and now I look in a
dictionary or ask a friend and now
I write exciting and scary stories
and now I have very good endings.
Now I use capitals I used to leave out
words and write short simple stories.

do not happen by themselves. By way of support, students need models of portfolios, as well as example of how others develop and reflect upon portfolios.

There are a considerable variety of portfolio assessment projects appearing in schools, reflecting the fact that portfolio assessment is a healthy and robust concept. We recommend, however, that when designing programs or purchasing commercial portfolio assessment materials, educators reflect on the eight aspects of the portfolio that we believe give the concept its power. We offer our list as a way of initiating thoughtful critiques.

A BROAD LOOK AT LEARNING

Portfolios offer a way of assessing student learning that is quite different from traditional methods. While achievement tests offer outcomes in units that can be counted and accounted, portfolio assessment offers the opportunity to serve students in a broader context: taking risks, developing creative solutions, and learning to make judgments about their own performances.

A portfolio, then, is a portfolio when it provides a complex and comprehensive view of student performance in context. It is a portfolio when the student is a participant in, rather than the object of, assessment. Above all, a portfolio is a portfolio when it provides a forum that encourages students to develop the abilities needed to become independent, self-directed learners.

Authors' note: We would like to thank Linda Lewis (Fort Worth Independent School District, Fort Worth, Texas), Jill Marienberg (Hillsboro High School, Hillsboro, Oregon), and Ronda Woodruff (West TV Elementary School, Beaverton School District, Beaverton, Oregon) for providing portfolio examples used in this article.

► CASES

Ms. Daniels
Strengths and Limitations in a Novice's Teaching

HILDA BORKO
University of Colorado, Boulder

This case describes two contrasting lessons taught by Ms. Daniels,[2] a novice teacher, toward the end of her student teaching experience. The case begins with background information about Ms. Daniels, her teacher education program, her final student teaching placement, and the research project from which these data are drawn. The two teaching episodes follow. They are described in detail and then analyzed for what they reveal about Ms. Daniels' pedagogical content knowledge of mathematics. Questions at the end suggest additional concepts and principles from educational psychology that can be used to further analyze the lessons and the insights they provide about Ms. Daniels's knowledge, beliefs, thinking, and practices.

BACKGROUND INFORMATION

Ms. Daniels

Ms. Daniels was a senior with a major in elementary education at a large southern university during the 1988–1989 academic year. In her final year of undergraduate education, she was a member of a cohort of 38 students in a year-long elementary teacher preparation program or "model." She completed the program and graduated with a bachelor's degree and K–8 teaching certification in June, 1989. Her goal upon graduation was to teach middle school mathematics. She was hired by a middle school to teach sixth grade mathematics and sev-

enth grade science beginning in the 1989–1990 academic year.

Ms. Daniels had the most extensive mathematics background of any of the students in her cohort group, having completed her first three years at the university as a mathematics major. She maintained a "C" average through two years of calculus, an introductory course in mathematical proof, a first course in modern algebra, and four computer science courses. Like many mathematics majors, she "hit the wall" in a second modern algebra course and an advanced calculus course, receiving very low grades in these courses. Further, as she reported to the researcher, "I got to my junior-level classes and ended up hating it. I thought about something else I would enjoy doing because I knew I would never enjoy math. So teaching is what I came up with." After being denied admittance into the secondary mathematics teacher education program due to her grades in mathematics, Ms. Daniels decided to major in elementary education with a mathematics concentration. She expressed a preference to teach "something that is a little higher than beginning math—something like algebra."

Although Ms. Daniels completed more courses in advanced mathematics than the other members of her cohort group, she had the fewest courses related to elementary mathematics. Most other participants completed a three-course sequence in Concepts in Mathematics that was developed specifically for elementary education majors. Ms. Daniels studied the content of the first two courses, those that dealt with number topics, on her own, and she earned credit for them by examination.

This route allowed her to miss opportunities provided by the courses to explore elementary number concepts and operations. She enrolled in the third course, which dealt with elementary geometric topics, and received a B in that course.

Ms. Daniels's Teacher Education Program

The senior year experience (model) in which Ms. Daniels participated was specifically intended for preservice teachers interested in middle school teaching. The model included professional course work and student teaching. Each cohort member had four different student teaching placements (7 weeks each; 2 each semester) in a city unified school district of approximately 15,000 students. At least two placements were in elementary school settings; at least one was in a middle school or junior high. During the first three placements, the cohort taught for half of the school day and took courses taught by University faculty; during the final placement, they taught the full school day. University faculty taught courses in mathematics, language arts, and reading methods during the first 12 weeks of the academic year (overlapping with the first student teaching placement and half of the second); during the second 12 weeks, they taught courses in science and social studies methods and diagnosis of student understanding.

Ms. Daniels's Fourth Student Teaching Placement

Ms. Daniels's fourth student teaching placement was in a self-contained sixth grade classroom in an elementary school. During the week in which she was observed as part of the Learning to Teach Mathematics project (see below) Ms. Daniels taught math twice a day: the regular math session from 11:30 AM to 12:30 PM and "Morning Math" from approximately 8:30 to 9:00 AM. Students were grouped for mathematics instruction during the regular session. Above average ("faster") students were in the Rectangle group; average ("slower") students were in the Circle group.

Morning Math was a time set aside by Mr. Blake, Ms. Daniels's cooperating teacher, for reviewing mathematics skills learned during the year, in preparation for the Survey of Basic Skills tests that were administered throughout the school district in early May. All students in the class participated in Morning Math sessions. A whole group instructional format was used.

The Learning to Teach Mathematics Project

Ms. Daniels, along with 7 other members of her cohort, was a participant in the Learning to Teach Mathematics project, a research project funded by the National Science Foundation to examine the process of becoming a middle school mathematics teacher by following a small number of novice teachers throughout their final year of teacher preparation and first year of teaching. As part of that project, Ms. Daniels was visited for one week near the end of her first, third, and fourth student teaching placements. A researcher observed her mathematics instruction on a daily basis; interviewed her about her planning for instruction and about her reactions to the lessons; and collected copies of written lesson plans, work sheets, and other handouts. This case is based on two teaching episodes that occurred during the researcher's visit to Ms. Daniels's classroom in her fourth student teaching placement. The episodes were selected because they provide contrasting examples of Ms. Daniels's knowledge, beliefs, thinking, and actions related to teaching and learning to teach.

THE TEACHING EPISODES

Ms. Daniels's Introduction to Volume

Ms. Daniels introduced the concept of volume to the Rectangle (above average) group in her sixth grade classroom on April 21, 1989, in a lesson that was part of the regularly scheduled mathematics program. She began the lesson by comparing volume to surface area, explaining that surface area is "the distance around the outside of a three-dimensional figure" or "the distance covering a three-dimensional object." Volume is "the space inside of ... a box, a rectangular prism." She then showed the students an empty cardboard box which they identified as a rectangular prism. She explained, "[It's a] rectangular prism. And it just so happens that this rectangular prism is filled with cubes or cubic units." Ms. Daniels held up a small wooden cube and said:

> "So, we can call it a cubic unit. Now, what I would like for you to do, I need a volunteer. OK, [Janice], I want you to somehow count how many cubic units cover the volume or the inside

of this box. Do that now. Somehow figure it out. If you have to, dump them out and count them."[3]

Ms. Daniels left the students to solve the problem on their own while she worked with the Circle (average) group. She returned on several occasions during the class session to check on their progress and to offer suggestions for how to approach the problem. For example, on one occasion Ms. Daniels asked the students how they were doing. They replied that several of them had gotten different numbers when they counted. Ms. Daniels then suggested, "Why don't you give ten to each person and see how many tens you've got." The students followed her suggestion.

The next time Ms. Daniels returned to the group, the students had agreed that the correct solution was 90 cubic units. She asked, "OK, now do you think there is an easier way to do this?" She told the students to "see if you can figure out what the pattern is." She then led a discussion in which the students shared their solutions and developed the formula for volume of a rectangular prism. As they explained, they first computed the number of cubes in one layer and then figured out the number of layers. From there, they were able to calculate the number of cubes that the box would hold. The discussion ended as follows:

> One student explained, "Six times 5 is 30. I know, 30 times 3." Ms. Daniels probed, "OK, you have got 6 this way and 5 that way. How did you figure out the 90, though?" Another student explained, "Multiply the 30 times 3." Ms. Daniels asked, "What, [Kent]?" Kent replied, "Five times 6 is 30 times 3 is 90." Ms. Daniels asked, "OK, where did you get the 3 from?" Kent responded, "Going down." Ms. Daniels concurred, "That's exactly right. There is a formula for volume. You take the length times the width times the depth or the height is what they call it. L times W times H." She concluded the lesson by writing the formula on the board.

Ms. Daniels's thinking about the lesson.
When asked about her planning for the lesson, Ms. Daniels indicated that the original idea to use a box and cubes to illustrate volume came from the students' textbook. However, the book used a two-dimensional representation of a box filled with cubes. The idea to use an actual box and cubes was Ms. Daniels's. She explained,

> [The students] know what the three dimensional shapes are, but they have trouble distinguishing . . . which one is length, which is width, and which is height. . . . So I think it's better for them to have an actual object for them to look at right in front of them, rather than flat on the paper, especially for volume because . . . that's on the inside anyway.

Ms. Daniels also considered her expectations for this particular group of students:

> I remember with my classes last placement, the upper level kids are real good at discovering things. And these kids are very upper, upper level, so I thought I'd try it with them to see if it worked.

When asked how she felt about the lesson, Ms. Daniels replied, "I think it went pretty well." She was particularly pleased that "the Rectangle group . . . noticed the formula right off the bat, so that didn't take much explaining on my part." She was not concerned about any aspect of the lesson and indicated that she would not do anything differently if she were to teach it again.

The Division of Fractions Episode*

The second lesson which we examine occurred on April 20, 1989, during Morning Math. At the beginning of the lesson, pupils worked independently for approximately 15 minutes on eight practice problems on subtraction and multiplication of fractions that Ms. Daniels had written on the board. She then reviewed the division of fractions algorithm using the problem, $3/4$ divided by $1/2$, as an example. She wrote on the board as she explained:

> "OK, you keep your first term the same. OK, $3/4$ remains $3/4$. When you divide fractions, it says well, to divide fractions we have to change the operation to multiplication and then flip or invert the second number. Not the first one, the second one. You look at the sign. It says change it to multiplication, and the number after the sign is the number that you invert. Does that make sense? OK, then it is just a matter of

*Activity taken from Borko, H. et al. "Learning to teach hard mathematics. Do novice teachers and their instructors give up too easily?" *Journal for Research in Mathematics Education.* 1992, vol. 23, no. 3, pp. 194–222. Reprinted with permission by the National Council of Teachers of Mathematics.

multiplication. Does anybody have problems with that part? Multiplication is very simple. You just multiply your two numerators together, 3 times 2 gives me what?"

Ms. Daniels answered several procedural questions. Then Elise asked, "I was just wondering why, up there when you go and divide it and down there you multiply it, why do you change over?" Ms. Daniels immediately recognized Elise's question as calling for a conceptual explanation, and she attempted to respond by providing a concrete example and accompanying diagram:

"Well, as you learned before, when you divide a fraction into a fraction, the process is to flip the second one and then multiply. And say we have a wall, OK, and we divide it into fourths. $^1/_4$ of it is already painted, OK. So we have $^3/_4$ of it left to paint. Right? You agree with me?" [Ms. Daniels drew a rectangle on the front board, drew three vertical lines to divide it into four congruent parts, and shaded one part.]

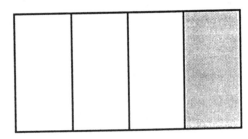

"But we have only enough paint to paint half of these three fourths. So half of $^3/_4$ would be between about right there. Right, do you agree with that?" [Ms. Daniels drew a line down the middle of the unshaded portion to divid it in half and shaded the portion that could be painted].

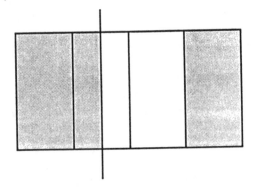

Elise replied, "Yes." Ms. Daniels continued: "There is $^1/_4$ on each side plus half of a fourth.

So now if we look at this, this fourth was divided in half, so we divide this fourth in half and this fourth in half. We are left with 1, 2, 3, 4, 5, 6." [She drew vertical lines to divide each of the remaining unshaded fourths in half.] "And if we had this fourth divided in half, it would be what kind of unit?" [She drew a vertical line to divide the shaded fourth in half.]

Ms. Daniels's completed drawing looked like this:

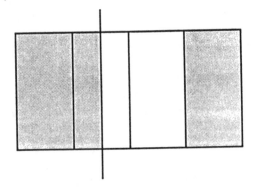

Ms. Daniels asked the students, "How many units is my wall divided into now? 1, 2, 3, 4, 5, 6, 7, 8. But $^2/_8$ is already covered. We see right here that we have enough paint to cover this many more eighths. Right? When we divide it into eighths, leaving us with how many eighths, 1, 2, 3. OK, oh wait. I did something wrong here."

Ms. Daniels realized that she had made an error. She paused for about 2 minutes, studying the board. She then decided to abandon the attempt to Provide a concrete example, saying:

"Well, I am just trying to show you so you can visualize what happens when you divide fractions, but it is kind of hard to see. We'll just use our rule for right now and let me see if I can think of a different way of explaining it to you. OK? But for right now, just invert the second number and then multiply."

Ms. Daniels stood at the board, working on the division problem. The students were working independently, apparently on the problems they had been given at the beginning of the lesson. After a few minutes, Ms. Daniels walked over to Mr. Blake's desk and looked at the presentation of division of fractions in the teacher's manual. She said to the researcher (who was sitting at Mr. Blake's desk),

"*I just did multiplication.*"[4] She did not indicate to the students that the example illustrated multiplication. Further, she did not attempt a correct representation on the following day.

For the remainder of the lesson, Ms. Daniels focused on computational procedures for division of fractions and related topics such as converting a mixed number to an improper fraction and visa versa. She demonstrated use of the algorithms and provided guided and independent practice. The Morning Math session lasted over one hour.

Ms. Daniels's thinking about the lesson.

The interview with Ms. Daniels conducted prior to the lesson reveals that she did not think about representations to use in demonstrating division of fractions when planning the lesson. In fact, she did not plan to provide a conceptual explanation at all. Instead, she planned to focus on review and practice of the division of fractions algorithm. As she explained to the researcher after the lesson, "I hadn't planned to have to give an explanation because I figured since it was a review, that, you know, we'd just have to review the process of it." Her planning, which was done the morning of the lesson, consisted of selecting a few problems from the appropriate chapter reviews and chapter tests in the text to give to the students to solve.

In discussing the episode with the researcher later that day, Ms. Daniels explained that when faced with Elise's question, "I attempted to do something I had learned about . . . in the methods course, but it didn't work because I did the wrong thing. . . . The example I had given was multiplication." However, although she "wasn't too happy with the explanation. . . . It wasn't very good," she was basically satisfied with the lesson. As she explained, "I think by the end of the time, that they had picked up on it." Also, "the kids participated and everything. And they were attentive, responded well." Her major concern was that "I just spent too much time on it. I mean, as a result, I had to cut short my other lessons, which I didn't want to have to do. . . ." She elaborated, "As far as time-wise, you just don't have time to reteach every single thing."

THINKING ABOUT MS. DANIELS'S TEACHING

There are many ways in which we can analyze Ms. Daniels's teaching in these two episodes, and many

concepts from educational psychology we can use to help us understand what she did and did not do in the lessons. Here I present one analysis in terms of Ms. Daniels's pedagogical content knowledge. I then provide a set of questions designed to help you think about other ways to analyze the lessons.

Pedagogical Content Knowledge

Pedagogical content knowledge, or knowledge of subject matter for teaching, is one of seven domains of teachers' professional knowledge identified by Lee Shulman (1987). Shulman defined pedagogical content knowledge as follows:

> *Within the category of pedagogical content knowledge I include, for the most regularly taught topics in one's subject area, the most useful forms of representation of those ideas, the most powerful analogies, illustrations, examples, explanations, and demonstrations—in a word, the ways of representing and formulating the subject that make it comprehensible to others. . . . Pedagogical content knowledge also includes an understanding of what makes the learning of specific topics easy or difficult; the conceptions and preconceptions that students of different ages and backgrounds bring with them to the learning of those most frequently taught topics and lessons. (Shulman, 1986, p. 9).*

What do the two episodes tell us about Ms. Daniels's pedagogical content knowledge?

Ms. Daniels's Introduction to Volume

The first teaching episode reveals reasonably strong pedagogical content knowledge on the part of Ms. Daniels. She selected an appropriate and powerful representation to use as a basis for the group activity. She drew upon her knowledge of students when making the decision to use a concrete example. She used the textbook for ideas; however, she modified its suggestions to better fit characteristics of the students and her objectives for the lesson.

There were also limitations in the pedagogical content knowledge Ms. Daniels demonstrated during the lesson. This assessment is based as much on what she did not say as what she said. For example, Ms. Daniels did not indicate that she considered alternative representations or other problems using the box and cubes representation when planning the lesson. When asked by the researcher whether the students had been introduced to volume previously, Ms. Daniels responded that she did not think so, revealing a lack of familiarity with the district's K–6 mathematics curriculum. She also seemed to jump from the box example to the formula very quickly, without explicitly helping the students to see that the representation of volume by a box filled with cubes leads to the derivation of the formula for the volume of a rectangular prism.

Ms. Daniels's Review of Division of Fractions

Ms. Daniels's selection of an incorrect application and visual representation in the review lesson on division of fractions indicates limitations in both her content knowledge and pedagogical content knowledge. She did not have a strong conceptual understanding of division of fractions. Therefore, when constructing the representation, she did not realize that she was giving a perfect example of the operator ("of") interpretation of multiplication. Her repertoire of powerful representations clearly was limited (in fact, non-existent). Ms. Daniels's knowledge of students, another component of pedagogical content knowledge, was also limited. She did not realize that her students were likely to have difficulty understanding the conceptual underpinnings of the division-of-fractions algorithm.

Novices' Teaching and Learning to Teach

This analysis is not meant as a negative assessment of Ms. Daniels's pedagogical content knowledge or her teaching. On the contrary, the first episode represents a reasonably strong mathematics lesson. Although the second episode reveals greater limitations in Ms. Daniels's professional knowledge, it illustrates some of her strengths as a teacher as well. For example, her procedural explanation of division of fractions was good, and she maintained student attention throughout the lesson. In fact, Ms. Daniels was considered by her cooperating teachers and university supervisors to be a strong student teacher, and she received high evaluations in all of her student teaching placements.

The episodes do suggest that pedagogical content knowledge should be a major focus of teacher preparation programs. As Shulman noted, pedagogical content knowledge is unique to the teaching profession. It is an area of knowledge that

novice teachers may not begin to develop until they are faced with actual teaching responsibilities. Therefore, we should not be surprised to find that novice teachers' pedagogical content knowledge is limited, and we should attempt to ensure that it is a major focus of their attention during initial teaching experiences (e.g., student teaching).

QUESTIONS TO GUIDE ADDITIONAL ANALYSES

1. What do these two teaching episodes suggest about other components of Ms. Daniels's knowledge base for teaching? For example, what do they suggest about her knowledge and beliefs about mathematics, about learners, and about general teaching strategies?

2. What do the teaching episodes suggest about Ms. Daniels's pedagogical thinking? What can you learn from them about her planning of instruction? About her thoughtfulness or reflectivity about teaching?

3. What do the teaching episodes suggest about the relationships among a teacher's knowledge, beliefs, thinking, and instructional practices?

4. This case provided no information about Ms. Daniels's teacher education program. Without having that information, what additional experiences would you recommend for a novice teacher such as Ms. Daniels, to help her acquire the knowledge, skills, and understandings that characterize expert teachers?

Information about Ms. Daniels's teacher education program is available in several articles and reports about the Learning to Teach Mathematics project; for example, Borko et al., 1992; Eisenhart, et al., 1991; Eisenhart, et al., 1992. These articles also offer recommendations for teacher education experiences based on our analyses of the role that teacher education played in Ms. Daniels' learning to teach. You may want to compare your answer to this question to ideas presented in the articles.

REFERENCES

Borko, H. (1991, October). The integration of content and pedagogy in teaching. Invited address at the National Conference on Critical Issues in Reforming Elementary Teacher Preparation in Mathematics and Science. University of Northern Colorado, Greeley, Colorado.

Borko, H., Eisenhart, M., Brown, C. A., Underhill, R. G., Jones, D., & Agard, P. C. (1992). Learning to teach hard mathematics: Do novice teachers and their instructors give up too easily? *Journal for Research in Mathematics Education, 23,* 194–222.

Eisenhart, M., Behm, L., & Romagnano, L. (1991). Learning to teach: Developing expertise or rite of passage? *Journal of Education for Teaching, 17,* 51–71.

Eisenhart, M., Borko, H., Underhill, R. G., Brown, C. A., Jones, D., & Agard, P. C. (1992). Conceptual knowledge falls through the cracks: Complexities of learning to teach mathematics for understanding. *Journal for Research in Mathematics Teaching.*

Shulman, L. (1986). Those who understand: Knowledge growth in teaching. *Educational Researcher, 15*(2). 4–14.

Shulman, L. (1987). Knowledge and teaching: Foundations of a new reform. *Harvard Educational Review, 57*(1), 1–22.

ENDNOTES

1. This case is based on research conducted as part of the Learning to Teach Mathematics project. The project was supported in part by the National Science Foundation under Grant No. MDR 865246. Any opinions, findings, and conclusions or recommendations expressed in this publication are those of the author and do not necessarily reflect the views of the National Science Foundation.

My colleagues on the Learning to Teach Mathematics project are Catherine Brown, Margaret Eisenhart, Robert Underhill, Doug Jones, and Patricia Agard. Several articles and presentations written by our research team feature Ms. Daniels and her teaching; portions of this case are taken from these documents (Borko, 1991; Borko, et al., 1992; Eisenhart, et al., 1992).

2. All names used in this case are pseudonyms.

3. In accord with anthropological usage, I am using the following conventions throughout this case: (a) extended excerpts from field notes are presented in block format, (b) verbatim statements by participants in the field notes are enclosed in quotation marks, (c) researchers' explanations and clarifications added to field notes when writing the case are enclosed in brackets, and (d) extended quotes from interviews are presented in block format without quotation marks.

4. (Editor's endnote) To understand why Ms. Daniels's explanation is really an example of multiplication, think of the problem as:

"If you have 3/4 of the wall left to paint and only enough paint to cover 1/2 of that 3/4, then how much of the wall can you paint?"

In other words, how much is 1/2 of 3/4? To solve this problem we multiply because **"of"** means multiply: $1/2 \times 3/4 = 3/8$

For one approach to explaining **division** using a diagram, see Figure 1 below:

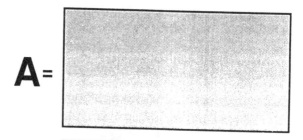

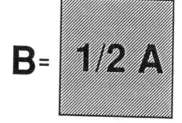

How many 1/2's are there in 3/4?

OR

How many B's are there in 3/4 of A?

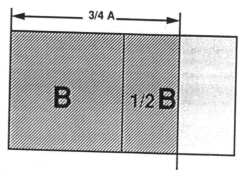

There are 1 1/2 B's in 3/4 of A; therefore, 3/4 divided by 1/2 =1 1/2.

FIGURE 1 **3/4 divided by 1/2 means how many sets of 1/2 are in 3/4.**

From Monocultural to Multicultural Teaching in an Inner-City Middle School

LYNNE T. DÍAZ-RICO
California State University, San Bernardino

THE CLASS

A stack of books slid off the desk and crashed to the floor as Bernardo took his seat in the 5th period eighth grade American history class. Ayala sprang to her feet, reaching across the empty desk between her desk and Bernardo's to take a swipe at his head before picking up her books. Bernardo, protesting his innocence loudly, appealed to Mrs. Winter for justice. Claudia Winter glanced up guiltily from her private conversation with another student, realizing that she had not seen the books fall and could not act as judge and jury. Of her five daily classes, the 5th period class took the longest to settle down; the students came directly from lunch, a period in which half of them seemed to look for trouble and the other half found trouble without even looking. Mrs. Winter stepped away from her desk, moving to the overhead projector at the front of the room to signal the students that class would begin soon. Ayala had not yet picked up the pile of books on the floor, and was two aisles away from her seat, sitting on another student's desk. The bell rang to begin the period, and students leisurely broke away from their social groups to take their seats.

"You have four minutes to complete the Warm-Up Activity." Mrs. Winter displayed a transparency on the overhead projector entitled "The Exploration of Coronado," with a map of the North American continent and ten geographic points labeled A, B, C

.. . . J. "Each place that Coronado explored is represented by a letter. On a sheet of paper, put the letters of the map in the proper order corresponding to the order in which Coronado explored them. Go ahead and get to work." Mrs. Winter pulled out her grade book to take attendance while the students squinted at the transparency. Eight of the 25 students registered for this class were absent. She had just finished noting the absent students when three students came to class late with an admission excuse from the counseling center. She motioned for them to take their seats. They were too late to understand and respond to the transparency.

As the class volunteered answers about Coronado's exploration, Mrs. Winter noticed that over half the class had not attempted the activity. She glanced down over her notes, looking for a topic that might spark a class discussion. She paused for a moment to frown at three girls at the back of the room who were whispering to each other. "Those of you who read the assigned chapter last night will recall that Coronado was looking for the Lost Cities of Eldorado. What cities did he actually find?" As she looked around expectantly, Marcie, a very shy girl who seldom volunteered, raised her hand reluctantly. Mrs. Winter nodded in her direction. "Yes, Marcie?" Marcie blurted out, "Mrs. Winter, they took my purse!" Two boys in the next aisle turned around quickly in their seats, pointing to two other boys behind Marcie. Everyone in the class looked at Marcie, who blushed and looked down at her hands, clenched in her lap. Mrs. Winter walked down the center aisle, between the rows of students' seats. The students in the center two rows shrank away from her as she passed. As she retrieved the purse from beneath a vacant desk, she felt a wave of desperation pass over her. American history was her favorite subject. Yet it did not take extra sensory perception to feel the hostility this class seemed to feel toward the topic. For a brief moment she imagined herself as The Old Woman Who Lived in a Shoe, grabbing twenty children one by one to pour castor oil down their throats. Me against Them, she thought glumly.

THE TEACHER

Claudia Winter was born in the same small town in Iowa as her parents and both sets of grandparents. Her father had been a teacher in the local high school until his recent retirement. Claudia had often considered teaching as a profession, until attending Iowa State University, where she switched her major to business management with a minor in history. She left Iowa after graduating from college, moving to Chicago and marrying an accounting major who took a job with a nationally prominent firm headquartered in a Chicago suburb. Claudia worked for several years as a management trainee with a meat products company, then switched to a cosmetics manufacturing company; but she found the world of business unfulfilling. She returned to graduate school when she was 26 years old to attain a teaching credential, and found, to her surprise, she was following in her father's footsteps.

Her first teaching position was at Riverview Junior High School, a large school in a part of Chicago that was undergoing rapid demographic change. Neighborhoods that until the 1970's had consisted of white, working class families employed in nearby meat packing plants were becoming neighborhoods in which Hispanic and African-American families were crowded into housing that had seen better days. Many households were supported by single parents who were not able to be home with their children after school, leaving teenagers unsupervised until dark. In Iowa, Claudia had grown up with very little experience with Hispanic or African-American cultures. Although she considered herself a conscientious teacher who tried hard to reach each

student, the student body at Riverview presented a distinct challenge. About one-third of the students were Hispanic, and many of these students had not learned enough English to complete written assignments. Another third of the students were African American. They seemed to treat her in a very distant manner, responding very little to her attempts to befriend them. The "Anglo" students in her classes—the remaining one-third— seem to be divided between students who showed little desire to succeed in school and those who seemed to want to earn just enough credits to graduate from high school. Claudia's approach was to be fair to everyone, and to try to interest all students in American history. The best way that she knew to be fair was to treat all students equally, and to try to ignore cultural and ethnic differences as much as possible. Unfortunately, the various racial and ethnic groups in her classrooms seemed to be pitted against one another, with constant sparring between groups and no visible attempts to form intercultural friendships. Part of Claudia's daily challenge was to keep the racial tensions and hostility from being voiced during class. Those students who vented any such feelings during class were sent to after-school detention as punishment.

In her first year of teaching, Claudia had struggled to maintain order as she taught. After several months, the students' behavior gradually improved, and Claudia no longer relied as heavily on discipline referrals to gain respect. She had achieved what she termed a "compromise" with students: If a class managed to complete a week's assignments and take a weekly Thursday quiz, Friday's class featured a movie. She found a video rental store where she could obtain cassettes of classic American movies such as Westerns, gangster movies about Al Capone, *Gone With the Wind,* and *Bonnie and Clyde.* In the name of American history, the films replaced formal lessons; there was little time for discussion of the content. Although Claudia felt somewhat guilty about bartering four days of good behavior for one day of cinema, the transaction kept students entertained and low-key on Friday afternoons. She tried to avoid films that featured very controversial topics that would inflame racial tensions among students. By using the videos to gain students' cooperation, and by using punishment to discourage students from voicing prejudice or ridicule for other students, Claudia had achieved a kind of workable truce that made the classroom tolerable.

THE INCIDENTS

Incidents in Claudia's second and third year of teaching upset this arrangement. First, the school district implemented a state-wide American History achievement test for eighth graders in Claudia's second year of teaching, and the scores that were returned in July revealed that her students had scored very poorly on the test. Despite her principal's assurance that the school in general was ranked among the lowest in the district (a fact that the teaching staff, fairly or unfairly, attributed to the large presence of minority students in the school whose "academic potential was poor"), Claudia felt exposed as a deficient teacher, and took her students' dismal showing on the test as an index of personal failure. She determined to work harder to instill in her students a love of American history and a desire to perform well academically. At present, her teaching consisted of a minimal transaction: students' going through the motions of learning in exchange for 20 percent of class time spent watching movies. This nagging sense of inadequacy was a source of chronic discomfort to Claudia as she taught.

A second incident presented a much more acute sense of failure. One day at lunch, racial tensions came to a head between members of an African-American teenage gang and a group of recently immigrated Puerto Rican youth. A fight between these groups in the cafeteria became a melee that raged throughout the school. An African-American boy was serious injured and windows were broken through the campus. Classes were canceled for the remainder of the day. The next day, when Claudia tried to call the 5th period class to order, a group of African-American girls talking loudly with one another in the back of the room refused to come to attention. Claudia walked to the back of the room and spoke with the group, requesting their attention so class could begin. The girls quieted, but resumed their loud talking as soon as Claudia reached the front of the room. Claudia again asked for their cooperation, without success. She wrote a discipline referral and asked the four to report to the office.

The next day, Claudia was called to the principal's office to face four angry mothers of the girls. In no uncertain terms, they called her a "racist" for targeting their daughters to discipline as a group, and demanded that she be fired. The principal, obviously uncomfortable, suggested as a compromise that Claudia attend an upcoming district-wide colloquium on multicultural education. Claudia was very angry that the principal did not staunchly defend her, and had subjected her to the confrontation with the parents. She was tempted to quit, but was afraid that she wouldn't find another teaching position because of the incident. She reluctantly agreed to attend the colloquium.

In the meantime, the four girls returned to class, but there was thick tension and hostility among the students and between the students and Claudia. There was very little time for learning history when the class persisted in petty behavioral disruptions and sullen, minimal cooperation. Claudia felt increasingly desperate and depressed that she could not succeed in covering the curriculum that would be on the year-end eighth grade achievement test. If the incident with the four students did not cost her the position at Riverview, the students abysmal test scores certainly would. Despite her resentment at being forced to attend the upcoming colloquium, Claudia secretly hoped that she would learn some techniques that would restore her faith in herself as a teacher and help her to engage the students in active learning.

THE SEMINAR

Justine Ellerman, the facilitator for the seminar, appeared to be about 55 years old, a dynamic African-American woman with a brisk handshake who got the colloquium underway immediately. Claudia recognized another teacher from Riverview, one of the two English-as-a-second-language specialists in the English department. About twenty other teachers and administrators from other schools in the district seemed eager and excited to be a part of the seminar. Participants were asked to write down their definitions of multicultural education and share these ideas with a small group.

When the groups had compared notes, Mrs. Ellerman asked for sample definitions. Claudia could tell there were some definitions that Mrs. Ellerman liked more than others. "Multicultural education is not about changing students to fit in with the American Ideal, so that everyone can adapt to middle class beliefs and behaviors," the facilitator stressed. "It is unfair and perhaps impossible for us to expect that students will leave their ethnic heritage behind when they enter our classrooms. Identity is not something that can be checked at the door and retrieved after class. Multicultural education is about all students having a full and equal opportunity to learn and to be respected."

As an exercise in awareness, each participant was asked briefly to profile four students whom they found most difficult to reach. Claudia chose four members of her 5th period American history class. Ayala, the shy but defiant Mexican-American girl who was fourteen but whose reading level in English was about the level of the fourth grade. Two periods of her day were taken up with ESL classes, but she was put in a regular American history class to "sink or swim." Jake, pudgy Anglo farm kid whose parents had moved to Chicago after selling their four acres in southern Illinois. Jake liked to talk—would start up a conversation with strangers on the street—but disliked to read, write, or study. Bernardo, "Mr. Macho," who lived with his mother, seeing his father only once or twice a year when he was able to return from Mexico. Bernardo's mother was 14 when he was born, and now that he was 14 he bossed her around at home and tried to do the same with Claudia in class. Marcie, a slender, never-vocal African-American girl who attracted bullies with her air of silent desperation; who was always prepared with homework that was almost never correct. When Claudia had written the short descriptions of each student, Mrs. Ellerman asked her to set these aside until the group had discussed the effect of culture on school behavior and attitudes.

"We're going to look at what I call a "monocultural" point of view about schooling," Mrs. Ellerman began. "Perhaps some of you will recognize your beliefs as we explore the "monocultural" belief system. I don't want you to think of these beliefs as *wrong*. They work well enough if your classroom is monocultural; if all your students are middle-class, if they are all raised in homes in which completing homework is a nightly ritual, if they all aspire to become investment brokers, English teachers, or school principals" (a few participants laughed). "But in a multicultural classroom, you're going to need a multicultural approach. Let's see what the research shows us about a contrast between these points of view."

Mrs. Ellerman wrote the following category titles on various flip charts around the room:

Motivation/values
Grades and motivation
Classroom behavior
Teacher/student relation
Teacher expectations

Peer relations
Learning styles
Covering the curriculum
Achievement, assessment

She called for volunteers to offer ideas about what motivation and values students should feel toward learning, and how teachers can motivate students. As the group called out ideas, Mrs. Ellerman wrote them on the first flip chart: "Learning for its own sake/ Good grades for college entrance/Working hard brings success/ Offer help before students have to ask for it/ Praise students' effort even if they fail/ "Ease up" on requirements so students can experience success.

"Before I let this go too far," cautioned Mrs. Ellerman, "I want to give you some feedback about offering unsolicited help. If a teacher offers help before a student asks for it, the student may read this as saying, 'You poor child, you don't have what it takes to get this on your own.' And reducing assignment requirements is equivalent to saying, 'A second-class education is good enough for you.' The child from a culturally different background needs to feel as competent and capable as the next student. They need to attribute their successes or failures to internal, controllable causes: their own efforts or their own insufficient knowledge, both factors that can be changed. A teacher's pity, unwarranted praise, or reduced expectations communicates that a students' failure is due to uncontrollable factors, such as their own inability. They begin to believe that nothing they do will change this. As the teacher of a multicultural classroom, your job is to use a deeper understanding of the student's needs and abilities to help them master the course content in their own way. And remember, grades may not be a prime motivator to some students. They may never have achieved good grades, and have learned not to expect them. Performing well in the eyes of their peers in class may be a more powerful motivator." As she spoke, she entered key phrases on another chart, entitled, "Multicultural approaches to values & motivation."

"Let's go on to students' classroom behavior," the facilitator invited. "Glance briefly at the student profiles that you have written. What behaviors on the part of these students make them difficult to teach?"

Claudia volunteered several behaviors: Bernardo's habit of calling out advice telling her how to deal with other students . . . Ayala's stubborn refusal to answer even easy questions when called on . . . Jake's incessant talking to other students during silent reading periods . . . Marcie's shyness, and helpless acceptance of harassment from bullies . . . Mrs. Ellerman asked, "Have you been viewing these behaviors as the characteristics—or faults—of individuals? How can we view these as examples of cultural traits? Can someone talk briefly about "shyness" as a cultural trait?"

The group had a lively discussion about cultural differences in behavior and interpersonal expectations. Claudia realized that she had often misinterpreted her students' attempts to give tokens of respect to her and to gain respect from her. For example, when Claudia gave Ayala verbal directions and Ayala did not give Claudia small signs of feedback, such as an occasional nod or "uh huh," Claudia assumed that Ayala did not understand her, and Claudia then often repeated her explanation in simplified language. Mrs. Ellerman explained that Ayala might be receiving signals that Claudia thought she was stupid. Although Claudia had not taught students of Asian background, several other teachers volunteered the difficulties they had experienced in drawing Chinese and Japanese students into increased verbal participation in class. Every culture seemed to have different rules about acceptable participation.

Complicating the students' cultural differences in participating in classroom discussion and interaction with her as the teacher were the various behaviors due to gender differences. Claudia asked herself if she had been guilty of giving the boys too much freedom to verbally dominate her class, while girls' voices were systematically silenced by insufficient "wait time" for their responses or by offering the girls questions that required lower-order thinking and pitching boys more complex verbal opportunities. "I wonder," she thought to herself, "If I should ask another teacher to observe my class. It might give me some useful feedback."

Throughout the morning Claudia took notes with her pen and with her heart. The group as a whole was sometimes open to Mrs. Ellerman's multicultural interpretation of teaching and learning, and sometimes very resistant. One fierce argument broke out over a remark Mrs. Ellerman made about high academic standards and rigorous teacher expectations. A high school English teacher objected. "Teachers who are critical, and do not hesitate to intervene with students whose work warrants correction: Would this engender a feeling of failure and low self-worth in students of low ability?"

"There is more to this issue than correcting errors," explained Mrs. Ellerman. "Part of the schooling that oppresses and silences a multicultural student is the idea that a teacher's standards are the only standards. This goes hand in hand with the belief that the teacher 'owns' the curriculum. Instead of all students moving in a lockstep together through a set curriculum, a wise teacher allows individual goal-setting. Meeting with students in goal-review conferences can encourage students to review their progress; to reflect on how they approach difficult assignments; to redo projects when they have learned more; and to revise projects for an improvement in their grade. Students' work can be kept in portfolios, so their progress is visible. Students can help one another in cooperative groups so they can share responsibility for their own improvement and that of their peers. Most importantly, learning can become a group goal. The teacher, after all, only 'owns' the *teaching* in a classroom. The students 'own' their *learning*." Mrs. Ellerman went on to describe a classroom in which students demonstrate self-regulated learning.

"Students are encouraged to reflect on their own answers. They are able to restate a problem in their own words, and explain their own thinking as they evaluate various solutions. Student autonomy is promoted, and students try to pose and solve problems independently of teacher direction. If students solve problems correctly, they build confidence by sharing their solutions with others." Claudia mulled over the emphasis on problem-solving. She asked Mrs. Ellerman directly, "Can you give me an example of problem-solving in an American history class?" The response was immediate: Require students to work together to prepare a defense of England's position in the Revolutionary War. What if the colonies were wrong in becoming independent?

In the early afternoon, Mrs. Ellerman asked various participants to describe how cooperative learning activities in their classrooms changed the atmosphere from a teacher-directed approach to an environment in which students helped to design and carry out learning activities. Claudia realized that many of the participants in the colloquium had attended previous seminars. Several had invited Mrs. Ellerman to give demonstrations in their classrooms. As one "veteran" expressed, "Multicultural education, for me, is a process that takes time to accomplish. Every time I think I know all about it, I am surprised to find myself learning more. My students teach me how to reach them better. I hope

I never again believe I know one best way to teach everyone."

In this colloquium, the various learning styles that students bring to the classroom was only superficially introduced, due to time constraints. Claudia vowed to pursue this to topic. She did find herself seeing Jake in a new light as a predominantly auditory learner, and promised herself that she would find materials which would make history more of an oral story for him. She saw Bernardo and Ayala in a new light, as field-dependent learners. Bernardo's relations with others preoccupied him, as his need to dominate others was paramount in importance over the content of instruction. Ayala's field dependence seemed to take other routes, as she evidently disliked labeling ideas as "right" and "wrong" and preferred to describe rather than evaluate history. Marcie's sense of helplessness might be due to her discomfort with verbal expression, a determined assertion of individuality in a social mileau that was dominated by very verbal and aggressive teenage peers. Claudia made a resolution to allow Marcie to express herself more often through projects that involved art and other forms of nonverbal expression.

As the colloquium drew to a close, Claudia felt that one big issue was being sidestepped: the need to cover a set curriculum so that students will perform well on standardized tests. In response to Claudia's inquiry, Mrs. Ellerman faced this issue squarely.

"Who writes the tests?" Mrs. Ellerman questioned. "If the tests are written to accompany a certain textbook, then the textbook authors are in charge of the curriculum. If the test is written by your district's social studies experts, then they are in charge of the curriculum. If the test is state-wide or national in scope, then the state or the national agencies are in charge of the curriculum. What is the purpose of these tests? Are they designed to showcase what your students know, or to show up their failure? A more important question than 'How can the students perform better on the standardized test?' is, 'How can we best demonstrate what our students know?'"

Assessing achievement is an important issue in multicultural education, according to Mrs. Ellerman, because of the associated issues of control over the curriculum and focus on curricular content that relates to a Eurocentric point of view. The traditional teaching of American history is an example of a story told from a Eurocentric standpoint. Students from other cultures may resent hearing about history as a list of conquests by Europeans. If this is what is taught, students may react with conscious or unconscious resentment and not wish to perform well on an assessment of this content.

Claudia remembered the Warm-Up Activity that consisted of a list of points conquered by Coronado. The activity, in retrospect, seemed irrelevant at best. She allowed herself to brainstorm about alternative ways in which the exploration of the New World could be introduced. Perhaps a skit in which Coronado and his advisors try to decide in which direction to travel next. Students might benefit from seeing the Southwest through fresh eyes, the way it appeared hundreds of years ago. Another possible dramatization might be the meeting of Coronado with the Zuñi chieftains. Students might also enjoy the chance to investigate Zuñi crafts and customs. This might give students like Marcie a chance to include nonverbal and artistic content in the history class.

"If you insist on standardized tests of achievement for your students," Mrs. Ellerman continued, "why not begin with a school academic club or extracurricular academic competition? Students who are especially motivated may enjoy competing in essay contests, or academic competitions such as decathlons or interschool challenge contests. If no such competition exists in your content field, why not start one? There is no better way to motivate excellence in students than to invest your own time in their growth and achievement. This may take the pressure off the classroom as a site in which students are forced to master a very particular and focused curriculum. If you do not feel you have to pressure your students to master a particular set of facts or solve a predetermined set of problems, you may find both yourself and your students open to much more self-directed learning and in-depth study of topics that are of interest to the students."

One of the school administrators mentioned the film *Stand and Deliver* as an example of the outcome that is possible if teachers have high expectations that students will master a predetermined curriculum. Mrs. Ellerman had high praise for the motion picture, with a few caveats: "Let's not forget that the protagonist, Jaime Escalante, was not exactly the Lone Ranger that the film depicts. In reality, the principal of Garfield High School was very supportive of Escalante's efforts, and national funding agencies such as the ARCO Foundation, National Science Foundation, and the Foundation for Advancements in Science and Education (FASE) supplied funds for summer attendance and correlated community college classes for his students. I recommend reading Escalante's article, with Jack Dinnann, in the *Journal of Negro Education* (1990, Vol. 59[3], 407–423), in which he details his model of achievement in math education."

After the colloquium, Claudia had much to reexamine. On Mrs. Ellerman's suggestion, she put herself in her students' place and asked a key question: "What class activities would I look forward to, that would make me come alive with excitement about the study of history?" Claudia decided to focus on three major changes in class procedure. First, students would be encouraged to take an active role in designing instruction and in carrying out instructional activities. Second, she would target various types of activities to include in the current unit on the early exploration of the North American continent. She could help students write and perform minidramas to recreate key scenes and personalities in the opening of the continent. She could encourage students to create puppet theater as an alternative to live drama to act out similar scenes. To promote another avenue of active learning, she could incorporate as much art into the curriculum as possible, to allow opportunities to explore the cultures of America. In addition to new types of activities, Claudia planned to institute self-regulated learning into the classroom. Every three weeks she would meet with students in small groups to plan their activities for the upcoming unit.

Over a period of several months, students began to reflect upon their own learning, and to actively plan to master content with a self-guided study plan. Claudia did not abandon the unit tests, but worked hard to develop a set of self-tutoring cards which students could use to master both fact-based and problem-solving test questions. She also allowed students who were auditory and oral learners to respond to essay questions by recording their answers on audiotape. Students complained at first that the Friday films were discontinued, but when Friday became Performance Day for the class's dramatic efforts, the films were forgotten.

A few surprising personalities began to unfold. Bernardo insisted on being the lead actor in several plays, until he discovered directing and stage management better suited his talents. He began to evolve from being domineering to being managerial. Ayala found that she learned best by being paired with another Mexican-American girl, whose thinking was similar to hers but whose English was better. During the fall semester, Ayala's command of English improved daily. Jake still disliked writing, but found he could express his ideas fluently into a tape recorder and was, in turn, willing to entertain Claudia's arguments about debatable points in history that she recorded onto the same tape. Claudia encouraged Marcie to create several art displays that featured Native American crafts; she found Marcie increasingly fascinated by textiles. She was able to check out several books for Marcie about Native American weaving from the public library. Claudia also found a free community craft class which taught simple hand loom techniques, and to her surprise, Marcie's mother agreed to enroll her daughter.

The best feeling came gradually to Claudia when she looked up from a busy class session one day and realized that a mixed group of African-American, Hispanic, and Anglo students were expecting her to stay after school and help them to rehearse the class play, *Bill and Ted's Excellent Romp through the Smithsonian*. Claudia thought to herself, "I've come a long way since the time when I would crawl home after school exhausted by the students' negativity. Would I rather stay and rehearse the play than do my Christmas shopping? You bet!"

QUESTIONS FOR DISCUSSION

Before attending the multicultural education workshop, Claudia Winter's teaching featured many aspects that may have undermined her students' motivation and learning. For each aspect of instruction listed below, describe how a culturally sensitive approach might differ from what could be considered "monocultural" teaching. Some examples of "monocultural" teaching assumptions and approaches have been provided. Try to find other examples for each category.

	"Monocultural" teaching	*Multicultural teaching*
Motivation/ values	Assume that a sense of success is more important than genuine content mastery	Alter students' ability, not academic goals; success = content mastery
	Assume students' cultural background is irrelevant	
Grades and motivation	Assume that good grades form basis for motivation	

Classroom behavior	Barter non-scholastic rewards for class cooperation
Teacher/student relations	Expect same response from all students to teacher's rapport attempts
Teacher expectations	Reduce expectations for students lacking academic preparation
Peer relations	Discipline groups of students who do not cooperate
Learning styles	
The curriculum	
Achievement assessment	

FOLLOW-UP/ EXPANSION ACTIVITIES

Teaching and learning: What other activities might interest a multicultural class in learning about the American revolution? For instance, can you describe a skit that the students could perform that would illustrate the difficulty that General Washington faced in equipping the Revolutionary Army?

The curriculum: What are some sources you might identify that would help to tell the story of America from a non-Eurocentric point of view? How could you use these materials to arouse debate on, for example, the issue of the "manifest destiny" of America?

Student interaction: Can you describe some activities that might reduce ethnic group conflict within the student body of a junior high school? Include activities that could prevent conflict before it occurs, as well as techniques to defuse hostility that have broken out between rival groups.

Learning styles: What are the consequences of a field-dependent versus field-independent learning style? What other individual differences can be considered "learning style" varieties?

Activities for self-regulation and assessment: What might be typical of the contents of a student portfolio in an American history class? Try to include some items that are not written work. How can learning contracts be used in conjunction with student self-assessment?

Analysis of Two Middle School Students' Cognitive Strategies, Memory, and Learning

PAUL R. PINTRICH and ALLISON J. YOUNG
Combined Program in Education and Psychology
The University of Michigan, Ann Arbor

The following two case studies are drawn from research on middle school students' learning in English, Social Studies, and Science classes. These two students took part in a study of how seventh graders read and attempt to understand information in a science textbook. We were interested in how seventh graders would approach the task, what cognitive strategies they might apply, and then how they would remember and "use" (or transfer) the information. The study involved the following steps:

1.   The students were asked to read four pages from their own science textbook on adaptation (see Box 1). They were told that they would be asked some questions about what they remembered and learned after they were done reading, although it was made clear that this was not a test. They were allowed as long as they wanted to read the passage (no one took more than 20 minutes) and they could take notes, make an outline, list important words, whatever they normally do when reading their science textbook.

2.   When the students signaled to the interviewer that they were done reading, they took a 5 minute break, left the room to get a drink of water and walked around a bit. When they came back, the interviewer asked the students to write down what they could remember and what they learned from reading the passage. The two students' verbatim responses to this free recall task are displayed in Table 1.

3.   After the students were done with this recall task, they were asked two questions about adaptation that required them to "go beyond the information given" in the actual passage and transfer or apply the information to a different situation. The questions were taken from the list of suggested discussion questions in the teacher's manual. The students' verbatim responses to these two questions are displayed in Table 2. The two "transfer" questions were:

> Q1: What if Ann Arbor became very cold and had snow year round like the North Pole? What might happen to the animals that live here now?
> Q2: What if a coyote that lives in the desert had a mutation that made his fur white? What might happen to this coyote?

4.   Finally, after the students answered these questions, they were asked some questions about how they went about reading and remembering the passage as well as how they answered the questions. The interview was designed to help us understand what the students were thinking as they attempted to read, remember, and comprehend the passage. The interviews are transcribed. The names of the students have been changed to insure their

BOX 1 Copy of Passage Students Read*

Organisms Adapt to Their Environments

Fossils indicate that changes have taken place in the past, but they do not tell us how. To find out how changes might have occurred in the past, life scientists study changes in living things. An **adaptation** (a′dap tā′shən) is the result of changes in the genetic makeup of an organism. These changes may be in body structure, body function, coloration, or behavior. Adaptations allow organisms to survive in certain environments. For example, the anteater shown below lives mostly on insects found in hard-to-reach places. To catch the insects it eats, the anteater has a long, sticky tongue. An organism whose tongue is not adapted to this type of food searching would find it much more difficult to live on these insects.

Sometimes an adaptation can involve more than one species. For example, one species can imitate another species for protection. The butterflies in the pictures above look alike, but they are different species. The monarch butterfly, shown on the left, contains a chemical that makes it distasteful to birds. Birds soon learn not to eat the bad-tasting monarchs. The viceroy, shown on the right, might taste fine to a bird. But it looks so much like the monarch that birds often stay away from the viceroy species too.

Mutations Can Cause Change

Sometimes changes in an organism come about through **mutations,** (myü tā′shənz), which are random changes in genes and chromosomes. Mutations occur naturally in the cells of organisms. Usually, mutations produce no noticeable changes in organisms. Some mutations, however, can lower an organism's chances of surviving and producing young.

The squirrel, shown to the right, is an **albino** (al bī′ nō). Albinos have a mutation in their genes that prevents them from having normal body colors. This mutation can be harmful to the squirrel since it will not blend with its surroundings. Therefore, the albino squirrel may be more visible to its enemies.

Other mutations can be an advantage for an organism. For example, some mosquitos sprayed by DDT probably had mutations that enabled them to resist the DDT poison. These mosquitoes lived and passed their DDT resistance on to their offspring.

Natural Selection

Over 150 years ago, an English naturalist by the name of Charles Darwin set off on a voyage around the world. On his trip, Darwin found organisms that he had never seen before. Yet he recognized that some of these unknown organisms looked like some of the plants and animals he was familiar with in England. Through careful observations, Darwin developed an idea that helps explain how groups of organisms change in the theory of evolution. This idea is called **natural selection** (nach′ər əl si lek′shən).

There were several observations that led Darwin to the idea of natural selection. First, Darwin saw that most species produce more offspring than the environment can support. Notice, for example, the many tadpoles in the picture to the left. There is only a limited amount of food and space for these developing frogs. Many will not survive.

Another observation Darwin made was that the members of any one species are not exactly alike. The second picture to the left shows adult frogs of the same species. Notice that some of their body colors are slightly different.

Darwin concluded that there must be a struggle for existence among organisms, such as tadpoles. He also realized that certain traits, such as a frog's color, make an organism better adapted to its environment. If an organism is better adapted, it stands a better chance of surviving and reproducing. For example, frogs with body colors that most closely match their environment will be better able to hide from their enemies. These frogs may then survive and produce offspring. Over many generations, certain inherited traits will be naturally selected by certain environments.

It should be mentioned that Darwin delayed publishing his ideas on natural selection for more than twenty years after his worldwide travels. In the meantime, another English naturalist, A. R. Wallace, had also come up with ideas about natural selection. In fairness to Darwin, however, Wallace generously waited to publish his views. Both Darwin's and Wallace's papers were finally presented together at a scientific meeting in 1858.

The organisms you see above are a famous example of Darwin's process of natural selection. About a hundred years ago, there was a species of moths in England called peppered moths. Almost all of the peppered moths were light-colored. When these light-colored moths rested on light-colored tree trunks, they blended in with the trees. The color made it hard for birds to spot and eat the moths. However, as more factories were built in England, soot began to blacken the trees. People soon discovered dark-colored peppered moths on the darkened bark of the trees. Within 75 years, there were more dark-colored moths than light-colored moths.

The color change in the moth species can be explained by the process of natural selection. When the tree trunks became blackened by soot, the light-colored moths were easily spotted and eaten by birds. The few moths with naturally occurring mutations for darker colors blended in with the dark soot on the bark. These dark-colored moths were eaten in lesser numbers. They then produced offspring which inherited the genes for the darker color. These dark-colored offspring also were eaten in lesser numbers. Gradually, the populations changed from mostly light-colored to mostly dark-colored moths.

*The students read the passage from the textbook, which included all the pictures, diagrams, etc.
LeVon Balzar et al.
Life Science. Copyright 1987, by Scott, Foresman and Co. Reprinted by permission.

anonymity, in accordance with standard research ethics.

SUGGESTED ISSUES TO DISCUSS/QUESTIONS TO CONSIDER IN ANALYZING CASE STUDY

1. Why were the students given a 5 minute break between the time they read the science text passage and when they were asked to do the free recall task? What do we know about the memory system (see Chapter(s) on Cognitive Theories in your Educational Psychology text) that would suggest a reason for this step? What implications does this have for the testing of children in classroom situations?

2. What are some other methodological issues to consider in the analysis of this case study? For example, do you think that interviews are appropriate for obtaining data on students' use of different types of learning strategies and their memory? If not, what other methods would you use? Are there any other questions the interviewer could have, or should have, asked to obtain valid data from the students? What would you have asked the students if you were their teacher?

3. Compare and contrast Sharon and Andrew in terms of the different cognitive strategies and tactics that they seem to use (see Chapter(s) on Cognitive Theories in your Educational Psychology text).

4. Compare and contrast Sharon and Andrew in terms of their metacognition and self-regulation skills (see Chapter(s) on Cognitive Theories in your Educational Psychology text).

5. Before you turn to Tables 1 and 2, but after you have read the interviews, try to predict which student is going to do better in remembering the information. In terms of your analysis, which student do you think is doing better in science specifically and in school in general? Why do you think that?

6. Examine their actual answers to the recall task (in Table 1) and their statements in the interview protocol to see if you can identify any examples of: (a) the influence of schemata, (b) the process of reconstructing memory, or (c) proactive or retroactive interference (see Chapter(s) on Cognitive Theories in your Educational Psychology text).

7. Examine their answers to the transfer task (in Table 2) and their statements in the interview pro-

tocol to see if you can identify any examples of: (a) low road transfer, (b) high road transfer, or (c) the influence of schemata (see Chapter(s) on Cognitive Theories in your Educational Psychology text). Why do you think the students did much worse on these transfer questions than on the free recall task?

8. Given your analysis of the interviews and the responses in Tables 1 and 2, what are the implications for your teaching behavior? What would you do if you were the teacher of these two students? Discuss these issues in terms of teaching for meaningful learning, teaching of self-regulatory skills and cognitive strategies, and teaching for positive transfer (see Chapter(s) on Cognitive Theories in your Educational Psychology text).

INTERVIEW WITH "SHARON"

Note: In the transcript, "I" stands for interviewer; "C" stands for child.

I: OK. This is the last thing we have to do. When you read these pages in the textbook, could you tell me what you were doing? When you read these 4 pages, what were you thinking? Start at the beginning and tell me everything you did.

C: I, um, I started reading and um, some of the definitions of the words in the black I couldn't understand. So I went over again and started from the beginning—started reading again. And with all the examples—like "adaptation"—I couldn't understand the meaning so with the examples—I used the examples to understand how, what it might be. I had an idea of what it was. Um. There was enough information I already knew. Before I started. I just used the context clue to understand the word and thought of some more examples that might be possible. . . . Um, like on this page, about Charles Darwin, I already knew about Charles Darwin, so, it helped me understand all the changes and how evolution occurred, um, and how the species may be different from the young ones. All the explanations—I understood these 2 pages really well. Better than these 2. I didn't really know them that well. Um. . . are you still. . . all I did was try to take the context clue and put it all together in my mind and see what I could do. And some things I still don't understand, but most of it I do.

I: OK. You said that you made some of your own examples, after you read about a definition. You made some of your own examples. Why did you do that?

C: Oh, well, using this example, if I could make some more examples it would make me understand more. Then I would know, "Yes, I do understand this." Because just using the example, they give a really good example about insects—using that, I thought of some different examples, I thought. And then if I thought I got it right, then I know that I understand the whole thing.

I: When you were writing all those things you could remember, tell me what you were thinking then.

C: I was trying to remember all the examples mainly. And from—because I didn't remember the exact definition of the word, so, just using the examples, I just put it in my own words. What it was. And I gave examples also. So if I don't understand, if I don't know the definition, I look back at the examples on the paper and then try to see. So. . .

I: Good. When I was asking you about Ann Arbor, and the coyote in the desert, what were you thinking about when you were answering those questions?

C: . . .Um . . . I thought about, . . first of all, I wanted to think about what you'd asked. And understand what you was ask—what you were asking me. And then I thought about all the things I read and if there was any relationship between the question you asked and the thing I read. I couldn't, I couldn't really mix them both up—the examples from the book and the questions up that well. I don't know why, but I just couldn't make them up that well. My answer might not have been that good. If I'd understood them that well.

I: You said that you tried to make connections and this between what you read and the questions I had—why did you do that?

C: Because, um, in the second question the word "mutation" came up. So I knew there was something about mutation in the book so I thought about all the things that were in the book and it helped me understand what mutation had to do with the coyote and with the change.

I: And then you said that you spent some time trying to understand what my question was—why did you do that?

C: Um . . . just to clear myself up about what you were asking. Cause at first I didn't understand. Then I looked at the question, stared at it, and think about what it's really asking me. I cannot just go on

read a question and then I know the question. Sometimes it's confusing so I'll read it over again and think about what it is saying and then go back to my text and look at that for answers.

I: OK

INTERVIEW WITH "ANDREW"

I: OK—this is the last thing we have to do today. When you were reading these pages in the textbook, what were you thinking? Could you tell me what you were doing? Start at the beginning and tell me everything you did.

C: When I was reading it I was wondering how the anteater worked and, what did it say? It had a sticky tongue. It was a nostril at first—I thought it sucked up the ants with it. I don't know. But that's how it was in cartoons. I didn't know—when I used to watch it.

I: OK. And what else did you do and think while you were reading?

C: I was wondering how they worked. It was pretty interesting how about the butterfly that blended into trees. That was closer to the end. Um . . . there was two butterflies that looked alike. That was pretty sweet, but they were, they really weren't. They had two different kinds of names and everything.

I: When you were writing down all the things that you could remember, what were you thinking while you were doing that?

C: Thinking what I could think—trying to remember what I had to remember. Cause sometimes, see, it comes back to me, but I don't know how to write it down on paper sometimes. It comes to me but, um, like I said, I don't know, sometimes I don't know how to write it down on paper, and sometimes I don't remember right after I read it. It comes to me by the time the test comes. Or something like that.

I: What do you do to make it come to you?

C: Just try to . . . sometimes I pray to help um, try and remember myself, what happened.

I: What happened, you mean in the book?

C: Yeah

I: How do you do that?

C: Well, I just, um . . . , say in my head sometimes, "Dear Lord, could you please help me with this test so I could pass it and try and help me to remember what I read in the book and I'll try to remember, too. In Jesus name, Amen".

I: OK, that's a strategy. When I asked you the questions about Ann Arbor and the White Coyote, what were you thinking about while you were answering those?

C: Well, I was, I don't like mosquitos but I'm glad like everything, it just came to me, everything on earth has to do with something. Like if the trees weren't here we wouldn't have this much oxygen, and if the mosquitos weren't here, the frogs couldn't eat them and they would die. And, um, I forgot what eats frogs but anyways, and it would go on like that and then eventually we would start dying cause we eat whatever, the frogs, see, wait a minute, that means. . . Oh forget it, but anyway, . . . That's weird.

I: So when I was asking about Ann Arbor and the coyotes in Ann Arbor, that's the kind of thing you were thinking about?

C: I was thinking how I wish everything could live. Like everything would live forever. That's what I was thinking and now what would happen if that did happen. And it would be colder on earth.

TABLE 1   **Verbatim Responses of Students to Recall Task**

Sharon's Response (as written by her)

I learned that adaptation is very important.

For example: a frog needs to eat insects. The frog has a special tongue for that insect. If the frog doesn't have that adaptation, it can not live on the insects.

I learned that Charles Darwin found the natural selting theory. He found that all species do not look the same as their young ones. The color of the young ones might be different from their parents. Also that evolution takes place gradually. This would be one of the reasons of the changes in the species. Another reason would be the environmental changes.

For example: A butterfly might be a lighter color a long time back because the trees were light colored. Now the butterfly became darker because the trees are darker. The cause of the tree becoming darker is because of the environmental changes. Thus there are two ways a specie might change over a period of time.

Mutation, I think is the changes occuring in the genes. Mutations can help a specie do a certain activity.

Andrew's Response (as written by him)

Adaption—is the result of _____ (left blank on sheet of paper)
Tadpoles and frogs are in the same species although they don't look the same.
There are two butterflies that look a like but aren't.
The anteater has a very sticky tongue and it is found in hard to reach areas. It eats insects not only ants.

TABLE 2 Students' Response to Transfer Questions

Sharon's response (as transcribed from a tape recording)

Q1: What if Ann Arbor became very cold and had snow year round like the North Pole? What might happen to the animals that live here now?

Mm, they might have to, mmm, in order to survive here they might have to build some more homes, different kinds of homes that would keep them warm. Or they might have to move, I don't know. (Interviewer probed for more information, but she said she didn't know.)

Q2: What if a coyote that lives in the desert had a mutation that made his fur white? What might happen to this coyote?

It wouldn't be, oh, Ok, since there was a lot of heat, it might not be able to protect itself. Mm, it might, um, it might have some special, um, because when the fur is not white it might have some chemicals or stuff which might help the coyote get some food or meet his survival needs which he might not be able to get since he changed. Maybe it's a different environment, I mean, maybe the coyote doesn't live in that kind of environment and is not used to the hot weather. It's all I can think of. (Interviewer probed, but she couldn't offer anything else.)

Andrew's response (as transcribed from a tape recording)

Q1: What if Ann Arbor became very cold and had snow year round like the North Pole? What might happen to the animals that live here now?

We would be able to have more pet shops, be more animals I guess to help them. Some animals can't live that long in cold weather. They can't survive. Bears will have to sleep all year round. They'd probably die. (I—What do you mean?) Since they have to sleep all year round and it, you know, you know how they, let's see, um, I don't know what it's called but they go to sleep in the winter I think. Is that true? I think they go to sleep in the winter and when it's winter, how are they going to survive? If it is cold all year round? (I—Ok, you said there would be more pet shops, why was that?) Because, like, little, well not for birds cause birds fly to where it's warm, so I'm talking about the animals that live, like the animals that don't fly. Probably bring in more animals instead of killing them. So they can have a good life. (I—Do you mean they can live in the pet shops?) Or, I mean, yeah, yeah, or they could, like people could bring them home. After they are trained and everything and get used to other people. Since they are wild animals.

Q2: What if a coyote that lives in the desert had a mutation that made his fur white? What might happen to this coyote?

Probably die, I'm not sure, I don't know that much about coyotes. (I—Tell me more about why you said, probably die.) The, like, I don't think coyotes get white fur, cause their fur is brown, I think. Sometimes, I'm not sure about this, but sometimes if their fur turns a different color, they're about to die. Like if our fingers turned blue or stayed like that for awhile, we might die.

Affect and Motivation in Secondary Mathematics

MARGARET R. MEYER and JAMES A. MIDDLETON
University of Wisconsin, Madison

Students bring more to class that books and pencils. They also bring with them wide ranges of prior knowledge, skills, work habits, attitudes, and beliefs. These factors interact with each other and with what goes on in the classroom and they influence students' learning of mathematics. The following two vignettes look at the interaction between selected student factors and teacher behaviors. The first one examines the origins and effects of differential treatment of students by the teacher and the second one focuses on how task characteristics influence student motivation.

Vignette Number 1

As her class works on the homework assignment during the fifteen minutes before the end of class, Ms. Evans is walking up and down the aisles to answer questions and help students when they have trouble with the assignment. Three girls sitting by the windows begin combing their hair and talking with one another. She frowns and heaves a sigh as she continues down the row. When she reaches Tom's desk he gets her attention and asks, "Ms. Evans, how do you do problem seven?"

She replies, "Come on, Tom, you know how to do that problem. Work on it a bit more before you ask me for help."

Ms. Evans looks up as Sarah slams her book shut and throws her pencil on her desk. As she approaches Sarah's desk, Ms. Evans interrupts a conversation between two boys and tells them to get busy.

"Sarah, are you okay?"

"Oh, Ms. Evans, I'm never going to get this stuff. I don't understand any of these problems!"

"Calm down, Sarah. It's not that bad. Let me see what you were working on. Number seven? Oh, that's easy. First you simplify the equation and then find the roots. Here, give me your pencil and I'll show you how to do it."

As the students leave the room when the bell rings, Ms. Evans intercepts Tom and says, "Tom, what did you get for number seven?" When he responds with the correct answer, she says "Good work, I knew that you could figure it out. Maybe tomorrow you could put that one on the board at the beginning of class."

ANALYSIS

Research has shown that the educational experience of males and females[1] is not always the same, even when they are sitting in the same classroom (Good, Sikes, & Brophy, 1973). In mathematics, differential treatment has been linked to differences in achievement and attitudes for males and females (Koehler, 1990).

[1]This vignette has focused on differential treatment of students based on gender. It could easily be changed so that the differential treatment was a function of race. The gap in achievement and participation in mathematics between white students and students of color is even greater than that between females and males. In so far as differential treatment contributes to this gap, it is worthy of our attention and concern.

Another look at the vignette will help to show how the experience of being a student in Ms. Evans' math class differs for males and females and how these experiences can result in differences in student outcomes.

Females

- Off-task behavior by the three girls is tolerated.
- Sarah is not encouraged to struggle with the problems.
- Sarah is shown how to get the correct answer to the problem.

Males

- Off-task behavior by the two boys is not tolerated.
- Tom is encouraged to struggle independently with the problem.
- Tom is rewarded for his performance with praise of his ability and public recognition.

Origins of Differential Treatment

What are the origins of the differential treatment patterns exhibited by Ms. Evans and many other teachers? Reyes and Stanic (1988) propose a model that links differential treatment in mathematics based on gender to teachers' beliefs; their beliefs about the aptitudes of males and females; and their beliefs about the appropriateness of achieving at high levels in mathematics for males and females.

If, consciously or unconsciously, Ms. Evans believes that males are naturally better at mathematics than females, then she will be more likely to encourage male students to struggle, to do their best and to give the answers to her female students. Despite her own success in mathematics, Ms. Evans could easily be a victim of the many articles appearing in the popular press that make claims for the mathematical superiority of males. She might also be responding to what she sees as differences in the way the girls and boys approach the learning of mathematics in her classroom. It could be that the boys are more responsive to her methods of teaching and get better grades than the girls.

What are some reasons why Ms. Evans might find the girls to be less responsive? Perhaps the girls feel that they are not supported by Ms. Evans as learners of mathematics. Perhaps they feel social pressures to achieve at lower levels than they are

capable of achieving. And perhaps they too believe the stereotype that math is for boys and girls can't do as well. The potential for a cycle of differential treatment, diminished student self-esteem, lowered student responsiveness, lowered achievement, and lowered teacher expectations is staggering. Learned helplessness, a critical psychological lowering of self-efficacy due to repeated failure, is more often reported for females in the domain of mathematics (Kloosterman, 1990).

The individual's perception of the appropriateness of achieving at high levels in mathematics has two dimensions: usefulness and sex role congruency. Usefulness is a perception that mathematics will be a benefit for students presently and in their future work. We know that males and females have different perceptions about the usefulness of mathematics: Males, more so than females, think that mathematics will be useful to them in their future (Meyer, 1989). Teachers can also have different perceptions regarding the usefulness of mathematics. It could be that Ms. Evans believes that because Sarah and the hair combers are girls (and therefore won't engage in technical occupations), they will not need as much mathematics as Tom and the other two boys.

Beliefs about usefulness are closely related to beliefs about sex role congruency. Sex role congruency refers to the perception that studying mathematics is an appropriate activity for an individual's stereotyped sex role. We know that males and females differ widely in this perception. Males hold more stereotypic beliefs than females, believing that mathematics is truly a male domain (Meyer, 1989) Despite being a woman in mathematics, Ms. Evans might feel that it is not feminine to achieve at high levels in mathematics. She might remember the social price that she had to pay to be good at mathematics when it was perceived by her peers to be a male domain.

Another way to explain Ms. Evans' response to Sarah might be to focus on Sarah's obvious frustration. It is easy for teachers, especially male teachers, to fall for the "tear trap." Teachers try to be sensitive to the needs of their students. They sometimes hold back from pushing a student to try harder because they don't want to cause frustration in students, because frustration can lead to tears, especially for girls. Boys might be equally frustrated, but they are less likely to show it. As a result teachers are sometimes too quick to show girls how to do the problems rather than insisting that they figure them out themselves.

Consequences of Differential Treatment

One needs to be cautious about making causal arguments regarding the effects of repeated patterns of differential treatment on the boys and girls in Ms. Evans class. However, there is considerable evidence that differential experiences are directly related to differences in student outcomes (Koehler, 1990) and it. is reasonable to speculate on what they might be.

What might Sarah and the other girls learn in Ms. Evans class besides mathematics? They might learn that it is not as important for girls to learn mathematics because Ms. Evans doesn't seem to mind when they goof off. The boys are often as uninterested in math as the girls are, but they are pushed beyond their initial reluctance while the girls are allowed to remain unengaged. The girls, and especially Sarah, are likely to learn that getting the answer is more important than understanding where it came from, that it is okay to be dependent on other people rather than becoming an autonomous learner, and that if you get emotional, you can get the teacher's attention. Also, since she is having difficulty with a problem that Ms. Evans says is easy, and because Ms. Evans gives her the answer, Sarah might conclude that she does not have the ability to do mathematics. Research shows that males and females differ in their confidence levels in mathematics (Meyer, 1989) even when they are achieving at the same level (Fennema & Sherman, 1977, 1978).

In contrast, what will the boys learn in Ms. Evans' classroom. They will learn, if they haven't already, that math is more important for boys to learn, because Ms. Evans always fusses at them when they don't pay attention. They will feel that Ms. Evans is supportive of them as learners of mathematics. Tom will learn that his ability and independent effort in the face of difficulty will lead to success, thereby reinforcing continued mastery-oriented behaviors (Dweck & Goetz, 1978; Kloosterman, 1990).

Is Ms. Evans aware that she treats the boys and girls in her class differently? If you were to ask her about this, she would probably reply that she treats all of her students the same and that she has the same high expectations for them to learn mathematics. Even if her behavior were pointed out to her, she probably would not see how these simple interactions could have any impact on her students. After all she hasn't said anything blatantly sexist like "It's okay if you can't do math, Sarah, because lots of girls have trouble with it and besides girls don't have to be able to do mathematics." And yet if Sarah has very many encounters like the one in this vignette, that is exactly the message that she will receive. The fact that the differential treatment is unintended will not lessen its impact on the boys and girls in Ms. Evans' classroom.

IMPLICATIONS FOR TEACHERS

The following suggestions for teachers are based on the not unreasonable assumption that there is a causal link between teachers' differential treatment of their students and the students' outcome differences in attitude and achievement.

- Monitor your behaviors: Are your expectations, feedback, and encouragement the same for males and females?
- Examine your own beliefs about the aptitudes of males and females and the appropriateness of them achieving at high levels.
- Monitor your students behaviors: Expect and encourage independent work and positive attitudes from both males and females.

Vignette Number 2

Motivation is considered both a necessary condition for learning and a factor which in part determines what is learned (Maier, 1949). In other words, a person must be in a condition ready for learning (i.e., motivated), and the material to be learned must have characteristics that fit the person's beliefs of what is worthwhile (i.e., motivating). As an example, consider the following vignette.

Individuals who have taken high school Algebra in the recent past will remember problems like the following:

A water tank can be filled by one pipe in 10 hours. Another pipe can empty the tank in 15 hours. If both pipes are open, how long will it take to fill the tank?

A class of 9th grade students were presented with a problem similar to the one above. As the teacher wrote the problem out on the board, students showed some initial interest in what the nature of the problem might be. However, as soon as the words, water tank *were written, the general affect and attitude of the class changed dramatically. Most students rolled their eyes and whispered, "How am I ever going to use this?" Some students immediately began writing down formulas and drawing pictures of bathtubs and watering troughs in an attempt to solve the problem, but soon became frustrated and quit. Several "math anxious" students recoiled in genuine horror as if encountering their worst nightmare: The water tank problem. One student actually got the answer.*

ANALYSIS

This scene, familiar to most teachers and all students, illustrates an important issue that is gaining prominence in the psychological study of education: the distinction between intrinsic motivation,[2] the tendency to do some activity "for its own sake," and extrinsic motivation, the tendency to perform a task in order to gain some reward (high grades and/or praise), or to escape some form of punishment (low grades and/or ridicule).

Motivational Characteristics of Tasks

It is clear that few if any of the students in the class described above were motivated intrinsically by the nature of the water tank problem. Their different responses to the task highlight recent findings by researchers in the area of motivation. For example, as soon as the words *water tank* were written on the board, the entire class understood the nature of the task, and they also knew that solving the problem would not be a particularly pleasing experience. The tendency for students to classify activities this way is a result of their previous experience with similar tasks in similar circumstances. Intrinsically motivating tasks are those that necessitate a moderately high degree of stimulation (cognitive/physiological arousal), and a concomitant degree of personal control (free choice, appropriate challenge).

If the level of cognitive stimulation is low, the task is perceived to be boring. If the level is high, the task is seen as confusing. If a student has little control over participation in an activity, the task will become perceived as being frustratingly difficult, or coercive. If the student has too much control, the task will be seen as being unchallenging and therefore not worthwhile. Therefore, an appropriate balance between arousal-producing aspects such as challenge, novelty, or fantasy, and opportunities for students to exercise their own control over task demands will encourage students to perceive mathematics activities as "fun" and they will want to engage in similar activities in the future (Middleton, 1992). However, if an educational task has no intrinsic worth to the student, the student must either rely on some extrinsic form of motivation in order to be induced to perform the task (Lepper, 1988; Covington & Beery, 1976), or avoid the task altogether by goofing off, or daydreaming (Covington & Beery, 1976).

Consequences of Task Characteristics

The motivational characteristics of tasks not only affect the individual's task engagement patterns, they also affect the nature and quality of what is actually learned. In the vignette, the students who actually attempted to solve the water tank problem quickly became frustrated with the difficulty of the task, and since it lacked applicability and personal interest, they gave up without solving the problem.

Lepper (1988) contrasted certain characteristics and repercussions of learning which involved either intrinsic or extrinsic motivational orientations. His thorough analysis of the literature clearly demonstrates the desirable qualities of the intrinsic orientation as it relates to students' learning strategies, tolerance for failure, and persistence. Benefits of intrinsic motivation include: (1) *Increased time on task* (Dweck, 1975; Dweck & Elliot, 1983; Dweck & Leggett, 1988); (2) *Persistence in the face of failure* (Dweck, 1975; Dweck & Elliot, 1983; Dweck & Leggett, 1988); (3) *Increased learning from an activity* (Grolnick & Ryan, 1987; McGraw, 1978); (4) *Higher creativity* (McGraw & McCullers, 1979); (5) *Increased metacognitive ability, elaborative processing, and monitoring of comprehension* (Markman, 1981); (6) *Selection of more difficult tasks* (Pittman, Emery & Boggiano, 1982), (7) *Greater risk taking* (Condry & Chambers, 1978); (8) *Selection of deeper and more efficient performance and learning strategies* (Nolen, 1988); (9) *Subsequent choice of an activity in the absence of an extrinsic reward* (Deci & Ryan, 1985); and (10)

[2]You may substitute the word "fun" for "intrinsic motivation" if you wish. "Fun" conjures up pleasant memories that epitomize the nature of intrinsic motivation as it is conceptualized here.

Increased efficiency in subsequent approaches to an activity (Harter, 1978; Pittman et. al., 1982).

It is important that the reader realizes that intrinsic and extrinsic motivation are not two independent aspects of the individual's motivational system. Rather, they interact significantly for nearly any task a person chooses to undertake (Middleton, in preparation). For example, when individuals who are engaged in an intrinsically motivating activity are offered a reward for their performance, their perceptions of the worth of the task can be severely eroded (Lepper & Greene, 1978). This relationship is more readily apparent when individuals are threatened with punishment if they don't do well on a task—they tend to do well, assuredly, but their level of enjoyment drops dramatically.

Students' lack of motivation for mathematics is a learned behavior, stemming from a paucity of experiences that promote intrinsic motivation in the classroom. By the time students reach the 6th or 7th grade, they have formed the basic motivational sets they will use for the rest of their school careers, and most likely for the rest of their lives. Unfortunately, in the United States, the general trend for students' developing attitudes is a downward spiral (Eccles, Wigfield & Reuman, 1987; Dossey, Mullis, Lindquist, & Chambers, 1988).

IMPLICATIONS FOR TEACHERS

The following recommendation for designing motivating activities may be of help to teachers who find it difficult to engage their students:[3]

- Make the activity stimulating by providing novelty, challenge and fantasy. Novelty in the form of different ways of looking at the phenomena of interest stimulates curiosity and the desire to understand. Challenge makes the effort required worthwhile and success in the activity meaningful. Opportunity for students to use their imagination through fantasy encourages planning, minimizes the risk of trial-and-error, and stimulates creativity.
- Give the students a sense of control by giving them plenty of choices. Students should be able to choose from alternative tasks those that most reflect their own interests and aptitudes. Once

[3]These recommendations are adapted from a chapter by the second author (Middleton, 1991, pp. 19–28). Reprinted with permission.

a task is selected there should be choices regarding solution strategies so that all students, regardless of their ability, can make progress on the task.
- Be aware of your students' interests. Try to give plenty of examples and problems that relate to the things that they like. This will increase the probability that the activity will provide both stimulation and a sense of control.
- Make sure that the motivating aspects of any educational activity are focused on the *learning* afforded by the activity. If the motivation is focused on aspects peripheral to learning, like on obtaining treats or getting out of class, then anything that is learned will also be peripheral to the content objectives.

QUESTIONS FOR STUDY

1. Think back on your own experiences in mathematics. Try to recall a situation in which you were definitely motivated intrinsically. Describe in detail the nature of the task you were performing in relationship to the domains of *arousal* and *control* as described above.

2. Think back on your own experiences in mathematics. Try to recall a situation in which you were definitely motivated extrinsically. Describe in detail the nature of the task you were performing in relationship to the domains of *arousal* and *control* as described above.

3. Think about the subject that you (will) teach, if it is not mathematics. What is one topic that is the equivalent of *The water tank problem* in eliciting negative student responses. Describe the nature of this topic and suggest modifications that would most likely result in higher student motivation.

REFERENCES

Condry, J., & Chambers, J. (1978). Intrinsic motivation and the process of learning. In M. R. Lepper & D. Greene (Eds.), *The hidden costs of reward* (pp. 61–84). Hillsdale, NJ: Lawrence Erlbaum Associates, Inc.

Covington, M. V., & Beery, R. G. (1976). *Self worth and school learning.* New York: Holt Rinehart and Winston.

Deci, E. L., & Ryan, R. M. (1985). *Intrinsic motivation and self-determination in human behavior.* New York: Plenum.

Dossey, J. A., Mullis, I. V. S., Lindquist, M. M., & Chambers, D. L. (1988). *The mathematics report card. Are we measuring up? Trends and achievement based on the 1986 national assessment.* Princeton, NJ: Educational Testing Service.

Dweck, C. S. (1975). The role of expectations and attributions in the alleviation of learned helplessness. *Journal of Personality and Social Psychology, 31,* 674–685.

Dweck, C. S., & Elliot, E. S. (1983). Achievement motivation. In E. M. Hetherington (Ed.), *Socialization, personality, and social development* pp.643–681). New York: Wiley.

Dweck, C. S., & Goetz, T. E. (1978). Attributions and learned helplessness. In J. H. Harvey, W. Ickes, & R. F. Kidd (Eds.), *New directions in attribution research* (Vol. 2) (pp. 157–179). Hillsdale, NJ: Lawrence Erlbaum.

Dweck, C. S., & Leggett, E. L. (1988). A social-cognitive approach to motivation and personality. *Psychological Review, 66,* 183–201.

Fennema, E., & Sherman, J. (1977). Sex-related differences in mathematics achievement, spatial visualization and affective factors. *American Educational Research Journal, 14*(1), 51–71.

Fennema, E., & Sherman, J. (1978). Sex-related differences in mathematics achievement and related factors: A further study. *Journal for Research in Mathematics Education, 9,* 189–203.

Good, T. L., Sikes, J. N., & Brophy, J. E. (1973). Effects of teacher sex and student sex on classroom interaction. *Journal of Educational Psychology, 65*(1), 74–87.

Grolnick, W. S., & Ryan, R. M. (1987). Autonomy in children's learning: An experimental and individual differences investigation. *Journal of Personality and Social Psychology, 52,* 890–898.

Harter, S. (1978). Effectance motivation reconsidered: Toward a developmental model. *Human Development, 1,* 34–64.

Kloosterman, P. (1990). Attributions, performance following failure, and motivation in mathematics. In E. Fennema & G. C. Leder (Eds.), *Mathematics and gender* (pp.96–127). New York: Teachers College Press.

Koehler, M. S. (1990). Classrooms, teachers, and gender differences in mathematics. In E. Fennema & G. C. Leder (Eds.), *Mathematics and gender* (pp. 128–148). New York: Teachers College Press.

Lepper, M. R. (1988). Motivational considerations in the study of instruction. *Cognition and Instruction, 5*(4), 289–309.

Lepper, M. R., & Greene, D. (Eds.), (1978). The hidden costs of reward. Hillsdale, NJ: Lawrence Erlbaum Associates, Inc.

McGraw, K. 0. (1978). The detrimental effects of reward on performance: A literature review and a prediction model. In M. R. Lepper & D. Greene (Eds.), *The hidden costs of reward* (pp. 33–60). Hillsdale, NJ: Lawrence Erlbaum Associates, Inc.

McGraw, K. O., & McCullers, J. C. (1979). Evidence of a detrimental effect of extrinsic incentives on breaking a mental set. *Journal of Experimental Social Psychology, 15,* 285–294.

Markman, E. M. (1981). Comprehension monitoring. In W. P. Dickson (Ed.), *Children's oral communication skills* (pp. 61–84). New York: Academic.

Meyer, M. R. (1989). Gender differences in mathematics. In M. M. Lindquist (Ed.), *Results from the fourth mathematics assessment of the national assessment of educational progress.* Reston, VA: The National Council of Teachers of Mathematics, 149–159.

Middleton, J. A. (1991). Designing fun activities for gifted students: A taxonomy of motivational objectives. In R. B. Clasen (Ed.), *Educating Able Learners. A Study Guide* (pp. 19–28). Madison, WI: Madison Education Extension Programs.

Middleton, J. A. (1991). *Motivation for achievement in mathematics: Findings, generalizations, and criticisms of the recent research.* University of Wisconsin—Madison: Manuscript in preparation for publication.

Middleton, J. A. (1992). *Teachers' versus students' beliefs regarding intrinsic motivation in the mathematics classroom: A personal constructs approach.* Paper presented at the annual meeting of the American Educational Research Association, San Francisco.

Nolen, S. B. (1988). Reasons for studying: Motivational orientation and study strategies. *Cognition and Instruction, 5*(4), 269–287.

Pittman, T. S., Emery, J., & Boggiano, A. K. (1982). Intrinsic and extrinsic motivational orientations: Reward-induced change in preference for complexity. *Journal of Personality and Social Psychology, 42,* 789–797.

Reyes, L. H., & Stanic, G. M. A. (1988). Race, sex, socioeconomic status, and mathematics. *Journal for Research in Mathematics Education, 19*(1), 26–43.

Motivation in First Grade Literacy

JULIANNE C. TURNER
Department of Educational Psychology
The Pennsylvania State University

MRS. O'CONNELL'S FIRST GRADE READING CLASS

It is a sunny day in March, and Mrs. O'Connell, the first grade teacher greets her class with a question, "Do you know what is special about today?" Shannon replies, "It's the first day of spring!" Mrs. O'Connell has planned some activities in the morning reading lesson around this theme. First, she reads the class a poem about spring she has written on the board. The children repeat as she points to the words. She tells the children that later their first seatwork assignment will be copying the poem. Next, Mrs. O'Connell wants to drill some phonics skills. She points to the word, *spring* and asks the children to suggest some words that rhyme with it. She says, "When I want to find rhyming words, I try different consonants and consonant blends in front of -ing." The children suggest some rhyming words like *fling* and *ring*. She advises the children that later they will be asked to write five words that rhyme with spring on their papers.

Next Mrs. O'Connell hands out two phonics worksheets. The first sheet provides more practice with rhyming words. She tells students that they are to unscramble the rhyming words on the sheet and arrange them so that they make sentences. She demonstrates by reviewing one sentence, "Can a _____ _____ in a _____? The three word choices are *boat, float,* and *goat*. She asks, "What makes sense? Can a float boat in a goat?" The children laugh, and one student gives the correct response. She tells the students to do the other sentences in the same way. Mike looks puzzled, but he continues to play with

his pencil, and doesn't ask a question. Last, she presents the second phonics worksheet to the children, a drill of the short *u* sound. She points out that the key words are "ugly duckling," words that remind children of the target vowel sound. In order to avoid later confusion, Mrs. O'Connell reviews all the pictures on the worksheet, such as cup, ruler, mule, sun, etc. Then she tells the children that there are 12 pictures representing both long and short *u* sounds, but that there are only 8 pictures of short *u* words. They should cut out all 8 short *u* words and paste them on the pictures of the 8 ugly ducklings. When they are finished, they should color their worksheets.

Just before the children are to begin their seatwork, Mrs. O'Connell reviews the assignments and her expectations. She reminds the children that the papers on which they copy the "spring" poems and write the rhyming words and the three sentences are to follow the standard format: write names at the top left, and skip a line before they begin. "Use your best handwriting," she reminds the class. She points out that, as usual, she has written the four seatwork assignments on the board in the order in which the children are to complete them. She asks if the children have any questions. Rhonda asks if they may share crayons when completing the worksheet assignment, and Mrs. O'Connell responds that she would rather they did not today. She reminds them that their morning work must be done by 11:15 if they are to go out to recess. Then Mrs. O'Connell calls the first reading group.

The children in Mrs. O'Connell's room are seated in groups of four. She has tried to compose the groups so that both boys and girls and able and less able learners can work together. She has told children that they can ask neighbors for help if they need it, but she also has stressed the need for quiet as she conducts reading group. The children at their desks begin their assignments by copying the poem. Jesse looks at the poem on the board and begins to copy the words, letter by letter. Five minutes later, when he gets to the end of the line, he realizes that the number of words on his first line does not match the model on the board. He erases his entire first line, ripping his paper, and starts over. Ten minutes after beginning the assignment, he is still struggling to fit the first line of the poem on the first line of his paper. By this time, the other children around him have completed this assignment and moved on. Unable to meet what he understands as the teacher's expectations ("Copy the poem exactly as you see it"), and uncertain about how to ask for help, Jesse abandons the assignment in frustration.

Samantha has easily copied the poem, saying it aloud word by word as she writes. When she begins to select rhyming words for spring, she quickly follows the strategy Mrs. O'Connell suggested. She chooses the first three appropriate consonants in the alphabet, combines them with -ing, and writes, *bing, ding* and *king*. She completes both activities in less than 10 minutes. She comments to Sara, "This work is easy. I finished mine before everyone else."

Across the room, Mike is staring at the worksheet requiring him to arrange the rhyming words to make a sentence. He seems unable to begin. He reads the word choices, *jam, ham,* and *Sam,* and the sentence stem: _____ put grape _____ on his _____. He doesn't understand how to select the words and looks to his neighbors for help, but they have moved on to other assignments. He fears that asking for help now will reveal that he doesn't understand. With a sigh, Mike simply fills in the words as they appeared in the list: *jam put grape ham on his Sam.* He hopes he got some correct.

Alisha begins the phonics sheet on short *u* by cutting and coloring. As she is coloring, she stares around the room to see what the other children are doing. Several minutes later, she goes into the hall for a minute, and then returns. She picks up her pencil and goes to the pencil sharpener. After a brief conversation with Jenny, she returns to her seat and starts coloring again. Fifteen minutes after beginning, she is still coloring. At that point, Mrs. O'Connell reminds the children that they have only five minutes left for morning work. Alicia hastily

scribbles some color on the remaining pictures so that all 12 are colored, then she quickly glances at Dana's worksheet. She puts 8 pictures in one pile and hurriedly pastes them on her worksheet. She hands in her paper, and gets in the line for recess.

MRS. ANDERSON'S FIRST GRADE READING CLASS

Across the hall, Mrs. Anderson has finished opening exercises and introduces the theme for the week in her first grade classroom. It is "Clifford's birthday party," based on the text of the same name. She asks the children to sit with her on the rug while she places an oversized copy of *Clifford's Birthday Party* (Bridwell, 1968) on her easel for all to see. Mrs. Anderson asks the children to contribute what they know about Clifford from previous stories and to predict what they think might happen in this story. She asks the children why they think the author wrote the book. Several children volunteer. She had placed small sticky notes over certain words in the text, and she requests the children's help in figuring out what those words might be. She reads the sentences, models some words that might fit, then asks children to suggest others. After each suggestion, she asks the children to explain the rationale for their suggestions. Then she gradually uncovers each word letter by letter. With each letter, she leads students to narrow their choices based on the sound/symbol clues. After they finish the book, she reviews the morning lesson by pointing out to children that when they encounter an unfamiliar word, they can use several strategies to decode it.

After the group lesson, the teacher explains that all the activities that week would be related to the theme of Clifford's birthday. The children were going to spend the week getting ready for his party, scheduled for Friday, and there were many things to do. On her easel paper, she had listed the activities and labeled each one as "reading," "writing," "planning," or "thinking." One activity, writing a story about Clifford's birthday party, was required. Mrs. Anderson points out that they were going to be authors and illustrators just like the ones who had created *Clifford.* There were many other activities children could choose as their interests dictated. Some of the choices included: writing invitations to Clifford's party, making a list of the things the children had to do to prepare for the party, designing and writing a birthday card for Clifford, listening to the taped version of the text while reading, reading another book about a birthday party, and playing a game with some of the sentences from a text read last week. Mrs. Anderson had arranged activities at centers around the classroom, designated as author's table, listening center, library, art center, etc. Children were to write down the three activities they would complete that morning and follow the schedule.

Some children move to the centers of their choice while others remain at their desks to begin their stories. Lauren takes out paper to begin her story. She thinks for a while, then begins saying her story aloud as she writes it. Almost immediately, she stops, unable to spell a word. She walks to the easel where the text is, copies "Clifford," and returns to her desk to continue. Several minutes later, she asks Megan, sitting across the table, how to spell *house*. Megan says the sounds out loud, and she and Lauren approximate the spelling, "hos." After she finishes, Lauren reads her story to Megan. She comments, "I want to be an author when I grow up."

In the library corner, Ian and Brett are reading *When Is My Birthday?* (Sipherd, 1988) together. They take turns reading pages. When Brett loses his place, Ian points out, "You need to go back and read what happens before that." Later on, Ian points to the picture and suggests Brett use it for a clue to the unknown word. He offers to re-read the page for Brett so he can "see how it sounds." Lauren has finished her story and sits down at the author's table with a group of other children who are working on writing party invitations. Before she begins, she glances around the table at the variety of invitations the children are composing. Rachel's invitation is mostly pictures with her name and phone number appended. Eric has written his invitation with great elaboration, noting what children should wear, what they should bring, and naming some of the games they would play at the party. Lauren decides she wants to tell the children where to come for the party and what they will do. She begins by drawing a picture of her house.

As the children work, Mrs. Anderson circulates from center to center, pausing to ask children how they are making decisions about activities, and participating briefly in small groups. At several points in the morning activities, she stops and reminds them that some are losing attention, and asks them to explain how they can stay focused. Then she sits down in the area where children are working with the sentence game. This is a new activity, and she wants to see which strategies the children can use

independently as well as provide some assistance for those who might have difficulty. The game consisted of four sentences from a text the class had studied the week before, written on oaktag, and cut up into individual words. Each sentence was color-coded. She was surprised to see Matthew attempting this activity, as he was not one of the most skilled or confident readers.

Matthew takes the words and thoughtfully arranges them: "she felled chairs. Then some" Mrs. Anderson asks him to read the sentence. With some hints, he decodes "some." Then he rearranges the sentence several times. Each time, Mrs. Anderson asks, "Does it make sense yet?" Matt shakes his head and tries again: "she felled some Then chairs." Finally, Mrs. Anderson asks, "What goes at the beginning of the sentence?" Matt quickly inserts "Then" at the beginning and proudly reads the sentence: "Then she felled some chairs." "I remember that from the story," Matt says. Then he asks to do another sentence. This time, in addition to re-reading for meaning, he uses the new strategies of starting with a capital letter and ending with a period. When he finishes, he surprises the teacher by asking to work with the longest and most difficult sentence. He works alone for a while, reading phrases each time to check for meaning. He starts with a capital letter this time, but still has the period in the middle of the sentence. "I've got the first part right," he beams. He continues to rearrange the words in the last part many times, each time re-reading for meaning. Finally, he places the period and has just two words left. "Where would these go?" Mrs. Anderson asks. He re-reads again, finally placing them correctly. Matt is exhilarated. The teacher reiterates for Matt the strategies he has used to construct the sentences and commends him on sticking with a difficult task until he has solved it. Because it was only 15 minutes until lunch, Mrs. Anderson calls the class back together to discuss the morning and to review with the children how they have managed their activities. She asks children how they made their choices, how they had handled difficulties like distractions and confusions, and what they might try next time. Then they line up for lunch.

Why did the children in these classrooms have different responses to their classwork? You may have noticed that the children in Mrs. Anderson's class showed more interest in their work, were more persistent when they encountered difficulty, and used more reading and learning strategies, such as re-reading, using the pictures, context, and text characteristics, and planning their work. They didn't give up or copy from others, although they did get useful help from their peers. It is likely that the children in Mrs. O'Connell's and Mrs. Anderson's students were very similar in September. In each room there were children who were very interested in reading and valued it, and some who had little interest or value. Similarly, some children thought of themselves as "readers" and "writers" before they came to school and some did not. By March, however, the children we observed in Mrs. Anderson's room, even the less able readers like Matt, were committed and engaged in reading activities. Clearly, teachers and the instructional decisions they make can have an influence on students' motivation for academic work.

THINKING ABOUT THE CLASSES

Think back to the two classrooms. How did they differ? We can note several differences such as the types of tasks, the opportunities for challenge, and the provisions for student choice, interests, and social interaction, and the teacher's approach to instruction.

Every day students complete many academic tasks, and the tasks they perform have a powerful influence on their motivation and learning. The tasks in the two classrooms differed in several ways. We might call the tasks in Mrs. O'Connell's room *closed*. That is, the teacher selected all the activities and there was only one right answer to most of the exercises. If the students didn't understand the task and they couldn't get help, they had few options. They could give up, like Jesse, fill in blanks mindlessly, like Mike, or copy from peers, like Alicia. When teachers provide only closed tasks, they may unwittingly send the message that what is important is completing the task, not learning from it. Mrs. O'Connell reinforced this interpretation when she reminded students that all work had to be finished by recess. In contrast, the tasks in Mrs. Anderson's room could be characterized as mostly *open*. In open tasks, children had some flexibility about what information to include and how they would use it. For example, children could compose their own story about Clifford and decide what to include in their invitation to the party. Thus children could respond at the level they were able. In this classroom, some children like Rachel were still

using drawing a great deal, while Eric was using mostly text in his writing.

Similarly, the children reading the book together had selected a book they were able to read. Mrs. Anderson had designed activities so that children could respond at a variety of levels and so that all could be successful. The "right" answers were varied and depended on the child.

Another important difference in the tasks in the two rooms concerned their purposes. The tasks in Mrs. O'Connell's room were selected with the goal of providing drill and practice in reading skills whereas those in Mrs. Anderson's room allowed practice but also provided opportunities to use reading and writing in *authentic* activities. Authentic activities are those in which children use reading and writing to solve a meaningful problem, such as writing an invitation; use cognitive and metacognitive skills, such as inference and self-monitoring; use multiple sources of information and involve others as resources (Resnick, 1987). If tasks are exclusively associated with drill and practice, children may come to associate literacy with the low-level tasks they complete every day (Doyle, 1983) rather than the real goals of literacy instruction, which are communication and enjoyment. Samantha had mistakenly interpreted her goal as completion and competition; Lauren was actively striving to construct meaning during her story.

A second way of distinguishing the classrooms is by examining the challenge of the reading and writing tasks. The most motivational tasks are those that provide an appropriate amount of challenge (Clifford, 1991). Moderately difficult tasks are motivating because they provide students with information about their own competence and help them measure their progress toward the goals of reading and writing. When tasks are at the appropriate level of difficulty, children become involved with the goal of increasing their own skills rather than worrying about how they compare to others (Ames & Archer, 1988). Think about Matt. The task he attempted was certainly challenging for him; he learned a great deal about using strategies for constructing meaning and felt a real sense of accomplishment at the end of the activity. Mike, however, was worried that the other children would consider him stupid, and so he didn't ask for the help he needed to learn; Samantha, too, showed less interest in learning than in looking smart.

It is not always easy to select tasks at the appropriate challenge level for students. Mike's task was too difficult for him, because he wasn't able to acquire the help he needed, so he became frustrated. Alisha's task was too easy for her, so she became bored. She spent most of her time socializing and coloring, activities more interesting to her than the stated purpose of the task. When the time was running out, she quickly selected the correct pictures and pasted them on. Alisha spent about 15 minutes coloring and 1 minute completing the task. She probably learned little that day. Because Mrs. O'Connell gave the same work to all the children, and because the tasks had only one right answer, it was likely that many children would become bored or frustrated rather than challenged (Csikszentmihalyi, 1990). Mrs. Anderson tried to address that problem by providing tasks that children could accomplish in a variety of ways. For example, Matt could have used the words to construct sentences of his own invention rather than the sentences from the book.

The two classrooms also differed in the number of choices the students were allowed to make about their work. In Mrs. O'Connell's room, students had no choices. They all completed the same work, in the same order, and at the same locations (their desks). In Mrs. Anderson's room, students were all required to do three activities, but they could select from an array of activities. In addition, students could complete the activities in the order they chose and they could move around the room from center to center. Mrs. Anderson had designed the activities so that no matter which choices the children made, they were meeting important instructional goals in reading or writing. But from the students' perspectives, being able to choose made them feel more autonomous and allowed them to select activities that interested them, thus insuring that they would probably work harder and persist longer at the tasks. Research on motivation has shown that when students are given choices, they report more interest in their school work, feel more competent, and have higher self-worth (Ryan & Grolnick, 1986). Alisha, by choosing to put more effort into coloring than matching the pictures to the sounds on her worksheet, was asserting her need to have some control over her task. It appears that the coloring aspect of the task motivated her, not the phonics. Students like Lauren, Eric, and Rachel had many choices in how they would execute their activities, and thus they were motivated to do the reading and writing inherent in their tasks.

Another way that teachers can make tasks motivating is by relating them to students' interests. Students engaged in reading tasks they perceived

as interesting processed text more deeply, used more learning strategies, invested more time and effort and reported higher intrinsic motivation and self-esteem (Schiefele, 1991). Mrs. O'Connell tried to pique students' interest by relating two of the morning's activities to the first day of spring. But the tasks themselves were not interesting, requiring just rote mechanical skills, and so she probably did not achieve her goal. Mrs. Anderson also tried using a thematic approach to her instructional activities. She organized her theme around two topics she felt would interest the children: Clifford, who was already a favorite storybook character, and a birthday party, something most 6-year-olds enjoy and understand. By centering all activities on these themes, Mrs. Anderson had a better chance of maintaining high interest.

A final way of increasing motivation is to promote social interaction. Interacting with other students is motivational for several reasons. First, students can communicate with each other about their tasks and gain greater understanding (Brown, Collins, & Duguid, 1989). Think about Ian and Lauren. Both were able to obtain the help they needed by consulting other children. Mrs. Anderson had taught the children that asking for assistance was a sign of a good student, because it demonstrated that they were trying hard and desirous of learning. In Mrs. O'Connell's class, students were unsure of whether seeking help was sanctioned. They needed to balance their need for help with the request for quiet, and since all the children were doing the same work at the same time, speed of completion became salient, and made the slower workers reluctant to expose their difficulties. Thus, available help was often not sought, as Jesse and Mike demonstrated. A second benefit of social interaction is that peers provide models of expertise that others can emulate. By observing how other students have progressed, children increase their belief in their own potential for progress, or self-efficacy (Bandura, 1982; Schunk, 1989). Finally, other students' accomplishments can help the children set proximal goals for their own progress. For example, Ian may have been able to use the example of Brett's expert use of reading strategies to set goals for himself.

A final comment should be made about the support structures that the teachers established in the classrooms. Mrs. Anderson had a more complex organizational structure in her classroom: the tasks were more complex and diverse and there was more movement and interaction. These factors required greater monitoring of activities than those in Mrs. O'Connell's room. Mrs. Anderson prepared her students for these responsibilities by teaching them a great variety of strategies and self-monitoring skills. For example, during the morning lesson, she demonstrated a variety of ways to decode words, and she modeled and asked students to explain their choices so that other students would understand how to use them. Secondly, she taught students self-monitoring strategies. She reminded students during the morning work period how to stay focused on their tasks and at the end of the day she discussed with students their successes and failures in maintaining attention, and organizing and completing their work. By allowing students to choose and order their tasks, she was providing opportunities for students to learn self-regulation skills. By discussing how students accomplished these tasks, she was helping them to reflect on what they did well and to improve on areas of weakness.

In summary, Mrs. Anderson's instruction was motivating because it combined elements such as more complex, authentic, and challenging tasks, opportunities for student choice, topics and themes that simultaneously tapped student interests while providing instruction in the curriculum objectives, and opportunities for social interaction.

QUESTIONS FOR STUDY

1. If you asked Jesse, Samantha, Eric, and Matt, "What are you supposed to learn from your reading activity?" how do you think they would respond? What do students' understandings of the purposes of instruction have to do with motivation? Support your answer with examples from the classroom descriptions.

2. Explain why you think Matt kept on trying at the sentence game while Mike, attempting a similar task, gave up.

3. Later in the afternoon of the day Mrs. O'Connell and Mrs. Anderson taught the lessons you read, they are conversing in the teacher's lounge. Mrs. O'Connell complains to Mrs. Anderson that her children are making many "careless"

errors, and some are so unprepared for first grade that they cannot even copy a poem off the board. [She adds that other students seem bored.] She laments the fact that she has such a wide range of abilities in her classroom, making students difficult to teach. She adds that her job is much more difficult because some parents never read with their children at home. She asks Mrs. Anderson how she copes with such issues in her class.

What do you think Mrs. O'Connell's theories of motivation are? How do you think Mrs. Anderson would reply to Mrs. O'Connell?

REFERENCES

Ames, C. & Archer, J. (1988). Achievement goals in the classroom: Students' learning strategies and motivation processes. *Journal of Educational Psychology, 80*, 260–267.

Bandura, A. (1982). Self-efficacy mechanism in human agency. *American Psychologist, 37*, 122–148.

Bridwell, J. (1968). *Clifford's birthday party*.

Brown, J. S., Collins, A., & Duguid, P. (1989). Situated cognition and the culture of learning. *Educational Researcher, 18*, 32–42.

Clifford, M. M. (1991). Risk taking: Theoretical, empirical and educational considerations. *Educational Psychologist, 26*, 263–297.

Csikszentmihalyi, M. (1990). Literacy and intrinsic motivation. *Daedalus, 119*, 115–140.

Doyle, W. (1983). Academic work. *Review of Educational Research, 53*, 159–199.

Resnick, L. B. (1987). Learning in school and out. *Educational Researcher, 16*, 13–20.

Ryan, R. M., & Grolnick, W. S. (1986). Origins and pawns in the classroom: Self-report and projective assessments of individual differences in children's perceptions. *Journal of Personality and Social Psychology, 50*, 550–558.

Schiefele, U. (1991). Interest, learning, and motivation. *Educational Psychologist, 26*, 299–323.

Schunk, D. H. (1989). Social cognitive theory and self-regulated learning. In B. J. Zimmerman & D. H. Schunk (Eds.), *Self-regulated learning and academic achievement* (pp. 83–110). New York: Springer-Verlag.

Sipherd, R. (1988). *When is my birthday?* Western Publishing Co.

18) Derry, S. J. (Dec. 1988/Jan. 1989). Putting learning strategies to work. *Educational Leadership, 46*, 4:4–10. Reprinted with permission of the Association for Supervision and Curriculum Development. Copyright 1989 by ASCD. All rights reserved.

19) Pressley, M. & Harris, K. (1990). What we really know about strategy instruction. *Educational Leadership, 48*, 1:31–34. Reprinted with permission of the Association for Supervision and Curriculum Development. Copyright 1990 by ASCD. All rights reserved.

20) Reprinted with permission from *The Harvard Education Letter,* July 1987 (Vol. III, No. 4, pages 5–6, Solving the arithmetic problem by Adria Steinberg. Copyright President and Fellows of Harvard College. All rights reserved.

21) Perkins, D. N. and G. Salomon. (1989). Are cognitive skills context-bound? *Educational Researcher, 18*, 1:16–25. Copyright 1989, by the American Educational Research Association. Reprinted by permission of the publisher.

22) Beane, J. A. (Sept. 1991). Sorting out the self-esteem controversy. *Educational Leadership 49*, 1:25–30. Reprinted with permission of the Association for Supervision and Curriculum Development. Copyright 1991 by ACSD. All rights reserved.

23) Clifford, M. (Sept. 1990). Students need challenge, not easy success. *Educational Leadership 48*, 1:22–26. Reprinted with permission of the Association for Supervision and Curriculum Development. Copyright 1990 by ASCD. All rights reserved.

24) Weiner, B. (1990). History of motivational research in education. *Journal of Emotional Psychology 82*, 4:616–622. Copyright 1990 by the American Psychological Association. Reprinted with permission.

25) Abi-Nader, J. (1991). Creating a vision of the future: Strategies for motivating minority students. *Phi Delta Kappan, 72*, 7:546–549. Copyright 1991, reprinted with permission of Phi Delta Kappa.

26) Reprinted with permission from *The Harvard Education Letter,* March 1987 (Vol. III, No. 2, page 2), "Some third graders are passing because I work with them." Copyright President and Fellows of Harvard College. All rights reserved.

27) Slavin, R. E. (February 1991). Synthesis of research on cooperative learning. *Educational Leadership, 48*, 5:71–82. Reprinted with permission of the Association for Supervision and Curriculum Development. Copyright 1991 by ASCD. All rights reserved.

28) Petty, R. (March 1989). Managing disruptive students. *Educational Leadership, 46*, 6:26–28. Reprinted with permission of the Association for Supervision and Curriculum Development. Copyright 1989 by ASCD. All rights reserved.

29a) Render, G., N. Padilla and H. M. Krank. (March 1989). What research really shows about assertive discipline. *Educational Leadership, 46*, 6:72–75. Reprinted with permission of the Association for Supervision and Curriculum Development. Copyright 1989 by ASCD. All rights reserved.

29b) McCormack, S. (March 1989). Response to Render, Padilla, and Krank: "But practitioners say it works!" *Educational Leadership, 46*, 6:77–79. Reprinted with permission of the Association for Supervision and Curriculum Development. Copyright 1989 by ASCD. All rights reserved.

30) Cuban, L. (Dec. 1990). Four stories about national goals for American education. *Phi Delta Kappan, 72,* 4:264–271. Copyright 1990, reprinted with permission of Phi Delta Kappa.

31) Slavin, R. E. (1990). IBM's writing to read: Is it right for reading? *Phi Delta Kappan, 72,* 3:214–216. Copyright 1990, reprinted with permission of Phi Delta Kappa.

32) Berg, C. A. and M. Clough. (Dec. 1990/Jan. 1991) Hunter lesson design: The wrong one for science teaching. *Educational Leadership, 48,* 4:73–78. Reprinted with permission of the Association for Supervision and Curriculum Development. Copyright 1991 by ASCD. All rights reserved.

33) Means, B. and M. S. Knapp. (Dec. 1991). Cognitive approaches to teaching advanced skills to educationally disadvantaged students. *Phi Delta Kappan, 73,* 4:282–289. Copyright 1991, reprinted with permission of Phi Delta Kappa.

34) Rosenshine, B. and C. Meister. (April 1992). The use of scaffolds for teaching higher-level cognitive strategies. *Educational Leadership, 49,* 7:26–33. Reprinted with permission of the Association for Supervision and Curriculum Development. Copyright 1992 by ASCD. All rights reserved.

35) Kirst, M. (1991a). Interview on assessment issues with Lorrie Shepard. *Educational Researcher, 20,* 2:21–23. Reprinted with permission by the American Educational Research Association. All rights reserved.

36) Kirst, M. (March 1991). Interview on assessment issues with James Popham. *Educational Researcher, 20,* 2:24–27. Reprinted with permission by the American Educational Research Association. All rights reserved.

37a) Cizek, G. J. (1991). Innovation or enervation? Performance assessment in perspective. *Phi Delta Kappan, 72,* 9:
695–699. Copyright 1991, reprinted with permission of Phi Delta Kappa.

37b) Wiggins, G. (1991). A response to Cizek. *Phi Delta Kappan, 72,* 9:700–703. Copyright 1991, reprinted with permission of Phi Delta Kappa.

38) Dempster, F. (April 1991). Synthesis of research on reviews and tests. *Educational Leadership, 48,* 7:71–76. Reprinted with permission of the Association for Supervision and Curriculum Development. Copyright 1991 by ASCD. All rights reserved.

39) Reprinted with permission from *The Harvard Education Letter,* May/June 1991 (Vol. VII, No. 3, pages 1–3). Retention: Can we stop failing kids? Copyright President and Fellows of Harvard College. All rights reserved.

40) Paulson, F. L., P. R. Paulson and C. A. Meyer. (Feb. 1991). What makes a portfolio a portfolio? *Educational Leadership, 48,* 5:60–63. Reprinted with permission of the Association for Supervision and Curriculum Development. Copyright 1991 by ASCD. All rights reserved.